# DERIVATIVES, ALTERNATIVE INVESTMENTS, PORTFOLIO MANAGEMENT

CFA® Program Curriculum
2023 • LEVEL 2 • VOLUME 5

WILEY

©2022 by CFA Institute. All rights reserved. This copyright covers material written expressly for this volume by the editor/s as well as the compilation itself. It does not cover the individual selections herein that first appeared elsewhere. Permission to reprint these has been obtained by CFA Institute for this edition only. Further reproductions by any means, electronic or mechanical, including photocopying and recording, or by any information storage or retrieval systems, must be arranged with the individual copyright holders noted.

CFA®, Chartered Financial Analyst®, AIMR-PPS®, and GIPS® are just a few of the trademarks owned by CFA Institute. To view a list of CFA Institute trademarks and the Guide for Use of CFA Institute Marks, please visit our website at www.cfainstitute.org.

This publication is designed to provide accurate and authoritative information in regard to the subject matter covered. It is sold with the understanding that the publisher is not engaged in rendering legal, accounting, or other professional service. If legal advice or other expert assistance is required, the services of a competent professional should be sought.

All trademarks, service marks, registered trademarks, and registered service marks are the property of their respective owners and are used herein for identification purposes only.

ISBN 978-1-953337-09-2 (paper)
ISBN 978-1-953337-33-7 (ebook)

2022

Please visit our website at
www.WileyGlobalFinance.com.

# CONTENTS

**How to Use the CFA Program Curriculum**     xi
     Errata     xi
     Designing Your Personal Study Program     xi
     CFA Institute Learning Ecosystem (LES)     xii
     Feedback     xii

## Derivatives

**Learning Module 1**     **Pricing and Valuation of Forward Commitments**     3
     Introduction     3
         Principles of Arbitrage-Free Pricing and Valuation of Forward Commitments     4
         Pricing and Valuing Generic Forward and Futures Contracts     5
     Carry Arbitrage     10
         Carry Arbitrage Model When There Are No Underlying Cash Flows     10
         Carry Arbitrage Model When Underlying Has Cash Flows     18
     Pricing Equity Forwards and Futures     21
         Equity Forward and Futures Contracts     21
         Interest Rate Forward and Futures Contracts     24
     Pricing Fixed-Income Forward and Futures Contracts     33
         Comparing Forward and Futures Contracts     38
     Pricing and Valuing Swap Contracts     39
         Interest Rate Swap Contracts     42
     Pricing and Valuing Currency Swap Contracts     48
     Pricing and Valuing Equity Swap Contracts     56
     *Summary*     *61*
     *Practice Problems*     *64*
     *Solutions*     *72*

**Learning Module 2**     **Valuation of Contingent Claims**     81
     Introduction     82
         Principles of a No-Arbitrage Approach to Valuation     82
     Binomial Option Valuation Model     84
     One-Period Binomial Model     86
     Two-Period Binomial Model: Call Options     93
     Two-Period Binomial Model: Put Options     97
     Two-Period Binomial Model: Role of Dividends     101
     Interest Rate Options and Multiperiod Model     107
         Multiperiod Model     110
     Black-Scholes-Merton (BSM) Option Valuation Model     110
         Introductory Material     111
         Assumptions of the BSM Model     111
     BSM Model: Components     113
     BSM Model: Carry Benefits and Applications     117
     Black Option Valuation Model and European Options on Futures     121

*indicates an optional segment*

|  |  |
|---|---:|
| European Options on Futures | 121 |
| Interest Rate Options | 123 |
| Swaptions | 127 |
| Option Greeks and Implied Volatility: Delta | 129 |
|     Delta | 130 |
| Gamma | 133 |
| Theta | 136 |
| Vega | 137 |
| Rho | 138 |
| Implied Volatility | 139 |
| *Summary* | *143* |
| *Practice Problems* | *146* |
| *Solutions* | *153* |

# Alternative Investments

**Learning Module 1** — **Overview of Types of Real Estate Investment** — **159**

|  |  |
|---|---:|
| *Summary* | *159* |
|     General Characteristics of Real Estate | 159 |
| Introduction | 160 |
| Basic Forms of Real Estate Investment | 161 |
|     Real Estate Investment: Basic Forms | 161 |
|     Characteristics | 165 |
|     Risk Factors | 167 |
| Economic Value Drivers, Role in Portfolio, and Risk/Return of Real Estate Investments Relative to Stocks and Bonds | 173 |
|     Economic Drivers | 173 |
|     Role of Real Estate in an Investment Portfolio | 176 |
|     Real Estate Risk and Return Relative to Stocks and Bonds | 178 |
|     Classifications | 180 |
|     Investment Characteristics by Property Type | 182 |
| Considerations in Analysis and Due Diligence | 187 |
| Indexes | 190 |
|     Appraisal-Based Indexes | 190 |
|     Transaction-Based Indexes | 192 |
|     Advantages and Disadvantages of Appraisal-Based and Transaction-Based Indexes | 193 |
|     Real Estate Security Indexes | 194 |

**Learning Module 2** — **Investments in Real Estate through Private Vehicles** — **197**

|  |  |
|---|---:|
| *Summary* | *197* |
| Introduction | 198 |
| Introduction to Valuation Approaches | 198 |
|     Highest and Best Use | 200 |
| The Income Approach to Valuation: Discount Rates and the Direct Capitalization of NOI and DCF Methods | 201 |
|     Similarities in Approaches | 201 |
|     The Direct Capitalization Method | 202 |

◘ indicates an optional segment

# Contents

|  |  |
|---|---|
| The DCF Method, the Relationship between Discount Rate and Cap Rate, and the Terminal Capitalization Rate | 206 |
|     The Relationship between the Discount Rate and the Cap Rate | 206 |
|     The Terminal Capitalization Rate | 207 |
| Private Market Real Estate Debt | 212 |
| *Practice Problems* | *216* |
| *Solutions* | *218* |

## Learning Module 3    Investments in Real Estate Through Publicly Traded Securities    221

|  |  |
|---|---|
| *Summary* | *221* |
| Introduction | 222 |
| Types of Publicly Traded Real Estate Securities | 223 |
|     REIT Structures | 224 |
|     Market Size | 224 |
|     Advantages and Disadvantages of Investing in REITs | 225 |
| Valuation: Net Asset Value Approach | 228 |
|     Introduction | 228 |
|     Accounting for Investment Properties | 229 |
|     Net Asset Value per Share: Calculation | 230 |
|     Net Asset Value per Share: Application | 232 |
| Valuation: Relative Value (Price Multiple) Approach | 234 |
|     Relative Value Approach to Valuing REIT Stocks | 234 |
|     Funds from Operations (FFO) and Adjusted Funds from Operations (AFFO) | 236 |
|     P/FFO and P/AFFO Multiples: Advantages and Disadvantages | 240 |
| REIT Mini Case Study: Example of Disclosures and Valuation Analysis | 241 |
|     Selection of Valuation Methods | 247 |
| Private vs. Public: A Comparison | 249 |
| *Practice Problems* | *252* |
| *Solutions* | *254* |

## Learning Module 4    Private Equity Investments    255

|  |  |
|---|---|
| Introduction | 255 |
| Valuation Techniques in Private Equity Transactions | 257 |
|     How Is Value Created in Private Equity? | 260 |
|     Using Market Data in Valuation | 263 |
| Contrasting Venture Capital and Buyout Investments | 264 |
| LBO model for valuation of Buyout Transactions | 265 |
|     The LBO Model | 266 |
| VC Method for valuation of Venture Capital Transactions | 269 |
|     Expected Exit Valuation | 270 |
|     Required Rate of Return | 270 |
|     Option Pools | 271 |
|     Stage Financing | 271 |
| Exit Routes: Return Cash to Investors | 274 |
|     Exit Routes: Summary | 275 |
| Risks and Costs of Private Equity | 276 |
|     What Are the Risks and Costs of Investing in Private Equity? | 276 |
| Private Equity Fund Structures and Terms | 277 |

*◉ indicates an optional segment*

| | | |
|---|---|---|
| | Economic Terms | 279 |
| | Corporate Governance Terms | 280 |
| | Due Diligence Investigations by Potential Investors | 282 |
| | Private Equity Fund Valuation | 282 |
| | Evaluating a Private Equity Fund | 283 |
| | Analysis of IRR since Inception | 283 |
| | Analysis of Return Multiples | 284 |
| | Concept in Action: Evaluating Private Equity Fund Performance | 286 |
| | *Summary* | *288* |
| | *References* | *290* |
| | *Practice Problems* | *291* |
| | *Solutions* | *297* |
| **Learning Module 5** | **Introduction to Commodities and Commodity Derivatives** | **301** |
| | Introduction | 301 |
| | Commodity Sectors | 302 |
| | Commodity Sectors | 304 |
| | Life Cycle of Commodities | 306 |
| | Energy | 307 |
| | Industrial/Precious Metals | 308 |
| | Livestock | 310 |
| | Grains | 310 |
| | Softs | 311 |
| | Valuation of Commodities | 312 |
| | Commodities Futures Markets: Participants | 314 |
| | Futures Market Participants | 314 |
| | Commodity Spot and Futures Pricing | 318 |
| | Theories of Futures Returns | 322 |
| | Theories of Futures Returns | 323 |
| | Components of Futures Returns | 329 |
| | Contango, Backwardation, and the Roll Return | 333 |
| | Commodity Swaps | 336 |
| | Total Return Swap | 337 |
| | Basis Swap | 338 |
| | Variance Swaps and Volatility Swaps | 338 |
| | Commodity Indexes | 340 |
| | S&P GSCI | 342 |
| | Bloomberg Commodity Index | 342 |
| | Deutsche Bank Liquid Commodity Index | 343 |
| | Thomson Reuters/CoreCommodity CRB Index | 343 |
| | Rogers International Commodity Index | 343 |
| | Rebalancing Frequency | 343 |
| | Commodity Index Summary | 344 |
| | *Summary* | *345* |
| | *Practice Problems* | *347* |
| | *Solutions* | *355* |

◉ indicates an optional segment

# Contents

## Portfolio Management

| Learning Module 1 | **Exchange-Traded Funds: Mechanics and Applications** | **361** |
|---|---|---|
| | Introduction | 361 |
| | ETF Mechanics | 362 |
| |     The Creation/Redemption Process | 363 |
| |     Trading and Settlement | 366 |
| | Understanding ETFs | 368 |
| |     Expense Ratios | 368 |
| |     Index Tracking/Tracking Error | 369 |
| |     Tax Issues | 375 |
| |     ETF Trading Costs | 376 |
| |     Total Costs of ETF Ownership | 381 |
| | ETF Risks | 383 |
| |     Counterparty Risk | 383 |
| |     Fund Closures | 385 |
| |     Investor-Related Risk | 386 |
| | ETFs in Portfolio Management | 388 |
| |     ETF Strategies | 388 |
| |     Efficient Portfolio Management | 389 |
| |     Asset Class Exposure Management | 390 |
| |     Active and Factor Investing | 392 |
| | *Summary* | *395* |
| | *Practice Problems* | *398* |
| | *Solutions* | *403* |
| | | |
| Learning Module 2 | **Using Multifactor Models** | **407** |
| | Background and Uses | 407 |
| |     Multifactor Models and Modern Portfolio Theory | 408 |
| | Arbitrage Pricing Theory and Multifactor Models | 409 |
| | Types of Multifactor Models | 414 |
| |     Factors and Types of Multifactor Models | 415 |
| |     The Structure of Fundamental Factor Models | 415 |
| |     Fixed-Income Multifactor Models | 417 |
| | Macroeconomic Factor Models | 421 |
| | Fundamental Factor Models | 425 |
| | Factor Models in Return Attribution | 427 |
| |     Factor Models in Return Attribution | 427 |
| | Factor Models in Risk Attribution | 430 |
| | Factor Models in Portfolio Construction | 435 |
| | Factor Models in Strategic Portfolio Decisions | 440 |
| | *Summary* | *441* |
| | *References* | *443* |
| | *Practice Problems* | *444* |
| | *Solutions* | *450* |
| | | |
| Learning Module 3 | **Measuring and Managing Market Risk** | **455** |
| | Introduction | 456 |
| |     Understanding Value at Risk | 456 |

◘ indicates an optional segment

| | | |
|---|---|---|
| | Estimating VaR | 459 |
| | The Parametric Method of VaR Estimation | 462 |
| | The Historical Simulation Method of VaR Estimation | 466 |
| | The Monte Carlo Simulation Method of VaR Estimation | 469 |
| | Advantages, Limitations, and Extensions of VaR | 472 |
| |     Advantages of VaR | 473 |
| |     Limitations of VaR | 474 |
| |     Extensions of VaR | 475 |
| | Other Key Risk Measures | 478 |
| |     Sensitivity Risk Measures | 478 |
| | Scenario Risk Measures | 483 |
| |     Historical Scenarios | 483 |
| |     Hypothetical Scenarios | 485 |
| | Sensitivity and Scenario Risk Measures and VaR | 488 |
| |     Advantages and Limitations of Sensitivity Risk Measures and Scenario Risk Measures | 489 |
| | Using Constraints in Market Risk Management | 492 |
| |     Risk Budgeting | 493 |
| |     Position Limits | 494 |
| |     Scenario Limits | 495 |
| |     Stop-Loss Limits | 495 |
| |     Risk Measures and Capital Allocation | 495 |
| | Market Participants and the Risk Measures They Use | 497 |
| |     Market Participants and the Different Risk Measures They Use | 497 |
| | Pension Funds and Insurers | 503 |
| |     Insurers | 504 |
| | *Summary* | *506* |
| | *References* | *509* |
| | *Practice Problems* | *510* |
| | *Solutions* | *520* |
| **Learning Module 4** | **Backtesting and Simulation** | **525** |
| | Introduction | 525 |
| | The Objectives of Backtesting | 526 |
| | The Backtesting Process | 527 |
| |     Step 1: Strategy Design | 527 |
| |     Step 2: Historical Investment Simulation | 530 |
| |     Step 3: Analysis of Backtesting Output | 531 |
| | Backtesting Multifactor Models | 534 |
| |     Step 1: Strategy Design | 535 |
| |     Step 2: Historical Investment Simulation | 536 |
| |     Step 3: Output Analysis | 537 |
| | Common Problems in Backtesting | 544 |
| |     Survivorship Bias | 544 |
| |     Look-Ahead Bias | 547 |
| |     Data Snooping | 550 |
| | Historical Scenario Analysis | 554 |
| | Simulation Analysis | 557 |
| |     Historical Simulation | 559 |

◎ indicates an optional segment

| | |
|---|---:|
| Monte Carlo Simulation | 563 |
| Sensitivity Analysis | 567 |
| *Summary* | *573* |
| *Practice Problems* | *574* |
| *Solutions* | *580* |
| **Glossary** | **G1** |

# How to Use the CFA Program Curriculum

The CFA® Program exams measure your mastery of the core knowledge, skills, and abilities required to succeed as an investment professional. These core competencies are the basis for the Candidate Body of Knowledge (CBOK™). The CBOK consists of four components:

- A broad outline that lists the major CFA Program topic areas (www.cfainstitute.org/programs/cfa/curriculum/cbok)
- Topic area weights that indicate the relative exam weightings of the top-level topic areas (www.cfainstitute.org/programs/cfa/curriculum)
- Learning Outcomes statements (LOS) that advise candidates about the specific knowledge, skills, and abilities they should acquire from curriculum content covering a topic area: LOS are provided in candidate study sessions and at the beginning of each block of related content and the specific lesson that covers them. We encourage you to review the information about the LOS on our website (www.cfainstitute.org/programs/cfa/curriculum/study-sessions), including the descriptions of LOS "command words" on the candidate resources page at www.cfainstitute.org.
- The CFA Program curriculum that candidates receive upon exam registration

Therefore, the key to your success on the CFA exams is studying and understanding the CBOK. You can learn more about the CBOK on our website: www.cfainstitute.org/programs/cfa/curriculum/cbok.

*The entire curriculum, including the practice questions, is the basis for all exam questions and is selected or developed specifically to teach the knowledge, skills, and abilities reflected in the CBOK.*

## ERRATA

The curriculum development process is rigorous and includes multiple rounds of reviews by content experts. Despite our efforts to produce a curriculum that is free of errors, there are instances where we must make corrections. Curriculum errata are periodically updated and posted by exam level and test date online on the Curriculum Errata webpage (www.cfainstitute.org/en/programs/submit-errata). If you believe you have found an error in the curriculum, you can submit your concerns through our curriculum errata reporting process found at the bottom of the Curriculum Errata webpage.

## DESIGNING YOUR PERSONAL STUDY PROGRAM

An orderly, systematic approach to exam preparation is critical. You should dedicate a consistent block of time every week to reading and studying. Review the LOS both before and after you study curriculum content to ensure that you have mastered the applicable content and can demonstrate the knowledge, skills, and abilities described by the LOS and the assigned reading. Use the LOS self-check to track your progress and highlight areas of weakness for later review.

Successful candidates report an average of more than 300 hours preparing for each exam. Your preparation time will vary based on your prior education and experience, and you will likely spend more time on some study sessions than on others.

## CFA INSTITUTE LEARNING ECOSYSTEM (LES)

Your exam registration fee includes access to the CFA Program Learning Ecosystem (LES). This digital learning platform provides access, even offline, to all of the curriculum content and practice questions and is organized as a series of short online lessons with associated practice questions. This tool is your one-stop location for all study materials, including practice questions and mock exams, and the primary method by which CFA Institute delivers your curriculum experience. The LES offers candidates additional practice questions to test their knowledge, and some questions in the LES provide a unique interactive experience.

## FEEDBACK

Please send any comments or feedback to info@cfainstitute.org, and we will review your suggestions carefully.

# Derivatives

# LEARNING MODULE 1

## Pricing and Valuation of Forward Commitments

by Adam Schwartz, PhD, CFA.

*Adam Schwartz, PhD, CFA is at Bucknell University (USA).*

*CFA Institute would like to thank Robert Brooks, PhD, CFA and Barbara Valbuzzi, CFA for their contributions to earlier versions of this reading.*

*[handwritten note: Lots of equations to memorize in this section]*

### LEARNING OUTCOMES

| Mastery | The candidate should be able to: |
|---|---|
| ☐ | describe how equity forwards and futures are priced, and calculate and interpret their no-arbitrage value |
| ☐ | describe the carry arbitrage model without underlying cashflows and with underlying cashflows |
| ☐ | describe how interest rate forwards and futures are priced, and calculate and interpret their no-arbitrage value |
| ☐ | describe how fixed-income forwards and futures are priced, and calculate and interpret their no-arbitrage value |
| ☐ | describe how interest rate swaps are priced, and calculate and interpret their no-arbitrage value |
| ☐ | describe how currency swaps are priced, and calculate and interpret their no-arbitrage value |
| ☐ | describe how equity swaps are priced, and calculate and interpret their no-arbitrage value |

## 1. INTRODUCTION

☐ describe how equity forwards and futures are priced, and calculate and interpret their no-arbitrage value

Forward commitments include forwards, futures, and swaps. A forward contract is a promise to buy or sell an asset at a future date at a price agreed to at the contract's initiation. The forward contract has a linear payoff function, with both upside and downside risk.

A swap is essentially a promise to undertake a transaction at a set price or rate at several dates in the future. The technique we use to price and value swaps is to identify and construct a portfolio with cash flows equivalent to those of the swap. Then, we can use tools, such as the law of one price, to determine swap values from simpler financial instruments, such as a pair of bonds with a cash flow pattern similar to those of our swap.

Look out for the big picture: value additivity, arbitrage, and the law of one price are important valuation concepts.

Forwards and swaps are widely used in practice to manage a broad range of market risks. As well, more complex derivative instruments can sometimes be understood in terms of their basic building blocks: forwards and option-based components. Here are just some of the many and varied uses for forwards, futures, and swaps that you might encounter in your investment career:

- Use of equity index futures and swaps by a private wealth manager to hedge equity risk in a low tax basis, concentrated position in his high-net-worth client's portfolio.
- Use of interest rate swaps by a defined benefits plan manager to hedge interest rate risk and to manage the pension plan's duration gap.
- Use of derivatives (total return swaps, equity futures, bond futures, etc.) overlays by a university endowment for tactical asset allocation and portfolio rebalancing.
- Use of interest rate swaps by a corporate borrower to synthetically convert floating-rate debt securities to fixed-rate debt securities (or vice versa).
- Use of VIX futures and inflation swaps by a firm's market strategist to infer expectations about market volatility and inflation rates, respectively.

## Principles of Arbitrage-Free Pricing and Valuation of Forward Commitments

In this section, we examine arbitrage-free pricing and valuation of forward commitments—also known as the no-arbitrage approach to pricing and valuing such instruments. We introduce some guiding principles that heavily influence the activities of arbitrageurs, who are price setters in forward commitment markets.

There is a distinction between the pricing and the valuation of forward commitments. Forward commitment pricing involves determining the appropriate forward commitment price or rate when initiating the forward commitment contract. Forward commitment valuation involves determining the appropriate value of the forward commitment, typically after it has been initiated.

Our approach to pricing and valuation is based on the assumption that prices adjust to prevent arbitrage profits. Hence, the material will be covered from an arbitrageur's perspective. Key to understanding this material is to think like an arbitrageur. Specifically, the arbitrageur seeks to make a profit following two rules:

Rule #1: Do not use your own money; and

Rule #2: Do not take any price risk.

To make a profit, subject to these restrictions, the arbitrageur may need to borrow or lend money and buy or sell assets. The no-arbitrage approach considers the contract's cash flows from contract initiation (Time 0) to contract maturity (Time T). If an initial investment requires an outflow of 100 euros, then we will present it as a –100 euro cash flow. Cash inflows to the arbitrageur have a positive sign, and outflows are negative.

# Introduction

Pricing and valuation tasks based on the no-arbitrage approach imply an inability to create a portfolio that earns a risk-free profit without making a positive net investment of capital. In other words, if cash and forward markets are priced correctly with respect to each other, we cannot create such a portfolio. That is, we cannot create money today with no risk or future liability. This approach is built on the **law of one price**, which states that if two investments have equivalent future cash flows regardless of what will happen in the future, then these two investments should have the same current price. Alternatively, if the law of one price is violated, someone could buy the cheaper asset and sell the more expensive asset, resulting in a gain at no risk and with no commitment of capital. The law of one price can be used with the value additivity principle, which states that the value of a portfolio is simply the sum of the values of each instrument held in the portfolio.

Throughout this discussion of forward commitments, the following key assumptions are made: (1) replicating instruments are identifiable and investable; (2) market frictions are nil; (3) short selling is allowed with full use of proceeds; and (4) borrowing and lending are available at a known risk-free rate.

Our analyses will rely on the **carry arbitrage model**, a no-arbitrage approach in which the underlying instrument is either bought or sold along with establishing a forward position—hence the term "carry." Carry arbitrage models are also known as cost-of-carry arbitrage models or cash-and-carry arbitrage models. Carry arbitrage models account for costs to carry/hold the underlying asset. Carry costs include financing costs plus storage and insurance costs (for physical underlying, like gold). The carry arbitrage model must also adjust for any carry benefits (i.e., negative carry costs), including dividends and interest (such as bond coupons) received. Typically, each type of forward commitment will result in a different model, but common elements will be observed. Carry arbitrage models are a great first approximation to explaining observed forward commitment prices in many markets.

The central theme here is that forward commitments are generally priced so as to preclude arbitrage profits. Section 3 demonstrates how to price and value equity, interest rate, fixed-income, and currency forward contracts. We also explain how these results apply to futures contracts.

## Pricing and Valuing Generic Forward and Futures Contracts

In this section, we examine the pricing of forward and futures contracts based on the no-arbitrage approach. The resulting carry arbitrage models are based on the replication of the forward contract payoff with a position in the underlying that is financed through an external source. Although the margin requirements, mark-to-market features, and centralized clearing in futures markets result in material differences between forward and futures markets in some cases, we focus mainly on cases in which the particular carry arbitrage model can be used in both markets.

### Forwards and Futures

Forward and futures contracts are similar in that they are both agreements in which one party is legally obligated to sell and the other party is legally obligated to buy an asset (financial or otherwise) at an agreed price at some specific date in the future. The main difference is that a futures contract is an exchange-traded financial instrument. Contracts trading on an organized exchange, such as the Chicago Mercantile Exchange (CME), incorporate standard features to facilitate trading and ensure both parties fulfill their obligations. For example, a gold futures contract traded on the CME (COMEX) features a standard contract size of 100 ounces, agreed upon deliverable assets (gold bars, perhaps), and a limited choice of maturity dates. To ensure performance of the long and the short parties, the futures exchange requires the posting and daily maintenance of a margin account.

A forward contract is an agreement to buy or sell a specific asset (financial or otherwise) at an agreed price at some specific date in the future. Forward contracts are bilateral non-exchange traded contracts, offering flexibility in terms of size, type of the underlying asset, expiration date, and settlement date. This customization comes at a price of potential credit risk and ability to unwind the position. Since the financial crisis, best practices for OTC contracts suggest daily settlement and margin requirements for forward contracts similar to those required by futures exchanges. Without daily settlement, a forward contract may accumulate (or may lose) value over time. Some of the differences and similarities between forwards and futures are summarized in Exhibit 1.

**Exhibit 1: Characteristics of Futures and Forward Contracts**

| Futures | Forwards |
|---|---|
| Exchange-traded | Negotiated between the contract counterparties |
| Standardized dates and deliverables | Customized dates and deliverables |
| Trades guaranteed by a clearinghouse | Trading subject to counterparty risk |
| Initial value = 0 | Initial value = 0 (Typically, but not required) |
| An initial margin deposit specified by the exchange is required. The margin account is adjusted for gains and losses daily. If daily losses cause the margin balance to drop below a limit set by the futures exchange (i.e., maintenance margin), additional funds must be deposited, or the position will be closed. | Margin requirements may be specified by the counterparties. |
| Daily settlement marks the contract price equal to the market price and contract value = 0. | Contract may outline a settlement schedule. The forward may accumulate (or lose) value between settlement periods or until maturity (if no early settlements are required). |

**Forward price** (F) or **futures price** (f) refers to the price that is negotiated between the parties to the forward or futures contract, respectively.

Our notation will be as follows, let:

$S_t$ represent spot price (cash price for immediate delivery) of the underlying instrument at any time t,

$F_t$ represent forward price at any time t, and

$f_t$ represent futures price at any time t.

Therefore, $S_0$, $F_0$, and $f_0$ denote, respectively, the spot, forward, and futures price, respectively, established at the initiation date, 0. The initial forward price is established to make the contract value zero for both the long and short parties. The forward (delivery) price does not change during the life of the contract. Time T represents the time at which the contract expires and the future transaction is scheduled to take place. Thus, $S_T$, $F_T$, and $f_T$ are the spot, forward, and futures price, respectively, at expiration time T. Between initiation at time 0 and expiration at time T, the spot price of the underlying asset may fluctuate to a new value, $S_t$. The price of a newly created forward or futures contract at time t with the same underlying and expiration (at time T) may differ from the price agreed to at time 0. So, our forward or futures contract established at time 0 may have a positive or negative value at time t. $V_t$ and $v_t$ will later be used to describe, respectively, the value of a forward and futures contract at any time t.

As we approach expiration, the price of a newly created forward or futures contract will approach the price of a spot transaction. At expiration, a forward or futures contract is equivalent to a spot transaction in the underlying. This property is often called **convergence**, and it implies that at time T, both the forward price and the futures price are equivalent to the spot price—that is,

Convergence property: $F_T = f_T = S_T$.

The convergence property is intuitive. For example, the one-year forward price of gold (that is, the price set today to purchase gold one year from now) might be very different from the spot price of gold. However, the price to buy gold one hour in the future should be very close to the spot price. As the maturity of the forward or futures contract approaches, the forward or futures price will converge to the spot price. If the forward or futures price were higher than the spot at maturity, an arbitrageur would:

1. Sell the forward or futures contract.
2. Borrow funds using a loan to buy the asset.
3. Make delivery at expiration of the contract, repay the loan, and keep the profit.

As market participants exploit this arbitrage opportunity, the forward or futures price will fall due to selling pressure.

If the futures price is below spot price, an arbitrageur would short sell the asset, invest the short-sale proceeds at the risk-free rate, and then enter into a long futures contract. He or she would take delivery of the asset at the futures contract expiration and use it to cover the short. The profit is simply the difference between the short-sale price and the futures price, after adjusting for carrying and financing costs. These actions on the part of arbitrageurs would act to enforce the convergence property.

Prior to expiration, the price of a newly created futures or forward contract will usually differ from the spot price. The forward and futures prices may even differ slightly from each other. For example, when the possibility of counterparty default exists or when the underlying asset price (such as a bond) is correlated with interest rates (which might impact the financing costs for daily settlement), the futures price might vary slightly from the forward price. For most cases, the generalist may assume the price of a futures contract and a forward contract will be same. That is $F_t = f_t$ before expiration.

Exhibit 2 shows the convergence property for a stock index futures/forward contact under continuous compounding and varying dividend yields. To carry a stock index, we must forego the interest rate that could be otherwise earned on our money, but we will collect dividend payments. As shown in Exhibit 2, the convergence path to the spot price at maturity depends on the costs and benefits of carrying the underlying asset. Here the stock index pays a dividend yield, which is a carry benefit. To hold the stock index, we must forego interest that could otherwise be earned on the investment. This financing rate (interest rate, $r_c$), assumed to be 2% in the following graph, is a cost to carry the index.

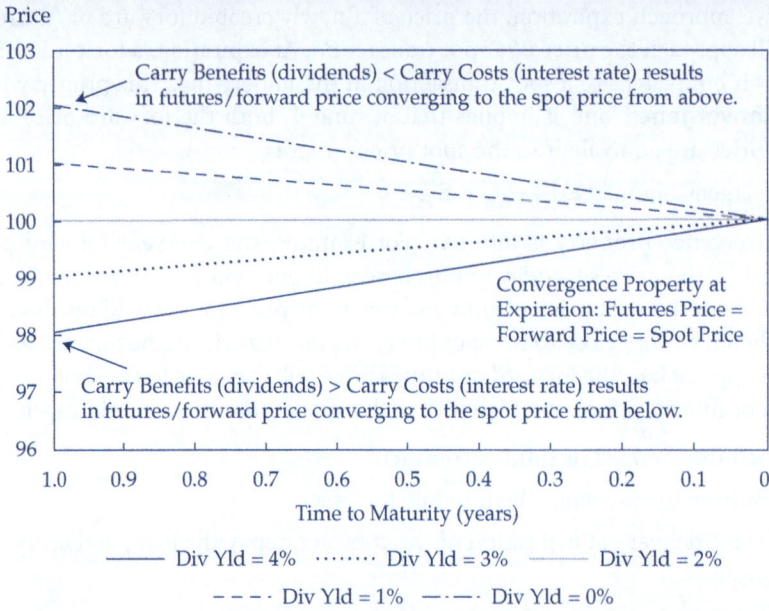

Exhibit 2: Convergence Property: Convergence of Forward Price to Spot Price ($r_c = 2\%$ and Index Level = 100)

As maturity of the contract approaches (at time = T), the price of a newly created forward or futures contract will approach the spot price so that at expiration $F_T = f_T = S_T$, according to the convergence property. Prior to expiration, the forward/futures prices may be above, below, or nearly equal to the current spot price $S_t$. For futures contracts, the difference between the spot price and the futures price is the **basis**. As the maturity date nears, the basis converges toward zero. According to the convergence property, the future price approaches the spot price as we move toward expiration. At expiration, the futures price is equal to the price today for delivery today (i.e., spot price). If the convergence property does not hold, arbitrage will force the prices to be equal at contract expiration. The nature of the pricing relationship between the spot and forward/futures prices shown here will be explained shortly using the carry arbitrage model. For example, carry arbitrage will help us understand why assets with carry benefits (dividends) greater than carry costs (costs to finance and store the underlying) will have forward prices that converge to the spot price from below.

As market prices change, the value of existing futures and forward positions will change also. The market value of the forward or futures contract, termed **forward value** or **futures value**, respectively, and sometimes just value, refers to the monetary value of an existing forward or futures contract. When the forward or futures contract is established, the price is negotiated so that the value of the contract on the initiation date is zero. Subsequent to the initiation date, the value can be significantly positive or negative.

For example, an industrial firm requires platinum to manufacture certain components used in automobile manufacturing. The firm enters a long forward contract on 10 March. Under the terms of the contract, the firm agrees to buy 4,500 ounces of platinum on 10 September for $900 per ounce from a metal producer. From the firm's point of view, this is effectively a six-month long forward contract at a price of $F_0 = \$900$. If the price (technically, the September forward price) of platinum increases to $1,100 in May, the firm will be happy to have locked in a purchase price of $900 (long forward contract value is positive). If the price of platinum decreases to $800, the firm must still honor the forward agreement to buy platinum at $900 (long forward contract value is negative). To describe the value of a forward contract, let $V_t$ be the value of the forward contract at any time t.

When the forward contract is established, the forward price is negotiated so that the market value of the forward contract on the initiation date is zero. Most forward contracts are structured this way and are referred to as **at market contracts**. Again, we assume no margin requirements. No money changes hands, meaning that the initial value is zero, so, $V_0 = 0$.

At expiration, the value of a forward contract $V_T$ is realized and, as shown next, is straightforward to compute. Remember, the profit on any completed transaction is the sale price minus the purchase price. The profit or value of the forward contract at expiration is also the sale price minus the purchase price. At initiation, a forward or futures contract allows for either a future purchase price or a future sale price, $F_0$, to be known at time 0. In a long forward, a buyer can lock in a purchase price, $F_0$. In a short forward, a seller can lock in a sale price, $F_0$. Again, a forward contract allows a buyer or a seller to fix an initial price $F_0$, either the purchase price (long forward) or the sale price (short forward). The party long the forward effectively agrees to buy an asset in the future (at time T) at a price set today (at time 0), $F_0$.

At expiration, the asset can be sold in the spot market at a price $S_T$. Therefore, a *long* position in a forward contract has a value at expiration of:

$$V_T = S_T - F_0.$$

A short position effectively locks in a sale price of $F_0$. It is the negative of the long position. Therefore, the value of a short forward position at expiration is the sale price minus the purchase price of the asset:

$$-V_T = -(S_T - F_0) = F_0 - S_T.$$

For example, in January a fund manager agrees to sell a bond portfolio in May for $F_0$ = £10,000,000. The fund manager locks in the sale price, $F_0$. If the spot price of the bond portfolio at expiration ($S_T$) is £9,800,000, then the short forward contract will have an expiration value to the fund manager of:

$$-V_T = £10,000,000 - £9,800,000 = £200,000.$$

The fund manager makes a profit by selling at a higher price than the market price at expiration.

Value may accumulate or diminish with the passage of time in forward contracts, which is why forward contracts require the posting of collateral. Futures contract values, on the other hand, are settled by margining at the end of each trading day when the contract is marked-to-market. The gains and losses in the position over time accumulate in the futures traders' margin accounts. Prior to daily settlement, during the trading hours the market value of a long position in a futures contract is the current futures price less the future price at the last time the contract was marked-to-market times the multiplier, $N_f$ (the multiplier is the standard contract size set by the futures exchange).

For a long futures contract, the value accumulated during the trading day ($v_t$) is:

$$v_t = \text{Multiplier} \times (\text{Current futures price} - \text{Previous settlement price}) \text{ or}$$

$$v_t = N_f \times (f_t - f_{t-1}).$$

Assume an investor is long one contract ($N_f$ = 100 ounces/contract) of June gold, which settled at $1,300/ounce on the previous trading day. So, the investor is effectively agreeing to purchase 100 ounces of gold in June for $1,300 per ounce or $130,000 total. The trader need not pay the entire $130,000 today but must post a deposit in a margin account to guarantee his/her performance. During the current trading day, the price of June gold increases to $1,310. Before marking-to-market, the value of the long contract is 100 × ($1,310 − $1,300) = +$1,000. After marking-to-market, the gain or loss is reflected in the trader's margin account and the new contract price is set equal to the settlement price. The futures contract value after daily settlement is 0 or $v_t = 0$.

## 2. CARRY ARBITRAGE

 describe the carry arbitrage model without underlying cashflows and with underlying cashflows

We first consider a generic forward contract, meaning that we do not specify the underlying as anything more than just an asset. As we move through this section, we will continue to address specific additional factors to bring each carry arbitrage model closer to real markets. Thus, we will develop several different carry arbitrage models, each one applicable to a specific forward commitment contract. We start with the simpler of the two base cases, carry of an asset without cash flows to the underlying, then move to the more complex case of forwards on assets with underlying cash flows, such as bonds with coupon payments or stocks that pay dividends.

### Carry Arbitrage Model When There Are No Underlying Cash Flows

Carry arbitrage models receive their name from the literal interpretation of carrying the underlying asset over the life of the forward contract. If an arbitrageur enters a forward contract to sell an underlying instrument for delivery at time T, then to offset this exposure, one strategy is to buy the underlying instrument at time 0 with borrowed funds and carry it to the forward expiration date (time T). The asset can then be sold (or even delivered) under the terms of a forward contract. The risks of this scenario are illustrated in Exhibit 3.

**Exhibit 3: Cash Flows from Carrying an Underlying Asset and Offsetting Short Forward Position**

|  | Time 0 | Time T |
|---|---|---|
| **Borrowing Funds to Purchase and Carry an Underlying Asset** | | |
| Underlying | $-S_0$ (purchase) | $+S_T$ (sale) |
| Borrowed funds | $+S_0$ (inflow) | $-FV(S_0)$ (repayment) |
| Net Cash Flow | $+S_0 - S_0 = 0$ | $+S_T - FV(S_0)$ |
| **Short Forward Position** | | |
| Short Forward | $V_0 = 0$ | $V_T = F_0 - S_T$ |
| **Overall Position: Long Asset + Borrowed Funds + Short Forward** | | |
|  | $+S_0 - S_0 + V_0 = 0$ | $+S_T - FV(S_0) + V_T = 0$ |
|  |  | $+S_T - FV(S_0) + (F_0 - S_T) = 0$ |
|  |  | $+F_0 - FV(S_0) = 0$ |
| **Net** | 0 | $F_0 = FV(S_0)$ |

The underlying asset is bought for $S_0$ with borrowed funds. The asset can be sold at time T for a price, $S_T$. At time T, the borrowed funds must be repaid at a cost of $FV(S_0)$; note that FV stands for the future value function. Clearly, when $S_T$ is below (above) $FV(S_0)$, our underlying transaction will suffer a loss (earn a profit). A short forward position can be added to our long position in the underlying asset to offset any profit or loss in the underlying. Both positions have no initial (time 0) cash flow. To prevent arbitrage, the overall portfolio (Asset + Borrowed funds + Short forward) should have a value of zero at time T. If the cost to finance the purchase of the asset, $FV(S_0)$, is equal to the initially agreed upon forward price, $F_0$, then there is no arbitrage profit. So, we should have $F_0 = FV(S_0)$.

For now, we will keep the significant technical issues to a minimum. When possible, we will just use FV and PV to denote future value and present value, respectively. At this point we are not yet concerned about compounding conventions, day count conventions, or even the appropriate risk-free interest rate proxy.

Carry arbitrage models rest on the no-arbitrage assumptions. Therefore, the arbitrageur does not use his or her own money to acquire positions but borrows to purchase the underlying. Borrowing (if the underlying asset is purchased) and lending the proceeds (if the underlying asset is sold) are done at the risk-free interest rate. Furthermore, the arbitrageur offsets all transactions, meaning he/she does not take any price risk. We do not consider other risks, such as liquidity risk and counterparty credit risk, as they would unnecessarily complicate our basic presentation.

If we assume continuous compounding ($r_c$), then $FV(S_0) = S_0 \exp^{r_c T}$. If we assume annual compounding (r), then $FV(S_0) = S_0(1 + r)^T$. Note that in practice, observed interest rates are derived from market prices. For example, a T-bill price implies the T-bill rate. Significant errors can occur if the quoted interest rate is used with the wrong compounding convention. When possible, we just use basic present value and future value representations to minimize confusion.

To help clarify, we first illustrate the price exposure solely from holding the underlying asset. Exhibit 4 shows the cash flows from carrying the underlying, a non-dividend-paying stock, assuming $S_0 = 100$, $r = 5\%$, and $T = 1$. For illustration purposes, we allow the stock price at expiration to go down to $S_T^- = 90$ or up to $S_T^+ = 110$. The initial transactions will generate cash flows shown at times 0 and T. In practice, the set of transactions (market purchases, bank transactions) are executed simultaneously at each time period, not sequentially. Here are the two transactions at time 0 that produce a levered equity purchase.

Step 1    Purchase one unit of the underlying at time 0 (an outflow).

Step 2    Borrow the purchase price at the risk-free rate (an inflow).

### Exhibit 4: Cash Flows for Long Financial Position

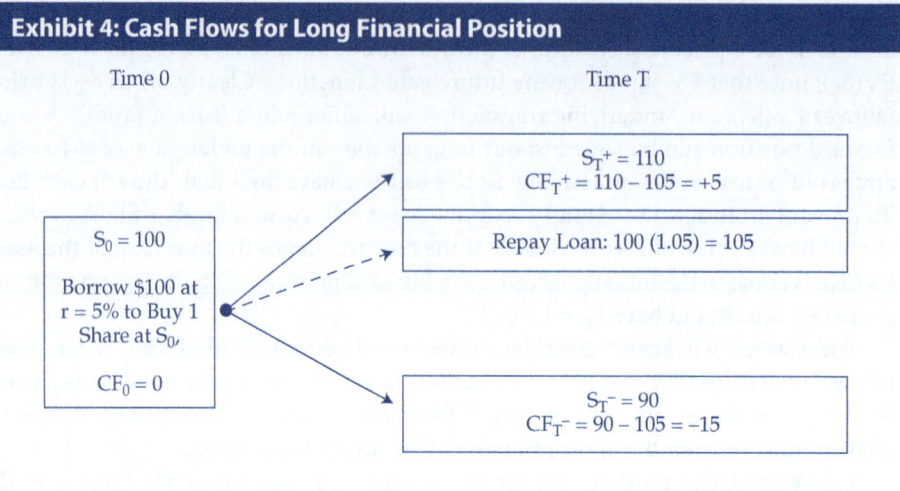

At time T (= 1), the stock price can jump up to $S_T^+ = 110$ or jump down to $S_T^- = 90$. Because the two outcomes are different, the strategy at this point has price risk. After the loan is repaid, the net cash flow will be +5 if the stock jumps up to 110 or −15 if the stock price jumps down to 90. To eliminate price risk, we must add another step to our list of simultaneous transactions. As suggested by Exhibit 3, we sell (go short) a forward contract to set a price today for the future sale of our underlying, and that price ($F_0 = FV(S_0)$) is 105.

Step 1      Sell a forward at $F_0 = 105$. For a short forward contract, $F_0$ is the price agreed to at time 0 to sell the asset at Time T.

The resulting portfolio with its offsetting transaction is illustrated in Exhibit 5.

### Exhibit 5: Cash Flow for Long Financial Position with Short Forward Contract

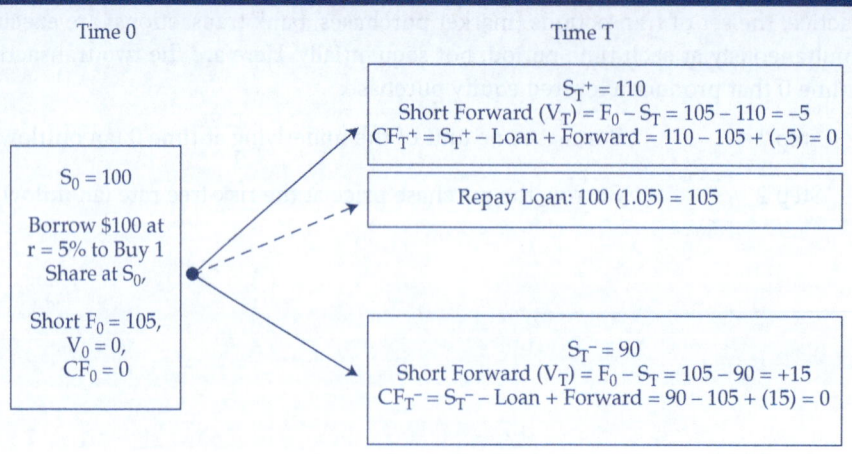

Regardless of the value of the underlying at maturity, we owe 105 on the loan. Notice that at expiration the underlying is worth 90 or 110. Since we agreed to sell the asset at 105, the forward contract value is either 15 or −5, respectively. If the asset is selling for 90 at time T, the forward contract allows us to sell our underlying position for 15 more (105 − 90) than in the spot market. The combination of the proceeds from the sale of the underlying and the value of the short forward at maturity is always 105 (=

## Carry Arbitrage

90 + 15 or 110 − 5), which is precisely the amount necessary to pay off the loan. So, there is zero net cash flow at expiration under any and all circumstances. Since this transaction has no risk (no uncertainty about value at time T), we require that the no-arbitrage forward price ($F_0$) is simply the future value of the underlying growing at the risk-free rate, or

$$F_0 = \text{Future value of underlying} = FV(S_0). \qquad (1)$$

In our example, $F_0 = FV(S_0) = 105$. In fact, with annual compounding and T = 1, we have simply $F_0 = S_0(1 + r)^T = 100(1 + 0.05)^1$. The future value refers to the amount of money equal to the spot price invested at the compounded risk-free interest rate during the time period. It is not to be confused with or mistaken for the mathematical expectation of the spot price at time T.

Without market frictions, arbitrage may be possible when mispricing occurs. To better understand the arbitrage mechanics, suppose that $F_0 = 106$. Based on the prior information, we observe that the forward price is higher than the price suggested by the carry arbitrage model—recall $F_0 = FV(S_0) = 105$. Because the carry arbitrage model value is lower than the market's forward price, we conclude that the market's forward price is too high and should be sold. An arbitrage opportunity exists, and it will involve selling the forward contract at 106 (Step 1). Step 2 occurs when a second transaction is needed to borrow funds to undertake Step 3, purchase of the underlying instrument so that gains (or losses) in the underlying will offset losses (or gains) on the forward contract. Note, the second step ensures the arbitrageur does not use his or her own money. The third transaction, the purchase of the underlying security, guarantees the arbitrageur does not take any market price risk. Note that all three transactions are done simultaneously. To summarize, the arbitrage transactions for $F_0 > FV(S_0)$ can be represented in the following three steps:

Step 1     Sell the forward contract on the underlying.

Step 2     Borrow the funds to purchase the underlying.

Step 3     Purchase the underlying.

Exhibit 6 shows the resulting cash flows from these transactions. This strategy is known as carry arbitrage because we are carrying—that is, we are long—the underlying instrument. At time T, we earn an arbitrage profit of +1. We do not use any of our own money and make a profit no matter the price of the underlying at maturity (i.e., 110, 90, or anything else). Since the profit of +1 at maturity occurs under every circumstance, it is considered risk-free. Any situation that allows a risk-free profit with no upfront cost will not be available for very long. It represents a clear arbitrage opportunity, one that will be pursued until forward prices fall and eliminate the arbitrage opportunity.

Note that if the forward price, $F_0$, were 106, the value of the forward contract at time 0 would be the PV of the +1 cash flow at Time T. Thus, at time 0, the value of our short forward is $V_0 = PV[F_0 − FV(S_0)] = (106 − 105)/(1 + 0.05)^1 = 0.9524$.

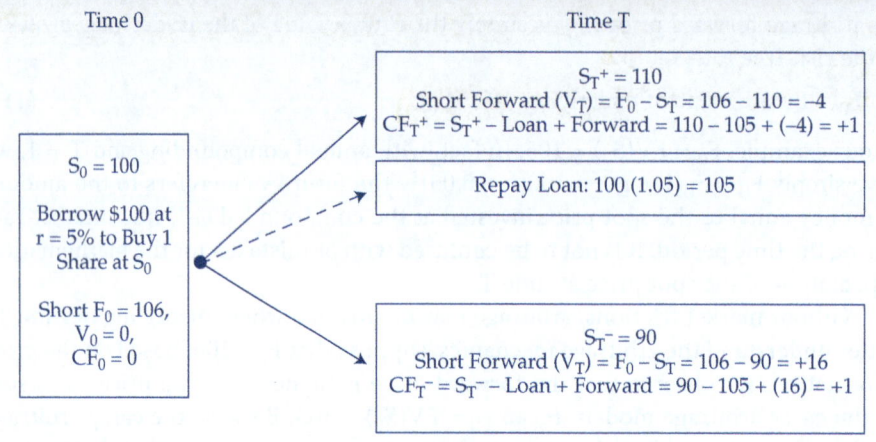

Exhibit 6: Cash Flow with Forward Price Greater Than Carry Arbitrage Model Price

Suppose instead we observe a lower forward price, $F_0 = 104$. Based on the prior information, we conclude that the forward price is too low when compared to the forward price determined by the carry arbitrage model of $F_0 = FV(S_0) = 105$. Since the forward price is too low, Step 1 is to buy the forward contract, and the value at T is $S_T - F_0$. The arbitrageur does not want any price risk, so Step 2 is to sell short the underlying instrument. To accomplish Step 2, we must borrow the asset and sell it. Note that when an arbitrageur needs to sell the underlying, it must be assumed that he/she does not hold it in inventory and thus must sell it short. If the underlying were held in inventory, the investment in it would not be accounted for in the analysis. When the transaction calls for selling a derivative instrument, such as a forward contract, it is always just selling—technically, not short selling.

The long forward contract will allow us to cover our short later. The arbitrageur will then lend the short sale proceeds of 100 at the risk-free rate (Step 3). The deposit of 100 will grow to 105 at time T. Clearly, we will have a profit of +1 when we buy the asset at 104 and deliver it to clear the short. Again, to summarize, the arbitrage transactions when the forward price is too low—that is, $F_0 < FV(S_0)$—involve the following three steps:

Step 1  Buy the forward contract on the underlying.

Step 2  Sell the underlying short.

Step 3  Lend the short sale proceeds.

We must replace the asset at a price of $S_T$, but we have +105 from the loan and a long forward at 104. Remember, the value of a long forward at time T is $V_T = S_T - F_0$. So, using the prior information, the value of the forward at expiration will be $90 - 104 = -14$ (if $S_T^- = 90$) or $110 - 104 = +6$ (if $S_T^+ = 110$). Thus, the cash flows at maturity will be $CF^- = +105 - 14 - 90 = +1$ or $CF^+ = +105 + 6 - 110 = +1$. Again, we make a profit equal to the mispricing of +1 regardless of the stock value at time T. It is an arbitrage profit, since it was done with no money invested and with no risk.

Note that this set of transactions is the exact opposite of the prior case in Exhibit 6. This strategy is known as **reverse carry arbitrage** because we are doing the opposite of carrying the underlying instrument; that is, we are selling short the underlying instrument.

Therefore, unless $F_0 = FV(S_0)$, there is an arbitrage opportunity. Notice that if $F_0 > FV(S_0)$, then the forward contract is sold and the underlying is purchased. Thus, arbitrageurs drive down the forward price and drive up the underlying price until $F_0 = FV(S_0)$ and a risk-free positive cash flow today (i.e., in PV terms) no longer exists. Further, if $F_0 < FV(S_0)$, then the forward contract is purchased and the underlying is sold short. In this case, the forward price is driven up and the underlying price is driven down. Absent market frictions, arbitrageurs' market activities will drive forward prices to equal the future value of the underlying, bringing the law of one price into effect once again. Most importantly, if the forward contract is priced at its equilibrium price, there will be no arbitrage profit.

### EXAMPLE 1

#### Forward Contract Price

An Australian stock paying no dividends is trading in Australian dollars for A$63.31, and the annual Australian interest rate is 2.75% with annual compounding.

1. Based on the current stock price and the no-arbitrage approach, which of the following values is *closest* to the equilibrium three-month forward price?

    A. A$63.31

    B. A$63.74

    C. A$65.05

#### Solution to 1:

B is correct. Based on the information given, $S_0$ = A$63.31, r = 2.75% (annual compounding), and T = 0.25. Therefore,

$F_0 = FV(S_0) = 63.31(1 + 0.0275)^{0.25}$ = A$63.7408.

2. If the interest rate immediately falls 50 bps to 2.25%, the three-month forward price will:

    A. decrease.

    B. increase.

    C. be unchanged.

#### Solution to 2:

A is correct, because the forward price is directly related to the interest rate. Specifically,

$F_0 = FV(S_0) = 63.31(1 + 0.0225)^{0.25}$ = A$63.6632.

Therefore, we see in this case that a decrease in interest rates resulted in a decrease in the forward price. This relationship between forward prices and interest rates will generally hold so long as the underlying is not also influenced by interest rates.

As we see in Example 1, the quoted forward price does not directly reflect expectations of future underlying prices. The only factors that matter are the current price ($S_0$), the interest rate and time to expiration, and, of course, the absence of arbitrage. Other factors will be included later as we make the carry arbitrage model more realistic, but we will not be including expectations of future underlying prices. So, if we can carry the asset, an opinion that the underlying will increase in value, perhaps even substantially, has no bearing on the forward price.

We now turn to the task of understanding the value of an existing forward contract. There are many circumstances in which, once a forward contract has been entered, one wants to know the contract's fair value. The goal is to calculate the position's value at current market prices. The need may arise from market-based accounting, for example, in which the accounting statements need to reflect the current fair value of various instruments. Finally, it is simply important to know whether a position in a forward contract is making money or losing money (that is, the profit or loss from exiting the contract early).

The forward value prior to maturity is based on arbitrage. A timeline to help illustrate forward valuation is shown in Exhibit 7. Suppose the first transaction involves buying a forward contract with a price of $F_0$ at Time 0 with expiration at Time T. Now consider selling a new forward contract with price $F_t$ at Time t, again with expiration at Time T. Exhibit 7 shows the potential cash flows. Remember the equivalence at expiration between the forward price, the futures price, and the underlying price will hold: $F_T = f_T = S_T$. Note that the middle of the timeline, "Time t" is the valuation date of the forward contract. Note also that we are seeking the forward value; therefore, this set of transactions would result in cash flows only if it is executed. We need not actually execute the transactions; we just need to see what they would produce if we did. This point is analogous to the fact that if we are holding a liquid asset, we need not sell it to determine its value; we can simply observe its market price, which gives us an estimate of the price at which we could sell the asset.

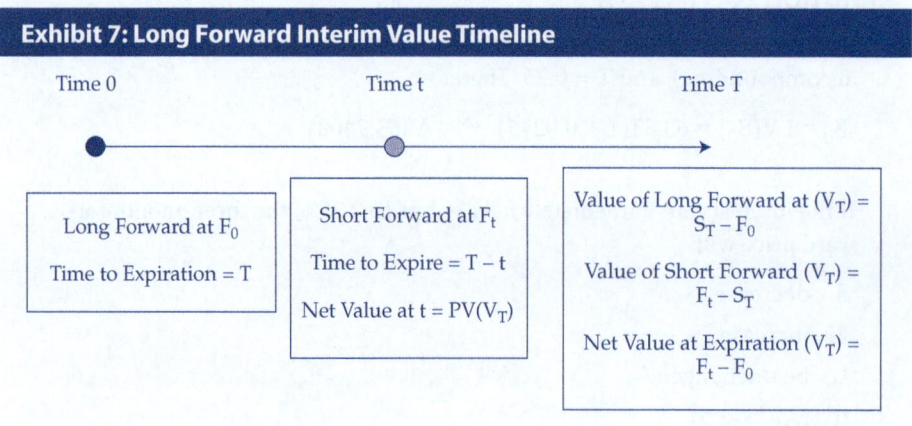

**Exhibit 7: Long Forward Interim Value Timeline**

Importantly, there are now three different points in time to consider: Time 0, Time t, and Time T. Note that once the offsetting forward is entered at time t, the net position is not subject to market risk. That is, the $S_T$ terms cancel (in Exhibit 7), so the cash flow at Time T is not influenced by what happens to the spot price. The position is completely hedged. Therefore, the value observed at Time t of the original forward contract initiated at Time 0 and expiring at Time T is simply the present value of the difference in the forward prices, $PV(F_t - F_0)$, at Time t. To be clear, the PV discounts the time T cash flow at the risk-free rate, r, to Time t. Equation 2 shows the long forward value at time t under annual compounding.

Value of Long Forward Contract Prior to Maturity (Time t) =

$V_t$ (long) = Present value of the difference in forward prices:

# Carry Arbitrage

$$V_t = PV[F_t - F_0] = \frac{[F_t - F_0]}{(1+r)^{T-t}}, \quad (2)$$

where $F_t$ is the current forward price and $F_0$ is the initial forward price.

Alternatively,

$$V_t = S_t - PV[F_0] = S_t - \frac{F_0}{(1+r)^{T-t}}. \quad (3)$$

Equation 3 can be derived from Equation 2. Assuming annual compounding,

$$F_t = S_t(1+r)^{(T-t)}, \text{ so } PV[F_t] = PV[S_t(1+r)^{(T-t)}]$$
$$= S_t(1+r)^{(T-t)} / (1+r)^{(T-t)} = S_t.$$

While both are correct, Equation 2 may be useful in cases when market frictions may cause the observed forward price, $F_t$, to differ slightly from the correct arbitrage-free price. Equation 3 may be more intuitive and has the advantage that the spot price, $S_t$, may be more readily observed than the forward price, $F_t$.

As in Equation 2, the long forward contract value can be viewed as the present value, determined using the given interest rate, of the difference in forward prices—the initial one and the new one that is priced at the point of valuation. If we know the underlying price at Time t, $S_t$, we can estimate the forward price, $F_t = FV(S_t)$, and we can then solve for the forward value as in Equation 2.

The interim valuation of a short forward contract is determined in a similar fashion. The short position value is also the present value of differences in forward prices and simply the negative of the long position value. So that,

Value of short forward contract prior to maturity (Time t) = $-V_t$

$$-V_t = PV[F_0 - F_t] = \frac{[F_0 - F_t]}{(1+r)^{T-t}},$$

or alternatively,

$$= PV[F_0] - S_t = \frac{F_0}{(1+r)^{T-t}} - S_t$$

### EXAMPLE 2

#### Forward Contract Value

1. Assume that at Time 0 we entered into a one-year long forward contract with price $F_0 = 105$. Nine months later, at Time t = 0.75, the observed price of the underlying stock is $S_{0.75} = 110$ and the interest rate is 5%. The value of the existing forward contract expiring in three months will be *closest* to:

   A. −6.34.
   B. 6.27.
   C. 6.34.

   **Solution:**

   B is correct. Note that, $S_{0.75} = 110$, r = 5%, and T − t = 0.25.

   Therefore, the three-month forward price at Time t is equal to $F_t = FV(S_t) = 110(1 + 0.05)^{0.25} = 111.3499$.

   Based on $F_0 = 105$, we find that the value of the existing forward entered at Time 0 and valued at Time t using the difference method (Equation 2) is:

> $V_t = PV[F_t - F_0] = (111.3499 - 105)/(1 + 0.05)^{0.25} = 6.2729.$
>
> Alternatively, using Equation 3 we have,
>
> $V_t = S_t - PV[F_0] = 110 - [105/(1 + 0.05)^{0.25}] = 6.2729.$

Now that we have the basics of forward pricing and forward valuation, we introduce some other realistic carrying costs that influence pricing and valuation.

## Carry Arbitrage Model When Underlying Has Cash Flows

We have seen that forward pricing and valuation are driven by arbitrageurs seeking to exploit mispricing by either carrying or reverse carrying the underlying instrument. Carry arbitrage, when $F_0 > FV(S_0)$, requires paying the interest cost from borrowing to fund purchase of the underlying, whereas reverse carry arbitrage, when $F_0 < FV(S_0)$, results in receiving the interest benefit from lending the proceeds from short-selling the underlying. For many instruments, there are other significant carry costs and benefits. We will now incorporate into forward pricing various costs and benefits related to the underlying instrument. For this reason, we need to introduce some notation.

Let CB denote the **carry benefits**: cash flows the owner might receive for holding the underlying assets (e.g., dividends, foreign currency interest, and bond coupon payments). Let $CB_T$ denote the future value of underlying carry benefits at time T and $CB_0$ denote the present value at time 0 of underlying carry benefits. Let CC denote the **carry costs**. For financial instruments, carry costs are essentially zero. For commodities, however, carrying costs include such factors as waste, storage, and insurance. Let $CC_T$ denote the future value of underlying carry costs at time T and $CC_0$ denote the present value of underlying carry costs at time 0. We do not cover commodities in this reading, but you should be aware of these costs. Moreover, you should note that carry costs are similar to financing costs. Holding a financial asset does not generate direct carry costs, but it does result in the opportunity cost of the interest that could be earned on the money tied up in carrying the spot asset. Remember, the financing costs at the risk-free rate are included in the calculation of $F_0 = FV[S_0]$. Other carrying costs that are common to physical assets (such as storage and insurance) are equivalent concepts. For example, to buy and hold gold, money is taken out of the bank (opportunity cost = r, the risk-free rate) to purchase the asset, and money must be paid to store and insure it. The cost to finance the spot asset purchase, the cost to store it, and any benefits that may result from holding the asset will all play a part in determination of the forward price.

The key forward pricing equation can be expressed as:

$F_0$ = Future value of the underlying adjusted for carry cash flows

$$= FV[S_0 + CC_0 - CB_0] \quad (4)$$

Equation 4 relates the forward price of an asset to the spot price by considering the cost of carry. It is sometimes referred to as the **cost of carry model** or future-spot parity. Carry costs and a positive rate of interest increase the burden of carrying the underlying instrument through time; hence, these costs are added in the forward pricing equation. Conversely, carry benefits decrease the burden of carrying the underlying instrument through time; hence, these benefits are subtracted in the forward pricing equation.

Based on Equation 4, $F_0 = FV(S_0 + CC_0 - CB_0)$, if there are no explicit carry costs ($CC_0 = 0$) as with many financial assets, then we have:

$F_0 = FV(S_0) - FV(CB_0) = FV(S_0) - FV(Benefits).$

# Carry Arbitrage

For a stock paying a dividend (D), a benefit, prior to maturity of the forward contract, we have the forward contract price ($F_0$):

$$F_0 = FV(S_0 - PV(D)) = FV(S_0) - FV(D).$$

In words, the initial forward price ($F_0$) is equal to the future value of carrying the underlying ($S_0$) minus the future value of any ownership benefits, (FV(D)), for a dividend paying stock, prior to expiration. Note the FV computation for the stock price will likely use a different time period than the FV computation for the dividends. This is because the dividend FV is only compounded from the time the dividend is collected until the expiration of the forward contract. So, FV(PV(D)) for a dividend collected at time t and held to expiration at time T would be $FV(PV(D)) = FV(D/(1+r)^t) = (1+r)^T \times [(D/(1+r)^t] = D(1+r)^{T-t}$. The calculation of $F_0$ for a dividend paying stock is illustrated in Example 3.

### EXAMPLE 3

#### Forward Contract Price with Underlying Cash Flows

A US stock paying a $10 dividend in two months is trading at $1,000. Assume the US interest rate is 5% with annual compounding.

1. Based on the current stock price and the no-arbitrage approach, which of the following values is *closest* to the equilibrium three-month forward price?

   A. $1,002.23
   B. $1,022.40
   C. $1,025.31

#### Solution to 1:

A is correct. Based on the information given, we know $S_0$ = $1,000, r = 5% (annual compounding), and T = 0.25. After 2 months, we will receive the benefit of a $10 dividend, which earns interest for 1 month. Therefore,

$$F_0 = FV(S_0) - FV(D) = 1,000(1 + 0.05)^{3/12} - 10(1 + 0.05)^{1/12}$$

$$= \$1,012.2722 - \$10.0407 = \$1,002.2315.$$

Using Equation 4, we could have arrived at the same result. Here $CC_0 = 0$, and $CB_0$ is the PV of the dividend at time 0 = $10/(1 + 0.05)^{2/12}$ = $9.919. Then,

$$F_0 = FV(S_0 + CC_0 - CB_0) = FV(1,000 + 0 - 9.919)$$

$$= (990.081) \times (1 + 0.05)^{3/12} = \$1,002.23.$$

2. If the dividend is instead paid in one month, the three-month forward price will:

   A. decrease.
   B. increase.
   C. be unchanged.

### Solution to 2:

A is correct. The benefit of the dividend occurs one month earlier, so we can collect interest for one additional month. The future value of the dividend would be slightly higher. So, the forward price would decrease slightly,

$$F_0 = FV(S_0) - FV(D) = 1,000(1 + 0.05)^{3/12} - 10(1 + 0.05)^{2/12}$$

$$= \$1,012.2722 - \$10.0816 = \$1,002.1906.$$

The value for a long forward position when the underlying has carry benefits or carry costs is found in the same way as described previously except that the new forward price ($F_t$), as well as the initial one ($F_0$), are adjusted to account for these benefits and costs. Specifically,

$V_t$ = Present value of the difference in forward prices adjusted for carry benefits and costs

$$= PV[F_t - F_0].$$

This equation is Equation 2. The forward value is equal to the present value of the difference in forward prices. The PV discounts the risk-free cash flow $[F_t - F_0]$ at time T to time t. The benefits and costs are reflected in this valuation equation because they are incorporated into the forward prices, where $F_t = FV(S_t + CC_t - CB_t)$ and $F_0 = FV(S_0 + CC_0 - CB_0)$. Again, the forward value is simply the present value of the difference in forward prices.

### EXAMPLE 4

### Forward Contract Price with Carry Costs and Benefits

1. A long one-year forward contract on a productive asset was entered at a forward price of ₡1,000. Now, seven months later, the underlying asset is selling for ₡1,050. The PV of the cost to store, insure, and maintain the asset for the next 5 months is ₡4.00, and the asset will generate income over the next 5 months with a PV of ₡28.00. Assume annual compounding for all costs and benefits and a risk-free rate of 2%.

   Based on the current spot price and the no-arbitrage approach, which of the following values is *closest* to the equilibrium five-month forward value?

   A. ₡34.22
   B. ₡33.50
   C. ₡35.94

### Solution to 1:

A is correct. Based on the information given, we know the following: $F_0 = 1,000$, $S_t = 1,050$, $CC_t = 4$, $CB_t = 28$, t = 7 months, T – t = 5 months, and r = 2%. The new forward price is $F_t = FV(S_t + CC_t - CB_t)$. So, with annual compounding, we have:

$$F_t = (1,050 + 4 - 28)(1 + 0.02)^{5/12} = ₡1,034.50 \text{ and}$$

$$V_t = PV[F_t - F_0] = [₡1,034.50 - ₡1000]/(1 + 0.02)^{5/12} = ₡34.22.$$

Now let us consider stock indexes, such as the EURO STOXX 50 or the US Russell 3000. With stock indexes, it is difficult to account for the numerous dividend payments paid by underlying stocks that vary in timing and amount. A **dividend index point** is a measure of the quantity of dividends attributable to a particular index. It is a useful measure of the amount of dividends paid, a very useful number for arbitrage trading. To simplify the problem, a continuous dividend yield is often assumed. This means it is assumed that dividends accrue continuously over the period in question rather than on specific discrete dates, which is not an unreasonable assumption for an index with a large number of component stocks.

The focus of the carry arbitrage model with continuous compounding is again the future value of the underlying adjusted for carry costs and benefits and can be expressed as:

$$F_0 = S_0 \exp^{(r_c + CC - CB)T} \qquad T \equiv \text{time to expiration} \qquad (5)$$

(Future value of the underlying adjusted for carry).

Note that in this context, $r_c$, CC, and CB are continuously compounded rates.

The carry arbitrage model can also be used when the underlying asset requires storage costs, needs to be insured, and suffers from spoilage. In these cases, rather than lowering the carrying burden, these costs make it more expensive to carry and hence the forward price is higher. We now apply these results to equity forward and futures contracts.

# PRICING EQUITY FORWARDS AND FUTURES   3

- ☐ describe how equity forwards and futures are priced, and calculate and interpret their no-arbitrage value
- ☐ describe how interest rate forwards and futures are priced, and calculate and interpret their no-arbitrage value

We now apply the concepts of arbitrage-free pricing and valuation to the specific types of forward and futures contracts typically used in investment management. We cover, in turn, equity, interest rate, fixed income, and currency forwards and futures. In doing so, we take account of the cash flows generated by the underlying (e.g., dividends, bond coupon payments, foreign currency interest) and the unique features of each of these contracts.

## Equity Forward and Futures Contracts

Although we alluded to equity forward pricing and valuation in the last section, we will now illustrate with concrete examples the application of carry arbitrage models to equity forward and futures contracts. Remember that here we assume that forward contracts and futures contracts are priced in the same way. Additionally, remember that it is vital to treat the compounding convention of interest rates appropriately.

If the underlying is a stock, then the carry benefit is the dividend payments as illustrated in the next two examples.

> **EXAMPLE 5**
>
> ### Equity Futures Contract Price with Continuously Compounded Interest Rates
>
> 1. The continuously compounded dividend yield on the EURO STOXX 50 is 3%, and the current stock index level is 3,500. The continuously compounded annual interest rate is 0.15%. Based on the carry arbitrage model, the three-month futures price will be *closest* to:
>
>    A. 3,473.85.
>    B. 3,475.15.
>    C. 3,525.03.
>
> **Solution:**
>
> B is correct. Based on the carry arbitrage model (see Equation 4), the futures price is
>
> $$f_0 = S_0 \exp^{(r_c + CC - CB)T}.$$
>
> We assume the carry costs (CC) are 0 for a financial asset, such as a stock index. The carry benefit (CB), in this case a 3% continuous dividend yield, is greater than the financing cost $r_c$ (0.15%), so the futures price will be below the spot price. The futures price, the future value of the underlying adjusted for carry (i.e., the dividend payments, over the next 3-months) is:
>
> $$f_0 = 3{,}500 \exp^{(0.0015 + 0 - 0.03)(3/12)} = 3{,}475.15.$$

> **EXAMPLE 6**
>
> ### Equity Forward Pricing and Forward Valuation with Discrete Dividends
>
> 1. Suppose Nestlé common stock is trading for CHF70 and pays a CHF2.20 dividend in one month. Further, assume the Swiss one-month risk-free rate is 1.0%, quoted on an annual compounding basis. Assume that the stock goes ex-dividend the same day the single stock forward contract expires. Thus, the single stock forward contract expires in one month.
>
>    The one-month forward price for Nestlé common stock will be *closest* to:
>
>    A. CHF66.80.
>    B. CHF67.86.
>    C. CHF69.94.
>
> **Solution:**
>
> B is correct. In this case, we have $S_0 = 70$, $r = 1.0\%$, $T = 1/12$, and $FV(CB_0) = 2.20 = CB_T$. Therefore,
>
> $$F_0 = FV(S_0 + CC_0 - CB_0) = FV(S_0) + FV(CC_0) - FV(CB_0)$$
>
> $$= 70(1 + 0.01)^{1/12} + 0 - 2.20 = CHF67.86.$$

# Pricing Equity Forwards and Futures

As shown in Equation 2a, the value of a forward contract is simply the present value (discounted from time T to time t) of the difference in the initial forward price and the current forward price, that is $V_t$ (long) = $PV[F_t - F_0]$. We will employ this basic principal to value various forward and swap contracts. Here, we find the current value (at time t) of an equity forward contract initially entered at time 0. To reiterate, the value prior to expiration is the present value of the difference in the initial equity forward price and the current equity forward price as illustrated in the next example.

### EXAMPLE 7

#### Equity Forward Valuation

Suppose we bought a one-year forward contract at 102, and there are now three months to expiration. The underlying is currently trading for 110, and interest rates are 5% on an annual compounding basis.

Suppose that instead of buying a forward contract, we buy a one-year *futures* contract at 102 and there are now three months to expiration. Today's futures price is 112.35. There are no other carry cash flows.

1. If there are no other carry cash flows, the <u>forward</u> value of the existing contract will be *closest* to:

    A. −10.00.

    B. 9.24.

    C. 10.35.

#### Solution to 1:

B is correct. For this case, we have $F_0 = 102$, $S_{0.75} = 110$, r = 5%, and $T - t = 0.25$. Note that the new forward price at t is simply $F_t = FV(S_t) = 110(1 + 0.05)^{0.25} = 111.3499$. Therefore, from Equation 2a we have:

$$V_t = PV[F_t - F_0] = (111.3499 - 102)/(1 + 0.05)^{0.25} = 9.2366, \text{ or}$$

alternatively, using Equation 2b,

$$V_t = S_t - PV[F_0] = 110 - 102/(1 + 0.05)^{0.25} = 9.2366.$$

Thus, we see that the current forward value is greater than the difference between the current underlying price of 110 and the initial forward price of 102 due to interest costs resulting in the new forward price being 111.35.

2. If a dividend payment is announced between the forward's valuation and expiration dates, assuming the news announcement does not change the current underlying price, the forward value will *most likely*:

    A. decrease.

    B. increase.

    C. be the same.

#### Solution to 2:

A is correct. The old forward price is fixed. The discounted difference in the new forward price and the old forward price is the value. If we impose a new dividend, it would lower the new forward price and thus lower the value of the old forward contract.

3. After marking to market, the futures value of the existing contract will be *closest* to:

   A. −10.35.
   B. 0.00.
   C. 10.35.

## Solution to 3:

B is correct. Futures contracts are marked to market daily, which implies that the market value, resulting in profits and losses, is received or paid at each daily settlement. Hence, the equity futures value is zero each day after settlement has occurred.

We turn now to the widely used interest rate forward and futures contracts.

## Interest Rate Forward and Futures Contracts

Historically, the most widely used interest rate that served as the underlying for many derivative instruments was Libor, the London Interbank Offered Rate. In 2008, financial regulators and many market participants began to suspect that the daily quoted Libor rates, which were compiled by the British Bankers Association, were being manipulated by certain banks. The manipulation of Libor by some participants resulted in its replacement by a new market reference rate (MRR) in 2021. Replacements for Libor as the MRR include SOFR (Secured Overnight Financing Rate), determined by the Federal Reserve Bank of New York and SONIA (Sterling Overnight Index Average), administered by the Bank of England. We use the generic term MRR for these and other Libor replacements.

Currently, there are active forward and futures markets for derivatives based on MRR. We will use the symbol $L_m$ to represent our spot MRR. Our focus will be on forward markets, as represented by forward rate agreements. In order to understand the forward market, however, let us first look at the MRR spot market.

Assume the following notation:

$L_m$ = MRR spot rate (set at time t = 0) for an m-day deposit

NA = notional amount, quantity of funds initially deposited

NTD = number of total days in a year, used for interest calculations (360 in the MRR market)

$t_m$ = accrual period, fraction of year for an m-day deposit—$t_m$ = m/NTD = m/360 (for the MRR market)

TA = terminal amount, quantity of funds repaid when the MRR deposit is withdrawn

For example, suppose we are considering a 90-day Eurodollar deposit (m = 90). Dollar MRR is quoted at 2%; thus, $L_{90}$ = 0.02. If $50,000 is initially deposited, then NA = $50,000. MRR is stated on an actual over 360-day count basis (often denoted ACT/360) with interest paid on an add-on basis. Add-on basis is the convention in the MRR market. The idea is that the interest is added on at the end—in contrast, for example, to the discount basis, in which the current price is discounted based on the amount paid at maturity. Hence, $t_m$ = 90/360 = 0.25. Accordingly, the terminal amount can be expressed as:

TA = NA × [1 + $L_m t_m$], and the interest paid is TA − NA = NA × [$L_m t_m$].

## Pricing Equity Forwards and Futures

In this example, TA = $50,000 × [1 + 0.02(90/360)] = $50,250 and the interest is $50,250 − $50,000 = $250.

Now let us turn to the forward market for MRR. A **forward rate agreement (FRA)** is an over-the-counter (OTC) forward contract in which the underlying is an interest rate on a deposit. An FRA involves two counterparties: the fixed-rate payer (long), who is also the floating-rate receiver, and the fixed-rate receiver (short), who is also the floating-rate payer. Thus, a fixed-payer (long) FRA will profit when the MRR rises. If the floating rate is above the rate in the forward agreement, the long position can be viewed as having the benefit of borrowing at below market rates. The long will receive a payment. A long FRA would be well suited for a firm planning to borrow in the future and wishing to hedge against rising rates. A fixed-receiver (short) FRA might be a bank or financial institution hoping to lock in a fixed lending rate in the future. The fixed receiver, as the name implies, receives an interest payment based on a fixed rate and makes an interest payment based on a floating rate. If we are the fixed receiver, then it is understood without saying that we also are the floating payer, and vice versa. Because there is no initial exchange of cash flows, to eliminate arbitrage opportunities, the FRA price is the fixed interest rate such that the FRA value is zero on the initiation date.

FRAs are identified in the form of "X × Y," where X and Y are months and the multiplication symbol, ×, is read as "by." To grasp this concept and the notion of exactly what is the underlying in an FRA, consider a 3 × 9 FRA, which is pronounced "3 by 9." The 3 indicates that the FRA expires in three months. After three months, we determine the FRA payoff based on an underlying rate. The underlying is implied by the difference in the 3 and the 9. That is, the payoff of the FRA is determined by a six-month (180-day) MRR when the FRA expires in three months. The notation 3 × 9 is market convention, though it can seem confusing at first. The rate on the FRA will be determined by the relationship between the spot rate on a nine-month MRR deposit and the spot rate on a three-month MRR deposit when the FRA is initiated. A long FRA will effectively replicate going long a nine-month MRR deposit and short a three-month MRR deposit. Note that although market convention quotes the time periods as months, the calculations use days based on the assumption of 30 days in a month.

The contract established between the two counterparties settles in cash the difference between a fixed interest payment established on the initiation date and a floating interest payment established on the FRA expiration date. The underlying of an FRA is neither a financial asset nor even a financial instrument; it is just an interest payment. It is also important to understand that the parties to an FRA are not necessarily engaged in a MRR deposit in the spot market. The MRR spot market is simply the benchmark from which the payoff of the FRA is determined. Although a party may use an FRA in conjunction with a MRR deposit, it does not have to do so any more than a party that uses a forward or futures on a stock index has to have a position in the stock index.

In Exhibit 8, we illustrate the key time points in an FRA transaction. The FRA is created and priced at Time 0, the initiation date, and expires h days later. The underlying instrument has m days to maturity as of the FRA expiration date. Thus, the FRA payoff is based on the spot m-day MRR observed in h days from FRA initiation. We can only observe spot market reference rates. To price the FRA, we require two spot rates: $L_h$, which takes us to the expiration of the FRA, and $L_T$, which takes us to the underlying maturity.

The FRA helps hedge single period interest rate risk for an m-day period beginning h days in the future. After the initial FRA rate ($FRA_0$) is established, we may also wish to determine a value for our FRA at a later date (Time g). As the MRR changes, our interest rate agreement may take on a positive or negative value.

### Exhibit 8: Important FRA Dates, Expressed in Days from Initiation

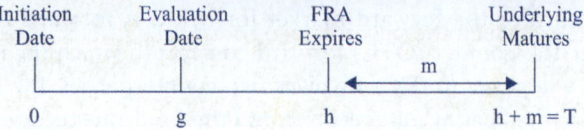

Using the notation in Exhibit 8, let $FRA_0$ denote the fixed forward rate set at Time 0 that expires at Time h wherein the underlying MRR deposit has m days to maturity at expiration of the FRA. Thus, the rate set at initiation of a contract expiring in 30 days in which the underlying is a 90-day MRR, denoted as a 1 × 4 FRA, will be such a number as 1% or 2.5%. Like all standard forward contracts, no money changes hands when an FRA is initiated, so our objective is to price the FRA, meaning to determine the fixed rate ($FRA_0$), such that the value of the FRA contract is zero on the initiation date.

When any interest rate derivative expires, there are technically two ways to settle at expiration: "advanced set, settled in arrears" and "advanced set, advanced settled." It is important to note that FRAs are typically settled based on "advanced set, advanced settled," whereas swaps and interest rate options are normally based on "advanced set, settled in arrears." Let us look at both approaches, because they are both used in the interest rate derivatives markets.

In the earlier example of a MRR deposit of $50,000 for 90 days at 2%, the rate was set when the money was deposited, and interest accrued over the life of the deposit. A payment of $50,250 (interest of $250 + principal of $50,000) was made at maturity, 90 days later. Here the term **advanced set** is used because the reference interest rate is set at the time the money is deposited. The advanced set convention is almost always used because most issuers and buyers of financial instruments want to know the rate on the instrument while they have a position in it.

In an FRA, the term "advanced" refers to the fact that the interest rate is set at Time h, the FRA expiration date, which is the time the underlying deposit starts. The term **settled in arrears** is used when the interest payment is made at Time h + m, the maturity of the underlying instrument. Thus, an FRA with advanced set, settled in arrears works the same way as a typical bank deposit as described in the previous example. At Time h, the interest rate is set at $L_m$, and the interest payment is made at Time T (h + m). Alternatively, when **advanced settled** is used, the settlement is made at Time h. Thus, in an FRA with the advanced set, advanced settled feature, the FRA expires and settles at the same time. Importantly, advanced set, advanced settled is almost always used in FRAs; although we will see advanced set, settled in arrears when we cover interest rate swaps, and it is also used in interest rate options. From this point forward in this discussion, all FRAs will be advanced set, advanced settled, as they are in practice.

The settlement amounts for advanced set, advanced settled are discounted in the following manner:

Settlement amount at h for receive-floating (Long):

$$NA \times \{[L_m - FRA_0] t_m\} / [1 + D_m t_m].$$

Again, the FRA is a forward contract on interest rates; long FRA (floating receiver) wins when rates increase. Note the floating rate (MRR perhaps, $L_m$) is received and thus has a positive sign. Since floating is received, the fixed rate ($FRA_0$) is paid (outflow). The FRA rate (fixed at t = 0 for the period m, which runs from time h to time T) is an outflow for the long and has a negative sign. For receive fixed (short), the FRA rate is an inflow and the floating rate $L_m$ is an outflow.

Settlement amount at h for receive-fixed (Short):

# Pricing Equity Forwards and Futures

$$NA \times \{[FRA_0 - L_m] t_m\} / [1 + D_m t_m].$$

The divisor, $1 + D_m t_m$, is a discount factor applied to the FRA payoff. It reflects the fact that the rate on which the payoff is determined, $L_m$, is obtained on day h from the spot market (advanced set), which uses settled in arrears. The discount factor is, therefore, appropriately applied to the FRA payment because the payment is received in advance, not in arrears. That is, the FRA payment is made early (advanced settled), but the interest on the loan is not due until later (settled in arrears). So, the settlement amount at time h is discounted to account for the fact that interest can be earned for m days on the advanced payment. Often it is assumed at time h that $D_m = L_m$, and we will commonly do so here, but it can be different.

Again, it is important to not be confused by the role played by an MRR spot market in an FRA. In the MRR spot market, deposits are made by various parties that are lending to banks. These rates are used as the benchmark for determining the payoffs of FRAs. The two parties to an FRA do not necessarily engage in any MRR spot transactions. Again, MRR spot deposits are settled in arrears, whereas FRA payoffs are settled in advance—hence the discounting.

### EXAMPLE 8

#### Calculating Interest on MRR Spot and FRA Payments

In 30 days, a UK company expects to make a bank deposit of £10,000,000 for a period of 90 days at 90-day MRR set 30 days from today. The company is concerned about a possible decrease in interest rates. Its financial adviser suggests that it negotiate today a 1 × 4 FRA, an instrument that expires in 30 days and is based on 90-day MRR. The company enters a £10,000,000 notional amount 1 × 4 receive-fixed FRA that is advanced set, advanced settled (note the company is the short-side of this FRA contract). The appropriate discount rate for the FRA settlement cash flows is 2.40%. After 30 days, 90-day MRR in British pounds is 2.55%.

1. The interest actually paid at maturity on the UK company's bank deposit will be *closest* to:

   A. £60,000.
   B. £63,750.
   C. £67,500.

#### Solution to 1:

B is correct. This is a simple deposit of £10,000,000 for 90 days at the prevailing 90-day MRR. Since m = 90, we use $L_{90}$ = 2.55%. Therefore, TA = 10,000,000 × [1 + 0.0255(0.25)] = £10,063,750. So, the interest paid at maturity is £63,750.

2. If the FRA was initially priced so that $FRA_0$ = 2.60%, the payment received to settle it will be *closest* to:

   A. −£2,485.08.
   B. £1,242.54.
   C. £1,250.00.

### Solution to 2:

B is correct. In this example, m = 90 (number of days in the deposit), $t_m$ = 90/360 (fraction of year until deposit matures observed at the FRA expiration date), and h = 30 (number of days initially in the FRA). The settlement amount of the 1 × 4 FRA at h for receive-fixed (the short) is:

$$NA \times \{[FRA_0 - L_m]t_m\}/[1 + D_m t_m]$$

$$= 10{,}000{,}000 \times \{[0.0260 - 0.0255](0.25)\}/[1 + 0.0240(0.25)]$$

$$= £1{,}242.54.$$

Since the short FRA involves paying floating, the short benefited from a decline in rates. Note $D_m$ does not equal $L_m$ in this example.

---

3. If the FRA was initially priced so that $FRA_0$ = 2.50%, the payment received to settle it will be *closest* to:

    A. −£1,242.54.
    B. £1,242.54.
    C. £1,250.00.

### Solution to 3:

A is correct. The data are similar to those in the previous question, but the initial FRA rate is now 2.50% and not 2.60%. Thus, the settlement amount of the 1 × 4 FRA at time h for receive-fixed (the short) is:

$$NA \times \{[FRA_0 - L_m]t_m\}/[1 + D_m t_m]$$

$$= 10{,}000{,}000 \times \{[0.0250 - 0.0255](0.25)\}/[1 + 0.0240(0.25)]$$

$$= -£1{,}242.54.$$

The short-side in the FRA suffered from a rise in rates because it is paying floating.

---

At this point, we highlight a few key concepts about FRAs and how to price and value them:

1. An FRA is a forward contract on interest rates. The long side of the FRA, fixed-rate payer (floating-rate receiver), incurs a gain when rates increase and incurs a loss when rates decrease. Conversely, the short side of the FRA, fixed-rate receiver (floating-rate payer), incurs a loss when rates increase and incurs a gain when rates decrease.

2. The FRA price, $FRA_0$, is the implied forward rate for the period beginning when the FRA expires to the underlying loan maturity. So, we require two spot rates to determine the initial forward rate. Therefore, pricing an FRA is like pricing a forward contract.

3. Although the interest on the underlying loan will not be paid until the end of the loan, the payoff on the FRA will occur at the expiration of the FRA (advanced settled). Therefore, the payoff of an FRA is discounted back to the expiration of the FRA.

As noted in point 2, the FRA price is the implied forward rate for the period beginning when the FRA expires at time h and running m days to the underlying loan maturity at time T. It is similar to any other forward contract. We wish to identify the appropriate $FRA_0$ rate that makes the value of the FRA equal to zero on the initiation date. The concept used to derive $FRA_0$ can be understood through a simple example.

# Pricing Equity Forwards and Futures

Recall that with simple interest, a one-period forward rate is found by solving the expression $[1 + y(1)][1 + F(1)] = [1 + y(2)]^2$, where $y(1)$ denotes the one-period yield to maturity and $y(2)$ the two-period yield to maturity. F denotes the forward rate in the next period. We can observe the spot rates $y(1)$ and $y(2)$. The forward rate is implied from those two rates. Borrowing or lending along the 2-year path must cost the same as borrowing or lending along the path using the 1-year spot and the 1-year forward. The solution for $F(1)$ is simply $F(1) = ([1 + y(2)]^2/[1 + y(1)]) - 1$. Assume the one-year spot rate is 3% and the two-year spot rate is 4%. To prevent arbitrage, $F(1) = ([1 + 0.04]^2/[1 + 0.03]) - 1 = 0.0501$. If the forward rate was not 5.01%, an arbitrageur could make a risk-free profit through borrowing along one path and lending along another.

As depicted in Exhibit 9, the rate for an FRA is computed in the same manner. We derive the forward rate (or FRA rate, $FRA_0$) from two spot rates (such as MRR): the longer rate $L_T$ and the shorter rate $L_h$. Borrowing or lending at $L_T$ for T days should cost the same as borrowing or lending for h days at $L_h$ and subsequently borrowing or lending for m days at $FRA_0$.

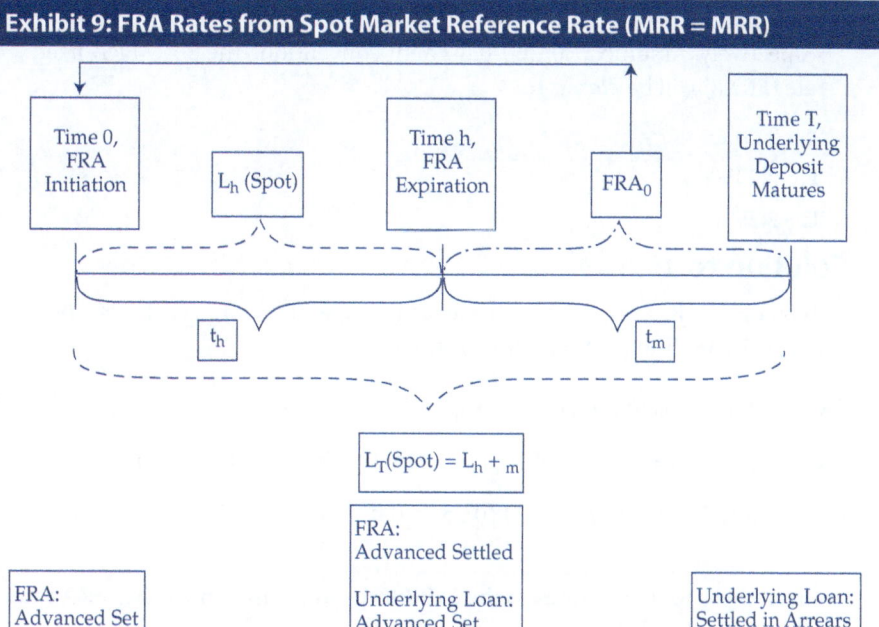

**Exhibit 9: FRA Rates from Spot Market Reference Rate (MRR = MRR)**

We can solve for the FRA rate by considering that the two paths must be equal to prevent arbitrage or:

$$[1 + L_h t_h][1 + FRA_0 t_m] = [1 + L_T t_T].$$

The solution in annualized form is shown in Equation 6:

$$FRA_0 = \{[1 + L_T t_T]/[1 + L_h t_h] - 1\}/t_m. \quad (6)$$

The result is the forward rate in the term structure.

So, if 180-day MRR is 2.0% and 90-day MRR is 1.5%, then the price of a 3 × 6 FRA would be:

$$FRA_0 = \{[1 + L_T t_{180}]/[1 + L_h t_{90}] - 1\}/t_{90}$$

$$= \{[1 + 0.02(180/360)]/[1 + 0.015(90/360)] - 1\}/(90/360)$$

$$= 0.024907 \text{ or } 2.49\%.$$

This result can be compared with the result from a simple approximation technique. Note that for this FRA, 90 is half of 180. Thus, we can use a simple arithmetic average equation—here, (1/2)1.5% + (1/2)X = 2.0%—and solve for the missing variable X: X = 2.5%. Knowing this approximation will always be biased slightly high, we know we are looking for an answer that is a little less than 2.5%. This is a helpful way to check your final answer.

### EXAMPLE 9

### FRA Fixed Rate

Now consider the following information for problems 2 and 3.

Assume a 30/360-day count convention and the following spot rates:

1-Month USD MRR is 2.48%, 3-Month USD MRR is 2.58%, 6-Month USD MRR is 2.62%, and 1-Year USD MRR is 2.72%.

1. Based on market quotes on Canadian dollar (C$) MRR, the six-month C$ MRR and the nine-month C$ MRR rates are presently at 1.5% and 1.75%, respectively. Assume a 30/360-day count convention. The 6 × 9 FRA fixed rate ($FRA_0$) will be *closest* to:

    **A.** 2.00%.

    **B.** 2.23%.

    **C.** 2.25%.

### Solution to 1:

B is correct. Based on the information given, we know $L_{180}$ = 1.50% and $L_{270}$ = 1.75%. The 6 × 9 FRA rate is thus:

$$FRA_0 = \{[1 + L_T t_T]/[1 + L_h t_h] - 1\}/t_m$$

$$FRA_0 = \{[1 + 0.0175(270/360)]/[1 + 0.015(180/360)] - 1\}/(90/360)$$

$$FRA_0 = [(1.013125/1.0075) - 1]/(0.25) = 0.022333, \text{ or } 2.23\%.$$

2. Given these four spot rates in the MRR term structure, how many FRA rates can be calculated?

    **A.** 4 FRA rates

    **B.** 6 FRA rates

    **C.** 12 FRA rates

### Solution to 2:

B is correct. Based on the four MRR spot rates given, we can compute six separate FRA rates as follows: 1 × 3, 1 × 6, 1 × 12, 3 × 6, 3 × 12, and 6 × 12 FRA rates.

3. The 1 × 3 FRA fixed rate will be *closest* to:

    **A.** 2.43%.

    **B.** 2.53%.

    **C.** 2.62%.

# Pricing Equity Forwards and Futures

> **Solution to 3:**
>
> C is correct. Based on the information given, we know $L_{30} = 2.48\%$ and $L_{90} = 2.58\%$. The 1 × 3 FRA rate is thus:
>
> $FRA_0 = \{[1 + L_T t_T]/[1 + L_h t_h] - 1\}/t_m$
>
> $FRA_0 = \{[1 + 0.0258(90/360)]/[1 + 0.0248(30/360)] - 1\}/(60/360)$
>
> $FRA_0 = [(1.00645/1.00207) - 1]/(0.1667) = 0.026220$, or $2.62\%$.

We can now value an existing FRA (with rate $FRA_0$) using the same general approach as we did with the forward contracts previously covered. Specifically, we can enter into an offsetting transaction at the new rate that would be set on an FRA that expires at the same time as our original FRA. By taking the opposite position, the new FRA offsets the old one. That is, if we are long the old FRA, we will pay fixed and receive the floating rate $L_m$ at h. We can go short a new FRA and receive fixed (with rate $FRA_g$) that will obligate us to pay $L_m$ at h.

Consider the following strategy. Let us assume that we initiate an FRA that expires in 90 days and is based on 90-day MRR (so, a 3 × 6 FRA). The fixed rate at initiation $FRA_0 = 2.49\%$ and $t_m = 90/360$. We are long the FRA, so we will pay the fixed rate of 2.49% and receive floating MRR. Having entered the long FRA, we wish to value our position 30 days later, at Time g, when there are 60 days remaining in the life of the FRA (note that this is now a 2 × 5 FRA, as one month has passed since FRA initiation). Assume, at this point, the rate on an FRA based on 90-day MRR that expires in 60 days ($FRA_g$) is 2.59%. Remember, the original FRA has a fixed rate set at 2.49% when it was initiated. Now, 30 days later, a new offsetting FRA can be created at 2.59%. To value the original FRA (at Time g), we short a new FRA that will receive fixed at 2.59% and pay floating MRR at time h. Effectively, we are now receiving fixed at 2.59% and paying fixed at 2.49%. The value of the offset position is 10 bps times (90/360), as follows, times the notional amount, which is then discounted to back to Time g:

10 bps: $FRA_g - FRA_0 = 2.59\% - 2.49\% = 0.10\%$

90/360: $t_m = m/NTD$, as $L_m$ is the 90-day MRR rate underlying both FRAs

Because the cash flows at T are now known with certainty at g, this offsetting transaction at Time g has eliminated any floating-rate risk at Time T. That is, we had a long FRA at time 0 and added a short FRA at time g. Since the notional amounts and times to maturity of the offsetting transaction are the same, the floating portion of the FRA cash flows ($L_m$) at time T will exactly cancel, $[L_m - FRA_0] + [FRA_g - L_m] = [FRA_g - FRA_0]$.

Our task, however, is to determine the fair value of the original FRA at Time g. Therefore, we need the present value of this Time T cash flow at Time g. That is, the value of the original FRA is the PV of the difference in the new FRA rate and the old FRA rate times the notional amount. Specifically, we let $V_g$ be the value at Time g of the original FRA that was initiated at Time 0, expires at Time h, and is based on m-day MRR, $L_m$. Note that discounting will be over the period $T - g$. With $D_{T-g}$ as the discount rate and NA as the notional amount. So,

Long FRA value at Time g: $V_g =$

$$NA \times \{[FRA_g - FRA_0] t_m\}/[1 + D_{(T-g)} t_{(T-g)}]. \quad (7)$$

Thus, the Time g value of the receive-floating FRA initiated at Time 0 ($V_g$) is just the present value of the difference in FRA rates, one entered at Time g and one entered at Time 0. Traditionally, it is assumed that the discount rate, $D_m$, is equal to the underlying floating rate, $L_m$, but that is not necessary. Note that here it is $D_{(T-g)}$.

The value of a receive-fixed or short FRA at time g is the negative of the long value ($-V_g$), so we have: $-V_g = -1 \times (NA \times \{[FRA_g - FRA_0] t_m\}/[1+ D_{(T-g)} t_{(T-g)}])$.

Short FRA value at Time g =

$$NA \times \{[FRA_0 - FRA_g] t_m\}/[1+ D_{(T-g)} t_{(T-g)}] \qquad (8)$$

### EXAMPLE 10

### FRA Valuation

1. Suppose we entered a receive-floating (long) 6 × 9 FRA with Canadian dollar notional amount of C$10,000,000 at Time 0. The six-month spot C$ MRR was 0.628%, and the nine-month C$ MRR was 0.712%. Also, assume the 6 × 9 FRA rate is quoted in the market at 0.877%. After 90 days have passed, the three-month C$ MRR is 1.25% and the six-month C$ MRR is 1.35%, which we will use as the discount rate to determine the value at g.

   Assuming the appropriate discount rate is C$ MRR, the value of the original receive-floating 6 × 9 FRA will be *closest* to:

   **A.** C$14,105.
   **B.** C$14,200.
   **C.** C$14,625.

### Solution:

A is correct. Initially, we have $L_{180} = 0.628\%$, $L_{270} = 0.712\%$, and $FRA_0 = 0.877\%$.

After 90 days (g = 90), we have $L_{90} = 1.25\%$ and $L_{180} = 1.35\%$. Interest rates rose during this period; hence, the FRA has gained value because the position is receive-floating. First, we compute the new FRA rate at Time g and then estimate the fair FRA value as the discounted difference in the new and old FRA rates. The new FRA rate at Time g, denoted $FRA_g$, is the rate on an FRA expiring in 90 days in which the underlying is 90-day C$ MRR (so, a 3 x 6 FRA). That rate is found using Equation 6. The shorter spot rate is now for h − g (180 − 90 = 90) days, which is the new time until both FRAs expire. The reference spot rate for the underlying maturity is now in T − g (270 − 90 = 180) days.

$FRA_g = \{[1 + L_{180} t_{(T-g)}]/[1 + L_{90} t_{(h-g)}] − 1\}/t_m$,

T − g = 180 days and h − g = 90 days, so we have:

$FRA_g = \{[1 + L_{180} (180/360)]/[1 + L_{90} (90/360)] − 1\}/(90/360)$.

Substituting the values given in this problem, we find:

$FRA_g = \{[1 + 0.0135 (180/360)]/[1 + 0.0125 (90/360)] − 1\}/(90/360) = [(1.006750/1.003125) − 1]/0.25$

= 0.014455, or 1.445%.

Therefore, using Equation 7, we have:

$V_g = 10{,}000{,}000 \times \{[0.01445 − 0.00877] (90/360)\}/[1 + 0.0135 (180/360)]$

= 14,105.

We now turn to the specific features of various forward and futures markets. The same general principles will apply, but the specifics will be different.

# PRICING FIXED-INCOME FORWARD AND FUTURES CONTRACTS

☐ describe how fixed-income forwards and futures are priced, and calculate and interpret their no-arbitrage value

Fixed-income forward and futures contracts have several unique issues that influence the specifics of the carry arbitrage model. First, in some countries the prices of fixed-income securities (termed "bonds" here) are quoted without the interest that has accrued since the last coupon date. The quoted price is sometimes known as the clean price. Naturally when buying a bond, one must pay the full price, which is sometimes called the dirty price, so the accrued interest is included. Nonetheless, it is necessary to understand how the quoted bond price and accrued interest compose the true bond price and the effect this convention has on derivatives pricing. The quotation convention for futures contracts, whether based on clean or dirty prices, usually corresponds to the quotation convention in the respective bond market. In this section, we will largely treat forwards and futures the same, except in certain places where noted.

In general, accrued interest is computed based on the following linear interpolation formula:

Accrued interest = Accrual period × Periodic coupon amount, or

AI = (NAD/NTD) × (C/n),

where NAD denotes the number of accrued days since the last coupon payment, NTD denotes the number of total days during the coupon payment period, n denotes the number of coupon payments per year (commonly n = 2 for semi-annual), and C is the stated annual coupon amount. For example, after two months (60 days), a 3% semi-annual coupon bond with par of 1,000 would have accrued interest of AI = (60/180) × (30/2) = 5. Note that accrued interest is expressed in currency units (not percent), and the number of total days (NTD) depends on the coupon payment frequency. As in the example, semi-annual indicates coupons are paid twice per year, so with 360 days per year, NTD = 360/2 = 180.

Second, fixed-income futures contracts often have more than one bond that can be delivered by the seller. Because bonds trade at different prices based on maturity and stated coupon, a mathematical adjustment to the amount required when settling a futures contract, known as the conversion factor (CF), is used to make all deliverable bonds approximately equal in price. According to the Chicago Mercantile Exchange, "A conversion factor is the approximate decimal price at which $1 par of a security would trade if it had a six percent yield-to-maturity." So, the CF adjusts each bond to an equivalent 6% coupon bond (i.e., benchmark bond). Other exchanges use different conversion factors, and these are illustrated later in the text and examples.

Third, when multiple bonds can be delivered for a particular futures contract, a cheapest-to-deliver bond typically emerges after adjusting for the conversion factor. The conversion factor adjustment, however, is not precise. Thus, if there are several candidates for delivery, the bond that will be delivered is the one that is least expensive for the seller to purchase in the open market to settle the obligation.

For bond markets in which the quoted price includes the accrued interest and in which futures or forward prices assume accrued interest is in the bond price quote, the futures or forward price simply conforms to the general formula we have previously discussed. Recall that the futures or forward price is simply the future value of the underlying in which finance costs, carry costs, and carry benefits are all incorporated, or

$F_0$ = Future value of underlying adjusted for carry cash flows

= $FV(S_0 + CC_0 - CB_0)$.

Let Time 0 be the forward contract trade initiation date and Time T be the forward contract expiration date, as shown in Exhibit 10. For the fixed-income bond, let Y denote the time to maturity of the bond at Time T, when the forward contract expires. Therefore, T + Y denotes the underlying instrument's current (Time 0) time to maturity. Let $B_0$ denote the quoted bond price observed at Time 0 of a fixed-rate bond that matures at Time T + Y and pays a fixed coupon rate.

### Exhibit 10: Timeline for Bond Futures and Forwards

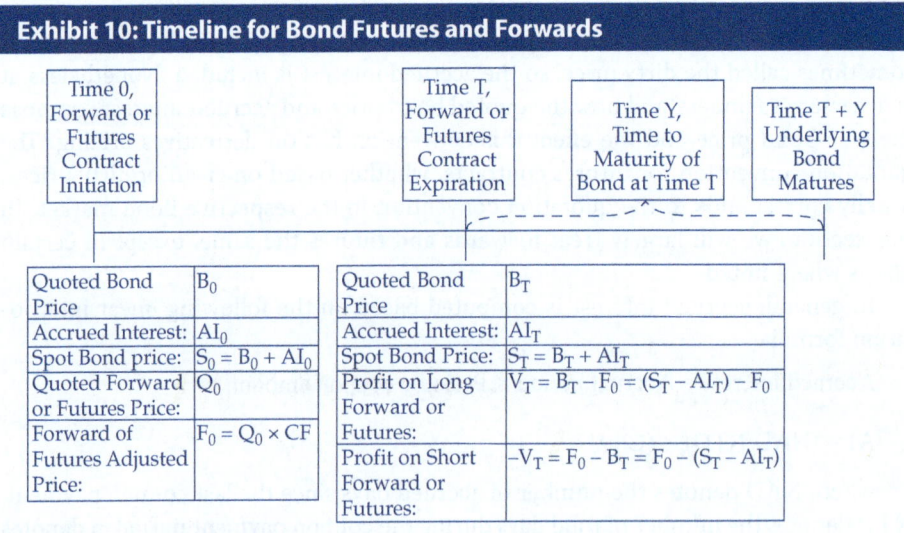

For bonds quoted without accrued interest, let $AI_0$ denote the accrued interest at Time 0. The carry benefits are the bond's fixed coupon payments, so $CB_0$ = PVCI, meaning the present value of all coupon interest (CI) paid over the forward contract horizon from Time 0 to Time T. The corresponding future value of these coupons paid over the contract horizon to time T is $CB_T$ = FVCI. Finally, there are no carry costs, and thus CC = 0. To be consistent with prior notation, we have:

$S_0$ = Quoted bond price + Accrued interest = $B_0 + AI_0$.

We could just insert this price ($S_0$) into the previous equation, letting $CB_0$ = PVCI, and thereby obtain the futures price the straightforward and traditional way. But fixed-income futures contracts often permit delivery of more than one bond and use the conversion factor system to provide this flexibility. In these markets, the futures price, $F_0$, is defined as the quoted futures price, $Q_0$, times the conversion factor, CF. Note that in this section, we will use the letter F to denote either the quoted forward price or the futures price times the conversion factor. In fact, the futures contract settles against the quoted bond price *without* accrued interest. Thus, as shown in Exhibit 10, the total profit or loss on a long position in fixed-income futures at expiration (Time T) is the quoted bond price minus the initial futures price or:

# Pricing Fixed-Income Forward and Futures Contracts

$v_T = B_T - F_0$. Moreover, based on our notation, we can also say,

$v_T = (S_T - AI_T) - F_0$.

The fixed-income forward or futures price including the conversion factor, termed the "adjusted price," can be expressed as:

$F_0 = Q_0 \times CF$

$= $ FV of underlying adjusted for carry cash flows from Times 0 to T

$= FV[S_0 + CC_0 - CB_0] = FV[S_0 + 0 - PVCI] = FV[B_0 + AI_0 - PVCI].$ (9)

In other words, the actual futures price is $F_0$, but in the market the availability of multiple deliverable bonds gives rise to the adjustment factor. Hence, the price you would see quoted is $Q_0$, where $Q_0 = F_0/CF$.

Recall that the bracketed term $B_0 + AI_0 - PVCI$ in Equation 9 is just the full spot price $S_0$ minus the present value of the coupons over the life of the forward or futures contract. The fixed-income forward or futures price ($F_0$) is thus the future value of the quoted bond price plus accrued interest less any coupon payments made during the life of the contract. Again, the quoted bond price plus the accrued interest is the spot price: It is in fact the price you would have to pay to buy the bond. Market conventions in some countries just happen to break this price out into the quoted price plus the accrued interest.

Why Equation 9 must hold is best understood by illustrating what happens when the futures price is not in equilibrium. In fact, in the following scenario, the futures are overpriced relative to the bond, giving rise to an arbitrage opportunity.

Assume we observe a 3-month forward contract, so T = 0.25, on a bond that expires at some time in the future, T + Y, and this bond is currently quoted ($B_0$) at 107% of par. There are no coupon payments for this bond over the life of the forward contract, so PVCI = 0.0. Other pertinent details of the bond and futures are presented in Exhibit 11.

### Exhibit 11: Bond and Futures Information for Illustrating Disequilibrium and Arbitrage Opportunity

| Bond | | |
|---|---|---|
| Quoted Bond Price | $B_0$ | 107.00 |
| PV of Coupon Interest | PVCI | 0 |
| Accrued Interest at Time 0 | $AI_0$ | 0.07 |
| Accrued Interest at Time T | $AI_T$ | 0.20 |
| **Futures** | | |
| Quoted Futures Price | $Q_0$ | 135.00 |
| Conversion Factor | CF | 0.80 |
| Adjusted Futures Price | $F_0 (= Q_0 \times CF)$ | 108.00 |
| **Interest Rate** | | |
| For Discounting/Compounding | r | 0.20% |

We observe that the full spot price of the bond is:

$S_0 = B_0 + AI_0 = 107 + 0.07 = 107.07$.

The futures price ($F_0$), which is the future value adjusted for carry cash flows (using Equation 9), is:

$$F_0 = FV[B_0 + AI_0 - PVCI] = (107 + 0.07 - 0)(1.002)^{0.25} = 107.12.$$

Note that the adjusted futures price using the quoted futures price ($Q_0 = 135$) and the conversion factor (CF = 0.80) is $F_0 = 108$. Adding the accrued interest at expiration ($AI_T = 0.20$) to the adjusted futures price gives 108.20. Remember, if you are selling a bond you receive the accrued interest; if you are buying a bond you pay the accrued interest. The adjusted futures price plus accrued interest should equal the future value of the full bond price adjusted for any carry cash flows given by Equation 9. Here, the adjusted futures price (including accrued interest) is 108.20, while the cost to buy and carry the bonds is 107.12. This implies that the futures contract is overpriced by (108.2 − 107.12) = 1.08, thus there is an arbitrage opportunity. In this case, we would simultaneously: 1) sell the overpriced futures contract; 2) borrow funds to purchase the bonds; and 3) buy the underpriced deliverable bonds.

So, to capture the 1.08 with no risk, an arbitrageur might wish to buy this bond and carry it and short the futures contract at 108. At maturity, the arbitrageur simply delivers the bond to cover the futures contract and repays the loan. Arbitrage should allow for the capture of any over (or under) pricing. Selling the futures contract at 108 involves no initial cash flow. The short futures locks in a sale price of 108 + 0.2 = 108.20 for the bond just purchased for 107.07. Since there are no carry benefits, it costs the arbitrageur 107.12, = FV(107.07) = (107.07)(1+0.002)$^{0.25}$, to carry the bond to expiration. The result is a risk-free profit at expiration of 1.08, = 108.00 + 0.2 − 107.12, for which the Time 0 PV is 1.0795, = 1.08(1.002)$^{-0.25}$.

The value of the Time 0 cash flows should be zero to prevent an arbitrage opportunity. This example shows the arbitrage profit as a 1.0795 cash flow at Time 0 or 1.08 at time T per bond. If the value had been negative—meaning the full bond price exceeded the adjusted future price plus accrued interest—then the arbitrageur would conduct the reverse carry arbitrage of short selling the bond, lending the proceeds, and buying the futures (termed reverse carry arbitrage because the underlying is not carried but is sold short).

In equilibrium, the adjusted futures price of the bond plus any accrued interest must equal the cost of buying and holding the spot bond until time T. That is, to eliminate an arbitrage opportunity:

$$F_0 + AI_T = FV[B_0 + AI_0 - PVCI], \text{ which implies, } F_0 = FV(S_0) - AI_T - FVCI.$$

In this example, equilibrium is not met. The adjusted futures price, $F_0 = 108$, promises a profit of (108 − 106.92) = 1.08 at expiration, since

$$FV(S_0) - AI_T - FVCI = 107.12 - 0.2 - 0 = 106.92.$$

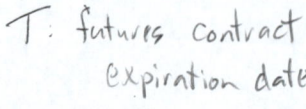
T: futures contract expiration date

==For clarity, substituting for $F_0$ and $S_0$ and solving for the quoted futures price ($Q_0$) results in Equation 10, the conversion factor adjusted futures price (i.e., quoted futures price):==

==$$Q_0 = [1/CF] \{FV[B_0 + AI_0] - AI_T - FVCI\} \tag{10}$$==

In this example we have,

$$Q_0 = [1/CF] \{FV[B_0 + AI_0] - AI_T - FVCI\}$$
$$= (1/0.8) \{(1 + 0.002)^{0.25}(107 + 0.07) - 0.20 - 0.0\} = 133.65.$$

Recall, a futures price of 135 was used as the quoted price, $Q_0$ (108 was the adjusted futures price). Any quoted futures price higher than the equilibrium futures price of 133.65 (106.92 adjusted) will present arbitrage opportunities; hence, the arbitrage transaction of selling the futures contract resulted in a riskless positive cash flow.

# Pricing Fixed-Income Forward and Futures Contracts

> **EXAMPLE 11**
>
> ## Estimating the Euro-Bund Futures Price
>
> 1. Euro-bund futures have a contract value of €100,000, and the underlying consists of long-term German debt instruments with 8.5 to 10.5 years to maturity. They are traded on the Eurex. Suppose the underlying 2% coupon (semi-annual payment) German bund is quoted at €108 and has accrued interest of €0.083 (15 days since last coupon paid). The euro-bund futures contract matures in one month (30 days). At contract expiration, the underlying bund will have accrued interest of €0.25; there are no coupon payments due until after the futures contract expires; and the current one-month risk-free rate is 0.1%. The conversion factor is 0.729535.
>
>    In this case, we have the following:
>
>    $T = 1/12$, $CF = 0.729535$, $B_0 = 108$, $FVCI = 0$, $AI_0 = (15/180 \times 2\%/2) = €0.083$, $AI_T = (45/180 \times 2\%/2) = €0.25$, and $r = 0.1\%$.
>
>    The equilibrium euro-bund quoted futures price ($Q_0$) based on the carry arbitrage model will be *closest* to:
>
>    **A.** €147.57.
>
>    **B.** €147.82.
>
>    **C.** €148.15.
>
> ## Solution:
>
> B is correct. The carry arbitrage model for forwards and futures is simply the future value of the underlying with adjustments for unique carry features. With bond futures, the unique features include the conversion factor, accrued interest, and any coupon payments. Thus, the equilibrium euro-bund futures price can be found using the carry arbitrage model (Equation 10):
>
> $Q_0 = [1/CF]\{FV[B_0 + AI_0] - AI_T - FVCI\}$.
>
> Thus, we have:
>
> $Q_0 = [1/0.729535][(1 + 0.001)^{1/12}(108 + 0.083) - 0.25 - 0] = 147.82$.
>
> Note that the same result can be found by $Q_0 = F_0/CF$, where:
>
> $F_0 = FV(S_0) - AI_T - FVCI = (1 + 0.001)^{1/12}(108 + 0.083) - 0.25 - 0 = 107.84$.
>
> In equilibrium, the quoted euro-bund futures price should be approximately €147.82 based on the carry arbitrage model.

Because of the mark-to-market settlement procedure, the value of a bond future is essentially the price change since the previous day's settlement. That value is captured at the settlement at the end of the day, at which time the value of the bond futures contract, like other futures contracts, resets to zero.

We now turn to the task of estimating the fair value of the bond forward contract at a point in time during its life. Without daily settlement, the value of a forward is not formally realized until expiration. Suppose the first transaction is buying (at Time 0) an at-market bond forward contract priced at $F_0$ with expiration of Time T. Later (at Time t) consider selling a new bond forward contract priced at $F_t$, again with expiration of Time T. At the maturity of the forward contracts, we take delivery of the bond under the long forward and use it to make delivery under the short forward. Assuming the same underlying, there is no price risk. The net cash flow at maturity is the difference in the price at which we sold, $F_t$, and the price we agreed to pay, $F_0$, or $(F_t - F_0)$. To confirm the price risk on the underlying bond is zero, we could also add the values of the long and the short forward positions at expiration $V_{Long} + V_{Short} = (B_T - F_0) + (F_t - B_T) = F_t - F_0$. Since the position is riskless, the value to the long at time t should be:

$$V_t = \text{Present value of difference in forward prices at time t} = PV[F_t - F_0].$$

As a simple example of bond forward contract valuation, assume that two forward contracts have been entered as follows: long forward at $F_0 = 119.12$ and short forward at $F_t = 119.92$. Time t is one month before expiration, and both forward contracts expire at Time T. Therefore, time to expiration in one-month is $T - t = 1/12$. Finally, assume the appropriate interest rate for discounting is $r = 0.5\%$.

The forward value observed at Time t for the Time T maturity bond forward contracts is simply the present value of the difference in their forward prices —denoted $PV_{t,T}(F_t - F_0)$. That is, we have:

$$V_t = (119.92 - 119.12)/(1 + 0.005)^{1/12} = 0.7997.$$

### EXAMPLE 12

### Estimating the Value of a Euro-Bund Forward Position

1. Suppose that one month ago, we purchased *five* euro-bund forward contracts with two months to expiration and a contract notional value of €100,000 each at a price of 145 (quoted as a percentage of par). The euro-bund forward contract now has one month to expiration. The current annualized one-month risk-free rate is 0.1%. Based on the current forward price of 148, the value of the euro-bund forward position will be *closest* to:

   **A.** €2,190.
   **B.** €14,998.
   **C.** €15,012.

### Solution:

B is correct. Because we are given both forward prices, the solution is simply the present value of the difference in forward prices at expiration.

$$V_t = PV[F_t - F_0] = (148 - 145)/(1 + 0.001)^{1/12} = 2.99975.$$

This is 2.9997 per €100 par value because this forward price was quoted as a percentage of par. Because five contracts each with €100,000 par were entered, we have $0.029997(€100,000)5 = €14,998.75$. Note that when interest rates are low and the forward contract has a short maturity, then the present value effect is minimal (about €1.25 in this example).

We conclude this section with some observations on the similarities and differences between forward and futures contracts.

## Comparing Forward and Futures Contracts

For every market considered here, the carry arbitrage model provides an approach for both pricing and valuing forward contracts. Recall the two generic expressions:

$$F_0 = FV(S_0 + CC_0 - CB_0) \text{ (Forward pricing)}$$

$V_t = PV[F_t - F_0]$ (Forward valuation)

Carry costs (CC) and financing costs increase the forward price, and carry benefits (CB) decrease the forward price. The arbitrageur is carrying the underlying, and costs increase the burden whereas benefits decrease the burden. The forward value can be expressed as either the present value of the difference in forward prices or as a function of the current underlying price adjusted for carry cash flows and the present value of the initial forward price.

Futures prices are generally found using the same model, but futures values are different because of the daily marking to market. Recall that the futures values are zero at the end of each trading day because profits and losses are taken daily.

In summary, the carry arbitrage model provides a compelling way to price and value forward and futures contracts. Stated concisely, the forward or futures price is simply the future value of the underlying adjusted for any carry cash flows. The forward value is simply the present value of the difference in forward prices at an intermediate time in the contract. The futures value is zero after marking to market. We turn now to pricing and valuing swaps.

## PRICING AND VALUING SWAP CONTRACTS 5

☐ describe how interest rate swaps are priced, and calculate and interpret their no-arbitrage value

Based on the foundational concepts we have studied on using the carry arbitrage model for pricing and valuing forward and futures contracts, we now apply this approach to pricing and valuing swap contracts.

A swap contract is an agreement to exchange (or swap) a series of cash flows at certain periodic dates. For example, an interest rate swap might exchange quarterly cash flows based on a floating rate for those based on a fixed rate. An interest rate swap is like an FRA except that it hedges multiperiod interest-rate risk, whereas an FRA only hedges single-period interest-rate risk. Similarly, in a currency swap the counterparties agree to exchange two series of interest payments, each denominated in a different currency, with the exchange of principal payments at inception and at maturity. Swap contracts can be synthetically created as either a portfolio of underlying instruments (such as bonds) or a portfolio of forward contracts (such as FRAs). Swaps are most easily understood as a portfolio of underlying bonds, so we will follow that approach.

Cash flows from a generic receive-floating and pay-fixed interest rate swap are shown in Exhibit 12. The cash flows are determined by multiplying a specified notional amount by a (fixed or floating) reference rate. In a fixed-for-floating interest rate swap (i.e., pay-fixed, receive-floating, also known as a plain vanilla swap), the fixed-rate payer in the swap would make a series of payments based on a fixed rate of interest applied to the notional amount. The counterparty would receive their fixed payments in return for making payments based on a floating rate applied to the same notional amount. The floating rate used as a reference will be referred to as the market reference rate (MRR). In our examples, we will use the MRR.

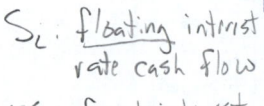

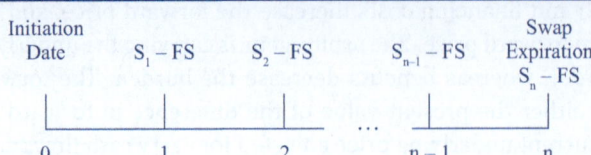

**Exhibit 12: Generic Swap Cash Flows: Pay-Fixed, Receive-Floating**

Our generic swap involves a series of n future cash flows at points in time represented simply here as 1, 2, ..., n. Let $S_i$ denote the floating interest rate cash flow based on some underlying, and let FS denote the cash flow based on some fixed interest rate. Notice how the cash flows are netted. If the floating rate $S_i$ increases above the agreed fixed rate FS, so $S_i > FS$, the fixed-rate payer (i.e., floating-rate receiver) will receive positive cash flow. If rates fall, so $S_i < FS$, the fixed-rate receiver (i.e., floating-rate payer) will receive the positive cash flow. We assume that the last cash flow occurs at the swap expiration. Later we will let $S_i$ denote the floating cash flows tied to currency movements or equity movements.

We again will rely on the arbitrage approach for determining the pricing of a swap. This procedure involves finding the fixed rate such that the value of the swap at initiation is zero. Recall that the goal of the arbitrageur is to generate positive cash flows with no risk and no investment of one's own capital. To understand swap valuation, we match the swap cash flows by synthetically creating a replicating portfolio from other instruments. The swap must have the same value as the synthetic portfolio, or arbitrage will result. A pay-fixed, receive-floating swap is equivalent to a short position (i.e., issuer) in a fixed-rate bond and a long position (i.e., investor) in a floating-rate bond. Assuming both bonds were initially priced at par, the initial cash flows are zero and the par payments at maturity offset each other. In other words, the **swap rate** is the rate at which the present value of all the expected floating-rate payments received over the life of the floating-rate bond equal the present value of all the expected fixed-rate payments made over the life of the fixed-rate bond. Thus, the fixed bond payment should be equivalent to the fixed swap payment. Exhibit 13 shows the view of a swap as a pair of bonds. Note that the coupon dates on the bonds match the settlement dates on the swap, and the maturity date matches the expiration date of the swap. As with all derivative instruments, numerous technical details have been simplified here. We will explore some of these details shortly.

### Exhibit 13: Receive-Floating, Pay-Fixed as a Portfolio of Bonds

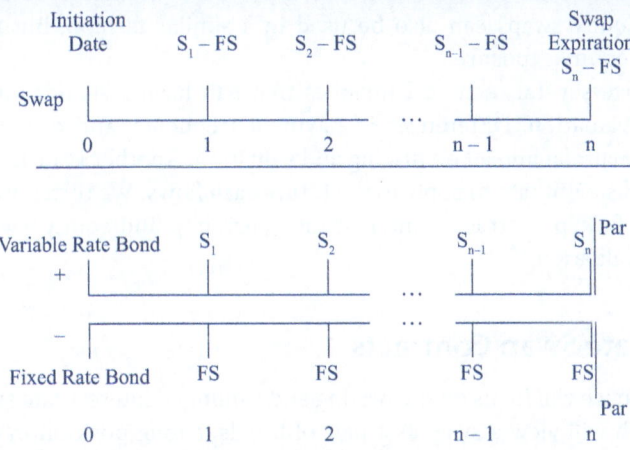

It is worth noting that our replicating portfolio did not need to use a pair of bonds. Swaps can also be viewed as a portfolio of forward or futures contracts. However, in practice futures have standardized characteristics, so there is rarely a set of futures contracts that can perfectly replicate a swap. In addition, because a single forward contract can be viewed as a portfolio of a call and a put (a long call and a short put at the same strike price equal to the swap's fixed rate would replicate the payoffs on a pay-fixed swap), a swap can also be viewed as a portfolio of options. The procedure is fairly straightforward in all cases. Just match the swap cash flows with the cash flows from a portfolio of marketable underlying instruments and rely on the law of one price and the absence of arbitrage to provide a value. Again, bonds are perhaps the best instruments to replicate a swap because they are easy to value.

Market participants often use swaps to transform one series of cash flows into another. For example, suppose that because of the relative ease of issuance, REB, Inc. sells a fixed-rate bond to investors. Based on careful analysis of the interest rate sensitivity of the company's assets, REB's leadership deems a MRR-based variable rate bond to be a more appropriate liability. By entering a receive-fixed, pay-floating interest rate swap, REB can create a synthetic floating-rate bond, as illustrated in Exhibit 15. REB issues fixed-rate bonds and thus must make periodic fixed-rate-based payments to the bond investors, denoted FIX. REB then enters a receive-fixed (FIX) and pay-floating (FLT) interest rate swap. The two fixed-rate payments cancel, leaving on net the floating-rate payments. Thus, we say that REB has created a synthetic floating-rate bond.

### Exhibit 14: REB's Synthetic Floating-Rate Bond Based on Fixed-Rate Bond Issuance with Receive-Fixed Swap

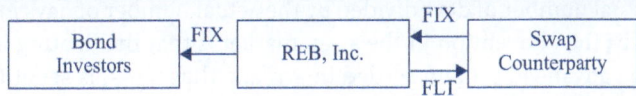

The example in Exhibit 14 is for a swap in which the underlying is an interest rate.

There are also currency swaps and equity swaps. Currency swaps can be used in a similar fashion, but the risks being addressed are both interest rate and currency exposures. Equity swaps can also be used in a similar fashion, but the risk being addressed is equity exposure.

Swaps have several technical nuances that can have a significant influence on pricing and valuation. Differences in payment frequency and day count methods often have a material impact on pricing and valuation. Another issue is identifying the appropriate discount rate to apply to the future cash flows. We turn now to examining three types of swap contracts—interest rate, currency, and equity—with a focus on pricing and valuation.

## Interest Rate Swap Contracts

In this section we will focus on the pricing and valuing of interest rate swap contracts. Our approach will view a swap as a pair of bonds, a long position in one bond and a short position in another bond. At inception of a fixed-for-floating swap, a fixed rate is selected so that the present value of the floating-rate payments is equal to the present value of the fixed-rate payments, meaning the swap value is zero for both parties at inception. The fixed rate (FS) is the swap rate. Determining the swap rate is equivalent to pricing the swap. As the market rates change and time passes over the term of the swap, the value of the swap changes. The swap value (the value of the two constituent bonds) can be positive (an asset) or negative (a liability) to the pay-fixed or receive-fixed swap holders.

Swaps are OTC products with many variations. For example, a plain vanilla MRR-based interest rate swap can involve different frequencies of cash flow settlements and day count conventions. In fact, a swap can have both semi-annual payments and quarterly payments as well as actual day counts and day counts based on 30 days per month. Unless stated otherwise, we will assume for simplicity that the notional amounts are all equal to one (NA = 1). Swap values per 1 notional amount can be simply multiplied by the actual notional amount to arrive at the swap's fair market value.

Interest rate swaps have two legs, typically a floating leg (FLT) and a fixed leg (FIX). The floating leg cash flow—denoted $S_i$ because the rate ($r_{FLT,i}$) may change (or float) during each period i—can be expressed as:

$$S_i = AP_{FLT} \times r_{FLT,i} = (NAD_{FLT}/NTD_{FLT}) \times r_{FLT,i}$$

and the fixed leg cash flow (denoted FS) can be expressed as:

$$FS = AP_{FIX} \times r_{FIX} = (NAD_{FIX}/NTD_{FIX}) \times r_{FIX}.$$

AP denotes the accrual period, $r_{FLT,i}$ denotes the observed floating rate appropriate for Time i, NAD denotes the number of accrued days during the payment period, NTD denotes the total number of days during the year applicable to each cash flow, and $r_{FIX}$ denotes the fixed swap rate. The accrual period accounts for the payment frequency and day count methods. The two most popular day count methods are known as 30/360 and ACT/ACT. As the name suggests, 30/360 treats each month as having 30 days; thus, a year has 360 days. ACT/ACT treats the accrual period as having the actual number of days divided by the actual number of days in the year (365 or 366). Finally, the convention in the swap market is that the floating interest rate is assumed to be advanced set and settled in arrears; thus, $r_{FLT,i}$ is set at the beginning of the period and paid at the end. If we assume constant and equal accrual periods (so, $AP_{FLT} = AP_{FIX}$), the receive-fixed, pay-floating *net* cash flow can be expressed as:

$$FS - S_i = AP \times (r_{FIX} - r_{FLT,i}),$$

and the pay-fixed, receive-floating *net* cash flow can be expressed as:

$$S_i - FS = AP \times (r_{FLT,i} - r_{FIX}).$$

# Pricing and Valuing Swap Contracts

As a simple example, if the fixed rate is 5%, the floating rate is 5.2%, and the accrual period is 30 days based on a 360-day year, the payment of a receive-fixed, pay-floating swap is calculated as:

$$FS - S_i = (30/360) \times (0.05 - 0.052) = -0.000167 \text{ per notional of } 1.$$

Because the floating rate exceeds the fixed rate, the receive-fixed (pay-floating) party would pay this amount (0.000167 per notional of 1) to the pay-fixed (receive-floating) party. In other words, only a single net payment is made by the receive-fixed party to the counterparty. The sign of the net payment is negative as it is an outflow (i.e., negative cash flow) for the receive-fixed (pay-floating) party. Moreover, assuming the notional amount (NA) is £100 million, the net payment made by the receive-fixed party is £16,700 (= –0.000167 x £100,000,000). Finally, if, instead, the fixed rate exceeds the floating rate, the sign of the net payment would be positive as it would be an inflow (i.e., positive cash flow) to the receive-fixed party from the pay-fixed counterparty.

We now turn to swap pricing. Exhibit 15 shows the cash flows for an interest rate swap along with a pair of bonds of equal par value. Suppose (at Step 1) the arbitrageur enters a receive-fixed, pay-floating interest rate swap with some initial value, $V_{swap}$. Replicating this swap with bonds would entail being long a fixed-rate bond (as the arbitrageur is receiving the fixed-rate coupon) and short a floating-rate bond (as she is paying the floating rate). Therefore, to price this swap, the arbitrageur creates the *opposite* of the replicating portfolio. So, at Step 2 she purchases a floating-rate bond whose value is denoted $V_{FLT}$. Note that the terms of the variable rate bond are selected to match exactly the floating payments of the swap. Next, a fixed-rate bond is sold short (Step 3)—equivalent to borrowing funds—with terms to match exactly the fixed payments of the swap.

### Exhibit 15: Cash Flows for Receive-Fixed, Pay-Floating Swap Offset with Bonds

| Position | Step | Time 0 | Time 1 | Time 2 | ... | Time n |
|---|---|---|---|---|---|---|
| **Swap** | Receive-fixed, pay-floating swap | $V_{swap}$ | $+FS - S_1$ | $+FS - S_2$ | ... | $+FS - S_n$ |
| **Offsetting Portfolio** | Buy floating-rate bond | $-V_{FLT}$ | $+S_1$ | $+S_2$ | ... | $+S_n + $ Par |
| | Short-sell fixed-rate bond | $+V_{FIX}$ | $-FS$ | $-FS$ | ... | $-(FS + $ Par$)$ |
| | **Net Cash Flows** | $V_{swap} = -V_{FLT} + V_{FIX} = 0$ | 0 | 0 | 0 | 0 |

This portfolio offsets the cash flows from the swap, so the net cash flows from Time 1 to Time n will all be equal to zero. So, in equilibrium we must have $V_{swap} = -V_{FLT} + V_{FIX} = 0$ to prevent an arbitrage opportunity. The value of a receive-fixed, pay-floating swap is:

$$V_{swap} = \text{Value of fixed bond} - \text{Value of floating bond} = V_{FIX} - V_{FLT}. \quad (11)$$

The value of a receive-fixed, pay-floating interest rate swap is simply the value of buying a fixed-rate bond and issuing (i.e., selling) a floating-rate bond. Remember, the fixed-rate and floating-rate bond values are just the PVs of all the expected interest and par payments. Pricing the swap means to determine the fixed rate ($r_{FIX}$) such that the value of the swap at initiation is zero. Said differently, to price the swap, the value of the fixed bond must equal the value of the floating bond in Equation 11.

As stated earlier, the value of a fixed bond ($V_{FIX}$) is the sum of the PV(All coupons) + PV(Par). If C is the coupon amount and par is 1, the value of a fixed-rate bond is, $V_{FIX}$ = sum of PV of all coupons (C) + PV of par value, or:

Value fixed bond rate: $V_{FIX} = C \sum_{i=1}^{n} PV_i(1) + PV_n(1)$. (12)

Notice the coupon amount in Equation 12 is multiplied by a summation term. This term includes the present value discount factors, PV(1), for each cash flow (or coupon payment). These PV factors are derived from the term structure of interest rates at the time of valuation. The summation adds up the PV factor for each coupon as it sequentially occurs. The sum of the PV of all the coupons is added to the PV of par at maturity (Time n). The present value expression is based on spot rates and is computed using the formula, $PV_i(1) = \dfrac{1}{1 + Rspot_i \left(\frac{NAD_i}{NTD}\right)}$. Spot interest rates ($Rspot_i$) will help us value each individual cash flow. As an illustration, consider the following term structure of rates for USD cash flows and the computation of their associated PV factors, as shown in Exhibit 16:

**Exhibit 16: Present Value Factors Using the Term Structure**

| Days to Maturity | US$ Spot Interest Rates (%) | Present Value (US$1) |
|---|---|---|
| 90 | 2.10 | 0.994777 |
| 180 | 2.25 | 0.988875 |
| 270 | 2.40 | 0.982318 |
| 360 | 2.54 | 0.975229 |
| | Sum: | 3.941199 |

The PV factors are computed for each rate in the term structure as:

$$PV_i(1) = \dfrac{1}{1 + Rspot_i \left(\frac{NAD_i}{NTD}\right)}.$$

Using this formula, we compute the PV factor for a unit cash flow of 1. For example, at 90 days, we have a spot rate of 2.10%, which implies a discount (PV) factor of 0.994777 = $1/[1 + 0.0210 (90/360)]. Similarly, for 360 days, we have a spot rate of 2.54%, which implies a PV factor of 0.975229 = 1/[1 + 0.0254(360/360)].

The present value factors make it straightforward to value a fixed-rate bond under a given term structure. For example, the value of a fixed 4% bond with quarterly interest payments and Par = 1 under the term structure in Exhibit 16 can be computed using Equation 12. The quarterly coupon payment, C, is 4%/4 on par of 1 or 0.01/quarter.

$$V_{FIX} = C \sum_{i=1}^{n} PV_i(1) + PV_n(1) = 0.01(3.941199) + 0.975229(1) = 1.014641.$$

So, using Equation 12 and the PV factors and their sum from Exhibit 16, we can quickly value the bond at 101.464% of par.

To find the fixed rate needed to price a swap, we first make a slight modification to the notation in Equation 12. Since the coupon C is just the fixed interest rate multiplied by Par (and Par is assumed to be 1), we can substitute $r_{FIX} = C$, so that:

$$V_{FIX} = r_{FIX} \sum_{i=1}^{n} PV_i(1) + PV_n(1).$$

# Pricing and Valuing Swap Contracts

The value of a floating-rate bond, $V_{FLT}$, at the reset date is 1 (par) because the interest payment is set to match the discount rate. Recall that when the YTM (discount rate) of a bond is equal to the coupon rate, the bond sells at par. Here, we assume par is 1. Because the floating rate and the discount rate are initially the same for our floating bond, at the reset date we have $V_{FLT}$ = par = 1.

Setting the value of the fixed bond in Equation 12 equal to 1 (the value of the floating bond at swap initiation, so $V_{FIX} = 1 = V_{FLT}$), we obtain:

$$V_{FIX} = r_{FIX} \sum_{i=1}^{n} PV_i(1) + PV_n(1) = 1.$$

This expression leads to the swap pricing equation, which sets $r_{FIX}$ for the fixed bond:

$$r_{FIX} = \frac{1 - PV_n(1)}{\sum_{i=1}^{n} PV_i(1)} \quad \text{(Swap Pricing Equation)}. \tag{13}$$

The fixed swap rate, the "price" that swap traders quote among one another, is simply one minus the *final* present value term divided by the sum of present values. The fixed swap leg cash flow (FS) for a unit of notional amount (NA) is simply the fixed swap rate adjusted for the accrual period, or:

$$FS = AP_{FIX} \times r_{FIX} \text{ (Fixed swap cash flow per unit of NA)}.$$

We can multiply FS times the notional amount later to find the cash flow for a swap in practice.

### EXAMPLE 13

### Solving for the Fixed Swap Rate Based on Present Value Factors

1. Suppose we are pricing a five-year MRR-based interest rate swap with annual resets (30/360 day count). The estimated present value factors, $PV_i(1)$, are given in the following table.

| Maturity (years) | Present Value Factors |
|---|---|
| 1 | 0.990099 |
| 2 | 0.977876 |
| 3 | 0.965136 |
| 4 | 0.951529 |
| 5 | 0.937467 |

The fixed rate of the swap ($r_{FIX}$) will be *closest* to:

A. 1.0%.
B. 1.3%.
C. 1.6%.

### Solution:

B is correct. Note that the sum of present values is:

$$\sum_{i=1}^{5} PV_i(1) = 0.990099 + 0.977876 + 0.965136 + 0.951529 + 0.937467$$

$$= 4.822107.$$

Since the final cash flow for a bond consists of the $n^{th}$ coupon plus par, we use the PV factor for the last cash flow, here cash flow 5, twice in Equation 11. We sum it with the other PV factors for the individual coupons in the denominator, and we apply it to Par in the numerator. Therefore, the solution for the fixed swap rate is:

$$r_{FIX} = \frac{1 - 0.937467}{4.822107} = 0.012968, \quad or \quad 1.2968\%.$$

From pricing a swap in Example 13, we now turn to interest rate swap valuation for a receive fixed (pay floating) swap. As noted previously, the fixed-rate receiver is effectively long a fixed bond and short a floating-rate bond. After initiation, this position will have a positive value when the fixed bond is trading at a premium to par (i.e., interest rates have fallen).

At any time after initiation, the market value of an existing swap can be understood by pricing a new offsetting swap. Assume $r_{FIX,0}$ is the swap rate at initiation. After initiation, the term structure of interest rates will likely imply a different swap rate, $r_{FIX,t}$.

The approach to value a multi-period swap is like the approach to valuing a single period FRA (i.e., multiplying the PV of the difference between the old FRA and the new FRA rates by a notional amount; Equation 6). Valuation is based on arbitrage transactions. Our initial swap position at Time 0 as a floating-rate payer would be offset by a position at Time t as a floating-rate receiver. The floating cash flows from paying and receiving will offset at each date (i), but the fixed payments will be different. We still receive the fixed rate, $r_{FIX,0}$, initially agreed to, but for the purposes of valuation we additionally assume the role as a fixed-rate payer at the new rate, $r_{FIX,t}$. The cash flows per unit of NA at each future date will always be based on the difference between the rate we initially received at Time 0 and the current rate paid at Time t, so $(FS_0 - FS_t) = AP(r_{FIX,0} - r_{FIX,t})$. Thus, the value of a *receive-fixed swap* at some future point in Time (t) is simply the sum of the present values of the difference in fixed swap rates times the stated notional amount (NA), or:

$$V_{SWAP,t} = NA \times (FS_0 - FS_t) \times \sum_{i=1}^{n} PV_i \quad \text{(Value of receive-fixed swap).} \quad (14)$$

In our valuation equation, n is the number of remaining cash flows from time t. Although this n may be different than the number of cash flows initially used to price the swap at time 0, we use the same notation. It is also important to be clear on which side of the swap this value applies. Notice the cash flow $FS_0$ in Equation 14 is positive. This is because the swap was initially set up (at Time 0) as a receive-fixed ($FS_0$), pay-floating swap. To establish a value, the swap is offset with a pay-fixed, receive-floating swap at Time t. Thus, when $FS_0$ has a positive sign, Equation 14 provides the value to the party initially receiving fixed. The negative of this amount is the value to the fixed-rate payer.

Now, since the *fixed-rate payer is effectively long a floating bond and short a fixed bond*, the position will have positive value when the fixed bond is trading at a discount to par (i.e., interest rates have risen). The fixed-rate payer is also the floating receiver and thus benefits as interest rates rise. At any date, the market value of a swap to the *fixed-rate payer* is based on the present value of the difference between the new offsetting fixed cash flow $FS_t$ to be received and the fixed cash flow $FS_0$ he or she originally agreed to pay. It will be the negative of the receive-fixed swap value ($V_{SWAP,t}$) given by Equation 14, and we can compute it as follows:

$$-V_{SWAP,t} = -1 \left[ NA \times (FS_0 - FS_t) \times \sum_{i=1}^{n} PV_i \right]$$

$$= NA \times (FS_t - FS_0) \times \sum_{i=1}^{n} PV_i \quad \text{(Value of pay-fixed swap).} \quad (15)$$

# Pricing and Valuing Swap Contracts

Exhibit 17 provides a summary of the swap legs and the associated replicating and offsetting portfolios for each swap leg. The replicating portfolio (at time 0) provides the same cash flows as our swap. The offsetting portfolio (at time t) will offset the cash flows from our replication of the swap and help us determine a value. Note that the floating cash flows at Time 0 and Time t cancel each other out. For valuation purposes, this allows us to focus on the difference in fixed swap rates. So, the value of a receive-fixed swap at time t is based on the difference between the initial fixed swap rate and the fixed swap rate at time t, or $r_{FIX,0} - r_{FIX,t}$, as shown in the last row of Exhibit 17.

### Exhibit 17: Swaps and Related Replicating and Offsetting Portfolios

| Swap | | Receive-Fixed, Pay-Floating | | Pay-Fixed, Receive-Floating | |
|---|---|---|---|---|---|
| | | Portfolio Position | Rates | Portfolio Position | Rates |
| Replicating Portfolio | Initiation t = 0 | Long Fixed-Rate Bond / Short Floating-Rate Bond | $r_{FIX,0} - r_{FLT,0}$ | Long Floating-Rate Bond / Short Fixed-Rate Bond | $r_{FLT,0} - r_{FIX,0}$ |
| Offsetting Portfolio | Time = t | Short Fixed-Rate Bond / Long Floating-Rate Bond | $r_{FLT,t} - r_{FIX,t}$ | Short Floating-Rate Bond / Long Fixed-Rate Bond | $r_{FIX,t} - r_{FLT,t}$ |
| Rates for Swap Valuation | Time = t | | $r_{FIX,0} - r_{FIX,t}$ | | $r_{FIX,t} - r_{FIX,0}$ |

The examples illustrated here show swap valuation only on a payment date. If a swap is being valued between payment dates, some adjustments are necessary. We do not pursue this topic here.

### EXAMPLE 14

#### Solving for Receive-Fixed Swap Value Based on Present Value Factors

Suppose two years ago we entered a €100,000,000 seven-year receive-fixed MRR-based interest rate swap with annual resets. The fixed rate in the swap contract entered two years ago was 2.0%. The estimated present value factors, $PV_i(1)$, are repeated from the previous example.

| Maturity (years) | Present Value Factors |
|---|---|
| 1 | 0.990099 |
| 2 | 0.977876 |
| 3 | 0.965136 |
| 4 | 0.951529 |
| 5 | 0.937467 |
| Sum | 4.822107 |

We know from the previous example that the current equilibrium fixed swap rate is close to 1.30% (two years after the swap was originally entered).

1. The value for the swap party receiving the fixed rate will be *closest* to:

   **A.** −€5,000,000.

   **B.** €3,375,000.

C. €4,822,000.

### Solution to 1:

B is correct. $r_{FIX,0} = 2.0\%$, and $r_{FIX,t} = 1.3\%$. We assume annual resets (AP = 360/360 = 1), so the cash flow per unit notional is $FS_0 = 2.0\%$ and $FS_t = 1.3\%$.

The swap value to the fixed-rate receiver is:

$$V_{SWAP,t} = NA \times (FS_0 - FS_t) \times \sum_{i=1}^{5} PV_i$$
$$= €100,000,000 \times (0.02 - 0.013) \times 4.822107 = €3,375,000.$$

2. The value for the swap party paying the fixed rate will be *closest* to:

   A. −€4,822,000.
   B. −€3,375,000.
   C. €5,000,000.

### Solution to 2:

B is correct. The equivalent pay-fixed swap value is simply the negative of the receive-fixed swap value:

$$-V_{SWAP,t} = NA \times (FS_t - FS_0) \times \sum_{i=1}^{5'} PV_i$$
$$= €100,000,000 \times (0.013 - 0.02) \times 4.822107$$
$$= -€3,375,000.$$

## 6. PRICING AND VALUING CURRENCY SWAP CONTRACTS

> describe how currency swaps are priced, and calculate and interpret their no-arbitrage value

A currency swap is a contract in which two counterparties agree to exchange future interest payments in different currencies. In a currency swap, one party is long a bond (fixed or floating) denominated in one currency and short a bond (fixed or floating) in another currency. The procedure for pricing and valuing currency swaps is like the pricing and valuation of interest rate swaps. Currency swaps come in a wide array of types and structures. We review a few key features:

1. Currency swaps often involve an exchange of notional amounts at both the initiation of the swap and at the expiration of the swap.
2. The payment on each leg of the swap is in a different currency unit, such as euros and Japanese yen, and the payments are not netted.
3. Each leg of the swap can be either fixed or floating.

Pricing a currency swap involves solving for three key variables: two fixed interest rates (each in a different currency) and one notional amount. We must determine the appropriate notional amount in one currency, given the notional amount in the other currency, as well as two fixed-interest rates such that the currency swap value is zero at initiation.

# Pricing and Valuing Currency Swap Contracts

We will focus on fixed-for-fixed currency swaps, so we essentially trade cash flows on a bond in one currency for cash flows on a bond in another currency. Let k be the currency units, such as euros and yen. Letters are used here rather than numbers to avoid confusion with calendar time. The value of a fixed-rate bond in currency k with par of 1 can be expressed generically as the present value of the coupons plus the present value of par, or:

$$V_k = C_k \sum_{i=1}^{n} PV_i(1) + PV_n(Par_k).$$

$C_k$ is the coupon in currency k, and $Par_k$ is the Par value paid at maturity in currency k. The value of a fixed-for-fixed currency swap, $V_{CS}$, is the difference in the price of two bonds. That is, the value of a currency swap is simply the value of a bond in currency a ($V_a$) less the value of a bond in currency b ($V_b$), expressed in terms of currency a, as follows:

$$V_{CS} = V_a - S_0 V_b.$$

Here, $S_0$ is the spot exchange rate at time 0. To make each party indifferent between the two bonds, the par or principal notional amounts are set to reflect the current spot exchange rate. This will lead to the swap having zero value ($V_{CS} = 0$) at inception (to prevent any arbitrage opportunity), so

$$V_a = S_0 V_b.$$

The swap value may change after initiation as the exchange rate and interest rates on the two currencies fluctuate. Currency swap valuation is best understood by considering an example. Exhibit 18 provides an illustration of an at-market 10-year receive-fixed US$ and pay-fixed € swap. The US$ bond has an annual coupon of US$30 and par of US$1,150. The annual coupon amount of the euro-denominated bond is €9 with par of €1,000. Both bonds are assumed to be trading at par (note, this is $1,150 for the US$ bond, not the usual $1,000) and have a 10-year maturity. We proceed as follows:

- Step 1: We enter the receive-fixed US$ and pay-fixed € swap.

  In Steps 2 and 3, we create a portfolio to offset the swap cash flows.

- Step 2 involves short-selling a US bond (so, paying the fixed US$ coupon on the bond) to offset the US dollar inflows from the swap.

- Step 3 involves purchasing a euro bond (so, receiving the fixed € coupon on the bond), which provides offsetting cash flows for the pay-fixed € portion of the swap.

### Exhibit 18: Numerical Example of Currency Swap Offset with Bonds

| Position | Step | Time 0 | Time 1 | Time 2 | ... | Time 10 |
|---|---|---|---|---|---|---|
| Swap | 1. Receive-fixed US$, pay-fixed euro swap | 0 | +$30 − ($1.5/€) x €9 = +$16.5 | +$30 − ($1.1/€) x €9 = +$20.1 | ... | +($30 + $1,150) − ($1.2/€) x (€9 + €1,000) = −$30.8 |
| Offsetting Bond Portfolio | 2. Short-sell US$ bond | +$1,150 | −$30 | −$30 | ... | −($30 + $1,150) |
| | 3. Buy euro bond | −($1.15/€) x €1,000 = −$1,150 | +($1.5/€) x €9 = +$13.5 | +($1.1/€) x €9 = +$9.9 | ... | +($1.2/€) x (€9 + €1,000) = $1,210.8 |

| Position | Step | Time 0 | Time 1 | Time 2 | ... | Time 10 |
|---|---|---|---|---|---|---|
| Offsetting Portfolio Cash Flows | | 0 | −$16.5 | −$20.1 | ... | +$30.8 |
| Overall Net Cash Flows | | 0 | 0 | 0 | 0 | 0 |

The cash flows from the bond portfolio will exactly offset the cash flows from the swap. This illustration assumes a current spot exchange rate ($S_0$) at which €1 trades for US$1.15, so $S_0 = \$1.15/€1$. Selected future spot exchange rates are $S_1 = \$1.50/€1$, $S_2 = \$1.10/€1$, and $S_{10} = \$1.20/€1$. These future spot exchange rates are used to show the conversion of future euro cash flows into US dollars, but notice that the overall net cash flows are all zero regardless of the future spot exchange rates. In other words, we could have used any numbers for $S_1$, $S_2$, and $S_{10}$. Regardless of exchange rates in the future, the bond portfolio and the swap always have offsetting cash flows. Since the portfolio and swap produce identical (although opposite) cash flows, the law of one price will allow us to determine a value for our swap in terms of a pair of bonds.

Since the net cash flows are 0 at every time t, the portfolio must be worth 0 initially. Exhibit 18 provides the intuition for solving for the notional amount (NA). For a zero cash flow at initiation, the NA (or par value) of the bond denominated in currency a ($NA_a$) must equal the spot exchange $S_0$ rate times the notional amount (or par value) of the bond denominated in currency b ($NA_b$). That is,

$$NA_a = S_0 \times NA_b.$$

The exchange rate is stated as number of units of currency a to buy one unit of currency b. The spot exchange rate in Exhibit 18 is $\$1.15/€1$, so currency a (in the numerator) is US\$. At the prevailing exchange rate $S_0$, it takes $1.15 to buy one euro. $NA_a = \$1,150$ and $S_0 = \$1.15/€1$, so $NA_b = \$1,150/(\$1.15/€1) = €1,000$. Therefore, the swap value at initiation is equal to zero, as it should be:

$$V_{CS} = V_a - S_0 V_b = \$1,150 - (\$1.15/€1) \times €1,000 = 0.$$

At any time during the life (tenor) of the swap shown in Exhibit 18, the opposite cash flows from the offsetting bond transactions result in a zero net cash flow. If the initial swap value is not at market or zero, then there are arbitrage opportunities. If the initial swap value is positive, then a set of arbitrage transactions would be implemented to capture the initial value with no net cash outflow. If the initial swap value is negative, then the opposite set of transactions would be implemented. The goal is to determine the fixed rates of the swap such that the current swap value is zero.

Because the fixed swap rate does not depend on the notional amounts, the fixed swap rates are found in the same manner as the fixed swap rate in an interest rate swap. For emphasis, we repeat the equilibrium fixed swap rate equations for each currency:

$$r_a = \frac{1 - PV_{n,a}(1)}{\sum_{i=1}^{n} PV_{i,a}(1)} \quad \text{and} \quad r_b = \frac{1 - PV_{n,b}(1)}{\sum_{i=1}^{n} PV_{i,b}(1)}. \tag{16}$$

We now have a solution for each of the three swap variables: one notional amount ($NA_a = S_0 \times NA_b$) and two fixed interest rates from Equation 16. Again, the fixed swap rate in each currency is simply one minus the final present value term divided by the sum of present values. We need to be sure that the present value terms are expressed in the appropriate currency. We illustrate currency swap pricing with spot rates by way of an example.

**Pricing and Valuing Currency Swap Contracts**

## EXAMPLE 15

### Currency Swap Pricing with Spot Rates

A US company needs to borrow 100 million Australian dollars (A$) for one year for its Australian subsidiary. The company decides to issue US$-denominated bonds in an amount equivalent to A$100 million. Then, the company enters into a one-year currency swap with quarterly reset (30/360 day count) and the exchange of notional amounts at initiation and at maturity. At the swap's initiation, the US company receives the notional amount in Australian dollars and pays to the counterparty, a swap dealer, the notional amount in US dollars. At the swap's expiration, the US company pays the notional amount in Australian dollars and receives from the counterparty the notional amount in US dollars. Based on interbank rates, we observe the following spot rates today, at Time 0, and compute their PV factors and sums:

| Days to Maturity | A$ Spot Interest Rates (%) | Present Value (A$1) | US$ Spot Interest Rates (%) | Present Value (US$1) |
|---|---|---|---|---|
| 90 | 2.50 | 0.993789[a] | 0.10 | 0.999750 |
| 180 | 2.60 | 0.987167 | 0.15 | 0.999251[b] |
| 270 | 2.70 | 0.980152 | 0.20 | 0.998502 |
| 360 | 2.80 | 0.972763 | 0.25 | 0.997506 |
|  | Sum: | 3.933870 | Sum: | 3.995009 |

[a] A$0.993789 = 1/[1 + 0.0250(90/360)].
[b] US$0.999251 = 1/[1 + 0.00150(180/360)].

Assume that the counterparties in the currency swap agree to an A$/US$ spot exchange rate of 1.140 (expressed as number of Australian dollars for US$1).

1. The annual fixed swap rates for Australian dollars and US dollars, respectively, will be *closest* to:

    A. 2.80% and 0.10%.
    B. 2.77% and 0.25%.
    C. 2.65% and 0.175%.

### Solution to 1:

B is correct. Since the PV factors are given, we do not need to compute them from the spot rates. Using Equation 16, the Australian dollar periodic fixed swap rate is:

$$r_{AUD} = \frac{1 - PV_{n,AUD}(1)}{\sum_{i=1}^{4} PV_{i,AUD}(1)} = \frac{1 - 0.972763}{3.933870}$$

= 0.00692381 or 0.692381%.

The US dollar periodic fixed swap rate is:

$$r_{USD} = \frac{1 - PV_{n,USD}(1)}{\sum_{i=1}^{4} PV_{i,USD}(1)} = \frac{1 - 0.997506}{3.995009}$$

= 0.00062422 or 0.062422%.

The annualized rate is simply (360/90) times the period results: 2.7695% for Australian dollars and 0.2497% for US dollars.

2. The notional amount (in US$ millions) will be *closest* to:

   A. 88.
   B. 100.
   C. 114.

### Solution to 2:

A is correct. The US dollar notional amount is calculated as A$100 million divided by the current spot exchange rate, A$1.140/US$1. From $NA_a = S_0 \times NA_b$, we have A$100,000,000 = A$1.14/US$1 × $N_b$. Solving for $N_b$ we have US$87,719,298 = A$100,000,000/(A$1.14/US$1).

3. The fixed swap quarterly payments in the currency swap will be *closest* to:

   A. A$692,000 and US$55,000.
   B. A$220,000 and US$173,000.
   C. A$720,000 and US$220,000.

### Solution to 3:

A is correct. The fixed swap quarterly payments in currency units equal the *periodic* swap rate times the appropriate notional amounts. From the answers to 1 and 2, we have

$FS_{A\$} = NA_{A\$} \times (AP) \times r_{A\$}$

= A$100,000,000 × (90/360) × (0.027695)

= A$692,375

and

$FS_{US\$} = NA_{US\$} \times (AP) \times r_{US\$}$

= US$87,719,298 × (90/360) × (0.002497)

= US$54,759.

One approach to pricing currency swaps is to view the swap as a pair of fixed-rate bonds. The main advantage of this approach is that all foreign exchange considerations are moved to the initial exchange rate. We do not need to address future foreign currency transactions. Also, note that a fixed-for-floating currency swap (i.e., pay-fixed currency a, receive-floating currency b) is simply a fixed-for-fixed currency swap (i.e., pay-fixed currency a, receive-fixed currency b) paired with a fixed-for-floating interest rate swap (i.e., pay-fixed currency b, receive-floating currency b). Also, we do not technically "price" a floating-rate swap because we do not designate a single coupon rate and because the value of such a swap is par on any reset date. Thus, we have the capacity to price any variation of currency swaps.

# Pricing and Valuing Currency Swap Contracts

We now turn to currency swap valuation. Recall that with currency swaps, there are two main sources of risk: interest rates associated with each currency and their exchange rate. The value of a fixed-for-fixed currency swap at some future point in time, say Time t, is simply the difference in a pair of fixed-rate bonds, one expressed in currency a and one expressed in currency b. To express the bonds in the same currency units, we convert the currency b bond into units of currency a through a spot foreign exchange transaction at a new rate, $S_t$. The value of a "receive currency a, pay currency b" (fixed-for-fixed) swap at any time t expressed in terms of currency a is the difference in bond values:

$$V_{CS} = V_a - S_t V_b.$$

Substituting the valuation equation for each of the bonds, we have:

$$V_{CS} = \left(FS_a \sum_{i=1}^{n} PV_i(1) + NA_a\, PV_n(1)\right) - S_t \left(FS_b \sum_{i=1}^{n} PV_i(1) + NA_b\, PV_n(1)\right).$$

Note that the fixed swap amount (FS) is the per-period fixed swap rate times the notional amount. Therefore, the currency swap valuation equation can be expressed as:

$$V_{CS} = NA_a \left(r_{Fix,a} \sum_{i=1}^{n} PV_i(1) + PV_n(1)\right) - S_t NA_b \left(r_{Fix,b} \sum_{i=1}^{n} PV_i(1) + PV_n(1)\right). \tag{17}$$

As mentioned, the terms in Equation 17 represent the difference in value of two fixed-rate bonds. The first term in braces is the value of a long position in a bond with face value of 1 unit of currency a, which is then multiplied by the notional amount of the swap in currency a ($NA_a$). This product represents the value of the cash inflows to the counterparty receiving interest payments in currency a. The second term (after the minus sign) implies outflows and represents the value of a short bond position with face value of 1 unit of currency b, which is multiplied by the product of the swap notional amount in currency b ($NA_b$) and the current (Time t) exchange rate, $S_t$ (stated in units of currency a per unit of currency b). This gives the value of the payments, in currency a terms, made by the party receiving interest in currency a and paying interest in currency b. $V_{CS}$ is then the value of the swap to the party receiving currency a, while the value of the swap to the party receiving currency b is simply the negative of that amount, $-V_{CS}$.

Equation 17 seems formidable, but it is a straightforward idea. We hold a bond in currency a, and we are short a bond in currency b (which we must express in terms of currency a). It is best understood by an example of a firm that has entered a currency swap and needs to determine the current value.

Example 16 continues the case of the company using a currency swap to effectively convert a bond issued in US dollars into a bond issued in Australian dollars. In studying the problem, take care to identify currency a (implied by how the exchange rate, $S_t$, is given) and the party receiving interest payments in currency a in the swap.

### EXAMPLE 16

#### Currency Swap Valuation with Spot Rates

This example builds on the previous example addressing currency swap pricing. Recall that a US company needed to borrow 100 million Australian dollars (A$) for one year for its Australian subsidiary. The company decided to borrow in US dollars (US$) an amount equivalent to A$100 million by issuing US-denominated bonds. The company then entered a one-year currency swap with a swap dealer. The swap uses quarterly reset (30/360 day count) and exchange of notional amounts at initiation and at maturity. At the swap's expiration, the US company pays the notional amount in Australian dollars and receives from the dealer the notional amount in US dollars. The fixed rates were found to be 2.7695% for Australian dollars and 0.2497% for US dollars. Initially, the notional amount in US dollars was determined to be US$87,719,298 with a spot exchange rate of A$1.14 for US$1.

Assume 60 days have passed since swap initiation and we now observe the following updated market information:

| Days to Maturity | A$ Spot Interest Rates (%) | Present Value (A$1) | US$ Spot Interest Rates (%) | Present Value (US$1) |
|---|---|---|---|---|
| 30 | 2.00 | 0.998336 | 0.50 | 0.999584 |
| 120 | 1.90 | 0.993707 | 0.40 | 0.998668 |
| 210 | 1.80 | 0.989609 | 0.30 | 0.998253 |
| 300 | 1.70 | 0.986031 | 0.20 | 0.998336 |
|  | Sum: | 3.967683 | Sum: | 3.994841 |

The currency spot exchange rate ($S_t$) is now A$1.13 for US$1.

1. The current value to the swap dealer in A$ of the currency swap entered 60 days ago will be *closest* to:

   A. −A$13,557,000.
   B. A$637,620.
   C. A$2,145,200.

## Solution to 1:

C is correct. The US firm issues $87.7 million of bonds and enters a swap with the swap dealer. The initial exchange rate is given as 1.14A$/1US$, so currency a is A$. The swap dealer is receiving quarterly interest payments in currency a (A$). The swap is diagrammed for Example 15 and Example 16 as shown below:

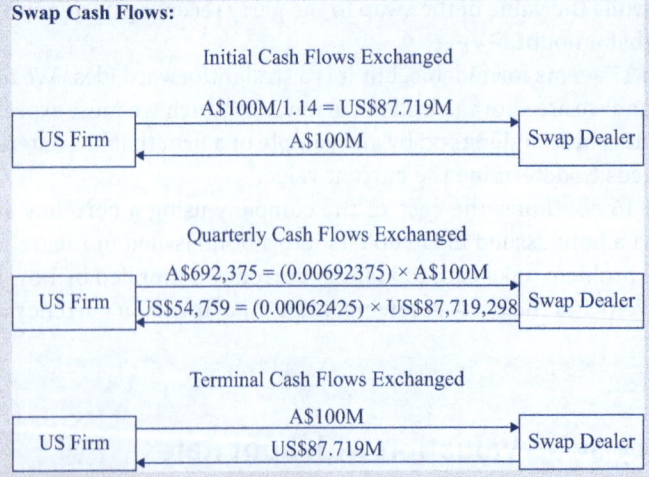

After 60 days, the new exchange rate is 1.13A$/1US$ and the term structure of interest rates has changed in both markets. Equation 17 gives the value of the swap at Time t, $V_{CS}$. This is the value of the swap to the party receiving interest payments in Australian dollars, which is the swap dealer. Thus, using Equation 14, the value to the swap dealer receiving A$ is:

$$V_{CS} = NA_a\left(r_{Fix,a}\sum_{i=1}^{n} PV_i(1) + PV_n(1)\right) - S_t NA_b\left(r_{Fix,b}\sum_{i=1}^{n} PV_i(1) + PV_n(1)\right)$$

$V_{CS}$ = A\$100,000,000 × [0.00692375 (3.967683) + 0.986031] − 1.13 (A\$/1US\$) × (US\$87,719,298) × [0.00062425 (3.994841) + 0.998336]

= A\$2,145,167.

The first term in Equation 17 represents the PV of the dealer's incoming cash flows in A\$, effectively a long position in an A\$ bond. Remember, the dealer is receiving quarterly interest payments in A\$ and will receive the A\$100M terminal payment at swap maturity. To compute the PV of the A\$ cash flows, the notional amount is multiplied by a term inside the braces, which represents the periodic interest rate multiplied by the sum of the PV factors for the four payments plus the PV factor for the terminal cash flow (where the PV factors reflect the new term structure). The second term is the PV of the dealer's US\$ outflows (effectively a short bond in currency b, here US\$). The PV of the quarterly interest payments and terminal payment are calculated using the new term structure and converted into A\$ at $S_t$. Thus, we have the value of the long A\$ bond minus the value of short US\$ bond (stated in A\$ terms). This gives $V_{CS}$, which is the value of the swap to the party receiving currency a and is the value from the perspective of the swap dealer.

2. The current value to the US firm in US\$ of the currency swap entered 60 days ago will be *closest* to:

   A. −\$2,673,705.
   B. −\$1,898,400.
   C. \$334,730.

## Solution to 2:

B is correct. In terms of Solution 1, the current value of the swap to the US firm is $-V_{CS}$. This represents the value to the firm making interest payments in currency a (A\$).

$-V_{CS}$ = −A\$2,145,167, which when converted to US\$ at $S_t$ is:

$-V_{CS}$ = −A\$2,145,167 × (1US\$/1.13A\$) = −US\$1,898,378.

Note that the US company initially issues a bond in US\$ in their home market and uses the swap to effectively convert to an A\$ bond issue. Understanding the swap as two bonds, the US firm is long a US\$ bond (US\$ is currency b in this example, which the US firm is receiving) and short a bond in A\$ (currency a, which the US firm is paying). The swap offsets the US firm's US\$ bond issue. The swap allows the US firm to make A\$ interest payments to the swap dealer, or to effectively issue a bond in A\$ (currency a). Alternatively, if the exchange rate had been stated as $S_t$ = 1US\$/1.13A\$ or equivalently as $S_t$ = \$0.885/A\$, then currency a would be US\$. In that case, the swap value, $V_{CS}$, can be understood in terms of the firm receiving US\$ since the swap gives the US firm the equivalent of a long position in a US\$ bond. The first term in the following equation represents the value of the US\$ bond to the US firm in the swap. The second term is the value of the A\$ bond position (short for the US firm) expressed in US\$ terms.

$$V_{CS} = NA_a\left(r_{Fix,a}\sum_{i=1}^{n}PV_i(1) + PV_n(1)\right) - S_t NA_b\left(r_{Fix,b}\sum_{i=1}^{n}PV_i(1) + PV_n(1)\right)$$

$V_{CS}$ = $87,719,298 x [0.00062422 (3.994841) + 0.998336] − (1US$/A$1.13) x (A$100,000,000) x [0.00692381 (3.967683) + 0.986031]

= −US$1,898,410.

The swap value is negative to the US firm due to changes in the term structure and exchange rate. The A$ has strengthened against the US$, so now the US firm must pay periodic interest and principal cash flows in A$ at a rate of 1.13A$/1US$. That is, for each US$ the US firm gets fewer A$ for making payments to the dealer. The new term structure now offers lower interest rates to A$ borrowers, and this also contributes to the negative swap value for the US firm. The firm had agreed to pay higher periodic A$ rates in the swap, but now the present value of those outflows has increased.

# 7  PRICING AND VALUING EQUITY SWAP CONTRACTS

☐ describe how equity swaps are priced, and calculate and interpret their no-arbitrage value

Drawing on our prior definition of a swap, we define an equity swap in the following manner: An **equity swap** is an OTC derivatives contract in which two parties agree to exchange a series of cash flows whereby one party pays a variable series that will be determined by an equity and the other party pays either (1) a variable series determined by a different equity or rate or (2) a fixed series. An equity swap is used to convert the returns from an equity investment into another series of returns, which, as noted, either can be derived from another equity series or can be a fixed rate. Equity swaps are widely used in equity portfolio investment management to modify returns and risks. Equity swaps allow parties to benefit from returns of an equity or index without owning any shares of the underlying equity. An equity swap may also be used to hedge risk exposure to an equity or index for a certain period.

We examine three types of equity swaps: 1) *receive-equity return, pay-fixed*; 2) *receive-equity return, pay-floating*; and 3) *receive-equity return, pay-another equity return*. Like interest rate swaps and currency swaps, equity swaps have several unique nuances. We highlight just a few. First, the underlying reference instrument for the equity leg of an equity swap can be an individual stock, a published stock index, or a custom portfolio. Second, the equity leg cash flow(s) can be with or without dividends. Third, all the interest rate swap nuances exist with equity swaps that have a fixed or floating interest rate leg.

We focus here on viewing an equity swap as a portfolio of an equity position and a bond. The equity swap cash flows can be expressed as follows:

NA(Equity return − Fixed rate) (for receive-equity, pay-fixed),

NA(Equity return − Floating rate) (for receive-equity, pay-floating), and

NA(Equity return$_a$ − Equity return$_b$) (for receive-equity, pay-equity),

# Pricing and Valuing Equity Swap Contracts

where a and b denote different equities. Note that an equity-for-equity swap can be viewed simply as a receive-equity a, pay-fixed swap combined with a pay-equity b, receive-fixed swap. The fixed payments cancel out, and we have synthetically created an equity-for-equity swap.

The cash flows for an equity leg ($S_i$) of an equity swap can be expressed as:

$S_i = NA_E \, R_E$,

where $R_E$ denotes the periodic return of the equity either with or without dividends as specified in the swap contract, and $NA_E$ denotes the notional amount. The cash flows for a fixed-interest rate leg (FS) of an equity swap are the same as those of an interest rate swap, or:

$FS = NA_E \times AP_{FIX} \times r_{FIX}$,    *AP: accrual period*

where $AP_{FIX}$ denotes the accrual period for the fixed leg (for which we assume the accrual period is constant) and $r_{FIX}$ here denotes the fixed rate on the equity swap.

### EXAMPLE 17

#### Equity Swap Cash Flows

Suppose we entered a receive-equity index and pay-fixed swap. It is quarterly reset, 30/360 day count, €5,000,000 notional amount, pay-fixed (1.6% annualized, quarterly pay, or 0.4% per quarter).

1. If the equity index return was 4.0% for the quarter (not annualized), the equity swap cash flow will be *closest* to:

    **A.** −€220,000.
    **B.** −€180,000.
    **C.** €180,000.

#### Solution to 1:

C is correct. Note that the equity index return is reported on a quarterly basis. It is not an annualized number. The fixed leg is often reported on an annual basis. Thus, one must carefully interpret the different return conventions. In this case, receive-equity index counterparty cash flows ($S_i$ − FS = $NA_E \times (R_E - r_{FIX})$) are as follows:

€5,000,000 × (0.040 − 0.004)

= €180,000 (Receive 4%, pay 0.4% for the quarter).

2. If the equity index return was −6.0% for the quarter (not annualized), the equity swap cash flow will be closest to:

    **A.** −€320,000.
    **B.** −€180,000.
    **C.** €180,000.

#### Solution to 2:

A is correct. Similar to 1, we have ($S_i$ − FS = $NA_E \times (R_E - r_{FIX})$):

€5,000,000 × (−0.060 − 0.004)

> = –€320,000 (Receive –6%, pay 0.4% for the quarter).
>
> When the equity leg of the swap is negative, then the receive-equity counterparty must pay both the equity return as well as the fixed rate (or whatever are the payment terms). Note also that equity swaps may cause liquidity problems. As seen here, if the equity return is negative, then the receive-equity return, pay-floating or pay-fixed swap may result in a large negative cash flow for the receive-equity return party.

For equity swaps, the equity position could be a wide variety of claims, including the return on a stock index with or without dividends and the return on an individual stock with or without dividends. For our objectives here, we ignore the influence of dividends with the understanding that the equity swap leg assumes all dividends are reinvested in the equity position. The arbitrage transactions for an equity swap when dividends are not included are extremely complex and beyond our objectives. The equity leg of the swap is produced by selling the equity position on a reset date and reinvesting the original equity notional amount ($NA_E$), leaving a remaining balance that is the cash flow required of the equity swap leg ($S_i$). Technically, we just sell off any equity value in excess of $NA_E$ or purchase additional shares to return the equity value to $NA_E$, effectively generating $S_i$. Exhibit 19 shows the cash flows from an equity swap offset with an equity and bond portfolio.

### Exhibit 19: Cash Flows for Receive-Fixed, Pay-Equity Swap Offset with Equity and Bond Portfolio

| Position | Steps | Time 0 | Time 1 | Time 2 | ... | Time n |
|---|---|---|---|---|---|---|
| Equity Swap | 1. Receive-fixed, pay-equity swap | $-V_{EQ}$ | $+FS - S_1$ | $+FS - S_2$ | ... | $+FS - S_n$ |
| Offset Portfolio | 2. Buy $NA_E$ of equity | $-NA_E$ | $+S_1$ | $+S_2$ | ... | $+S_n + NA_E$ |
| | 3. Short sell fixed-rate bond | $+V_{FIX}$, (C = FS) | $-FS$ | $-FS$ | ... | $-(FS + Par)$ |
| | Net cash flows | $-V_{EQ} - NA_E + V_{FIX}$ | 0 | 0 | 0 | $NA_E - Par$ |

Assume a portfolio manager has a large position in a stock that he/she expects to underperform in the future. Perhaps for liquidity or tax reasons, the manager prefers not to sell the stock but considers a receive-fixed, pay equity swap. Exhibit 19 shows the cash flows from such a swap as well as the offsetting portfolio (to eliminate arbitrage), which will assist us in valuing the swap. In Step 1, we enter a receive-fixed, pay equity swap. Steps 2 and 3 provide the offsetting cash flows to those of the swap, which are buy $NA_E$ worth of equity and short sell a fixed-rate bond (with coupon equal to the fixed interest rate leg cash flows), respectively. Notice that from Time 1 to n – 1 the sum of these three transactions is always zero. Note also that the final (Time n) cash flow for the long position in the equity includes the periodic return ($S_n$) plus the sale proceeds of the underlying equity position ($NA_E$). For the terminal cash flows to equal zero, we must either set the bond par value to equal the initial equity position ($NA_E$ = Par) or finance this difference. In this latter case, the bond par value could be different from the notional amount of equity.

As shown, the swap and pair of offsetting transactions produce 0 net cash flow from period 1 to period n – 1. In equilibrium, we require $-V_{EQ} - NA_E + V_{FIX} - PV(Par - NA_E) = 0$. That is, if the portfolio has initial value with no required cash outflow, then arbitrage will be possible. Hence, the equity swap value is:

$$V_{EQ} = V_{FIX} - NA_E - PV(Par - NA_E).$$

# Pricing and Valuing Equity Swap Contracts

Assuming equilibrium ($V_{EQ} = 0$), the fixed swap rate can be expressed as the $r_{FIX}$ rate such that $V_{FIX} = NA_E + PV(Par - NA_E)$. Note that assuming $NA_E = Par = 1$ and using our fixed bond pricing (Equation 10), we have the pricing equation for an equity swap:

$$r_{FIX} = \frac{1 - PV_n(1)}{\sum_{i=1}^{n} PV_i(1)}.$$

You should recognize that the pricing of an equity swap is identical to Equation 11 for the pricing of a comparable interest rate swap, even though the future cash flows are dramatically different. If the swap required a floating payment, there would be no need to price the swap; the floating side effectively prices itself at par automatically at the start. If the swap involves paying one equity return against another, there would also be no need to price it. You could effectively view this arrangement as *paying equity "a" and receiving the fixed rate* as specified and *receiving equity "b" and paying the same fixed rate*. The fixed rates would cancel.

Finding the value of an equity swap after the swap is initiated, say at Time t (so, $V_{EQ,t}$), is similar to valuing an interest rate swap except that rather than adjusting the floating-rate bond for the last floating rate observed (remember, advanced set), we adjust the value of the notional amount of equity, as shown in Equation 18:

$$V_{EQ,t} = V_{FIX}(C_0) - (S_t/S_{t-1})NA_E - PV(Par - NA_E), \qquad (18)$$

where $V_{FIX}(C_0)$ denotes the value at Time t of a fixed-rate bond initiated with coupon $C_0$ at Time 0, $S_t$ denotes the current equity price, $S_{t-1}$ denotes the equity price observed at the last reset date, and PV() denotes the present value function from the swap maturity date to Time t.

### EXAMPLE 18

### Equity Swap Pricing

1. In Examples 13 and 14 related to interest rate swaps, we considered a five-year, annual reset, 30/360 day count, MRR-based swap. The following table provides the present values per €1, $PV_i(1)$.

| Maturity (years) | Present Value Factors |
|---|---|
| 1 | 0.990099 |
| 2 | 0.977876 |
| 3 | 0.965136 |
| 4 | 0.951529 |
| 5 | 0.937467 |

Assume an annual reset Libor floating-rate bond trading at par. The fixed rate was previously found to be 1.2968% (see Example 13). Given these same data (just shown), the fixed interest rate in the EURO STOXX 50 equity swap is *closest* to:

A. 0.0%.

B. 1.1%.

C. 1.3%.

## Solution:

C is correct. The fixed rate on an equity swap is the same as that on an interest rate swap, or 1.2968% as in Example 13. That is, the fixed rate on an equity swap is simply the fixed rate on a comparable interest rate swap.

$$\sum_{i=1}^{5} PV_i(1) = 0.990099 + 0.977876 + 0.965136 + 0.951529 + 0.937467$$
$$= 4.822107.$$

Using Equation 11, the solution for the fixed swap rate is:

$$r_{FIX} = \frac{1 - 0.937467}{4.822107} = 0.012968, \quad or \quad 1.2968\%.$$

## EXAMPLE 19

### Equity Swap Valuation

Suppose six months ago we entered a receive-fixed, pay-equity five-year annual reset swap in which the fixed leg is based on a 30/360 day count. At the time the swap was entered, the fixed swap rate was 1.5%, the equity was trading at 100, and the notional amount was 10,000,000. Now all spot interest rates have fallen to 1.2% (a flat term structure), and the equity is trading for 105. Assume the Par value of the bond is equal to $NA_E$.

1. The current fair value of this equity swap is *closest* to:

    A. –€300,000.
    
    B. –€500,000.
    
    C. €500,000.

### Solution to 1:

A is correct. Because we have not yet passed the first reset date, there are five remaining cash flows for this equity swap. The fair value of this swap is found by solving for the fair value of the implied fixed-rate bond. We then adjust for the equity value. The fixed rate of 1.5% results in fixed cash flows of 150,000 at each settlement. Applying the respective present value factors, which are based on the new spot rates of 1.2% (i.e., new term structure is flat), gives us the following:

| Date (Years) | Present Value Factors (PV) | Fixed Cash Flow | PV (Fixed Cash Flow) |
|---|---|---|---|
| 0.5 | 0.994036 | 150,000 | 149,105 |
| 1.5* | 0.982318 | 150,000 | 147,348 |
| 2.5 | 0.970874 | 150,000 | 145,631 |
| 3.5 | 0.959693 | 150,000 | 143,954 |
| 4.5 | 0.948767 | 10,150,000 | 9,629,981 |
|  |  | Total: | 10,216,019 |

*Answers may differ due to rounding: PV(1.5) = 1/(1 + 3 × (0.012/2)) = 0.982318.

Using Equation 18, we have,

$$V_{EQ,t} = V_{FIX}(C_0) - (S_t/S_{t-1})NA_E - PV(Par - NA_E).$$

Therefore, the fair value of this equity swap is:

# Pricing and Valuing Equity Swap Contracts

$V_{EQ,t} = 10{,}216{,}019 - [(105/100) \times 10{,}000{,}000] - 0 = -283{,}981.$

2. The value of the equity swap will be *closest* to zero if the stock price is:

   A. 100.
   B. 102.
   C. 105.

## Solution to 2:

B is correct. The value of the fixed leg of the swap is 102.16% of par, = $(10{,}216{,}019/10{,}000{,}000) \times 100]$. Therefore, a stock price ($S_t$) of 102.1602 will result in a value of zero for the swap, as follows:

$V_{EQ,t} = 10{,}216{,}019 - [(102.1602/100) \times 10{,}000{,}000] - 0 = 0.$

# SUMMARY

This reading on forward commitment pricing and valuation provides a foundation for understanding how forwards, futures, and swaps are both priced and valued.

Key points include the following:

- The arbitrageur would rather have more money than less and abides by two fundamental rules: Do not use your own money, and do not take any price risk.

- The no-arbitrage approach is used for the pricing and valuation of forward commitments and is built on the key concept of the law of one price, which states that if two investments have the same future cash flows, regardless of what happens in the future, these two investments should have the same current price.

- Throughout this reading, the following key assumptions are made:
  - Replicating and offsetting instruments are identifiable and investable.
  - Market frictions are nil.
  - Short selling is allowed with full use of proceeds.
  - Borrowing and lending are available at a known risk-free rate.

- Carry arbitrage models used for forward commitment pricing and valuation are based on the no-arbitrage approach.

- With forward commitments, there is a distinct difference between pricing and valuation. Pricing involves the determination of the appropriate fixed price or rate, and valuation involves the determination of the contract's current value expressed in currency units.

- Forward commitment pricing results in determining a price or rate such that the forward contract value is equal to zero.

- Using the carry arbitrage model, the forward contract price ($F_0$) is:

$F_0 = FV(S_0) = S_0(1 + r)^T$ (assuming annual compounding, r)

$F_0 = FV(S_0) = S_0 \exp^{r_c T}$ (assuming continuous compounding, $r_c$)

- The key forward commitment pricing equations with carry costs (CC) and carry benefits (CB) are:

$F_0 = FV[S_0 + CC_0 - CB_0]$ (with discrete compounding)

$F_0 = S_0 \exp^{(r_c + CC - CB)T}$ (with continuous compounding)

Futures contract pricing in this reading can essentially be treated the same as forward contract pricing.

- The value of a forward commitment is a function of the price of the underlying instrument, financing costs, and other carry costs and benefits.
- The key forward commitment valuation equations are:

Long Forward: $V_t = PV[F_t - F_0] = \dfrac{[F_t - F_0]}{(1+r)^{T-t}}$

and

Short Forward: $-V_t = PV[F_0 - F_t] = \dfrac{[F_0 - F_t]}{(1+r)^{T-t}}$,

With the PV of the difference in forward prices adjusted for carry costs and benefits. Alternatively,

Long Forward: $V_t = S_t - PV[F_0] = S_t - \dfrac{F_0}{(1+r)^{T-t}}$

and

Short Forward: $-V_t = PV[F_0] - S_t = \dfrac{F_0}{(1+r)^{T-t}} - S_t$

- With equities and fixed-income securities, the forward price is determined such that the initial forward value is zero.
- A forward rate agreement (FRA) is a forward contract on interest rates. The FRA's fixed interest rate is determined such that the initial value of the FRA is zero.
- FRA settlements amounts at Time h are:

Pay-fixed (Long): $NA \times \{[L_m - FRA_0] t_m\}/[1 + D_m t_m]$ and

Receive-fixed (Short): $NA \times \{FRA_0 - L_m] t_m\}/[1 + D_m t_m]$.

- The FRA's fixed interest rate (annualized) at contract initiation is:

$FRA_0 = \{[1 + L_T t_T]/[1 + L_h t_h] - 1\}/t_m$.

- The Time g value of an FRA initiated at Time 0 is:

Long FRA: $V_g = NA \times \{[FRA_g - FRA_0] t_m\}/[1 + D_{(T-g)} t_{(T-g)}]$ and

Short FRA: $-V_g = NA \times \{[FRA_0 - FRA_g] t_m\}/[1 + D_{(T-g)} t_{(T-g)}]$.

- The fixed-income forward (or futures) price including conversion factor (i.e., adjusted price) is:

$F_0 = Q_0 \times CF = FV[S_0 + CC_0 - CB_0] = FV[B_0 + AI_0 - PVCI]$,

## Pricing and Valuing Equity Swap Contracts

and the conversion factor adjusted futures price (i.e., quoted futures price) is:

$Q_0 = [1/CF] \{FV [B_0 + AI_0] - AI_T - FVCI\}$.

- The general approach to pricing and valuing swaps as covered here is using a replicating portfolio or offsetting portfolio of comparable instruments, typically bonds for interest rate and currency swaps and equities plus bonds for equity swaps.
- The swap pricing equation, which sets $r_{FIX}$ for the implied fixed bond in an interest rate swap, is:

$$r_{FIX} = \frac{1 - PV_n(1)}{\sum_{i=1}^{n} PV_i(1)}.$$

- The value of an interest rate swap at a point in Time t after initiation is the sum of the present values of the difference in fixed swap rates times the stated notional amount, or:

$$V_{SWAP,t} = NA \times (FS_0 - FS_t) \times \sum_{i=1}^{n} PV_i \quad \text{(Value of receive-fixed swap)}$$

and

$$-V_{SWAP,t} = NA \times (FS_t - FS_0) \times \sum_{i=1}^{n} PV_i \quad \text{(Value of pay-fixed swap)}.$$

- With a basic understanding of pricing and valuing a simple interest rate swap, it is a straightforward extension to pricing and valuing currency swaps and equity swaps.
- The solution for each of the three variables, one notional amount ($NA_a$) and two fixed rates (one for each currency, a and b), needed to price a fixed-for-fixed currency swap are:

$$NA_a = S_0 \times NA_b; \quad r_a = \frac{1 - PV_{n,a}(1)}{\sum_{i=1}^{n} PV_{i,a}(1)} \quad \text{and} \quad r_b = \frac{1 - PV_{n,b}(1)}{\sum_{i=1}^{n} PV_{i,b}(1)}.$$

- The currency swap valuation equation, for valuing the swap at time t (after initiation), can be expressed as:

$$V_{CS} = NA_a \left( r_{Fix,a} \sum_{i=1}^{n} PV_i(1) + PV_n(1) \right) - S_t NA_b \left( r_{Fix,b} \sum_{i=1}^{n} PV_i(1) + PV_n(1) \right).$$

- For a receive-fixed, pay equity swap, the fixed rate ($r_{FIX}$) for the implied fixed bond that makes the swap's value ($V_{EQ}$) equal to "0" at initiation is:

$$r_{FIX} = \frac{1 - PV_n(1)}{\sum_{i=1}^{n} PV_i(1)}.$$

- The value of an equity swap at Time t ($V_{EQ,t}$), after initiation, is:

$$V_{EQ,t} = V_{FIX}(C_0) - (S_t/S_{t-1})NA_E - PV(Par - NA_E)$$

where $V_{FIX}(C_0)$ is the Time t value of a fixed-rate bond initiated with coupon $C_0$ at Time 0, $S_t$ is the current equity price, $S_{t-1}$ is the equity price at the last reset date, and PV() is the PV function from the swap maturity date to Time t.

# PRACTICE PROBLEMS

## The following information relates to questions 1-6

Tim Doyle is a portfolio manager at BestFutures Group, a hedge fund that frequently enters into derivative contracts either to hedge the risk of investments it holds or to speculate outside of those investments. Doyle works alongside Diane Kemper, a junior analyst at the hedge fund. They meet to evaluate new investment ideas and to review several of the firm's existing investments.

**Carry Arbitrage Model**

Doyle and Kemper discuss the carry arbitrage model and how they can take advantage of mispricing in bond markets. Specifically, they would like to execute an arbitrage transaction on a Eurodollar futures contract in which the underlying Eurodollar bond is expected to make an interest payment in two months. Doyle makes the following statements:

Statement 1   If the Eurodollar futures price is less than the price suggested by the carry arbitrage model, the futures contract should be purchased.

Statement 2   Based on the cost of carry model, the futures price would be higher if the underlying Eurodollar bond's upcoming interest payment was expected in five months instead of two.

**Three-Year Treasury Note Futures Contract**

Kemper then presents two investment ideas to Doyle. Kemper's first investment idea is to purchase a three-year Treasury note futures contract. The underlying 1.5%, semi-annual three-year Treasury note is quoted at a clean price of 101. It has been 60 days since the three-year Treasury note's last coupon payment, and the next coupon payment is payable in 120 days. Doyle asks Kemper to calculate the full spot price of the underlying three-year Treasury note.

**10-Year Treasury Note Futures Contract**

Kemper's second investment idea is to purchase a 10-year Treasury note futures contract. The underlying 2%, semi-annual 10-year Treasury note has a dirty price of 104.17. It has been 30 days since the 10-year Treasury note's last coupon payment. The futures contract expires in 90 days. The quoted futures contract price is 129. The current annualized three-month risk-free rate is 1.65%. The conversion factor is 0.7025. Doyle asks Kemper to calculate the equilibrium quoted futures contract price based on the carry arbitrage model.

**Japanese Government Bonds**

After discussing Kemper's new investment ideas, Doyle and Kemper evaluate one of their existing forward contract positions. Three months ago, BestFutures took a long position in eight 10-year Japanese government bond (JGB) forward contracts, with each contract having a contract notional value of 100 million yen. The contracts had a price of JPY153 (quoted as a percentage of par) when the contracts were purchased. Now, the contracts have six months left to expiration and have a price of JPY155. The annualized six-month interest rate is 0.12%. Doyle asks Kemper to value the JGB forward position.

**Interest Rate Swaps**

Additionally, Doyle asks Kemper to price a one-year plain vanilla swap. The spot rates and days to maturity at each payment date are presented in Exhibit 1.

### Exhibit 1: Selected US Spot Rate Data

| Days to Maturity | Spot Interest Rates (%) |
|---|---|
| 90 | 1.90 |
| 180 | 2.00 |
| 270 | 2.10 |
| 360 | 2.20 |

Finally, Doyle and Kemper review one of BestFutures's pay-fixed interest rate swap positions. Two years ago, the firm entered into a JPY5 billion five-year interest rate swap, paying the fixed rate. The fixed rate when BestFutures entered into the swap two years ago was 0.10%. The current term structure of interest rates for JPY cash flows, which are relevant to the interest rate swap position, is presented in Exhibit 2.

### Exhibit 2: Selected Japanese Interest Rate Data

| Maturity (Years) | Yen Spot Interest Rates (%) | Present Value Factors |
|---|---|---|
| 1 | 0.03 | 0.9997 |
| 2 | 0.06 | 0.9988 |
| 3 | 0.08 | 0.9976 |
| Sum | | 2.9961 |

Doyle asks Kemper to calculate the value of the pay-fixed interest rate swap.

1. Which of Doyle's statements regarding the Eurodollar futures contract price is correct?

    A. Only Statement 1

    B. Only Statement 2

    C. Both Statement 1 and Statement 2

2. The full spot price of the three-year Treasury note is:

    A. 101.00.

    B. 101.25.

    C. 101.50.

3. The equilibrium 10-year Treasury note quoted futures contract price is *closest* to:

    A. 147.94.

    B. 148.89.

    C. 149.78.

4. The value of the JGB long forward position is *closest* to:

   A. JPY15,980,823.

   B. JPY15,990,409.

   C. JPY16,000,000.

5. Based on Exhibit 1, the fixed rate of the one-year plain vanilla swap is *closest* to:

   A. 0.12%.

   B. 0.55%.

   C. 0.72%.

6. Based on Exhibit 2, the value of the pay-fixed interest rate swap is *closest* to:

   A. −JPY6,491,550.

   B. −JPY2,980,500.

   C. −JPY994,793.

# The following information relates to questions 7-11

Donald Troubadour is a derivatives trader for Southern Shores Investments. The firm seeks arbitrage opportunities in the forward and futures markets using the carry arbitrage model.

Troubadour identifies an arbitrage opportunity relating to a fixed-income futures contract and its underlying bond. Current data on the futures contract and underlying bond are presented in Exhibit 1. The current annual compounded risk-free rate is 0.30%.

| Exhibit 1: Current Data for Futures and Underlying Bond | | | |
|---|---|---|---|
| **Futures Contract** | | **Underlying Bond** | |
| Quoted futures price | 125.00 | Quoted bond price | 112.00 |
| Conversion factor | 0.90 | Accrued interest since last coupon payment | 0.08 |
| Time remaining to contract expiration | Three months | Accrued interest at futures contract expiration | 0.20 |
| Accrued interest over life of futures contract | 0.00 | | |

Troubadour next gathers information on a Japanese equity index futures contract, the **Nikkei 225 Futures Contract**:

Troubadour holds a long position in a Nikkei 225 futures contract that has a remaining maturity of three months. The continuously compounded dividend yield on the Nikkei 225 Stock Index is 1.1%, and the current stock index level is 16,080. The continuously compounded annual interest rate is 0.2996%.

Troubadour next considers an equity forward contract for Texas Steel, Inc. (TSI). Information regarding TSI common shares and a TSI equity forward contract is

# Practice Problems

presented in Exhibit 2.

### Exhibit 2: Selected Information for TSI

- The price per share of TSI's common shares is $250.
- The forward price per share for a nine-month TSI equity forward contract is $250.562289.
- Assume annual compounding.

Troubadour takes a short position in the TSI equity forward contract. His supervisor asks, "Under which scenario would our position experience a loss?"

Three months after contract initiation, Troubadour gathers information on TSI and the risk-free rate, which is presented in Exhibit 3.

### Exhibit 3: Selected Data on TSI and the Risk-Free Rate (Three Months Later)

- The price per share of TSI's common shares is $245.
- The risk-free rate is 0.325% (quoted on an annual compounding basis).
- TSI recently announced its regular semiannual dividend of $1.50 per share that will be paid exactly three months before contract expiration.
- The market price of the TSI equity forward contract is equal to the no-arbitrage forward price.

7. Based on Exhibit 1 and assuming annual compounding, the arbitrage profit on the bond futures contract is *closest* to:

   A. 0.4158.

   B. 0.5356.

   C. 0.6195.

8. The current no-arbitrage futures price of the Nikkei 225 futures contract is *closest* to:

   A. 15,951.81.

   B. 16,047.86.

   C. 16,112.21.

9. Based on Exhibit 2, Troubadour should find that an arbitrage opportunity relating to TSI shares is

   A. not available.

   B. available based on carry arbitrage.

   C. available based on reverse carry arbitrage.

10. The *most appropriate* response to Troubadour's supervisor's question regarding the TSI forward contract is:

    A. a decrease in TSI's share price, all else equal.

    B. an increase in the risk-free rate, all else equal

C. a decrease in the market price of the forward contract, all else equal.

11. Based on Exhibits 2 and 3, and assuming annual compounding, the per share value of Troubadour's short position in the TSI forward contract three months after contract initiation is *closest* to:

   A. $1.6549.

   B. $5.1561.

   C. $6.6549.

## The following information relates to questions 12-20

Sonal Johnson is a risk manager for a bank. She manages the bank's risks using a combination of swaps and forward rate agreements (FRAs).

Johnson prices a three-year MRR-based interest rate swap with annual resets using the present value factors presented in Exhibit 1.

### Exhibit 1: Present Value Factors

| Maturity (years) | Present Value Factors |
|---|---|
| 1 | 0.990099 |
| 2 | 0.977876 |
| 3 | 0.965136 |

Johnson also uses the present value factors in Exhibit 1 to value an interest rate swap that the bank entered into one year ago as the pay-fixed (receive-floating) party. Selected data for the swap are presented in Exhibit 2. Johnson notes that the current equilibrium two-year fixed swap rate is 1.12%.

### Exhibit 2: Selected Data on Fixed for Floating Interest Rate Swap

| | |
|---|---|
| Swap notional amount | $50,000,000 |
| Original swap term | Three years, with annual resets |
| Fixed swap rate (since initiation) | 3.00% |

One of the bank's investments is exposed to movements in the Japanese yen, and Johnson desires to hedge the currency exposure. She prices a one-year fixed-for-fixed currency swap involving yen and US dollars, with a quarterly reset. Johnson uses the interest rate data presented in Exhibit 3 to price the currency swap.

## Exhibit 3: Selected Japanese and US Interest Rate Data

| Days to Maturity | Yen Spot Interest Rates | US Dollar Spot Interest Rates |
|---|---|---|
| 90 | 0.05% | 0.20% |
| 180 | 0.10% | 0.40% |
| 270 | 0.15% | 0.55% |
| 360 | 0.25% | 0.70% |

Johnson next reviews an equity swap with an annual reset that the bank entered into six months ago as the receive-fixed, pay-equity party. Selected data regarding the equity swap, which is linked to an equity index, are presented in Exhibit 4. At the time of initiation, the underlying equity index was trading at 100.00.

## Exhibit 4: Selected Data on Equity Swap

| | |
|---|---|
| Swap notional amount | $20,000,000 |
| Original swap term | Five years, with annual resets |
| Fixed swap rate | 2.00% |

The equity index is currently trading at 103.00, and relevant US spot rates, along with their associated present value factors, are presented in Exhibit 5.

## Exhibit 5: Selected US Spot Rates and Present Value Factors

| Maturity (years) | Spot Rate | Present Value Factors |
|---|---|---|
| 0.5 | 0.40% | 0.998004 |
| 1.5 | 1.00% | 0.985222 |
| 2.5 | 1.20% | 0.970874 |
| 3.5 | 2.00% | 0.934579 |
| 4.5 | 2.60% | 0.895255 |

Johnson reviews a 6 × 9 FRA that the bank entered into 90 days ago as the pay-fixed/receive-floating party. Selected data for the FRA are presented in Exhibit 6, and current MRR data are presented in Exhibit 7. Based on her interest rate forecast, Johnson also considers whether the bank should enter into new positions in 1 × 4 and 2 × 5 FRAs.

## Exhibit 6: 6 × 9 FRA Data

| | |
|---|---|
| FRA term | 6 × 9 |
| FRA rate | 0.70% |
| FRA notional amount | US$20,000,000 |
| FRA settlement terms | Advanced set, advanced settle |

| Exhibit 7: Current MRR (Market Reference Rate) | |
| --- | --- |
| 30-day MRR | 0.75% |
| 60-day MRR | 0.82% |
| 90-day MRR | 0.90% |
| 120-day MRR | 0.92% |
| 150-day MRR | 0.94% |
| 180-day MRR | 0.95% |
| 210-day MRR | 0.97% |
| 270-day MRR | 1.00% |

Three months later, the 6 × 9 FRA in Exhibit 6 reaches expiration, at which time the three-month US dollar MRR is 1.10% and the six-month US dollar MRR is 1.20%. Johnson determines that the appropriate discount rate for the FRA settlement cash flows is 1.10%.

12. Based on Exhibit 1, Johnson should price the three-year MRR-based interest rate swap at a fixed rate *closest* to:

    A. 0.34%.

    B. 1.16%.

    C. 1.19%.

13. From the bank's perspective, using data from Exhibit 1, the current value of the swap described in Exhibit 2 is *closest* to:

    A. −$2,951,963.

    B. −$1,849,897.

    C. −$1,943,000.

14. Based on Exhibit 3, Johnson should determine that the annualized equilibrium fixed swap rate for Japanese yen is *closest* to:

    A. 0.0624%.

    B. 0.1375%.

    C. 0.2496%.

15. From the bank's perspective, using data from Exhibits 4 and 5, the fair value of the equity swap is *closest* to:

    A. −$1,139,425.

    B. −$781,322.

    C. −$181,323.

16. Based on Exhibit 5, the current value of the equity swap described in Exhibit 4 would be zero if the equity index was currently trading the *closest* to:

    A. 97.30.

    B. 99.09.

**Practice Problems**

C. 100.00.

17. From the bank's perspective, based on Exhibits 6 and 7, the value of the 6 × 9 FRA 90 days after inception is *closest* to:

    A. $14,820.

    B. $19,647.

    C. $29,635.

18. Based on Exhibit 7, the no-arbitrage fixed rate on a new 1 × 4 FRA is *closest* to:

    A. 0.65%.

    B. 0.73%.

    C. 0.98%.

19. Based on Exhibit 7, the fixed rate on a new 2 × 5 FRA is *closest* to:

    A. 0.61%.

    B. 1.02%.

    C. 1.71%.

20. Based on Exhibit 6 and the three-month US dollar MRR at expiration, the payment amount that the bank will receive to settle the 6 × 9 FRA is *closest* to:

    A. $19,945.

    B. $24,925.

    C. $39,781.

# SOLUTIONS

1. C is correct. Doyle's first statement is correct. Unless the Eurodollar futures contract's quoted price is equal to the no-arbitrage futures price, there is an arbitrage opportunity. Moreover, if the quoted futures price is less than the no-arbitrage futures price, then to take advantage of the arbitrage opportunity, the Eurodollar futures contract should be purchased and the underlying Eurodollar bond should be sold short. Doyle would then lend the short sale proceeds at the risk-free rate. The strategy that comprises those transactions is known as reverse carry arbitrage.

   Doyle's second statement is also correct. Based on the cost of carry model, the futures price is calculated as the future value of the sum of the underlying plus the underlying carry costs minus the future value of any ownership benefits. If the Eurodollar bond's interest payment was expected in five months instead of two, the benefit of the cash flow would occur three months later, so the future value of the benefits term would be slightly lower. Therefore, the Eurodollar futures contract price would be slightly higher if the Eurodollar bond's interest payment was expected in five months instead of two months.

   A is incorrect because Doyle's Statement 2 is correct (not incorrect). Based on the cost of carry model, the futures price would be higher if the underlying Eurodollar bond's interest payment took place in five months instead of two months.

   B is incorrect because Doyle's Statement 1 is correct (not incorrect). If the Eurodollar's futures contract price is less than the price suggested by the carry arbitrage model, the futures contract should be purchased.

2. B is correct. The full spot price of the three-year Treasury note is calculated as

   $S_0$ = Quoted bond price + Accrued interest = $B_0 + AI_0$.

   Accrued interest (AI) = Accrural period × Periodic coupon amount
   $= \left(\frac{NAD}{NTD}\right) \times \left(\frac{C}{n}\right)$.

   AI = (60/180) × (0.015/2) = 0.25.

   $S_0$ = 101 + 0.25 = 101.25.

   A is incorrect because 101 is the quoted clean (not the full spot) price of the three-year Treasury note. The clean price excludes accrued interest; the full price, also referred to as the dirty price, includes accrued interest.

   C is incorrect because the number of days until the next coupon payment (instead of the accrual period) is incorrectly used to compute accrued interest:

   AI = (120/180) × (0.015/2) = 0.50.

   $S_0$ = 101 + 0.50 = 101.50.

3. A is correct. The equilibrium 10-year quoted futures contract price based on the carry arbitrage model is calculated as

   $Q_0 = (1/CF) \times [FV(B_0 + AI_0) - AI_T - FVCI]$.

   CF = 0.7025.

   $B_0$ = 104.00.

   $AI_0$ = 0.17.

$AI_T = (120/180 \times 0.02/2) = 0.67$.

$FVCI = 0$.

$Q_0 = (1/0.7025) \times [(1 + 0.0165)^{3/12}(104.17) - 0.67 - 0] = 147.94$.

B is incorrect because accrued interest at expiration is not subtracted in the equilibrium quoted futures contract price formula:

$Q_0 = (1/0.7025) \times [(1 + 0.0165)^{3/12}(104.17) - 0] = 148.89$.

C is incorrect because the future value is incorrectly calculated (the exponent of 3/12 is omitted):

$Q_0 = (1/0.7025) \times [(1 + 0.0165)(104.17) - 0.67 - 0] = 149.78$.

4. B is correct. The value of the JGB forward position is calculated as

$V_t = PV[F_t - F_0] = (155 - 153)/(1 + 0.0012)^{\frac{6}{12}} = 1.9988$.

Therefore, the value of the long forward position is 1.9988 per JPY100 par value. For the long position in eight contracts with each contract having a par value of 100 million yen, the value of the position is calculated as

$0.019988 \times (JPY100,000,000) \times 8 = JPY15,990,409$.

A is incorrect because the present value of the difference between the price when the contracts were purchased and the current price of the contracts was incorrectly computed (the exponent of 6/12 is omitted):

$V_t = F_t - F_0 = (155 - 153)/(1 + 0.0012) = 1.9980$.

$0.019980 \times (JPY100,000,000) \times 8 = JPY15,980,823$.

C is incorrect because the absolute difference (not the present value of the difference) between the price when the contracts were purchased and the current price of the contracts was computed:

$V_t = F_t - F_0 = (155 - 153) = 2$.

$0.02 \times (JPY100,000,000) \times 8 = JPY16,000,000$.

5. B is correct. The swap's fixed rate is calculated as

$r_{FIX} = [1 - PV_n(1)] / \sum_{i=1}^{n} PV_i(1)$.

$PV_i(1) = 1/[1 + Rspot_i (NAD_i/NTD)]$.

$90 - \text{day PV factor} = 1/[1 + 0.019 \times (90/360)] = 0.9953$.

$180 - \text{day PV factor} = 1/[1 + 0.020 \times (180/360)] = 0.9901$.

$270 - \text{day PV factor} = 1/[1 + 0.021 \times (270/360)] = 0.9845$.

$360 - \text{day PV factor} = 1/[1 + 0.022 \times (360/360)] = 0.9785$.

$$\sum_{i=1}^{4} PV_i(1) = 0.9953 + 0.9901 + 0.9845 + 0.9785 = 3.9483.$$

$r_{FIX} = (1 - 0.9785)/3.9483 = 0.0055 = 0.55\%.$

A is incorrect because the 90-day PV factor is incorrectly used in the numerator of the swap pricing equation instead of the final present value term:

$$r_{FIX} = [1 - PV_n(1)] / \sum_{i=1}^{n} PV_i(1).$$

$r_{FIX} = (1 - 0.9953)/3.9483 = 0.0012 = 0.12\%.$

C is incorrect because the sum of the present value terms excludes the final present value term:

$$\sum_{i=1}^{3} PV_i(1) = 0.9953 + 0.9901 + 0.9845 = 2.9699.$$

$$r_{FIX} = [1 - PV_n(1)] / \sum_{i=1}^{n} PV_i(1).$$

$r_{FIX} = (1 - 0.9785)/2.9699 = 0.0072 = 0.72\%.$

6. B is correct. The value of the pay-fixed interest rate swap is calculated as

$$-V_{SWAP,t} = NA \times (FS_t - FS_0) \times \sum_{i=1}^{n} PV_i.$$

$$FS_t = r_{FIX} = [1 - PV_n(1)] / \sum_{i=1}^{3} PV_i(1) = (1 - 0.9976)/2.9961 = 0.000801$$

$= 0.08\%.$

$-V_{SWAP,t} = NA \times (FS_t - FS_0) \times \sum_{i=1}^{3} PV_i$
$= JPY5billion \times (0.000801 - 0.001) \times 2.9961$
$= -JPY2,980,500.$

Given that rates have declined since the inception of the swap, the value of the pay-fixed, receive-floating position is currently a loss of JPY2,980,500.

A is incorrect because the arithmetic average of the yen spot rates (instead of the current fixed swap rate) was incorrectly used to calculate the value of the pay-fixed swap:

Arithmetic average of yen spot rates = $(0.0003 + 0.0006 + 0.0008)/3 = 0.0006.$

$-V_{SWAP,t} = NA \times (FS_t - FS_0) \times \sum_{i=1}^{3} PV_i$
$= JPY5billion \times (0.0006 - 0.001) \times 2.9961$
$= -JPY6,491,550.$

C is incorrect because the product of the notional amount and the difference between the initial swap fixed rate and the current swap fixed rate was not multiplied by the sum of the present values:

$-V_{SWAP,t} = NA \times (FS_t - FS_0) = JPY5billion \times (0.0008 - 0.001)$
$= -JPY994,793.$

7. B is correct.

The no-arbitrage futures price is equal to the following:

$F_0 = FV[B_0 + AI_0 - PVCI]$

$F_0 = (1 + 0.003)^{0.25}(112.00 + 0.08 - 0) = 112.1640$.

The adjusted price of the futures contract is equal to the conversion factor multiplied by the quoted futures price:

$F_0 = CF \times Q_0$

$F_0 = (0.90)(125) = 112.50$.

Adding the accrued interest of 0.20 in three months (futures contract expiration) to the adjusted price of the futures contract gives a total price of 112.70.

This difference means that the futures contract is overpriced by 112.70 − 112.1640 = 0.5360. The available arbitrage profit is the present value of this difference: $0.5360/(1.003)^{0.25} = 0.5356$.

8. B is correct. The no-arbitrage futures price is

$F_0 = S_0 \exp^{(r_c + CC - CB)T}$

$F_0 = 16{,}080 \exp^{(0.002996 + 0 - 0.011)(3/12)} = 16{,}047.86$.

9. A is correct. The carry arbitrage model price of the forward contract is

$FV(S_0) = S_0(1 + r)^T = \$250(1 + 0.003)^{0.75} = \$250.562289$.

The market price of the TSI forward contract is $250.562289. A carry or reverse carry arbitrage opportunity does not exist because the market price of the forward contract is equal to the carry arbitrage model price.

10. B is correct. From the perspective of the long position, the forward value is equal to the present value of the difference in forward prices:

$V_t = PV[F_t - F_0]$,

where

$F_t = FV(S_t + CC_t - CB_t)$.

All else equal, an increase in the risk-free rate before contract expiration would cause the forward price, $F_t$, to increase. This increase in the forward price would cause the value of the TSI forward contract, from the perspective of the short, to decrease. Therefore, an increase in the risk-free rate would lead to a loss on the short position in the TSI forward contract.

11. C is correct. The no-arbitrage price of the forward contract, three months after

contract initiation, is

$$F_{0.25} = FV_{0.25}(S_{0.25} + CC_{0.25} - CB_{0.25})$$

$$F_{0.25} = [\$245 + 0 - \$1.50/(1 + 0.00325)^{(0.5 - 0.25)}](1 + 0.00325)^{(0.75 - 0.25)} = \$243.8966.$$

Therefore, from the perspective of the long, the value of the TSI forward contract is

$$V_{0.25} = PV_{0.25}[F_{0.25} - F_0]$$

$$V_{0.25} = (\$243.8966 - \$250.562289)/(1 + 0.00325)^{0.75 - 0.25} = -\$6.6549.$$

Because Troubadour is short the TSI forward contract, the value of his position is a gain of $6.6549.

12. C is correct. The swap pricing equation is

$$r_{FIX} = \frac{1 - PV_n(1)}{\sum_{i=1}^{n} PV_i(1)}.$$

That is, the fixed swap rate is equal to 1 minus the final present value factor (in this case, Year 3) divided by the sum of the present values (in this case, the sum of Years 1, 2, and 3). The sum of present values for Years 1, 2, and 3 is calculated as

$$\sum_{i=1}^{n} PV_i(1) = 0.990099 + 0.977876 + 0.965136 = 2.933111.$$

Thus, the fixed-swap rate is calculated as

$$r_{FIX} = \frac{1 - 0.965136}{2.933111} = 0.01189 \text{ or } 1.19\%.$$

13. B is correct. The value of a swap from the perspective of the receive-fixed (pay-floating) party is calculated as

$$V = NA \times (FS_0 - FS_t) \times \sum_{i=1}^{n} PV_i.$$

The swap has two years remaining until expiration. The sum of the present values for Years 1 and 2 is

$$\sum_{i=1}^{n} PV_i = 0.990099 + 0.977876 = 1.967975.$$

Given the current equilibrium two-year swap rate of 1.12% and the fixed swap rate at initiation of 3.00%, the swap value per dollar notional is calculated as

$$V = 1 \times (0.03 - 0.0112) \times 1.967975 = 0.036998.$$

The current value of the swap, from the perspective of the receive-fixed party, is $50,000,000 × 0.036998 = $1,849,897.

From the perspective of the bank, as the pay-fixed party, the value of the swap is −$1,849,897.

14. C is correct. The equilibrium swap fixed rate for yen is calculated as

$$r_{JPY} = \frac{1 - PV_{n,JPY}(1)}{\sum_{i=1}^{4} PV_{i,JPY}(1)}.$$

The yen present value factors are calculated as

$$PV(1)_{i,JPY} = \frac{1}{1 + Rspo\, t_{i,JPY}\left(\frac{NAD_i}{NTD}\right)},$$

where

90-day PV factor = 1/[1 + 0.0005(90/360)] = 0.999875

180-day PV factor = 1/[1 + 0.0010(180/360)] = 0.999500

270-day PV factor = 1/[1 + 0.0015(270/360)] = 0.998876

360-day PV factor = 1/[1 + 0.0025(360/360)] = 0.997506

Sum of present value factors = 3.995757

Therefore, the yen periodic rate is calculated as

$$r_{JPY} = \frac{1 - PV_n(1)}{\sum_{i=1}^{4} PV_i(1)} = \frac{1 - 0.997506}{3.995757} = 0.000624 = 0.0624\%.$$

The annualized rate is (360/90) times the periodic rate of 0.0624%, or 0.2496%.

15. B is correct. The value of an equity swap at time t is calculated as

$$V_{EQ,t} = V_{FIX}(C_0) - (S_t/S_{t-1})NA_E - PV(Par - NA_E).$$

The swap was initiated six months ago, so the first reset has not yet passed; thus, there are five remaining cash flows for this equity swap. The fair value of the swap is determined by comparing the present value of the implied fixed-rate bond with the return on the equity index. The fixed swap rate of 2.00%, the swap notional amount of $20,000,000, and the present value factors in Exhibit 5 result in a present value of the implied fixed-rate bond's cash flows of $19,818,678:

| Date (in years) | PV Factors | Fixed Cash Flow | PV (fixed cash flow) |
|---|---|---|---|
| 0.5 | 0.998004 or 1/[1 + 0.0040(180/360)] | $400,000 | $399,202 |
| 1.5 | 0.985222 or 1/[1 + 0.0100(540/360)] | $400,000 | $394,089 |
| 2.5 | 0.970874 or 1/[1 + 0.0120(900/360)] | $400,000 | $388,350 |
| 3.5 | 0.934579 or 1/[1 + 0.0200(1,260/360)] | $400,000 | $373,832 |
| 4.5 | 0.895255 or 1/[1 + 0.0260(1,620/360)] | $20,400,000 | $18,263,205 |
| Total | | | $19,818,678 |

The value of the equity leg of the swap is calculated as (103/100)($20,000,000) = $20,600,000.

Note the swap's notional amount and the implied fixed-rate bond's par value are both $20,000,000; therefore, the term − PV(Par − $NA_E$) reduces to zero.

The swap was designed to profit if rates fell or equities declined. Neither happened, so the swap value will be negative for the bank. The fair value of the equity swap, from the perspective of the bank (receive-fixed, pay-equity party) is calculated as

$V_{EQ}$ = $19,818,678 - $20,600,000 = −$781,322.

16. B is correct. The equity index level at which the swap's fair value would be zero can be calculated by setting the swap valuation formula equal to zero and solving for $S_t$:

$V_{EQ,t} = V_{FIX}(C_0) - (S_t/S_{t-1})NA_E = 0.$

The value of the fixed leg of the swap has a present value of $19,818,678, or 99.0934% of par value:

| Date (years) | PV Factors | Fixed Cash Flow | PV (fixed cash flow) |
|---|---|---|---|
| 0.5 | 0.998004 | $400,000 | $399,202 |
| 1.5 | 0.985222 | $400,000 | $394,089 |
| 2.5 | 0.970874 | $400,000 | $388,350 |
| 3.5 | 0.934579 | $400,000 | $373,832 |
| 4.5 | 0.895255 | $20,400,000 | $18,263,205 |
| Total | | | $19,818,678 |

Treating the swap notional value as par value and substituting the present value of the fixed leg and $S_0$ into the equation yields

$$0 = 99.0934 - \left(\frac{S_t}{100}\right) 100$$

Solving for $S_t$ yields

$S_t = 99.0934.$

17. A is correct. The current value of the 6 × 9 FRA is calculated as

$V_g = NA \times \{[FRA_g - FRA_0]t_m\}/[1 + D_{(T-g)} t_{(T-g)}].$

The 6 × 9 FRA expires six months after initiation. The bank entered into the FRA 90 days ago; thus, the FRA will expire in 90 days. To value the FRA, the first step is to compute the new FRA rate, which is the rate on Day 90 of an FRA that expires in 90 days in which the underlying is the 90-day MRR:

$FRA_g = \{[1 + L_T t_T]/[1+L_h t_h] - 1\}/t_m$

$FRA_g = \{[1 + L_{180}(180/360)]/[1 + L_{90}(90/360)] - 1\}/(90/360)$

Exhibit 7 indicates that $L_{90} = 0.90\%$ and $L_{180} = 0.95\%$, so

$FRA_g = \{[1 + 0.0095(180/360)]/[1 + 0.0090(90/360)] - 1\}/(90/360)$

$FRA_g = \{[1.00475/1.00225] - 1]\} \times 4 = 0.009978$, or 0.9978%.

Therefore, given the FRA rate at initiation of 0.70% and notional principal of $20 million from Exhibit 1, the current value of the forward contract is calculated as

$V_g = \$20,000,000 \times [(0.009978 - 0.0070)(90/360)]/[1 + 0.0095(180/360)].$

$= \$14,890.00/1.00475 = \$14,819.61.$

18. C is correct. The no-arbitrage fixed rate on the 1 × 4 FRA is calculated as

$FRA_0 = \{[1 + L_T t_T]/[1 + L_h t_h] - 1\}/t_m$.

For a 1 × 4 FRA, the two rates needed to compute the no-arbitrage FRA fixed rate are $L_{30} = 0.75\%$ and $L_{120} = 0.92\%$. Therefore, the no-arbitrage fixed rate on the 1 × 4 FRA rate is calculated as

$FRA_0 = \{[1 + 0.0092(120/360)]/[1 + 0.0075(30/360)] - 1\}/(90/360).$

$FRA_0 = \{[1.003066/1.000625] - 1\} \times 4 = 0.009761$, or 0.98% rounded.

# Solutions

19. B is correct. The fixed rate on the 2 × 5 FRA is calculated as

    $FRA_0 = \{[1 + L_T t_T]/[1 + L_h t_h] - 1\}/t_m$.

    For a 2 × 5 FRA, the two rates needed to compute the no-arbitrage FRA fixed rate are $L_{60} = 0.82\%$ and $L_{150} = 0.94\%$. Therefore, the no-arbitrage fixed rate on the 2 × 5 FRA rate is calculated as

    $FRA_0 = \{[1 + 0.0094(150/360)]/[1 + 0.0082(60/360)] - 1\}/(90/360)$

    $FRA_0 = \{[(1.003917/1.001367) - 1\} \times 4 = 0.010186$, or 1.02% rounded.

20. A is correct. Given a three-month US dollar MRR of 1.10% at expiration, the settlement amount for the bank as the pay-fixed (receive-floating) party is calculated as

    Settlement amount pay-fixed (receive floating)

    $= NA \times \{[L_m - FRA_0]t_m\}/[1 + D_m t_m]\}$.

    Settlement amount pay-fixed (receive floating)

    $= \$20{,}000{,}000 \times \{[0.011 - 0.0070] \times (90/360)]/[1 + 0.011(90/360)]\}$.

    Settlement amount pay-fixed (receive floating)

    $= \$20{,}000{,}000 \times (0.001)/1.00275 = \$19{,}945.15$.

    Therefore, the bank will receive $19,945 (rounded) as the receive-floating party.

# LEARNING MODULE 2

## Valuation of Contingent Claims

by Robert E. Brooks, PhD, CFA, and David Maurice Gentle, MEc, BSc, CFA.

*Robert E. Brooks, PhD, CFA, is at the University of Alabama (USA). David Maurice Gentle, MEc, BSc, CFA, is at Omega Risk Consulting (Australia).*

*(handwritten note: Lots of equations to memorize)*

### LEARNING OUTCOMES

| Mastery | The candidate should be able to: |
|---|---|
| ☐ | describe and interpret the binomial option valuation model and its component terms |
| ☐ | describe how the value of a European option can be analyzed as the present value of the option's expected payoff at expiration |
| ☐ | identify an arbitrage opportunity involving options and describe the related arbitrage |
| ☐ | calculate the no-arbitrage values of European and American options using a two-period binomial model |
| ☐ | calculate and interpret the value of an interest rate option using a two-period binomial model |
| ☐ | identify assumptions of the Black–Scholes–Merton option valuation model |
| ☐ | interpret the components of the Black–Scholes–Merton model as applied to call options in terms of a leveraged position in the underlying |
| ☐ | describe how the Black–Scholes–Merton model is used to value European options on equities and currencies |
| ☐ | describe how the Black model is used to value European options on futures |
| ☐ | describe how the Black model is used to value European interest rate options and European swaptions |
| ☐ | interpret each of the option Greeks |
| ☐ | describe how a delta hedge is executed |
| ☐ | describe the role of gamma risk in options trading |
| ☐ | define implied volatility and explain how it is used in options trading |

# 1. INTRODUCTION

A contingent claim is a derivative instrument that provides its owner a right but not an obligation to a payoff determined by an underlying asset, rate, or other derivative. Contingent claims include options, the valuation of which is the objective of this reading. Because many investments contain embedded options, understanding this material is vital for investment management.

Our primary purpose is to understand how the values of options are determined. Option values, as with the values of all financial instruments, are typically obtained using valuation models. Any financial valuation model takes certain inputs and turns them into an output that tells us the fair value or price. Option valuation models, like their counterparts in the forward, futures, and swaps markets, are based on the principle of no arbitrage, meaning that the appropriate price of an option is the one that makes it impossible for any party to earn an arbitrage profit at the expense of any other party. The price that precludes arbitrage profits is the value of the option. Using that concept, we then proceed to introduce option valuation models using two approaches. The first approach is the binomial model, which is based on discrete time, and the second is the Black–Scholes–Merton (BSM) model, which is based on continuous time.

The reading is organized as follows. Section 2 introduces the principles of the no-arbitrage approach to pricing and valuation of options. In Section 3, the binomial option valuation model is explored, and in Section 4, the BSM model is covered. In Section 5, the Black model, being a variation of the BSM model, is applied to futures options, interest rate options, and swaptions. Finally, in Section 6, the Greeks are reviewed along with implied volatility. Section 7 provides a summary.

## Principles of a No-Arbitrage Approach to Valuation

Our approach is based on the concept of arbitrage. Hence, the material will be covered from an arbitrageur's perspective. Key to understanding this material is to think like an arbitrageur. Specifically, like most people, the arbitrageur would rather have more money than less. The arbitrageur, as will be detailed later, follows two fundamental rules:

Rule # 1    Do not use your own money.

Rule # 2    Do not take any price risk.

Clearly, if we can generate positive cash flows today and abide by both rules, we have a great business—such is the life of an arbitrageur. If traders could create a portfolio with no future liabilities and positive cash flow today, then it would essentially be a money machine that would be attractive to anyone who prefers more cash to less. In the pursuit of these positive cash flows today, the arbitrageur often needs to borrow to satisfy Rule #1. In effect, the arbitrageur borrows the arbitrage profit to capture it today and, if necessary, may borrow to purchase the underlying. Specifically, the arbitrageur will build portfolios using the underlying instrument to synthetically replicate the cash flows of an option. The underlying instrument is the financial instrument whose later value will be referenced to determine the option value. Examples of underlying instruments include shares, indexes, currencies, and interest rates. As we will see, with options we will often rely on a specific trading strategy that changes over time based on the underlying price behavior.

Based on the concept of comparability, the no-arbitrage valuation approach taken here is built on the concept that if two investments have the same future cash flows regardless of what happens, then these two investments should have the same current price. This principle is known as the **law of one price**. In establishing these

## Introduction

foundations of option valuation, the following key assumptions are made: (1) Replicating instruments are identifiable and investable. (2) There are no market frictions, such as transaction costs and taxes. (3) Short selling is allowed with full use of proceeds. (4) The underlying instrument follows a known statistical distribution. (5) Borrowing and lending at a risk-free interest rate is available. When we develop the models in this reading, we will be more specific about what these assumptions mean, in particular what we mean by a known statistical distribution.

In an effort to demonstrate various valuation results based on the absence of arbitrage, we will rely heavily on cash flow tables, which are a representation of the cash flows that occur during the life of an option. For example, if an initial investment requires €100, then from an arbitrageur's perspective, we will present it as a −€100 cash flow. If an option pays off ¥1,000, we will represent it as a +¥1,000 cash flow. That is, cash outflows are treated as negative and inflows as positive.

We first demonstrate how to value options based on a two-period binomial model. The option payoffs can be replicated with a dynamic portfolio of the underlying instrument and financing. A dynamic portfolio is one whose composition changes over time. These changes are important elements of the replicating procedure. Based on the binomial framework, we then turn to exploring interest rate options using a binomial tree. Although more complex, the general approach is shown to be the same.

The multiperiod binomial model is a natural transition to the BSM option valuation model. The BSM model is based on the key assumption that the value of the underlying instrument follows a statistical process called geometric Brownian motion. This characterization is a reasonable way to capture the randomness of financial instrument prices while incorporating a pre-specified expected return and volatility of return. Geometric Brownian motion implies a lognormal distribution of the return, which implies that the continuously compounded return on the underlying is normally distributed.

We also explore the role of carry benefits, meaning the reward or cost of holding the underlying itself instead of holding the derivative on the underlying.

Next we turn to Fischer Black's futures option valuation model (Black model) and note that the model difference, versus the BSM model, is related to the underlying futures contract having no carry costs or benefits. Interest rate options and swaptions are valued based on simple modifications of the Black model.

Finally, we explore the Greeks, otherwise known as delta, gamma, theta, vega, and rho. The Greeks are representations of the sensitivity of the option value to changes in the factors that determine the option value. They provide comparative information essential in managing portfolios containing options. The Greeks are calculated based on an option valuation model, such as the binomial model, BSM model, or the Black model. This information is model dependent, so managers need to carefully select the model best suited for their particular situation. In the last section, we cover implied volatility, which is a measure derived from a market option price and can be interpreted as reflecting what investors believe is the volatility of the underlying.

The models presented here are useful first approximations for explaining observed option prices in many markets. The central theme is that options are generally priced to preclude arbitrage profits, which is not only a reasonable theoretical assumption but is sufficiently accurate in practice.

We turn now to option valuation based on the binomial option valuation model.

## 2  BINOMIAL OPTION VALUATION MODEL

☐ describe and interpret the binomial option valuation model and its component terms

The binomial model is a valuable tool for financial analysts. It is particularly useful as a heuristic device to understand the unique valuation approach used with options. This model is extensively used to value path-dependent options, which are options whose values depend not only on the value of the underlying at expiration but also how it got there. The path-dependency feature distinguishes this model from the Black–Scholes–Merton option valuation model (BSM model) presented in the next section. The BSM model values only path-independent options, such as European options, which depend on only the values of their respective underlyings at expiration. One particular type of path-dependent option that we are interested in is American options, which are those that can be exercised prior to expiration. In this section, we introduce the general framework for developing the binomial option valuation models for both European and American options.

The binomial option valuation model is based on the no-arbitrage approach to valuation. Hence, understanding the valuation of options improves if one can understand how an arbitrageur approaches financial markets. An arbitrageur engages in financial transactions in pursuit of an initial positive cash flow with no possibility of a negative cash flow in the future. As it appears, it is a great business if you can find it.[1]

To understand option valuation models, it is helpful to think like an arbitrageur. The arbitrageur seeks to exploit any pricing discrepancy between the option price and the underlying spot price. The arbitrageur is assumed to prefer more money compared with less money, assuming everything else is the same. As mentioned earlier, there are two fundamental rules for the arbitrageur.

Rule # 1   Do not use your own money. Specifically, the arbitrageur does not use his or her own money to acquire positions. Also, the arbitrageur does not spend proceeds from short selling transactions on activities unrelated to the transaction at hand.

Rule # 2   Do not take any price risk. The focus here is only on market price risk related to the underlying and the derivatives used. We do not consider other risks, such as liquidity risk and counterparty credit risk.

We will rely heavily on these two rules when developing option valuation models. Remember, these rules are general in nature, and as with many things in finance, there are nuances.

In Exhibit 1, the two key dates are the option contract initiation date (identified as Time 0) and the option contract expiration date (identified as Time T). Based on the no-arbitrage approach, the option value from the initiation date onward will be estimated with an option valuation model.

---

1 There is not a one-to-one correspondence between arbitrage and great investment opportunities. An arbitrage is certainly a great investment opportunity because it produces a risk-free profit with no investment of capital, but all great investment opportunities are not arbitrage. For example, an opportunity to invest €1 today in return for a 99% chance of receiving €1,000,000 tomorrow or a 1% chance of receiving €0 might appear to be a truly great investment opportunity, but it is not arbitrage because it is not risk free and requires the investment of capital.

## Exhibit 1: Illustration of Option Contract Initiation and Expiration

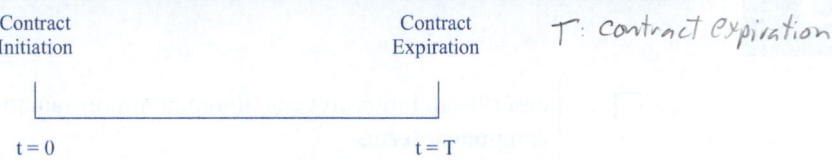

Let $S_t$ denote the underlying instrument price observed at Time t, where t is expressed as a fraction of a year. Similarly, $S_T$ denotes the underlying instrument price observed at the option expiration date, T. For example, suppose a call option had 90 days to expiration when purchased (T = 90/365), but now only has 35 days to expiration (t = 55/365). Further, let $c_t$ denote a European-style call price at Time t and with expiration on Date t = T, where both t and T are expressed in years. Similarly, let $C_t$ denote an American-style call price. At the initiation date, the subscripts are omitted, thus $c = c_0$. We follow similar notation with a put, using the letter p, in place of c. Let X denote the exercise price.[2]

For example, suppose on 15 April a 90-day European-style call option contract with a 14 July expiration is initiated with a call price of c = €2.50 and T = 90/365 = 0.246575.

At expiration, the call and put values will be equal to their intrinsic value or exercise value. These **exercise values** can be expressed as

$c_T = Max(0, S_T - X)$ and

$p_T = Max(0, X - S_T)$,

respectively. If the option values deviate from these expressions, then there will be arbitrage profits available. The option is expiring, there is no uncertainty remaining, and the price must equal the market value obtained from exercising it or letting it expire.

Technically, European options do not have exercise values prior to expiration because they cannot be exercised until expiration. Nonetheless, the notion of the value of the option if it could be exercised, $Max(0, S_t - X)$ for a call and $Max(0, X - S_t)$ for a put, forms a basis for understanding the notion that the value of an option declines with the passage of time. Specifically, option values contain an element known as time value, which is just the market valuation of the potential for higher exercise value relative to the potential for lower exercise value. The time value is always non-negative because of the asymmetry of option payoffs at expiration. For example, for a call, the upside is unlimited, whereas the downside is limited to zero. At expiration, time value is zero.

Although option prices are influenced by a variety of factors, the underlying instrument has a particularly significant influence. At this point, the underlying is assumed to be the only uncertain factor affecting the option price. We now look in detail at the one-period binomial option valuation model. The one-period binomial model is foundational for the material that follows.

---

[2] In financial markets, the exercise price is also commonly called the strike price.

# 3 ONE-PERIOD BINOMIAL MODEL

☐ describe and interpret the binomial option valuation model and its component terms

☐ describe how the value of a European option can be analyzed as the present value of the option's expected payoff at expiration

Exhibit 2 illustrates the one-period binomial process for an asset priced at S. In the figure on the left, each dot represents a particular outcome at a particular point in time in the binomial lattice. The dots are termed nodes. At the Time 0 node, there are only two possible future paths in the binomial process, an up move and a down move, termed arcs. The figure on the right illustrates the underlying price at each node. At Time 1, there are only two possible outcomes: $S^+$ denotes the outcome when the underlying goes up, and $S^-$ denotes the outcome when the underlying goes down.

**Exhibit 2: One-Period Binomial Lattice with Underlying Distribution Illustrated**

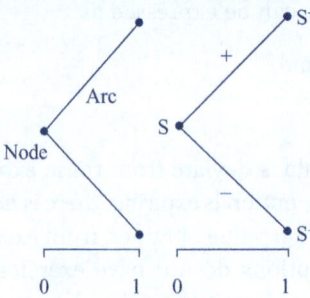

At Time 1, there are only two possible outcomes and two resulting values of the underlying, $S^+$ (up occurs) and $S^-$ (down occurs). Although the one-period binomial model is clearly unrealistic, it will provide key insights into the more realistic multiperiod binomial as well as the BSM model.

We further define the total returns implied by the underlying movements as

$u = \frac{S^+}{S}$ (up factor) and

$d = \frac{S^-}{S}$ (down factor).

The up factors and down factors are the total returns; that is, one plus the rate of return. The magnitudes of the up and down factors are based on the volatility of the underlying. In general, higher volatility will result in higher up values and lower down values.

We briefly review option valuation within a one-period binomial tree. With this review, we can move quickly to option valuation within a two-period binomial lattice by performing the one-period exercise three times.

# One-Period Binomial Model

We consider the fair value of a two-period call option value measured at Time 1 when an up move occurs, that is $c^+$. Based on arbitrage forces, we know this option value at expiration is either

$$c^{++} = \text{Max}(0, S^{++} - X) = \text{Max}(0, u^2 S - X), \text{ or}$$

$$c^{+-} = \text{Max}(0, S^{+-} - X) = \text{Max}(0, udS - X).$$

At this point, we assume that there are no costs or benefits from owning the underlying instrument. Now consider the transactions illustrated in Exhibit 3. These transactions are presented as cash flows. Thus, if we write a call option, we receive money at Time Step 0 and may have to pay out money at Time Step 1. Suppose the first trade is to write or sell one call option within the single-period binomial model. The value of a call option is positively related to the value of the underlying. That is, they both move up or down together. Hence, by writing a call option, the trader will lose money if the underlying goes up and make money if the underlying falls. Therefore, to execute a hedge, the trader will need a position that will make money if the underlying goes up. Thus, the second trade needs to be a long position in the underlying. Specifically, the trader buys a certain number of units, h, of the underlying. The symbol h is used because it represents a hedge ratio.

Note that with these first two trades, neither arbitrage rule is satisfied. The future cash flow could be either $-c^- + hS^-$ or $-c^+ + hS^+$ and can be positive or negative. Thus, the cash flows at the Time Step 1 could result in the arbitrageur having to pay out money if one of these values is less than zero. To resolve both of these issues, we set the Time Step 1 cash flows equal to each other—that is, $-c^+ + hS^+ = -c^- + hS^-$—and solve for the appropriate hedge ratio:

$$h = \frac{c^+ - c^-}{S^+ - S^-} \geq 0 \tag{1}$$

We determine the hedge ratio such that we are indifferent to the underlying going up or down. Thus, we are hedged against moves in the underlying. A simple rule for remembering this formula is that the hedge ratio is the value of the call if the underlying goes up minus the value of the call if the underlying goes down divided by the value of the underlying if it goes up minus the value of the underlying if it goes down. The up and down patterns are the same in the numerator and denominator, but the numerator contains the option and the denominator contains the underlying.

Because call prices are positively related to changes in the underlying price, we know that h is non-negative. As shown in Exhibit 3, we will buy h underlying units as depicted in the second trade, and we will finance the present value of the net cash flows as depicted in the third trade. If we assume r denotes the per period risk-free interest rate, then the present value calculation, denoted as PV, is equal to $1/(1 + r)$. We need to borrow or lend an amount such that the future net cash flows are equal to zero. Therefore, we finance today the present value of $-hS^- + c^-$ which also equals $-hS^+ + c^+$. At this point we do not know if the finance term is positive or negative, thus we may be either borrowing or lending, which will depend on c, h, and S.

**Exhibit 3: Writing One Call Hedge with h Units of the Underlying and Finance**

| Strategy | Time Step 0 | Time Step 1 Down Occurs | Time Step 1 Up Occurs |
|---|---|---|---|
| 1) Write one call option | +c | $-c^-$ | $-c^+$ |
| 2) Buy h underlying units | $-hS$ | $+hS^-$ | $+hS^+$ |

| Strategy | Time Step 0 | Time Step 1 Down Occurs | Time Step 1 Up Occurs |
|---|---|---|---|
| 3) Borrow or lend | $-PV(-hS^- + c^-)$ $= -PV(-hS^+ + c^+)$ | $-hS^- + c^-$ | $-hS^+ + c^+$ |
| Net Cash Flow | $+c - hS$ $-PV(-hS^- + c^-)$ | 0 | 0 |

The value of the net portfolio at Time Step 0 should be zero or there is an arbitrage opportunity. If the net portfolio has positive value, then arbitrageurs will engage in this strategy, which will push the call price down and the underlying price up until the net is no longer positive. We assume the size of the borrowing will not influence interest rates. If the net portfolio has negative value, then arbitrageurs will engage in the opposite strategy—buy calls, short sell the underlying, and lend—pushing the call price up and the underlying price down until the net cash flow at Time 0 is no longer positive. Therefore, within the single-period binomial model, we have

$$+c - hS - PV(-hS^- + c^-) = 0$$

or, equivalently,

$$+c - hS - PV(-hS^+ + c^+) = 0.$$

Therefore, the **no-arbitrage approach** leads to the following single-period call option valuation equation:

$$c = hS + PV(-hS^- + c^-) \qquad (2)$$

or, equivalently, $c = hS + PV(-hS^+ + c^+)$. In words, long a call option is equal to owning h shares of stock partially financed, where the financed amount is $PV(-hS^- + c^-)$, or using the per period rate, $(-hS^- + c^-)/(1 + r)$.[3]

We will refer to Equation 2 as the no-arbitrage single-period binomial option valuation model. This equation is foundational to understanding the two-period binomial as well as other option valuation models. The option can be replicated with the underlying and financing, a point illustrated in the following example.

### EXAMPLE 1

### Long Call Option Replicated with Underlying and Financing

1. Identify the trading strategy that will generate the payoffs of taking a long position in a call option within a single-period binomial framework.

    A. Buy $h = (c^+ + c^-)/(S^+ + S^-)$ units of the underlying and financing of $-PV(-hS^- + c^-)$

    B. Buy $h = (c^+ - c^-)/(S^+ - S^-)$ units of the underlying and financing of $-PV(-hS^- + c^-)$

    C. Short sell $h = (c^+ - c^-)/(S^+ - S^-)$ units of the underlying and financing of $+PV(-hS^- + c^-)$

### Solution:

B is correct. The following table shows the terminal payoffs to be identical between a call option and buying the underlying with financing.

---

[3] Or, by the same logic, $PV(-hS^+ + c^+)$, which is $(-hS^+ + c^+)/(1 + r)$.

# One-Period Binomial Model

| Strategy | Time Step 0 | Time Step 1 Down Occurs | Time Step 1 Up Occurs |
|---|---|---|---|
| Buy 1 call option | $-c$ | $+c^-$ | $+c^+$ |
| OR A REPLICATING PORTFOLIO | | | |
| Buy h underlying units | $-hS$ | $+hS^-$ | $+hS^+$ |
| Borrow or lend | $-PV(-hS^- + c^-)$ $= -PV(-hS^+ + c^+)$ | $-hS^- + c^-$ | $-hS^+ + c^+$ |
| Net | $-hS - PV(-hS^- + c^-)$ | $+c^-$ | $+c^+$ |

Recall that by design, h is selected such that $-hS^- + c^- = -hS^+ + c^+$ or $h = (c^+ - c^-)/(S^+ - S^-)$. Therefore, a call option can be replicated with the underlying and financing. Specifically, the call option is equivalent to a leveraged position in the underlying.

Thus, the no-arbitrage approach is a replicating strategy: A call option is synthetically replicated with the underlying and financing. Following a similar strategy with puts, the no-arbitrage approach leads to the following no-arbitrage single-period put option valuation equation:

$$p = hS + PV(-hS^- + p^-) \tag{3}$$

or, equivalently, $p = hS + PV(-hS^+ + p^+)$ where

$$h = \frac{p^+ - p^-}{S^+ - S^-} \leq 0 \tag{4}$$

Because $p^+$ is less than $p^-$, the hedge ratio is negative. Hence, to replicate a long put position, the arbitrageur will short sell the underlying and lend a portion of the proceeds. Note that a long put position would be replicated by trading h units of the underlying. With h negative, this trade is a short sale, and because $-h$ is positive, the value $-hS$ results in a positive cash flow at Time Step 0.

### EXAMPLE 2

### Long Put Option Replicated with Underlying and Financing

1. Identify the trading strategy that will generate the payoffs of taking a long position in a put option within a single-period binomial framework.

   **A.** Short sell $-h = -(p^+ - p^-)/(S^+ - S^-)$ units of the underlying and financing of $-PV(-hS^- + p^-)$

   **B.** Buy $-h = (p^+ - p^-)/(S^+ - S^-)$ units of the underlying and financing of $-PV(-hS^- + p^-)$

   **C.** Short sell $h = (p^+ - p^-)/(S^+ - S^-)$ units of the underlying and financing of $+PV(-hS^- + p^-)$

### Solution:

A is correct. Before illustrating the replicating portfolio, we make a few observations regarding the hedge ratio. Note that by design, h is selected such that $-hS^- + p^- = -hS^+ + p^+$ or $h = (p^+ - p^-)/(S^+ - S^-)$. Unlike calls, the put hedge ratio is not positive (note that $p^+ < p^-$ but $S^+ > S^-$). Remember that taking a position in $-h$ units of the underlying is actually short selling the underlying rather than buying it. The following table shows the terminal payoffs to be identical between a put option and a position in the underlying with financing.

| Strategy | Time Step 0 | Time Step 1 Down Occurs | Time Step 1 Up Occurs |
|---|---|---|---|
| Buy 1 Put Option | $-p$ | $+p^-$ | $+p^+$ |
| OR A REPLICATING PORTFOLIO | | | |
| Short sell $-h$ Underlying Units | $-hS$ | $+hS^-$ | $+hS^+$ |
| Borrow or Lend | $-PV(-hS^- + p^-)$ $= -PV(-hS^+ + p^+)$ | $-hS^- + p^-$ | $-hS^+ + p^+$ |
| Net | $-hS - PV(-hS^- + p^-)$ | $+p^-$ | $+p^+$ |

Therefore, a put option can be replicated with the underlying and financing. Specifically, the put option is simply equivalent to a short position in the underlying with financing in the form of lending.

What we have shown to this point is the no-arbitrage approach. Before turning to the expectations approach, we mention, for the sake of completeness, that the transactions for replicating the payoffs for writing options are the reverse for those of buying them. Thus, for writing a call option, the writer will be selling stock short and investing proceeds (i.e. lending), whereas for a put, the writer will be purchasing stock on margin (i.e. borrowing). Once again, we see the powerful result that the same basic conceptual structure is used for puts and calls, whether written or purchased. Only the exercise and expiration conditions vary.

The no-arbitrage results that have been presented can be expressed as the present value of a unique expectation of the option payoffs.[4] Specifically, the **expectations approach** results in an identical value as the no-arbitrage approach, but it is usually easier to compute. The formulas are viewed as follows:

$$c = PV[\pi c^+ + (1 - \pi)c^-] \text{ and} \tag{5}$$

$$p = PV[\pi p^+ + (1 - \pi)p^-] \tag{6}$$

where the probability of an up move is

$$\pi = [FV(1) - d]/(u - d)$$

Recall the future value is simply the reciprocal of the present value or $FV(1) = 1/PV(1)$. Thus, if $PV(1) = 1/(1 + r)$, then $FV(1) = (1 + r)$. Note that the option values are simply the present value of the expected terminal option payoffs. The expected terminal option payoffs can be expressed as

$$E(c_1) = \pi c^+ + (1 - \pi)c^- \text{ and}$$

$$E(p_1) = \pi p^+ + (1 - \pi)p^-$$

where $c_1$ and $p_1$ are the values of the options at Time 1. The present value and future value calculations are based on the risk-free rate, denoted r.[5] Thus, the option values based on the expectations approach can be written and remembered concisely as

$$c = PV_r[E(c_1)] \text{ and}$$

---

[4] It takes a bit of algebra to move from the no-arbitrage expression to the present value of the expected future payoffs, but the important point is that both expressions yield exactly the same result.
[5] We will suppress "r" most of the time and simply denote the calculation as PV. The "r" will be used at times to reinforce that the present value calculation is based on the risk-free interest rate.

$p = PV_r[E(p_1)]$

The expectations approach to option valuation differs in two significant ways from the discounted cash flow approach to securities valuation. First, the expectation is not based on the investor's beliefs regarding the future course of the underlying. That is, the probability, π, is objectively determined and not based on the investor's personal view. This probability has taken several different names, including risk-neutral (RN) probability. Importantly, we did not make any assumption regarding the arbitrageur's risk preferences: The expectations approach is a result of this arbitrage process, not an assumption regarding risk preferences. Hence, they are called risk-neutral probabilities. Although we called them probabilities from the very start, they are not the true probabilities of up and down moves.

Second, the discount rate is *not* risk adjusted. The discount rate is simply based on the estimated risk-free interest rate. The expectations approach here is often viewed as superior to the discounted cash flow approach because both the subjective future expectation as well as the subjective risk-adjusted discount rate have been replaced with more objective measures.

### EXAMPLE 3

### Single-Period Binomial Call Value

A non-dividend-paying stock is currently trading at €100. A call option has one year to mature, the periodically compounded risk-free interest rate is 5.15%, and the exercise price is €100. Assume a single-period binomial option valuation model, where u = 1.35 and d = 0.74.

1. The optimal hedge ratio will be *closest* to:

    A. 0.57.

    B. 0.60.

    C. 0.65.

### Solution to 1:

A is correct. Given the information provided, we know the following:

$S^+ = uS = 1.35(100) = 135$

$S^- = dS = 0.74(100) = 74$

$c^+ = Max(0, uS - X) = Max(0, 135 - 100) = 35$

$c^- = Max(0, dS - X) = Max(0, 74 - 100) = 0$

With this information, we can compute both the hedge ratio as well as the call option value. The hedge ratio is:

$$h = \frac{c^+ - c^-}{S^+ - S^-} = \frac{35 - 0}{135 - 74} = 0.573770$$

2. The call option value will be *closest* to:

    A. €13.

    B. €15.

    C. €17.

### Solution to 2:

C is correct. The risk-neutral probability of an up move is

$$\pi = [FV(1) - d]/(u - d) = (1.0515 - 0.74)/(1.35 - 0.74) = 0.510656,$$

where $FV(1) = (1 + r) = 1.0515$.

Thus the call value by the expectations approach is

$$c = PV[\pi c^+ + (1 - \pi)c^-] = 0.951022[(0.510656)35 + (1 - 0.510656)0]$$
$$= €16.998,$$

where $PV(1) = 1/(1 + r) = 1/(1.0515) = 0.951022$.

Note that the call value by the no-arbitrage approach yields the same answer:

$$c = hS + PV(-hS^- + c^-) = 0.573770(100) + 0.951022[-0.573770(74) + 0] = €16.998.$$

The value of a put option can also be found based on put–call parity. Put–call parity can be remembered as simply two versions of portfolio insurance, long stock and long put or lend and long call, where the exercise prices for the put and call are identical. Put–call parity with symbols is

$$S + p = PV(X) + c \tag{7}$$

Put–call parity holds regardless of the particular valuation model being used. Depending on the context, this equation can be rearranged. For example, a call option can be expressed as a position in a stock, financing, and a put, or

$$c = S - PV(X) + p$$

### EXAMPLE 4

### Single-Period Binomial Put Value

1. You again observe a €100 price for a non-dividend-paying stock with the same inputs as the previous box. That is, the call option has one year to mature, the periodically compounded risk-free interest rate is 5.15%, the exercise price is €100, u = 1.35, and d = 0.74. The put option value will be *closest* to:

    A. €12.00.

    B. €12.10.

    C. €12.20.

### Solution:

B is correct. For puts, we know the following:

$$p^+ = \text{Max}(0, 100 - uS) = \text{Max}(0, 100 - 135) = 0$$

$p^- = Max(0, 100 - dS) = Max(0, 100 - 74) = 26$

With this information, we can compute the put option value based on risk-neutral probability from the previous example or [recall that PV(1) = 0.951022]

$p = PV[\pi p^+ + (1 - \pi)p^-] = 0.951022[(0.510656)0 + (1 - 0.510656)26] = €12.10$

Therefore, in summary, option values can be expressed either in terms of replicating portfolios or as the present value of the expected future cash flows. Both expressions yield the same valuations.

# TWO-PERIOD BINOMIAL MODEL: CALL OPTIONS

4

- ☐ describe and interpret the binomial option valuation model and its component terms
- ☐ identify an arbitrage opportunity involving options and describe the related arbitrage

The two-period binomial lattice can be viewed as three one-period binomial lattices, as illustrated in Exhibit 4. Clearly, if we understand the one-period model, then the process can be repeated three times. First, we analyze Box 1 and Box 2. Finally, based on the results of Box 1 and Box 2, we analyze Box 3.

**Exhibit 4: Two-Period Binomial Lattice as Three One-Period Binomial Lattices**

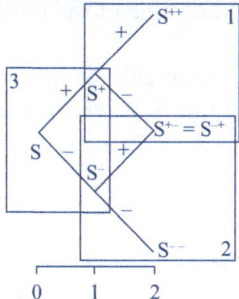

At Time 2, there are only three values of the underlying, $S^{++}$ (an up move occurs twice), $S^{--}$ (a down move occurs twice), and $S^{+-} = S^{-+}$ (either an up move occurs and then a down move or a down move occurs and then an up move). For computational reasons, it is extremely helpful that the lattice recombines—that is, $S^{+-} = S^{-+}$, meaning that if the underlying goes up and then down, it ends up at the same price as if it goes down and then up. A recombining binomial lattice will always have just one more ending node in the final period than the number of time steps. In contrast, a non-recombining lattice of n time steps will have $2^n$ ending nodes, which poses a tremendous computational challenge even for powerful computers.

For our purposes here, we assume the up and down factors are constant throughout the lattice, ensuring that the lattice recombines—that is $S^{+-} = S^{-+}$. For example, assume u = 1.25, d = 0.8, and $S_0$ = 100. Note that $S^{+-}$ = 1.25(0.8)100 = 100 and $S^{-+}$ = 0.8(1.25)100 = 100. So the middle node at Time 2 is 100 and can be reached from either of two paths.

The two-period binomial option valuation model illustrates two important concepts, self-financing and dynamic replication. Self-financing implies that the replicating portfolio will not require any additional funds from the arbitrageur during the life of this dynamically rebalanced portfolio. If additional funds are needed, then they are financed externally. Dynamic replication means that the payoffs from the option can be exactly replicated through a planned trading strategy. Option valuation relies on self-financing, dynamic replication.

Mathematically, the no-arbitrage approach for the two-period binomial model is best understood as working backward through the binomial tree. At Time 2, the payoffs are driven by the option's exercise value.

For calls:

$$c^{++} = \text{Max}(0, S^{++} - X) = \text{Max}(0, u^2 S - X),$$

$$c^{+-} = \text{Max}(0, S^{+-} - X) = \text{Max}(0, udS - X), \text{ and}$$

$$c^{--} = \text{Max}(0, S^{--} - X) = \text{Max}(0, d^2 S - X)$$

For puts:

$$p^{++} = \text{Max}(0, X - S^{++}) = \text{Max}(0, X - u^2 S),$$

$$p^{+-} = \text{Max}(0, X - S^{+-}) = \text{Max}(0, X - udS), \text{ and}$$

$$p^{--} = \text{Max}(0, X - S^{--}) = \text{Max}(0, X - d^2 S)$$

At Time 1, the option values are driven by the arbitrage transactions that synthetically replicate the payoffs at Time 2. We can compute the option values at Time 1 based on the option values at Time 2 using the no-arbitrage approach based on Equations 1 and 2. At Time 0, the option values are driven by the arbitrage transactions that synthetically replicate the value of the options at Time 1 (again based on Equations 1 and 2).

We illustrate the no-arbitrage approach for solving the two-period binomial call value. Suppose the annual interest rate is 3%, the underlying stock is S = 72, u = 1.356, d = 0.541, and the exercise price is X = 75. The stock does not pay dividends. Exhibit 5 illustrates the results.

# Two-Period Binomial Model: Call Options

### Exhibit 5: Two-Period Binomial Tree with Call Values and Hedge Ratios

**Time 0:**

| Item | Value |
|---|---|
| Underlying | 72 |
| Call | 19.47407 |
| Hedge Ratio | 0.56971 |

**Time 1, up (p = P(u)):**

| Item | Value |
|---|---|
| Underlying | 97.632 |
| Call | 33.43048 |
| Hedge Ratio | 0.72124 |

**Time 1, down (p = P(d)):**

| Item | Value |
|---|---|
| Underlying | 38.952 |
| Call | 0 |
| Hedge Ratio | 0 |

**Time 2, up-up (p = P(uu)):**

| Item | Value |
|---|---|
| Underlying | 132.389 |
| Call | 57.389 |

**Time 2, up-down / down-up (p = P(ud) = P(du)):**

| Item | Value |
|---|---|
| Underlying | 52.81891 |
| Call | 0 |

**Time 2, down-down (p = P(dd)):**

| Item | Value |
|---|---|
| Underlying | 21.07303 |
| Call | 0 |

---

We now verify selected values reported in Exhibit 5. At Time Step 2 and assuming up occurs twice, the underlying stock value is $u^2S = (1.356)^2 72 = 132.389$, and hence, the call value is 57.389 [= Max(0,132.389 − 75)]. The hedge ratio at Time Step 1, assuming up occurs once, is

$$h^+ = \frac{c^{++} - c^{+-}}{S^{++} - S^{+-}} = \frac{57.389 - 0}{132.389 - 52.819} = 0.72124$$

The RN probability of an up move throughout this tree is [RN: risk-neutral]

$$\pi = [FV(1) - d]/(u - d) = (1.03 - 0.541)/(1.356 - 0.541) = 0.6$$

With this information, we can compute the call price at Time 1 when an up move occurs as

$$c = PV[\pi c^{++} + (1 - \pi)c^{+-}] = (1/1.03)[(0.6)57.389 + (1 - 0.6)0] = 33.43048$$

and at Time Step 0,

$$h = \frac{c^+ - c^-}{S^+ - S^-} = \frac{33.43048 - 0}{97.632 - 38.952} = 0.56971$$

Thus, the call price at the start is

$$c = PV[\pi c^+ + (1 - \pi)c^-] = (1/1.03)[(0.6)33.43048 + (1 - 0.6)0] = 19.47$$

From the no-arbitrage approach, the call payoffs can be replicated by purchasing h shares of the underlying and financing $-PV(-hS^- + c^-)$. Therefore, we purchase 0.56971 shares of stock for 41.019 [= 0.56971(72)] and borrow 21.545 {or in cash flow terms, $-21.545 = (1/1.03)[-0.56971(38.952) + 0]$}, replicating the call values at Time 0. We then illustrate Time 1 assuming that an up move occurs. The stock position will now be worth 55.622 [= 0.56971(97.632)], and the borrowing must be repaid with interest or 22.191 [= 1.03(21.545)]. Note that the portfolio is worth 33.431 (55.622 − 22.191), the same value as the call except for a small rounding error. Therefore, the portfolio of stock and the financing dynamically replicates the value of the call option.

The final task is to demonstrate that the portfolio is self-financing. Self-financing can be shown by observing that the new portfolio at Time 1, assuming an up move occurs, is equal to the old portfolio that was formed at Time 0 and liquidated at Time 1. Notice that the hedge ratio rose from 0.56971 to 0.72124 as we moved from Time 0 to Time 1, assuming an up move occurs, requiring the purchase of additional shares. These additional shares will be financed with additional borrowing. The total borrowing is 36.98554 {= −PV(−hS$^{+-}$ + c$^{+-}$) = − (1/1.03)[−0.72124(52.81891) +0]}. The borrowing at Time 0 that is due at Time 1 is 22.191. The funds borrowed at Time 1 grew to 36.98554. Therefore, the strategy is self-financing.

The two-period binomial model can also be represented as the present value of an expectation of future cash flows. Based on the one-period results, it follows by repeated substitutions that

$$c = PV[\pi^2 c^{++} + 2\pi(1-\pi)c^{+-} + (1-\pi)^2 c^{--}] \quad (8)$$

and

$$p = PV[\pi^2 p^{++} + 2\pi(1-\pi)p^{+-} + (1-\pi)^2 p^{--}] \quad (9)$$

Therefore, the two-period binomial model is again simply the present value of the expected future cash flows based on the RN probability. Again, the option values are simply the present value of the expected terminal option payoffs. The expected terminal option payoffs can be expressed as

$$E(c_2) = \pi^2 c^{++} + 2\pi(1-\pi)c^{+-} + (1-\pi)^2 c^{--}$$

and

$$E(p_2) = \pi^2 p^{++} + 2\pi(1-\pi)p^{+-} + (1-\pi)^2 p^{--}$$

Thus, the two-period binomial option values based on the expectations approach can be written and remembered concisely as

$$c = PV_r[E\pi(c_2)] \text{ and}$$

$$p = PV_r[E\pi(p_2)]$$

It is vital to remember that this present value is over two periods, so the discount factor with discrete rates is PV = [1/(1 + r)$^2$]. Recall the subscript "r" just emphasizes the present value calculation and is based on the risk-free interest rate.

> **EXAMPLE 5**
>
> ### Two-Period Binomial Model Call Valuation
>
> You observe a €50 price for a non-dividend-paying stock. The call option has two years to mature, the periodically compounded risk-free interest rate is 5%, the exercise price is €50, u = 1.356, and d = 0.744. Assume the call option is European-style.
>
> 1. The probability of an up move based on the risk-neutral probability is *closest* to:
>
>     **A.** 30%.
>
>     **B.** 40%.
>
>     **C.** 50%.
>
> ### Solution to 1:
>
> C is correct. Based on the RN probability equation, we have:
>
> π = [FV(1) − d]/(u − d) = [(1 + 0.05) − 0.744]/(1.356 − 0.744) = 0.5 or 50%
>
> 2. The current call option value is *closest* to:
>
>     **A.** €9.53.
>
>     **B.** €9.71.
>
>     **C.** €9.87.

## Solution to 2:

B is correct. The current call option value calculations are as follows:

$c^{++} = \text{Max}(0, u^2 S - X) = \text{Max}[0, 1.356^2 (50) - 50] = 41.9368$

$c^{-+} = c^{+-} = \text{Max}(0, udS - X) = \text{Max}[0, 1.356(0.744)(50) - 50] = 0.44320$

$c^{--} = \text{Max}(0, d^2 S - X) = \text{Max}[0, 0.744^2 (50) - 50] = 0.0$

With this information, we can compute the call option value:

$c = PV[E(c_2)] = PV[\pi^2 c^{++} + 2\pi(1 - \pi)c^{+-} + (1 - \pi)^2 c^{--}]$

$= [1/(1 + 0.05)]^2 [0.5^2 41.9368 + 2(0.5)(1 - 0.5)0.44320 + (1 - 0.5)^2 0.0]$

$= 9.71$

It is vital to remember that the present value is over two periods, hence the single-period PV is squared. Thus, the current call price is €9.71.

3. The current put option value is *closest* to:

   A. €5.06.
   B. €5.33.
   C. €5.94.

## Solution to 3:

A is correct. The put option value can be computed simply by applying put–call parity or $p = c + PV(X) - S = 9.71 + [1/(1 + 0.05)]^2 50 - 50 = 5.06$. Thus, the current put price is €5.06.

# TWO-PERIOD BINOMIAL MODEL: PUT OPTIONS

☐ describe and interpret the binomial option valuation model and its component terms

☐ calculate the no-arbitrage values of European and American options using a two-period binomial model

We now turn to consider American-style options. It is well-known that call options on non-dividend-paying stock will not be exercised early because the minimum price of the option exceeds its exercise value. To illustrate by example, consider a call on a US$100 stock, with an exercise price of US$10 (that is, very deep in the money). Suppose the call is worth its exercise value of only US$90. To get stock exposure, one could fund and pay US$100 to buy the stock, or fund and pay only US$90 for the call and pay the last US$10 at expiration only if the stock is at or above US$100 at that time. Because the latter choice is preferable, the call must be worth more than the US$90 exercise value. Another way of looking at it is that it would make no sense to exercise this call because you do not believe the stock can go any higher and you would thus simply be obtaining a stock that you believe would go no higher. Moreover, the stock would require that you pay far more money than you have tied up in the call. It is always better to just sell the call in this situation because it will be trading for more than the exercise value.

The same is not true for put options. By early exercise of a put, particularly a deep in-the-money put, the sale proceeds can be invested at the risk-free rate and earn interest worth more than the time value of the put. Thus, we will examine how early exercise influences the value of an American-style put option. As we will see, when early exercise has value, the no-arbitrage approach is the only way to value American-style options.

Suppose the periodically compounded interest rate is 3%, the non-dividend-paying underlying stock is currently trading at 72, the exercise price is 75, u = 1.356, d = 0.541, and the put option expires in two years. Exhibit 6 shows the results for a European-style put option.

### Exhibit 6: Two-Period Binomial Model for a European-Style Put Option

| Item | Value |
|---|---|
| Underlying | 72 |
| Put | 18.16876 |
| Hedge Ratio | −0.43029 |

| Item | Value |
|---|---|
| Underlying | 97.632 |
| Put | 8.61401 |
| Hedge Ratio | −0.27876 |

| Item | Value |
|---|---|
| Underlying | 38.952 |
| Put | 33.86353 |
| Hedge Ratio | −1 |

| Item | Value |
|---|---|
| Underlying | 132.389 |
| Put | 0 |

| Item | Value |
|---|---|
| Underlying | 52.81891 |
| Put | 22.18109 |

| Item | Value |
|---|---|
| Underlying | 21.07303 |
| Put | 53.92697 |

The Time 1 down move is of particular interest. The exercise value for this put option is 36.048 [= Max(0,75 − 38.952)]. Therefore, the exercise value is higher than the put value. So, if this same option were American-style, then the option would be worth more exercised than not exercised. Thus, the put option should be exercised. Exhibit 7 illustrates how the analysis changes if this put option were American-style. Clearly, the right to exercise early translates into a higher value.

## Exhibit 7: Two-Period Binomial Model for an American-Style Put Option

| Item | Value |
|---|---|
| Underlying | 72 |
| Put | ~~18.16876~~ 19.01710 |
| Hedge Ratio | ~~−0.43029~~ −0.46752 |

| Item | Value |
|---|---|
| Underlying | 97.632 |
| Put | 8.61401 |
| Hedge Ratio | −0.27876 |

| Item | Value |
|---|---|
| Underlying | 38.952 |
| Put | ~~33.86353~~ 36.04800 |
| Hedge Ratio | −1 |

| Item | Value |
|---|---|
| Underlying | 132.389 |
| Put | 0 |

| Item | Value |
|---|---|
| Underlying | 52.81891 |
| Put | 22.18109 |

| Item | Value |
|---|---|
| Underlying | 21.07303 |
| Put | 53.92697 |

American-style option valuation requires that one work backward through the binomial tree and address whether early exercise is optimal at each step. In Exhibit 7, the early exercise premium at Time 1 when a down move occurs is 2.18447 (36.048 − 33.86353). Also, if we replace 33.86353 with 36.048—in bold below for emphasis—in the Time 0 calculation, we obtain a put value of

$$p = PV[\pi p^+ + (1 − \pi)p^−] = (1/1.03)[(0.6)8.61401 + (1 − 0.6)\mathbf{36.048}] = 19.02$$

Thus, the early exercise premium at Time 0 is 0.85 (19.02 − 18.17). From this illustration, we see clearly that in a multiperiod setting, American-style put options cannot be valued simply as the present value of the expected future option payouts, as shown in Equation 9. American-style put options can be valued as the present value of the expected future option payout in a single-period setting. Hence, when early exercise is a consideration, we must address the possibility of early exercise as we work backward through the binomial tree.

### EXAMPLE 6

### Two-Period Binomial American-Style Put Option Valuation

1. Suppose you are given the following information: $S_0 = 26$, $X = 25$, $u = 1.466$, $d = 0.656$, $n = 2$ (time steps), $r = 2.05\%$ (per period), and no dividends. The tree is provided in Exhibit 8.

### Exhibit 8: Two-Period Binomial American-Style Put Option

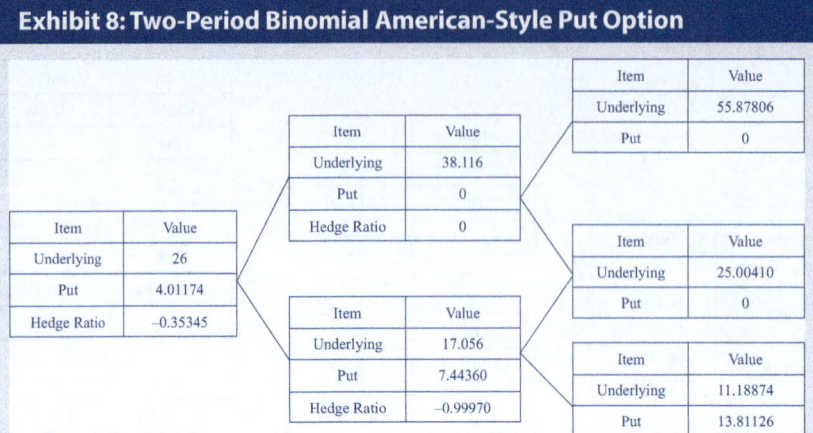

The early exercise premium of the above American-style put option is *closest* to:

A. 0.27.

B. 0.30.

C. 0.35.

## Solution:

A is correct. The exercise value at Time 1 with a down move is 7.944 [= Max(0,25 − 17.056)]. Thus, we replace this value in the binomial tree and compute the hedge ratio at Time 0. The resulting put option value at Time 0 is thus 4.28143 (see Exhibit 9).

### Exhibit 9: Solution

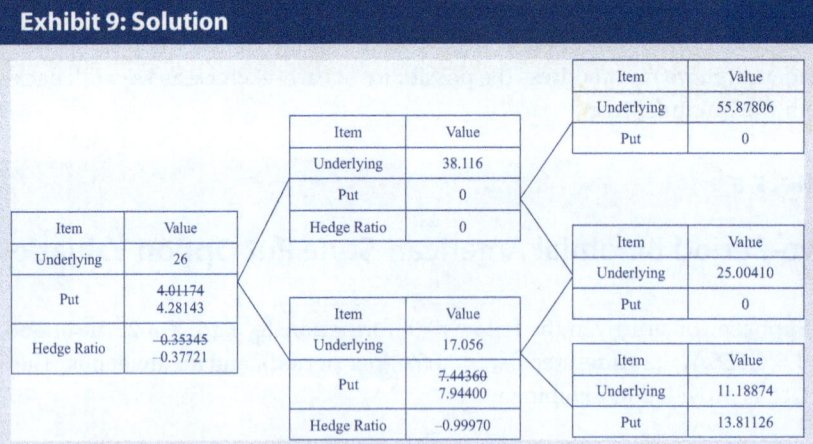

In Exhibit 9, the early exercise premium at Time 1 when a down move occurs is 0.5004 (7.944 − 7.44360). Thus, if we replace 7.44360 with 7.944—in bold below for emphasis—in the Time 0 calculation, we have the put value of

$$p = PV[\pi p^+ + (1 − \pi)p^−] = (1/1.0205)[(0.45)0 + (1 − 0.45)\mathbf{7.944}] = 4.28$$

Thus, the early exercise premium at Time 0 when a down move occurs 0.27 (= 4.28 − 4.01).

# TWO-PERIOD BINOMIAL MODEL: ROLE OF DIVIDENDS

☐ describe and interpret the binomial option valuation model and its component terms

We now briefly introduce the role of dividend payments within the binomial model. Our approach here is known as the escrow method. Because dividends lower the value of the stock, a call option holder is hurt. Although it is possible to adjust the option terms to offset this effect, most option contracts do not provide protection against dividends. Thus, dividends affect the value of an option. We assume dividends are perfectly predictable; hence, we split the underlying instrument into two components: the underlying instrument without the known dividends and the known dividends.[6] For example, the current value of the underlying instrument without dividends can be expressed as

$$\hat{S} = S - \gamma$$

where γ denotes the present value of dividend payments. We use the ^ symbol to denote the underlying instrument without dividends. In this case, we model the uncertainty of the stock based on $\hat{S}$ and not S. At expiration, the underlying instrument value is the same, $\hat{S}_T = S_T$, because we assume any dividends have already been paid. The value of an investment in the stock, however, would be $S_T + \gamma_T$, which assumes the dividend payments are reinvested at the risk-free rate.

To illustrate by example, consider a call on a US$100 stock with exercise price of US$95. The periodically compounded interest rate is 1.0%, the stock will pay a US$3 dividend at Time Step 1, u = 1.224, d = 0.796, and the call option expires in two years. Exhibit 10 shows some results for an American-style call option. The computations in Exhibit 10 involve several technical nuances that are beyond the scope of our objectives. The key objective here is to see how dividend-motivated early exercise influences American options.

The Time 1 up move is particularly interesting. At Time 0, the present value of the US$3 dividend payment is US$2.970297 (= 3/1.01). Therefore, 118.7644 = (100 − 2.970297)1.224 is the stock value without dividends at Time 1, assuming an up move occurs. The exercise value for this call option, including dividends, is 26.7644 [= Max(0,118.7644 + 3 − 95)], whereas the value of the call option per the binomial model is 24.9344. In other words, the stock price just before it goes ex-dividend is 118.7644 + 3 = 121.7644, so the option can be exercised for 121.7644 − 95 = 26.7644. If not exercised, the stock drops as it goes ex-dividend and the option becomes worth 24.9344 at the ex-dividend price. Thus, by exercising early, the call buyer acquires the stock just before it goes ex-dividend and thus is able to capture the dividend. If the call is not exercised, the call buyer will not receive this dividend. The American-style call option is worth more than the European-style call option because at Time Step 1 when an up move occurs, the call is exercised early, capturing additional value.

---

6 The reading focuses on regular, "known" dividends. In the case of large, special dividends, option exchanges may adjust the exercise price.

### Exhibit 10: Two-Period Binomial Model for an American-Style Call Option with Dividends

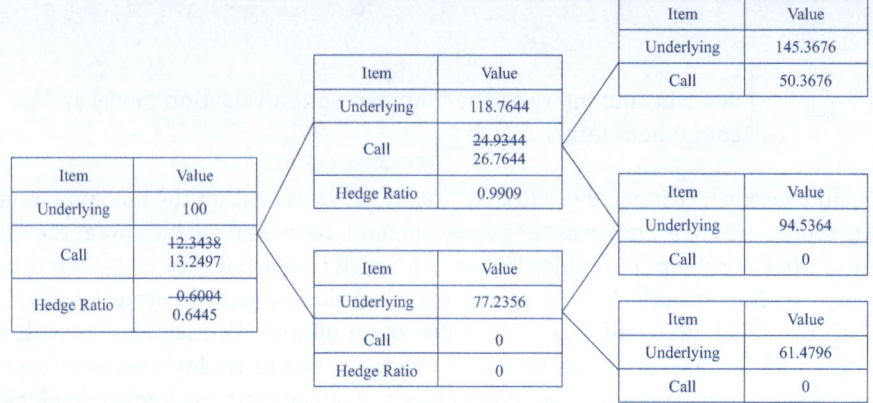

We now provide a comprehensive binomial option valuation example. In this example, we contrast European-style exercise with American-style exercise.

### EXAMPLE 7

## Comprehensive Two-Period Binomial Option Valuation Model Exercise

Suppose you observe a non-dividend-paying Australian equity trading for A$7.35. The call and put options have two years to mature, the periodically compounded risk-free interest rate is 4.35%, and the exercise price is A$8.0. Based on an analysis of this equity, the estimates for the up and down moves are u = 1.445 and d = 0.715, respectively.

## Two-Period Binomial Model: Role of Dividends

1. Calculate the European-style call and put option values at Time Step 0 and Time Step 1. Describe and interpret your results.

### Solution to 1:

The expectations approach requires the following preliminary calculations:

RN probability: $\pi = [FV(1) - d]/(u - d)$  *right after eqs (5); (6)*

$= [(1 + 0.0435) - 0.715]/(1.445 - 0.715) = 0.45$

$c^{++} = \text{Max}(0, u^2S - X)$

$= \text{Max}[0, 1.445^2(7.35) - 8.0] = 7.347$

$c^{+-} = \text{Max}(0, udS - X)$

$= \text{Max}[0, 1.445(0.715)7.35 - 8.0] = 0$

$c^{--} = \text{Max}(0, d^2S - X)$

$= \text{Max}[0, 0.715^2(7.35) - 8.0] = 0$

$p^{++} = \text{Max}(0, X - u^2S)$

$= \text{Max}[0, 8.0 - 1.445^2(7.35)] = 0$

$p^{+-} = \text{Max}(0, X - udS)$

$= \text{Max}[0, 8.0 - 1.445(0.715)7.35] = 0.406$

$p^{--} = \text{Max}(0, X - d^2S)$

$= \text{Max}[0, 8.0 - 0.715^2(7.35)] = 4.24$

Therefore, at Time Step 1, we have (note that $c_2|^+_1$ is read as the call value expiring at Time Step 2 observed at Time Step 1, assuming an up move occurs)

$E(c_2|^+_1) = \pi c^{++} + (1 - \pi)c^{+-} = 0.45(7.347) + (1 - 0.45)0 = 3.31$

$E(c_2|^-_1) = \pi c^{-+} + (1 - \pi)c^{--} = 0.45(0.0) + (1 - 0.45)0.0 = 0.0$

$E(p_2|^+_1) = \pi p^{++} + (1 - \pi)p^{+-} = 0.45(0.0) + (1 - 0.45)0.406 = 0.2233$

$E(p_2|^-_1) = \pi p^{-+} + (1 - \pi)p^{--} = 0.45(0.406) + (1 - 0.45)4.24 = 2.51$

Thus, because $PV_{1,2}(1) = 1/(1 + 0.0435) = 0.958313$, we have the Time Step 1 option values of

$c^+ = PV_{1,2}\left[E\left(c_2|^+_1\right)\right] = 0.958313(3.31) = 3.17$

$c^- = PV_{1,2}\left[E\left(c_2|^-_1\right)\right] = 0.958313(0.0) = 0.0$

$p^+ = PV_{1,2}\left[E\left(p_2|^+_1\right)\right] = 0.958313(0.2233) = 0.214$

$p^- = PV_{1,2}\left[E\left(p_2|^-_1\right)\right] = 0.958313(2.51) = 2.41$

At Time Step 0, we have

$E(c_2|_0) = \pi^2 c^{++} + 2\pi(1 - \pi)c^{+-} + (1 - \pi)^2 c^{--}$

$= 0.45^2(7.347) + 2(0.45)(1 - 0.45)0 + (1 - 0.45)^2 0 = 1.488$

$$E(p_2|_0) = \pi^2 p^{++} + 2\pi(1-\pi)p^{+-} + (1-\pi)^2 p^{--}$$
$$= 0.45^2(0) + 2(0.45)(1-0.45)0.406 + (1-0.45)^2 4.24 = 1.484$$

Thus,

$$c = PV_{rf,0,2}\left[E(c_2|_0)\right] = 0.91836(1.488) = 1.37 \text{ and}$$
$$p = PV_{rf,0,2}\left[E(p_2|_0)\right] = 0.91836(1.484) = 1.36$$

With the two-period binomial model, the call and put values based on the expectations approach are simply the present values of the expected payoffs. The present value of the expected payoffs is based on the risk-free interest rate and the expectations approach is based on the risk-neutral probability. The parameters in this example were selected so that the European-style put and call would have approximately the same value. Notice that the stock price is less than the exercise price by roughly the present value factor or $7.35 = 8.0/1.0435^2$. One intuitive explanation is put–call parity, which can be expressed as $c - p = S - PV(X)$. Thus, if $S = PV(X)$, then $c = p$.

2. Calculate the European-style call and put option hedge ratios at Time Step 0 and Time Step 1. Based on these hedge ratios, interpret the component terms of the binomial option valuation model.

### Solution to 2:

The computation of the hedge ratios at Time Step 1 and Time Step 0 will require the option values at Time Step 1 and Time Step 2. The terminal values of the options are given in Solution 1.

$S^{++} = u^2 S = 1.445^2(7.35) = 15.347$

$S^{+-} = udS = 1.445(0.715)7.35 = 7.594$

$S^{--} = d^2 S = 0.715^2(7.35) = 3.758$

$S^{+} = uS = 1.445(7.35) = 10.621$

$S^{-} = dS = 0.715(7.35) = 5.255$

Therefore, the hedge ratios at Time 1 are

$$h_c^+ = \frac{c^{++} - c^{+-}}{S^{++} - S^{+-}} = \frac{7.347 - 0.0}{15.347 - 7.594} = 0.9476$$

$$h_c^- = \frac{c^{-+} - c^{--}}{S^{+-} - S^{--}} = \frac{0.0 - 0.0}{7.594 - 3.758} = 0.0$$

$$h_p^+ = \frac{p^{++} - p^{+-}}{S^{++} - S^{+-}} = \frac{0.0 - 0.406}{15.347 - 7.594} = -0.05237$$

$$h_p^- = \frac{p^{-+} - p^{--}}{S^{+-} - S^{--}} = \frac{0.406 - 4.24}{7.594 - 3.758} = -1.0$$

In the last hedge ratio calculation, both put options are in the money ($p^{-+}$ and $p^{--}$). In this case, the hedge ratio will be $-1$, subject to a rounding error. We now turn to interpreting the model's component terms. Based on the no-arbitrage approach, we have for the call price, assuming an up move has occurred, at Time Step 1,

$$c^+ = h_c^+ S^+ + PV_{1,2}\left(-h_c^+ S^{+-} + c^{+-}\right)$$
$$= 0.9476(10.621) + (1/1.0435)[-0.9476(7.594) + 0.0] = 3.1684$$

Thus, the call option can be interpreted as a leveraged position in the stock. Specifically, long 0.9476 shares for a cost of 10.0645 [= 0.9476(10.621)] partially financed with a 6.8961 {= (1/1.0435)[−0.9476(7.594) + 0.0]} loan. Note that the loan amount can be found simply as the cost of the position in shares less the option value [6.8961 = 0.9476(10.621) − 3.1684]. Similarly, we have

$$c^- = h_c^- S^- + PV_{1,2}\left(-h_c^- S^{--} + c^{--}\right)$$
$$= 0.0(5.255) + (1/1.0435)[-0.0(3.758) + 0.0] = 0.0$$

Specifically, long 0.0 shares for a cost of 0.0 [= 0.0(5.255)] with no financing. For put options, the interpretation is different. Specifically, we have

$$p^+ = PV_{1,2}\left(-h_p^+ S^{++} + p^{++}\right) + h_p^+ S^+$$
$$= (1/1.0435)[-(-0.05237)15.347 + 0.0] + (-0.05237)10.621 = 0.2140$$

Thus, the put option can be interpreted as lending that is partially financed with a short position in shares. Specifically, short 0.05237 shares for a cost of 0.55622 [= (−0.05237)10.621] with financing of 0.77022 {= (1/1.0435)[−(−0.05237)15.347 + 0.0]}. Note that the lending amount can be found simply as the proceeds from the short sale of shares plus the option value [0.77022 = (0.05237)10.621 + 0.2140]. Again, we have

$$p^- = PV_{1,2}\left(-h_p^- S^{-+} + p^{-+}\right) + h_p^- S^-$$
$$= (1/1.0435)[-(-1.0)7.594 + 0.406] + (-1.0)5.255 = 2.4115$$

Here, we short 1.0 shares for a cost of 5.255 [= (−1.0)5.255] with financing of 7.6665 {= (1/1.0435)[−(−1.0)7.594 + 0.406]}. Again, the lending amount can be found simply as the proceeds from the short sale of shares plus the option value [7.6665 = (1.0)5.255 + 2.4115].

Finally, we have at Time Step 0

$$h_c = \frac{c^+ - c^-}{S^+ - S^-} = \frac{3.1684 - 0}{10.621 - 5.255} = 0.5905$$

$$h_p = \frac{p^+ - p^-}{S^+ - S^-} = \frac{0.2140 - 2.4115}{10.621 - 5.255} = -0.4095$$

The interpretations remain the same at Time Step 0:

$c = h_c S + PV_{0,1}(-h_c S^- + c^-)$

$= 0.5905(7.35) + (1/1.0435)[-0.5905(5.255) + 0.0] = 1.37$

Here, we are long 0.5905 shares for a cost of 4.3402 [=0.5905(7.35)] partially financed with a 2.97 {= (1/1.0435)[−0.5905(5.255) + 0.0] or = 0.5905(7.35) − 1.37} loan.

$p = PV_{0,1}(-h_p S^+ + p^+) + h_p S$

$= (1/1.0435)\{-[-0.4095(10.621)] + 0.214\} + (-0.4095)7.35 = 1.36$

Here, we short 0.4095 shares for a cost of 3.01 [= (−0.4095)7.35] with financing of 4.37 (= (1/1.0435){−[−0.4095(10.621)] + 0.214} or = (0.4095)7.35 + 1.36).

3. Calculate the American-style call and put option values and hedge ratios at Time Step 0 and Time Step 1. Explain how your results differ from the European-style results.

## Solution to 3:

We know that American-style call options on non-dividend-paying stock are worth the same as European-style call options because early exercise will not occur. Thus, as previously computed, $c^+ = 3.17$, $c^- = 0.0$, and $c = 1.37$. Recall that the call exercise value (denoted with EV) is simply the maximum of zero or the stock price minus the exercise price. We note that the EVs are less than or equal to the call model values; that is,

$c_{EV}^+ = Max(0, S^+ - X) = Max(0, 10.621 - 8.0) = 2.621\ (< 3.1684)$

$c_{EV}^- = Max(0, S^- - X) = Max(0, 5.255 - 8.0) = 0.0\ (= 0.0)$

$c_{EV} = Max(0, S - X) = Max(0, 7.35 - 8.0) = 0.0\ (< 1.37)$

Therefore, the American-style feature for non-dividend-paying stocks has no effect on either the hedge ratio or the option value. The binomial model for American-style calls on non-dividend-paying stocks can be described and interpreted the same as a similar European-style call. This point is consistent with what we said earlier. If there are no dividends, an American-style call will not be exercised early.

This result is not true for puts. We know that American-style put options on non-dividend-paying stock may be worth more than the analogous European-style put options. The hedge ratios at Time Step 1 will be the same as European-style puts because there is only one period left. Therefore, as previously shown, $p^+ = 0.214$ and $p^- = 2.41$.

The put exercise values are

$p_{EV}^+ = Max(0, X - S^+) = Max(0, 8.0 - 10.621) = 0\ (< 0.214)$

$p_{EV}^- = Max(0, X - S^-) = Max(0, 8.0 - 5.255) = 2.745\ (> 2.41)$

Because the exercise value for the put at Time Step 1, assuming a down move occurred, is greater than the model value, we replace the model value with the exercise value. Hence,

$p^- = 2.745$

and the hedge ratio at Time Step 0 will be affected. Specifically, we now have

$$h_p = \frac{p^+ - p^-}{S^+ - S^-} = \frac{0.2140 - 2.745}{10.621 - 5.255} = -0.4717$$

and thus the put model value is

$p = (1/1.0435)[0.45(0.214) + 0.55(2.745)] = 1.54$

Clearly, the early exercise feature has a significant impact on both the hedge ratio and the put option value in this case. The hedge ratio goes from −0.4095 to −0.4717. The put value is raised from 1.36 to 1.54.

We see through the simple two-period binomial model that an option can be viewed as a position in the underlying with financing. Furthermore, this valuation model can be expressed as the present value of the expected future cash flows, where the expectation is taken under the RN probability and the discounting is at the risk-free rate.

Up to this point, we have focused on equity options. The binomial model can be applied to any underlying instrument though often requiring some modifications. For example, currency options would require incorporating the foreign interest rate. Futures options would require a binomial lattice of the futures prices. Interest rate options, however, require somewhat different tools that we now examine.

# INTEREST RATE OPTIONS AND MULTIPERIOD MODEL

7

☐ calculate and interpret the value of an interest rate option using a two-period binomial model

In this section, we will briefly illustrate how to value interest rate options. There are a wide variety of approaches to valuing interest rate options. We do not delve into how arbitrage-free interest rate trees are generated. The particular approach used here assumes the RN probability of an up move at each node is 50%.

Exhibit 11 presents a binomial lattice of interest rates covering two years along with the corresponding zero-coupon bond values. The rates are expressed in annual compounding. Therefore, at Time 0, the spot rate is (1.0/0.970446) − 1 or 3.04540%.[7] Note that at Time 1, the value in the column labeled "Maturity" reflects time to maturity not calendar time. The lattice shows the rates on one-period bonds, so all bonds have a maturity of 1. The column labeled "Value" is the value of a zero-coupon bond with the stated maturity based on the rates provided.

---

7 The values in the first box from the left are observed at t = 0. The values in the remainder of the lattice are derived by using a technique that is outside the scope of this reading.

### Exhibit 11: Two-Year Binomial Interest Rate Lattice by Year

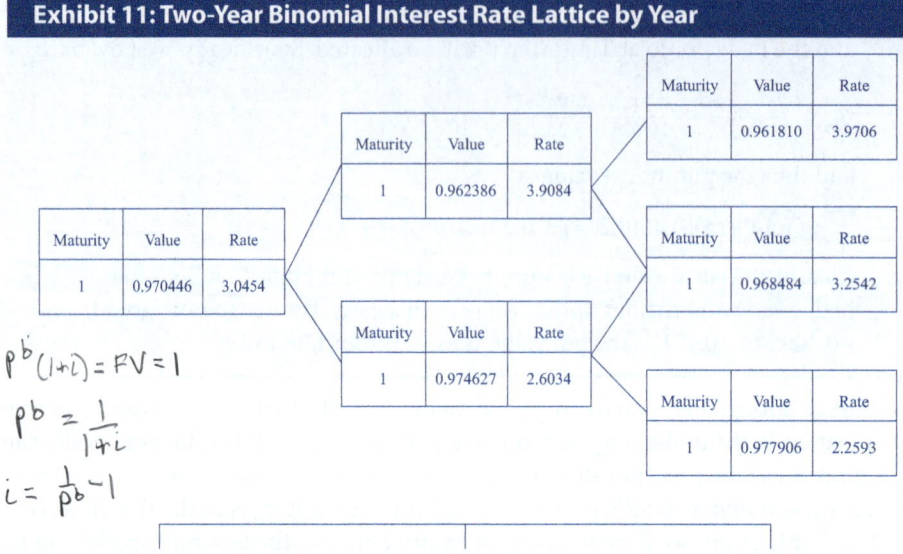

The underlying instrument for interest rate options here is the spot rate. A call option on interest rates will be in the money when the current spot rate is above the exercise rate. A put option on interest rates will be in the money when the current spot rate is below the exercise rate. Thus, based on the notation in the previous section, the current spot rate is denoted S. Option valuation follows the expectations approach discussed in the previous section but taken only one period at a time. The procedure is illustrated with an example.

### EXAMPLE 8

### Option on Interest Rates

1. This example is based on Exhibit 11. Suppose we seek to value two-year European-style call and put options on the periodically compounded one-year spot interest rate (the underlying). Assume the notional amount of the options is US$1,000,000 and the call and put exercise rate is 3.25% of

# Interest Rate Options and Multiperiod Model

par. Assume the RN probability is 50% and these option cash settle at Time 2 based on the observed rates.[8]

## Solution:

Using the expectations approach introduced in the last section, we have (per US$1) at Time Step 2

$c^{++} = \text{Max}(0, S^{++} - X) = \text{Max}[0, 0.039706 - 0.0325] = 0.007206$

$c^{+-} = \text{Max}(0, S^{+-} - X) = \text{Max}[0, 0.032542 - 0.0325] = 0.000042$

$c^{--} = \text{Max}(0, S^{--} - X) = \text{Max}[0, 0.022593 - 0.0325] = 0.0$

$p^{++} = \text{Max}(0, X - S^{++}) = \text{Max}[0, 0.0325 - 0.039706] = 0.0$

$p^{+-} = \text{Max}(0, X - S^{+-}) = \text{Max}[0, 0.0325 - 0.032542] = 0.0$

$p^{--} = \text{Max}(0, X - S^{--}) = \text{Max}[0, 0.0325 - 0.022593] = 0.009907$

At Time Step 1, we have

$c^{+} = PV_{1,2}[\pi c^{++} + (1 - \pi)c^{+-}]$

$= 0.962386[0.5(0.007206) + (1 - 0.5)0.000042]$

$= 0.003488$

$c^{-} = PV_{1,2}[\pi c^{+-} + (1 - \pi)c^{--}]$

$= 0.974627[0.5(0.000042) + (1 - 0.5)0.0]$

$= 0.00002$

$p^{+} = PV_{1,2}[\pi p^{++} + (1 - \pi)p^{+-}]$

$= 0.962386[0.5(0.0) + (1 - 0.5)0.0]$

$= 0.0$

$p^{-} = PV_{1,2}[\pi p^{+-} + (1 - \pi)p^{--}]$

$= 0.974627[0.5(0.0) + (1 - 0.5)0.009907]$

$= 0.004828$

Notice how the present value factors are different for the up and down moves. At Time Step 1 in the + outcome, we discount by a factor of 0.962386, and in the − outcome, we discount by the factor 0.974627. Because this is an option on interest rates, it should not be surprising that we have to allow the interest rate to vary.

---

[8] In practice, interest rate options usually have a settlement procedure that results in a deferred payoff. The deferred payoff arises from the fact that the underlying interest rate is based on an instrument that pays interest at the end of its life. For the instrument underlying the interest rate, the interest payment occurs after the interest has accrued. To accommodate this reality in this problem, we would have to introduce an instrument that matures at time three. The purpose of this example is merely to illustrate the procedure for rolling backward through an multinterest rate tree when the underlying is the interest rate. We simplify this example by omitting this deferred settlement. In Section 5.2, we discuss in detail the deferred settlement procedure and incorporate it into the pricing model.

> Therefore, at Time Step 0, we have
>
> $c = PV_{rf,0,1}[\pi c^+ + (1 - \pi)c^-]$
>
> $= 0.970446[0.5(0.003488) + (1 - 0.5)0.00002]$
>
> $= 0.00170216$
>
> $p = PV_{rf,0,1}[\pi p^+ + (1 - \pi)p^-]$
>
> $= 0.970446[0.5(0.0) + (1 - 0.5)0.004828]$
>
> $= 0.00234266$
>
> Because the notional amount is US$1,000,000, the call value is US$1,702.16 [= US$1,000,000(0.00170216)] and the put value is US$2,342.66 [= US$1,000,000(0.00234266)]. The key insight is to just work a two-period binomial model as three one-period binomial models.

We turn now to briefly generalize the binomial model as it leads naturally to the Black–Scholes–Merton option valuation model.

## Multiperiod Model

The multiperiod binomial model provides a natural bridge to the Black–Scholes–Merton option valuation model presented in the next section. The idea is to take the option's expiration and slice it up into smaller and smaller periods. The two-period model divides the expiration into two periods. The three-period model divides expiration into three periods and so forth. The process continues until you have a large number of time steps. The key feature is that each time step is of equal length. Thus, with a maturity of T, if there are n time steps, then each time step is T/n in length.

For American-style options, we must also test at each node whether the option is worth more exercised or not exercised. As in the two-period case, we work backward through the binomial tree testing the model value against the exercise value and always choosing the higher one.

The binomial model is an important and useful methodology for valuing options. The expectations approach can be applied to European-style options and will lead naturally to the BSM model in the next section. This approach simply values the option as the present value of the expected future payoffs, where the expectation is taken under the risk-neutral probability and the discounting is based on the risk-free rate. The no-arbitrage approach can be applied to either European-style or American-style options because it provides the intuition for the fair value of options.

## 8   BLACK-SCHOLES-MERTON (BSM) OPTION VALUATION MODEL

☐ identify assumptions of the Black–Scholes–Merton option valuation model

The BSM model, although very complex in its derivation, is rather simple to use and interpret. The objective here is to illustrate several facets of the BSM model with the objective of highlighting its practical usefulness. After a brief introduction, we examine the assumptions of the BSM model and then delve into the model itself.

## Introductory Material

Louis Bachelier published the first known mathematically rigorous option valuation model in 1900. By the late 1960s, there were several published quantitative option models. Fischer Black, Myron Scholes, and Robert Merton introduced the BSM model in 1973 in two published papers, one by Black and Scholes and the other by Merton. The innovation of the BSM model is essentially the no-arbitrage approach introduced in the previous section but applied with a continuous time process, which is equivalent to a binomial model in which the length of the time step essentially approaches zero. It is also consistent with the basic statistical fact that the binomial process with a "large" number of steps converges to the standard normal distribution. Myron Scholes and Robert Merton won the 1997 Nobel Prize in Economics based, in part, on their work related to the BSM model.[9] Let us now examine the BSM model assumptions.

## Assumptions of the BSM Model

The key assumption for option valuation models is how to model the random nature of the underlying instrument. This characteristic of how an asset evolves randomly is called a stochastic process. Many financial instruments enjoy limited liability; hence, the values of instruments cannot be negative, but they certainly can be zero. In 1900, Bachelier proposed the normal distribution. The key advantages of the normal distribution are that zero is possible, meaning that bankruptcy is allowable, it is symmetric, it is relatively easy to manipulate, and it is additive (which means that sums of normal distributions are normally distributed). The key disadvantage is that negative stock values are theoretically possible, which violates the limited liability principal of stock ownership. Based on research on stock prices in the 1950s and 1960s, a preference emerged for the lognormal distribution, which means that log returns are distributed normally. Black, Scholes, and Merton chose to use the lognormal distribution.

Recall that the no-arbitrage approach requires self-financing and dynamic replication; we need more than just an assumption regarding the terminal distribution of the underlying instrument. We need to model the value of the instrument as it evolves over time, which is what we mean by a stochastic process. The stochastic process chosen by Black, Scholes, and Merton is called geometric Brownian motion (GBM).

Exhibit 12 illustrates GBM, assuming the initial stock price is S = 50. We assume the stock will grow at 3% ($\mu$ = 3% annually, geometrically compounded rate). This GBM process also reflects a random component that is determined by a volatility ($\sigma$) of 45%. This volatility is the annualized standard deviation of continuously compounded percentage change in the underlying, or in other words, the log return. Note that as a particular sample path drifts upward, we observe more variability on an absolute basis, whereas when the particular sample path drifts downward, we observe less variability on an absolute basis. For example, examine the highest and lowest lines shown in Exhibit 12. The highest line is much more erratic than the lowest line. Recall that a 10% move in a stock with a price of 100 is 10 whereas a 10% move in a stock with a price of 10 is only 1. Thus, GBM can never hit zero nor go below it. This property is

---

9 Fischer Black passed away in 1995 and the Nobel Prize is not awarded posthumously.

appealing because many financial instruments enjoy limited liability and cannot be negative. Finally, note that although the stock movements are rather erratic, there are no large jumps—a common feature with marketable financial instruments.

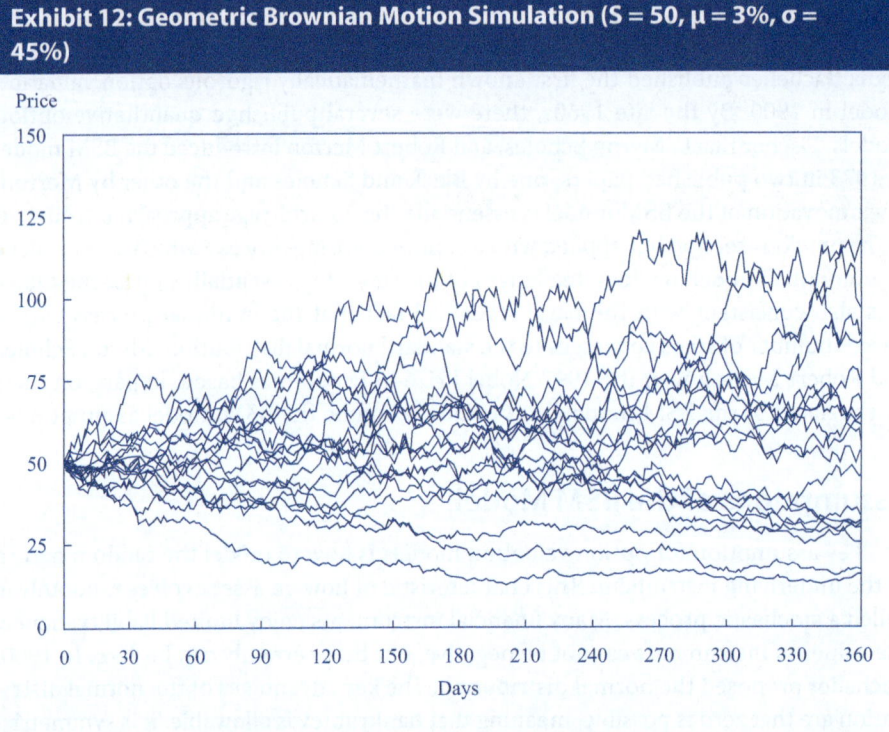

**Exhibit 12: Geometric Brownian Motion Simulation (S = 50, μ = 3%, σ = 45%)**

Within the BSM model framework, it is assumed that all investors agree on the distributional characteristics of GBM except the assumed growth rate of the underlying. This growth rate depends on a number of factors, including other instruments and time. The standard BSM model assumes a constant growth rate and constant volatility.

The specific assumptions of the BSM model are as follows:

- The underlying follows a statistical process called geometric Brownian motion, which implies that the continuously compounded return is normally distributed.
- Geometric Brownian motion implies continuous prices, meaning that the price of underlying instrument does not jump from one value to another; rather, it moves smoothly from value to value.
- The underlying instrument is liquid, meaning that it can be easily bought and sold.
- Continuous trading is available, meaning that in the strictest sense one must be able to trade at every instant.
- Short selling of the underlying instrument with full use of the proceeds is permitted.
- There are no market frictions, such as transaction costs, regulatory constraints, or taxes.
- No arbitrage opportunities are available in the marketplace.
- The options are European-style, meaning that early exercise is not allowed.

- The continuously compounded risk-free interest rate is known and constant; borrowing and lending is allowed at the risk-free rate.
- The volatility of the return on the underlying is known and constant.
- If the underlying instrument pays a yield, it is expressed as a continuous known and constant yield at an annualized rate.

Naturally, the foregoing assumptions are not absolutely consistent with real financial markets, but, as in all financial models, the question is whether they produce models that are tractable and useful in practice, which they do.

### EXAMPLE 9

### BSM Model Assumptions

1. Which is the *correct* pair of statements? The BSM model assumes:

   A. the return on the underlying has a normal distribution. The price of the underlying can jump abruptly to another price.
   
   B. brokerage costs are factored into the BSM model. It is impossible to trade continuously.
   
   C. volatility can be predicted with certainty. Arbitrage is non-existent in the marketplace.

### Solution:

C is correct. All four of the statements in A and B are incorrect within the BSM model paradigm.

# BSM MODEL: COMPONENTS

interpret the components of the Black–Scholes–Merton model as applied to call options in terms of a leveraged position in the underlying

We turn now to a careful examination of the BSM model.

The BSM model is a continuous time version of the discrete time binomial model. Given that the BSM model is based on continuous time, it is customary to use a continuously compounded interest rate rather than some discretely compounded alternative. Thus, when an interest rate is used here, denoted simply as r, we mean solely the annualized continuously compounded rate.[10] The volatility, denoted as σ, is also expressed in annualized percentage terms. Initially, we focus on a non-dividend-paying stock. The BSM model, with some adjustments, applies to other underlying instruments, which will be examined later.

The BSM model for stocks can be expressed as

$$c = SN(d_1) - e^{-rT}XN(d_2) \quad (10)$$

and

$$p = e^{-rT}XN(-d_2) - SN(-d_1) \quad (11)$$

---

10 Note $e^r = 1 + r_d$, where $r_d$ is the annually compounded rate.

where

$$d_1 = \frac{\ln(S/X) + (r + \sigma^2/2)T}{\sigma\sqrt{T}}$$

$$d_2 = d_1 - \sigma\sqrt{T}$$

N(x) denotes the standard normal cumulative distribution function, which is the probability of obtaining a value of less than x based on a standard normal distribution. In our context, x will have the value of $d_1$ or $d_2$. N(x) reflects the likelihood of observing values less than x from a random sample of observations taken from the standard normal distribution.

Although the BSM model appears very complicated, it has straightforward interpretations that will be explained. N(x) can be estimated by a computer program or a spreadsheet or approximated from a lookup table. The normal distribution is a symmetric distribution with two parameters, the mean and standard deviation. The standard normal distribution is a normal distribution with a mean of 0 and a standard deviation of 1.

Exhibit 13 illustrates the standard normal probability density function (the standard bell curve) and the cumulative distribution function (the accumulated probability and range of 0 to 1). Note that even though GBM is lognormally distributed, the N(x) functions in the BSM model are based on the standard normal distribution. In Exhibit 13, we see that if x = −1.645, then N(x) = N(−1.645) = 0.05. Thus, if the model value of d is −1.645, the corresponding probability is 5%. Clearly, values of d that are less than 0 imply values of N(x) that are less than 0.5. As a result of the symmetry of the normal distribution, we note that N(−x) = 1 − N(x).

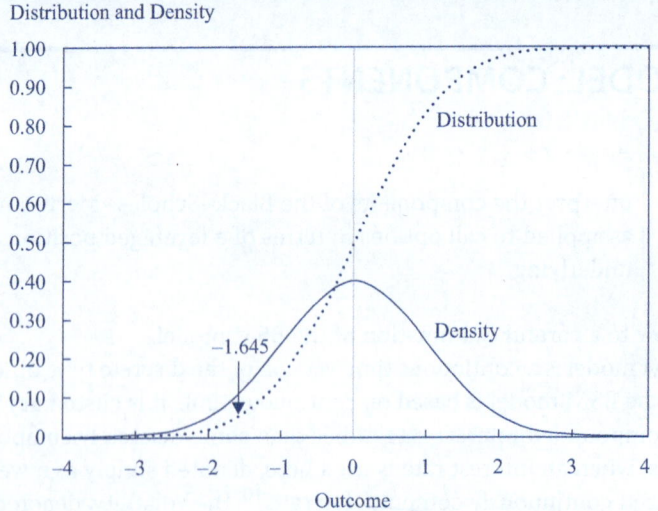

**Exhibit 13: Standard Normal Distribution**

The BSM model can be described as the present value of the expected option payoff at expiration. Specifically, we can express the BSM model for calls as c = $PV_r[E(c_T)]$ and for puts as p = $PV_r[E(p_T)]$, where $E(c_T) = Se^{rT}N(d_1) - XN(d_2)$ and $E(p_T) = XN(-d_2) - Se^{rT}N(-d_1)$. The present value term in this context is simply $e^{-rT}$. As with most valuation tasks in finance, the value today is simply the present value of the expected future cash flows. It is important to note that the expectation is based on the risk-neutral probability measure defined in Section 3.1. The expectation is not based

## BSM Model: Components

on the investor's subjective beliefs, which reflect an aversion to risk. Also, the present value function is based on the risk-free interest rate not on the investor's required return on invested capital, which of course is a function of risk.

Alternatively, the BSM model can be described as having two components: a stock component and a bond component. For call options, the stock component is $SN(d_1)$ and the bond component is $e^{-rT}XN(d_2)$. The BSM model call value is the stock component minus the bond component. For put options, the stock component is $SN(-d_1)$ and the bond component is $e^{-rT}XN(-d_2)$. The BSM model put value is the bond component minus the stock component.

The BSM model can be interpreted as a dynamically managed portfolio of the stock and zero-coupon bonds.[11] The goal is to replicate the option payoffs with stocks and bonds. For both call and put options, we can represent the initial cost of this replicating strategy as

Replicating strategy cost = $n_S S + n_B B$

where the equivalent number of underlying shares is $n_S = N(d_1) > 0$ for calls and $n_S = -N(-d_1) < 0$ for puts. The equivalent number of bonds is $n_B = -N(d_2) < 0$ for calls and $n_B = N(-d_2) > 0$ for puts. The price of the zero-coupon bond is $B = e^{-rT}X$. Note, if n is positive, we are buying the underlying and if n is negative we are selling (short selling) the underlying. The cost of the portfolio will exactly equal either the BSM model call value or the BSM model put value.

For calls, we are simply buying stock with borrowed money because $n_S > 0$ and $n_B < 0$. Again the cost of this portfolio will equal the BSM model call value, and if appropriately rebalanced, then this portfolio will replicate the payoff of the call option. Therefore, a call option can be viewed as a leveraged position in the stock.

Similarly, for put options, we are simply buying bonds with the proceeds from short selling the underlying because $n_S < 0$ and $n_B > 0$. The cost of this portfolio will equal the BSM model put value, and if appropriately rebalanced, then this portfolio will replicate the payoff of the put option. Note that a short position in a put will result in receiving money today and $n_S > 0$ and $n_B < 0$. Therefore, a short put can be viewed as an over-leveraged or over-geared position in the stock because the borrowing exceeds 100% of the cost of the underlying.

Exhibit 14 illustrates the direct comparison between the no-arbitrage approach to the single-period binomial option valuation model and the BSM option valuation model. The parallel between the h term in the binomial model and $N(d_1)$ is easy to see. Recall that the term hedge ratio was used with the binomial model because we were creating a no-arbitrage portfolio. Note for call options, $-N(d_2)$ implies borrowing money or short selling $N(d_2)$ shares of a zero-coupon bond trading at $e^{-rT}X$. For put options, $N(-d_2)$ implies lending money or buying $N(-d_2)$ shares of a zero-coupon bond trading at $e^{-rT}X$.

### Exhibit 14: BSM and Binomial Option Valuation Model Comparison

| Option Valuation Model Terms | Call Option | | Put Option | |
|---|---|---|---|---|
| | Underlying | Financing | Underlying | Financing |
| Binomial Model | hS | $PV(-hS^- + c^-)$ | hS | $PV(-hS^- + p^-)$ |
| BSM Model | $N(d_1)S$ | $-N(d_2)e^{-rT}X$ | $-N(-d_1)S$ | $N(-d_2)e^{-rT}X$ |

---

[11] When covering the binomial model, the bond component was generically termed financing. This component is typically handled with bank borrowing or lending. With the BSM model, it is easier to understand as either buying or short selling a risk-free zero-coupon bond.

If the value of the underlying, S, increases, then the value of $N(d_1)$ also increases because S has a positive effect on $d_1$. Thus, the replicating strategy for calls requires continually buying shares in a rising market and selling shares in a falling market.

Within the BSM model theory, the aggregate losses from this "buy high/sell low" strategy, over the life of the option, adds up exactly to the BSM model option premium received for the option at inception.[12] This result must be the case; otherwise there would be arbitrage profits available. Because transaction costs are not, in fact, zero, the frequent rebalancing by buying and selling the underlying adds significant costs for the hedger. Also, markets can often move discontinuously, contrary to the BSM model's assumption that prices move continuously, thus allowing for continuous hedging adjustments. Hence, in reality, hedges are imperfect. For example, if a company announces a merger, then the company's stock price may jump substantially higher, contrary to the BSM model's assumption.

In addition, volatility cannot be known in advance. For these reasons, options are typically more expensive than they would be as predicted by the BSM model theory. In order to continue using the BSM model, the volatility parameter used in the formula is usually higher (by, say, 1% or 2%, but this can vary a lot) than the volatility of the stock actually expected by market participants. We will ignore this point for now, however, as we focus on the mechanics of the model.

### EXAMPLE 10

### Illustration of BSM Model Component Interpretation

Suppose we are given the following information on call and put options on a stock: $S = 100$, $X = 100$, $r = 5\%$, $T = 1.0$, and $\sigma = 30\%$. Thus, based on the BSM model, it can be demonstrated that $PV(X) = 95.123$, $d_1 = 0.317$, $d_2 = 0.017$, $N(d_1) = 0.624$, $N(d_2) = 0.507$, $N(-d_1) = 0.376$, $N(-d_2) = 0.493$, $c = 14.23$, and $p = 9.35$.

1. The initial trading strategy required by the no-arbitrage approach to replicate the call option payoffs for a buyer of the option is:

    A. buy 0.317 shares of stock and short sell –0.017 shares of zero-coupon bonds.

    B. buy 0.624 shares of stock and short sell 0.507 shares of zero-coupon bonds.

    C. short sell 0.317 shares of stock and buy 0.017 shares of zero-coupon bonds.

### Solution to 1:

B is correct. The no-arbitrage approach to replicating the call option involves purchasing $n_S = N(d_1) = 0.624$ shares of stock partially financed with $n_B = -N(d_2) = -0.507$ shares of zero-coupon bonds priced at $B = Xe^{-rT} = 95.123$ per bond. Note that by definition the cost of this replicating strategy is the BSM call model value or $n_S S + n_B B = 0.624(100) + (-0.507)95.123 = 14.17$. Without rounding errors, the option value is 14.23.

2. Identify the initial trading strategy required by the no-arbitrage approach to replicate the put option payoffs for a buyer of the put.

    A. Buy 0.317 shares of stock and short sell –0.017 shares of zero-coupon bonds.

---

[12] The validity of this claim does not rest on the validity of the BSM model assumptions; rather the validity depends only on whether the BSM model accurately predicts the replication cost.

> **B.** Buy 0.624 shares of stock and short sell 0.507 shares of zero-coupon bonds.
>
> **C.** Short sell 0.376 shares of stock and buy 0.493 shares of zero-coupon bonds.
>
> ### Solution to 2:
>
> C is correct. The no-arbitrage approach to replicating the put option is similar. In this case, we trade $n_S = -N(-d_1) = -0.376$ shares of stock—specifically, short sell 0.376 shares—and buy $n_B = N(-d_2) = 0.493$ shares of zero-coupon bonds. Again, the cost of the replicating strategy is $n_S S + n_B B = -0.376(100) + (0.493)95.123 = 9.30$. Without rounding errors, the option value is 9.35. Thus, to replicate a call option based on the BSM model, we buy stock on margin. To replicate a put option, we short the stock and buy zero-coupon bonds.

Note that the $N(d_2)$ term has an additional important interpretation. It is a unique measure of the probability that the call option expires in the money, and correspondingly, $1 - N(d_2) = N(-d_2)$ is the probability that the put option expires in the money. Specifically, the probability based on the RN probability of being in the money, not one's own estimate of the probability of being in the money nor the market's estimate. That is, $N(d_2) = \text{Prob}(S_T > X)$ based on the unique RN probability.

# BSM MODEL: CARRY BENEFITS AND APPLICATIONS

## 10

☐ describe how the Black–Scholes–Merton model is used to value European options on equities and currencies

We now turn to incorporating various carry benefits into the BSM model. Carry benefits include dividends for stock options, foreign interest rates for currency options, and coupon payments for bond options. For other underlying instruments, there are carry costs that can easily be treated as negative carry benefits, such as storage and insurance costs for agricultural products. Because the BSM model is established in continuous time, it is common to model these carry benefits as a continuous yield, denoted generically here as $\gamma^c$ or simply $\gamma$.

The BSM model requires a few adjustments to accommodate carry benefits. The carry benefit-adjusted BSM model is

$$c = Se^{-\gamma T} N(d_1) - e^{-rT} X N(d_2) \tag{12}$$

and

$$p = e^{-rT} X N(-d_2) - Se^{-\gamma T} N(-d_1) \tag{13}$$

where

$$d_1 = \frac{\ln(S/X) + (r - \gamma + \sigma^2/2)T}{\sigma\sqrt{T}}$$

Note that $d_2$ can be expressed again simply as $d_2 = d_1 - \sigma\sqrt{T}$. The value of a put option can also be found based on the carry benefit-adjusted put–call parity:

$$p + Se^{-\gamma T} = c + e^{-rT} X \tag{14}$$

The carry benefit-adjusted BSM model can again be described as the present value of the expected option payoff at expiration. Now, however, $E(c_T) = Se^{(r-\gamma)T}N(d_1) - XN(d_2)$ and $E(p_T) = XN(-d_2) - Se^{(r-\gamma)T}N(-d_1)$. The present value term remains simply $e^{-rT}$. Carry benefits will have the effect of lowering the expected future value of the underlying

Again, the carry benefit adjusted BSM model can be described as having two components, a stock component and a bond component. For call options, the stock component is $Se^{-\gamma T}N(d_1)$ and the bond component is again $e^{-rT}XN(d_2)$. For put options, the stock component is $Se^{-\gamma T}N(-d_1)$ and the bond component is again $e^{-rT}XN(-d_2)$. Although both $d_1$ and $d_2$ are reduced by carry benefits, the general approach to valuation remains the same. An increase in carry benefits will lower the value of the call option and raise the value of the put option.

Note that $N(d_2)$ term continues to be interpreted as the RN probability of a call option being in the money. The existence of carry benefits has the effect of lowering $d_1$ and $d_2$, hence the probability of being in the money with call options declines as the carry benefit rises. This RN probability is an important element to describing how the BSM model is used in various valuation tasks.

For stock options, $\gamma = \delta$, which is the continuously compounded dividend yield. The dividend-yield BSM model can again be interpreted as a dynamically managed portfolio of the stock and zero coupon bonds. Based on the call model above applied to a dividend yielding stock, the equivalent number of units of stock is now $n_S = e^{-\delta T}N(d_1) > 0$ and the equivalent number of units of bonds remains $n_B = -N(d_2) < 0$. Similarly with puts, the equivalent number of units of stock is now $n_S = -e^{-\delta T}N(-d_1) < 0$ and the equivalent number of units of bonds again remains $n_B = N(-d_2) > 0$.

With dividend paying stocks, the arbitrageur is able to receive the benefits of dividend payments when long the stock and has to pay dividends when short the stock. Thus, the burden of carrying the stock is diminished for a long position. The key insight is that dividends influence the dynamically managed portfolio by lowering the number of shares to buy for calls and raising the number of shares to short sell for puts. Higher dividends will lower the value of $d_1$, thus lowering $N(d_1)$. Also, higher dividends will lower the number of bonds to short sell for calls and raise the number of bonds to buy for puts.

### EXAMPLE 11

### BSM Model Applied to Equities

Suppose we are given the following information on an underlying stock and options: $S = 60$, $X = 60$, $r = 2\%$, $T = 0.5$, $\delta = 2\%$, and $\sigma = 45\%$. Assume we are examining European-style options.

1. Which answer *best* describes how the BSM model is used to value a call option with the parameters given?

    A. The BSM model call value is the exercise price times $N(d_1)$ less the present value of the stock price times $N(d_2)$.

    B. The BSM model call value is the stock price times $e^{-\delta T}N(d_1)$ less the exercise price times $e^{-rT}N(d_2)$.

    C. The BSM model call value is the stock price times $e^{-\delta T}N(-d_1)$ less the present value of the exercise price times $e^{-rT}N(-d_2)$.

### Solution to 1:

B is correct. The BSM call model for a dividend-paying stock can be expressed as $Se^{-\delta T}N(d_1) - Xe^{-rT}N(d_2)$.

2. Which answer *best* describes how the BSM model is used to value a put option with the parameters given?

   **A.** The BSM model put value is the exercise price times $N(d_1)$ less the present value of the stock price times $N(d_2)$.

   **B.** The BSM model put value is the exercise price times $e^{-\delta T}N(-d_2)$ less the stock price times $e^{-rT}N(-d_2)$.

   **C.** The BSM model put value is the exercise price times $e^{-rT}N(-d_2)$ less the stock price times $e^{-\delta T}N(-d_1)$.

## Solution to 2:

C is correct. The BSM put model for a dividend-paying stock can be expressed as $Xe^{-rT}N(-d_2) - Se^{-\delta T}N(-d_1)$.

3. Suppose now that the stock does not pay a dividend—that is, $\delta = 0\%$. Identify the correct statement.

   **A.** The BSM model option value is the same as the previous problems because options are not dividend adjusted.

   **B.** The BSM model option values will be different because there is an adjustment term applied to the exercise price, that is $e^{-\delta T}$, which will influence the option values.

   **C.** The BSM model option value will be different because $d_1$, $d_2$, and the stock component are all adjusted for dividends.

## Solution to 3:

C is correct. The BSM model option value will be different because $d_1$, $d_2$, and the stock component are all adjusted for dividends.

### EXAMPLE 12

### How the BSM Model Is Used to Value Stock Options

1. Suppose that we have some Bank of China shares that are currently trading on the Hong Kong Stock Exchange at HKD4.41. Our view is that the Bank of China's stock price will be steady for the next three months, so we decide to sell some three-month out-of-the-money calls with exercise price at 4.60 in order to enhance our returns by receiving the option premium. Risk-free government securities are paying 1.60% and the stock is yielding HKD 0.24%. The stock volatility is 28%. We use the BSM model to value the calls.

   Which statement is correct? The BSM model inputs (underlying, exercise, expiration, risk-free rate, dividend yield, and volatility) are:

   **A.** 4.60, 4.41, 3, 0.0160, 0.0024, and 0.28.

   **B.** 4.41, 4.60, 0.25, 0.0160, 0.0024, and 0.28.

   **C.** 4.41, 4.41, 0.3, 0.0160, 0.0024, and 0.28.

### Solution:

B is correct. The spot price of the underlying is HKD4.41. The exercise price is HKD4.60. The expiration is 0.25 years (three months). The risk-free rate is 0.016. The dividend yield is 0.0024. The volatility is 0.28.

For foreign exchange options, γ = r$^f$, which is the continuously compounded foreign risk-free interest rate. When quoting an exchange rate, we will give the value of the domestic currency per unit of the foreign currency. For example, Japanese yen (¥) per unit of the euro (€) will be expressed as the euro trading for ¥135 or succinctly 135¥/€. This is called the foreign exchange spot rate. Thus, the foreign currency, the euro, is expressed in terms of the Japanese yen, which is in this case the domestic currency. This is logical, for example, when a Japanese firm would want to express its foreign euro holdings in terms of its domestic currency, Japanese yen.

With currency options, the underlying instrument is the foreign exchange spot rate. Again, the carry benefit is the interest rate in the foreign country because the foreign currency could be invested in the foreign country's risk-free instrument. Also, with currency options, the underlying and the exercise price must be quoted in the same currency unit. Lastly, the volatility in the model is the volatility of the log return of the spot exchange rate. Each currency option is for a certain quantity of foreign currency, termed the notional amount, a concept analogous to the number of shares of stock covered in an option contract. The total cost of the option would be obtained by multiplying the formula value by the notional amount in the same way that one would multiply the formula value of an option on a stock by the number of shares the option contract covers.

The BSM model applied to currencies can be described as having two components, a foreign exchange component and a bond component. For call options, the foreign exchange component is $Se^{-r^f T}N(d_1)$ and the bond component is $e^{-rT}XN(d_2)$, where r is the domestic risk-free rate. The BSM call model applied to currencies is simply the foreign exchange component minus the bond component. For put options, the foreign exchange component is $Se^{-r^f T}N(-d_1)$ and the bond component is $e^{-rT}XN(-d_2)$. The BSM put model applied to currencies is simply the bond component minus the foreign exchange component. Remember that the underlying is expressed in terms of the domestic currency.

### EXAMPLE 13

### BSM Model Applied to Value Options on Currency

A Japanese camera exporter to Europe has contracted to receive fixed euro (€) amounts each quarter for his goods. The spot price of the currency pair is 135¥/€. If the exchange rate falls to, say, 130¥/€, then the yen will have strengthened because it will take fewer yen to buy one euro. The exporter is concerned that the yen will strengthen because in this case, his forthcoming fixed euro will buy fewer yen. Hence, the exporter is considering buying an at-the-money spot euro put option to protect against this fall; this in essence is a call on yen. The Japanese risk-free rate is 0.25% and the European risk-free rate is 1.00%.

1. What are the underlying and exercise prices to use in the BSM model to get the euro put option value?

    **A.** 1/135; 1/135
    **B.** 135; 135
    **C.** 135; 130

### Solution to 1:

B is correct. The underlying is the spot FX price of 135 ¥/€. Because the put is at-the-money spot, the exercise price equals the spot price.

2. What are the risk-free rate and the carry rate to use in the BSM model to get the euro put option value?

   A. 0.25%; 1.00%
   B. 0.25%; 0.00%
   C. 1.00%; 0.25%

## Solution to 2:

A is correct. The risk-free rate to use is the Japanese rate because the Japanese yen is the domestic currency unit per the exchange rate quoting convention. The carry rate is the foreign currency's risk-free rate, which is the European rate.

# BLACK OPTION VALUATION MODEL AND EUROPEAN OPTIONS ON FUTURES

11

☐ describe how the Black model is used to value European options on futures

We turn now to examine a modification of the BSM model when the underlying is a forward or futures contract.

In 1976, Fischer Black introduced a modified version of the BSM model approach that is applicable to options on underlying instruments that are costless to carry, such as options on futures contracts—for example, equity index futures—and options on forward contracts. The latter include interest rate-based options, such as caps, floors, and swaptions.

## European Options on Futures

We assume that the futures price also follows geometric Brownian motion. We ignore issues like margin requirements and marking to market. Black proposed the following model for European-style futures options:

$$c = e^{-rT}[F_0(T)N(d_1) - XN(d_2)] \qquad (15)$$

and

$$p = e^{-rT}[XN(-d_2) - F_0(T)N(-d_1)] \qquad (16)$$

where

$$d_1 = \frac{\ln[F_0(T)/X] + (\sigma^2/2)T}{\sigma\sqrt{T}} \text{ and}$$

$$d_2 = d_1 - \sigma\sqrt{T}$$

Note that $F_0(T)$ denotes the futures price at Time 0 that expires at Time T, and $\sigma$ denotes the volatility related to the futures price. The other terms are as previously defined. Black's model is simply the BSM model in which the futures contract is assumed to reflect the carry arbitrage model. Futures option put–call parity can be expressed as

$$c = e^{-rT}[F_0(T) - X] + p \qquad (17)$$

As we have seen before, put–call parity is a useful tool for describing the valuation relationship between call and put values within various option valuation models.

The Black model can be described in a similar way to the BSM model. The Black model has two components, a futures component and a bond component. For call options, the futures component is $F_0(T)e^{-rT}N(d_1)$ and the bond component is again $e^{-rT}XN(d_2)$. The Black call model is simply the futures component minus the bond component. For put options, the futures component is $F_0(T)e^{-rT}N(-d_1)$ and the bond component is again $e^{-rT}XN(-d_2)$. The Black put model is simply the bond component minus the futures component.

Alternatively, futures option valuation, based on the Black model, is simply computing the present value of the difference between the futures price and the exercise price. The futures price and exercise price are appropriately adjusted by the N(d) functions. For call options, the futures price is adjusted by $N(d_1)$ and the exercise price is adjusted by $-N(d_2)$ to arrive at difference. For put options, the futures price is adjusted by $-N(-d_1)$ and the exercise price is adjusted by $+N(-d_2)$.

### EXAMPLE 14

### European Options on Futures Index

The S&P 500 Index (a spot index) is presently at 1,860 and the 0.25 expiration futures contract is trading at 1,851.65. Suppose further that the exercise price is 1,860, the continuously compounded risk-free rate is 0.2%, time to expiration is 0.25, volatility is 15%, and the dividend yield is 2.0%. Based on this information, the following results are obtained for options on the futures contract.[13]

| Options on Futures | |
|---|---|
| **Calls** | **Puts** |
| $N(d_1) = 0.491$ | $N(-d_1) = 0.509$ |
| $N(d_2) = 0.461$ | $N(-d_2) = 0.539$ |
| c = US$51.41 | p = US$59.76 |

1. Identify the statement that *best* describes how the Black model is used to value a European call option on the futures contract just described.

    **A.** The call value is the present value of the difference between the exercise price times 0.461 and the current futures price times 0.539.

    **B.** The call value is the present value of the difference between the current futures price times 0.491 and the exercise price times 0.461.

    **C.** The call value is the present value of the difference between the current spot price times 0.491 and the exercise price times 0.461.

### Solution to 1:

B is correct. Recall Black's model for call options can be expressed as $c = e^{-rT}[F_0(T)N(d_1) - XN(d_2)]$.

---

13 We ignore the effect of the multiplier. As of this writing, the S&P 500 futures option contract chas a multiplier of 250. The prices reported here have not been scaled up by this amount. In practice, the option cost would by 250 times the option value.

> 2. Which statement *best* describes how the Black model is used to value a European put options on the futures contract just described?
>
>    A. The put value is the present value of the difference between the exercise price times 0.539 and the current futures price times 0.509.
>
>    B. The put value is the present value of the difference between the current futures price times 0.491 and the exercise price times 0.461.
>
>    C. The put value is the present value of the difference between the current spot price times 0.491 and the exercise price times 0.461.
>
> **Solution to 2:**
>
> A is correct. Recall Black's model for put options can be expressed as $p = e^{-rT}[XN(-d_2) - F_0(T)N(-d_1)]$.
>
> 3. What are the underlying and exercise prices to use in the Black futures option model?
>
>    A. 1,851.65; 1,860
>
>    B. 1,860; 1,860
>
>    C. 1,860; 1,851.65
>
> **Solution to 3:**
>
> A is correct. The underlying is the futures price of 1,851.65 and the exercise price was given as 1,860.

# INTEREST RATE OPTIONS

☐ describe how the Black model is used to value European interest rate options and European swaptions

With interest rate options, the underlying instrument is a reference interest rate, such as three-month MRR. An interest rate call option gains when the reference interest rate rises and an interest rate put option gains when the reference interest rate falls. Interest rate options are the building blocks of many other instruments.

For an interest rate call option on three-month MRR with one year to expiration, the underlying interest rate is a forward rate agreement (FRA) rate that expires in one year. This FRA is observed today and is the underlying rate used in the Black model. The underlying rate of the FRA is a 3-month MRR deposit that is investable in 12 months and matures in 15 months. Thus, in one year, the FRA rate typically converges to the three-month spot MRR.

Interest rates are typically set in advance, but interest payments are made in arrears, which is referred to as advanced set, settled in arrears. For example, with a bank deposit, the interest rate is usually set when the deposit is made, say $t_{j-1}$, but the interest payment is made when the deposit is withdrawn, say $t_j$. The deposit, therefore, has $t_m = t_j - t_{j-1}$ time until maturity. Thus, the rate is advanced set, but the payment is settled in arrears. Likewise with a floating rate loan, the rate is usually set and the interest accrues at this known rate, but the payment is made later. Similarly, with some interest rate options, the time to option expiration ($t_{j-1}$) when the interest rate is set does not correspond to the option settlement ($t_j$) when the cash payment is made, if any. For example, if an interest rate option payment based on three-month MRR is US$5,000 determined on January 15th, the actual payment of the US$5,000 would occur on April 15.

Interest rates are quoted on an annual basis, but the underlying implied deposit is often less than a year. Thus, the annual rates must be adjusted for the accrual period. Recall that the accrual period for a quarterly reset 30/360 day count FRA is 0.25 (= 90/360). If the day count is on an actual (ACT) number of days divided by 360 (ACT/360), then the accrual period may be something like 0.252778 (= 91/360), assuming 91 days in the period. Typically, the accrual period in FRAs is based on 30/360 whereas the accrual period based on the option is actual number of days in the contract divided by the actual number of days in the year (identified as ACT/ACT or ACT/365).

The model presented here is known as the standard market model and is a variation of Black's futures option valuation model. Again, let $t_{j-1}$ denote the time to option expiration (ACT/365), whereas let $t_j$ denote the time to the maturity date of the underlying FRA. Note that the interest accrual on the underlying begins at the option expiration (Time $t_{j-1}$). Let $FRA(0,t_{j-1},t_m)$ denote the fixed rate on a FRA at Time 0 that expires at Time $t_{j-1}$, where the underlying matures at Time $t_j$ (= $t_{j-1} + t_m$), with all times expressed on an annual basis. We assume the FRA is 30/360 day count. For example, $FRA(0,0.25,0.5) = 2\%$ denotes the 2% fixed rate on a forward rate agreement that expires in 0.25 years with settlement amount being paid in 0.75 (= 0.25 + 0.5) years.[14] Let $R_X$ denote the exercise rate expressed on an annual basis. Finally, let $\sigma$ denote the interest rate volatility. Specifically, $\sigma$ is the annualized standard deviation of the continuously compounded percentage change in the underlying FRA rate.

Interest rate options give option buyers the right to certain cash payments based on observed interest rates. For example, an interest rate call option gives the call buyer the right to a certain cash payment when the underlying interest rate exceeds the exercise rate. An interest rate put option gives the put buyer the right to a certain cash payment when the underlying interest rate is below the exercise rate.

With the standard market model, the prices of interest rate call and put options can be expressed as

$$c = (AP)e^{-r(t_{j-1}+t_m)}\left[FRA(0,t_{j-1},t_m)N(d_1) - R_X N(d_2)\right] \quad (18)$$

and

$$p = (AP)e^{-r(t_{j-1}+t_m)}\left[R_X N(-d_2) - FRA(0,t_{j-1},t_m)N(-d_1)\right] \quad (19)$$

where

AP denotes the accrual period in years

$$d_1 = \frac{\ln\left[FRA(0,t_{j-1},t_m)/R_X\right] + (\sigma^2/2)t_{j-1}}{\sigma\sqrt{t_{j-1}}}$$

$$d_2 = d_1 - \sigma\sqrt{t_{j-1}}$$

The formulas here give the value of the option for a notional amount of 1. In practice, the notional would be more than one, so the full cost of the option is obtained by multiplying these formula amounts by the notional amount. Of course, this point is just the same as finding the value of an option on a single share of stock and then multiplying that value by the number of shares covered by the option contract.

---

14 Note that in other contexts the time periods are expressed in months. For example with months, this FRA would be expressed as FRA(0,3,6). Note that the third term in parentheses denotes the maturity of the underlying deposit from the expiration of the FRA.

Immediately, we note that the standard market model requires an adjustment when compared with the Black model for the accrual period. In other words, a value such as $FRA(0,t_{j-1},t_m)$ or the strike rate, $R_X$, as appearing in the formula given earlier, is stated on an annual basis, as are interest rates in general. The actual option premium would have to be adjusted for the accrual period. After accounting for this adjustment, this model looks very similar to the Black model, but there are important but subtle differences. First, the discount factor, $e^{-r(t_{j-1}+t_m)}$, does not apply to the option expiration, $t_{j-1}$. Rather, the discount factor is applied to the maturity date of the FRA or $t_j$ (= $t_{j-1} + t_m$). We express this maturity as ($t_{j-1} + t_m$) rather than $t_j$ to emphasize the settlement in arrears nature of this option. Second, rather than the underlying being a futures price, the underlying is an interest rate, specifically a forward rate based on a forward rate agreement or $FRA(0,t_{j-1},t_m)$. Third, the exercise price is really a rate and reflects an interest rate, not a price. Fourth, the time to the option expiration, $t_{j-1}$, is used in the calculation of $d_1$ and $d_2$. Finally, both the forward rate and the exercise rate should be expressed in decimal form and not as percent (for example, 0.02 and not 2.0). Alternatively, if expressed as a percent, then the notional amount adjustment could be divided by 100.

As with other option models, the standard market model can be described as simply the present value of the expected option payoff at expiration. Specifically, we can express the standard market model for calls as $c = PV[E(c_{tj})]$ and for puts as $p = PV[E(p_{tj})]$, where $E(c_{tj}) = (AP)[FRA(0,t_{j-1},t_m)N(d_1) - R_X N(d_2)]$ and $E(p_{tj}) = (AP)[R_X N(-d_2) - FRA(0,t_{j-1},t_m)N(-d_1)]$. The present value term in this context is simply $e^{-rt_j} = e^{-r(t_{j-1}+t_m)}$. Again, note we discount from Time $t_j$, the time when the cash flows are settled on the FRA.

There are several interesting and useful combinations that can be created with interest rate options. We focus on a few that will prove useful for understanding swaptions in the next section. First, if the exercise rate is selected so as to equal the current FRA rate, then long an interest rate call option and short an interest rate put option is equivalent to a receive-floating, pay-fixed FRA.

Second, if the exercise rate is again selected so it is equal to the current FRA rate, then long an interest rate put option and short an interest rate call option is equivalent to a receive-fixed, pay-floating FRA. Note that FRAs are the building blocks of interest rate swaps.

Third, an interest rate cap is a portfolio or strip of interest rate call options in which the expiration of the first underlying corresponds to the expiration of the second option and so forth. The underlying interest rate call options are termed caplets. Thus, a set of floating-rate loan payments can be hedged with a long position in an interest rate cap encompassing a series of interest rate call options.

Fourth, an interest rate floor is a portfolio or strip of interest rate put options in which the expiration of the first underlying corresponds with the expiration of the second option and so forth. The underlying interest rate put options are termed floorlets. Thus, a floating-rate bond investment or any other floating-rate lending situation can be hedged with an interest rate floor encompassing a series of interest rate put options.

Fifth, applying put–call parity as discussed earlier, long an interest rate cap and short an interest rate floor with the exercise prices set at the swap rate is equivalent to a receive-floating, pay-fixed swap. On a settlement date, when the underlying rate is above the strike, both the cap and the swap pay off to the party. When the underlying rate is below the strike on a settlement date, the party must make a payment on the short floor, just as the case with a swap. For the opposite position, long an interest rate floor and short an interest rate cap result in the party making a payment when the underlying rate is above the strike and receiving one when the underlying rate is below the strike, just as is the case for a pay-floating, receive-fixed swap.

Finally, if the exercise rate is set equal to the swap rate, then the value of the cap must be equal to the value of the floor at the start. When an interest rate swap is initiated, its current value is zero and is known as an at-market swap. When an exercise rate is selected such that the cap value equals the floor value, then the initial cost of being long a cap and short the floor is also zero. This occurs when the cap and floor strike are equal to the swap rate.

> ### EXAMPLE 15
>
> ### European Interest Rate Options
>
> Suppose you are a speculative investor in Singapore. On 15 May, you anticipate that some regulatory changes will be enacted, and you want to profit from this forecast. On 15 June, you intend to borrow 10,000,000 Singapore dollars to fund the purchase of an asset, which you expect to resell at a profit three months after purchase, say on 15 September. The current three-month SORA (that is, Singapore MRR) is 0.55%. The appropriate FRA rate over the period of 15 June to 15 September is currently 0.68%. You are concerned that rates will rise, so you want to hedge your borrowing risk by purchasing an interest rate call option with an exercise rate of 0.60%.
>
> 1. In using the Black model to value this interest rate call option, what would the underlying rate be?
>
>    **A.** 0.55%
>
>    **B.** 0.68%
>
>    **C.** 0.60%
>
> ### Solution to 1:
>
> B is correct. In using the Black model, a forward or futures price is used as the underlying. This approach is unlike the BSM model in which a spot price is used as the underlying.
>
> 2. The discount factor used in pricing this option would be over what period of time?
>
>    **A.** 15 May–15 June
>
>    **B.** 15 June–15 September
>
>    **C.** 15 May–15 September
>
> ### Solution to 2:
>
> C is correct. You are pricing the option on 15 May. An option expiring 15 June when the underlying is three-month Sibor will have its payoff determined on 15 June, but the payment will be made on 15 September. Thus, the expected payment must be discounted back from 15 September to 15 May.

Interest rate option values are linked in an important way with interest rate swap values through caps and floors. As we will see in the next section, an interest rate swap serves as the underlying for swaptions. Thus, once again, we see that important links exist between interest rate options, swaps, and swaptions.

# SWAPTIONS

☐ describe how the Black model is used to value European interest rate options and European swaptions

A swap option or swaption is simply an option on a swap. It gives the holder the right, but not the obligation, to enter a swap at the pre-agreed swap rate—the exercise rate. Interest rate swaps can be either receive fixed, pay floating or receive floating, pay fixed. A payer swaption is an option on a swap to pay fixed, receive floating. A receiver swaption is an option on a swap to receive fixed, pay floating. Note that the terms "call" and "put" are often avoided because of potential confusion over the nature of the underlying. Notice also that the terminology focuses on the fixed swap rate.

A payer swaption buyer hopes the fixed rate goes up before the swaption expires. When exercised, the payer swaption buyer is able to enter into a pay-fixed, receive-floating swap at the predetermined exercise rate, $R_X$. The buyer can then immediately enter an offsetting at-market receive-fixed, pay-floating swap at the current fixed swap rate. The floating legs of both swaps will offset, leaving the payer swaption buyer with an annuity of the difference between the current fixed swap rate and the swaption exercise rate. Thus, swaption valuation will reflect an annuity.

Swap payments are advanced set, settled in arrears. Let the swap reset dates be expressed as $t_0, t_1, t_2, ..., t_n$. Let $R_{FIX}$ denote the fixed swap rate starting when the swaption expires, denoted as before with T, quoted on an annual basis, and $R_X$ denote the exercise rate starting at Time T, again quoted on an annual basis. As before, we will assume a notional amount of 1.

Because swap rates are quoted on an annual basis, let AP denote the accrual period. Finally, we need some measure of uncertainty. Let $\sigma$ denote the volatility of the forward swap rate. More precisely, $\sigma$ denotes annualized, standard deviation of the continuously compounded percentage changes in the forward swap rate.

The swaption model presented here is a modification of the Black model. Let the present value of an annuity matching the forward swap payment be expressed as

$$\text{PVA} = \sum_{j=1}^{n} PV_{0,t_j} \quad (1)$$

This term is equivalent to what is sometimes referred to as an annuity discount factor. It applies here because a swaption creates a series of equal payments of the difference in the market swap rate at expiration and the chosen exercise rate. Therefore, the payer swaption valuation model is

$$\text{PAY}_{SWN} = (AP)PVA[R_{FIX}N(d_1) - R_X N(d_2)] \quad (20)$$

and the receiver swaption valuation model

$$\text{REC}_{SWN} = (AP)PVA[R_X N(-d_2) - R_{FIX}N(-d_1)] \quad (21)$$

where

$$d_1 = \frac{\ln(R_{FIX}/R_X) + (\sigma^2/2)T}{\sigma\sqrt{T}}, \text{ and as always,}$$

$$d_2 = d_1 - \sigma\sqrt{T}$$

As noted with interest rate options, the actual premium would need to be scaled by the notional amount. Once again, we can see the similarities to the Black model. We note that the swaption model requires two adjustments, one for the accrual period and one for the present value of an annuity. After accounting for these adjustments, this model looks very similar to the Black model but there are important subtle differences.

First, the discount factor is absent. The payoff is not a single payment but a series of payments. Thus, the present value of an annuity used here embeds the option-related discount factor. Second, rather than the underlying being a futures price, the underlying is the fixed rate on a forward interest rate swap. Third, the exercise price is really expressed as an interest rate. Finally, both the forward swap rate and the exercise rate should be expressed in decimal form and not as percent (for example, 0.02 and not 2.0).

As with other option models, the swaption model can be described as simply the present value of the expected option payoff at expiration. Specifically, we can express the payer swaption model value as

$$PAY_{SWN} = PV[E(PAY_{SWN,T})]$$

and the receiver swaption model value as

$$REC_{SWN} = PV[E(REC_{SWN,T})],$$

where

$$E(PAY_{SWN,T}) = e^{rT}PAY_{SWN} \text{ and}$$

$$E(REC_{SWN,T}) = e^{rT}REC_{SWN}.$$

The present value term in this context is simply $e^{-rT}$. Because the annuity term embedded the discounting over the swaption life, the expected swaption values are the current swaption values grossed up by the current risk-free interest rate.

Alternatively, the swaption model can be described as having two components, a swap component and a bond component. For payer swaptions, the swap component is $(AP)PVA(R_{FIX})N(d_1)$ and the bond component is $(AP)PVA(R_X)N(d_2)$. The payer swaption model value is simply the swap component minus the bond component. For receiver swaptions, the swap component is $(AP)PVA(R_{FIX})N(-d_1)$ and the bond component is $(AP)PVA(R_X)N(-d_2)$. The receiver swaption model value is simply the bond component minus the swap component.

As with nearly all derivative instruments, there are many useful equivalence relationships. Recall that long an interest rate cap and short an interest rate floor with the same exercise rate is equal to a receive-floating, pay-fixed interest rate swap. Also, short an interest rate cap and long an interest rate floor with the same exercise rate is equal to a pay-floating, receive-fixed interest rate swap. There are also equivalence relationships with swaptions. In a similar way, long a receiver swaption and short a payer swaption with the same exercise rate is equivalent to entering a receive-fixed, pay-floating forward swap. Long a payer swaption and short a receiver swaption with the same exercise rate is equivalent to entering a receive-floating, pay-fixed forward swap. Note that if the exercise rate is selected such that the receiver and payer swaptions have the same value, then the exercise rate is equal to the at-market forward swap rate. Thus, there is again a put–call parity relationship important for valuation.

In addition, being long a callable fixed-rate bond can be viewed as being long a straight fixed-rate bond and short a receiver swaption. A receiver swaption gives the buyer the right to receive a fixed rate. Hence, the seller will have to pay the fixed rate when this right is exercised in a lower rate environment. Recall that the bond issuer has the right to call the bonds. If the bond issuer sells a receiver swaption with similar terms, then the bond issuer has essentially converted the callable bond into a straight bond. The bond issuer will now pay the fixed rate on the underlying swap and the floating rate received will be offset by the floating-rate loan created when the bond was refinanced. Specifically, the receiver swaption buyer will benefit when rates fall and the swaption is exercised. Thus, the embedded call feature is similar to a receiver swaption.

## EXAMPLE 16

### European Swaptions

1. Suppose you are an Australian company and have ongoing floating-rate debt. You have profited for some time by paying at a floating rate because rates have been falling steadily for the last few years. Now, however, you are concerned that within three months the Australian central bank may tighten its monetary policy and your debt costs will thus increase. Rather than lock in your borrowing via a swap, you prefer to hedge by buying a swaption expiring in three months, whereby you will have the choice, but not the obligation, to enter a five-year swap locking in your borrowing costs. The current three-month forward, five-year swap rate is 2.65%. The current five-year swap rate is 2.55%. The current three-month risk-free rate is 2.25%.

   With reference to the Black model to value the swaption, which statement is correct?

   **A.** The underlying is the three-month forward, five-year swap rate.
   **B.** The discount rate to use is 2.55%.
   **C.** The swaption time to expiration, T, is five years.

### Solution:

A is correct. The current five-year swap rate is not used as a discount rate with swaptions. The swaption time to expiration is 0.25, not the life of the swap.

# OPTION GREEKS AND IMPLIED VOLATILITY: DELTA

☐ interpret each of the option Greeks
☐ describe how a delta hedge is executed

With option valuation models, such as the binomial model, BSM model, and Black's model, we are able to estimate a wide array of comparative information, such as how much the option value will change for a small change in a particular parameter.[15] We will explore this derived information as well as implied volatility in this section. These topics are essential for those managing option positions and in general in obtaining a solid understanding of how option prices change. Our discussion will be based on stock options, though the material covered in this section applies to all types of options.

The measures examined here are known as the Greeks and include, delta, gamma, theta, vega, and rho. With these calculations, we seek to address how much a particular portfolio will change for a given small change in the appropriate parameter. These measures are sometimes referred to as static risk measures in that they capture movements in the option value for a movement in one of the factors that affect the option value, while holding all other factors constant.

---

15 Parameters in the BSM model, for example, include the stock price, exercise price, volatility, time to expiration, and the risk-free interest rate.

Our focus here is on European stock options in which the underlying stock is assumed to pay a dividend yield (denoted δ). Note that for non-dividend-paying stocks, δ = 0.

## Delta

**Delta** is defined as the change in a given instrument for a given small change in the value of the stock, holding everything else constant. Thus, the delta of long one share of stock is by definition +1.0, and the delta of short one share of stock is by definition −1.0. The concept of the option delta is similarly the change in an option value for a given small change in the value of the underlying stock, holding everything else constant. The option deltas for calls and puts are, respectively,

$$\text{Delta}_c = e^{-\delta T} N(d_1) \tag{22}$$

and

$$\text{Delta}_p = -e^{-\delta T} N(-d_1) \tag{23}$$

Note that the deltas are a simple function of $N(d_1)$. The delta of an option answers the question of how much the option will change for a given change in the stock, holding everything else constant. Therefore, delta is a static risk measure. It does not address how likely this particular change would be. Recall that $N(d_1)$ is a value taken from the cumulative distribution function of a standard normal distribution. As such, the range of values is between 0 and 1. Thus, the range of call delta is 0 and $e^{-\delta T}$ and the range of put delta is $-e^{-\delta T}$ and 0. As the stock price increases, the call option goes deeper in the money and the value of $N(d_1)$ is moving toward 1. As the stock price decreases, the call option goes deeper out of the money and the value of $N(d_1)$ is moving toward zero. When the option gets closer to maturity, the delta will drift either toward 0 if it is out of the money or drift toward 1 if it is in the money. Clearly, as the stock price changes and as time to maturity changes, the deltas are also changing.

Delta hedging an option is the process of establishing a position in the underlying stock of a quantity that is prescribed by the option delta so as to have no exposure to very small moves up or down in the stock price. Hence, to execute a single option delta hedge, we first calculate the option delta and then buy or sell delta units of stock. In practice, rarely does one have only one option position to manage. Thus, in general, delta hedging refers to manipulating the underlying portfolio delta by appropriately changing the positions in the portfolio. A delta neutral portfolio refers to setting the portfolio delta all the way to zero. In theory, the delta neutral portfolio will not change in value for small changes in the stock instrument. Let $N_H$ denote the number of units of the hedging instrument and $\text{Delta}_H$ denote the delta of the hedging instrument, which could be the underlying stock, call options, or put options. Delta neutral implies the portfolio delta plus $N_H \text{Delta}_H$ is equal to zero. The optimal number of hedging units, $N_H$, is

$$N_H = -\frac{\text{Portfolio delta}}{\text{Delta}_H}$$

Note that if $N_H$ is negative, then one must short the hedging instrument, and if $N_H$ is positive, then one must go long the hedging instrument. Clearly, if the portfolio is options and the hedging instrument is stock, then we will buy or sell shares to offset the portfolio position. For example, if the portfolio consists of 100,000 shares of stock at US$10 per share, then the portfolio delta is 100,000. The delta of the hedging instrument, stock, is +1. Thus, the optimal number of hedging units, $N_H$, is −100,000 (= −100,000/1) or short 100,000 shares. Alternatively, if the portfolio delta is 5,000 and a particular call option with delta of 0.5 is used as the hedging instrument, then to arrive at a delta neutral portfolio, one must sell 10,000 call options (= −5,000/0.5).

Alternatively, if a portfolio of options has a delta of −1,500, then one must buy 1,500 shares of stock to be delta neutral [= −(−1,500)/1]. If the hedging instrument is stock, then the delta is +1 per share.

### EXAMPLE 17

### Delta Hedging

1. Apple stock is trading at US$125. We write calls (that is, we sell calls) on 1,000 Apple shares and now are exposed to an increase in the price of the Apple stock. That is, if Apple rises, we will lose money because the calls we sold will go up in value, so our liability will increase. Correspondingly, if Apple falls, we will make money. We want to neutralize our exposure to Apple. Say the call delta is 0.50, which means that if Apple goes up by US$0.10, a call on one Apple share will go up US$0.05. We need to trade in such a way as to make money if Apple goes up, to offset our exposure. Hence, we buy 500 Apple shares to hedge. Now, if Apple goes up US$0.10, the sold calls will go up US$50 (our liability goes up), but our long 500 Apple hedge will profit by US$50. Hence, we are delta hedged.

   Identify the *incorrect* statement:

   **A.** If we sell Apple puts, we need to buy Apple stock to delta hedge.
   **B.** Call delta is non-negative (≥ 0); put delta is non-positive (≤ 0).
   **C.** Delta hedging is the process of neutralizing exposure to the underlying.

### Solution:

A is the correct answer because statement A is incorrect. If we sell puts, we need to short sell stock to delta hedge.

One final interpretation of option delta is related to forecasting changes in option prices. Let $\hat{c}$, $\hat{p}$, and $\hat{S}$ denote some new value for the call, put, and stock. Based on an approximation method, the change in the option price can be estimated with a concept known as a delta approximation or

$$\hat{c} - c \cong \text{Delta}_c \left(\hat{S} - S\right) \text{ for calls and}$$
$$\hat{p} - p \cong \text{Delta}_p \left(\hat{S} - S\right) \text{ for puts.}[16]$$

We can now illustrate the actual call values as well as the estimated call values based on delta. Exhibit 15 illustrates the call value based on the BSM model and the call value based on the delta approximation,

$$\hat{c} = c + \text{Delta}_c \left(\hat{S} - S\right).$$

Notice for very small changes in the stock, the delta approximation is fairly accurate. For example, if the stock value rises from 100 to 101, notice that both the call line and the call (delta) estimated line are almost the same value. If, however, the stock value rises from 100 to 150, the call line is now significantly above the call (delta) estimated line. Thus, we see that as the change in the stock increases, the estimation error also increases. The delta approximation is biased low for both a down move and an up move.

---

[16] The symbol $\cong$ denotes approximately. The approximation method is known as a Taylor series. Also note that the put delta is non-positive (≤ 0).

**Exhibit 15: Call Values and Delta Estimated Call Values (S = 100 = X, r = 5%, σ = 30%, δ = 0)**

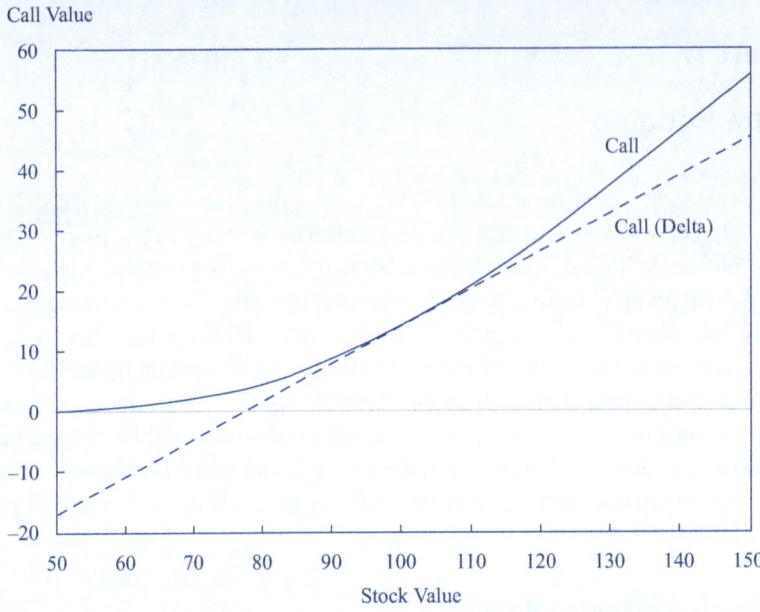

We see that delta hedging is imperfect and gets worse as the underlying moves further away from its original value of 100. Based on the graph, the BSM model assumption of continuous trading is essential to avoid hedging risk. This hedging risk is related to the difference between these two lines and the degree to which the underlying price experiences large changes.

### EXAMPLE 18

### Delta Hedging

Suppose we know S = 100, X = 100, r = 5%, T = 1.0, σ = 30%, and δ = 5%. We have a short position in put options on 10,000 shares of stock. Based on this information, we note $Delta_c = 0.532$, and $Delta_p = -0.419$. Assume each stock option contract is for one share of stock.

1. The appropriate delta hedge, assuming the hedging instrument is stock, is executed by which of the following transactions? Select the *closest* answer.

    **A.** Buy 5,320 shares of stock.

    **B.** Short sell 4,190 shares of stock.

    **C.** Buy 4,190 shares of stock.

### Solution to 1:

B is correct. Recall that $N_H = -\frac{\text{Portfolio delta}}{\text{Delta}_H}$. The put delta is given as −0.419, thus the short put delta is 0.419. In this case, Portfolio delta = 10,000(0.419) = 4,190 and $Delta_H$ = 1.0. Thus, the number of number of hedging units is −4,190 [= −(4,190/1)] or short sell 4,190 shares of stock.

2. The appropriate delta hedge, assuming the hedging instrument is calls, is executed by which of the following transactions? Select the *closest* answer.

   A. Sell 7,876 call options.
   B. Sell 4,190 call options.
   C. Buy 4,190 call options.

**Solution to 2:**

A is correct. Again the Portfolio delta = 4,190 but now Delta$_H$ = 0.532. Thus, the number of hedging units is −7,875.9 [= −(4,190/0.532)] or sell 7,876 call options.

3. Identify the correct interpretation of an option delta.

   A. Option delta measures the curvature in the option price with respect to the stock price.
   B. Option delta is the change in an option value for a given small change in the stock's value, holding everything else constant.
   C. Option delta is the probability of the option expiring in the money.

**Solution to 3:**

B is correct. Delta is defined as the change in a given portfolio for a given small change in the stock's value, holding everything else constant. Option delta is defined as the change in an option value for a given small change in the stock's value, holding everything else constant.

# GAMMA

## 15

- interpret each of the option Greeks
- describe the role of gamma risk in options trading

Recall that delta is a good approximation of how an option price will change for a small change in the stock. For larger changes in the stock, we need better accuracy. **Gamma** is defined as the change in a given instrument's delta for a given small change in the stock's value, holding everything else constant. Option gamma is similarly defined as the change in a given option delta for a given small change in the stock's value, holding everything else constant. Option gamma is a measure of the curvature in the option price in relationship to the stock price. Thus, the gamma of a long or short position in one share of stock is zero because the delta of a share of stock never changes. A stock always moves one-for-one with itself. Thus, its delta is always +1 and, of course, −1 for a short position in the stock. The gamma for a call and put option are the same and can be expressed as

$$\text{Gamma}_c = \text{Gamma}_p = \frac{e^{-\delta T}}{S_0 \sigma \sqrt{T}} n(d_1) \quad (24)$$

where n(d$_1$) is the standard normal probability density function. The lowercase "n" is distinguished from the cumulative normal distribution—which the density function generates—and that we have used elsewhere in this reading denoted by uppercase "N". The gamma of a call equals the gamma of a similar put based on put–call parity or $c - p = S_0 - e^{-rT}X$. Note that neither $S_0$ nor $e^{-rT}X$ is a direct function of delta. Hence, the right-hand side of put–call parity has a delta of 1. Thus, the right-hand side delta is not sensitive to changes in the underlying. Therefore, the gamma of a call must equal the gamma of a put.

Gamma is always non-negative. Gamma takes on its largest value near at the money. Options deltas do not change much for small changes in the stock price if the option is either deep in or deep out of the money. Also, as the stock price changes and as time to expiration changes, the gamma is also changing.

Gamma measures the rate of change of delta as the stock changes. Gamma approximates the estimation error in delta for options because the option price with respect to the stock is non-linear and delta is a linear approximation. Thus, gamma is a risk measure; specifically, gamma measures the non-linearity risk or the risk that remains once the portfolio is delta neutral. A gamma neutral portfolio implies the gamma is zero. For example, gamma can be managed to an acceptable level first and then delta is neutralized as a second step. This hedging approach is feasible because options have gamma but a stock does not. Thus, in order to modify gamma, one has to include additional option trades in the portfolio. Once the revised portfolio, including any new option trades, has the desired level of gamma, then the trader can get the portfolio delta to its desired level as step two. To alter the portfolio delta, the trader simply buys or sells stock. Because stock has a positive delta, but zero gamma, the portfolio delta can be brought to its desired level with no impact on the portfolio gamma.

One final interpretation of gamma is related to improving the forecasted changes in option prices. Again, let $\hat{c}$, $\hat{p}$, and $\hat{S}$ denote new values for the call, put, and stock. Again based on an approximation method, the change in the option price can be estimated by a delta-plus-gamma approximation or

$$\hat{c} - c \approx \text{Delta}_c(\hat{S} - S) + \frac{\text{Gamma}_c}{2}(\hat{S} - S)^2 \text{ for calls and}$$

$$\hat{p} - p \approx \text{Delta}_p(\hat{S} - S) + \frac{\text{Gamma}_p}{2}(\hat{S} - S)^2 \text{ for puts.}$$

Exhibit 16 illustrates the call value based on the BSM model; the call value based on the delta approximation,

$$\hat{c} = c + \text{Delta}_c(\hat{S} - S);$$

and the call value based on the delta-plus-gamma approximation,

$$\hat{c} = c + \text{Delta}_c(\hat{S} - S) + \frac{\text{Gamma}_c}{2}(\hat{S} - S)^2.$$

Notice again that for very small changes in the stock, the delta approximation and the delta-plus-gamma approximations are fairly accurate. If the stock value rises from 100 to 150, the call line is again significantly above the delta estimated line but is below the delta-plus-gamma estimated line. Importantly, the call delta-plus-gamma estimated line is significantly closer to the BSM model call values. Thus, we see that even for fairly large changes in the stock, the delta-plus-gamma approximation is accurate. As the change in the stock increases, the estimation error also increases. From Exhibit 16, we see the delta-plus-gamma approximation is biased low for a down move but biased high for an up move. Thus, when estimating how the call price changes when the underlying changes, we see how the delta-plus-gamma approximation is an improvement when compared with using the delta approximation on its own.

### Exhibit 16: Call Values, Delta Estimated Call Values, and Delta-Plus-Gamma Estimated Call Values (S = 100 = X, r = 5%, σ = 30%, δ = 0)

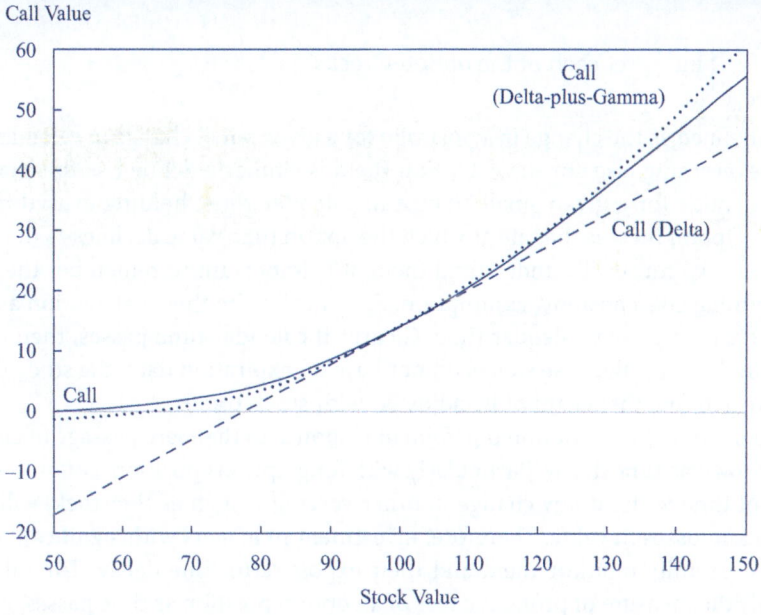

If the BSM model assumptions hold, then we would have no risk in managing option positions. In reality, however, stock prices often jump rather than move continuously and smoothly, which creates "gamma risk." Gamma risk is so-called because gamma measures the risk of stock prices jumping when hedging an option position, and thus leaving us suddenly unhedged.

### EXAMPLE 19

### Gamma Risk in Option Trading

1. Suppose we are options traders and have only one option position—a short call option. We also hold some stock such that we are delta hedged. Which one of the following statements is true?

   **A.** We are gamma neutral.

   **B.** Buying a call will increase our overall gamma.

   **C.** Our overall position is a positive gamma, which will make large moves profitable for us, whether up or down.

### Solution:

B is correct. Buying options (calls or puts) will always increase net gamma. A is incorrect because we are short gamma, not gamma neutral. C is also incorrect because we are short gamma. We can only become gamma neutral from a short gamma position by purchasing options.

## 16. THETA

☐ interpret each of the option Greeks

**Theta** is defined as the change in a portfolio for a given small change in calendar time, holding everything else constant. Option theta is similarly defined as the change in an option value for a given small change in calendar time, holding everything else constant. Option theta is the rate at which the option time value declines as the option approaches expiration. To understand theta, it is important to remember the "holding everything else constant" assumption. Specifically, the theta calculation assumes nothing changes except calendar time. Clearly, if calendar time passes, then time to expiration declines. Because stocks do not have an expiration date, the stock theta is zero. Like gamma, theta cannot be adjusted with stock trades.

The gain or loss of an option portfolio in response to the mere passage of calendar time is known as time decay. Particularly with long options positions, often the mere passage of time without any change in other variables, such as the stock, will result is significant losses in value. Therefore, investment managers with significant option positions carefully monitor theta and their exposure to time decay. Time decay is essentially the measure of profit and loss of an option position as time passes, holding everything else constant.

Note that theta is fundamentally different from delta and gamma in the sense that the passage of time does not involve any uncertainty. There is no chance that time will go backward. Time marches on, but it is important to understand how your investment position will change with the mere passage of time.

Typically, theta is negative for options. That is, as calendar time passes, expiration time declines and the option value also declines. Exhibit 17 illustrates the option value with respect to time to expiration. Remember, as calendar time passes, the time to expiration declines. Both the call and the put option are at the money and eventually are worthless if the stock does not change. Notice, however, how the speed of the option value decline increases as time to expiration decreases.

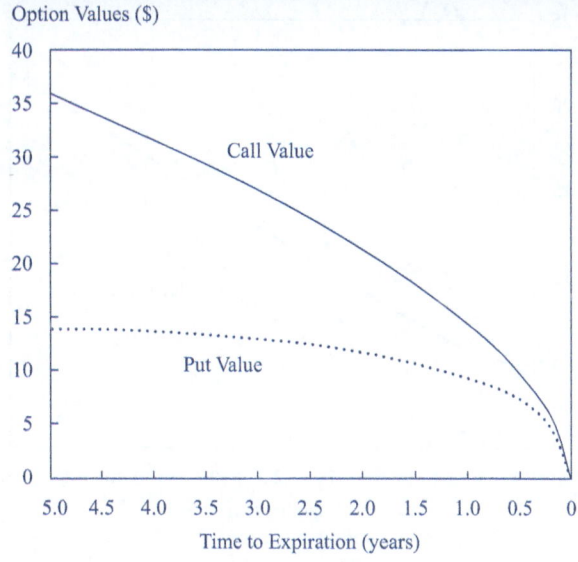

**Exhibit 17: Option Values and Time to Expiration (S = 100 = X, r = 5%, σ = 30%, δ = 0)**

# VEGA

17

☐ interpret each of the option Greeks

**Vega** is defined as the change in a given portfolio for a given small change in volatility, holding everything else constant. Vega measures the sensitivity of a given portfolio to volatility. The vega of an option is positive. An increase in volatility results in an increase in the option value for both calls and puts.

The vega of a call equals the vega of a similar put based on put–call parity or $c - p = S_0 - e^{-rT}X$. Note that neither $S_0$ nor $e^{-rT}X$ is a direct function of volatility. Therefore, the vega of a call must offset the vega of a put so that the vega of the right-hand side is zero.

Unlike the Greeks we have already discussed, vega is based on an unobservable parameter, future volatility. Although historical volatility can be calculated, there is no objective measure of future volatility. Similar to the concept of expected value, future volatility is subjective. Thus, vega measures the sensitivity of a portfolio to changes in the volatility used in the option valuation model. Option values are generally quite sensitive to volatility. In fact, of the five variables in the BSM, an option's value is most sensitive to volatility changes.

At extremely low volatility, the option values tend toward their lower bounds. The lower bound of a European-style call option is zero or the stock less the present value of the exercise price, whichever is greater. The lower bound of a European-style put option is zero or the present value of the exercise price less the stock, whichever is greater. Exhibit 18 illustrates the option values with respect to volatility. In this case, the call lower bound is 4.88 and the put lower bound is 0. The difference between the call and put can be explained by put–call parity.

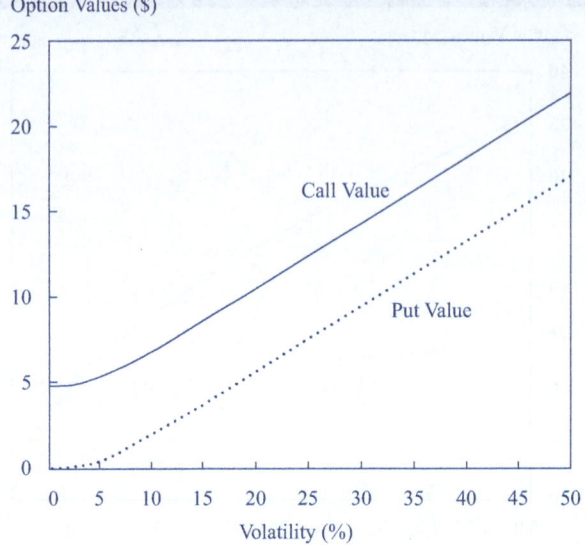

**Exhibit 18: Option Values and Volatility (S = 100 = X, r = 5%, T = 1, δ = 0)**

Vega is very important in managing an options portfolio because option values can be very sensitive to volatility changes. Vega is high when options are at or near the money. Volatility is usually only hedged with other options and volatility itself can be quite volatile. Volatility is sometimes considered a separate asset class or a separate risk factor. Because it is rather exotic and potentially dangerous, exposure to volatility needs to be managed, bearing in mind that risk managers, board members, and clients may not understand or appreciate losses if volatility is the source.

# 18 RHO

☐ interpret each of the option Greeks

**Rho is defined as the change in a given portfolio for a given small change in the risk-free interest rate, holding everything else constant. Thus, rho measures the sensitivity of the portfolio to the risk-free interest rate.**

The rho of a call is positive. Intuitively, buying an option avoids the financing costs involved with purchasing the stock. In other words, purchasing a call option allows an investor to earn interest on the money that otherwise would have gone to purchasing the stock. The higher the interest rate, the higher the call value.

The rho of a put is negative. Intuitively, the option to sell the stock delays the opportunity to earn interest on the proceeds from the sale. For example, purchasing a put option rather than selling the stock deprives an investor of the potential interest that would have been earned from the proceeds of selling the stock. The higher the interest rate, the lower the put value.

When interest rates are zero, the call and put option values are the same for at-the-money options. Recall that with put–call parity, we have $c - p = S_0 - e^{-rT}X$, and when interest rates are zero, then the present value function has no effect. As interest rates rise, the difference between call and put options increases as illustrated in Exhibit 19. The impact on option prices when interest rates change is relatively small when compared with that for volatility changes and that for changes in the stock. Hence, the influence of interest rates is generally not a major concern.[17]

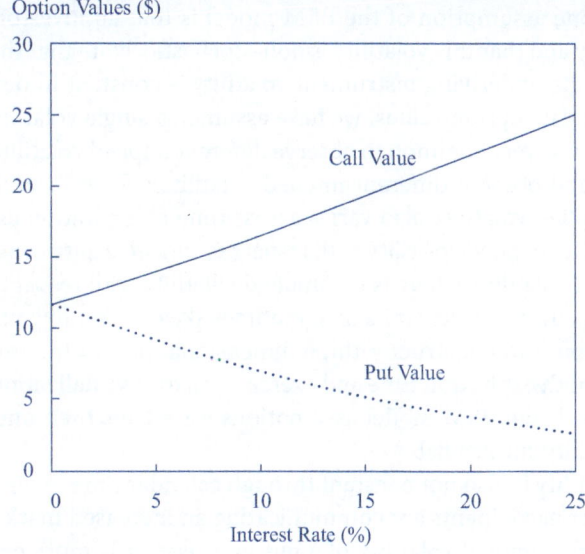

Exhibit 19: Option Values and Interest Rates (S = 100 = X, r = 5%, T = 1, δ = 0)

## IMPLIED VOLATILITY

19

☐ define implied volatility and explain how it is used in options trading

As we have already touched on in Section 6.4, for most options, the value is particularly sensitive to volatility. Unlike the price of the underlying, however, volatility, is not an observable value in the marketplace. Volatility can be, and often is estimated, based on a sample of historical data. For example, for a three-month option, we might look back over the last three months and calculate the actual historical stock volatility. We can then use this figure as an estimate of volatility over the next three months. The volatility parameter in the BSM model, however, is the *future* volatility. As we know, history is a very frail guide of the future, so the option may appear to be "mispriced" with respect to the actual future volatility experienced. Different investors will have different views of the future volatility. The one with the most accurate forecast will have the most accurate assessment of the option value.

Much like yield to maturity with bonds, volatility can be inferred from option prices. This inferred volatility is called the **implied volatility**. Thus, one important use of the BSM model is to invert the model and estimate implied volatility. The key advantage

---

17 An exception to this rule is that with interest rate options, the interest rate is not constant and serves as the underlying. The relationship between the option value and the underlying interest rate is, therefore, captured by the delta, not the rho. Rho is really more generally the relationship between the option value and the rate used to discount cash flows.

is that implied volatility provides information regarding the perceived uncertainty going forward and thereby allows us to gain an understanding of the collective opinions of investors on the volatility of the underlying and the demand for options. If the demand for options increases and the no-arbitrage approach is not perfectly reflected in market prices—for example, because of transaction costs—then the preference for buying options will drive option prices up, and hence, the observed implied volatility. This kind of information is of great value to traders in options.

Recall that one assumption of the BSM model is that all investors agree on the value of volatility and that this volatility is non-stochastic. Note that the original BSM model assumes the underlying instrument volatility is constant in our context. That is, when we calculate option values, we have assumed a single volatility number, like 30%. In practice, it is very common to observe different implied volatilities for different exercise prices and observe different implied volatilities for calls and puts with the same terms. Implied volatility also varies across time to expiration as well as across exercise prices. The implied volatility with respect to time to expiration is known as the term structure of volatility, whereas the implied volatility with respect to the exercise price is known as the volatility smile or sometimes skew depending on the particular shape. It is common to construct a three dimensional plot of the implied volatility with respect to both expiration time and exercise prices, a visualization known as the volatility surface. If the BSM model assumptions were true, then one would expect to find the volatility surface flat.

Implied volatility is also not constant through calendar time. As implied volatility increases, market participants are communicating an increased market price of risk. For example, if the implied volatility of a put increases, it is more expensive to buy downside protection with a put. Hence, the market price of hedging is rising. With index options, various volatility indexes have been created, and these indexes measure the collective opinions of investors on the volatility in the market. Investors can now trade futures and options on various volatility indexes in an effort to manage their vega exposure in other options.

Exhibit 20 provides a look at a couple of decades of one such volatility index, the Chicago Board Options Exchange S&P 500 Volatility Index, known as the VIX. The VIX is quoted as a percent and is intended to approximate the implied volatility of the S&P 500 over the next 30 days. VIX is often termed the fear index because it is viewed as a measure of market uncertainty. Thus, an increase in the VIX index is regarded as greater investor uncertainty. From this figure, we see that the implied volatility of the S&P 500 is not constant and goes through periods when the VIX is low and periods when the VIX is high. In the 2008 global financial crisis, the VIX was extremely high, indicating great fear and uncertainty in the equity market. Remember that implied volatility reflects both beliefs regarding future volatility as well as a preference for risk mitigating products like options. Thus, during the crisis, the higher implied volatility reflected both higher expected future volatility as well as increased preference for buying rather than selling options.

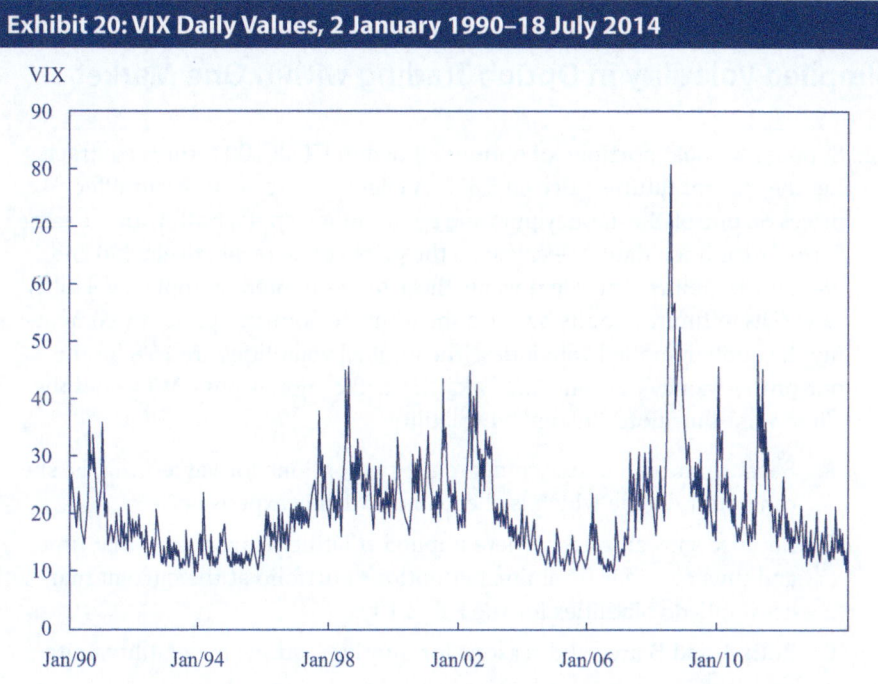

Exhibit 20: VIX Daily Values, 2 January 1990–18 July 2014

Implied volatility has several uses in option trading. An understanding of implied volatility is essential in managing an options portfolio. This reading explains the valuation of options as a function of the value of the underlying, the exercise price, the expiration date, the risk-free rate, dividends or other benefits paid by the underlying, and the volatility of the underlying. Note that each of these parameters is observable except the volatility of the underlying over the option term looking ahead. This volatility has to be estimated in some manner, such as by calculating historical volatility. But as noted, historical volatility involves looking back in time. There are, however, a vast number of liquid options traded on exchanges around the world so that a wide variety of option prices are observable. Because we know the price and all the parameters except the volatility, we can back out the volatility needed by the option valuation model to get the known price. This volatility is the implied volatility.

Hence, implied volatility can be interpreted as the market's view of how to value options. In the option markets, participants use volatility as the medium in which to quote options. The price is simply calculated by the use of an agreed model with the quoted volatility. For example, rather than quote a particular call option as trading for €14.23, it may be quoted as 30.00, where 30.00 denotes in percentage points the implied volatility based on a €14.23 option price. Note that there is a one-to-one relationship between the implied volatility and the option price, ignoring rounding errors.

The benefit of quoting via implied volatility (or simply volatility), rather than price, is that it allows volatility to be traded in its own right. Volatility is the "guess factor" in option pricing. All other inputs—value of the underlying, exercise price, expiration, risk-free rate, and dividend yield—are agreed.[18] Volatility is often the same order of magnitude across exercise prices and expiration dates. This means that traders can compare the values of two options, which may have markedly different exercise prices and expiration dates, and therefore, markedly different prices in a common unit of measure, specifically implied volatility.

---

18 The risk-free rate and dividend yield may not be entirely agreed, but the impact of variations to these parameters is generally very small compared with the other inputs.

### EXAMPLE 20

#### Implied Volatility in Option Trading within One Market

1. Suppose we hold portfolio of options all tied to FTSE 100 futures contracts. Let the current futures price be 6,850. A client calls to request our offer prices on out-of-the-money puts and at-the-money puts, both with the same agreed expiration date. We calculate the prices to be respectively, 190 and 280 futures points. The client wants these prices quoted in implied volatility as well as in futures points because she wants to compare prices by comparing the quoted implied volatilities. The implied volatilities are 16% for the out-of-the-money puts and 15.2% for the at-the-money puts. Why does the client want the quotes in implied volatility?

    **A.** Because she can better compare the two options for value—that is, she can better decide which is cheap and which is expensive.

    **B.** Because she can assess where implied volatility is trading at that time, and thus consider revaluing her options portfolio at the current market implied volatilities for the FTSE 100.

    **C.** Both A and B are valid reasons for quoting options in volatility units.

**Solution:**

C is correct. Implied volatility can be used to assess the relative value of different options, neutralizing the moneyness and time to expiration effects. Also, implied volatility is useful for revaluing existing positions over time.

### EXAMPLE 21

#### Implied Volatility in Option Trading Across Markets

1. Suppose an options dealer offers to sell a three-month at-the-money call on the FTSE index option at 19% implied volatility and a one-month in-the-money put on Vodaphone (VOD) at 24%. An option trader believes that based on the current outlook, FTSE volatility should be closer to 25% and VOD volatility should be closer to 20%. What actions might the trader take to benefit from her views?

    **A.** Buy the FTSE call and the VOD put.

    **B.** Buy the FTSE call and sell the VOD put.

    **C.** Sell the FTSE call and sell the VOD puts.

**Solution:**

B is correct. The trader believes that the FTSE call volatility is understated by the dealer and that the VOD put volatility is overstated. Thus, the trader would expect FTSE volatility to rise and VOD volatility to fall. As a result, the FTSE call would be expected to increase in value and the VOD put would be expected to decrease in value. The trader would take the positions as indicated in B.

Regulators, banks, compliance officers, and most option traders use implied volatilities to communicate information related to options portfolios. This is because implied volatilities, together with standard pricing models, give the "market consensus" valuation, in the same way that other assets are valued using market prices.

In summary, as long as all market participants agree on the underlying option model and how other parameters are calculated, then implied volatility can be used as a quoting mechanism. Recall that there are calls and puts, various exercise prices, various maturities, American and European, and exchange-traded and OTC options. Thus, it is difficult to conceptualize all these different prices. For example, if two call options on the same stock had different prices, but one had a longer expiration and lower exercise price and the other had a shorter expiration and higher exercise, which should be the higher priced option? It is impossible to tell on the surface. But if one option implied a higher volatility than the other, we know that after taking into account the effects of time and exercise, one option is more expensive than the other. Thus, by converting the quoted price to implied volatility, it is easier to understand the current market price of various risk exposures.

## SUMMARY

This reading on the valuation of contingent claims provides a foundation for understanding how a variety of different options are valued. Key points include the following:

- The arbitrageur would rather have more money than less and abides by two fundamental rules: Do not use your own money and do not take any price risk.
- The no-arbitrage approach is used for option valuation and is built on the key concept of the law of one price, which says that if two investments have the same future cash flows regardless of what happens in the future, then these two investments should have the same current price.
- Throughout this reading, the following key assumptions are made:
  - Replicating instruments are identifiable and investable.
  - Market frictions are nil.
  - Short selling is allowed with full use of proceeds.
  - The underlying instrument price follows a known distribution.
  - Borrowing and lending is available at a known risk-free rate.
- The two-period binomial model can be viewed as three one-period binomial models, one positioned at Time 0 and two positioned at Time 1.
- In general, European-style options can be valued based on the expectations approach in which the option value is determined as the present value of the expected future option payouts, where the discount rate is the risk-free rate and the expectation is taken based on the risk-neutral probability measure.
- Both American-style options and European-style options can be valued based on the no-arbitrage approach, which provides clear interpretations of the component terms; the option value is determined by working backward through the binomial tree to arrive at the correct current value.
- For American-style options, early exercise influences the option values and hedge ratios as one works backward through the binomial tree.
- Interest rate option valuation requires the specification of an entire term structure of interest rates, so valuation is often estimated via a binomial tree.

- A key assumption of the Black–Scholes–Merton option valuation model is that the return of the underlying instrument follows geometric Brownian motion, implying a lognormal distribution of the price.
- The BSM model can be interpreted as a dynamically managed portfolio of the underlying instrument and zero-coupon bonds.
- BSM model interpretations related to $N(d_1)$ are that it is the basis for the number of units of underlying instrument to replicate an option, that it is the primary determinant of delta, and that it answers the question of how much the option value will change for a small change in the underlying.
- BSM model interpretations related to $N(d_2)$ are that it is the basis for the number of zero-coupon bonds to acquire to replicate an option and that it is the basis for estimating the risk-neutral probability of an option expiring in the money.
- The Black futures option model assumes the underlying is a futures or a forward contract.
- Interest rate options can be valued based on a modified Black futures option model in which the underlying is a forward rate agreement (FRA), there is an accrual period adjustment as well as an underlying notional amount, and that care must be given to day-count conventions.
- An interest rate cap is a portfolio of interest rate call options termed caplets, each with the same exercise rate and with sequential maturities.
- An interest rate floor is a portfolio of interest rate put options termed floorlets, each with the same exercise rate and with sequential maturities.
- A swaption is an option on a swap.
- A payer swaption is an option on a swap to pay fixed and receive floating.
- A receiver swaption is an option on a swap to receive fixed and pay floating.
- Long a callable fixed-rate bond can be viewed as long a straight fixed-rate bond and short a receiver swaption.
- Delta is a static risk measure defined as the change in a given portfolio for a given small change in the value of the underlying instrument, holding everything else constant.
- Delta hedging refers to managing the portfolio delta by entering additional positions into the portfolio.
- A delta neutral portfolio is one in which the portfolio delta is set and maintained at zero.
- A change in the option price can be estimated with a delta approximation.
- Because delta is used to make a linear approximation of the non-linear relationship that exists between the option price and the underlying price, there is an error that can be estimated by gamma.
- Gamma is a static risk measure defined as the change in a given portfolio delta for a given small change in the value of the underlying instrument, holding everything else constant.
- Gamma captures the non-linearity risk or the risk—via exposure to the underlying—that remains once the portfolio is delta neutral.
- A gamma neutral portfolio is one in which the portfolio gamma is maintained at zero.
- The change in the option price can be better estimated by a delta-plus-gamma approximation compared with just a delta approximation.

# Implied Volatility

- Theta is a static risk measure defined as the change in the value of an option given a small change in calendar time, holding everything else constant.
- Vega is a static risk measure defined as the change in a given portfolio for a given small change in volatility, holding everything else constant.
- Rho is a static risk measure defined as the change in a given portfolio for a given small change in the risk-free interest rate, holding everything else constant.
- Although historical volatility can be estimated, there is no objective measure of future volatility.
- Implied volatility is the BSM model volatility that yields the market option price.
- Implied volatility is a measure of future volatility, whereas historical volatility is a measure of past volatility.
- Option prices reflect the beliefs of option market participant about the future volatility of the underlying.
- The volatility smile is a two dimensional plot of the implied volatility with respect to the exercise price.
- The volatility surface is a three dimensional plot of the implied volatility with respect to both expiration time and exercise prices.
- If the BSM model assumptions were true, then one would expect to find the volatility surface flat, but in practice, the volatility surface is not flat.

# PRACTICE PROBLEMS

## The following information relates to questions 1-9

Bruno Sousa has been hired recently to work with senior analyst Camila Rocha. Rocha gives him three option valuation tasks.

**Alpha Company**

Sousa's first task is to illustrate how to value a call option on Alpha Company with a one-period binomial option pricing model. It is a non-dividend-paying stock, and the inputs are as follows.

- The current stock price is 50, and the call option exercise price is 50.
- In one period, the stock price will either rise to 56 or decline to 46.
- The risk-free rate of return is 5% per period.

Based on the model, Rocha asks Sousa to estimate the hedge ratio, the risk-neutral probability of an up move, and the price of the call option. In the illustration, Sousa is also asked to describe related arbitrage positions to use if the call option is overpriced relative to the model.

**Beta Company**

Next, Sousa uses the two-period binomial model to estimate the value of a European-style call option on Beta Company's common shares. The inputs are as follows.

- The current stock price is 38, and the call option exercise price is 40.
- The up factor ($u$) is 1.300, and the down factor ($d$) is 0.800.
- The risk-free rate of return is 3% per period.

Sousa then analyzes a put option on the same stock. All of the inputs, including the exercise price, are the same as for the call option. He estimates that the value of a European-style put option is 4.53. Exhibit 1 summarizes his analysis. Sousa next must determine whether an American-style put option would have the same value.

# Practice Problems

### Exhibit 1: Two-Period Binomial European-Style Put Option on Beta Company

**Time = 0**

| Item | Value |
|---|---|
| Underlying | 38 |
| Put | 4.5346 |
| Hedge Ratio | −0.4307 |

**Time = 1**

| Item | Value |
|---|---|
| Underlying | 49.4 |
| Put | 0.2517 |
| Hedge Ratio | −0.01943 |

| Item | Value |
|---|---|
| Underlying | 30.4 |
| Put | 8.4350 |
| Hedge Ratio | −1 |

**Time = 2**

| Item | Value |
|---|---|
| Underlying | 64.22 |
| Put | 0 |

| Item | Value |
|---|---|
| Underlying | 39.52 |
| Put | 0.48 |

| Item | Value |
|---|---|
| Underlying | 24.32 |
| Put | 15.68 |

Sousa makes two statements with regard to the valuation of a European-style option under the expectations approach.

- Statement 1     The calculation involves discounting at the risk-free rate.

- Statement 2     The calculation uses risk-neutral probabilities instead of true probabilities.

Rocha asks Sousa whether it is ever profitable to exercise American options prior to maturity. Sousa answers, "I can think of two possible cases. The first case is the early exercise of an American call option on a dividend-paying stock. The second case is the early exercise of an American put option."

**Interest Rate Option**

The final option valuation task involves an interest rate option. Sousa must value a two-year, European-style call option on a one-year spot rate. The notional value of the option is 1 million, and the exercise rate is 2.75%. The risk-neutral probability of an up move is 0.50. The current and expected one-year interest rates are shown in Exhibit 2, along with the values of a one-year zero-coupon bond of 1 notional value for each interest rate.

**Exhibit 2: Two-Year Interest Rate Lattice for an Interest Rate Option**

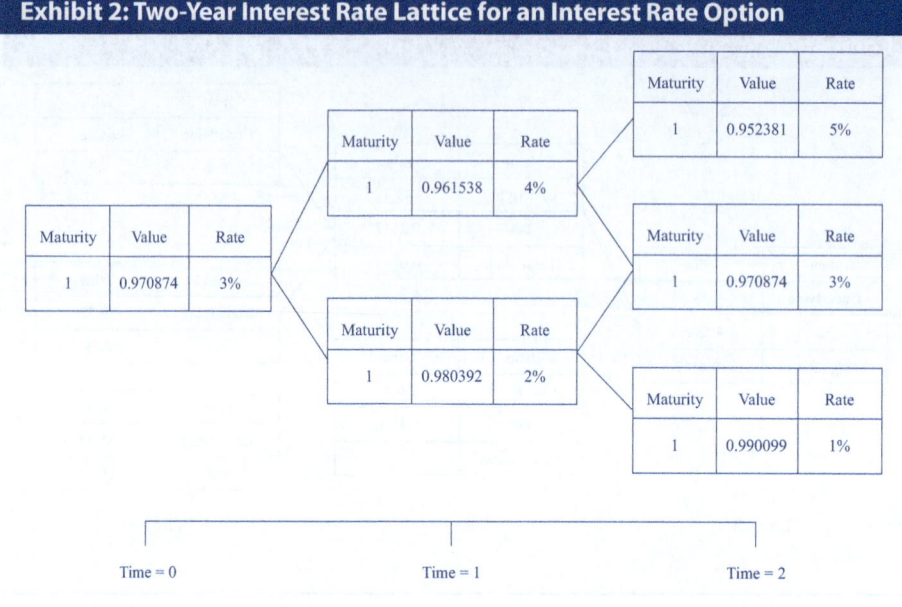

Rocha asks Sousa why the value of a similar in-the-money interest rate call option decreases if the exercise price is higher. Sousa provides two reasons.

Reason 1      The exercise value of the call option is lower.

Reason 2      The risk-neutral probabilities are changed.

1. The optimal hedge ratio for the Alpha Company call option using the one-period binomial model is *closest* to:

    A. 0.60.

    B. 0.67.

    C. 1.67.

2. The risk-neutral probability of the up move for the Alpha Company stock is *closest* to:

    A. 0.06.

    B. 0.40.

    C. 0.65.

3. The value of the Alpha Company call option is *closest* to:

    A. 3.71.

    B. 5.71.

    C. 6.19.

4. For the Alpha Company option, the positions to take advantage of the arbitrage opportunity are to write the call and:

    A. short shares of Alpha stock and lend.

## Practice Problems

   B. buy shares of Alpha stock and borrow.

   C. short shares of Alpha stock and borrow.

5. The value of the European-style call option on Beta Company shares is *closest* to:

   A. 4.83.

   B. 5.12.

   C. 7.61.

6. The value of the American-style put option on Beta Company shares is *closest* to:

   A. 4.53.

   B. 5.15.

   C. 9.32.

7. Which of Sousa's statements about binomial models is correct?

   A. Statement 1 only

   B. Statement 2 only

   C. Both Statement 1 and Statement 2

8. Based on Exhibit 2 and the parameters used by Sousa, the value of the interest rate option is *closest* to:

   A. 5,251.

   B. 6,236.

   C. 6,429.

9. Which of Sousa's reasons for the decrease in the value of the interest rate option is correct?

   A. Reason 1 only

   B. Reason 2 only

   C. Both Reason 1 and Reason 2

# The following information relates to questions 10-17

Trident Advisory Group manages assets for high-net-worth individuals and family trusts.

Alice Lee, chief investment officer, is meeting with a client, Noah Solomon, to discuss risk management strategies for his portfolio. Solomon is concerned about recent volatility and has asked Lee to explain options valuation and the use of options in risk management.

**Options on Stock**

Lee uses the BSM model to price TCB, which is one of Solomon's holdings.

Exhibit 1 provides the current stock price (S), exercise price (X), risk-free interest rate (r), volatility (σ), and time to expiration (T) in years as well as selected outputs from the BSM model. TCB does not pay a dividend.

### Exhibit 1: BSM Model for European Options on TCB

**BSM Inputs**

| S | X | r | σ | T | |
|---|---|---|---|---|---|
| $57.03 | 55 | 0.22% | 32% | 0.25 | |

**BSM Outputs**

| $d_1$ | $N(d_1)$ | $d_2$ | $N(d_2)$ | BSM Call Price | BSM Put Price |
|---|---|---|---|---|---|
| 0.3100 | 0.6217 | 0.1500 | 0.5596 | $4.695 | $2.634 |

### Options on Futures

The Black model valuation and selected outputs for options on another of Solomon's holdings, the GPX 500 Index (GPX), are shown in Exhibit 2. The spot index level for the GPX is 187.95, and the index is assumed to pay a continuous dividend at a rate of 2.2% (δ) over the life of the options being valued, which expire in 0.36 years. A futures contract on the GPX also expiring in 0.36 years is currently priced at 186.73.

### Exhibit 2: Black Model for European Options on the GPX Index

**Black Model Inputs**

| GPX Index | X | r | σ | T | δ Yield |
|---|---|---|---|---|---|
| 187.95 | 180 | 0.39% | 24% | 0.36 | 2.2% |

| Black Model Call Value | Black Model Put Value | Market Call Price | Market Put Price |
|---|---|---|---|
| $14.2089 | $7.4890 | $14.26 | $7.20 |

**Option Greeks**

| Delta (call) | Delta (put) | Gamma (call or put) | Theta (call) daily | Rho (call) per % | Vega per % (call or put) |
|---|---|---|---|---|---|
| 0.6232 | −0.3689 | 0.0139 | −0.0327 | 0.3705 | 0.4231 |

After reviewing Exhibit 2, Solomon asks Lee which option Greek letter best describes the changes in an option's value as time to expiration declines.

Solomon observes that the market price of the put option in Exhibit 2 is $7.20. Lee responds that she used the historical volatility of the GPX of 24% as an input to the BSM model, and she explains the implications for the implied volatility for the GPX.

### Options on Interest Rates

Solomon forecasts the three-month MRR will exceed 0.85% in six months and is considering using options to reduce the risk of rising rates. He asks Lee to value an interest rate call with a strike price of 0.85%. The current three-month MRR is 0.60%, and an FRA for a three-month MRR loan beginning in six months is currently 0.75%.

**Hedging Strategy for the Equity Index**

Solomon's portfolio currently holds 10,000 shares of an exchange-traded fund (ETF) that tracks the GPX. He is worried the index will decline. He remarks to Lee, "You have told me how the BSM model can provide useful information for reducing the risk of my GPX position." Lee suggests a delta hedge as a strategy to protect against small moves in the GPX Index.

Lee also indicates that a long position in puts could be used to hedge larger moves in the GPX. She notes that although hedging with either puts or calls can result in a delta-neutral position, they would need to consider the resulting gamma.

10. Based on Exhibit 1 and the BSM valuation approach, the initial portfolio required to replicate the long call option payoff is:

   A. long 0.3100 shares of TCB stock and short 0.5596 shares of a zero-coupon bond.

   B. long 0.6217 shares of TCB stock and short 0.1500 shares of a zero-coupon bond.

   C. long 0.6217 shares of TCB stock and short 0.5596 shares of a zero-coupon bond.

11. To determine the long put option value on TCB stock in Exhibit 1, the correct BSM valuation approach is to compute:

   A. 0.4404 times the present value of the exercise price minus 0.6217 times the price of TCB stock.

   B. 0.4404 times the present value of the exercise price minus 0.3783 times the price of TCB stock.

   C. 0.5596 times the present value of the exercise price minus 0.6217 times the price of TCB stock.

12. What are the correct spot value ($S$) and the risk-free rate ($r$) that Lee should use as inputs for the Black model?

   A. 186.73 and 0.39%, respectively

   B. 186.73 and 2.20%, respectively

   C. 187.95 and 2.20%, respectively

13. Which of the following is the correct answer to Solomon's question regarding the option Greek letter?

   A. Vega

   B. Theta

   C. Gamma

14. Based on Solomon's observation about the model price and market price for the put option in Exhibit 2, the implied volatility for the GPX is *most likely*:

   A. less than the historical volatility.

B. equal to the historical volatility.

C. greater than the historical volatility.

15. The valuation inputs used by Lee to price a call reflecting Solomon's interest rate views should include an underlying FRA rate of:

    A. 0.60% with six months to expiration.

    B. 0.75% with nine months to expiration.

    C. 0.75% with six months to expiration.

16. The strategy suggested by Lee for hedging small moves in Solomon's ETF position would *most likely* involve:

    A. selling put options.

    B. selling call options.

    C. buying call options.

17. Lee's put-based hedge strategy for Solomon's ETF position would *most likely* result in a portfolio gamma that is:

    A. negative.

    B. neutral.

    C. positive.

# SOLUTIONS

1. A is correct. The hedge ratio requires the underlying stock and call option values for the up move and down move. $S^+ = 56$, and $S^- = 46$. $c^+ = \text{Max}(0, S^+ - X) = \text{Max}(0, 56 - 50) = 6$, and $c^- = \text{Max}(0, S^- - X) = \text{Max}(0, 46 - 50) = 0$. The hedge ratio is

$$h = \frac{c^+ - c^-}{S^+ - S^-} = \frac{6 - 0}{56 - 46} = \frac{6}{10} = 0.60$$

2. C is correct. For this approach, the risk-free rate is $r = 0.05$, the up factor is $u = S^+/S = 56/50 = 1.12$, and the down factor is $d = S^-/S = 46/50 = 0.92$. The risk-neutral probability of an up move is

$\pi = [FV(1) - d]/(u - d) = (1 + r - d)/(u - d)$

$\pi = (1 + 0.05 - 0.92)/(1.12 - 0.92) = 0.13/0.20 = 0.65$

3. A is correct. The call option can be estimated using the no-arbitrage approach or the expectations approach. With the no-arbitrage approach, the value of the call option is

$c = hS + PV(-hS^- + c^-)$.

$h = (c^+ - c^-)/(S^+ - S^-) = (6 - 0)/(56 - 46) = 0.60$.

$c = (0.60 \times 50) + (1/1.05) \times [(-0.60 \times 46) + 0]$.

$c = 30 - [(1/1.05) \times 27.6] = 30 - 26.286 = 3.714$.

Using the expectations approach, the risk-free rate is $r = 0.05$, the up factor is $u = S^+/S = 56/50 = 1.12$, and the down factor is $d = S^-/S = 46/50 = 0.92$. The value of the call option is

$c = PV \times [\pi c^+ + (1 - \pi)c^-]$.

$\pi = [FV(1) - d]/(u - d) = (1.05 - 0.92)/(1.12 - 0.92) = 0.65$.

$c = (1/1.05) \times [0.65(6) + (1 - 0.65)(0)] = (1/1.05)(3.9) = 3.714$.

Both approaches are logically consistent and yield identical values.

4. B is correct. You should sell (write) the overpriced call option and then go long (buy) the replicating portfolio for a call option. The replicating portfolio for a call option is to buy $h$ shares of the stock and borrow the present value of $(hS^- - c^-)$.

$c = hS + PV(-hS^- + c^-)$.

$h = (c^+ - c^-)/(S^+ - S^-) = (6 - 0)/(56 - 46) = 0.60$.

For the example in this case, the value of the call option is 3.714. If the option is overpriced at, say, 4.50, you short the option and have a cash flow at Time 0 of +4.50. You buy the replicating portfolio of 0.60 shares at 50 per share (giving you a cash flow of −30) and borrow $(1/1.05) \times [(0.60 \times 46) - 0] = (1/1.05) \times 27.6 = 26.287$. Your cash flow for buying the replicating portfolio is $-30 + 26.287 = -3.713$. Your net cash flow at Time 0 is $+4.50 - 3.713 = 0.787$. Your net cash flow at Time 1 for either the up move or down move is zero. You have made an arbitrage profit of 0.787.

In tabular form, the cash flows are as follows:

| Transaction | Time Step 0 | Time Step 1 Down Occurs | Time Step 1 Up Occurs |
|---|---|---|---|
| Sell the call option | 4.50 | 0 | −6.00 |
| Buy $h$ shares | −0.6 × 50 = −30 | 0.6 × 46 = 27.6 | 0.6 × 56 = 33.6 |
| Borrow −PV(−$hS^-$ + $c^-$) | −(1/1.05) × [(−0.6 × 46) + 0] = 26.287 | −0.6 × 46 = −27.6 | −0.6 × 46 = −27.6 |
| Net cash flow | 0.787 | 0 | 0 |

5. A is correct. Using the expectations approach, the risk-neutral probability of an up move is

$$\pi = [FV(1) - d]/(u - d) = (1.03 - 0.800)/(1.300 - 0.800) = 0.46.$$

The terminal value calculations for the exercise values at Time Step 2 are

$$c^{++} = \text{Max}(0, u^2 S - X) = \text{Max}[0, 1.30^2(38) - 40] = \text{Max}(0, 24.22) = 24.22.$$

$$c^{-+} = \text{Max}(0, udS - X) = \text{Max}[0, 1.30(0.80)(38) - 40] = \text{Max}(0, -0.48) = 0.$$

$$c^{--} = \text{Max}(0, d^2 S - X) = \text{Max}[0, 0.80^2(38) - 40] = \text{Max}(0, -15.68) = 0.$$

Discounting back for two years, the value of the call option at Time Step 0 is

$$c = PV[\pi^2 c^{++} + 2\pi(1 - \pi)c^{-+} + (1 - \pi)^2 c^{--}].$$

$$c = [1/(1.03)]^2 [0.46^2 (24.22) + 2(0.46)(0.54)(0) + 0.54^2 (0)].$$

$$c = [1/(1.03)]^2 [5.1250] = 4.8308.$$

6. A is correct. Using the expectations approach, the risk-neutral probability of an up move is

$$\pi = [FV(1) - d]/(u - d) = (1.03 - 0.800)/(1.300 - 0.800) = 0.46.$$

An American-style put can be exercised early. At Time Step 1, for the up move, $p^+$ is 0.2517 and the put is out of the money and should not be exercised early ($X < S$, 40 < 49.4). However, at Time Step 1, $p^-$ is 8.4350 and the put is in the money by 9.60 ($X - S = 40 - 30.40$). So, the put is exercised early, and the value of early exercise (9.60) replaces the value of not exercising early (8.4350) in the binomial tree. The value of the put at Time Step 0 is now

$$p = PV[\pi p^+ + (1 - \pi)p^-] = [1/(1.03)][0.46(0.2517) + 0.54(8.4530)] = 4.54.$$

Following is a supplementary note regarding Exhibit 1.
The values in Exhibit 1 are calculated as follows.

## Solutions

At Time Step 2:

$p^{++} = \text{Max}(0, X - u^2 S) = \text{Max}[0, 40 - 1.300^2(38)] = \text{Max}(0, 40 - 64.22) = 0.$

$p^{-+} = \text{Max}(0, X - udS) = \text{Max}[0, 40 - 1.300(0.800)(38)] = \text{Max}(0, 40 - 39.52) = 0.48.$

$p^{--} = \text{Max}(0, X - d^2 S) = \text{Max}[0, 40 - 0.800^2(38)] = \text{Max}(0, 40 - 24.32) = 15.68.$

At Time Step 1:

$p^+ = \text{PV}[\pi p^{++} + (1 - \pi) p^{-+}] = [1/(1.03)][0.46(0) + 0.54(0.48)] = 0.2517.$

$p^- = \text{PV}[\pi p^{-+} + (1 - \pi) p^{--}] = [1/(1.03)][0.46(0.48) + 0.54(15.68)] = 8.4350.$

At Time Step 0:

$p = \text{PV}[\pi p^+ + (1 - \pi) p^-] = [1/(1.03)][0.46(0.2517) + 0.54(8.4350)] = 4.5346.$

7. C is correct. Both statements are correct. The expected future payoff is calculated using risk-neutral probabilities, and the expected payoff is discounted at the risk-free rate.

8. C is correct. Using the expectations approach, per 1 of notional value, the values of the call option at Time Step 2 are

$c^{++} = \text{Max}(0, S^{++} - X) = \text{Max}(0, 0.050 - 0.0275) = 0.0225.$

$c^{+-} = \text{Max}(0, S^{+-} - X) = \text{Max}(0, 0.030 - 0.0275) = 0.0025.$

$c^{--} = \text{Max}(0, S^{--} - X) = \text{Max}(0, 0.010 - 0.0275) = 0.$

At Time Step 1, the call values are

$c^+ = \text{PV}[\pi c^{++} + (1 - \pi) c^{+-}]$.

$c^+ = 0.961538[0.50(0.0225) + (1 - 0.50)(0.0025)] = 0.012019.$

$c^- = \text{PV}[\pi c^{+-} + (1 - \pi) c^{--}]$.

$c^- = 0.980392[0.50(0.0025) + (1 - 0.50)(0)] = 0.001225.$

At Time Step 0, the call option value is

$c = \text{PV}[\pi c^+ + (1 - \pi) c^-]$.

$c = 0.970874[0.50(0.012019) + (1 - 0.50)(0.001225)] = 0.006429.$

The value of the call option is this amount multiplied by the notional value, or $0.006429 \times 1{,}000{,}000 = 6{,}429.$

9. A is correct. Reason 1 is correct: A higher exercise price does lower the exercise value (payoff) at Time 2. Reason 2 is not correct because the risk-neutral probabilities are based on the paths that interest rates take, which are determined by the market and not the details of a particular option contract.

10. C is correct. The no-arbitrage approach to creating a call option involves buying Delta = $N(d_1)$ = 0.6217 shares of the underlying stock and financing with $-N(d_2)$ = −0.5596 shares of a risk-free bond priced at $\exp(-rt)(X) = \exp(-0.0022 \times 0.25)(55)$ = \$54.97 per bond. Note that the value of this replicating portfolio is $n_S S + n_B B = 0.6217(57.03) - 0.5596(54.97) = \$4.6943$ (the value of the call option with slight rounding error).

11. B is correct. The formula for the BSM price of a put option is $p = e^{-rt}XN(-d_2) - SN(-d_1)$. $N(-d_1) = 1 - N(d_1) = 1 - 0.6217 = 0.3783$, and $N(-d_2) = 1 - N(d_2) = 1 - 0.5596 = 0.4404$.

    Note that the BSM model can be represented as a portfolio of the stock ($n_S S$) and zero-coupon bonds ($n_B B$). For a put, the number of shares is $n_S = -N(-d_1) < 0$ and the number of bonds is $n_B = -N(d_2) > 0$. The value of the replicating portfolio is $n_S S + n_B B = -0.3783(57.03) + 0.4404(54.97) = \$2.6343$ (the value of the put option with slight rounding error). B is a risk-free bond priced at $\exp(-rt)(X) = \exp(-0.0022 \times 0.25)(55) = \$54.97$.

12. A is correct. Black's model to value a call option on a futures contract is $c = e^{-rT}[F_0(T)N(d_1) - XN(d_2)]$. The underlying $F_0$ is the futures price (186.73). The correct discount rate is the risk-free rate, $r = 0.39\%$.

13. B is correct. Lee is pointing out the option price's sensitivity to small changes in time. In the BSM approach, option price sensitivity to changes in time is given by the option Greek theta.

14. A is correct. The put is priced at $7.4890 by the BSM model when using the historical volatility input of 24%. The market price is $7.20. The BSM model overpricing suggests the implied volatility of the put must be lower than 24%.

15. C is correct. Solomon's forecast is for the three-month MRR to exceed 0.85% in six months. The correct option valuation inputs use the six-month FRA rate as the underlying, which currently has a rate of 0.75%.

16. B is correct because selling call options creates a short position in the ETF that would hedge his current long position in the ETF.

    Exhibit 2 could also be used to answer the question. Solomon owns 10,000 shares of the GPX, each with a delta of +1; by definition, his portfolio delta is +10,000. A delta hedge could be implemented by selling enough calls to make the portfolio delta neutral:

    $$N_H = -\frac{\text{Portfolio delta}}{\text{Delta}_H} = -\frac{+10,000}{+0.6232} = -16,046 \text{ calls.}$$

17. C is correct. Because the gamma of the stock position is 0 and the put gamma is always non-negative, adding a long position in put options would most likely result in a positive portfolio gamma.

    Gamma is the change in delta from a small change in the stock's value. A stock position always has a delta of +1. Because the delta does not change, gamma equals 0.

    The gamma of a call equals the gamma of a similar put, which can be proven using put–call parity.

# Alternative Investments

# LEARNING MODULE 1

## Overview of Types of Real Estate Investment

by Steven G. Bloom, CFA, Jeffrey D. Fisher, PhD, David Kruth, CFA, Bryan D. MacGregor, PhD, MRICS, MRTPI, Ian Rossa O'Reilly, CFA, and Anthony Paolone, CFA.

*Steven G. Bloom, CFA, is at ARC Fiduciary (USA). Jeffery D. Fisher, PhD. David Kruth, CFA. Bryan MacGregor, PhD, MRICS, MRTPI. Ian Rossa O'Reilly, CFA (Canada). Anthony Paolone, CFA.*

| LEARNING OUTCOMES | |
|---|---|
| Mastery | The candidate should be able to: |
| ☐ | compare the characteristics, classifications, principal risks, and basic forms of public and private real estate investments |
| ☐ | explain portfolio roles and economic value determinants of real estate investments |
| ☐ | discuss commercial property types, including their distinctive investment characteristics |
| ☐ | explain the due diligence process for both private and public equity real estate investments |
| ☐ | discuss real estate investment indexes, including their construction and potential biases |

# SUMMARY

## General Characteristics of Real Estate

- Real estate investments can occur in four basic forms: private equity (direct ownership), publicly traded equity (indirect ownership claim), private debt (direct mortgage lending), and publicly traded debt (securitized mortgages).
- Many motivations exist for investing in real estate income property. The key ones are current income, price appreciation, inflation hedge, diversification, and tax benefits.

- Adding equity real estate investments to a traditional portfolio will potentially have diversification benefits because of the less-than-perfect correlation of equity real estate returns with returns to stocks and bonds.
- If the income stream can be adjusted for inflation and real estate prices increase with inflation, then equity real estate investments may provide an inflation hedge.
- Debt investors in real estate expect to receive their return from promised cash flows and typically do not participate in any appreciation in value of the underlying real estate. Thus, debt investments in real estate are similar to other fixed-income investments, such as bonds.
- Regardless of the form of real estate investment, the value of the underlying real estate property can affect the performance of the investment with location being a critical factor in determining the value of a real estate property.
- Real estate property has some unique characteristics compared with other investment asset classes. These characteristics include heterogeneity and fixed location, high unit value, management intensiveness, high transaction costs, depreciation, sensitivity to the credit market, illiquidity, and difficulty of value and price determination.
- There are many different types of real estate properties in which to invest. The main commercial (income-producing) real estate property types are office, industrial and warehouse, retail, and multi-family. Other types of commercial properties are typically classified by their specific use.
- Certain risk factors are common to commercial property, but each property type is likely to have a different susceptibility to these factors. The key risk factors that can affect commercial real estate include business conditions, lead time for new development, excess supply, cost and availability of capital, unexpected inflation, demographics, lack of liquidity, environmental issues, availability of information, management expertise, and leverage.
- Location, lease structures, and economic factors—such as economic growth, population growth, employment growth, and consumer spending—affect the value of each property type.

## 1. INTRODUCTION

Real estate property is an asset class that plays a significant role in many investment portfolios and is an attractive source of current income. Investor allocations to public and private real estate have increased significantly over the last 20 years. Because of the unique characteristics of real estate property, real estate investments tend to behave differently from other asset classes—such as stocks, bonds, and commodities—and thus have different risks and diversification benefits. Private real estate investments are further differentiated because the investments are not publicly traded and require analytic techniques different from those of publicly traded assets. Because of the lack of directly comparable transactions, an appraisal process is required to value real estate property. Many of the indexes and benchmarks used for private real estate also rely on appraisals, and because of this characteristic, they behave differently from indexes for publicly traded equities, such as the S&P 500, MSCI Europe, FTSE Asia Pacific, and many other regional and global indexes.

# BASIC FORMS OF REAL ESTATE INVESTMENT

☐ compare the characteristics, classifications, principal risks, and basic forms of public and private real estate investments

Real estate offers investors long-term stable income, some protection from inflation, and generally low correlations with stocks and bonds. High-quality, well-managed properties with low leverage are generally expected to provide higher returns than high-grade corporate debt (albeit with higher risk) and lower returns and risk than equity. Real estate investment can be an effective means of diversification in many balanced investment portfolios. Investors can choose to have the equity, or ownership, position in properties, or they may prefer to have exposure to real estate debt as a lender or owner of mortgage-backed securities.

Private real estate investments often hold the greatest appeal for investors with long-term investment horizons and the ability to accept relatively lower liquidity. Pension funds, sovereign wealth funds, insurance companies, and high-net-worth individuals have been among the largest investors in private real estate. Securitized real estate ownership—shares of publicly traded, pooled real estate investments, such as real estate operating companies (REOCs), real estate investment trusts (REITs), and mortgage-backed securities (MBS)—has historically provided smaller investors with ready access to the asset class because of low share prices and the benefits of higher liquidity and professional management. Institutional investors also pursue securitized real estate when the market capitalization of the vehicles can accommodate large investor demand.

Regardless of vehicle type, the risk profile of the underlying investment can vary significantly. High-quality properties in leading markets with long-term leases and low leverage have a relatively conservative risk profile, as do those **mortgages** that represent only slightly more than half of the asset's value. Older properties with short-term leases in suburban markets with ample room for new development and higher leverage constitute higher-risk properties. Below-investment-grade, non-rated, and mezzanine debt similarly carries higher risk. Development property is often considered the riskiest because of long lead times and the dependence on contractors, suppliers, regulators, and future tenants for success.

## Real Estate Investment: Basic Forms

There are many different types of real estate *property*, *capital position*, and *investment vehicle* classifications.

### *Property Type:*

One simple way to classify property type distinguishes between *residential* and *non-residential*—typically, commercial—properties. Real estate can be categorized as either *owner occupied* or for *rent*. Exhibit 1 presents the various property types along these two lines of classification.

**Exhibit 1: Residential vs. Commercial Real Estate**

|  | Owner Occupied | For Rent (Commercial) |
|---|---|---|
| **Residential*** | Single-family homes, apartments/condominiums, manufactured housing | Single-family homes and multi-family buildings |
| **Non-Residential** | Office, shopping centers, manufacturing facilities, warehouses, agricultural, other specialty real estate | Office, shopping centers, industrial warehouse/distribution, hotels, agricultural, other specialty real estate |

*A later section on classifications will further discuss various types of residential real estate. Multi-family properties contain individual for-rent apartments or flats. Condominiums refer to owner-occupied units in multi-unit buildings.

Senior housing/assisted living properties represent a specialized real estate use. Other specialized and niche property types include medical offices and facilities, self-storage, data centers, manufactured housing communities, casinos, cell towers, movie theaters, billboards, and just about any other type of for-rent real property. These other property types would fit a non-core investment strategy.

*Capital position*

Capital position describes whether the investment is structured as equity or debt.

An equity investor has an ownership interest in the property or properties. An equity investor may be the sole or a joint owner of the real estate property or may invest in securities of a company that owns the real estate property. The owner of the real estate property controls such decisions as whether to obtain a mortgage loan on the real estate, who should handle property management, and when to sell the real estate. In the case of a REIT, that control is delegated to the managers of the REIT by the shareholders.

A debt investor is in a position of lender to the owner of the property or properties. A debt investor may loan funds to the entity acquiring the real estate property or may invest in securities that are based on real estate lending. Typically, the real estate property is used as collateral for a mortgage loan. In such cases, the mortgage lender has a priority claim on the real estate. The value of the equity investor's interest in the real estate is equal to the value of the real estate less the amount owed to the mortgage lender.

*Investment Vehicles:*

Real estate investment can be made through a private or public vehicle and take the form of either equity or debt. Combining the two dimensions, we have four quadrants as illustrated in Exhibit 2.

# Basic Forms of Real Estate Investment

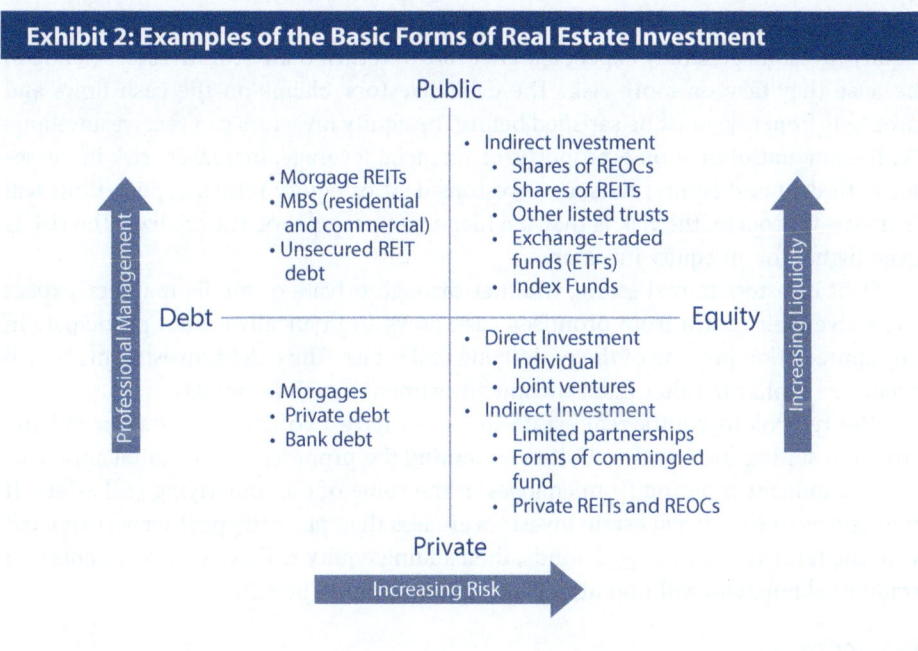

Exhibit 2: Examples of the Basic Forms of Real Estate Investment

**Private vs. Public**

Private investment can be as simple as buying a property outright. Commercial property owners, whether as the sole owner or joint owner, are more likely to use a special vehicle to limit their liability. Property owners who accept capital from passive investors will form partnerships with the real estate professionals acting as the general partners (GPs) and the passive investors being admitted to the partnership as limited partners (LPs). The model commonly has the entrepreneur/real estate professional taking the GP role and managing the partnership for the LPs. The LPs typically consist of insurance companies, pension funds, sovereign wealth funds, foundations, endowments, and high-net-worth individuals.

Public investors can purchase common stock, partnership units, or trust units in entities that are listed on public exchanges and freely traded. By definition, investments in corporations, REITs, and other vehicles that, in turn, own properties are indirect investments. The key benefits to investing in publicly traded securities include liquidity, access to professional management, and a portfolio of properties combined with low minimum-purchase requirements.

Real estate operating companies (REOCs) are taxable corporations that operate and manage commercial real estate with few corporate-structure restrictions. They commonly own and often develop real estate.

In contrast, REITs are restricted to primarily owning and operating rental properties and mortgages and are required to distribute nearly all or all of their earnings to investors to avoid paying corporate income.

Mortgage-backed securities are classified as public investments when there are active secondary trading markets. There are some restrictions as to who is eligible to purchase the MBS and minimum trade sizes. MBS are indirect investments. The trust certificates typically own the right to receive cash flow from an underlying pool of mortgages, which, in turn, are secured by real property, rather than owning the mortgage outright.

### Equity versus Debt

Equity investors generally expect a higher rate of return than debt investors (lenders) because they take on more risk. The debt investors' claims on the cash flows and proceeds from sale must be satisfied before the equity investors can receive anything. As the amount of debt on a property, or financial leverage, increases, risk increases for both debt and equity; thus, an investor's debt or equity return expectations will increase. Of course, the risk is that the higher return will not materialize. The risk is even higher for an equity investor.

Debt investors in real estate, whether through private or public markets, expect to receive their return from promised cash flows and typically do not participate in any appreciation in value of the underlying real estate. Thus, debt investments in real estate are similar to other fixed-income investments, such as bonds.

The returns to equity real estate investors have two components: an income stream resulting from such activities as renting the property and a capital appreciation component resulting from changes in the value of the underlying real estate. If the returns to equity real estate investors are less than perfectly positively correlated with the returns to stocks and bonds, then adding equity real estate investments to a traditional portfolio will potentially have diversification benefits.

### Categorization

The categorization of real estate investment into the four quadrants helps investors identify the forms that best fit their objectives. For example, some investors may prefer to own and manage real estate. Other investors may prefer the greater liquidity and professional management associated with purchasing publicly traded REITs. Other investors may prefer mortgage lending because it involves less risk than equity investment or unsecured lending; the mortgage lender has a priority claim on the real estate used as collateral for the mortgage. Still other investors may want to create a portfolio of investors.

Each quadrant offers differences in risk and expected return, including the impact of taxes on the return. So, investors should explore the risk and return characteristics of each quadrant as part of their investment decisions.

> **KNOWLEDGE CHECK**
>
> ## Form of Investment
>
> An investor is interested in adding real estate to her portfolio of equity and fixed-income securities for the first time. She has no previous real estate experience but believes adding real estate will provide some diversification benefits. She is concerned about liquidity because she may need the money in a year or so.
>
> 1. Which form of investment is *most likely* appropriate for her?
>
>    **A.** Shares of REITs
>
>    **B.** Mortgage-backed securities
>
>    **C.** Direct ownership of commercial real estate property
>
>    **Solution**
>
>    A is correct. She is probably better off investing in shares of publicly traded REITs, which provide liquidity, have professional management, and require a smaller investment than direct ownership of real estate. Using REITs, she may be able to put together a diversified real estate investment portfolio. Although REITs are more correlated with stocks than direct ownership of real estate is, direct ownership is much less liquid and a lot of properties are needed to have a diversified real estate portfolio. Also, adding shares of REITs to her current portfolio should provide more diversification benefits

# Basic Forms of Real Estate Investment

> than adding debt in the form of mortgage-backed securities and will allow her to benefit from any appreciation of the real estate.
>
> Debt investments in real estate, such as MBS, are similar to other fixed-income investments, such as bonds, and can be highly sensitive to changes in interest rates. The difference is that their income streams are secured on real estate assets, which means that the risks are default risks linked to the performance of the real estate assets and the ability of mortgagees to pay interest. In contrast, adding equity real estate investments to a traditional portfolio (of equity and fixed-income investments) will potentially have diversification benefits.

## Characteristics

Some of the main characteristics of real estate investment that distinguish it from listed equity or fixed-income investments include the following:

| | |
|---|---|
| **Unique Asset & Fixed Location** | No two real estate properties are the same. |
| **High Unit Value** | The price of a unit of real estate property is high compared with the price of a single stock or bond. |
| **Management Intensive** | Owning real estate requires maintenance, contracting, and collecting rent. Owning a stock or bond doesn't require such efforts. |
| **High Transaction Costs** | Buying/selling real estate is costly in time and money with multiple parties involved. Trading in stocks/bonds is much more straightforward. |
| **Depreciation** | Real estate investments are directly subject to depreciation as buildings are subject to "wear and tear". |
| **Illiquidity** | Real estate investments require time to sell, and the bid/ask spread is much wider than that for stocks and bonds. |
| **Need for debt capital** | Real estate investments typically require debt capital. |
| **Price Determination** | Real estate prices are typically determined by appraisals and estimates rather than by market transactions readily visible in the market as each property is unique. |

- *Unique asset and fixed location*: Whereas all bonds of a particular issue are identical, as are stocks of a particular type in a specific company, no two properties are the same. Buildings differ in use, size, location, age, type of construction, quality, and tenant and leasing arrangements. Even identically constructed buildings with the same tenants and leases will be at different locations.
- *High unit value*: The unit value to purchase one private real estate property is large compared to a single share of stock or a bond. The amount required to make an investment in private real estate limits the number of potential investors and the ability to construct a diversified real estate portfolio. This contributed to the development of publicly traded securities, such as REITs, which allow partial ownership of an indivisible asset.

- *Management intensive*: A private real estate equity investor or direct owner of real estate has responsibility for management of the real estate, including maintaining the properties, negotiating leases, and collecting rents. This active management, whether carried out by the owner or by hired property managers, creates additional costs when projecting returns.
- *High transaction costs*: Buying and selling real estate is also costly and time consuming because others—such as brokers, appraisers, lawyers, lenders, and construction professionals—are likely to be involved in the process until a transaction is completed.
- *Depreciation*: Buildings depreciate as a result of use and the passage of time. A building's value may also change as the desirability of its location and its design changes from the perspective of end users.
- *Need for debt capital*: Real estate values are sensitive to the cost and availability of debt capital because of the large amounts required to purchase and develop real estate properties. The ability to access funds and the cost of funds in the credit markets are important.
- *Illiquidity*: Real estate properties are relatively illiquid. They may take a significant amount of time to market and to sell at a price that is close to the owner's perceived fair market value. The initial spread between bid and asked prices is generally wide.
- *Price determination*: As a result of the wide differences in the characteristics of real estate properties and the low volume of transactions, estimates of value or appraisals rather than transaction prices are usually necessary to assess changes in value or expected selling price over time. The limited number of participants in the market for a property, combined with the importance of local knowledge, makes it harder to know the market value of a property.

These characteristics slowed widespread investor allocations to real estate. Securitization helped overcome some of these problems, especially investment size and illiquidity. In the United States, REITs were originally conceived of as a type of mutual fund to provide small investors with access to the asset class. Similar to mutual funds, this vehicle does not pay income taxes and instead distributes dividends to investors. REITs typically allow exposure to a diversified portfolio of real estate. In regions without REIT structures or if property companies want greater flexibility, REOCs could also raise public capital. REIT and REOC shares are typically liquid, and active trading results in prices that are more likely to reflect market value. It is much easier to sell the shares of a listed company that owns real estate than to sell the underlying real estate.

### KNOWLEDGE CHECK

## Investment Characteristics

1. An investor states that he likes investing in private real estate because he believes the market is less efficient than other liquid asset classes and, therefore, expects to earn a return premium. What are some of the sources of real estate market inefficiency?

**Solution**

It can be difficult to readily establish fair market value in real estate. Infrequent transactions, high transaction costs, and low transparency reduce market efficiency. Market players who recognize the impact of new information on underlying property value cannot readily buy real estate when it is priced below intrinsic value and sell real estate when prices move above intrinsic value. In a less efficient market, an investor with superior knowledge and information or a better understanding of the appropriate price to pay for properties (superior valuation skills) may earn a higher return by making more informed investment decisions, provided that they can wait until market prices adjust to intrinsic values. However, there is also mounting evidence that real estate is becoming more efficient.

Online data services provide real-time pricing transparency based on property location, type, size, and age. There is also information about commercial tenants, rents, lease terms, and lease expiration schedules. The large number and large size of real estate private equity funds with ample capital to deploy suggest numerous professional investors are scouring markets for the best opportunities. An investor buying relatively few properties may be able to take advantage of market inefficiencies.

However, larger investors with broad real estate exposure are more likely to see diversification reduce idiosyncratic opportunities for above-market returns. Private real estate investors should expect to earn a return premium for illiquidity. Earning excess returns from market inefficiency becomes increasingly difficult as the number of knowledgeable, well-capitalized participants competing for acquisitions and spurring transaction activity increases.

2. A portfolio manager believes the entire real estate sector is trading at cyclically depressed levels because of prior overbuilding, a jump in interest rates, and a recession. The manager wants tactical exposure to real estate for what the manager expects to be a three-year recovery cycle. What would be a good real estate investment strategy for the manager?

**Solution**

The portfolio manager could purchase the shares of a large, diversified REIT or REOC. REIT shares would provide exposure to underlying real estate, and REOCs could offer exposure to a combination of rental income, property management and brokerage income, and development profits. By investing in the shares of a larger, presumably liquid company, the portfolio manager should be able to exit the position if the sector recovers as expected or if the portfolio manager decides to raise cash. Geography- and sector-focused real estate companies (e.g., companies that own shopping centers in Australia) should be considered if the portfolio manager's views extend to specific markets.

Investing in private funds or companies may not offer as much liquidity, and entry/exit costs could be higher.

## Risk Factors

In this section, we consider risk factors associated with investing in commercial real estate. Most of the risk factors that follow affect the income and/or value of the real estate property and, if investing indirectly, the income and value of the equity or debt investment.

Risks that are identified can be, to some extent, planned for and incorporated in investors' expectations. In some cases, a risk can be converted to a known dollar amount through insurance. In other cases, risk can be reduced through diversification or shifted to another party through contractual arrangements. For example, the risk of expenses increasing can be shifted to tenants by including expense reimbursement clauses in their leases. The risk that remains must be evaluated and reflected in contractual terms (e.g., rental prices) such that the expected return is equal to or greater than the required return necessary to make the investment.

The following are characteristic sources of risk or risk factors of real estate investment:
- Property demand and supply
- Valuation
- Property operations

*Property Demand and Supply*

| Feature | Description |
|---|---|
| Business conditions | General economic conditions, such as GDP, employment, interest rates, and business cycle, impact demand for real estate. |
| Demographics | Demographic factors, such as population, age, and income level, impact demand for real estate. |
| Real estate cycle | Long-lead times and a relatively long real estate cycle contribute to a buildup of excess supply based on the assumption of high rents. |

- *Business conditions*: Fundamentally, the commercial real estate business involves renting space to users. The demand for space depends on a myriad of international, national, regional, and local economic conditions. GDP, employment, household income, interest rates, and inflation are particularly relevant to real estate. Changes in macroeconomic conditions will affect real estate investments because both current and expected income and real estate values may be affected.
- *Demographics*: The size and age distribution of the population in the local market, the distribution of socioeconomic groups, and rates of new household formation are demographic factors that affect the demand for real estate.
- *Excess supply*: The real estate cycle is generally long, lasting approximately 17–18 years *on average*, albeit with a great deal of variance. Increases in the demand for space, which usually accompany the business cycle, will lead to higher occupancy, which, in turn, can support higher rents. New development usually begins once rents and property income increase to levels high enough to meet investor return requirements. Construction costs and property operating expenses generally increase later in the real estate cycle as increased competition for labor, materials, and land contribute to rising development costs, thereby increasing the minimum rent threshold required to justify new construction.

New development requires long lead times to secure capital, land, designs, permits, and zoning approval; to start and complete construction; to lease space; and to have tenants move in. If additions to real estate supply do not keep up with demand, rents will continue to rise, which encourages even more development. As the business cycle ages, recession risks increase. When the inevitable contraction in business activity occurs and demand for space moderates or declines, new supply continuing to come to market will contribute to a decline in market occupancy, which is accompanied by falling rents and declining returns to real estate investment. Rent price swings between the lows and highs can be dramatic. When rents and returns drop, new supply will contract and remain low until space demand rises high enough to absorb the excess space and contribute to higher rents.

## Valuation

| Feature | Description |
| --- | --- |
| Cost and availability of capital | Real estate must compete with other assets for debt and equity capital. Real estate investors would be willing to pay more in a low interest rate environment |
| Availability of information | If information on a property is limited, it is more difficult to make an informed decision on investing in that property. |
| Lack of liquidity | Real estate takes time (and money) to sell and buy. |
| Interest rate environment | The interest rate environment effects supply, demand, and prices of real estate. |

- *Cost and availability of capital*: Real estate must compete with other assets for debt and equity capital. The willingness of investors to invest in real estate depends on the availability of debt capital and the cost of that capital, as well as the expected return on other investments, such as stocks and bonds, which affects the availability of equity capital. A shortage of debt capital as well as high interest rates can significantly reduce the demand for real estate and reduce prices. Alternatively, an environment of low interest rates and easy access to debt capital can decrease investors' weighted average cost of capital and increase the amount investors are willing to pay for real estate investments.

- *Availability of information*: A lack of information to conduct the property analysis adds to the risk of the investment. The amount of data available on real estate space and capital markets has improved considerably. Although some countries have much more information available to investors than others, in general, the availability of information has been increasing on a global basis as investors want to evaluate investment alternatives on a comparable basis. Real estate indexes have become available in many countries around the world. These indexes allow investors to benchmark their properties' performance against that of peers and also provide a better understanding of the risk and return for real estate compared with other asset classes. Indexes are discussed in more detail elsewhere.

- *Lack of liquidity*: Liquidity is the ability to convert an asset to cash quickly without a significant price discount or loss of principal. Real estate is considered to have low liquidity (high liquidity risk) because of the large value of an individual investment and the time and cost it takes to sell a property at its current value. Buyers are unlikely to make large investments without conducting adequate due diligence, which takes both time and money. Therefore, buyers are not likely to agree to a quick purchase without a significant discount to the price.

- *Interest rate environment.* Fixed-income securities are usually negatively affected by higher interest rates because higher discount rates reduce the present value of the instrument. Real estate values may also decline initially when interest rates rise. Unlike a fixed-rate bond with a fixed maturity price, however, property income, land prices, and real estate values may increase over time or at least through the latter part of the real estate cycle.

*Property Operations*

| Feature | Description |
| --- | --- |
| Management | Real estate requires "asset management" (managing/monitoring the investment) and "property management" (maintenance, day-to-day operations). |
| Lease Provisions | Real estate investments include legal contracts that can add to or detract from the value of the investment. |
| Leverage | Real estate investments typically include more leverage for the equity holder than other types of investments. This leverage affects the risk/return profile. |
| ESG Considerations | Real estate values can be directly impacted by environment-, social-, and governance-related issues. |
| Obsolescence | Real estate investments can become obsolete due to changing technology, tenant preferences, and other factors. |
| Ongoing market disruption | Online shopping, remote working, and other disruptions continue to change the face of real estate markets globally |

- *Management*: Investment management can be categorized into two levels: asset management and property management. Asset management involves monitoring the investment's financial performance and making changes as needed. Property management is exclusive to real estate investments. It involves the overall day-to-day operation of the property and the physical maintenance of the property, including the buildings. Management risk reflects the ability of the property and asset managers to make the right decisions regarding the operation of the property, such as negotiating leases, maintaining the property, marketing the property, and making renovations when necessary.

- *Lease provisions:* Landlords use lease provisions to partially or fully recover loss in purchasing power from inflation through a combination of contractual rent increases and expense passthroughs. Predetermined contractual rent step-ups can move in line with unexpected inflation if they are tied to a consumer price or other inflation-linked index. Even then, increases in operating expenses, especially real estate taxes and insurance costs, can rise faster than general inflation. Real rental income after expenses would be penalized in such a scenario unless leases also require lessees to reimburse landlords for property operating expenses. Expense caps, which limit how much of the annual increase is passed along to the tenant, would not perfectly protect the lessor against unforeseen increases in expenses. Short-term leases (typically six months to two years) and leases in markets that allow the property owner to require periodic rent reviews present the landlord with the opportunity to frequently reset rents in response to changing market conditions. The longer the lease or the longer the period between rent reviews, the more difficult it is to anticipate rising costs and, therefore, the more important it is for lessors to require expense reimbursements from tenants. Following a real estate market downturn, however, high vacancy rates and low rents may prevent landlords from raising rents on new leases in line with inflation.

- *Leverage*: Leverage affects returns on investments in real estate but not the value of the underlying real estate property at any given point. Leverage is the use of borrowed funds to finance some of the purchase price of an

# Basic Forms of Real Estate Investment

investment. The ratio of borrowed funds to total purchase price is known as the loan-to-value (LTV) ratio. Higher LTV ratios mean greater amounts of leverage. Real estate transactions can be more highly leveraged than most other types of investments. But increasing leverage also increases risk because the lender has the first claim on the cash flow and on the value of the property if there is default on the loan. A small change in property income can result in a relatively large change in the amount of cash flow available to the equity investor after making the mortgage payment.

- *ESG considerations*: Real estate values can be affected by environmental conditions, including soil and groundwater contaminants related to a prior owner, prior tenants, or an adjacent property owner. Such problems can significantly reduce the value because of the costs incurred to correct them. In addition, social- and governance-related issues can have an impact on the development and management of real estate.

- *Obsolescence:* Changes in tenant preferences, regulations, and technology affect space demand. Ceiling heights in older buildings may not be high enough to accommodate warehouse stacking requirements or office communication networking cables and equipment. Distribution facility docks may not work with larger trucks, and paved lots may not be deep enough to allow room for large trucks to turn. Internet shopping, department store closures and consolidation, and other retail shopping trends, especially in the United States, which has the largest amount of per capita retail space, have constrained demand for large shopping center space. It may not be economically viable to upgrade, reconfigure, or repurpose older buildings to comply with energy efficiency and other modernization requirements or changing business and consumer preferences.

- *Ongoing market disruption*: Rising use of the internet, cloud computing services, and offsite IT backup systems have spurred the growth of data centers while reducing the space businesses need for onsite computer and server systems. Internet sales and delivery combined with increased attention to companies' carbon footprint are contributing to shifting trade and distribution patterns. Companies may prefer to locate warehouse distribution facilities closer to customers for faster and even same-day delivery. Large shopping center owners have been partially successful at replacing former department store anchor tenants with restaurants and other forms of entertainment to attract consumer traffic and converting retail space to local distribution space.

- *Other risk factors*: Many other risk factors exist, such as unobserved physical defects in the property, natural disasters (e.g., earthquakes and hurricanes, for which insurance and repair costs can be expensive), pandemics, acts of terrorism, and climate change. Unfortunately, the biggest risk may be one that was unidentified as a risk at the time of purchasing the property. Unidentified, difficult-to-forecast, and catastrophic risks can cause major disruptions and be devastating to investors.

**EXAMPLE 1**

The COVID-19 pandemic caused tremendous shocks to the global economy. The quarantine and stay-at-home policies inflicted great pain on the lodging and brick-and-mortar retail sectors in particular and accelerated such trends as retail consolidation and the rise of internet retailing. The prevalence of working from home during the pandemic may have helped the data center sector by increasing internet communication traffic and forcing companies to rely on business continuity services. At the same time, many employers realized they can get by with less office space by permitting some employees to work from home regularly, and many employees have grown accustomed to working from home and do not look to return to the office full time, at least until the pandemic ends. There is also evidence that urban residents are leaving large, expensive cities for suburban living. Rents across the residential, office, and retail sectors declined more than 10% in many gateway cities. Such events as the COVID-19 pandemic make it difficult to predict by how much and how fast demand for space will change during the next 2 to 10 years.

**KNOWLEDGE CHECK**

## Commercial Real Estate Risk

1. An investor wants to add real estate to her portfolio to benefit from its diversifying characteristics. She decides to buy a commercial property, financing at most 30% of the asset with debt in order to avoid incurring financial risk due to interest rate changes. This strategy is *most likely* to:
    **A.** limit the risk due to leverage.
    **B.** mitigate the risk due to inflation.
    **C.** eliminate the risk due to interest rate changes.
   **Solution**

   A is correct. If less money is borrowed, there is less risk of cash flow and equity value volatility due to the use of financial leverage.

   C is not correct because the risk related to changes in interest rates remains. The investor may be able to accept slightly more leverage and mitigate the interest rate risk associated with debt by locking in the current interest rate with a long-term, fixed-rate amortizing loan. If interest rates rise, however, the value of real estate will likely be affected even if the investor did not borrow any money. Higher interest rates mean investors require a higher rate of return on all assets. In addition, the resale price of the property will likely depend on the cost of debt to the next buyer, who may be more likely to rely on higher leverage to finance the purchase.

   B is not correct because there is still risk of inflation, although real estate tends to have a low amount of inflation risk. But borrowing less money doesn't necessarily mean the property is less affected by inflation. Furthermore, inflation benefits fixed-rate borrowers who are able to repay debt in the future with cash that is worth less than cash borrowed today.

# ECONOMIC VALUE DRIVERS, ROLE IN PORTFOLIO, AND RISK/RETURN OF REAL ESTATE INVESTMENTS RELATIVE TO STOCKS AND BONDS

3

☐ explain portfolio roles and economic value determinants of real estate investments

☐ discuss commercial property types, including their distinctive investment characteristics

## Economic Drivers

Real estate return drivers are straightforward. Cash flow is a function of rental income, operating expenses, leverage, and capital spending. The contributors to cash flow are, in turn, driven by the supply of space, demand for space, and other economic factors. Investment vehicle valuation depends on the risk premium investors expect from real estate.

Long-term demographic trends, along with population growth, are major drivers of real estate demand. College graduates and non-child households moving to urban centers, new families moving to suburban markets, and elderly people moving to assisted living facilities are just a few of the demand drivers that have been widely discussed.

Exhibit 3 shows major economic factors that affect demand for the major property types.

### Exhibit 3: Major Factors Affecting Real Estate Demand by Sector

| | | Multi-Family | Retail | Hotel | Office | Industrial |
|---|---|---|---|---|---|---|
| **Macro Factors (affect all sectors)** | GDP growth | ✓ | ✓ | ✓ | ✓ | ✓ |
| | Population growth | ✓ | ✓ | ✓ | ✓ | ✓ |
| | Job creation | ✓ | ✓ | ✓ | ✓ | ✓ |
| | Wage growth | ✓ | ✓ | ✓ | ✓ | ✓ |
| | Regulatory | ✓ | ✓ | ✓ | ✓ | ✓ |
| | Taxes | ✓ | ✓ | ✓ | ✓ | ✓ |
| **Individual (Consumer)** | Household formations | ✓ | ✓ | | | |
| | Personal income | ✓ | ✓ | ✓ | | |
| | Consumer confidence | ✓ | ✓ | ✓ | | |
| | Consumer credit | ✓ | ✓ | ✓ | | |
| **Business Environment** | Retail sales growth | | ✓ | | | ✓ |
| | Consumer spending | | ✓ | ✓ | | ✓ |
| | Business formations | ✓ | | ✓ | ✓ | ✓ |
| | Business investment | | | ✓ | ✓ | ✓ |
| | Business confidence | | | ✓ | ✓ | ✓ |

|  | | Multi-Family | Retail | Hotel | Office | Industrial |
|---|---|---|---|---|---|---|
| Industrial | Industrial production | | | | | ✓ |
|  | Trade, transport, and logistics | | | | | ✓ |
|  | Changing supply routes | | | | | ✓ |

The list is by no means exhaustive. The relative importance of each measure can vary by market, property type, and timing of the business and real estate cycle, especially for rapid, extreme changes in the economic factors. Over the course of a full business cycle, however, each factor's relative importance for a market or property type tends to remain stable.

Risks tend to be greatest for those property-type sectors in which tenant/occupant demand for space can fluctuate most widely in the short term (notably, hotels), leases are shorter, and dislocations between supply and demand are most likely to occur (notably, office and hotel). However, the quality and locations of properties, leasing success, and financing status/access to capital are also extremely important factors in determining the investment risk profile.

*Macro Factors*

Several macro factors affect all major real estate sectors. These macro factors include: GDP growth, population growth, job creation, wage growth, regulations, and taxes. GDP growth is generally the most important single economic factor affecting the outlook for all property types.

*Job creation* tends to be reflected in increased demand for office space and in requirements for more retail space to cater to related increases in spending. Job creation also tends to be reflected in the following:

1. increased demand for multi-family accommodation as newly employed people gain the financial means to rent their own accommodations;
2. greater hotel room demand as both leisure and business travel increase in response to an expanded workforce.

Job creation is also a driver for many of the specialty sectors, including self-storage and data centers.

*Wage growth*, increases in disposable income, and increased consumer spending generally will support retail sales growth. Even as retail sales rise, online retailers have continued to pick up market share. During the 2019 holiday season, for example, US retail sales increased 4.1% annually, whereas online and non-store sales rose 14.6% (excluding automobile dealers, gas stations, and restaurants, according to the National Retail Federation). Large regional shopping centers and department stores experienced the greatest pressure. Retailers' success or failure and landlords' ability to replace weak tenants with stronger tenants or reposition properties influence rental income and occupancy directly (through rental rates based on a percentage of sales) and indirectly (through tenants' ability to pay rent).

*Individual (Consumer) Factors*

*Household formation* is one of the largest drivers of apartment demand. Income, wage growth, and consumer confidence all determine whether residents can afford to move to larger, higher-quality, better-located units or buy a home.

### Industrial Factors

Industrial manufacturing and warehouse distribution centers have seen increased demand from global trade in and near port cities. Online sales are shifting traditional transportation patterns as retailers look to store inventory closer to customers to speed delivery times. In addition, some brick-and-mortar retailers are allocating more retail space to holding inventory for delivery of online sales.

### Real Estate Cycles

As discussed elsewhere, the supply side of the real estate economic cycle is driven by the following types of periods:

- *oversupply*—when occupancy and rental rates are low; and
- *undersupply*—when occupancy and rents are high.

Property types with long development and construction periods are more prone to supply–demand dislocations for the following reasons:

1. new construction typically commences in a booming economy when demand for space cannot be accommodated by existing supply and rents rise high enough to provide developers with an attractive return;
2. properties already under development continue to be completed for two or three years after a recession eventually arrives and depresses demand; and
3. the large size of many facilities (especially, landmark office properties), complicated mixed-use properties, or convention center hotels further exacerbate excess supply on completion.

---

**KNOWLEDGE CHECK**

## Economic Value Drivers

1. Which of the following statistics is likely to be most relevant for all of the following: office, industrial, and hotel properties?

   **A.** Business confidence

   **B.** Household formation

   **C.** Industrial production

   **Solution**

   A is correct. Companies are more likely to expand their business and engage in business travel when business confidence is rising. Household formations have an indirect effect on these sectors and are most relevant to the multi-family sector. Changes in industrial production are less directly tied to the office and hotel markets.

2. In addition to the market and property-specific analysis of occupancy, rental rate, lease expiry, and financing statistics, analysts of office properties are *most likely* to pay particular attention to trends in:

   **A.** retail sales growth.

   **B.** household formation.

   **C.** job creation.

   **Solution**

   C is correct. Job creation is most significant for office REITs. Household formations are more significant for multi-family and retail REITs than for office

REITs, whereas retail sales growth is more significant for shopping center/retail and industrial REITs than for office REITs.

3. Which of the following property sectors would be expected to experience the *greatest* cash flow volatility?

   **A.** Industrial
   **B.** Hotel
   **C.** Shopping center

   **Solution**

   B is correct. Hotel room demand fluctuates with economic activity and business and consumer confidence; there are no long-term leases on hotel rooms to protect hotel REITs' revenue streams from changes in demand. Industrial and shopping center REITs benefit from long-term leases on their properties and from the relatively mild dislocations between supply and demand caused by the construction of new space in these subsectors.

## Role of Real Estate in an Investment Portfolio

In addition to the core property types, a **core real estate investment style** or strategy is further defined as investing in high-quality, well-leased, core property types with low leverage (no more than 30% of asset value) in the largest markets with strong, diversified economies. It is a conservative strategy designed to minimize real estate–specific risks, including leasing, development, and speculation in favor of steady returns. Hotel properties are excluded from the core categories because of the higher cash flow volatility resulting from single-night leases and the greater importance of property operations, brand, and marketing.

There are many different types of equity real estate investors, ranging from individual investors to large pension funds, sovereign wealth funds, and publicly traded real estate companies. Hereafter, for simplicity, the term *investor* will refer to an equity investor in real estate. Investors typically invest in real estate for one or more of the following five reasons:

1. current income;
2. capital appreciation;
3. inflation hedge;
4. diversification; and
5. tax benefits.
6. *Current income*: Investors may expect to earn current income on the property through letting, leasing, or renting the property. Investors expect that market demand for space in the property will be sufficient to produce net income after collecting rents and paying operating expenses. This income constitutes part of an investor's return. The amount available to the investor will be affected by taxes and financing costs. Historically, income has been the largest component of investor return.
7. *Capital appreciation*: Any price increase also contributes to an investor's total return. Investors may anticipate selling properties after holding them for a period of time and realizing the capital appreciation.

8. *Inflation hedge*: Investors may expect both rents and real estate prices to rise in an inflationary environment. If rents and prices do, in fact, increase with inflation, then equity real estate investments provide investors with an inflationary hedge. This means that the real rate of return may be less volatile than the nominal rate of return for equity real estate investments.

9. *Diversification*: Investors may anticipate diversification benefits. Real estate performance has not typically been highly correlated with the performance of other asset classes—such as stocks, bonds, or cash—so adding real estate to a portfolio may lower the overall risk of the portfolio (that is, the volatility of returns) relative to the expected return.

   Correlation data suggest that real estate property exposure, both private and listed, provides significant diversification benefits. Exhibit 4 shows correlations of annual returns for the 10-year period from 2010 through 2019 that are based on property indexes as well as fixed income, global equities, and global consumer price index (CPI) data.

**Exhibit 4: 10-Year Asset Class Correlations, 2010–2019**

| Indices | Global CPI | Bloomberg Barclays Global Agg. USD Unhedged | Private RE GREFI | Public RE FTSE EPRA Nareit Developed | MSCI Global World Equities |
|---|---|---|---|---|---|
| Annualized Return | 2.6% | 2.5% | 5.9% | 9.2% | 10.3% |
| Global CPI | 1 | 0.42 | −0.53 | 0.05 | −0.22 |
| Bloomberg Barclays Global Agg. USD Unhedged | | 1 | −0.46 | 0.50 | 0.28 |
| Private RE: GREFI | | | 1 | −0.47 | −0.34 |
| Public RE: FTSE EPRA Nareit Developed | | | | 1 | 0.67 |
| MSCI Global World Equities | | | | | 1 |

Note that the correlation matrix indicates potential for diversification benefits of adding private equity real estate investment to a stock and bond portfolio; it shows negative correlations of −0.34 versus global equity and −0.46 versus global bonds. When real estate is publicly traded, it tends to behave more like the stock market than the real estate market, at least in the short run, as evidenced by a positive correlation of +0.67 versus global equity and +0.50 versus global bonds. Several studies have shown that listed real estate can perform similarly to private real estate in the medium term after adjusting for leverage and the lagged and smoothed performance of private real estate. Some argue that because private real estate indexes are based on infrequent appraisals or market transactions, however, their performance lags changes in the listed markets, which dampens price volatility and correlations with stock indexes.

10. *Tax benefits*: A final reason for investing in real estate for some investors is the preferential tax benefits that may result. Private real estate investments may receive favorable tax treatment compared with other investments. For example, the preferential tax treatment in the United States comes from the fact that real estate can be depreciated for tax purposes over a shorter period (i.e., faster) than the period over which the property actually deteriorates. In many countries, REIT structures also offer tax benefits because

in those countries, REITs do not pay corporate income taxes on real estate income as long as the income is distributed to shareholders. Exhibit 5 shows the minimum profit distribution obligation for various markets, typically 90% or more.

### Exhibit 5: Most REITs Required to Distribute at Least 90% of Income

| Market | Minimum Profit Distribution Obligation |
|---|---|
| United States | 90% of taxable ordinary income |
| Japan | 90% of distributable profits |
| Hong Kong SAR | 90% of net income |
| United Kingdom | 90% of property rental profits |
| Germany | 90% of annual net income |
| Australia | 100% of trust income |
| Singapore | 90% of tax transparent income |
| Canada | 100% of income |
| Sweden | No REIT regime |
| France | 100% of taxable profit |
| Netherlands | 100% of taxable profit |

*Notes:* Ordered by market capitalization based on the FTSE EPRA Nareit Global Developed Real Estate Index Series, as of 31 December 2019. Exhibit 5 represents a simple view of dividend distribution requirements. Rates may vary depending on the source of income, such as capital gains on property sales, income from real estate securities, and non-real estate income.
*Source:* European Public Real Estate Association, "EPRA Global REIT Survey 2019" (2019).

> **KNOWLEDGE CHECK**
>
> ## Motivations for Investing in Real Estate
>
> 1. Why would an investor want to include real estate equity investments in a portfolio that already has a diversified mixture of stocks and bonds?
>
> **Solution**
>
> Real estate equity offers diversification benefits because it is less than perfectly correlated with stocks and bonds—for direct ownership (private equity investment) in particular. In other words, there are times when stocks and bonds may perform poorly while private equity real estate investments perform well, and vice versa. Thus, adding real estate equity investments may improve the risk-adjusted return of the portfolio.

## Real Estate Risk and Return Relative to Stocks and Bonds

Total returns from investing in real estate have proved attractive on an absolute basis. Real estate investment has appealed to investors for providing income with the possibility for income growth. The structure of leases, which are legal agreements requiring the tenant to make periodic payments to the space owner, and exposure to underlying tenant credits give real estate its bond-like characteristics. Like bond prices, real estate values are sensitive to changes in interest rates, inflation, and associated risk premiums.

At the end of the lease term, however, there will be uncertainty as to whether the tenant will renew the lease or the landlord will be required to find a new tenant and what the rental rate will be at that time. These issues depend on the availability of competing space and also on factors that affect the profitability of the companies leasing the space and the strength of the overall economy, in much the same way that stock prices are affected by the same factors. These factors give a stock market characteristic to the risk of real estate.

On balance, because of these two influences (bond-like and stock-like characteristics), core real estate, as an asset class, is expected to have a risk and return profile that falls between the risk and return profiles of stocks and bonds.

By this, we mean the risk and return characteristics of a portfolio of real estate versus a portfolio of large-cap stocks and a portfolio of investment-grade bonds. Individual real estate investments or portfolios could certainly have risk that is greater or less than that of an individual stock or bond holdings or portfolios. The more aggressive real estate investment strategies, such as accepting high financial leverage or development risk, carry higher return expectations accompanied by higher volatility. Exhibit 6 illustrates the basic expected risk–return relationships of stocks, bonds, and core private real estate investments. In Exhibit 6, expected risk is measured by the standard deviation of expected returns. Given different correlations with stock and bond returns, it should be evident that adding real estate to a multi-asset-class portfolio expands the efficient frontier.

**Exhibit 6: Expected Returns and Risks of Core Private Real Estate Compared with Stocks and Investment-Grade Bonds**

### KNOWLEDGE CHECK

### Investment Risk

1. Which is a riskier investment: core private real estate or investment-grade bonds? Explain why.

   **Solution**

   Historically, core private equity real estate with modest leverage is riskier than investment-grade bonds. Although real estate leases offer income streams somewhat like those of bonds, the income expected when leases

> renew can be uncertain and will depend on market conditions at that time—unlike the more certain face value of a bond at maturity.

## Classifications

Commercial property types include the following:

- *Residential properties*—multi-family and single-family properties that are non-owner occupied, purchased with the intent to rent out in order to produce income.
- *Non-Residential properties*—commercial properties typically described by their end use, such as:
    - *Office buildings*—high-rise buildings, office parks, etc.
    - *Industrial and warehouse*—factories, show rooms, warehouses, industrial parks, etc.
    - *Retail*—shopping centers, malls, etc.
    - *Hospitality*—hotels, restaurants, recreational facilities, etc.
    - *Other*—a large variety of custom projects

Details of the various commercial property types are provided below.

**Residential properties** include *single-family detached houses* and *multi-family properties*, such as apartments. Residential real estate properties, particularly multi-family properties, purchased with the intent to let, lease, or rent (in other words, produce income) are typically included in the category of **commercial real estate properties** (sometimes called income-producing real estate properties).

Multi-family properties contain multiple residential units. The names given to the individual units, such as apartments or flats, vary by region. A multi-unit building may be owned by one investor, or each unit may be owned by a separate investor, who may occupy or rent the unit. Multi-family housing is usually differentiated by location (urban or suburban), structure height (high-rise, mid-rise, low-rise, or garden apartments or townhouses), and amenities (pool, balcony, exercise facilities, concierge services, etc.).

**Non-residential properties** include commercial properties other than multi-family properties, farmland, and timberland. Commercial real estate is by far the largest class of real estate for investment and is the focus of this reading. Commercial real estate properties are typically classified by end use. In addition to multi-family properties, core institutional commercial real estate properties include office, industrial and warehouse, and retail properties. Hospitality is sometimes included among the major commercial categories, but the higher cash flow volatility and the much greater importance of operations exclude it from being described as one of the core real estate sectors.

Note, however, that the same *building* can serve more than one end use and can contain residential as well as non-residential uses of space. A property that has a combination of end users is usually referred to as a *mixed-use development*. Thus, the classifications should be viewed mainly as a convenient way of categorizing the use of space for the purpose of analyzing the determinants of supply and demand and economic performance for each type of space.

- *Office* properties range from major multi-tenant office buildings found in the central business districts of most large cities to single-tenant office buildings. They are often built with the needs of specific tenants in mind (known in real estate terms as *build to suit* if it is for one occupant). Examples of properties developed and built considering the needs of prospective tenants would be a medical office building near a hospital or the office headquarters of a large company.

At other times, new construction will begin after an anchor tenant has committed to occupy a large portion of the building and reduced the lease-up risk for the developer. Developments that are preleased to some or all of the tenants are easier to finance than "speculative" construction, which proceeds without tenant commitments.

In some markets, speculative development is the norm. In general, speculative construction increases as the property cycle heats up. After a real estate bust, lenders may require preleasing as a condition for financing new development. As the cycle recovers, restrictions generally ease.

- *Industrial and warehouse* properties include wholesale and retail distribution centers, combination warehouse/showroom and office buildings, and light or heavy manufacturing facilities as well as associated warehouse space. Also included are special purpose buildings designed specifically for industrial use that would be difficult to convert to another use. Older buildings that originally had one use may be converted to another use.

  For example, office space may be converted to warehouse or light industrial space, and warehouse or light industrial space may be converted to residential or office space. Frequently, the conversion is based on the desirability of the area for the new use.

- *Retail* properties vary significantly in size and include the following: large regional shopping centers and malls with large department stores or big-box retailers as anchors and numerous smaller in-line stores between the anchors; neighborhood shopping centers with smaller anchor tenants and many in-line tenants; and standalone properties, such as a grocery store or restaurant. As indicated earlier, it is also common to find retail space combined with office space, particularly on the ground floor of office buildings in major cities, or residential space. Office tenants appreciate having restaurants, exercise facilities, and convenience stores in close proximity, and retailers benefit from the daily office-worker traffic.

- *Hospitality* properties vary considerably in size and available amenities. Motels and smaller hotels are used primarily as a place for business travelers and families to spend a night. These properties may have limited amenities and are often located very close to a major highway. Hotels designed for tourists who plan to stay longer usually have a restaurant, a swimming pool, and other amenities. They are also typically located near other attractions that tourists visit.

  Hotels at "destination resorts" provide the greatest number of amenities. Facilities at these resort hotels can be quite luxurious, with several restaurants, swimming pools, nearby golf courses, and so on. Hotels that cater to convention business may be either in a popular destination resort or located near the center of a major city.

- *Other specialty types* of commercial real estate are available for investors. Examples include a large variety of investment opportunities, such as hospitals, bioscience laboratories, self-storage, student housing, cell towers, data centers, parking facilities marinas, and sports complexes. The physical structure of a building intended for a specific use may be similar to the physical structure of buildings intended for other uses; for example, government office space is similar to other office space. In other cases, buildings intended for one use may not easily be adapted for other uses. For example, buildings used by universities and hospitals may not easily be adapted to other uses.

Some commercial property types are more management intensive than others. Of the main commercial property types, hotels require the most day-to-day management and are more like operating a business than multi-family, office, or retail space. Shopping centers (shopping malls) are also relatively management intensive because it is important for the owner to maintain the right tenant mix and promote the mall. Usually, investors consider properties that are more management intensive to be riskier because of the operational risks. Therefore, investors typically require a higher rate of return on these management-intensive properties.

> **KNOWLEDGE CHECK**
>
> ## Commercial Real Estate Segments
>
> 1. Commercial real estate properties are *most likely* to include:
>    - **A.** residential, industrial, hospitality, retail, and office.
>    - **B.** multi-family, industrial, warehouse, retail, and office.
>    - **C.** multi-family, industrial, hospitality, retail, and timberland.
>
> **Solution**
>
> B is correct. Commercial real estate properties include multi-family, industrial, warehouse, retail, and office, as well as hospitality and other. Residential properties include single-family, owner-occupied homes and income-producing (commercial) residential properties. Timberland is a unique category of real estate.

## Investment Characteristics by Property Type

In this section, the main factors that influence property supply and demand and typical lease terms are discussed. It is important to discuss lease terms because they affect a property's value and the risk/return profile of the investment.

High-quality, well-leased office, retail, industrial/warehouse, and multi-family properties in strong markets are often considered the *core* property types used to create a portfolio that is relatively low risk. Hotels are usually considered riskier because there are no leases and their performance may be highly correlated with the business cycle—especially if they have a restaurant and depend on convention business. Specialty properties are excluded because the substitutability of the space is relatively low. It does not matter much what type of tenant occupies an office, retail, or distribution facility as long as the tenant blends well with the overall tenant mix and its credit quality is acceptable. Hospitals and cell towers have only one type of tenant, and the facilities are not easily converted to other uses.

For each property type, location is the critical factor in determining value. Properties with the highest value per unit of space are in the best locations and have modern features and functionality. Moderately valued properties are typically in adequate but not prime locations and/or have slightly outdated features. Properties with the lowest values per unit of space are in poor locations and have outdated features.

*Common Types of Leases*

An important consideration in commercial leases is whether the owner or tenant incurs the risk of operating expenses, such as utilities, increasing in the future. A **net lease** requires the tenant to be responsible for paying operating expenses, whereas a **gross lease** requires the owner to pay the operating expenses. Many apartment leases are gross leases, meaning the tenant pays one amount for use of the space and the property owner is responsible for operating expenses, including utilities and real estate taxes. It is also common to see residential tenants be responsible for their own energy (gas and electric) and telephone utilities, cable television costs, and internet access, in addition to the apartment's quoted rent.

Non-residential commercial properties that are net leased require tenants to pay a portion or all of the property's operating expenses in addition to the base or initial fixed rent. The amount varies by region and type of lease and is subject to negotiation. **Triple-net leases** (or NNN leases) require each tenant to pay its share of the following three operating expenses: common area maintenance (CAM) and repair expenses; property taxes; and building insurance costs. Such tenants are also responsible for insuring their own furnishings, equipment, systems, and so on, against fire, water damage, and other perils.

A long-term single-tenant net lease requires the tenant to pay all the operating expenses directly and a base rent to the property owner. This setup is common with a **sale-leaseback** and other types of long-term real estate financings. In a sale-leaseback, a company sells the building it owns and occupies to a real estate investor and the company then signs a long-term lease with the buyer to continue to occupy the building. The tenant is responsible for all aspects of property ownership while it leases the space, including major repairs, such as roof replacement. At the end of the lease, use of the property reverts to the landlord. The tenant is not responsible for normal property depreciation.

The base rent for net leases is lower than that for an equivalent gross lease because the tenant must bear the operating expenses and the risk of expenses being higher than expected. Alternatively, the landlord must charge a higher rent to earn a profit when it is responsible for all property operating expenses.

Not all leases are structured as net or gross leases. For example, a lease may be structured such that in the first year of the lease, the owner is responsible for paying the operating expenses; then, for every year of the lease after that, the owner pays for expenses up to the amount paid in the first year. Any increase in expenses above that amount is passed through to the tenant as an expense reimbursement. That is, the tenant bears the risk of any increase in expenses, although the owner benefits from any decline in expenses. In a multi-tenant building, the expenses may be prorated among the tenants on the basis of the amount of space they are leasing. Although having a small number of tenants can simplify managing a property, it increases risk. If one tenant gets into financial trouble or decides not to renew a lease, it can have a significant effect on cash flows.

> **KNOWLEDGE CHECK**
>
> ## Net and Gross Leases
>
> 1. What is the net rent equivalent for an office building where the gross rent is $20 per square foot and operating expenses are currently $8 per square foot?
>
>    **Solution**
>
>    On a gross lease, the owner pays the operating expense, whereas on a net lease, the tenant pays. So, we might expect the rent on a net lease to be $12 per square foot (or $20 psf – $8 psf). With the gross lease, the owner bears

> the risk of rising operating expenses, whereas the same is true of the tenant with net leases. If expenses decline, the benefit under a gross lease accrues to the owner through improved operating margins because the tenant still would pay $20. With the net lease, the tenant would benefit from a decline in operating expenses by paying a lower amount to the landlord, thereby reducing the tenant's total cost of occupancy.

Medium- to long-term leases frequently include contractual increases in rents known as rent bumps, rent step-ups, or step-up rents. The lease may specify a given step-up each year, such as 1% of the prior-period rent; a period step-up of, for example, 3% of the prior-period rent every five years; or occasionally an adjustment to mark rents to then-prevailing market rates. It is common to specify step-ups tied to inflation, either annually or cumulatively after several years. The higher a country's inflation rate, the more likely the tenant will pay a base rent plus annual inflation.

Long-term leases provide greater cash flow stability than short-term leases, especially when market-level rents are changing. When market vacancy is low and rents are rising, property owners benefit more from short-term leases because they can raise rents more frequently. The marking to market of rents hurts owners of properties with short-term leases when market rents decline. As above-market rent leases expire, tenants have greater ability to negotiate lower rates. Rental declines presumably occur when market vacancy increases, providing tenants with more space alternatives. When market rents decline, tenants cannot walk away from their leases in most countries unless they file for bankruptcy. When market rents increase, landlords cannot raise rents on existing leases (unless they negotiated a clause to reset rents from time to time on the basis of market conditions). Investors may prefer properties with long-term leases if they are risk averse or are concerned about declining market rents. Similarly, investors will expect greater returns from owning hotel properties, for example, than from a ground lease, at the other extreme, whereby a tenant has the right to develop and use the land property improvements for an extended period, with, say, 40 years remaining until lease expiration.

### Office

The demand for office properties depends heavily on employment growth. The typical amount of space used per employee is also important because it tends to increase when the economy is strong and decline when the economy is weak. There also has been a tendency for the average amount of space per employee to decrease over time as technology has allowed more employees to spend more time working away from the office and less permanent space is needed.

The average length of an office building lease varies. Lease terms may depend on the desirability of the property and the financial strength of the tenant, as well as other terms in the lease, such as provisions for future rent changes and whether there are options to extend the lease. Smaller tenants tend to sign 3- to 5-year leases, whereas larger tenants more commonly sign 5- to 10-year leases. Lease length, rent, renewal rights, and the tenant's ability to exit the lease vary by country, regulations, and culture and even through cycles and over time.

For example, in the United Kingdom since the early 1990s, lease terms have fallen. Rents are typically fixed for five years and then set at the higher of the then-market rent or contract rent upon review; these are known as upward-only rent reviews. Leases are typically on a full repairing and insuring (FRI) basis; the tenant is responsible for most costs. Therefore, detailed cost (expense) analysis is much less important in deriving net operating income—a critical measure in estimating the value of a commercial property—in the United Kingdom than in markets where operating costs are typically the responsibility of the owner.

*Industrial and Warehouse*

The demand for industrial and warehouse space heavily depends on the overall strength of the economy and economic growth. The demand for warehouse space also depends on import and export activity in the economy. Industrial leases are often long-term net leases, especially when the property is built specifically for the tenant, although gross leases or leases with expense reimbursements, as described for office properties, also exist.

Industrial and warehouse property values have shifted along with changing domestic and international trade routes. Developed economies outsourcing to low-cost manufacturing centers have supported the growth of global trade centers. The opening of the wider Panama Canal in 2016, which can accommodate the much larger neo-Panamax container ships, has allowed US Gulf Coast and East Coast ports to accept more shipments from eastern Asia and has taken some of the trade share from US West Coast ports. In 2019 and 2020, various trade restrictions disrupted global trade and COVID-19 accelerated the penetration of online retail sales and e-commerce. The retail trend has increased demand for space closer to population centers. CBRE Research reported that in 2019 approximately 13.8 million square feet of retail shopping space had been or was in the process of being converted to 15.5 million square feet of warehouse space. If developed economies continue to increase domestic manufacturing, commodity and goods distribution routes will shift again.

*Retail*

The demand for retail space depends heavily on trends in consumer spending. Consumer spending, in turn, depends on the health of the economy, population growth, job growth, consumer confidence, and savings rates.

Retail lease terms, including length of leases and rental rates, vary not only on the basis of the quality of the property but also by the size and the importance of the tenant. For example, in the United States, the length of leases is typically shorter (three to five years) for smaller tenants in a shopping center and is longer for larger, anchor tenants, such as department stores. Anchor tenants may be offered extremely favorable rental terms designed to attract them to the property. The quality of anchor tenants is often a key factor in attracting other tenants.

A unique aspect of many retail leases is the requirement that the tenants pay additional rent once their sales reach a certain level. This type of lease is referred to as a "percentage lease." The lease will typically specify a "minimum rent" or base rent that must be paid regardless of the tenant's sales and the basis for calculating percentage rent once the tenant's sales reach a certain level or breakpoint. For example, the lease may specify a minimum rent of $30 per square foot plus 10% of sales over $300 per square foot. Note that at the breakpoint of $300 per square foot in sales, we obtain the same rent per square foot based on either the minimum rent of $30 or 10% of $300. This is a typical way of structuring the breakpoint, and the sales level of $300 would be referred to as a "natural breakpoint."

> **KNOWLEDGE CHECK**
>
> ### Retail Rents
>
> 1. A retail lease specifies that the minimum rent is $40 per square foot plus 5% of sales revenue over $800 per square foot. What will the rent be if the tenant's sales are $1,000 per square foot?
>
> **Solution**
>
> The rent per square foot will be $40 + 5% × ($1,000 − $800), or $40 + $10 = $50. We get the same answer by multiplying 5% × $1,000 (= $50) because $800 is the "natural breakpoint," meaning that 5% of $800 results in the minimum rent of $40. A lease may not have the breakpoint set at this natural level; in which case, it is important that the lease clearly define how to calculate the rent.

*Multi-Family*

The demand for multi-family space depends on population growth, especially for the age segment most likely to rent apartments. The relevant age segment can be very broad or very narrow, depending on the particular culture's propensity to rent. Homeownership rates vary from country to country. The relevant age segment for renters can also vary by type of property being rented or by locale. For example, the average age of a property renter in an area attractive to retirees may be higher.

Demand also depends on how the cost of renting compares with the cost of owning—that is, the ratio of home prices to rents. As home prices rise and become less affordable, more people will rent. Similarly, as home prices fall, there may be a shift from renting to owning. Mortgage markets also influence rental property and homeownership costs. Countries with well-developed or subsidized mortgage markets will see greater use of leverage. Home ownership usually receives greater subsidies and permits more leverage than investment properties. Higher interest rates will make homeownership more expensive: For owners that partially finance the purchase with debt, the financing cost will be higher, whereas for other homeowners, the opportunity cost of having funds tied up in a home will increase. This increase in the cost of ownership may cause a shift toward renting. If interest rates decrease, there may be a shift toward homeownership.

Multi-family rental properties typically have leases that range from six months to two years, with one year being most common. The tenant may or may not be responsible for paying expenses, such as utilities, depending on whether each unit has a separate meter. The owner is typically responsible for the upkeep of common property, insurance, repair, and maintenance of the property. The tenant is typically responsible for cleaning the space rented and for insurance on personal property.

> **KNOWLEDGE CHECK**
>
> ### Economic Value Determinants
>
> 1. The primary economic driver of the demand for office space is most likely:
>
>    **A.** job growth.
>
>    **B.** population growth.

> **C.** growth in savings rates.
>
> **Solution**
>
> A is correct. Job growth is the main economic driver of office demand, especially for jobs in industries that are heavy users of office space, such as finance and insurance. As the number of jobs increases, companies need to provide office space for the new employees. Population growth may indirectly affect the demand for office space because it affects demand and job growth. Growth in savings rates affects consumer spending and the demand for retail space.
>
> 2. The demand for which of the following types of real estate is likely most affected by population demographics?
>
>    **A.** Office
>
>    **B.** Multi-family
>
>    **C.** Industrial and warehouse
>
>    **Solution**
>
>    B is correct. Population demographics are a primary determinant of the demand for multi-family space.

# CONSIDERATIONS IN ANALYSIS AND DUE DILIGENCE

☐ explain the due diligence process for both private and public equity real estate investments

Direct real estate investors, their advisers, appraisers, and lenders should perform thorough due diligence before acquiring properties or making secured loans. Property value will be based on several factors, such as cash flow outlook, market conditions, and prices paid for recent properties. Therefore, due diligence should include an analysis of all the cash flow drivers and liabilities. In addition, other qualitative factors must be considered. For example, whether the seller/borrower has clear title to the property.

Indirect investors should also perform due diligence on REITS and REOCs to determine whether the share valuation is appropriate before making investment decisions. Much of the information about public companies can be found in public filings of annual audited financial statements, quarterly reports, and investor presentations.

The purpose of due diligence is to identify potential problems that have not been disclosed by the seller that could negatively impact value.

Property due diligence should include an examination of the following.

### Market review

- Understand market trends, including local market population, job, and income growth.
- Understand expected additions to supply and space absorption rates (how much net space is leased each year).
- Understand tenant preferences; building amenities; market rents; and expense trends.

**Lease and rent review**

- Compare the tenant rents with market rent forecasts and lease length to determine how much rents will change when leases expire.
- Review the lease expiration timeline for all tenants. A landlord may see approximately 20% of the leases expire in any given year. Or there may be some years with large lease expirations.
- Analyze the history of rental payments, late payments, and any defaults for the major tenants.

**Review costs of re-leasing**

- Review costs and incentives provided to both renewing and new tenants.
- Costs typically include commissions paid to real estate brokers and downtime between leases.
- Incentives typically include a period of free rent and allowances for tenants' improvements to their space
- These costs are typically not included in annual operating income. Instead, these expenses are capitalized and amortized over the length of the lease.

**Review documentation**

- Review copies of bills for operating expenses, for example, utility bills and real estate taxes.
- Review multiple years of *audited financial statements*. The cash flow statements will provide perspective on operating expenses and revenue trends.
- Look for evidence of overstated income (underspending on capital expenditures) or overstated occupancy (tenant incentives)

**Property inspections and service agreements**

- Conduct an *environmental inspection* to be sure there are no issues, such as a contaminant material, at the site. Leaking fuel tanks can be a common problem.
- Conduct a *physical/engineering inspection* to be sure the property has no structural issues. Check the condition of the building systems, structures, and foundation and the adequacy of utilities.
- Review *service and maintenance agreements* to determine whether recurring problems exist.
- Conduct a *property survey* to determine whether the planned physical improvements are in the boundary lines of the site and to find out if any easements would affect the value.

**Legal documentation and tax compliance**

- Conduct a *title search* by reviewing the ownership history. Make sure there are no issues related to the property title and that the property is not subject to any previously unidentified liens.
- Verify that the property is compliant with *zoning laws, environmental regulations*, parking ratios, and so on.

- Verify that *property taxes, insurance, special assessments*, and so on, have been paid.

During the due diligence process, if differences in income, liabilities, property structural problems, legal issues, or other issues are discovered, the investor should adjust the valuation model accordingly. Then, the potential investor can try to renegotiate a lower price or look for another investment opportunity.

> **KNOWLEDGE CHECK**
>
> ## Due Diligence
>
> 1. What is the primary purpose of due diligence?
>    **Solution**
>    Due diligence is done to identify legal, environmental, physical, and other unanticipated problems that have not been disclosed by the seller that could be costly to remediate or that could negatively affect value. If identified, an issue or issues could result in negotiating a lower price or allow the investor to walk away from the transaction.

> **EXAMPLE 2**
>
> ## IFC Sustainable Investments in Hotels
>
> The International Finance Corporation (IFC), a member of the World Bank Group, is the largest global development institution focused exclusively on leveraging the power of the private sector to tackle the world's most pressing development challenges. Working with private enterprises in more than 100 countries, IFC uses its capital, expertise, and influence to help eliminate extreme poverty and promote shared prosperity.
>
> Tourism is a major contributor to employment, foreign exchange earnings, and tax revenues for developing countries. Hotels and tourism generate economic activity for small and medium-sized enterprises (SMEs) , which supply goods and services during both construction and operations. The IFC has made many investments in hotels in countries around the world. Here, we highlight some ESG impacts of three such investments:
>
> - Ghana—Movenpick Ambassador Hotel;
> - Mali—Azalai Grand Hotel;
> - Maldives—Villingili Hotel (part of Shangri-La group).
>
> ## Social and Environmental Impacts of These Investments
>
> *Mali—Azalai Grand Hotel*
>
> - The hotel has implemented several corporate responsibility initiatives, for example, participating in the United against Malaria (UAM) campaign.
> - The hotel has implemented international standards in such areas as sewage treatment, waste disposal, power and water conservation, and employee safety.

> ### Ghana—Movenpick Ambassador Hotel
>
> - The hotel has been awarded a Green Globe certificate, an industry certification program for sustainable tourism
> - Engages with local artists to produce original artwork for the hotel and established an art academy. The hotel decorates with over 800 pieces of Ghanaian art, including wood carvings, textile weavings, and paintings.
>
> ### Maldives—Villingili Hotel (part of Shangri-La group)
>
> - Globally known for its commitment to bio-diversity and environmental sustainability through its Eco Centre, which sponsors the Reef Care project and other activities.
> - Maintains an excellent record of managing environmental, health, and safety measures.
>
> *Source:* https://www.ifc.org/wps/wcm/connect/industry_ext_content/ifc_external_corporate_site/trp/news/restored_tourism_casestudy_hotels_2016

## 5. INDEXES

discuss real estate investment indexes, including their construction and potential biases

An investor will find a variety of real estate indexes to choose from and may find one that seems representative of the market of interest to them. There are real estate indexes that measure:

- property income performance,
- property total return,
- investment fund performance, and
- listed security returns.

Investors should be aware, however, of how the index is constructed and the inherent limitations resulting from the construction method. Investors should also be aware that the apparent low correlation of real estate with other asset classes may be due to limitations in real estate index construction.

### Appraisal-Based Indexes

Many indexes rely on appraisals to estimate how the value of a portfolio of properties or the real estate market in general is changing over time. Property and private real estate investment indexes often rely on appraisals to estimate values because there usually are not sufficient transactions of the same property to rely on transactions to indicate value. Even though real estate transactions may be occurring, they are not for the same property; differences in sale prices (transaction prices) can be due to changes in the market or differences in the characteristics of the property (size, age, location, and so on). Appraisal-based indexes combine valuation information from individual properties and provide a measure of market movements.

For example, a well-known index that measures the change in values of real estate held by institutional investors in the United States is the NCREIF Property Index (NPI). Members of NCREIF (National Council of Real Estate Investment Fiduciaries) who are investment managers and pension fund plan sponsors contribute to NCREIF every quarter information on appraised values, along with **net operating income (NOI)**, capital expenditures, and other information, such as occupancy. This information is then used to create an index that measures the performance of these properties quarterly. The return for all the properties is calculated as follows:

$$\text{Return} = \frac{\text{NOI} - \text{Capital expenditures} + (\text{Ending market value} - \text{Beginning market value})}{\text{Beginning market value}}$$

In this calculation, the beginning and ending market values are based on the appraisals of the properties.

The return calculated with this formula is commonly known as the *holding period return* and is equivalent to a single-period internal rate of return, or IRR (the IRR if the property were purchased at the beginning of the quarter at its beginning market value and sold at the end of the quarter at its ending market value). A similar equation is used to calculate the returns on stocks and bonds, but in those cases, an actual transaction price is typically used. Because this is not possible for real estate, the appraised value is used.

Note that the income return is not the same as cash flow, because cash flow is calculated after capital expenditures.

An index like the one described allows us to compare the performance of real estate with other asset classes, such as stocks and bonds. The quarterly returns are also important for measuring risk, which is often measured as the volatility or standard deviation of the quarterly returns. A major drawback, however, is that *the income component of real estate returns does not represent distributions to investors in real estate funds or REITs*. The total return for equities is based on capital appreciation plus dividends, not on the underlying company's operating income. The index does succeed, however, as a benchmark to compare returns among individual real estate funds.

The Global Real Estate Fund Index (GREFI) is a capitalization-weighted index incorporating local currency returns launched in 2014, with values going back to 2009. The GREFI is published quarterly. The GREFI combines data from three organizations as follows:

- The NCREIF, which began aggregating data and reporting property index-level returns in 1978, produces a variety of US real estate indexes based on such factors as property type and location.

- The European Association for Investors in Non-Listed Real Estate Vehicles (INREV) launched in 2003 and performs similar functions.

- The Asian Association for Investors in Non-Listed Real Estate Vehicles (ANREV) was formed in 2007 as a sister organization to INREV.

In addition to the ones discussed here, several other appraisal-based indexes are also available. For example, MSCI publishes a wide range of property indexes that cover markets worldwide, including emerging markets. These MSCI indexes, formerly called the MSCI IPD (Investment Property Databank) indexes, are calculated in a manner similar to that of the NPI.

> **KNOWLEDGE CHECK**
>
> ### Appraisal-Based Indexes
>
> 1. Why are appraisals often used to create real estate performance indexes?
>    **Solution**
>    Because properties do not transact very frequently, it is more difficult to create transaction-based indexes as is done for publicly traded securities. Appraisal-based indexes can be constructed even when there are no transactions by relying on quarterly or annual appraisals of the property. Of course, when no transactions occur, it is also difficult for appraisers to estimate value.

## Transaction-Based Indexes

Some indexes are based on actual transactions rather than appraised values. These indexes have been made possible by companies that collect information on enough transactions to create an index based only on transactions. In fact, both NCREIF and MSCI have transaction information that can be used for this purpose. When creating a transaction-based index, the fact that the same property does not sell very frequently is still an issue. So, to develop an index that measures changes in value on a quarterly basis as discussed for appraisal indexes, the fact that different properties sell every quarter needs to be controlled for. Some econometric techniques, usually involving regression analysis, are used to address the issue and to create the index in two main ways. One is to create what is referred to as a **repeat sales index**, and the other is to create what is referred to as a **hedonic index**.

A *repeat sales index*, as the name implies, relies on repeat sales of the same property. A particular property may sell only twice during the entire period of the index. But if at least some properties have sold each quarter, the repeat sales regression methodology can use this information to create an index. Of course, the more sales, the more reliable the index. In general, the idea supporting this type of index is that because it is the same property that sold twice, the change in value between the two sale dates indicates how market conditions have changed over time. Property and tenant credit quality, the lease maturity schedule, and market conditions may have changed, depending on the amount of time between sales. The regression methodology allocates this change in value to each time period—that is, each quarter on the basis of the information from sales that occurred that quarter. The details of how the regression works are beyond the scope of this reading. An example of a repeat sales index for commercial real estate in the United States is the suite of RCA Commercial Property Price Indices (RCA CPPI).

A *hedonic index* does not require repeat sales of the same property. It requires only one sale. The way it controls for the fact that different properties are selling each quarter is to include variables in the regression that control for differences in the characteristics of the property, such as size, age, quality of construction, and location. These independent variables in the regression reflect how differences in characteristics cause values to differ so that they can be separated from the differences in value due to changes in market conditions from quarter to quarter. Again, the details of this regression are beyond the scope of this reading. The point is that indexes based only on transactions can be constructed. They require a lot of data and are usually most reliable at the national level for the major property types, but sometimes they are reliable at the regional level within a country if sufficient transactions are available.

> **KNOWLEDGE CHECK**
>
> **Transaction-Based Indexes**
>
> 1. Describe two main ways of creating transaction-based indexes.
>
>    **Solution**
>
>    The two main ways are (1) a repeat sales index and (2) a hedonic index. A repeat sales index requires repeat sales of the same property; because it is the same property, controls for differences in property characteristics, such as its size and location, are not required. A hedonic index requires only one sale of a property and thus can usually include more properties than a repeat sales index; however, it must control for "hedonic" characteristics of the property, such as its size and location.

## Advantages and Disadvantages of Appraisal-Based and Transaction-Based Indexes

Appraisal-based indexes are often criticized for having appraisal lag, which results from appraised values tending to lag when there are sudden shifts in the market.

### Appraisal lags in rising and falling markets

In a rising market, transaction prices usually start to rise first. Then as these higher prices are reflected in comparable sales and investor surveys, they are captured in appraised values. Thus, appraisal-based indexes will tend to lag behind a rising market and may not capture the price increase until a quarter or more after it is reflected in transactions.

In a falling market, transaction prices would fall first. Later, these lower prices would be reflected in appraised values. Thus, appraisal-based indexes will tend to lag behind a falling market.

### Infrequent appraisals

Another cause of appraisal lag is that all properties in an appraisal-based index may not be appraised every quarter. A manager may assume the value has stayed the same for several quarters until he or she goes through the appraisal process to estimate a new value. Within a pooled fund, a manager may have a subset of properties appraised each quarter with the aim that each will be appraised at least annually. This situation causes a lag in the index.

### Impact on performance measurement and asset allocation

If the investment managers are all using appraised values to measure returns and if the index is based on appraised values, then it is an "apples to apples" comparison and less of a concern from a performance measurement perspective. If the purpose of the index is for comparison with other asset classes that are publicly traded, however, appraisal lag is more of an issue. Appraisal lag tends to smooth the index, meaning that it has less volatility. Thus, appraisal-based indexes may underestimate the volatility of real estate returns. Because of the lag in appraisal-based real estate indexes, they will also tend to have a lower correlation with other asset classes. (Exhibit 4 provides public and private real estate return correlations with fixed income and equities.) The smoothing effect will also overstate Sharpe ratios, which is problematic if the index is used in asset allocation models to determine how much of a portfolio should be allocated to real estate versus other asset classes. The appropriate allocation to and benefits from private real estate would likely be overestimated.

### Adjustment for appraisal lag

Appraisal lag can be adjusted for in two ways. The first is to "unsmooth" the appraisal-based index. Several techniques have been developed to do this, but they are beyond the scope of this reading. In general, the resulting unsmoothed index will have more volatility and more correlation with other asset classes. The second way of adjusting for appraisal lag is to use a transaction-based index when comparing real estate with other asset classes.

Transaction-based indexes tend to lead appraisal-based indexes for the reasons discussed, but they can be noisy (that is, they include random elements in the observations) because of the need to use statistical techniques to estimate the index. So, there may be upward or downward movements from quarter to quarter that are somewhat random even though in general (viewed over a year or longer) the index is capturing the correct movements in the market. The challenge for those creating these indexes is to try to keep the noise to a minimum through the use of appropriate statistical techniques and collecting as much data as possible.

> **KNOWLEDGE CHECK**
>
> ## Comparing Appraisal-Based and Transaction-Based Indexes
>
> 1. What are the main differences between the performance of appraisal-based and transaction-based indexes?
>
> **Solution**
>
> An appraisal-based index will tend to have less volatility and lag a transaction-based index, resulting in a lower correlation with other asset classes being reported.

## Real Estate Security Indexes

There are a wide variety of real estate security indexes available developed by index providers, stock exchanges, and trade organizations. These indexes include real estate equity security indexes, real estate debt security indexes, and other real estate indexes. Some examples are as follows:

- Real estate equity security indexes: Bloomberg, FTSE Russell, MSCI, Nikkei, and S&P Dow Jones.
- Real estate debt security indexes: CMBX
- Other real estate indexes: US REITs—FTSE and Nareit
- European and Asia Pacific listed real estate company indexes: FTSE, EPRA, and Nareit
- Various global real estate securities indexes: FTSE, EPRA, and Nareit

# Indexes

Depending on the split between REITs and REOCs, the indexes available from the various providers may contain equity REITs only, equity REITs and REOCs, or just REOCs. There are indexes based on market cap, country, property type, exchange listing, and major diversified index membership (e.g., S&P 500 REITs). In addition to total return, some indexes track capital appreciation and dividend yields.

# LEARNING MODULE

# 2

# Investments in Real Estate through Private Vehicles

by Steven G. Bloom, CFA, Jeffrey D. Fisher, PhD, David Kruth, CFA, Bryan D. MacGregor, PhD, MRICS, MRTPI, Ian Rossa O'Reilly, CFA, and Anthony Paolone, CFA.

*Steven G. Bloom, CFA, is at ARC Fiduciary (USA). Jeffery D. Fisher, PhD. David Kruth, CFA. Bryan MacGregor, PhD, MRICS, MRTPI. Ian Rossa O'Reilly, CFA (Canada). Anthony Paolone, CFA.*

| LEARNING OUTCOMES | |
|---|---|
| Mastery | The candidate should be able to: |
| ☐ | discuss the income, cost, and sales comparison approaches to valuing real estate properties |
| ☐ | compare the direct capitalization and discounted cash flow valuation methods |
| ☐ | estimate and interpret the inputs (for example, net operating income, capitalization rate, and discount rate) to the direct capitalization and discounted cash flow valuation methods |
| ☐ | calculate the value of a property using the direct capitalization and discounted cash flow valuation methods |
| ☐ | calculate and interpret financial ratios used to analyze and evaluate private real estate investments |

# SUMMARY

- Generally, three different valuation approaches are used by appraisers: income, cost, and sales comparison.
- The income approach includes direct capitalization and discounted cash flow methods. Both methods focus on net operating income as an input to the value of a property and indirectly or directly factor in expected growth.
- The cost approach estimates the value of a property based on adjusted replacement cost. This approach is typically used for unusual properties for which market comparables are difficult to obtain.

- The sales comparison approach estimates the value of a property based on what price comparable properties are selling for in the current market.
- When debt financing is used to purchase a property, additional ratios and returns calculated and interpreted by debt and equity investors include the loan-to-value ratio, the debt service coverage ratio, and leveraged and unleveraged internal rates of return.

# 1 INTRODUCTION

Direct property ownership and investment through private vehicles has long been the preferred choice of institutional investors, including insurance companies, pension funds, sovereign wealth funds, foundations, endowments, and high-net-worth families and individuals. Investors consider private real estate for capital gain, income, tax benefits, and low correlation with other asset classes. Long-term investors expect to earn an illiquidity premium, as same-property transactions are relatively rare. Direct property ownership allows owners to decide where and when to invest and when to sell.

# 2 INTRODUCTION TO VALUATION APPROACHES

discuss the income, cost, and sales comparison approaches to valuing real estate properties

In general, appraisers, or surveyors as they are known in the United Kingdom, use three different approaches to estimate real estate value: the **income approach**, the **cost approach**, and the **sales comparison approach**.

The *income approach* considers what price an investor would pay for a property based on forecasted cash flows discounted by an expected rate of return that is commensurate with the risk of the investment. It commonly relies on a discounted cash flow (DCF) analysis to calculate the present value of the expected future income from the property, including proceeds from resale at the end of a typical investment holding period, although there are other methods. The concept is that value depends on the expected rate of return that investors would require to invest in the property.

The *cost approach* considers what it would cost to reproduce or replicate the asset and deducts depreciation and other factors that reduce the value of the property. **Replacement cost** includes the expense of buying the land and constructing a new property on the site that has the same utility or functionality as the property being appraised (referred to as the subject property). Adjustments are made if the subject property is older or not of a modern design, if the location of the property is not ideal for its current use, or if it is not feasible (due to ordinance restrictions such as building codes, historical protections, etc.) to construct a new property in the current market. The concept is that you should not pay more for a property than the cost of buying vacant land and developing a comparable property. The development cost should include the developer's expected profit that would compensate the developer for development risk, including time and complexity, and the cost of financing development.

The *sales comparison approach* considers what similar or comparable properties (comparables) transacted for in the current market. It is also referred to as the market approach. Recent property sales serve as the basis for establishing market comparables

# Introduction to Valuation Approaches

(market comps), or units of comparison. Price per square meter or square foot of leasable area or total area is the most common measure. The UK-based RICS (Royal Institute of Chartered Surveyors), which promotes international valuation standards, identifies other common units of measurement, such as price per gross or net rent per square meter, price-to-revenue, and price-to-earnings before interest, taxes, depreciation, and amortization. Adjustments are made to reflect comparables' differences from the subject property, such as size, age, location, and condition of the property, and to adjust for differences in market conditions at the times of sale. The most recent transactions should carry more weight than prior-period sales. The concept is that you would not pay more than others are paying for similar properties.

### KNOWLEDGE CHECK

## London Office Property Valuation

You have been asked to appraise an office property in London. The following table provides some characteristics about the property and details on three other properties that sold in the past three months.

| Property/Market | Target Property | Taller Towers/City of London | Fairview Ally/Mayfair | Real Estate Road/Knightsbridge |
|---|---|---|---|---|
| Size (square feet) | 100,000 | 500,000 | 25,000 | 200,000 |
| Occupancy | 75% | 85% | 80% | 80% |
| Market Net Rent | £80 psf | £65 psf | £90 psf | £75 psf |
| Property Net Rent | £72 psf | £75 psf | £95 psf | £65 psf |
| Annual Net Rent for Property | £5,400,000 | £31,875,000 | £1,900,000 | £10,400,000 |
| Annual Operating Income | £4,590,000 | £28,687,500 | £1,710,000 | £8,840,000 |
| Age | 22 years | 5 years | 10 years | 15 years |
| Quality | Class B | Class A | Class A | Class B |
| Market Rent Trend | Flat | +2% | +5% | Flat |
| **Valuation Metrics** | | | | |
| Selling Price | ? | £725,000,000 | £40,000,000 | £175,000,000 |
| Price Per Square Foot | | £1,450 | £1,600 | £875 |
| Price/Rental Revenue | | 22.7× | 21.1× | 16.8× |
| Price/Operating Income | | 25.3× | 23.4× | 19.8× |

*Notes:* Figures are rounded. Values are hypothetical.

1. How would you estimate the property value using the information given, and what is your estimate?

   **Solution**

   The target property has more in common with the other Class B property based on quality, age, and rents trailing the market average. In contrast, the two Class A, or Grade A, properties, rent at a premium to the local market, and Taller Towers has the highest occupancy.

> As the appraiser, you may come up with a range of values based on the property in its current condition, with the in-place tenant leases and occupancy, and what the property would be worth if occupancy and income were higher.
>
> Using the most comparable property valuation metrics without any adjustments, values would range from a low of £87.5 million, based on a purchase price of £875 per square foot, to a high of £90.7 million using the same price-to-revenue multiple of 16.8×. A discount to these multiples may be warranted because the target property is older. Alternatively, if the target property's occupancy were to readily increase to 80%, the upper range of the valuation could move higher.
>
> It is beyond the scope of this example to consider how much it would cost to raise occupancy by spending capital to improve the vacant space and pay broker leasing commissions, nor are we considering the property potential if larger amounts were invested in renovating the property. If you were to estimate the property value following such a renovation, you would subtract the cost of the renovation from the post-renovation value.

These approaches are unlikely to result in the same value because they rely on different assumptions and availability of data to estimate the value. The idea is to try to triangulate on the market value by approaching the estimate three different ways. The appraiser may have more confidence in one or two of the approaches depending on the availability of data for each approach. Part of the appraisal process is trying to reconcile the differences in the estimates of value from each approach and coming up with a final estimate of value for the subject property.

## Highest and Best Use

Before we elaborate on the three approaches to estimating value, it is helpful to understand an important concept known as **highest and best use**. The highest and best use of a vacant site is the use that would result in the highest value (risk adjusted) for the land. Presumably, the developer that could earn the highest risk-adjusted profit based on time, effort, construction and development cost, leasing, and exit value would be the one to pay the highest price for the land.

Developers commonly back into the cost of land by estimating the expected exit price for the to-be-completed property, subtracting the all-in development costs, exit costs, and their minimum profit requirement. The amount that remains represents the most the developer would be willing to pay for the land. Developers would consider all possible uses given zoning constraints or incorporating the cost paid and time spent securing rezoning approval. Developers might consider the potential profit and risk associated with residential, office, retail, mixed-use, and other property types. Note that the highest and best use is not necessarily the use with the highest total value; it is the use that provides the developer with the highest profit based on the return required to compensate it for all the risks associated with the project.

The theory is that the land value is based on its highest and best use *as if vacant* even if an existing building is on the site. If an existing building is on the site that is not the highest and best use of the site, then the value of the building—not the land—will be lower.

> **KNOWLEDGE CHECK**
>
> ### Highest and Best Use
>
> Two uses have been identified for a property. One is an office building that would have a value after construction of $20 million. Development costs would be $16 million, including a profit for the developer. The second use is an apartment building that would have a value after construction of $25 million. Development costs, including a profit to the developer, would be $22 million.
>
> 1. What is the highest and best use of the site and the implied land value?
>    **Solution**
>
>    |  | Office | Apartment |
>    | --- | --- | --- |
>    | Value on completion | $20,000,000 | $25,000,000 |
>    | Cost to construct building | (16,000,000) | (22,000,000) |
>    | Implied land value | $4,000,000 | $3,000,000 |
>
>    An investor/developer could pay up to $4 million for the land to develop an office building but only $3 million for the land to develop an apartment building. The highest and best use of the site is an office building with a land value of $4 million. Of course, this answer assumes a competitive market with several potential developers who would bid for the land to develop an office building.

We will now discuss each of the approaches to estimating value in more detail and provide examples of each.

# 3 THE INCOME APPROACH TO VALUATION: DISCOUNT RATES AND THE DIRECT CAPITALIZATION OF NOI AND DCF METHODS

☐ compare the direct capitalization and discounted cash flow valuation methods

The **direct capitalization method** and the **discounted cash flow (DCF) method** are income approaches used to appraise or estimate the value of a commercial (income-producing) property. The direct capitalization method estimates the value of an income-producing property based on the level and quality of its net operating income. The DCF method discounts future projected cash flows to arrive at a present value of the property. Net operating income (NOI), a measure of income and a *proxy for cash flow*, is a focus of both approaches.

## Similarities in Approaches

Both income approaches focus on net operating income generated from a property. Recall, NOI is a measure of the income from the property after deducting operating expenses for such items as property taxes, insurance, maintenance, utilities, and repairs but before deducting any costs associated with financing (leverage) and before deducting federal income taxes. NOI in a real estate property context is similar to earnings before interest, taxes, depreciation, and amortization (EBITDA) in a financial reporting context. Note that neither property NOI nor EBITDA includes capital spending, financing costs, or taxes, and therefore, neither represents actual cash flow. That is not to say these considerations are unimportant. NOI is just the starting point.

Both income approaches consider growth and property quality. The first, the direct capitalization method, capitalizes the current NOI using an *implicit* growth **capitalization rate**, or "cap rate." That is, properties expected to generate faster growth will use a capitalization rate that results in a higher value, and properties with slower growth will use a capitalization rate that results in a lower value. When the capitalization rate is applied to the forecasted first-year NOI for the property, the implicit assumption is that the first-year NOI is representative of what the typical first-year NOI would be for similar properties.

The second approach, the DCF method, applies an explicit growth rate to construct an NOI stream from which a present value can be derived. As we will see, there is some overlap because even for the second method, we generally estimate a terminal value by capitalizing NOI at some future date. Income can be projected either for the entire economic life of the property or for a typical holding period with the assumption that the property will be sold at the end of the holding period. The discount rate should reflect the risk characteristics of the property. It can be derived from market comparisons or from specific analysis; we will examine both cases.

## The Direct Capitalization Method

The direct capitalization method capitalizes the current or expected NOI to calculate real estate value. If we think about the inverse of the cap rate as a multiplier, the approach is analogous to an income multiplier. The direct capitalization method differs from the DCF method, in which future operating income (a proxy for cash flow) is discounted at a discount rate to produce a present value.

### The Capitalization Rate and the Discount Rate

The cap and discount rates are closely linked but are not the same. Briefly, the discount rate is the return required from an investment and comprises the risk-free rate plus a risk premium specific to the investment. The cap rate is lower than the discount rate because it is calculated using the current NOI. So, the cap rate is like a current yield for the property. The discount rate is applied to current and future NOI, which may be expected to grow. In general, when income and value are growing at a constant compound growth rate, we have

$$\text{Cap rate} = \text{Discount rate} - \text{Growth rate}. \tag{1}$$

The growth rate is implicit in the cap rate in that the buyer incorporates cash flow growth into the value the buyer is willing to pay for the property, but we have to make it explicit for a DCF valuation. If the growth rate were negative, the cap rate would exceed the discount rate.

### Defining the Capitalization Rate

The capitalization rate is a very important measure for valuing income-producing real estate property. The cap rate is defined as follows:

$$\text{Cap rate} = \text{NOI/Value}, \tag{2}$$

where NOI is usually based on what is expected during the current or first year of ownership of the property. Sometimes the term *going-in cap rate* is used to clarify that it is based on the first year of ownership when the investor is *going into* the deal. (Later, we will explain that the *terminal cap rate* is based on expected income for the year after the anticipated sale of the property.)

The value used in Equation 2 is an estimate of what the property is worth at the time of purchase. If we rearrange Equation 2 and solve for value, we get the following equation:

Value = NOI/Cap rate. (3)

So, if we know the appropriate cap rate, we can estimate the value of the property by dividing its first-year NOI by the cap rate.

Where does the cap rate come from? The simple answer is that it is based on observing what other similar or comparable properties are selling for. Assuming that the sale price for a comparable property is a good indication of the value of the subject property, we have

Cap rate of comparable = NOI of comparable/Sale price of comparable. (4)

The cap rate is like a snapshot at a point in time of the relationship between NOI and value. It is somewhat analogous to the price–earnings (PE) multiple for a stock except that it is the reciprocal. The reciprocal of the cap rate is price divided by NOI. In the United Kingdom, the reciprocal of the cap rate is called the "years purchase" (YP). It is the number of years that it would take for income at the current level to be equal to the original purchase price. Just as stocks with greater earnings growth potential tend to have higher price–earnings multiples and, inversely, lower earnings yields, properties with greater income growth potential have higher ratios of price to current NOI and thus lower cap rates.

It is preferrable to observe several sales of similar properties before drawing conclusions about what cap rates investors are willing to accept for a property. As we will discuss later, there are also reasons why we would expect the cap rate to differ for different properties, such as what the future income potential is for the property—that is, how it is expected to change after the first year. This is important because the cap rate is only explicitly based on the first-year income. But the cap rate that investors are willing to accept depends on how they expect the income to change in the future and the risk of that income. These expectations are said to be implicit in the cap rate that investors are willing to accept at the time of purchase.

It is often necessary to make adjustments based on specific lease terms and characteristics of a market. For example, a similar approach is common in the United Kingdom, where the term "fully let property" is used to refer to a property that is leased at market rent because either it has a new tenant or the rent has just been reviewed. In such cases, the appraisal is undertaken by applying a capitalization rate to this rent rather than to NOI because leases usually require the tenant to pay all costs. The cap rate derived by dividing rent by the recent sale prices of comparables is often called the all-risks yield (ARY) and is shown in the following formula:

ARY = Rent/Recent sale prices of comparables. (5)

Note that the term "yield" in this case is used like a "current yield" based on first-year NOI. It is a cap rate and will differ from the total return that an investor might expect to get from future growth in NOI and value. If it is assumed, however, that the rent will be level in the foreseeable future (like a perpetuity), then the cap rate will be the same as the return and the all-risks yield will be an internal rate of return or yield to maturity.

In simple terms, the valuation is

Market value = Rent/ARY. (6)

Again, this valuation is essentially the same as dividing NOI by the cap rate as discussed earlier except the occupant is assumed to be responsible for all expenses, so the rent is divided by the ARY. In practice, management costs should also be considered—although operating costs falling on the landlord are typically much lower than in the United States. ARY is a cap rate and will differ from the required total return (the discount rate) an investor might expect to receive from future growth in NOI and value. When rents are expected to increase after every rent review, the investor's expected return will be higher than the cap rate. If rents are expected to increase at a constant compound rate, then the investor's expected return (discount rate) will equal the cap rate plus the growth rate, as was shown with Equation 1.

> **KNOWLEDGE CHECK**
>
> ## Capitalizing NOI
>
> 1. A property has just been let at an NOI of £250,000 for the first year, and the capitalization rate on comparable properties is 5%. What is the value of the property?
>
> **Solution**
>
> Value = NOI/Cap rate = £250,000/0.05 = £5,000,000.

Suppose the rent review for the property in Question Set 17 occurs every year and rents are expected to increase 2% each year. *An approximation of the IRR would simply be the cap rate plus the growth rate;* in this case, a 5% cap rate plus 2% rent growth results in a 7% IRR. Of course, if the rent review were less frequent, as in the United Kingdom where it is typically every five years, then we could not simply add the growth rate to the cap rate to get the IRR. But the IRR would still be higher than the cap rate if rents were expected to increase.

### Stabilized NOI

When the cap rate is applied to the forecasted first-year NOI for the property, the implicit assumption is that the first-year NOI is representative of what the typical first-year NOI would be for similar properties. In some cases, the appraiser might project an NOI to be used to estimate value that is different from what might actually be expected for the first year of ownership for the property if what is actually expected is not typical.

An example of this situation might be when a property is undergoing a renovation and has a temporarily higher-than-typical amount of vacancy until the renovation is complete. The purpose of the appraisal might be to estimate what the property will be worth once the renovation is complete. A cap rate will be used from properties that are not being renovated because they are more typical. Thus, the appraiser projects what is referred to as a **stabilized NOI**, which is what the NOI would be once the renovation is complete. This NOI is used to estimate the value. Of course, if the property is being purchased before the renovation is complete, a slightly lower price will be paid because the purchaser has to wait for the renovation to be complete to get the higher NOI. Applying the cap rate to the lower NOI of the renovation period will understate the value of the property because it implicitly assumes that the lower NOI is expected to continue.

> **KNOWLEDGE CHECK**
>
> ### Value of a Property to Be Renovated
>
> A property is being purchased that requires some renovation to be competitive with otherwise comparable properties. Renovations satisfactory to the purchaser will be completed by the seller at the seller's expense. If it were already renovated, it would have NOI of ¥9 million next year, which would be expected to increase by 3% per year thereafter. Investors would normally require a 12% IRR (discount rate) to purchase the property after it is renovated. Because of the renovation, the NOI will be only ¥4 million next year. But thereafter, the NOI is expected to be the same as it would be if it had already been renovated at the time of purchase.
>
> 1. What is the value of or the price a typical investor is willing to pay for the property?
>
>    **Solution**
>
>    If the property were already renovated (and the NOI had stabilized), the value would be as follows:
>
>    Value if renovated = ¥9,000,000/(0.12 − 0.03) = ¥100,000,000.
>
>    But because of the renovation, there is a loss in income of ¥5 million during the first year. If for simplicity we assume that this amount would have been received at the end of the year, then the present value of the lost income at a 12% discount rate is as follows:
>
>    Loss in value = ¥5,000,000/(1.12) = ¥4,464,286.
>
>    Thus, the value of the property is as follows:
>
>    | | |
>    |---|---|
>    | Value if renovated | ¥100,000,000 |
>    | Less loss in value | − ¥4,464,286 |
>    | = Value | ¥95,535,714 |
>
>    An alternative approach is to get the present value of the first year's income and the value in a year when renovated:
>
>    {¥4,000,000 + [¥9,000,000(1.03)]/(0.12 − 0.03)}/(1.12) = ¥95,535,714.

### Other Forms of the Income Approach

Direct capitalization usually uses NOI and a cap rate. However, there are some alternatives to the use of NOI and a cap rate. For example, a *gross income multiplier* might be used in some situations. The gross income multiplier is the ratio of the sale price to the gross income expected from the property in the first year after sale. It may be obtained from comparable sales in a way similar to what was illustrated for cap rates. The problem with using a gross income multiplier is that it does not explicitly consider vacancy rates and operating expenses. Thus, it implicitly assumes that the ratio of vacancy and expenses to gross income is similar for the comparable and subject properties. But if, for example, expenses were expected to be lower on one property versus another because it was more energy efficient, an investor would pay more for the same rent. Thus, its gross income multiplier should be higher. The use of a gross rent multiplier is also considered a form of direct capitalization but is generally not considered as reliable as using a capitalization rate.

# 4  THE DCF METHOD, THE RELATIONSHIP BETWEEN DISCOUNT RATE AND CAP RATE, AND THE TERMINAL CAPITALIZATION RATE

☐ estimate and interpret the inputs (for example, net operating income, capitalization rate, and discount rate) to the direct capitalization and discounted cash flow valuation methods

☐ calculate the value of a property using the direct capitalization and discounted cash flow valuation methods

The direct capitalization method typically estimates value by capitalizing the first-year NOI at a cap rate derived from market evidence. The DCF method (sometimes referred to as a yield capitalization method) involves projecting income beyond the first year and discounting that income at a discount rate (yield rate). The terms *yield rate* and *discount rate* are used synonymously in this discussion, as are the terms *yield capitalization* and *discounted cash flow analysis*.

## The Relationship between the Discount Rate and the Cap Rate

If the income and value for a property are expected to change over time at the same compound rate—for example, 3% per year—then the relationship between the cap rate and the discount rate is the same as in Equation 1:

Cap rate = Discount rate − Growth rate.

To see the intuition behind this, let us solve for the discount rate, which is the return that is required to invest in the property:

Discount rate = Cap rate + Growth rate.

Recall that the cap rate is based on first-year NOI. The growth rate captures how NOI will change in the future along with the property value. Thus, we can say that the investor's return (discount rate) comes from the return on first-year income (cap rate) plus the growth in income and value over time (growth rate). Although income and value may not always change at the same compound rate each year, this formula gives us insight into the relationship between the discount rate and the cap rate. Essentially, the difference between the discount and cap rates has to do with growth in income and value.

Intuitively, given that both methods start from the same NOI in the first year, you would pay more for an income stream that will grow than for one that will be constant. So, the price is higher and the cap rate is lower when the NOI is growing, which is what is meant by the growth being *implicit* in the cap rate. If the growth rate is constant, we can extend Equation 3 using Equation 1 to give

$$\text{Value of property} = NOI/(r - g), \tag{7}$$

where

$r$ = the discount rate (required return)

$g$ = the growth rate for income (given constant growth in income, value will grow at the same rate)

This equation is analogous to the dividend growth model applied to stocks. If NOI is not expected to grow at a constant rate, then NOIs are projected into the future and each period's NOI is discounted to arrive at a value of the property. Rather than project NOIs into infinity, NOIs typically are projected for a specified holding period, and a terminal value (estimated sale price) at the end of the holding period is estimated.

> **KNOWLEDGE CHECK**
>
> ## Growth Explicit Appraisal
>
> 1. NOI is expected to be $100,000 the first year, and after that, NOI is expected to increase at 2% per year for the foreseeable future. The property value is also expected to increase by 2% per year. Investors expect to get a 12% IRR given the level of risk; therefore, the value is estimated using a 12% discount rate. What is the value of the property today (at the beginning of the first year)?
>
>    **Solution**
>
>    $V = NOI/(r - g)$
>
>    $= \$100,000/(0.12 - 0.02)$
>
>    $= \$100,000/0.10$
>
>    $= \$1,000,000.$
>
>    The property value growth rate is not required to calculate the value of the property after the first year. However, it would be used in a DCF calculation to determine the property's terminal value.

## The Terminal Capitalization Rate

When a DCF methodology is used to value a property, one of the important inputs is generally the estimated sale price of the property at the end of a typical holding period. This input is often referred to as the estimated terminal value. Estimating the terminal value of a property can be quite challenging in practice, especially given that the purpose of the analysis is to estimate the value of the property today. But if we do not know the value of the property today, how can we know what it will be worth in the future when sold to another investor? We must also use some method for estimating what the property will be worth when sold in the future.

In theory, this value is based on the present value of income to be received by the *next* investor. But we usually do not try to project NOI for another holding period beyond the initial one. Rather, we rely on the direct capitalization method using the NOI of the first year of ownership for the next investor and a cap rate. The cap rate used to estimate the resale price or terminal value is referred to as a *terminal cap rate* or *residual cap rate*. It is a cap rate that is selected at the time of valuation to be applied to the NOI earned in the first year after the property is expected to be sold to a new buyer.

Selecting a terminal cap rate is challenging. Recall that the cap rate equals the discount rate less the growth rate when income and value are growing constantly at the same rate. Whether constant growth is realistic or not, we know that the cap rate will be higher (lower) if the discount rate is higher (lower). Similarly, the cap rate will be lower if the growth rate is expected to be higher, and vice versa. These relationships also apply to the terminal cap rate and the going-in cap rate.

The terminal cap rate could be the same, higher, or lower than the going-in cap rate, depending on the expected discount and growth rates at the time of sale. If interest rates are expected to be higher in the future, pushing up discount rates, then terminal cap rates might be higher. The growth rate is often assumed to be a little lower because the property is older at the time of sale and may not be as competitive. This situation would result in a slightly higher terminal cap rate. Uncertainty about what the NOI will be in the future may also result in selecting a higher terminal cap rate. The point is that the terminal cap rate is not necessarily the same as the going-in cap rate at the time of the appraisal.

### KNOWLEDGE CHECK

## Appraisal with a Terminal Value

1. Net operating income is expected to be level at $100,000 per year for the next five years because of existing leases. Starting in Year 6, the NOI is expected to increase to $120,000 because of lease rollovers and thereafter to increase at 2% per year. The property value is also expected to increase at 2% per year after Year 5. The investors in the property require a 12% return and expect to hold the property for five years. What is the current value of the property?

**Solution**

Exhibit 1 shows the projected NOI for this example. Because NOI and property value are expected to grow at the same constant rate after Year 5, we can calculate the cap rate at that time based on the discount rate less the growth rate. That gives us a terminal cap rate that can be used to estimate the value that the property could be sold for at the end of Year 5 (based on the income a buyer would get after that). We can then discount this value along with the income for Years 1–5 to get the present value.

### Exhibit 1: Projected Income

### Step 1:

Estimate resale price after five years.

Resale (residual) or "terminal" cap rate = 12% − 2% = 10%.

Apply this to NOI in Year 6:

Resale = $120,000/0.10 = $1,200,000.

Note that the value that can be obtained by selling the property at some point in the future is often referred to as the "reversion" by real estate professionals.

### Step 2:

Discount the level NOI for the first five years and the resale price.

PMT = $100,000.

FV = $1,200,000.

$n$ = 5.

$i$ = 12%.

Solving for PV, the current value of the property is estimated to be $1,041,390. Note that the implied going-in cap rate is ($100,000/$1,041,390) = 9.60%.

In Question Set 20, the going-in cap rate (9.6%) is lower than the terminal cap rate (10.0%). Investors would be willing to pay a higher price for the current NOI because they know that it will increase when the lease is renewed at market rents in five years. The expected rent jump on lease renewal is implicit in the cap rate.

As noted earlier, we often expect the terminal cap rate to be higher than the going-in cap rate because it is being applied to income that is more uncertain. Also, the property will be older and may have less growth potential or require increased spending. Finding a lower implied going-in cap rate in this example is consistent with this. At certain times, however, we would expect the terminal cap rate to be lower than the going-in cap rate—for example, if we think that interest rates and thus discount rates will be lower when the property is sold in the future or we expect markets to be a lot stronger in the future, with expectations for higher rental growth than in the current market. In general, the higher the risk, the higher the cap rate required to lift the investment return commensurately.

> **KNOWLEDGE CHECK**
>
> ## Appraisal with Level NOI
>
> 1. Suppose the NOI from a property is expected to be level at $600,000 per year for a long period of time such that, for all practical purposes, it can be assumed to be a perpetuity. What is the value of the property assuming investors want a 12% rate of return?
>
>    **Solution**
>
>    In this case, the growth rate is zero, so we have
>
>    Value = NOI/Discount rate.
>
>    Value = $600,000/0.12 = $5,000,000.
>
>    Note that in this case, the cap rate will be the same as the discount rate. This is true when there is no expected change in income and value over time.

> **KNOWLEDGE CHECK**
>
> ## Discounted Cash Flow Analysis
>
> You work for a real estate investment firm that has been presented with the opportunity to purchase a 10-year-old warehouse distribution facility in Perth, Australia. The property contains 20,000 square meters (m²) of leasable area that is 100% leased to three tenants. Two of the tenants have 10 years remaining on their respective leases. The third tenant has only three years left on its lease and has already indicated it will not renew the lease at expiration. One of the other tenants has indicated it would like to lease the space as soon as it becomes available as long as the property owner makes material improvements to the building.
>
> ### Part 1
>
> 1. Your manager has asked you to prepare a discounted cash flow analysis to determine whether the acquisition would meet the company's return targets. Based on the assumptions provided, calculate the first-year NOI, the

purchase price, and the terminal value. Note that the rent presented is net of all operating expenses.

| Assumptions | | | |
|---|---|---|---|
| Annual Net Rent per Square Meter | AUD 145.00 | Initial Cap Rate | 6.0% |
| Leasable Area (square meters) | 20,000 | Terminal Cap Rate | 7.0% |
| Lease 1 (m$^2$) | 6,897 | Exit Year | 7 |
| Lease 2 (m$^2$) | 6,897 | NOI in Year 9 (millions) | AUD 3.79 |
| Lease 3 (m$^2$) | 6,207 | | |

**Solution**

First-year NOI = AUD145/m$^2$ × 20,000 m$^2$ of leasable area

= AUD2.9 million.

Purchase price = Year 1 NOI/Cap rate = AUD2.9 million/6.0%

= AUD48.3 million.

Terminal value at the end of Year 7 = AUD3.79 million/7.0%

= AUD54.1 million.

## Part 2:

1. Why do you think your manager asked you to use a 6.0% acquisition cap rate and a 7.0% terminal cap rate?

**Solution**

The 6.0% cap rate would be based on the cap rate from recent property sales adjusted for location, property age and quality, and tenant/lease composition. The 7.0% terminal cap rate is 100 bps higher than the initial cap rate because of a combination of the following: The property will be older and, besides the renovation of one building, will have continued to depreciate; and a measure of conservatism is advisable. A higher cap rate implies a lower *relative* price based on future earnings.

## Part 3:

This part of the example illustrates the cash flow forecast, the DCF, and NPV/return analysis. Net property income increases at a 3.0% annual rate based on lease terms, which is consistent with the market. Additional capital spending and other below-the-line expenses that are not reported on the income statement are estimated at 3.5% of NOI. The forecast includes the large renovation during Year 4 to prepare the space vacated by the tenant whose lease expires at the end of Year 3 for one of the remaining tenants. Year 4 NOI includes a 20% increase above the 3.0% trend, which was negotiated with the tenant for the new lease, offset by six months of forgone rent during the renovation as incentive for the expanding tenant. Capital spending is also assumed to be lower in the year immediately preceding and the year following the renovation before returning to the steady-state trend. Recall that the NOI forecast needs to extend one year past the exit year to calculate the forward income that the next property buyer would use to value the property and present its own bid.

# The DCF Method, the Relationship between Discount Rate and Cap Rate, and the Terminal Capitalization Rate

## Cash Flow Forecast (AUD thousands)

| Property Net Operating Income: | Year 0 | Year 1 | Year 2 | Year 3 | Year 4 | Year 5 | Year 6 | Year 7 | Year 8 |
|---|---|---|---|---|---|---|---|---|---|
| Lease 1 | | 1,000.0 | 1,030.0 | 1,060.9 | 1,092.7 | 1,125.5 | 1,159.3 | 1,194.1 | 1,229.9 |
| Lease 2 | | 1,000.0 | 1,030.0 | 1,060.9 | 1,092.7 | 1,125.5 | 1,159.3 | 1,194.1 | 1,229.9 |
| Lease 3 | | 900.0 | 927.0 | 954.8 | 590.1 | 1,215.5 | 1,242.0 | 1,289.6 | 1,328.3 |
| Net Property NOI | | 2,900.0 | 2,987.0 | 3,076.6 | 2,775.5 | 3,466.6 | 3,570.6 | 3,677.7 | 3,788.0 |
| Capital Spending and Leasing Expense | | (101.5) | (104.5) | (74.3) | (1,094.4) | (78.8) | (125.0) | (128.7) | (132.6) |
| Property Cash Flow | | 2,798.5 | 2,882.5 | 3,002.3 | 1,681.2 | 3,387.8 | 3,445.6 | 3,549.0 | 3,655.4 |

The next table presents the unlevered discounted cash flow. Your manager suggests using a 7.0% discount rate for the investment based on the attractive, lower-risk-location, 10-year leases; the likelihood that an existing tenant will expand into the to-be-vacated space; and strong market fundamentals. The present value of the future cash flows is then compared with the acquisition price. (It is only a coincidence that the discount rate equals the terminal cap rate.) If the net present value is positive, the investment would create some value over the hurdle rate of return represented by the discount rate.

## Discounted Cash Flow Analysis (AUD thousands)

| | Year 0 | Year 1 | Year 2 | Year 3 | Year 4 | Year 5 | Year 6 | Year 7 |
|---|---|---|---|---|---|---|---|---|
| Initial outlay | −48,333 | | | | | | | |
| Annual property cash flow | | 2,799 | 2,882 | 3,002 | 1,681 | 3,388 | 3,446 | 3,549 |
| Exit value | | | | | | | | 54,114 |
| Total cash flow | (48,333) | 2,799 | 2,882 | 3,002 | 1,681 | 3,388 | 3,446 | 57,663 |
| Discount rate (input) | 7.0% | $1/(1+0.07)^1$ | $1/(1+0.07)^2$ | $1/(1+0.07)^3$ | $1/(1+0.07)^4$ | $1/(1+0.07)^5$ | $1/(1+0.07)^6$ | $1/(1+0.07)^7$ |
| Present value factor | | 0.9346 | 0.8734 | 0.8163 | 0.7629 | 0.7130 | 0.6663 | 0.6227 |
| Present value of property cash flows | | 2,615 | 2,518 | 2,451 | 1,283 | 2,415 | 2,296 | 35,910 |

### NPV and Return Analysis

| | | |
|---|---|---|
| Sum of present value of cash inflows | | 49,488 |
| Cash outlay | | (48,333) |
| Net present value of future CF | | 1,154 |
| IRR (Output) | | 7.4% |

The NPV of the property exceeds the acquisition price by AUD1.154 million. The positive net present value demonstrates that the investment would create value and excess return relative to the risk-adjusted cost of capital. The 7.4% expected IRR further confirms that the forecasted return would exceed the 7.0% discount rate.

## Part 4:

This part of the example provides an example of sensitivity analysis of price and NPV to various cap rates. There are two sensitivity tables: (1) a sensitivity analysis on the entry cap rate and (2) a sensitivity analysis on the exit cap rate.

### Sensitivity Tables (AUD thousands)

| | \multicolumn{5}{c}{Initial Capitalization Rate} | | | | |
|---|---|---|---|---|---|
| | 7.0% | 6.5% | 6.0% | 5.5% | 5.0% |
| Purchase price | 41,429 | 44,615 | 48,333 | 52,727 | 58,000 |
| NPV | 3,847 | 2,626 | 1,154 | (647) | (2,896) |

| | \multicolumn{5}{c}{Terminal Capitalization Rate} | | | | |
|---|---|---|---|---|---|
| | 8.0% | 7.5% | 7.0% | 6.5% | 6.0% |
| Exit price | 47,350 | 50,507 | 54,114 | 58,277 | 63,134 |
| NPV | (3,058) | (1,092) | 1,154 | 3,747 | 6,771 |

The preceding sensitivity tables present the range of net present values in thousands of Australian dollars for several entry and exit cap rates. The corresponding purchase and exit prices, also in thousands, are presented alongside the cap rates. The acquisition table is presented from lower asset price/higher cap rate to higher asset price/lower cap rate. The table indicates that the investor could pay more than AUD48.3 million, or the 6.0% cap rate on Year 1 NOI, and still exceed the cost of capital but not as much as AUD52.7 million, which equates to a 5.5% cap rate. In fact, the investor could pay approximately AUD51.1 million, the equivalent of a 5.67% cap rate, and still break even on the basis of the given discount rate. The breakeven purchase price represents the maximum value the investor could pay for the acquisition while holding all other factors constant without the net present value turning negative.

## 5. PRIVATE MARKET REAL ESTATE DEBT

> calculate and interpret financial ratios used to analyze and evaluate private real estate investments

Thus far, our focus has been on analyzing a property without considering whether debt financing would be on the property or whether it would be purchased on an all-cash basis. The reason is that the way a property is financed should not affect the property's value. This does not mean that the overall level of interest rates and the availability of debt in the market do not affect values. It means that for a given property, the investor paying all cash should be paying the same price as one who decides to use some debt financing.

Of course, investors who do use debt financing will normally expect to earn a higher rate of return on their equity investment because they expect to earn a greater return on the property than what they will be paying the lender. Thus, there will be positive financial leverage. By borrowing money, the investor is taking on more risk in anticipation of a higher return on equity invested. The risk is higher because with debt comes more uncertainty as to what return the investor will actually earn on equity, because the investor gets what is left over after paying the lender. A small drop in property value can result in a large decrease in the investor's return if a high amount

## Private Market Real Estate Debt

of debt was used to finance the property. When a property is valued without explicitly considering financing, the discount rate can be thought of as a weighted average of the rate of return an equity investor would want and the interest rate on the debt.

The maximum amount of debt that an investor can obtain on commercial real estate is usually limited by either the ratio of the loan to the appraised value of the property (loan to value, or LTV) or the debt service coverage ratio (DSCR), depending on which measure results in the lowest loan amount. The debt service coverage ratio is the ratio of the first-year NOI to the loan payment (referred to as debt service for commercial real estate). That is,

$$\text{DSCR} = \text{NOI}/\text{Debt service}. \tag{8}$$

The debt service includes both interest and principal payments on the mortgage. The principal payments are the portion of the loan payment that amortizes the loan over the loan term. An interest-only loan is one that has no principal payments, so the loan balance will remain constant over time. Interest-only loans typically either revert to amortizing loans at some point or have a specified maturity date. For example, an interest-only loan might be made that requires the entire balance of the loan to be repaid after 7–10 years (referred to as a "balloon payment"). Lenders typically require a DSCR of 1.25–1.5 depending on the property type to provide a margin of safety that the NOI from the property can cover the debt service.

### KNOWLEDGE CHECK

### Loans on Real Estate

1. A property has been appraised for $5 million and is expected to have NOI of $400,000 in the first year. The lender is willing to make an interest-only loan at an 8% interest rate as long as the loan-to-value ratio does not exceed 80% and the DSCR is at least 1.25. The balance of the loan will be due after seven years. How much of a loan can be obtained?

   **Solution**

   Based on the loan-to-value ratio, the loan would be 80% of $5 million, or $4 million. With a DSCR of 1.25, the maximum debt service would be $400,000/1.25 = $320,000. This amount is the mortgage payment that would result in a 1.25 DSCR for an interest-only loan.

   If the loan is interest only, then we can obtain the loan amount by simply dividing the mortgage payment by the interest rate. Therefore, the loan amount would be $320,000/0.08 = $4,000,000.

   In this case, we obtain the same loan amount from either the LTV or the DSCR requirements of the lender. If one ratio had resulted in a lower loan amount, that would normally be the maximum that could be borrowed.

When financing is used on a property, equity investors often look at their first-year return on equity or the "equity dividend rate" as a measure of how much cash flow they are getting as a percentage of their equity investment. This measure is sometimes referred to as a *cash-on-cash return* because it measures how much cash they are receiving as a percentage of the cash equity they put into the investment.

> **KNOWLEDGE CHECK**
>
> ## Equity Dividend Rate
>
> 1. Using the information in Question Set 23, what is the equity dividend rate, or cash-on-cash return, assuming the property is purchased at its appraised value?
>
>    **Solution**
>
>    The first-year cash flow is the NOI less the mortgage payment.
>
>    | | |
>    |---|---|
>    | NOI | $400,000 |
>    | Debt service | $320,000 |
>    | Cash flow | $80,000 |
>
>    The amount of equity is the purchase price less the loan amount.
>
>    | | |
>    |---|---|
>    | Price | $5,000,000 |
>    | Mortgage | $4,000,000 |
>    | Equity | $1,000,000 |
>
>    The equity yield rate is the cash flow divided by equity: $80,000/$1,000,000 = 8%. Keep in mind that this is not an IRR that would be earned over a holding period until the property is sold. The equity investor does not share any of the price appreciation in the value of the property with the lender. For loans called "participation" loans, the lender might receive some of the price appreciation, but it would be in exchange for a lower interest rate on the loan.

> **KNOWLEDGE CHECK**
>
> ## Leveraged IRR
>
> 1. Refer to Question Sets 23 and 24. Suppose the same property is sold for $6 million after five years. What IRR will the equity investor receive on his or her investment?
>
>    **Solution**
>
>    The cash flow received by the equity investor from the sale will be the sale price less the mortgage balance, or $6 million – $4 million = $2 million. Using a spreadsheet:
>
>    | **Levered IRR** | | |
>    |---|---|---|
>    | | Amount ($) | Year |
>    | Invested Capital | (1,000,000) | 0 |
>    | Cash flow | 80,000 | 1 |
>    | Cash flow | 80,000 | 2 |
>    | Cash flow | 80,000 | 3 |
>    | Cash flow | 80,000 | 4 |
>    | Cash flow | 2,080,000 | 5 |

| Levered IRR | |
|---|---|
| IRR | 21.14% |

This IRR is based on the equity invested in the property.

## KNOWLEDGE CHECK

## Unleveraged IRR

1. Refer to Question Sets 23, 24, and 25. What would the IRR be if the property were purchased on an all-cash basis (no loan)?

   **Solution**

   Now the equity investor will receive all the cash flow from the sale ($6 million) and the NOI ($400,000). The initial investment will be $5 million. Using a spreadsheet:

   | Unlevered IRR | | |
   |---|---|---|
   | | Amount ($) | Year |
   | Invested Capital | (5,000,000) | 0 |
   | Cash flow | 400,000 | 1 |
   | Cash flow | 400,000 | 2 |
   | Cash flow | 400,000 | 3 |
   | Cashflow | 400,000 | 4 |
   | Cashflow | 6,400,000 | 5 |
   | IRR | | 11.20% |

   This IRR is based on an unleveraged (all-cash) investment in the property. The difference between this IRR (11.20%) and the IRR the equity investor receives with the loan calculated in Question Set 25 (21.14%) reflects positive financial leverage. The property earns 11.20% before adding a loan, and the loan is at 8%. So, the investor is benefiting from the spread between 11.20% and 8%.

# PRACTICE PROBLEMS

## The following information relates to questions 1-5

Jane Lee is the new chief investment officer of the Eastland University Endowment Fund (the "Fund"). Historically, the Fund has invested based on a 60% equity/40% fixed-income allocation. However, Lee seeks to change the Fund's investment strategy by shifting a large amount of assets from traditional investments to alternative investments, including real estate, to increase portfolio diversification and the Fund's risk-adjusted return.

Lee recently hired Jon Tarrow as the Fund's new head of real estate. During a recent meeting, Tarrow and Lee concluded that the initial real estate investment strategy would be to acquire stabilized office buildings located in primary markets. Tarrow has been working on the potential acquisition of a 100% occupied, Class A office building located in New York City. Tarrow and his junior analyst will conduct an independent valuation analysis of the office building; however, Tarrow has also hired an appraiser to value the building and provide valuation support. The appraiser will use three different approaches to estimate the building's value but will place emphasis on both the direct capitalization and the discounted cash flow methods.

During an internal meeting, the junior analyst makes the following three statements about the appraiser's two primary valuation methods:

**Statement 1:** The direct capitalization method requires an estimation of a terminal value.

**Statement 2:** Properties expected to generate faster growth will require a capitalization rate that results in a higher value.

**Statement 3:** The direct capitalization and the discounted cash flow methods both consider growth and property quality.

The appraiser has concluded that net operating income (NOI) for the New York City office building is expected to be $15,600,000 for the first year, and after that, NOI is expected to increase at 0.50% annually for the foreseeable future. The building's value is also expected to increase by 0.50% annually, and investors expect to achieve a 5.75% internal rate of return given the level of risk.

Lee then tells Tarrow that the Fund can procure a loan with an interest-only 5.25% coupon provided that the loan-to-value (LTV) ratio does not exceed 65% and the debt service coverage ratio (DSCR) is at least 1.65x. The balance of the loan would be due after 10 years.

1. Which of the following three valuation approaches *best* represents the one the appraiser will place the most emphasis on?

    A. Cost approach

    B. Income approach

    C. Sales comparison approach

2. Which of the junior analyst's three statements regarding the appraiser's two primary valuation methods is *incorrect*?

    A. Statement 1

**Practice Problems**

    **B.** Statement 2

    **C.** Statement 3

3. Which of the following will lead to a decrease in the appraiser's value of the New York City office building?

    **A.** Increase in building NOI

    **B.** Decrease in discount rate

    **C.** Decrease in NOI and building value growth rates

4. Based on the direct capitalization method, the appraiser's current value of the New York City office building is *closest* to:

    **A.** $249,600,000.

    **B.** $271,300,000.

    **C.** $297,100,000.

5. The maximum loan amount that the Fund can obtain on the New York City office building is *closest* to:

    **A.** $117,100,000.

    **B.** $180,100,000.

    **C.** $193,100,000.

## SOLUTIONS

1. B is correct. The direct capitalization method and the discounted cash flow method are income approaches used to appraise or estimate the value of a commercial (income-producing) property.

   A is incorrect because the cost approach considers what reproducing or replicating a property would cost and deducts depreciation and other factors that reduce the property's value. Replacement cost includes the expense of buying the land and constructing a new property on the site that has the same utility or functionality as the property being appraised.

   C is incorrect because the sales comparison approach considers what similar or comparable properties (comparables) were transacted for in the current market. It is also referred to as the market approach.

2. A is incorrect. The discounted cash flow method (not direct capitalization method) requires a terminal value by capitalizing NOI at some future date.

   B is correct because properties expected to generate faster growth will use a capitalization rate that results in a higher value, and properties with slower growth will use a capitalization rate that results in a lower value.

   C is correct because both income approaches consider growth and property quality.

3. C is correct. The value of a property = $NOI/(r - g)$, where $r$ = the discount rate (required return) and $g$ = the growth rate for income (given constant growth in income, value will grow at the same rate). Therefore, a decrease in the NOI and building value growth rates will lead to a decrease in the property's value.

   A is incorrect because an increase in building NOI will lead to a higher property value.

   B is incorrect because a decrease in the discount rate will lead to a higher property value.

4. C is correct. The value of a property = $NOI/(r - g)$, where $r$ = the discount rate (required return) and $g$ = the growth rate for income (given constant growth in income, value will grow at the same rate). Therefore, the building's value is calculated as follows:

   $15,600,000/(5.75\% - 0.50\%) = \$297,142,857$ ($297,100,000 rounded).

   A is incorrect because a property value of $249,600,000 is incorrectly calculated as follows:

   $15,600,000/(5.75\% + 0.50\%) = \$249,600,000$.

   B is incorrect because a property value of $271,300,000 is incorrectly calculated as follows:

   $15,600,000/5.75\% = \$271,300,000$.

5. B is correct. Based on the LTV ratio, the maximum loan amount would be 65% of $297,100,000, or $193,115,000 ($193,100,000 rounded). With a minimum DSCR of 1.65x, the maximum debt service would be $15,600,000/1.65 = $9,454,545. This amount is the mortgage payment that would result in a 1.65x DSCR for an interest-only loan. If the loan is interest only, then we can obtain the loan amount by simply dividing the mortgage payment by the interest rate. Therefore, the loan amount would be $9,454,545/0.0525 = $180,086,580 ($180,100,000 rounded). Because the loan amount based on the minimum DSCR results in a lower loan amount, that would be the maximum amount that could be borrowed.

   A is incorrect because $117,100,000 is incorrectly calculated as follows:

$15,600,000/0.0525/1.65 = $180,086,580.

$180,086,580 × 65% = $117,056,277 ($117,100,000 rounded).

C is incorrect because $193,100,000 is the rounded loan amount based on the maximum LTV of 65%. Because the loan amount based on the minimum DSCR results in a lower loan amount, $180,086,580 ($180,100,000 rounded) would be the maximum loan amount that could be borrowed.

# LEARNING MODULE 3

## Investments in Real Estate Through Publicly Traded Securities

by Steven G. Bloom, CFA, Jeffrey D. Fisher, PhD, David Kruth, CFA, Bryan D. MacGregor, PhD, MRICS, MRTPI, Ian Rossa O'Reilly, CFA, and Anthony Paolone, CFA.

*Steven G. Bloom, CFA, is at ARC Fiduciary (USA). Jeffery D. Fisher, PhD. David Kruth, CFA. Bryan MacGregor, PhD, MRICS, MRTPI. Ian Rossa O'Reilly, CFA (Canada). Anthony Paolone, CFA.*

| LEARNING OUTCOMES | |
|---|---|
| Mastery | The candidate should be able to: |
| ☐ | discuss types of publicly traded real estate securities |
| ☐ | justify the use of net asset value per share (NAVPS) in valuation of publicly traded real estate securities and estimate NAVPS based on forecasted cash net operating income |
| ☐ | describe the use of funds from operations (FFO) and adjusted funds from operations (AFFO) in REIT valuation |
| ☐ | calculate and interpret the value of a REIT share using the net asset value, relative value (price-to-FFO and price-to-AFFO), and discounted cash flow approaches |
| ☐ | explain advantages and disadvantages of investing in real estate through publicly traded securities compared to private vehicles |

## SUMMARY

- The principal types of publicly traded real estate securities include real estate investment trusts (REITs), real estate operating companies (REOCs), and residential and commercial mortgage-backed securities (RMBS and CMBS).
- Compared with other publicly traded shares, REITs typically offer higher-than-average yields and greater stability of income and returns. They are amenable to a net asset value approach to valuation because of the existence of active private markets for their real estate assets.

- Compared with REOCs, REITs offer higher yields and income tax exemptions but have less operating flexibility to invest in a broad range of real estate activities and less potential for growth from reinvesting their operating cash flows because of their high income-to-payout ratios.
- In assessing the investment merits of REITs, investors analyze the effects of trends in general economic activity, retail sales, job creation, population growth, and new supply and demand for specific types of space. Investors also pay particular attention to occupancies, leasing activity, rental rates, remaining lease terms, in-place rents compared with market rents, costs to maintain space and re-lease space, tenants' financial health and tenant concentration in the portfolio, financial leverage, debt maturities and costs, and the quality of management and governance.
- Analysts make adjustments to the historical cost-based financial statements of REITs and REOCs to obtain better measures of current income and net worth. The three principal figures they calculate and use are (1) funds from operations or accounting net earnings, excluding depreciation, deferred tax charges, and gains or losses on sales of property and debt restructuring; (2) adjusted funds from operations, or funds from operations adjusted to remove straight-line rent and to provide for maintenance-type capital expenditures and leasing costs, including leasing agents' commissions and tenants' improvement allowances; and (3) net asset value or the difference between a real estate company's asset and liability ranking prior to shareholders' equity, all valued at market values instead of accounting book values.
- REITs and some REOCs generally return a significant portion of their income to their investors as required by law and, as a result, tend to pay high dividends. Thus, dividend discount or discounted cash flow models for valuation are also applicable. These valuation approaches are applied in the same manner as they are for shares in other industries. Usually, investors use two- or three-step dividend discount models with near-term, intermediate-term, and/or long-term growth assumptions. In discounted cash flow models, investors often use intermediate-term cash flow projections and a terminal value based on historical cash flow multiples.

# INTRODUCTION

Historically real estate investing was reserved for the wealthy and institutions. REITs were initially conceived of as a way for small investors to gain exposure to a professionally managed, diversified real estate portfolio. REITs were viewed as a type of (closed-end) mutual fund and income passthrough vehicle through which the portfolio manager would acquire attractively valued properties, occasionally sell fully valued properties, and distribute property earnings to the trust's investors. Legislation was passed in the United States in 1960 to authorize REITs, and the Netherlands followed suit in 1969. The US model and other types of tax-advantaged real estate investment vehicles have been adopted worldwide. The S&P 500 Index added REITs as a separate GICS sector in 2016.

As of October 2020, more than 35 countries have REITs or REIT-like structures, more are considering adopting similar vehicles, and REITs are held by individuals and institutions alike.

## TYPES OF PUBLICLY TRADED REAL ESTATE SECURITIES

☐ discuss types of publicly traded real estate securities

Publicly traded real estate securities allow investors to gain indirect exposure to real estate equity and debt by purchasing shares of companies that own real estate, real estate loans, or both. Securitization makes it possible for investors of all sizes to access an asset class that was once available only to the largest investors. Globally, the principal types of publicly traded real estate securities are REITs, REOCs, and MBS.

- **Real estate investment trusts (REITs)** are companies that own, finance, and—to a limited extent—develop income-producing real estate across a range of property sectors. REITs must meet a number of requirements in order to qualify as REITs. Most REITs are required to distribute 90%–100% of their taxable income to shareholders.

- REITs that own real estate are called **equity REITs**. Those that make or invest in loans secured by real estate are categorized as mortgage REITs. The companies' tax advantages result from being allowed to deduct dividends paid from income, which effectively exempts REITs from corporate income tax in many countries. In many jurisdictions, qualifying REITs are simply exempt from corporate income tax.

- **Real estate operating companies (REOCs)** are ordinary taxable real estate ownership companies. Businesses are organized as REOCs, as opposed to REITs, if the following is true:

    - they are located in countries that do not have a tax-advantaged REIT regime in place,
    - they engage to a large extent in the development of for-sale real estate properties, or
    - they offer other non-qualifying services, such as brokerage and third-party property management.

    The primary cash inflows for merchant developers are from sales of developed or improved properties rather than from recurring lease or rental income. The more flexible operating company structure may be preferred, even when a company develops, owns, and operates qualifying rental properties, because the REIT prohibitions are too restrictive or they prefer to retain earnings for reinvestment.

- Mortgage-backed securities are asset-backed securitized debt obligations that represent rights to receive cash flows from portfolios of mortgage loans—mortgage loans on commercial properties in the case of commercial mortgage-backed securities (CMBS) and mortgage loans on residential properties in the case of residential mortgage-backed securities (RMBS). Whereas residential mortgage pools often contain thousands of loans, commercial mortgage pools typically range from around 100 loans to as few as 1 loan when the asset is very large.

The market capitalization of publicly traded real estate equity securities is greatly exceeded by the market value of real estate debt securities—in particular, RMBS. In addition to publicly traded real estate securities, there are privately held real estate securities, including private REITs and REOCs, privately held mortgages, private debt issues, and bank debt. Many real estate private equity partnerships create private REITs to own income-producing properties.

## REIT Structures

REITs are tax-efficient conduits for distributing earnings from rental income to shareholders. Most are structured as corporations or trusts. There are numerous requirements for a company to qualify as a REIT. In most countries, REITs are required to:

- distribute 90%–100% of their otherwise taxable earnings,
- invest at least 75% of their assets in real estate, and
- derive at least 75% of income from real estate rental income or interest on mortgages.

Countries may specify a minimum number of shareholders, maximum share ownership by a single shareholder, a minimum number of properties/ maximum asset concentration, a maximum level of non-rental income, a maximum amount of development, and limits on leverage and types of loans. In the United States, a REIT must have at least 100 shareholders, and no fewer than 5 shareholders can own more than 50% of the shares (the five-or-fewer rule). There are numerous other requirements as well. The restrictions effectively bar an individual or small group from creating REITs to own individual real estate assets.

Most REITs in the United States are self-managed and self-advised. Senior executives are company employees who report to trustees or the board of directors, who, in turn, are elected by shareholders. Fully integrated REITs generally have fewer conflicts than REITs that are externally advised or externally managed. Externally managed REITs pay asset management fees to the third-party adviser, which has an inherent incentive to increase the size of the REIT if fees are based on total assets. External managers may require REITs to pay for other services that are provided by affiliates of the manager, such as property management, acquisitions, and debt placement.

That is not to say all externally managed REITs should be avoided. Management quality, governance, alignment, reputation, and transparency clearly matter. Several services rate the quality of governance, transparency, and so forth, to assist in the investment valuation, for both externally managed and self-managed REITs.

## Market Size

Details about the market's relative size by geographic area and security type are shown in Exhibit 1.

### Exhibit 1: Relative Size and Composition of Publicly Traded Real Estate Equity Security Markets

*A. Percentage of market value of publicly traded real estate equity securities (REITs and REOCs) in developed markets as of 31 May 2019*

| By Region (%) | | By Market (%) | |
|---|---|---|---|
| North America | 56.7 | United States | 53.9 |
| Asia Pacific | 26.4 | Japan | 11.3 |
| Europe | 16.8 | Hong Kong SAR | 7.9 |
| Middle East, Africa | 0.1 | Australia | 4.7 |

**A. Percentage of market value of publicly traded real estate equity securities (REITs and REOCs) in developed markets as of 31 May 2019**

| By Region (%) | By Market (%) | |
|---|---|---|
| | Germany | 4.7 |
| | United Kingdom | 4.6 |
| | Canada | 2.8 |
| | Singapore | 2.5 |
| | Sweden | 1.7 |
| | Netherlands | 1.6 |
| | France | 1.5 |
| | Others | 2.8 |

**B. Percentage of market value of publicly traded equity real estate equity securities in developed markets by type of structure as of 29 March 2019**

| | Global | North America | Europe | Asia Pacific |
|---|---|---|---|---|
| REITs | 68 | 96 | 43 | 42 |
| Non-REITs, REOCs | 32 | 4 | 57 | 58 |

*Sources:* www.ftserussell.com and www.epra.com. Based on data from the FTSE EPRA Nareit Developed Index.

Note that, as evidenced in Exhibit 9, Panel B, REIT structures are relatively more common in North America than in Europe or Asia Pacific due to the favorable tax structure afforded to REIT structures in North America versus other parts of the world where REOC structures are relatively more common. As an investment asset class, income-producing real estate offers the advantages of stable income based on its contractual revenue from leases and a measure of long-term inflation protection because, over the long term, rents tend to rise with inflation.

## Advantages and Disadvantages of Investing in REITs

The advantages and disadvantages of investing in public real estate companies as compared with private real estate investments include the following:

**Advantages of REITs**

1. *Liquidity*: Ability to buy and sell shares of almost any amount on major exchanges
2. *Transparency*: Readily available share prices and transaction histories
3. *Diversification of property holdings*: By property type, geography, and underlying tenant credit
4. *High-quality portfolios*: Many companies own high-quality assets in leading markets.
5. *Active professional management*: Most companies have strong executive management overseeing dedicated property management teams with economies of scale.
6. *Potentially stable income*: Well-occupied properties subject to long-term leases generate predictable property income, sometimes with distributions occurring monthly.

7. *Tax efficiency*: REIT and passthrough structures avoid corporate income taxation, leaving only the investor to pay taxes on dividends received.

**Disadvantages of REITs**

1. *Lack of retained earnings*: As REITs are required to pay 90%+ of earnings to shareholders, REITs must access capital markets to fund growth. The faster the expansion, the more often the company must raise new capital.
2. *Regulatory costs*: REITs have the cost burden of maintaining a corporate structure of a publicly trading company and complying with regulatory filings.
3. *Reduced portfolio diversification benefits*: As shares of the REIT are publicly traded, the pricing is partially determined by stock market movements and liquidity rather than only by underlying value. This reduces the diversification benefits for the overall portfolio as compared to private real estate.
4. *Limited in types of assets owned*: REITs are also constrained in the types of assets they own. Consequently, many REITs form **taxable REIT subsidiaries** (TRS), which pay income taxes on earnings from non-REIT-qualifying activities, such as merchant development or third-party property management.

> **KNOWLEDGE CHECK**
>
> ## Publicly Traded Real Estate Investments
>
> 1. Which of the following assets requires the *most* expertise in real estate on the part of the investor?
>     - **A.** A REOC share
>     - **B.** An equity REIT share
>     - **C.** A direct investment in a single property
>
>    **Solution**
>
>    C is correct. Direct investment in a single property requires a high level of real estate expertise. Investment in publicly traded equity investments (in REITs or REOCs) requires much less expertise because investors benefit from having their property interests actively managed on their behalf by professional managers and from having their business interests overseen and guided by boards of directors, as in the case of all public corporations.
>
> 2. Which of the following has the *most* operating and financial flexibility?
>     - **A.** A REOC
>     - **B.** An equity REIT
>     - **C.** A direct investment in a single property
>
>    **Solution**
>
>    A is correct. REOCs are free to invest in any kind of real estate or related activity without limitation. This freedom gives management the opportunity to create more value in development activity and in trading real estate and to retain as much of their income as they believe is appropriate. A wider range of capital structures and degrees of financial leverage may be used in the process. In contrast to REOCs, REITs face restrictions on the amount of income and assets accounted for by activities other than collecting rent and

interest payments. Direct investment is less liquid and divisible than REOC and REIT shares, which limits the operational flexibility of such investment.

3. Investors seeking broad diversification would invest in the securities of which of the following companies?

    **A.** A company that owns multi-family rental properties in Hong Kong SAR

    **B.** A company that owns large office properties in New York City, San Francisco, Los Angeles, and Chicago

    **C.** A company with a mix of office and retail properties in urban and suburban markets

**Solution**

C is correct. It should be clear that a company with a mix of assets—office and retail—with exposure to urban and suburban markets offers the best diversification. A is incorrect because the company has only one type of asset, multi-family rentals, in one market, Hong Kong SAR. The systematic risk is high for that portfolio. B is incorrect because the company owns only one asset type, office properties, and the economic activity correlation may be high among urban cities with exposure to global trade and the financial sector.

Alternatively, investors looking for property and market diversification might, instead of the solutions provided, consider investing in a few large companies that own different asset types in multiple cities or several pure-play companies, each of which concentrates on a single asset type in its given region, as long as the companies' regions and product type do not overlap to a large extent.

### KNOWLEDGE CHECK

## Publicly Traded Real Estate Investments

1. Which of the following best represents an advantage of REITs over a direct investment in an income-producing property?

    **A.** Diversification—of property holdings
    **B.** Operating flexibility
    **C.** Diversification—of overall portfolio

**Solution**

A is correct. REITs provide diversification of property holdings. B is incorrect because REITs do face restrictions on the amount of income and assets accounted for by activities other than collecting rent and interest payments; these restrictions can prevent a REIT from maximizing its returns. C is incorrect because as shares of REITs are publicly traded, their price is partly determined by stock market movements and market liquidity, reducing the diversification benefits to an overall portfolio as compared with private real estate.

> **KNOWLEDGE CHECK**
>
> **Investment Objectives**
>
> 1. Two real estate investors are each choosing from among the following investment types: a REOC, an equity REIT, or a direct investment in an income-producing property. Investor A's primary objective is liquidity, and Investor B's primary objective is maximum growth/capital gain potential. State and explain which real estate investment type best suits:
>
>     1. Investor A.
>     2. Investor B.
>
> **Solution**
>
> For Investor A, with a liquidity objective, REOC and REIT investments are most appropriate because REOCs and REITs are traded on stock exchanges and are more liquid. Direct investments in income-producing property are generally less liquid.
>
> For Investor B, with a maximum growth objective, REOCs and direct property investment are most appropriate because REOCs and direct investors are free to invest in any kind of real estate or related activity without limitation and to reinvest as much of their income as they believe is appropriate for their objectives. This freedom gives them the opportunity to create more value in development activity and in trading real estate. REITs' constraints prevent them from retaining earnings to reinvest, so their growth opportunities are more limited.
>
> There are several caveats to note for each generalized solution. Shares of closely held listed companies with low market float that trade infrequently may not offer the desired liquidity. Management quality, corporate governance, balance-sheet capacity and leverage, attractive investment and reinvestment opportunities, and many other considerations matter greatly when it comes to selecting the vehicle and company that are best at delivering growth and value to shareholders.

## 3. VALUATION: NET ASSET VALUE APPROACH

☐ justify the use of net asset value per share (NAVPS) in valuation of publicly traded real estate securities and estimate NAVPS based on forecasted cash net operating income

### Introduction

The approaches analysts take in valuing equity include those based on the following:

- asset value estimates,
- price multiple comparisons,
- discounted cash flow.

## Valuation: Net Asset Value Approach

Two possible measures of value that analysts might use are

- book value per share (BVPS)—based on reported accounting values
- net asset value per share (NAVPS) based on market values for assets.

Note: In this reading, BVPS refers to depreciated real estate value rather than total shareholders' equity per share. NAVPS is the relevant market-based valuation measure for valuing REITs and REOCs.

NAVPS is a fundamental benchmark for the value of a REIT or REOC. In Europe and Asia, the price-to-NAV multiple is the primary measure that analysts use to value real estate companies. (US analysts more commonly report on price multiples of gross cash flow) Real estate NAV may be viewed as the largest component of the intrinsic value of a REIT or REOC. NAVPS should also include the following:

- assessments of the value of any non-asset-based income streams (e.g., fee or management income);
- the value of non–real estate assets, including cash;
- net of the value of any contingent liabilities;
- the value added by management of the REIT or REOC.

Shares priced at discounts to NAVPS suggest potential undervaluation, and shares priced at premiums to NAVPS suggest potential overvaluation. However, this discount or premium might be justified by indications of future events, such as a missed property development completion or expected high value creation by a management team These assessments must be made in the context of the stock market's tendency to be forward looking in its valuations and at times to have different investment criteria from property markets. In addition, the stock price discount or premium to NAVPS may be explained by investors' view of management's added value, leverage, and company governance.

REITs whose shares trade below NAVPS or have high leverage may have a more difficult time raising new capital to fund acquisitions and development, which, in turn, may limit long-term growth, in contrast to REITs that trade at or above NAVPS. Selling equity below NAVPS can be dilutive for investors.

## Accounting for Investment Properties

If accounting is on a fair value basis, accounting values may be relevant for asset-based valuation. If historical cost values are used, however, accounting values are generally not relevant and must be adjusted.

Under International Financial Reporting Standards (IFRS), companies are allowed to value investment properties using either a *cost model* or a *fair value model.*

- cost model is identical to the cost model used for property, plant, and equipment
- fair value model all changes in the asset's fair value affect net income To use the fair value model, a company must be able to reliably determine the property's fair value on a continuing basis. In general, a company must consistently apply its chosen model (cost or fair value) to all of its investment property. If a company chooses the fair value model for its investment property, it must continue to use the fair value model until it disposes of the property or changes its use such that it is no longer considered investment property (e.g., it becomes owner-occupied property or part of inventory). The company must continue to use the fair value model for that property even if transactions on comparable properties, used to estimate fair value, become less frequent.

Investment property appears as a separate line item on the balance sheet. Companies are required to disclose whether they use the fair value model or the cost model for their investment property. If the company uses the fair value model, it must make additional disclosures about how it determines fair value and must provide reconciliation between the beginning and ending carrying amounts of the investment property. If the company uses the cost model, it must make additional disclosures—for example, the depreciation method and useful life estimates must be disclosed. In addition, if the company uses the cost model, it must also disclose the fair value of investment property.

In contrast to IFRS, under US GAAP, most US real estate owners use the historical cost accounting model, which values an asset at its original purchase price plus capital investment less historical depreciation. This model does not accurately represent the economic values of assets and liabilities in environments of significant operating income and asset price changes or long-term inflation. US GAAP historical cost accounting practices tend to distort the measure of economic income and asset value by (1) understating carrying values on long-held property assets that are often appreciating in value because of general price inflation or other property-specific reasons and (2) overstating depreciation when companies use accelerated depreciation.

## Net Asset Value per Share: Calculation

As a result of shortcomings in accounting reported values, investment analysts and investors use estimates of **net asset value per share (NAVPS)**. NAVPS is the difference between a real estate company's assets and its liabilities, *all taken at current market values instead of accounting book values*, divided by the number of shares outstanding.

NAVPS = (Market Value of Assets − Market Value of Liabilities)/number of shares

NAVPS is a superior measure of a company's net worth compared with historical book value per share.

In valuing a REIT's or REOC's real estate portfolio, analysts will look for the results of existing appraisals if they are available (such as those provided by companies reporting under IFRS). If such appraisals are unavailable or if they disagree with the assumptions or methodology of those appraisals, analysts will often capitalize the rental streams—represented by net operating income—produced by a REIT's or REOC's properties, using a market-required rate of return.

NOI is defined as gross rental revenue minus operating costs (which include estimated vacancy and collection losses, insurance costs, taxes, utilities, and repair and maintenance expenses)

NOI = (Gross rental revenue − Operating costs)

*before deducting depreciation, general and administration (G&A) expenses, and interest expense.

After deducting G&A expenses from NOI, the figure obtained is analogous to earnings before interest, depreciation, and amortization (EBITDA).

EBITDA = (NOI − G&A expenses)

Recall that this approach is similar to the valuation of private real estate covered earlier. These estimated asset values will be substituted for the book values of the properties on the balance sheet and adjustments made to any related accounting assets, such as capitalized leases, to avoid double counting.

Generally, goodwill, deferred financing expenses, and deferred tax assets will be excluded to arrive at a "hard" economic value for total assets. Liabilities will be similarly adjusted to replace the face value of debt with market values if these are significantly different (e.g., as a result of changes in interest rates), and any such "soft" liabilities as

## Valuation: Net Asset Value Approach

deferred tax liabilities will be removed. The revised net worth of the company divided by the number of shares outstanding is the NAV. Although this figure is calculated before provision for any income or capital gains taxes that might be payable on liquidation, the inability to predict how the company or its assets might be sold and the prospect that it might be kept intact in an acquisition cause investors to look to the pre-tax asset value as their primary net worth benchmark. If a company has held its assets for many years and has a very low remaining depreciable value for its assets for tax purposes, it can affect investors' perspectives on valuation. Quantifying the effects of a low adjusted cost base, however, is impeded by lack of knowledge of the tax circumstances and strategies of a would-be acquirer.

Exhibit 2 provides an example of the calculations involved in estimating NAV based on capitalizing rental streams. Because the book values of assets are based on historical costs, the analyst estimates NAVPS. First, by capitalizing NOI with certain adjustments, the analyst obtains an estimate of the value of rental properties; then, the value of other tangible assets is added, and the total is netted of liabilities. This net amount, NAV, is then divided by the number of shares outstanding to obtain NAVPS.

### Exhibit 2: Analyst Adjustments to REIT Financials to Obtain NAVPS

| | |
|---|---|
| Last-12-month real estate NOI | $270,432 |
| Less: Non-cash rent | 7,667 |
| Plus: Adjustment for full impact of acquisitions (1) | 4,534 |
| Pro forma cash NOI for last 12 months | $267,299 |
| Plus: Next-12-month growth in NOI (2) | $4,009 |
| Estimated next-12-month cash NOI | $271,308 |
| Assumed cap rate (3) | 7.00% |
| Estimated value of operating real estate | $3,875,829 |
| Plus: Cash and equivalents | 65,554 |
| Plus: Land held for future development | 34,566 |
| Plus: Accounts receivable | 45,667 |
| Plus: Prepaid/other assets (4) | 23,456 |
| Estimated gross asset value | $4,045,072 |
| Less: Total debt | 1,010,988 |
| Less: Other liabilities | 119,886 |
| Net asset value | $2,914,198 |
| Shares outstanding | 55,689 |

1. An incremental 50% of the annual expected return on acquisitions that were completed midway through the previous year.
2. Growth is estimated at 1.5%.
3. Cap rate is based on recent comparable transactions in the property market.
4. This figure does not include intangible assets.

NAVPS is calculated to be $2,914,198 divided by 55,689 shares, which equals $52.33 per share.

The second line in Exhibit 2 shows the adjustment to remove **non-cash rent**; this adjustment is the result of the accounting practice of "straight lining" the rental revenue from long-term leases with contractual step-ups. When the real estate company reports the average contractual rent it expects to receive over the course of each lease, rent received from the tenant is less than the average revenue booked during the early years of the lease, and the tenant pays more rent than the company reports during the latter years of the lease term. (The amount of this deduction is the difference between the average contractual rent over the leases' terms and the cash rent actually paid.) NOI is also increased to reflect a full year's rent for properties acquired during the course of the year, resulting in pro forma "cash NOI" for the previous 12 months of $267,299,000. This amount is then increased to include expected growth for the next 12 months at 1.5%, resulting in expected next-12-month cash NOI of $271,308,000.

An appropriate capitalization rate is then estimated on the basis of recent transactions for comparable properties in the property market. An estimated value for the REIT's operating real estate is obtained by dividing expected next-12-month cash NOI by the decimalized capitalization rate (in this case, 0.07). The book values of the REIT's other tangible assets, including cash, accounts receivable, land for future development, and prepaid expenses, are added to obtain estimated gross asset value. (Land is sometimes taken at market value if this amount can be determined reliably; but because land is often difficult to value and of low liquidity, analysts tend to use book values.) From this figure, debt and other liabilities (but not deferred taxes, because this item is an accounting provision rather than an economic liability) are subtracted to obtain net asset value. Division by the number of shares outstanding produces NAVPS.

## Net Asset Value per Share: Application

NAVPS can be reasonably estimated when there are ample market transactions to provide property comparables. Investors can make observations about how such properties trade on the basis of the price per square foot or on the basis of capitalization rate (the rate obtained by dividing net operating income by total value). Broker reports and private real estate research companies also track rental rates by property and other tenant incentives, such as free rent or capital to improve the space, and then apply these valuations to the assets of a public company. As of 2020, close to 15% of commercial real estate is held by publicly traded REITs in the United States (www.epra.com). In Europe, only 7% of the commercial real estate market is owned by listed real estate companies (REITs and REOCs), and in Singapore, 34% of the commercial market is owned by listed real estate companies

### *Important Considerations in a NAV-Based Approach to Valuing REITs*

Although NAV estimates provide investors with a specific value, several important considerations should be taken into account when using this approach to value REITs and REOCs. First, investors must understand the implications of using a private market valuation tool on a publicly traded security. In this context, it is useful to examine how NAVs are calculated.

The methods most commonly used to calculate NAV are:

1. using the cap rate approach to valuing the NOI of a property or portfolio of properties,
2. applying value per square foot (or unit) to a property or portfolio of properties, and
3. using appraised values disclosed in the company's financial statements.

An analyst may adjust these appraised values reported by the company if she does not agree with the underlying assumptions and if there is sufficient information to do so. In the first two instances, the cap rates and values per square foot are derived from observing transactions that have occurred in the marketplace. In contrast, most sophisticated direct purchasers of commercial real estate arrive at a purchase price after performing detailed forecasting of the cash flows they expect to achieve from owning and operating a specific property over their investment time horizon. These cash flows are then discounted to a present value or purchase price.

Whatever that present value or purchase price is, an analyst can estimate value by dividing an estimate of NOI by the cap rate—essentially, the required rate of current return for income streams of that risk. In addition, an analyst can take the present value or purchase price and divide by the property's rentable area for a value per square foot. The point is that cap rates and values per square foot result from a more detailed analysis and discounted cash flow process. The discount rate used by a private owner/operator of commercial real estate could differ from the discount rate used by investors purchasing shares of REITs.

**Premium or discount to NAV**

Real estate stocks can trade at either premiums and or discounts to NAV. Over time, REITs and REOCs globally have at times traded at premiums to NAV of more than 25% and at other times at discounts to NAV exceeding 25%. Thus, if the NAV of a REIT were $20 per share, the stock might trade as low as $15 per share or as high as $25 per share, depending on a range of factors.

The price-to-NAV ratio will vary by market, sector, outlook, and perceived quality of management and governance. Private property investors may or may not value individual assets the same way public equity investors value listed real estate companies. Property buyers frequently consider the long-term prospects and valuation for an asset when making an investment. Appraisal-based NAV estimates, however, often lag changes in market conditions.

Stock investors tend to focus more on the near-term projected outlook for changes in income and asset value. These factors help explain why share valuation may differ from NAV. As alluded to earlier, it is possible that REITs and REOCs can trade at some premium or discount to NAV until the premium/discount becomes wide enough for market forces to close the arbitrage gap.

Another factor to consider when using a NAV approach to REIT or REOC valuation is that NAV implicitly treats a company as an individual asset or static pool of assets. In reality, such treatment is not consistent with a going-concern assumption. Management teams have different track records and abilities to produce value over time, assets can be purchased and sold, and capital market decisions can add or subtract value. An investor must thus consider how much value a management team can add to (or subtract from) current NAV.

For instance, an investor may be willing to purchase REIT A trading at a 10% premium to NAV versus REIT B trading at a small discount to NAV because the management team of REIT A has a stronger track record and better opportunities to grow the NAV compared with REIT B, thus justifying the premium at which REIT A trades relative to REIT B.

NAV estimates can also become quite subjective when property markets become illiquid and few transactions are observable or when REITs and REOCs own hundreds of properties, making it difficult for an investor to estimate exactly how much the portfolio would be worth if the assets were sold individually. There may also be a large-portfolio premium in good economic environments when prospective strategic purchasers may be willing to pay a premium to acquire a large amount of desired property at once or a large-portfolio discount when there are few buyers for the kind of property in question. In addition, such assets as undeveloped land, very large properties with few comparable assets, properties with specific uses, service businesses, and joint ventures complicate the process of estimating NAV with accuracy and confidence.

*Further Observations on NAV*

Among institutional investors, the most common view is that if REIT management is performing well in the sense of creating value, REITs and REOCs should trade at premiums to underlying NAVPS. This rationale is based on the following:

1. Investors in the stocks have liquidity on a day-to-day basis, whereas a private investor in real estate does not, thus warranting a lower required return rate (higher value) in the public market than in the private market for the same assets.

2. The competitive nature of the public markets and the size of the organizations should attract above-average management teams, which should produce better real estate operating performance and lead to better investment decisions than the average private real estate concern.

In conclusion, although NAV is by its nature an absolute valuation metric, in practice it is often more useful as a relative valuation tool. If all REITs are trading above or below NAV, selecting individual REITs could become a relative exercise—that is, purchasing the REIT stock trading at the smallest premium to NAV when REITs are trading above NAV or selling the REIT trading at the smallest discount to NAV when REITs are all trading at a discount to NAV. In practice, NAV is also used as a relative metric by investors looking at implied cap rates. To calculate the implied cap rate of a REIT or REOC, the current price is used in a NAV model to work backward and solve for the cap rate. By doing so, an investor looking at two similar portfolios of real estate could ascertain whether the market is valuing these portfolios differently on the basis of the implied cap rates.

## 4. VALUATION: RELATIVE VALUE (PRICE MULTIPLE) APPROACH

> describe the use of funds from operations (FFO) and adjusted funds from operations (AFFO) in REIT valuation

Conventional equity valuation approaches, including market-based or relative value approaches, are used with some adaptations to value REITs and REOCs. Such multiples as the price-to-funds from operations ratio (P/FFO), the price-to-adjusted funds from operations ratio (P/AFFO), and the enterprise value-to-EBITDA ratio (EV/EBITDA) are used for valuing shares of REITs and REOCs in much the same way as for valuing shares in other industries.

### Relative Value Approach to Valuing REIT Stocks

REIT analysts and investors make extensive use of two measures of operating performance that are specific to REITs. **Funds from operations (FFO)** is defined as net income plus depreciation and amortization less gains or losses on the sale of real property.

$$FFO = (Net\ income + depreciation + amortization) - (Net\ gains\ on\ sale\ of\ real\ property)$$

FFO is one of the most commonly used metrics in the United States. (In Europe and Asia, NAVPS is more commonly used, as discussed earlier.)

**Adjusted funds from operations (AFFO)** subtracts from FFO recurring capital expenditure and the difference between reported rents and cash rents

AFFO = (FFO − Non-cash rent − Recurring capex)

AFFO better approximates a company's sustainable dividend-paying capacity. These definitions are discussed in greater detail in a later section.

P/E ratio and P multiples are commonly used to value equities. For REITs, the relative value measures most frequently are P/FFO and P/AFFO. The ratio EV/EBITDA is used to a lesser extent. The use of P/FFO and P/AFFO multiples allows investors to quickly ascertain the value of a given REIT's shares compared with that of other REIT shares or to compare the current valuation level of a REIT's shares with historical levels. Within the REIT sector, P/FFO and P/AFFO multiples are also often compared with the average multiple of companies owning similar properties—for example, comparing the P/FFO multiple of a REIT that owns office properties with the average P/FFO multiple for all REITs owning office properties. These multiples are typically calculated using current stock prices and year-ahead estimated FFO or AFFO.

FFO and AFFO are based on net income available to equity and thus represent levered income. P/FFO multiples are generally lower for companies with higher leverage, all things equal. EBITDA, by definition, measures income before the leveraging effect of debt. Not only do EV/EBITDA multiples facilitate like-for-like valuation comparisons; they also better approximate how investors evaluate real estate. Recall that the inverse of the multiple, EBITDA/EV, closely approximates the real estate capitalization rate formula (NOI/market value).

There are three main drivers that differentiate P/FFO, P/AFFO, and EV/EBITDA multiples among most REITs and REOCs:

1. *Expectation for growth in FFO and AFFO*: The higher the expected growth, the higher the multiple or relative valuation. Growth can be driven by the following:

    a. business model (e.g., REITs and REOCs successful in real estate development often generate above-average FFO and AFFO growth over time);

    b. geography (e.g., having a concentration of properties in primary, supply-constrained markets, such as New York City or London, can give landlords more pricing power and higher cash flow growth than can be obtained in secondary markets); and

    c. other factors (e.g., management skill or lease structure).

2. *Risk associated with the underlying real estate*: Cash flow volatility related to asset type, quality, and age; market conditions; lease types; and submarket location also affect valuation.

    a. Example 1: Owning apartments is viewed as having less cash flow variability than owning hotels. As such, apartment-focused REITs tend to trade at relatively high multiples compared with hotel REITs.

    b. Example 2: Shares of companies with young, well-maintained portfolios generally trade at higher multiples than stocks of companies with older or out-of-date properties with deferred maintenance that will require higher capital expenditures to sustain rent growth.

3. *Risks associated with the company's capital structures and access to capital*: As financial leverage increases, equities' FFO and AFFO multiples decrease because required return increases as risk increases. Higher leverage

constrains a company's incremental borrowing capacity and may create a stock overhang if investors avoid buying shares in anticipation of future equity offerings.

There are many other factors that affect valuation, as with any investment, including investor perceptions of management, asset types or markets being in or out of favor, complexity, quality of financial disclosure, transparency, and governance.

FFO is, in essence, the REIT sector equivalent of P/E. Investors can derive a quick "cash flow" multiple by looking at P/AFFO because AFFO makes a variety of adjustments to FFO that result in an approximation of cash earnings.

## Funds from Operations (FFO) and Adjusted Funds from Operations (AFFO)

FFO has long been the standard measure of REIT performance. The National Association of Real Estate Investment Trusts (Nareit) took steps to standardize and promote the definition. FFO is an SEC-accepted non-GAAP financial measure (as is EBITDA), which, according to the SEC and as specified in updated guidance from Nareit (2018), must be reconciled with GAAP net income. The SEC also recommends that companies that report adjustments to FFO reconcile those figures with the Nareit-defined FFO, sometimes referred to as Nareit FFO.

FFO attempts to approximate continuing operating performance. The more complete definition of FFO is as follows:

> net income (computed in accordance with GAAP) plus losses (minus gains) from sales of properties, plus depreciation and amortization related to real estate, plus real estate impairments and write-downs unrelated to depreciation.

Why is depreciation added back to net income? Investors believe that real estate maintains its value to a greater extent than other business assets, often appreciating in value over the long term, and that depreciation deductions under IFRS and US GAAP do not represent economic reality. A taxable REOC that uses a moderate degree of leverage and regularly chooses to reinvest most of its income in its business usually will be able to defer a large part of its annual tax liability—that is, its cash income taxes will be low as a result of the accelerated depreciation rates for tax purposes permitted in most countries, and reinvesting continues to add to the depreciable real estate base.

Net income is adjusted for gains and losses from sales of previously depreciated operating properties on the grounds that they do not represent sustainable, normal income. The amortization add-back includes amortization of leasing commissions, tenant improvements, and tenant allowances.

Similar to cash flow from operations, FFO is not a measure of cash flow. It does not include investment and spending necessary to sustain cash flow growth or cash flow related to financing activities. FFO also includes FFO from unconsolidated businesses.

Adjusted funds from operations, also known as **funds available for distribution (FAD)** or **cash available for distribution**, is a refinement of FFO that is designed to be a more accurate measure of current economic income. AFFO is most often defined as FFO adjusted to remove any non-cash rent and to subtract maintenance-type capital expenditures and leasing costs (including leasing agents' commissions and tenants' improvement allowances). So-called **straight-line rent** is the average contractual rent over a lease term, and this figure is recognized as revenue under IFRS and US GAAP. The difference between this figure and the cash rent paid during the period is the amount of the non-cash rent or **straight-line rent adjustment**. Because most long-term leases contain escalating rental rates, this difference in rental revenue recognition can be significant. Also, deductions from FFO for capital expenditures related to maintenance and for leasing the space in properties reflect costs that need to be incurred to maintain the value of properties.

The purpose of the adjustments to net earnings made in computing FFO and AFFO is to obtain a more tangible, cash-focused measure of sustainable economic income that reduces reliance on non-cash accounting estimates and excludes non-economic, non-cash charges.

AFFO is superior to FFO as a measure of economic income and thus economic return because it considers the capital expenditures necessary to maintain the economic income of a property portfolio. AFFO is also more reflective of a REIT's dividend-paying ability than FFO. It is open, however, to more variation and error in estimation than FFO.

The precise annual provision required to maintain and lease the space in a property is difficult to predict, and the actual expense in any single year may be significantly more or less than the norm because of the timing of capital expenditure programs and the uneven expiration schedule of leases. Consequently, estimates of FFO are more frequently referenced measures, although analysts and investors will tend to base their investment judgments to a significant degree on their AFFO estimates. Although many REITs and REOCs compute and refer to AFFO in their disclosures, their methods of computation and their assumptions vary. Firms that compile statistics and estimates of publicly traded enterprises for publications, such as Bloomberg and Refinitiv, tend not to gather AFFO estimates because of the absence of a universally accepted methodology for computing AFFO and inconsistent corporate reporting of actual AFFO figures, which hinders corroboration of analysts' estimates.

Exhibit 3 illustrates the most straightforward, convenient way of calculating FFO and AFFO for a hypothetical firm, Office Equity REIT Inc.

**Exhibit 3: Calculation of FFO and AFFO for Office Equity REIT Inc. (SGD thousands, except per-share data)**

| A. Calculation of funds from operations | |
|---|---|
| Net income | 160,638 |
| Add: Depreciation and amortization | 76,100 |
| Add: (Gains)/losses from sale of depreciable real estate | 25,000 |
| Funds from operations | 261,738 |
| FFO per share (55,689 shares outstanding) | 4.70 |
| **B. Calculation of adjusted funds from operations** | |
| Funds from operations | 261,738 |
| Less: Non-cash (straight-line) rent adjustment | 21,103 |
| Less: Recurring maintenance-type capital expenditures and leasing commissions | 55,765 |
| Adjusted funds from operations | 184,870 |
| AFFO per share (55,689 shares outstanding) | 3.32 |

**KNOWLEDGE CHECK**

## Analyst Adjustments (I)

1. Which of the following is the *best* measure of a REIT's current economic return to shareholders?

   **A.** FFO

   **B.** AFFO

   **C.** Net income

   **Solution**

   B is correct. AFFO is calculated from FFO by deducting non-cash rent, capital expenditures for maintenance, and leasing costs.

   A is incorrect because it does not account for non-cash rent, capital expenditures for maintenance, and leasing costs. C is incorrect because it includes non-cash depreciation and amortization expense and does not account for non-cash rent, capital expenditures, and capitalized leasing costs, which are appropriate adjustments to net income in calculating current economic return.

2. An analyst gathers the following information for a REIT:

   | | |
   |---|---:|
   | Net operating income | $115 million |
   | Book value of properties | $1,005 million |
   | Market value of debt outstanding | $505 million |
   | Market cap rate | 7% |
   | Shares outstanding | 100 million |

   The REIT's NAV per share is *closest* to:

   **A.** $10.05.

   **B.** $11.38.

   **C.** $16.42.

   **Solution**

   B is correct. NAVPS estimates real estate values by capitalizing NOI. Valuing $115 million of NOI with a capitalization rate of 7% yields a value for the properties of $1,642,857,000. After deducting $505 million of debt at market value, NAV is $1,137,857,000; NAVPS equals NAV divided by 100 million shares outstanding, or $11.38.

   A is incorrect because it is the book value of the assets (not the net assets) per share: $1,005 million divided by 100 million shares = $10.05 per share. It does not take into account the market value of the assets and does not deduct debt. C is incorrect because it is the market value of the real estate—that is, NOI capitalized at 7%, divided by 100 million shares: $1,642,857,000/100,000,000 = $16.42. This calculation excludes the liabilities of the entity.

3. All else equal, estimated NAV per share will decrease with an increase in the:

   **A.** capitalization rate.

# Valuation: Relative Value (Price Multiple) Approach

   B. estimated growth rate.
   C. deferred tax liabilities.

   **Solution**

   A is correct. The capitalization rate is used to calculate the estimated value of operating real estate because it is the NOI as a percentage of the value of operating real estate: NOI/Capitalization rate = Estimated value. As the capitalization rate increases, the estimated value of operating real estate and thus NAV will decrease.

   B is incorrect because an increase in the estimated growth rate would increase the estimated NOI and the estimated value of operating income. C is incorrect because deferred liabilities are not counted as "hard" liabilities and are not subtracted from the NAV.

## KNOWLEDGE CHECK

## Analyst Adjustments (II)

1. An increase in the capitalization rate will *most likely* decrease a REIT's:

   A. cost of debt.
   B. estimated NOI.
   C. estimated NAV.

   **Solution**

   C is correct. The capitalization rate is used to estimate the market value of real estate, which is then used to calculate NAV.

   A is incorrect because a higher capitalization rate does not decrease the REIT's cost of debt. B is incorrect because the estimated NOI is based on income growth, not the capitalization rate.

2. An analyst gathers the following information for a REIT:

   | | |
   |---|---|
   | Non-cash (straight-line) rent | €207,430 |
   | Depreciation | €611,900 |
   | Recurring maintenance-type capital expenditures and leasing commissions | €550,750 |
   | Adjusted funds from operations | €3,320,000 |
   | AFFO per share | €3.32 |

   The REIT's FFO per share is *closest* to:

   A. €3.93.
   B. €4.08.
   C. €4.48.

   **Solution**

   B is correct. FFO = AFFO + Non-cash (straight-line) rent + Recurring maintenance-type capital expenditures and leasing commissions = 3,320,000 + 550,750 + 207,430 = €4,078,180. The number of shares outstanding = 3,320,000/3.32 = 1,000,000. FFO per share = 4,078,180/1,000,000 ≈ €4.08.

   A is incorrect because it adds depreciation to AFFO (3,320,000 + 611,900 = €3,931,900; 3,931,900/1,000,000 ≈ €3.93 per share). C is incorrect because it also adds depreciation to AFFO + Non-cash (straight-line) rent + Recurring maintenance-type capital expenditures and leasing commissions.

3. Which of the following estimates is *least likely* to be compiled by firms that publish REIT analysts' estimates?

    A. FFO
    B. AFFO
    C. NAV

    **Solution**

    B is correct. Firms that compile statistics and estimates of REITs tend not to gather AFFO estimates because of the absence of a universally accepted methodology for computing AFFO and inconsistent corporate reporting of actual AFFO figures. FFO is commonly tracked in the United States, and NAV is the standard measure in Europe and Asia.

## P/FFO and P/AFFO Multiples: Advantages and Disadvantages

The key advantages and disadvantages of using P/FFO and P/AFFO multiples in the valuation of REITs and REOCs are as follows:

**Advantages**

1. Multiples of earnings measures of this kind are widely accepted in evaluating shares across global stock markets and industries.
2. In light of this acceptance, portfolio managers can put the valuation of REITs and REOCs into context with other investment alternatives.
3. FFO estimates are readily available through market data providers, such as Bloomberg and Refinitiv, which facilitates calculating P/FFO multiples.
4. Multiples can be used in conjunction with such items as expected growth and leverage levels to deepen the relative analysis among REITs and REOCs. Because FFO and AFFO do not take into account differences in leverage, leverage ratios can be used to adjust for leverage differences among REITs when using these multiples to compare valuations.

**Disadvantages**

1. Applying a multiple to FFO or AFFO may not capture the intrinsic value of all real estate assets held by the REIT or REOC, such as non-income-producing assets (for example, land held for development, vacant buildings, and properties under development), underused assets (current use may not represent highest and best use), or assets with below-market rents.
2. P/FFO does not adjust for the impact of recurring capital expenditures needed to keep properties operating smoothly. Although P/AFFO should do so, wide variations in estimates and assumptions are incorporated into the calculation of AFFO.
3. An increased level of such one-time items as gains and accounting charges, as well as new revenue recognition rules, has affected the income statement, thus making P/FFO and P/AFFO more difficult to compute and complicating comparisons between companies.

# REIT MINI CASE STUDY: EXAMPLE OF DISCLOSURES AND VALUATION ANALYSIS

☐ calculate and interpret the value of a REIT share using the net asset value, relative value (price-to-FFO and price-to-AFFO), and discounted cash flow approaches

In this section, we undertake the valuation of a REIT by using the previously outlined approaches for valuation. The REIT in our example is Capitol Shopping Center REIT Inc. (CSC), a fictitious company that owns and operates retail shopping centers primarily in the Washington, DC, metropolitan area. The following are CSC's income statements, balance sheets, and cash flow statements for Year 1 and Year 2.

### Exhibit 4: Capitol Shopping Center REIT Inc. Financial Statements (USD thousands, except per-share data)

**A. Income statements**

|  | Three Months Ending 31 December | | Year Ending 31 December | |
|---|---|---|---|---|
|  | Year 2 | Year 1 | Year 2 | Year 1 |
| Rental revenue | 133,700 | 130,300 | 517,546 | 501,600 |
| Other property income | 3,600 | 2,100 | 14,850 | 13,450 |
| Total property revenue | 137,300 | 132,400 | 532,396 | 515,050 |
| Rental expenses | 29,813 | 28,725 | 112,571 | 109,775 |
| Property taxes | 15,050 | 14,850 | 57,418 | 55,375 |
| Total property expenses | 44,863 | 43,575 | 169,989 | 165,150 |
| Property net operating income | 92,437 | 88,825 | 362,407 | 349,900 |
| Other income | 450 | 385 | 1,840 | 1,675 |
| General and administrative expenses | 6,150 | 7,280 | 23,860 | 26,415 |
| EBITDA | 86,737 | 81,930 | 340,387 | 325,160 |
| Depreciation and amortization | 28,460 | 27,316 | 115,110 | 111,020 |
| Net interest expense | 25,867 | 25,015 | 100,823 | 99,173 |
| Net income available to common | 32,410 | 29,599 | 124,454 | 114,967 |
| Weighted average common shares | 61,100 | 60,100 | 60,600 | 60,100 |
| Earnings per share | 0.53 | 0.49 | 2.05 | 1.91 |

**B. Balance sheets**

|  | Year Ending 31 December | |
|---|---|---|
|  | Year 2 | Year 1 |
| *Assets* | | |
| Real estate, at cost | | |

### B. Balance sheets

|  | Year Ending 31 December | |
|---|---|---|
|  | Year 2 | Year 1 |
| Operating real estate | 3,627,576 | 3,496,370 |
| Land held for future development | 133,785 | 133,785 |
|  | 3,761,361 | 3,630,155 |
| Less accumulated depreciation | (938,097) | (822,987) |
| Net real estate | 2,823,264 | 2,807,168 |
| Cash and equivalents | 85,736 | 23,856 |
| Accounts receivable, net | 72,191 | 73,699 |
| Deferred rent receivable, net | 38,165 | 33,053 |
| Prepaid expenses and other assets | 106,913 | 101,604 |
| *Total assets* | 3,126,269 | 3,039,380 |
| *Liabilities and shareholders' equity* | | |
| Liabilities | | |
| Mortgages payable | 701,884 | 647,253 |
| Notes payable | 1,090,745 | 1,090,745 |
| Accounts payable and other liabilities | 219,498 | 200,439 |
| Total liabilities | 2,012,127 | 1,938,437 |
| Common shares and equity | 1,114,142 | 1,100,943 |
| Total liabilities and shareholders' equity | 3,126,269 | 3,039,380 |

### C. Cash flow statements

|  | Year Ending 31 December | |
|---|---|---|
|  | Year 2 | Year 1 |
| *Operating activities* | | |
| Net income | 124,454 | 114,967 |
| Depreciation and amortization | 115,110 | 111,020 |
| Change in accounts receivable | 1,508 | 452 |
| Change in deferred rents | (5,112) | (4,981) |
| Change in prepaid expenses and other assets | (5,309) | 1,237 |
| Change in accounts payable and other liabilities | 19,059 | (11,584) |
| Net cash provided by operating activities | 249,710 | 211,111 |
| *Investing activities* | | |
| Acquisition of real estate | (111,200) | (22,846) |
| Capital expenditures on operating real estate | (20,006) | (18,965) |
| Net cash used in investing activities | (131,206) | (41,811) |
| *Financing activities* | | |
| Issuance of mortgages | 54,631 | 14,213 |

## C. Cash flow statements

|  | Year Ending 31 December | |
|---|---|---|
|  | Year 2 | Year 1 |
| Issuance of common shares | 58,425 | 0 |
| Dividends paid to common shareholders | (169,680) | (165,275) |
| Net cash used in financing activities | (56,624) | (151,062) |
| Increase (decrease) in cash and equivalents | 61,880 | 18,238 |
| Cash and cash equivalents, beginning of year | 23,856 | 5,618 |
| Cash and cash equivalents, end of year | 85,736 | 23,856 |

CSC also publishes a supplemental investor packet that provides further disclosures used by the investment community to analyze the company. Exhibit 5 shows its adjustments to arrive at FFO and AFFO, as well as its calculation of dividend payouts based on dividends paid.

### Exhibit 5: Capitol Shopping Center REIT Inc. FFO, AFFO, and Dividend Payouts (USD thousands, except per-share data)

|  | Three Months Ending 31 December | | Year Ending 31 December | |
|---|---|---|---|---|
|  | Year 2 | Year 1 | Year 2 | Year 1 |
| Funds from operations |  |  |  |  |
| Net income | 32,410 | 29,599 | 124,454 | 114,967 |
| Depreciation and amortization | 28,460 | 27,316 | 115,110 | 111,020 |
| Funds from operations | 60,870 | 56,915 | 239,564 | 225,987 |
| FFO/share | 1.00 | 0.95 | 3.95 | 3.76 |
| Adjusted funds from operations |  |  |  |  |
| Funds from operations | 60,870 | 56,915 | 239,564 | 225,987 |
| Less non-cash rents (1) | (1,469) | (1,325) | (5,112) | (4,981) |
| Less recurring capital expenditures (2) | (5,638) | (5,101) | (20,006) | (18,965) |
| Adjusted funds from operations | 53,763 | 50,489 | 214,446 | 202,041 |
| AFFO/share | 0.88 | 0.84 | 3.54 | 3.36 |
| Dividends/share | 0.70 | 0.69 | 2.80 | 2.75 |
| *Dividend payout ratios* |  |  |  |  |
| On FFO | 70.0% | 72.6% | 70.9% | 73.1% |
| On AFFO | 79.6% | 82.1% | 79.1% | 81.8% |

|  | Three Months Ending 31 December | | Year Ending 31 December | |
| --- | --- | --- | --- | --- |
|  | Year 2 | Year 1 | Year 2 | Year 1 |
| Weighted average common shares | 61,100 | 60,100 | 60,600 | 60,100 |

1. Non-cash rents include the impact of straight lining contractual rent increases in leases, per accounting rules. The change in deferred rents can often provide the impact of this accounting on rental revenues.
2. Recurring capital expenditures include those costs needed to maintain the revenue-producing ability of existing assets, such as leasing commissions to keep or attract new tenants, such maintenance items as roofs and parking lot repairs, and basic buildouts of space as an inducement to attract tenants.

The historical stock price and the company's financial statements, including disclosures, are used to complete a simple analysis of the balance sheet, as shown in Exhibit 6.

### Exhibit 6: Capitol Shopping Center REIT Inc. Balance Sheet Analysis (USD thousands, except per-share data)

|  | Year Ending 31 December | |
| --- | --- | --- |
|  | Year 2 | Year 1 |
| Ending debt | 1,792,629 | 1,737,998 |
| Ending stock price | 72.36 | 61.50 |
| Ending shares | 61,100 | 60,100 |
| Ending market capitalization | 4,421,196 | 3,696,150 |
| *Debt/total market capitalization* | *40.5%* | *47.0%* |
| Peer group debt/total market capitalization | 47.1% | 56.7% |
| All REITs debt/total market capitalization | 42.8% | 49.6% |
| EBITDA | 340,387 | 325,160 |
| Interest expense | 100,823 | 99,173 |
| *Interest coverage* | *3.38x* | *3.28x* |
| Peer group interest coverage | 2.35× | 2.16× |
| All REITs interest coverage | 2.58× | 2.27× |
| Ending net debt | 1,706,893 | 1,714,142 |
| EBITDA | 340,387 | 325,160 |
| *Net debt-to-EBITDA* | *5.01×* | *5.27×* |
| Peer group net debt-to-EBITDA | 7.10× | 8.60× |
| All REITs net debt-to-EBITDA | 6.70× | 7.80× |
| Ending net debt | 1,706,893 | 1,714,142 |
| Ending gross real estate | 3,761,361 | 3,630,155 |
| *Net debt/gross real estate (book)* | *45.4%* | *47.2%* |
| Peer group net debt/gross real estate (book) | 52.8% | 55.1% |
| All REITs net debt/gross real estate (book) | 49.6% | 52.6% |

The exhibits provide a historical picture of CCS's financial performance and balance sheet. Some key points about the company's properties, operations, dividend policy, recent business activity, and historical trading attributes follow.

- CSC owns properties that are generally considered defensive in the commercial real estate sector because many of its properties are tenanted by basic necessity goods retailers, such as grocery stores and drug stores.

- CSC's location in the Washington, DC, metropolitan area is generally viewed as favorable for two key reasons: (1) Washington, DC, is the capital of the United States, and the government is the largest driver of employment and has historically provided more stability than the private sector; and (2) the city is a fairly dense area with strict zoning restrictions that make new construction of shopping centers difficult, which limits competing new supply.

- CSC has been able to increase its rents and net operating income by 2%–3% each year, on average, in the past decade.

- The past two reported years (Year 1 and Year 2) were difficult for the broader commercial real estate markets. CSC was able to achieve positive growth while many of its peers saw FFO and AFFO decline. Because forecasts now call for improving fundamental property-level conditions, CSC's portfolio may not have as much "upside" because it did not experience the decline in occupancy and rents that other REITs did.

- In the middle of Year 2, the company purchased a portfolio of three shopping centers from a local developer for a total price of $111.2 million. The return on these assets in the first year is an estimated 6.75%. The company was able to achieve a better going-in cap rate on this acquisition than the market averages of 6.0%–6.25% because of its strong relationships and reputation with tenants, commercial property brokers, and competitors, as well as its ability to act quickly because of its strong balance sheet. In addition, the property is not fully leased, leaving the potential to increase net operating income if CSC can attract additional tenants. CSC funded the purchase with a $54.6 million mortgage at a 6% interest rate and cash from a common stock offering of 1 million shares and from cash on hand.

- The company intends to make additional acquisitions in the future as part of its growth plan. It intends to use a combination of debt, common equity, and internally generated cash to make these purchases. It typically requires the properties it acquires to generate an unleveraged internal rate of return of 9.5% in the form of current yield and capital appreciation over time.

- CSC's balance sheet strategy is to operate at less than 50% debt/market capitalization, with a preference for leverage to be closer to 40%. At year-end 2018, CSC's debt/market capitalization was 40.5% and its interest coverage was 3.38×. The company's current in-place average debt cost is 5.7%. In comparison, CSC's peers operate at an average leverage level of 47.1% and have an interest coverage ratio of 2.35×.

- CSC's board has chosen a dividend policy that provides an approximate 80% payout of cash flow, or AFFO. This level allows the company to pay an attractive dividend to shareholders, retain some cash flow, provide a cushion in the event of a downturn, and remain in compliance with REIT payout requirements in the United States. It is easily able to meet these REIT payout requirements because the requirements are based on taxable net income, which is calculated after deducting depreciation. In fact, CSC's dividend level has run well in excess of taxable net income, according to comments made by its management.

- Over the last decade, CSC has traded between 9× and 19× FFO, while its peers have traded between 8× and 18×, and all REITs have traded between 7× and 20×. On an AFFO basis, CSC's historical multiple has been 10×–21×, with its peers trading between 9×–19× and all REITs being in the 9×–24× range.
- Currently, shopping center REITs are estimated to be trading at 7.6% above analyst estimates of NAV. The overall REIT sector is estimated to be trading at a 14.8% premium to estimated NAV.
- CSC's historical beta to the broader equity market is 0.80. The current risk-free rate of return is 4.0%, and the market risk premium is estimated at 5.0%.

Investors and analysts who cover CSC have published estimates for its FFO per share, AFFO per share, and dividends per share for the next three years. Putting the average, or "consensus," of these estimates together with the company's reported results reveals the FFO/AFFO and dividend snapshot shown in Exhibit 7.

### Exhibit 7: Capitol Shopping Center REIT Inc. Actual and Estimated Earnings and Dividends (all amounts are per share)

|  | Year Ending 31 December | | | | |
|---|---|---|---|---|---|
|  | Yr1A | Yr2A | Yr3E | Yr4E | Yr5E |
| CSC's FFO/share | $3.76 | $3.95 | $4.23 | $4.59 | $4.80 |
| Growth | — | 5.1% | 7.1% | 8.5% | 4.6% |
| Peer group FFO/share growth | — | 3.4% | 6.8% | 8.2% | 4.2% |
| All REITs FFO/share growth | — | 1.2% | 7.9% | 9.8% | 10.2% |
| CSC's AFFO/share | $3.36 | $3.54 | $3.76 | $4.09 | $4.31 |
| Growth | — | 5.4% | 6.2% | 8.8% | 5.4% |
| Peer group AFFO/share growth | — | −1.0% | 6.2% | 9.1% | 4.8% |
| All REITs AFFO/share growth | — | −3.0% | 8.1% | 9.7% | 10.8% |
| CSC's dividends/share | $2.75 | $2.80 | $2.98 | $3.25 | $3.40 |
| Growth | — | 1.8% | 6.4% | 9.1% | 4.6% |
| Peer group dividends/share growth | — | −2.0% | 5.6% | 7.9% | 5.1% |
| All REITs dividends/share growth | — | −5.0% | 7.8% | 8.9% | 6.0% |
| CSC's dividend payout on AFFO | 81.8% | 79.1% | 79.3% | 79.5% | 78.9% |

Taking the recent stock price of $69.85 per share and focusing on the next two years (as most analysts looking at multiples do), we can determine comparative FFO and AFFO multiples for CRE. Exhibit 8 also includes the multiples of its direct peers and the entire REIT industry.

### Exhibit 8: Comparative Multiple Analysis

|  | P/FFO | | P/AFFO | |
|---|---|---|---|---|
|  | Yr3E | Yr4E | Yr3E | Yr4E |
| Capitol Shopping Center REIT Inc. (CSC)[a] | 16.5× | 15.2× | 18.6× | 17.1× |
| Shopping center–oriented REITs | 14.5× | 13.3× | 16.1× | 14.5× |

# REIT Mini Case Study: Example of Disclosures and Valuation Analysis

|  | P/FFO | | P/AFFO | |
|---|---|---|---|---|
|  | Yr3E | Yr4E | Yr3E | Yr4E |
| All REITs | 14.2× | 12.8× | 16.5× | 14.6× |
| *CSC's premium/(discount) to:* | | | | |
| Shopping center REITs | 13.8% | 14.3% | 15.5% | 17.9% |
| All REITs | 16.2% | 18.8% | 12.7% | 17.1% |

<sup>a</sup>Based on a current stock price of $69.85.

## Selection of Valuation Methods

As this discussion demonstrates, different valuation methods can yield different results. Under such circumstances, an analyst should re-examine the assumptions made to investigate why the approaches are generating such different results. The methods selected by an analyst may depend on which ones the analyst believes use the most reliable assumptions, which ones the analyst believes will be used by other investors, or which ones best reflect the analyst's own investment philosophy or view of value. The analyst may choose to use a single valuation approach, a midpoint in the range of values obtained by using several approaches, or a weighted average of the values obtained based on the analyst's view of the relative reliability of the models used to arrive at the values.

> **KNOWLEDGE CHECK**
>
> ## Valuation (I)
>
> 1. If the outlook for economic growth turns negative and property market transaction volumes decline, it is *least likely* that CSC's:
>
>    **A.** P/FFO and P/AFFO would be lower.
>
>    **B.** relative P/FFO and P/AFFO multiples would be higher than those of peers.
>
>    **C.** NAV becomes the most useful valuation method.
>
>    **Solution**
>
>    C is correct. NAV becomes more subjective in a negative and less liquid market with fewer observable transactions, and thus this basis of valuation becomes less useful and reliable.
>
>    A and B are incorrect because P/FFO and P/AFFO are likely to fall in a negative economic environment, but investors may be willing to pay a relative premium for CSC's stock based on its superior stability in economically challenging times. Thus, P/FFO and P/AFFO are likely to be higher than those of peers.
>
> 2. If other REITs have no land on their balance sheets, how is CSC's "Land held for future development" *best* factored into a relative P/FFO or P/AFFO multiple valuation?
>
>    **A.** There should be no impact on multiples as a result of land value.
>
>    **B.** CSC would warrant lower multiples to account for land value.

**C.** CSC would warrant higher multiples to account for land value.

**Solution**

C is correct. Although it may not produce income that contributes to FFO or AFFO, the land has value and represents a source of greater internal growth potential. For that reason, A and B are incorrect.

3. An analyst speaks with private market real estate investors and learns that because interest rates have just increased 200 bps, buyers will require future property acquisitions to have going-in cap rates that are 100 bps to 200 bps higher than those on recent property market transactions. The analyst's estimate of NAV for CSC *most likely*:

    **A.** increases as cap rates are higher.

    **B.** decreases as cap rates are higher.

    **C.** remains the same unless CSC has debt maturing in the near term.

    **Solution**

    B is correct. Estimated real estate value decreases as the cap rate increases. Because NAV is derived directly from estimated real estate value, it also decreases. For this reason, A is incorrect. C is incorrect because an increase in cap rates decreases asset values. The fact that CSC has debt maturing in the near term is not a key factor influencing NAV.

4. An analyst determines that CSC purchased its "Land held for future development" 15 years ago and that on average, land values at that time were one-third of what they are today. Which of the following *best* adjusts NAV to reflect this consideration?

    **A.** The cap rate on operating assets should be changed.

    **B.** Land value and thus NAV should be adjusted higher to reflect today's valuations.

    **C.** NAV is still mainly a representation of book values; thus, there should be no adjustments.

    **Solution**

    B is correct. An analyst tries to attribute market values to real property owned.

    A is incorrect because the cap rate used by analysts in calculating NAVs represents the return on only the income-producing asset portfolio and does not relate to land holdings that are not currently producing any income. C is incorrect because NAV is not a representation of book values, which rely on accounting methodology rather than market values.

5. Zoning in CSC's real estate markets is changed to allow more new space in the future, dampening CSC's long-term FFO growth by about 0.5%. The effect on CSC's valuation using a dividend discount model is *most likely* that the present value of the dividend stream:

    **A.** decreases because of lower growth.

    **B.** remains the same.

    **C.** increases because of the new supply.

    **Solution**

    A is correct. Lower growth affects the projected dividend stream, decreasing its present value. For that reason, B and C are incorrect.

> **KNOWLEDGE CHECK**
>
> ## Valuation (II)
>
> 1. An analyst gathers the following information for two REITs:
>
>    |        | Price/NAV | Capitalization Rate Used in NAV |
>    |--------|-----------|--------------------------------|
>    | REIT A | 100%      | 6%                             |
>    | REIT B | 99%       | 8%                             |
>
>    If the REITs have similar property portfolio values, interest expense, and corporate overhead, which REIT *most likely* has the higher price/FFO?
>
>    **A.** REIT A
>
>    **B.** REIT B
>
>    **C.** They will have similar P/FFO because their ratios of price to NAV are almost identical.
>
>    **Solution**
>
>    A is correct. If both companies have similar portfolio values as indicated in the text and by the similar P/NAV, then the company with the lower capitalization rate is more expensive, which results in lower FFO and hence a higher P/FFO. If each company were worth ¥100, then REIT A, which is valued at a 6% cap rate, would have ¥6 of NOI and REIT B would have ¥8 of NOI. Because interest expense and overhead are similar for both companies, REIT A would also have lower FFO and a correspondingly higher P/FFO multiple.
>
>    B is incorrect because A has a lower capitalization rate, implying a lower FFO and hence a higher P/FFO if P/NAV for each company is similar, which is the case here.
>
>    C is incorrect because it neglects the effect of the lower capitalization rate of REIT A.

# PRIVATE VS. PUBLIC: A COMPARISON

☐ explain advantages and disadvantages of investing in real estate through publicly traded securities compared to private vehicles

Large institutional and high-net-worth investors have historically pursued private real estate investments through direct ownership, joint ventures, and private fund investments, whereas individual investors, without the resources to invest directly, typically invested in listed property companies. As more real estate companies went public and continued to issue equity to fund acquisitions, developments, and mergers, the market cap of the publicly listed real estate sector rose significantly. This larger market float and liquidity permitted institutional investors to add to their real estate exposure by creating allocations to public real estate companies

Should investors with the ability to pursue both public *and* private real estate investments choose one over the other? The answer depends on investor objectives, including total return requirements, volatility (risk) tolerance, diversification goals, and the expected returns from each investment. Many institutional investors such as pension funds and endowments have chosen to allocate to both.

Both public and private real estate equity investments provide exposure to real estate properties, potentially hedge inflation, deliver attractive risk-adjusted returns, and provide some diversification benefits to stock and bond portfolios.

Listed real estate can play a complementary role in private real estate. Listed real estate's liquidity makes it easier to express a short-term view, such as when markets become too negative on retail and drive shares of public companies below net asset value. When there are sustained valuation differences between public and private real estate, fund and company managers can capture opportunities. If public companies trade well below net asset value, the public companies may choose to go private or sell to private real estate funds. When real estate values are high, public companies can sell real estate to realize gains and private funds may seek exits through the IPO market.

Private real estate investors have the ability to pursue a variety of strategies, such as merchant (for sale) development, which is highly restricted for REITs. In some countries, REITs were early movers in specialty sectors, such as self-storage and data centers. Investors wanting exposure to some of these niches had to seek out listed company exposure until the private funds moved into these sectors, often in the search for higher yield.

Private and public real estate investments both have something to offer investors, and each has its drawbacks. Exhibit 9 summarizes some of the key differences, advantages, and disadvantages of public and private real estate investing.

**Exhibit 9: Advantages and Disadvantages of Private and Public Real Estate**

| Private Real Estate (Direct Investment) | Public Real Estate (Equity REITs and Real Estate Operating Companies) |
|---|---|
| *Advantages* | |

## Private vs. Public: A Comparison

| Private Real Estate (Direct Investment) | Public Real Estate (Equity REITs and Real Estate Operating Companies) |
|---|---|
| ▪ Direct exposure to real estate fundamentals | ▪ Tracks real estate fundamentals over the long term |
| ▪ Stable returns/low volatility | ▪ Liquidity |
| ▪ Property performance drives returns | ▪ Access to professional management |
| ▪ Low correlations with other asset classes | ▪ Potential inflation hedge |
| ▪ Potential inflation hedge | ▪ Potential for strong alignment of interests |
| ▪ Control (direct real estate and separate accounts) | ▪ Tax-efficient structure avoids double taxation (REITs only) |
| ▪ Potential to earn illiquidity premium | ▪ Potential for exposure to diversified portfolios |
| ▪ Wide variety of strategies/few restrictions | ▪ Access to diverse sectors, including data centers, medical offices, and self-storage |
| ▪ Tax benefits (e.g., accelerated depreciation, deferred taxes in some markets when sales are reinvested in other real estate) | ▪ Low investment requirements |
| | ▪ Low entry/exit costs |
| | ▪ No special investor qualifications beyond equity investing generally |
| | ▪ Limited liability |
| | ▪ Greater regulation and investor protections |
| | ▪ High transparency |
| *Disadvantages* | |
| ▪ Low liquidity | ▪ High volatility (compared with private real estate) |
| ▪ Difficult-to-exit funds' redemption activity is high | ▪ Equity market correlation is high in short term |
| ▪ High fees and expenses | ▪ REIT structure limits possible activities |
| ▪ Appraisal valuations commonly lag changes in market conditions | ▪ Stock prices may not reflect underlying property values (i.e., trade at discount to NAV) |
| ▪ Fewer regulations to protect investors | |
| ▪ Some managers focus on asset gathering over high profitability | ▪ Dividends taxed at high current income tax rates |
| ▪ High investment minimums and high net-worth requirements | ▪ Regulatory compliance costs are prohibitive for small companies |
| ▪ Low transparency | ▪ Poor governance/mis-aligned interests can penalize stock performance |
| ▪ High returns often derived from leverage | ▪ Equity markets often penalize companies with high leverage |

# PRACTICE PROBLEMS

## The following information relates to questions 1–4

Maitha Smith is the CIO of the Westland Pension Fund (the "Fund"). Smith and her junior analyst are analyzing Bay Realty Corp. ("Bay"), a publicly traded REIT based in San Francisco, for a potential investment. Bay currently owns and operates 40 office buildings totaling 8 million square feet. These properties exhibit an average LTV (loan-to-value) ratio of 40%. Bay owns no other real estate–related assets. Bay's senior executives are company employees who report to the board of directors, whose members are elected by shareholders.

Smith first instructs her junior analyst to conduct a NAVPS (net asset value per share) analysis on Bay. The junior analyst makes the following three statements:

**Statement 1:** NAVPS should not include investors' assessments of the value of any non-asset-based income streams, the value of non–real estate assets, or the value added by management.

**Statement 2:** REITs whose shares trade below NAVPS or have high leverage might have a more difficult time raising new capital to fund acquisitions and development, which could limit long-term growth.

**Statement 3:** Shares priced at discounts to NAVPS are interpreted as indications of potential overvaluation.

To complement the NAVPS, Smith instructs her junior analyst to also calculate FFO and AFFO measures for Bay. The junior analyst then makes the following three statements as part of the ongoing discussion:

**Statement 4:** AFFO better approximates a company's sustainable dividend-paying capacity than FFO.

**Statement 5:** FFO and AFFO are based on net income available to equity and thus represent levered income.

**Statement 6:** FFO is superior to AFFO as a measure of economic income and thus economic return because it takes into account the capital expenditures necessary to maintain the economic income of a property portfolio.

After the discussion, the junior analyst obtains selected information on Bay, which is shown in Exhibit 1:

| Exhibit 1 | |
|---|---:|
| Non-cash (straight-line) rent | $215,000 |
| Recurring maintenance–type capital expenditures and leasing commissions | $700,000 |
| Adjusted funds from operations | $4,000,000 |
| AFFO per share | $5.00 |
| Current stock price | $80.00 |

1. Which of the following *best* describes Bay?

    **A.** Mortgage REIT

# Practice Problems

   B. Internally managed REIT

   C. Real estate operating company (REOC)

2. Which of the junior analyst's three statements regarding NAVPS is correct?

   A. Statement 1

   B. Statement 2

   C. Statement 3

3. Which of the junior analyst's three statements regarding FFO and AFFO is *incorrect*?

   A. Statement 4

   B. Statement 5

   C. Statement 6

4. Based on Exhibit 1, Bay's P/FFO is *closest* to:

   A. 14.3x

   B. 13.0x.

   C. 20.7x.

# SOLUTIONS

1. B is correct. Bay is internally managed, or self-managed. Bay's senior executives are company employees who report to the board of directors, whose members are elected by shareholders. Fully integrated REITs, such as Bay, generally have fewer conflicts than REITs that are externally advised or externally managed.

   A is incorrect because Bay is an equity REIT, not a mortgage REIT. Bay currently owns and operates 40 office buildings totaling 8 million square feet.

   C is incorrect because REOCs are ordinary taxable real estate ownership companies, which are different from REITs. Businesses are organized as REOCs, as opposed to REITs, if they are located in countries that do not have a tax-advantaged REIT regime in place, if they engage to a large extent in the development of for-sale real estate properties, or if they offer other non-qualifying services, such as brokerage and third-party property management.

2. B is correct. REITs whose shares trade below NAVPS or have high leverage might have a more difficult time raising new capital to fund acquisitions and development, which in turn could limit long-term growth, in contrast to REITs that trade at or above NAVPS.

   A is incorrect because NAVPS should include investors' assessments of the value of any non-asset-based income streams, the value of non–real estate assets, and the value added by management.

   C is incorrect because shares priced at discounts to NAVPS are interpreted as indications of potential undervaluation.

3. C is incorrect. AFFO is superior to FFO (not the other way around) as a measure of economic income and thus economic return because it takes into account the capital expenditures necessary to maintain the economic income of a property portfolio.

   A is correct because AFFO better approximates a company's sustainable dividend-paying capacity than FFO.

   B is correct because both FFO and AFFO are based on net income available to equity and thus represent levered income.

4. B is correct. FFO = AFFO + Non-cash (straight-line) rent + Recurring maintenance–type capital expenditures and leasing commissions = $4,000,000 + $215,000 + $700,000 = $4,915,000. The number of shares outstanding = 4,000,000/5.00 = 800,000. FFO per share = 4,915,000/800,000 = $6.14.

   Current stock price = $80.00 per share

   P/FFO = $80.00/$6.14 = 13.0x

   A is incorrect because 14.3x is incorrectly calculated as follows:

   $4,000,000 − $215,000 + $700,000 = $4,485,000. The number of shares outstanding = 4,000,000/5.00 = 800,000. FFO per share = 4,485,000/800,000 = $5.61.

   Current stock price = $80.00 per share

   P/FFO = $80.00/$5.61 = 14.3x

   C is incorrect because 20.7x is incorrectly calculated as follows:

   $4,000,000 − $215,000 − $700,000 = $3,085,000. The number of shares outstanding = 4,000,000/5.00 = 800,000. FFO per share = 3,085,000/800,000 = $3.86.

   Current stock price = $80.00 per share

   P/FFO = $80.00/$3.86 = 20.7x

# LEARNING MODULE 4

## Private Equity Investments

by Yves Courtois, CMT, MRICS, CFA, and Tim Jenkinson, PhD.

Yves Courtois, CMT, MRICS, CFA, is at KPMG (Luxembourg). Tim Jenkinson, PhD, is at Saïd Business School, Oxford University (United Kingdom).

| LEARNING OUTCOMES | |
|---|---|
| Mastery | The candidate should be able to: |
| ☐ | explain sources of value creation in private equity |
| ☐ | explain how private equity firms align their interests with those of the managers of portfolio companies |
| ☐ | compare and contrast characteristics of buyout and venture capital investments |
| ☐ | interpret LBO model and VC method output |
| ☐ | explain alternative exit routes in private equity and their impact on value |
| ☐ | explain risks and costs of investing in private equity |
| ☐ | explain private equity fund structures, terms, due diligence, and valuation in the context of an analysis of private equity fund returns |
| ☐ | interpret and compare financial performance of private equity funds from the perspective of an investor |
| ☐ | calculate management fees, carried interest, net asset value, distributed to paid in (DPI), residual value to paid in (RVPI), and total value to paid in (TVPI) of a private equity fund |

## 1. INTRODUCTION

Private equity's shift from a niche activity to a critical component of the financial system is evident from investors' financial commitment: around $2.8 trillion globally as of mid-2018. And that's just the equity portion. The use of debt means transaction value is often two or three times the actual equity raised. Blackstone, Carlyle, and KKR are household names and publicly traded companies of significant size. Private equity funds may account for 15%–18% of the value of all mergers and acquisitions, and the market capitalization of Alibaba, Amazon, Facebook, and Google has raised the profile of venture capital investing.

We take two approaches to illuminate our subject: In Section 2 the perspective is primarily that of the private equity firm evaluating potential investments. Valuing acquisitions is particularly complex; except for public-to-private transactions, there will be no market prices to refer to, and the challenges are considerable. In Section 3 we take the perspective of an outside investor investing in a fund sponsored by the private equity firm.

Definitions of private equity differ, but here we include the entire asset class of equity investments that are not quoted on stock markets. Private equity stretches from venture capital (VC)—working with early-stage companies that may be without revenues but that possess good ideas or technology—to growth equity, providing capital to expand established private businesses often by taking a minority interest, all the way to large buyouts (leveraged buyouts, or LBOs), in which the private equity firm buys the entire company. When the target is publicly traded, the private equity fund performs a public-to-private transaction, removing the target from the stock market. But buyout transactions usually involve private companies and very often a particular division of an existing company.

Some exclude venture capital from the private equity universe because of the higher risk profile of backing new companies as opposed to mature ones. For this reading, we refer simply to *venture capital* and *buyouts* as the two main forms of private equity.

Many classifications of private equity are available. Classifications proposed by the European and Private Equity Venture Capital Association (EVCA) are displayed in Exhibit 1.

### Exhibit 1: Classification of Private Equity in Terms of Stage and Type of Financing of Portfolio Companies

| Broad Category | Subcategory | Brief Description |
| --- | --- | --- |
| Venture capital | Seed stage | Financing provided to research business ideas, develop prototype products, or conduct market research |
| | Start-up stage | Financing to recently created companies with well-articulated business and marketing plans |
| | Later (expansion) stage | Financing to companies that have started their selling effort and may already be covering costs: Financing may serve to expand production capacity, product development, or provide working capital. |
| | Replacement capital | Financing provided to purchase shares from other existing venture capital investors or to reduce financial leverage. |
| Growth | Expansion capital | Financing to established and mature companies in exchange for equity, often a minority stake, to expand into new markets and/or improve operations |
| Buyout | Acquisition capital | Financing in the form of debt, equity, or quasi-equity provided to a company to acquire another company |
| | Leveraged buyout | Financing provided by an LBO firm to acquire a company |
| | Management buyout | Financing provided to the management to acquire a company, specific product line, or division (carve-out) |

| Broad Category | Subcategory | Brief Description |
|---|---|---|
| Special situations | Mezzanine finance | Financing generally provided in the form of subordinated debt and an equity kicker (warrants, equity, etc.) frequently in the context of LBO transactions |
| | Distressed/turnaround | Financing of companies in need of restructuring or facing financial distress |
| | One-time opportunities | Financing in relation to changing industry trends and new government regulations |
| | Other | Other forms of private equity financing are also possible—for example, activist investing, funds of funds, and secondaries. |

Private equity funds may also be classified geographically, by sector, or both. Certain specialists target real asset classes, such as real estate, infrastructure, energy, and timber, or they seek out emerging or niche sectors, such as agribusiness or royalties in pharmaceuticals, music, film, or TV.

US private equity enjoyed a far larger market size historically than private equity in other regions, with few restrictions on hostile takeovers. Buyouts subsequently expanded to Europe and then Asia as friendly deals became commonplace. In broad terms, around four-fifths of the money has been flowing into buyout, growth, and other types of private equity in both the United States and Europe, with buyout amounts far exceeding other types. The sheer scale of buyouts means that an individual deal can absorb billions of dollars in capital. Buyout funds have benefited from increased allocations given their ability to absorb far higher capital amounts and to deliver historically higher-than-average returns.

Venture capital deals, in contrast, tend to drip, providing small amounts of feed money. Still, advances in technology and communications are causing the number of venture capital funds and the availability of start-up capital to grow. Investor attention started to shift to China in 2015, an especially active year for raising capital. VC funds targeting Asia had more than US$200 billion in 2017, up from US$50 billion in 2010.

Most private equity money comes from institutional investors, such as pension funds, sovereign wealth funds, endowments, and insurance companies, although many family offices and high-net-worth individuals also invest directly or through fund-of-funds intermediaries. Venture capital investors include government agencies and corporations seeking to promote regional investment or gain insight into, and possibly control of, emerging businesses and technologies.

Private equity investment is characterized by a buy-to-sell orientation: Investors typically expect their money to be returned, with a handsome profit, within 10 years of committing their funds. The economic incentives of the funds are aligned with this goal.

# VALUATION TECHNIQUES IN PRIVATE EQUITY TRANSACTIONS

2

- [ ] explain sources of value creation in private equity
- [ ] explain how private equity firms align their interests with those of the managers of portfolio companies

This reading is not intended to be a comprehensive review of valuation techniques. Instead, we highlight some essential considerations specific to private equity. Private equity firms serve as a rich laboratory for applying the principles of asset and equity valuation.

First and foremost, we must distinguish between the price paid for a private equity stake and the valuation of that same private equity stake. The price paid for a private equity stake is the outcome of a negotiation process in which each party may assign a different value to the same stake. Whereas public company shares are traded on a regulated market and their prices are transparent, the buyers and sellers of private equity interests generally make greater efforts to uncover their value. Private equity valuation is thus time-bound and dependent on the respective motives of buyers and sellers.

Selecting a valuation methodology for a private equity (PE) portfolio company depends largely on its stage of development. Common methodologies appear in Exhibit 2, along with the stages in which they may apply.

### Exhibit 2: Overview of Selected Valuation Methodologies and Their Possible Application in Private Equity

| Valuation Technique | Brief Description | Application |
| --- | --- | --- |
| Income approach: discounted cash flow (DCF) | Value is obtained by discounting expected future cash flows at an appropriate cost of capital. | Generally applies across the broad spectrum of company stages.<br>Given the emphasis on expected cash flows, DCF provides the most relevant results when applied to companies with a sufficient operating history. It is most applicable to companies operating from the expansion phase up to the maturity phase. |
| Relative value: earnings multiples | Application of an earnings multiple to the earnings of a portfolio company. The earnings multiple is frequently obtained from the average of a group of public companies operating in a similar business and of comparable size.<br>Commonly used multiples include price/earnings (P/E), enterprise value/EBITDA, enterprise value/sales. | Generally applies to companies with a significant operating history and a predictable stream of cash flows.<br>May also apply (with caution) to companies operating at the expansion stage.<br>Rarely applies to early-stage or start-up companies. |
| Real option | The right to undertake a business decision (call or put option). Requires judgmental assumptions about key option parameters. | Generally applies to situations in which the management or shareholders have significant flexibility in making radically different strategic decisions (i.e., option to undertake or abandon a high-risk, high-return project). Therefore, generally applies to some companies operating at the seed or start-up phase. |
| Replacement cost | Estimated cost to recreate the business as it stands as of the valuation date. | Generally applies to early-stage (seed and start-up) companies, companies operating at the development stage and generating negative cash flows, or asset-rich companies.<br>Rarely applies to mature companies because it is difficult to estimate the cost to recreate a company with a long operating history. For example, it would be difficult to estimate the cost to recreate a long-established brand, such as Coca-Cola, whereas the replacement cost methodology may be used to estimate the brand value for a recently launched beverage (R&D expenses, marketing costs, etc.). |

## Valuation Techniques in Private Equity Transactions

In a vibrant and booming private equity market, there is a natural tendency among participants to focus on the earnings approach to determine value. The benchmark value it offers is perceived as corresponding best to the market's present state, but given the lack of liquidity of private equity investments, the concurrent use of other metrics is strongly recommended.

In most transactions, private equity investors are faced with a set of investment decisions that are based on an assessment of prospective returns and associated probabilities. Private equity firms are confronted generally with a large flow of information arising from detailed due diligence investigations and from complex financial models. It is essential to understand the potential upside and downside impact of internal and external factors on the business, net income, and cash flows. The interplay between exogenous factors (such as favorable and unfavorable macroeconomic conditions, interest rates, and exchange rates) and value drivers for the business (such as sales margins and required investments) should also be considered carefully. For example, what will be the sales growth if competition increases or if competing new technologies are introduced?

When building financial forecasts, variables in the financial projections should be linked to key business drivers with assigned subjective probabilities. The use of Monte Carlo simulation can further enhance the analysis and identify significant financial upsides and downsides to the business. In a Monte Carlo simulation, the analyst must model the fundamental value drivers of the portfolio company, which are in turn linked to a valuation model. The objective is to ensure that the simulation is as close as possible to the realities of the business and encompasses the range of possible outcomes, including base case, worst case, and best case scenarios (sometimes called a triangular approach).

Other key considerations when evaluating a private equity transaction include the value of control, the impact of illiquidity, and the extent of any country risk. Estimating the discount for illiquidity and marketability and a premium for control are among the most subjective decisions in private equity valuation. The control premium is an incremental value associated with a bloc of shares that will be instrumental in gaining control of a company. In most buyouts, the entire equity capital is acquired by the private equity purchasers. But in venture capital deals, investors often acquire minority positions. In this case, the control premium (if any) largely depends on the relative strength and alignment of interest of shareholders willing to gain control. For example, in a situation with only a limited number of investors able to acquire control, the control premium is likely to be much more significant relative to a situation with a dominant controlling shareholder invested along with a large number of much smaller shareholders.

The distinction between marketability and liquidity is more subtle. The cost of illiquidity may be defined as the cost of finding prospective buyers and represents the speed of conversion of the assets to cash, whereas the cost of marketability is closely related to the right to sell the assets. In practice, the marketability and liquidity discounts are frequently lumped together.

The cost for illiquidity and premium for control may be closely related because illiquidity may be more acute when there is a fierce battle for control. But there are many dimensions to illiquidity. The size of the illiquidity discount may be influenced by such factors as the shareholding structure, the level of profitability and its expected sustainability, the possibility of an initial public offering (IPO) in the near future, and the size of the private company. Because determining the relative importance of each factor may be difficult, the illiquidity discount is frequently assessed overall on a judgmental basis. In practice, the discount for illiquidity and premium for control are both adjustments to the preliminary value estimate instead of being factored into the cost of capital.

When valuing private equity portfolio companies in emerging markets, country and currency risk represent additional sources of risk frequently added to a modified version of the standard CAPM. Estimating the appropriate country risk premium represents a significant challenge in emerging market private equity valuation, and numerous estimation approaches exist.

All of this is to say that PE valuation is highly challenging and valuation does not simply involve a net present value calculation based on a static set of future profit projections. Using a combination of valuation methodologies, supplemented by stress testing and scenario analysis, provides the strongest support to estimating value. One of the key ways private equity firms add value is by challenging the way businesses are run. Should the PE firm manage to improve the business's finances, operations, management, or marketing, we can expect additional value.

## How Is Value Created in Private Equity?

How private equity funds actually create value has been the subject of much debate. Rather than ownership and control being separate, as in most publicly quoted companies, private equity concentrates ownership and control. Many view the combining of ownership and control as a fundamental source of the returns earned by the best private equity funds. The survival of the private equity governance model depends on economic advantages it may have over the public equity governance model, including (1) the ability to re-engineer the private firm to generate superior returns, (2) financial leverage and the ability to access credit markets on favorable terms, and (3) a better alignment of interests between private equity firm owners and the managers of the firms they control.

Do private equity houses have a superior ability to re-engineer companies and therefore generate superior returns? Some of the largest private equity organizations, such as Ardian, Blackstone Group, Carlyle Group, CVC Capital Partners, KKR, and Partners Group, have developed high-end consulting capabilities supported frequently by seasoned industry veterans, such as former CEOs, chief financial officers, and senior advisers. They have proven their ability to execute deals on a global basis. Irrespective of their size, some of the very best firms have developed effective re-engineering capabilities to add value to their investments. But it is hard to believe that this factor, all else being equal, is the main driver of added value. Assuming that private equity houses have a superior ability to re-engineer companies, this would mean that public companies have inherently less ability to do so. Many public companies, however, such as Apple, Berkshire Hathaway, Samsung, Tencent Holdings, Toyota, and Unilever, have long track records of creating value through organizational changes and re-engineering. Only a portion of the value added by private equity houses may be explained by superior capabilities in this sphere.

Is financial leverage the main driver of private equity returns in buyouts? In private equity, target companies are rarely purchased using only the equity of the buyout company. Relative to comparable publicly quoted companies, there is a much greater use of debt in a typical buyout transaction. The use of debt is central to the structure and feasibility of buyouts, and private equity firms use significant proportions of debt to finance each deal. The leverage increases equity returns and the number of transactions a particular fund can make. A private equity firm may invest equity representing 30% of the buyout purchase price and raise the rest in the debt markets. It may use a combination of bank loans—often called leveraged loans because of the prominent proportion of the company's capital structure they represent—and high-yield bonds.

> **Leveraged Loan Covenants**
>
> To protect investors, leveraged loans often carry covenants that may require or restrict certain actions. For instance, the covenants may require the company (1) to maintain specified financial ratios, (2) within certain limits, to submit information regularly so that the bank can monitor performance, or (3) to operate within certain parameters. The covenants may restrict the company from further borrowing (in other words, no additional bonds can be issued and no additional funds can be borrowed from banks or other sources), or they may impose limits on paying dividends or even making certain operating decisions.
>
> Similarly, bond terms may include covenants intended to protect the bondholders. One of the key differences between leveraged loans and high-yield bonds, however, is that leveraged loans are generally senior secured debt whereas the bonds are unsecured in the case of bankruptcy. Even given covenants on the bonds, the bonds issued to finance an LBO are usually high-yield bonds that receive low-quality ratings and must offer high coupons to attract investors because of the amount of leverage used.

The ample availability of credit at favorable terms—think low credit spreads and fewer covenants—before the 2007 global financial crisis (GFC) and a resumption of covenant-lite terms combined with low interest rates during much of the 2010s contributed to a significant increase in available leverage for buyouts. Borrowing six to eight times EBITDA has been common for large buyout transactions. Note that in private equity, leverage is typically measured as a multiple of EBITDA instead of equity.

When considering the impact of leverage on value, we should naturally turn to one of the foundations of modern finance: the Modigliani–Miller (1958) theorem. This theorem, in its basic form, states that in the absence of taxes, asymmetric information, and bankruptcy costs and assuming efficient markets, the value of a firm is not affected by how the firm is financed. In other words, it should not matter if the firm is financed by equity or debt as far as firm value is concerned. The relaxing of the no-tax assumption raises interesting questions in leveraged buyouts, as the tax shield on the acquisition debt creates value because of the tax-deductibility of interest. One would also expect that the financial leverage of a firm would be set at a level where bankruptcy costs do not outweigh these tax benefits. Private equity firms may have a better ability than public companies to raise high levels of debt as a result of their better control over management but also as a result of their reputation for having raised and repaid such high levels of debt in previous transactions.

Such debt financing is raised initially from the syndicated loan market but then is frequently repackaged via sophisticated structured products, such as collateralized loan obligations (CLOs), which typically consist of a portfolio of secured floating-rate leveraged loans issued by non-investment-grade companies. In some cases, the private equity funds issue high-yield bonds as a way of financing the portfolio company, and these often are sold to funds that create collateralized debt obligations (CDOs).

This raises the question of whether a massive transfer of risk to the credit markets is taking place in private equity. If the answer to this question is yes, then one would expect that it will self-correct during the next economic downturn. During early 2008, the CDO and CLO markets were undergoing a significant slowdown as a result of the credit market turmoil that started in the summer of 2007, triggered by the subprime mortgage crisis. As a result, the LBO market for very large transactions ("mega-buyouts") was affected by a lack of financing. Global equity market declines beginning in mid- to late 2015, which accompanied or responded to the Brexit referendum, the Asian currency weakness, and changing regulatory capital rules, further interrupted LBO and leveraged debt activity. The pause ended up being short-lived; market volumes resumed their upward growth in 2017.

Additional leverage is also gained by means of equity-like instruments at the acquisition vehicle level, which are frequently located in a favorable jurisdictions, such as Luxembourg, the Channel Islands, the Cayman Islands, the British Virgin Islands, or Malta. Acquisitions by large buyout private equity firms are generally held by a top holding company in a favorable tax jurisdiction. The top holding company's share capital and equity-like instruments are held in turn by investment funds run by a general partner who is controlled by the private equity buyout firm. These instruments are treated as debt for tax purposes in certain jurisdictions.

The effect of leverage may be analyzed through Jensen's (1986, 1989) free cash flow hypothesis. According to Jensen, low-growth companies generating high free cash flows tend to invest in projects that destroy value (i.e., with a negative net present value) instead of distributing excess cash to shareholders. This is a possible explanation for why an LBO transaction generates value, because excess cash is used to repay the senior debt tranche, effectively removing management's discretionary use of cash. Here, too, financial leverage may explain part of the value added by private equity investment.

Examining the value created via the re-engineering of private firms and the availability and effects of leverage is informative. Now we turn to the alignment of economic interests between private equity owners and the managers of the companies they control to ensure the latter's efforts to achieve the ambitious milestones set by the former. Results-driven pay packages and contractual clauses ensure that managers are incentivized to reach their targets and that they will not be left behind after the private equity house exits the investment. One common clause stipulates that any offer made by a future acquirer of the company be extended to all shareholders, including company management.

Consider the managers of public companies subsequently acquired by private equity groups. Empirical evidence shows that managers tend to acknowledge an increased level of directness and intensity of input after the takeover, which enables them to conduct higher-value-added projects. Crucially, these projects can be implemented over a longer time frame after the buyout; this situation is in contrast to the short-termism that prevailed during their public market period. This short-termism is mostly driven by shareholders' expectations, the analyst community, and market participants more broadly who place significant emphasis on meeting quarterly earnings targets. Private equity firms have a longer time horizon, so they attract talented managers with the ability to implement sometimes profound restructuring plans, isolated against short-term market consequences.

Private equity firms are not, however, the sole catalysts of change at large companies. Some large organizations, such as Google, SAP, and Tencent, have proven their ability to inspire entrepreneurship at all levels within their ranks while generating substantial value over the long term.

A balance of rights and obligations between the private equity firm and the management team requires effective structuring. The following matters are covered by the contractual clauses that private equity firms use to ensure that the management team is focused on achieving the business plan. If the agreed objectives are not met, the control and equity allocation held by the private equity firm may increase.

- *Corporate board seats*: A seat ensures some degree of private equity control in the case of major corporate events, such as a company sale, takeover, restructuring, IPO, bankruptcy, or liquidation.
- *Noncompete clause*: This is generally imposed on founders, preventing them from restarting the same activity during a predefined period of time.
- *Preferred dividends and liquidation preference*: Private equity firms generally come first when distributions take place, and they may be guaranteed a minimum multiple of their original investment before other shareholders receive their returns.

- *Reserved matters*: Some domains of strategic importance (such as changes in the business plan, acquisitions, or divestitures) are subject to approval or veto by the private equity firm.
- *Earnouts (mostly in venture capital)*: These are agreements that the acquisition price paid by the private equity firm is contingent on company management achieving predefined financial performance over a specified future time period (e.g., over one or two years). Earnouts are not specific to private equity.

How the PE firm structures the investment contract can have a major bearing on the returns. Venture capital firms, in particular, whose investee companies face considerable uncertainties, can set terms that increase their level of control over time or can even seize control if too many targets are missed.

## Using Market Data in Valuation

With the exception of public-to-private transactions, there is no direct market evidence of company valuation with most private equity deals. But virtually all valuation techniques use evidence from the market at different stages in the calculation rather than relying entirely on accounting data and management forecasts.

The two most important ways in which market data are used to infer the value of the entity being acquired are (1) by analyzing publicly traded comparison companies and (2) by considering the valuations that are implied by recent transactions involving similar entities. Typically, these techniques involve trading or acquisition multiples. Suppose we need a valuation for a privately owned company in the food-retail sector. The comparison-company approach would look at the trading multiples—such as enterprise value to EBITDA—of comparable public food-retail companies and use this multiple to value the target. Similarly, the transaction multiples that were paid in recent food-retail M&A transactions can inform the market value of our target. It is very important, of course, to make sure that the comparisons are appropriate, and this is simply not always possible, especially for niche businesses or targets that are pioneering products and services.

Market data come into play for DCF approaches, in particular when estimating the discount rate. The same weighted average cost of capital (WACC) formula we use for public companies is used to establish the cost of capital for private companies. We face a serious challenge, however, in assessing the cost of equity in PE settings: the lack of public historical data on share prices and returns. Therefore, beta ($\beta$), which represents the relative exposure of company shares to the market, must be estimated by means of a proxy. Typically the proxy is the result of estimating the beta for comparable companies and then adjusting it for financial and operating leverage. This benchmark exercise calls for analyst judgment: To what extent are the comparable public firms genuinely comparable to the target firm? Should outlying companies be excluded? What is the target debt-to-equity ratio of the target firm versus the industry average? What comparable public companies are appropriate if the target firm operates in several business segments?

Given that forecasts of future financial performance are usually only available for a few years ahead, when it comes to DCF valuation it is almost always necessary to estimate the terminal value of the company beyond this forecasting horizon. It is possible to apply a perpetual growth rate assumption, although small changes in the assumed growth rate, which itself is very difficult to predict, can have a significant impact on the valuation. An alternative is to use a trading multiple that exists (or is predicted to exist) in public markets and apply this to the final-year forecasted values.

For instance, if the average enterprise-value-to-EBITDA ratio for comparable publicly quoted companies is 10, then this might be applied to the private target's final forecast EBITDA value as a way of estimating the terminal value.

## 3. CONTRASTING VENTURE CAPITAL AND BUYOUT INVESTMENTS

☐ compare and contrast characteristics of buyout and venture capital investments

Our two main categories of private equity investments, buyout and venture capital funds, dominate in terms of number of funds and invested amounts. Whereas a VC firm may have a specialized industry focus—seeking the next rising star in technology or life sciences—LBO firms generally invest in a portfolio of firms with more predictable cash flow. VC firms seek revenue growth from new enterprise and technology; buyout firms focus more on EBIT or EBITDA growth by established companies. Valuation is thus fundamentally different, and Exhibit 3 presents certain key distinctions.

### Exhibit 3: Characteristics of Buyout and Venture Capital Investments

| Buyout Investments: | Venture Capital Investments: |
|---|---|
| Steady and predictable cash flows | Low cash flow predictability; cash flow projections may not be realistic |
| Excellent market position (can be a niche player) | Lack of market history; new market and possibly an unproven future market (early-stage venture) |
| Significant asset base (may serve as a basis for collateral lending) | Weak asset base |
| Strong and experienced management team | Newly formed management team with strong individual track record as entrepreneurs |
| Extensive use of leverage consisting of a large proportion of senior debt and a significant layer of junior and/or mezzanine debt | Primarily equity funded; the use of leverage is rare and very limited |
| Risk is measurable; investments are in mature businesses with long operating histories | The assessment of risk is difficult because of new technologies, new markets, and a lack of operating history |
| Predictable exit (secondary buyout, sale to a strategic buyer, IPO) | Exits are difficult to anticipate (secondary venture sale, sale to strategic/financial buyer, IPO) |
| Established products | Technological breakthrough but the route to market is yet unproven |
| Potential for restructuring and cost reduction | Significant cash burn rate required to ensure company development and commercial viability |
| Low working capital requirement | Expanding capital requirement if in the growth phase |
| Buyout firms typically conduct full-blown due diligence before investing in the target firm (financial, strategic, commercial, legal, tax, environmental) | VC firms tend to conduct technology and commercial due diligence before investing; financial due diligence is limited as portfolio companies have no or very little operating history |
| Buyout firms monitor cash flow management and strategic and business planning | VC firms monitor the achievement of milestones defined in the business plan |

| Buyout Investments: | Venture Capital Investments: |
|---|---|
| • Investment portfolio returns are generally characterized by a lower variance across returns from underlying investments; bankruptcies are rare | • Investment portfolio returns are generally characterized by very high returns from a limited number of highly successful investments and a significant number of write-offs from poor-performing investments or failures |
| • Large buyout firms are generally significant players in the capital markets | • VC firms tend to be much less active in the capital markets |
| • Most transactions are auctions involving multiple potential acquirers | • Many transactions are "proprietary," arising from relationships between venture capitalists and entrepreneurs |
| • High-performing buyout firms tend to have a better ability to secure larger pools of financing given their track record | • VC firms tend to be less scalable relative to buyout firms; the increase in size of subsequent funds tends to be less significant |
| • Variable revenue to the general partner (GP) at buyout firms generally comes in the form of carried interest, transaction fees, and monitoring fees | • Carried interest (participation in profits) is generally the main source of variable revenue to the general partner at VC firms; transaction and monitoring fees are rare in practice |

# LBO MODEL FOR VALUATION OF BUYOUT TRANSACTIONS

4

☐ interpret LBO model and VC method output

When the buyer in a private equity transaction acquires from the seller a controlling stake in the equity capital of a target company, it is called a buyout. The generic term "buyout" refers explicitly to the notion of acquiring control. It denotes a wide range of techniques, including but not limited to management buyouts (MBOs), leveraged buyouts (LBOs), and takeovers. In this reading, we focus on LBOs: using borrowed money to finance a significant portion of the acquisition price.

Given their target sector, private equity firms look for characteristics that make a company particularly attractive as an LBO target:

*Undervalued/depressed stock price.* The private equity firm perceives that the company's intrinsic value exceeds its market price. Firms are therefore willing to pay a premium to the market price in order to secure approval by the seller's shareholders. In other circumstances, firms see a chance to make an acquisition cheaply, and the stock prices of out-of-favor public companies may make them attractive.

*Willing management and shareholders.* Company management is looking for a deal. They may have opportunities to increase value, but they lack the resources to make investments in the processes, personnel, equipment, and so on, that would drive long-term growth. Company shareholders may have insufficient access to capital and so welcome a private equity partner. Family business owners may want to cash out. PE firms can provide the time and capital to expand a company or turn it around.

*Inefficient companies.* Private equity firms seek to generate attractive returns by identifying companies that are inefficiently managed and have the potential to perform well if managed better.

*Strong and sustainable cash flow.* Companies that generate strong cash flow are attractive because LBO transactions have the target company taking on significant debt. Cash flow is necessary to make interest payments.

*Low leverage.* Private equity firms focus on target companies that have no significant debt on their balance sheets because then it's easier to use debt to finance a large portion of the purchase price.

*Assets.* Private equity managers like companies that have a significant amount of unencumbered physical assets. These physical assets can be used as security, and secured debt is cheaper than unsecured debt.

Earlier we considered a typical LBO capital structure that entailed 30% equity along with leveraged loans and high-yield bonds to make up the rest of the purchase price. Leveraged loans are often the source of a larger amount of capital than either equity or high-yield bonds. As an alternative to high-yield bonds, mezzanine financing may be used. Mezzanine financing refers to debt or preferred shares with a relationship to common equity that results from a feature such as attached warrants or conversion options. Being subordinate to both senior and high-yield debt, mezzanine financing typically pays a higher coupon rate. In addition to interest or dividends, this type of financing offers a potential return based on increases in the value of common equity and is generally customized to fit the specific requirements of the transaction in question.

## The LBO Model

The LBO model is not a separate valuation technique but, rather, a way of determining the impact of the capital structure, purchase price, and other parameters on the returns expected by the private equity firm from the deal.

The LBO model has three main input parameters: the cash flow forecasts of the target company, the return that the providers of financing (equity, senior debt, high-yield bonds, mezzanine) are expecting, and the amount of financing available for the transaction. The free cash flow forecasts of the target company are generally prepared by its management and are subject to an extensive due diligence process (strategic, commercial, financial, legal, and environmental) to determine their reliability. The forecasts assume an explicit horizon that generally corresponds to the expected holding period (i.e., investment period) of the private equity firm.

The exit year is typically considered to determine the expected IRR sensitivity of the equity capital around the anticipated exit date. The exit value is determined most frequently by reference to an expected range of exit multiples determined on the basis of a peer group of comparable companies (enterprise value-to-EBITDA ratio).

Given the significant predictability of cash flows in buyout transactions, the income-based approach (discounted cash flows, adjusted present value, LBO model, target IRR) is frequently used as a primary method to determine the value of equity, considering the expected change in leverage until the time of exit of the investment. The initial high and declining financial leverage is the main technical valuation issue that needs to be adequately factored into the income approach when applied to a buyout valuation. The value is also frequently corroborated by an analysis of the peer group of comparable publicly traded companies.

On the basis of the input parameters, the LBO model provides the maximum price that can be paid to the seller while satisfying the target returns for the providers of financing. This is why the LBO model is not a valuation methodology per se. It is a negotiation tool that helps develop a range of acceptable prices to conclude the transaction.

Exhibit 4 is a value-creation chart that illustrates the sources of the additional value between the original cost and the exit value. Value creation comes from a combination of factors: earnings growth arising from operational improvements and enhanced corporate governance, multiple expansion depending on pre-identified potential exits, and the optimization of financial leverage and repayment of part of the debt with operational cash flows before the exit. Each component of the value creation chart should be carefully considered and backed by supporting analyses, which frequently come from the lengthy due diligence process (especially commercial, tax, and financial analysis) and also from a strategic review that quantifies the range of plausible value creation.

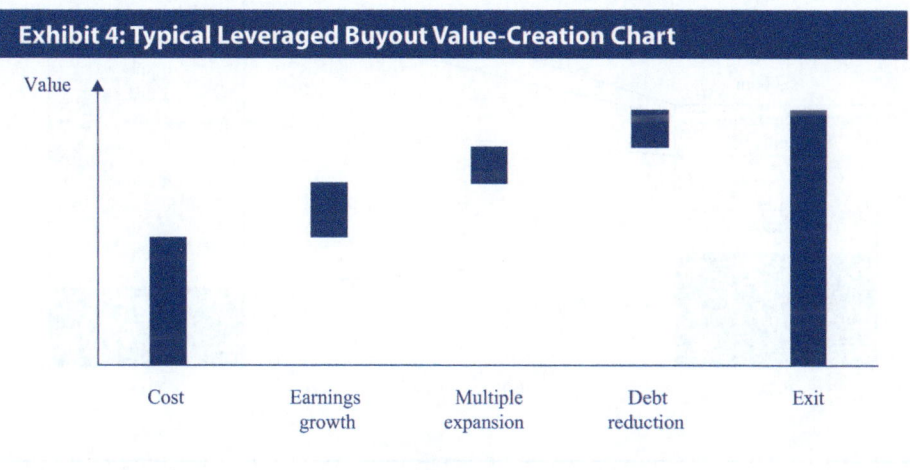

Exhibit 4: Typical Leveraged Buyout Value-Creation Chart

Exhibit 5 provides an example of a €5,000 (amounts in millions) investment in a private equity transaction. The transaction is financed with 50% debt and 50% equity. The €2,500 equity investment is further broken into €2,400 of preference shares owned by the private equity fund, €95 of equity owned by the private equity fund, and €5 of management equity. The preference shares are promised a 12% annual return (paid at exit). The private equity fund's equity is promised 95% of the residual value of the firm after creditors and preference shares are paid, and management equity holders are promised the remaining 5%.

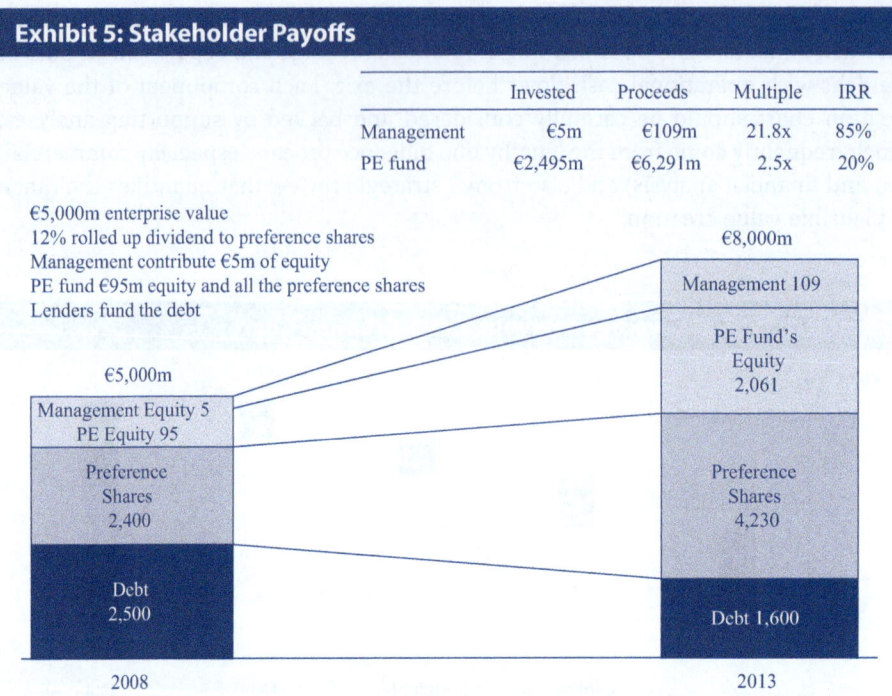

**Exhibit 5: Stakeholder Payoffs**

Assume that the exit value, five years after investment, is 1.6 times the original cost. The initial investment of €5,000 has an exit value of €8,000. The specific payoffs for the four claimants are as follows:

- Senior debt has been partially retired with operational cash flows, reducing debt from €2,500 to €1,600. So debtholders get €1,600.
- Preference shares are paid a 12% return for five years, so they receive €2,400 × $(1.12)^5$ = €4,230.
- PE fund equity receives 95% of the terminal equity value, or 0.95 × [8,000 − (4,230 + 1,600)] = €2,061.
- Management equity receives 5% of the terminal equity value, or 0.05 × [8,000 − (4,230 + 1,600)] = €109.

As you can see, preference shares increase in value over time as a result of their preferred dividend being capitalized, and the equity held by the PE fund and by the management is expected to increase significantly depending on the total enterprise value upon exit. Both the equity sold to managers, frequently known as the management equity program (MEP), and the equity held by the private equity firm are most sensitive to the level of the exit. The larger the exit multiple, the larger the upside potential for both the MEP and the equity held by the private equity firm. In the example, assuming that an exit of 1.6 times cash may be achieved at the anticipated exit date (five years from investment), the management would realize an IRR of 85% per annum on its investment and the private equity fund equity holders an IRR of 20% per annum. The preference shares component of the private equity fund earns an IRR of 12% per annum.

This chart also demonstrates the critical importance of leverage in buyout transactions. A reduction in financial leverage over time is instrumental in magnifying the returns available to shareholders. Note that the bulk of financial leverage in LBOs consists of senior debt, much of which will be amortizing. Therefore, the reduction in financial leverage gradually increases over time as a proportion of principal is paid back to senior lenders on an annual or semi-annual basis depending on the terms of the senior debt. As a result of the gradual repayment of senior debt over time, a larger proportion of operating cash flows becomes available to equity holders. Of course, this mechanism works well as long as no significant adverse economic factors impact the business of the target LBO company and also as long as a successful exit can be secured in the foreseeable future. It should be remembered that these high levels of debt increase the risks borne by the equity investors significantly. Such risks should be accounted for when comparing the expected returns with alternative investment classes, such as investments in the stock market.

Typically, a series of scenarios with varying levels of cash exits, growth assumptions, and debt levels are engineered with the use of an LBO model, using as inputs the required rate of return from each stakeholder (equity, mezzanine, senior debtholders) to gain a sound understanding of the buyout firm's flexibility in conducting the deal.

# VC METHOD FOR VALUATION OF VENTURE CAPITAL TRANSACTIONS[1]

☐ interpret LBO model and VC method output

The primary difficulty of venture capital investing is the substantial uncertainty about the company's future prospects. Traditional valuation tools, such as discounted cash flow, earnings multiples, and the LBO model, are not usually practical in the VC context. Moreover, due to the uncertainty, VC financing is done in stages—financing rounds referred to as Series A, Series B, and so on—and it is essential to understand the effects of ownership dilution. So, we turn to the VC method.[1]

Imagine a start-up company is worth $16 million, and its shareholders own 100% of the equity. The company decides to raise $4 million in additional equity capital from a venture capital firm. The value of the start-up company after the financing is $20 million (= $16 million + $4 million).

According to the VC method, $16 million is known as the pre-money (i.e., pre-financing) valuation, $4 million is the amount of new equity Series A investment, and $20 million is known as the post-money (i.e., post-financing) valuation. That is,

Pre-money valuation + New equity investment = Post-money valuation.

What is the total equity stake owned by the VC firm if it were to make the $4 million investment? After the transaction, the VC firm will own 20% (= $4 million/$20 million) of the equity stake or, in VC terms, will have 20% fractional ownership of the start-up. The original shareholder equity stake gets diluted to 80%. This basic example is central to understanding the VC Method.

The central challenge of the VC method is determining the pre-money valuation. The closer you are to the inception date of the company, the harder it is to assess its pre-money valuation. Indeed, in early-stage venture capital, the investor might be backing an idea with no tangible proof of commercial viability. At the heart of a successful VC investment is a fundamentally novel and uncertain idea; otherwise, existing firms would easily replicate it. It is hard to envision a comparable company

---

1 Authored by Victoria Ivashina, PhD, Harvard Business School.

in the public domain or even comparable VC investments when you are early in the process. So the VC Method works backwards to come up with the pre-money valuation, taking as inputs the expected exit valuation and the required return on investment.

## Expected Exit Valuation

VC investments are typically financed through a closed-end fund with a finite life horizon; 10 years is very common in private equity. The average holding period for individual investments within the fund is between five and eight years. Performance metrics for the firm, measuring its progress toward commercial success, are identified at the end of the expected investment period. The performance metric could be, for example, revenues or number of users. For early-stage VC investments, it might be ambitious to expect that the company becomes profitable, but if that is the expectation, one could also use earnings per share or EBITDA. Choosing the right multiple to apply depends on the specifics of the industry, and the general idea is that, whatever the performance metrics, the value of the VC investment at exit can be determined based on projected performance metrics at anticipated exit and an appropriate industry multiple.

## Required Rate of Return

VC firms target an expected hurdle return. The failure rate of VC investments, especially early-stage VC investments, is much higher than that of growth equity or buyouts. Thus, the target return on investment tends to be 10× to 30×, compared with 2.0× to 2.5× in the buyout space.

Armed with the hurdle return and the value of the equity at exit, we can compute the post-money valuation:

$$\text{ROI} = \frac{\text{Value of equity at exit}}{\text{Post-money valuation}},$$

so,

$$\text{Post-money valuation} = \frac{\text{Value of equity at exit}}{\text{ROI}}.$$

Given the capital needs of the company, we know that the pre-money valuation is as follows:

Pre-money valuation = Post-money valuation − New equity injection.

Take an entrepreneur who is looking to raise $500,000. Given the size of its market and the industry, the entrepreneur's company expects to reach sales of $80 million over the investment horizon. A typical revenue multiple for a revenue-generating business in its industry is 2×. If the VC firm's ROI is 20× and the entrepreneur's company has no debt, then what is the pre-money valuation? And what is the VC firm's fractional ownership?

$$\text{Pre-money valuation} = \frac{\$80 \text{ million} \times 2}{20} - \$0.5 \text{ million} = \$7.5 \text{ million}.$$

$$\text{VC fractional ownership} = \frac{\$0.5 \text{ million}}{\$7.5 \text{ million} + \$0.5 \text{ million}} = 6.25\%.$$

These numbers are sensitive to the revenue figure. The required ROI will be dictated by the competition and the cost of capital. Although ROI is not sensitive to the length of the holding period, an expected holding period of five to eight years is generally the assumption in the VC fund structure. The previous example could also be reframed in terms of required internal rate of return (IRR) to equity. Over a five-year period, 20× ROI is equivalent to an 82% IRR. In general,

# VC Method for valuation of Venture Capital Transactions

$$(1 + \text{IRR})^t = \text{ROI} = \frac{\text{Value of equity at exit}}{\text{Post-money valuation}},$$

or in this case,

$$(1 + \text{IRR})^5 = 20 = \frac{\$80 \text{ million} \times 2}{\$8 \text{ million}}.$$

## Option Pools

Returning to the first example, if the start-up were owned by the founders, they held a total of 10 million shares, and there is no option pool, what is number of new shares that the company needs to issue? And at what price?

We know that

$$\frac{N(\text{new shares})}{N(\text{total shares after financing})} = \frac{N(\text{new shares})}{N(\text{old shares}) + N(\text{new shares})} = 20\%.$$

This means that 2.5 million new shares [= (0.2 × 10 million)/0.8] will have to be issued. Based on the $4 million of new equity raised, the shares would be issued at $4 million/2.5 million = $1.60 per share.

Scenarios without an outstanding option pool, however, are unrealistic. To attract and incentivize employees, start-ups grant their employees the option to purchase shares. When these options are exercised, they will naturally have a dilutive effect, so VC firms tend to calculate the per-share price on a fully diluted basis.

The basis of the dilution is contractually defined. The central question is about who assumes the effect of future dilution: original shareholders or new investors? There is tension between what benefits the VC investors and what benefits the founders, which is why this is important. By calculating the share price on a fully diluted basis, VC investors are effectively left untouched by the dilution effect. Instead, the original shareholders, our founders, absorb the effects of dilution. We will return to this concept when we examine follow-up financing series.

Back to our start-up example, let's say that in addition to the founders holding 10 million shares, there is an outstanding option pool of 2 million shares. How many shares need to be issued? And at what price per share? (Recall that the default is to make calculations on a fully diluted basis.) What is the starting equity stake of the VC firm? What is the VC firm's equity stake after dilution?

- The number of existing or original shares on a fully diluted basis now is 12 million. This means that 3 million new shares [= (0.2 × 12 million)/0.8] will have to be issued.
- The new price per share is $4 million/3 million = $1.33.
- The VC firm's starting ownership is 3 million/13 million = 23.08%, but as options are exercised, this ownership will be diluted to 20%.
- The VC fractional ownership on a post-dilution basis is not affected and is equal to 20% = $4 million/$20 million. The ownership structure should not affect the value of the assets—the key insight of the Modigliani–Miller theorem. If the pre-money valuation is $4 million, it should remain at $4 million regardless of how many options the firm issues.

## Stage Financing

We've established that VC financing is usually executed in stages, largely due to the uncertainty that surrounds VC investments.

As an example, let's take Facebook and its initial financing rounds. The first external investment in the company took place in 2004, shortly after the platform launched, in the amount of $500,000. Just a year later, Facebook raised $12.7 million. In 2006, it raised $27.5 million, followed by $300 million in 2007. Behind this astonishing growth in fundraising sits an even more impressive rise in company valuation. So what changed for Facebook in the three years between 2004 and 2007? Why were the initial rounds so small by comparison? The answer is uncertainty about the company's future, and this illustrates that even one year out, company valuation can fluctuate dramatically. This is despite the fact that Facebook was a sought-after company with multiple veteran VC investors pursuing it. As the Facebook user base grew, so did their investment and investors' visibility into the company's future commercial success. Stage financing, thus, is a key mitigator of the risk that is fundamental to venture capital: significant uncertainty about growth and profitability prospects.

How do the different series of financing relate to each other? Because the earlier-stage investors take on higher risk, the return for those investors has to be higher. Valuations, specifically pre-money valuations, at which later rounds of financing are raised, provide insight into the performance of an otherwise illiquid asset class.

Let's assume that our earlier example—a VC firm raising $500,000 for a start-up company in exchange for a 6.25% stake—describes a Series A financing. Imagine that one year later the firm raises $2 million in a Series B financing at 10× ROI. The exit of all investors is expected to occur simultaneously, and Series B investors were projecting an exit valuation of $300 million. We can compute the ownership structure in each of the financing rounds along with the implied ROI for the Series A and B financings.

For Series B investors,

$$\text{Post-money valuation} = \frac{\$300 \text{ million}}{10} = \$30 \text{ million}.$$

$$\text{Pre-money valuation} = \frac{\$300 \text{ million}}{10} - \$2 \text{ million} = \$28 \text{ million}.$$

$$\text{VC fractional ownership} = \frac{\$2 \text{ million}}{\$28 \text{ million} + \$2 \text{ million}} = 6.67\%.$$

$$\text{ROI} = (1 + \text{IRR})^5 = 10 = \frac{\$300 \text{ million}}{\$30 \text{ million}}.$$

These figures are summarized in Exhibit 6.

**Exhibit 6: Stage Financing Example**

| (in thousands) | Series A | Series B |
|---|---|---|
| Required ROI | 20.0 | 10.0 |
| Investment | 500 | 2,000 |
| Exit valuation | 160,000 | 300,000 |
| | | |
| Post-money valuation | 8,000 | 30,000 |
| Pre-money valuation | 7,500 | 28,000 |
| Fractional ownership required | 6.25% | 6.67% |
| | | |
| Ownership: | | |
| Entrepreneurs | 93.75% | 87.50% |
| Series A investors | 6.25% | 5.83% |
| Series B investors | — | 6.67% |

| (in thousands) | Series A | Series B |
|---|---|---|
| Total | 100.00% | 100.00% |
| | | |
| Implied ROI | | |
| Series A investors | 20.0 | 35.0 |
| Series B investors | — | 10.0 |

This example illustrates that the pre-money valuation implied by Series B indicates a substantial appreciation of the Series A investment. Instead of 20× ROI, Series A now has an implied ROI of 35×, although no exits occurred, and despite dilution of the Series A stake from 6.25% to 5.83%.

For Series A investors, the implied ROI, which was originally 20×, or

$$\text{ROI} = 20 = \frac{\$160 \text{ million} \times 6.25\%}{\$0.5 \text{ million}},$$

increases to 35× at the time of the Series B financing one year later, or

$$\text{ROI} = 35 = \frac{\$300 \text{ million} \times 5.83\%}{\$0.5 \text{ million}}.$$

The entry of new investors with Series B dilutes ownership for both Series A investors and the entrepreneurs on a proportionate basis. That is,

Entrepreneurs' ownership = [(1 − 6.67%) × 87.50%].

Series A investors' ownership = [(1 − 6.67%) × 6.25%] = 5.83%.

Venture capital investments tend to be minority stake investments. This is partly because the founders might not be willing to give up control but also because entrepreneurs are essential in the initial stages of business development. So, the dilution of initial investors through the subsequent financing rounds is common. In the previous example, the dilution from Series B was absorbed pro rata by the entrepreneurs and the Series A investors. Because control is not essential, this arrangement is typical. If an alternative economic arrangement is sought, however—as in the earlier example of employees' stock options—designing an arrangement whereby the dilution is absorbed disproportionately by entrepreneurs is possible.

Whereas our example treated Series A and Series B shares as common stock, it is typical to use convertible preferred equity in later-stage financing. The capital that comes in later stages is less risky than earlier-stage financing. In addition, to mitigate risk further, later-stage capital tends to have a preferred dividend. Series B shares could entitle shareholders to a preferred dividend of 5%, for example. On an investment of $2 million over three years, the cumulative dividend is $315,250. If the investee company performance is as expected and the returns are high, the preference shares will be irrelevant. However, if things do not go as planned, the accumulated dividend is treated as junior debt, diminishing the value held by earlier equity investors while preserving the value for Series B. Clearly, this makes Series B more valuable than if it had been just common equity. Importantly, the value comes at the expense of earlier investors. These adjustments are rarely accounted for in practice, however.

## 6. EXIT ROUTES: RETURN CASH TO INVESTORS

☐ explain alternative exit routes in private equity and their impact on value

The exit is a critical mechanism for unlocking value in private equity. Most private equity firms consider their exit options prior to investing, and they factor their assessment of the exit outcome into their IRR analysis.

Generally, PE investors have access to the following four exit routes:

- *Initial public offering (IPO)*: Going public offers significant advantages, including higher valuation multiples as a result of enhanced liquidity, access to large amounts of capital, and the possibility of attracting higher-caliber managers. But the process is cumbersome and less flexible and entails significant costs. Therefore, an IPO is an appropriate exit route for private companies that are of a sufficient size with an established operating history and excellent growth prospects. Timing is important and heavily dependent on public equity market conditions. IPO markets have shut down for long periods following major events, such as the internet bubble collapse that began in March 2000 and the GFC, starting in 2007. Regional economic concerns and regulatory issues, such as uncertainty around Britain's plan to exit the European Union, have had negative ramifications for equity and IPO markets worldwide. In fact, any extended market downturn can limit the ability of new companies to come to market. IPO exits are more common for VC-backed companies, but they are not the largest divestment alternative.

- *Secondary market*: The sale of an investor's stake to other financial investors or to strategic investors (think companies that operate in the same sector or are keen to try). As private equity has become increasingly segmented, secondary market transactions tend to occur within each segment—that is, buyout firms tend to sell to other buyout firms (secondary buyouts) and venture firms to other venture firms (secondary venture capital transactions). These secondary market transactions account for a significant proportion of exits, especially in the buyout segment. Venture capital exits by means of a buyout are also possible but are rare in practice, because buyout firms are reluctant to finance development-stage companies with a significant amount of leverage. The main advantages of secondary market transactions are (1) the possibility of achieving the highest valuation multiples in the absence of an IPO and (2) the fact that given the segmentation of private equity firms, specialized firms have the skill to bring their portfolio companies to the next level—say, through a restructuring or merger or by bringing them to a new market—and then to sell, either to a strategic investor seeking to exploit synergies or to another private equity firm with another set of skills to further add value to the portfolio company.

- *Management buyout (MBO)*: These takeovers by company management use significant amounts of leverage to finance the acquisition. Alignment of interest between management and investors is optimal under this exit scenario, but it may come at the expense of excessive leverage that significantly reduces the company's flexibility.

- *Liquidation*: Controlling shareholders have the power to liquidate the company if it is no longer viable. This exit mechanism generally results in a floor value for the company but may come at a cost of very negative publicity for the private equity firm if the company is large and the employee count is significant.

Timing the exit and determining the optimal exit route are important. Even carefully planned exits face the unexpected, however, and may be delayed or accelerated depending on market conditions or purely opportunistic circumstances.

Suppose, for example, that an LBO firm is planning to exit one of its portfolio companies, but the public market and economic conditions have collapsed, rendering any exit via a trade sale or an IPO unprofitable. Instead, the LBO firm exploits the depressed pricing environment to conduct another acquisition and merges the target with the original portfolio company in order to strengthen its market position and product range. Then it waits for better market conditions before conducting the sale. Such flexibility is critical for private equity firms during hard times and underlines the importance of PE firms maintaining sufficient financial strength.

There seems to be no boundary to the size of buyout transactions, as expectations have consistently been exceeded. Three of the largest buyout transactions—TXU Energy ($32.1 billion), First Data ($25.7 billion), and Alltel ($25.1 billion)—all took place in 2007 immediately prior to the GFC. Strength in capital markets combined with the increasing prevalence of megafunds suggest even larger transactions may be in store for the biggest buyout firms. Private equity firms appear to be moving into uncharted territory by managing exits at such levels. The central question about these mega-buyout transactions is how the exits will take place given that the possibilities are much more limited relative to smaller deals. IPOs, for example, raise significantly more challenges, restricting sellers to a gradual exit (only a single block of shares can be sold initially) and proving excessively risky when market conditions are suboptimal. And a real challenge exists for large, unified companies for which a single exit is the only way out. This is in contrast to the type of large companies that may be viewed as holding companies for a portfolio of real assets, which can be sold in tranches.

When an exit is anticipated within one or two years, the multiples observed from comparable publicly quoted firms provide good guidance for an expected exit multiple, and stress tests on that value may be conducted for small incremental changes and based on market knowledge. When the exit horizon is much further out, these multiples are less reliable, and stress tests may be performed on valuation model inputs, such as discount factor and terminal growth rates, and on financial forecasts, such as sales growth and operating margins.

## Exit Routes: Summary

Valuation is the most critical aspect of private equity transactions. The investment decision-making process typically flows from the screening of investment opportunities to preparing a proposal, appraising the investment, and structuring the deal and finally to the negotiating phase. Along with the various due diligence investigations (commercial or strategic, financial, legal, tax, environmental) that are generally conducted on private equity investment opportunities, valuation serves to assess a company's ability to generate superior cash flows from a distinctive competitive advantage and as a benchmark for negotiations with the seller. Because of the difficulties in valuing private companies, a variety of alternative valuation methods are typically used to provide guidance. Private equity valuation is a process that starts as a support for decision making at the transaction phase but also serves as a monitoring tool to capture new opportunities, create value, or protect from losses during the investment period and as a performance reporting tool for investors.

## 7. RISKS AND COSTS OF PRIVATE EQUITY

☐ explain risks and costs of investing in private equity

We turn now to the perspective of a private equity fund investor.

### What Are the Risks and Costs of Investing in Private Equity?

Most jurisdictions restrict private equity investing to "qualified investors"—typically, institutions and high-net-worth individuals who meet certain criteria. These restrictions are a product of the high levels of risk associated with private equity investing, which are generally subject to disclosure in the private equity fund prospectus. Such risks may be categorized as general private equity risk factors, investment strategy–specific risk factors (buyout, venture capital, mezzanine), industry-specific risk factors, risk factors specific to the investment vehicle, or regional or emerging market risks when applicable.

The following are some general private equity risk factors:

- *Illiquidity of investments*: Because private equity investments are generally not traded on any securities market, the exit of investments may not end up being conducted on a timely basis.
- *Unquoted investments*: Investing in unquoted securities may be risky relative to investing in securities quoted on a regulated securities exchange.
- *Competition for attractive investment opportunities*: Competition for investment opportunities on attractive terms may be high.
- *Reliance on the management of investee companies (agency risk)*: There is no assurance that the management of the investee companies will run the company in the best interests of the private equity firm, particularly in earlier-stage deals in which the management retains a controlling stake in the company and enjoys certain private benefits of control.
- *Loss of capital*: High business and financial risks may result in a substantial loss of capital.
- *Government regulations*: Investee companies' products and services may be subject to changes in government regulations that adversely affect their business model.
- *Taxation risk*: The tax treatment of capital gains, dividends, or limited partnerships may change over time.
- *Valuation of investments*: The valuation of private equity investments is subject to significant judgment. When valuations are not conducted by an independent party, they may be subject to bias.
- *Lack of investment capital*: Investee companies may require additional future financing that may not be available.
- *Lack of diversification*: Highly concentrated investment portfolios may be exposed to significant losses. Instead, private equity investors should consider a mix of funds of different vintage, portfolio companies at different stages of development, and investing across private equity strategies, such as large and mid-market buyouts, venture capital, mezzanine finance, and restructuring.

- *Market risk*: Changes in general market conditions (interest rates, currency exchange rates) may adversely affect private equity investments. The impact of market risk is, however, long-term in nature given the long-term horizon of private equity funds. Temporary short-term market fluctuations are generally irrelevant.

The costs associated with private equity are substantially higher than the costs of public market investing. We break them down here:

- *Transaction fees*: These arise from due diligence work, bank financing costs, the legal fees of arranging an acquisition, and the costs of arranging the sale of an investee company.
- *Fund setup costs*: These are mainly the legal costs of setting up the investment vehicle, and they are typically amortized over the life of the investment vehicle.
- *Administrative costs*: Custodian, accounting, and transfer-agent costs are generally charged yearly as a fraction of the investment vehicle's net asset value.
- *Audit costs*: This is a fixed annual fee.
- *Management and performance fees*: 2% management fees and 20% performance fees, which are generally more significant than the fees charged by regular investment funds.
- *Dilution*: A more subtle cost—from our preceding examples we know that dilution comes from the stock options granted to management and the PE firm itself, as well as from additional rounds of financing.
- *Placement fees*: Fundraising fees may be charged up front—2% is not uncommon in private equity—or by means of a trailer fee. A trailer fee is generally charged annually and figures as a fraction of the amount invested by limited partners as long as these amounts remain invested in the investment vehicle.

# PRIVATE EQUITY FUND STRUCTURES AND TERMS | 8

☐ explain private equity fund structures, terms, due diligence, and valuation in the context of an analysis of private equity fund returns

When analyzing an investment in a private equity fund, a solid understanding of PE fund structures, terms of investment, due diligence, and PE fund valuation are an absolute prerequisite for investors. When interpreting financial performance, private equity raises many more challenges than public equities do. In addition to the structure and terms, two of the main differentiating characteristics relate to the nature of the subscriptions investors make in private equity structures and to the J-curve effect. Investors initially commit a certain amount to the private equity fund that is subsequently drawn by the fund as the fund's capital is deployed to portfolio companies. This contrasts with public market investing in which investment orders are typically fully disbursed at the time the orders are settled on the markets. The J-curve effect refers to the typical profile of reported PE fund returns, whereby low or negative returns are reported in the early years of a private equity fund (in large part as a result of the fees' impact on net returns), followed by increased returns thereafter as the private equity firm manages portfolio companies toward the exit.

The limited partnership has emerged as the dominant form in most jurisdictions. Funds that are structured as limited partnerships are governed by a limited partnership agreement between the fund manager, called the general partner (GP), and the fund's investors, called limited partners (LPs). Whereas the GP has management control over the fund and is jointly liable for all debts, LPs have limited liability; that is, they do not risk more than the amount of their investment in the fund.

The main alternative to the limited partnership is a corporate structure called a company limited by shares, which mirrors in its functioning the limited partnership but offers better legal protection to the GP and to some extent the LPs, depending on the jurisdiction. Some fund structures are subject to light regulatory oversight, which offers enhanced protection to LPs.

The vast majority of these private equity fund structures are closed-end, meaning they restrict existing investors from redeeming their shares over the lifetime of the fund and limit new investors to entering the fund at predefined time periods, at the discretion of the GP.

Private equity firms operate effectively in two spheres: the business of managing private equity investments and the business of raising funds. Their marketing efforts tend to be planned well in advance of the launch of their funds to ensure that the announced target fund size will be met once the fund is effectively started. The marketing phase of a private equity fund, depending on whether it is a first fund or a following fund, may take between one and two years. Once investors have committed their investment to the fund, private equity managers draw on investors' commitments—this action is called a drawdown or capital call—as the fund is being deployed and invested in portfolio companies. After commitment, private equity funds tend to have a duration of 10–12 years, generally extendable to an additional 2–3 years. Exhibit 7 illustrates structuring and stages in the life cycle for a PE fund.

### Exhibit 7: Structuring and Life Cycle Stages for a Private Equity Fund

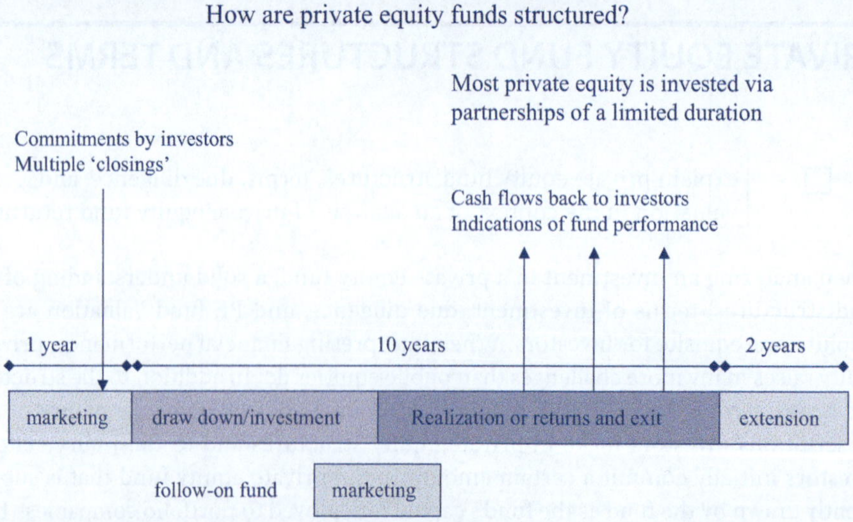

How are private equity funds structured?

Most private equity is invested via partnerships of a limited duration

Commitments by investors
Multiple 'closings'

Cash flows back to investors
Indications of fund performance

1 year — 10 years — 2 years

marketing | draw down/investment | Realization or returns and exit | extension

follow-on fund — marketing

Fund terms are contractually defined in a fund prospectus or limited partnership agreement, which is available to qualified prospective investors. The definition of qualified investors depends on the jurisdiction. Typically, wealth criteria (e.g., exceeding

**Private Equity Fund Structures and Terms**

US$1 million) and/or a minimum subscription threshold (e.g., a minimum of €125,000) apply. The terms are frequently the result of the balance of negotiation power between GPs and LPs. Although the balance of negotiation power shifted in favor of LPs during and immediately following the GFC, it turned back in favor of GPs as the largest sponsor continued to increase in size and gain market share. Any significant downturn in private equity's fortunes may change the balance of power in favor of LPs once again. In any event, the negotiation of terms informs an alignment of interests between the GP and LPs and defines GP incentives, such as transaction fees and profit sharing. The most significant fund terms may be categorized into economic and corporate governance terms.

## Economic Terms

- *Management fees* represent an annual percentage of committed capital, which is paid quarterly to the GP during the fund investment period. Fees of 1.5%–2.5% are common, and some of the most successful funds charge even more. After the investment period, fees may decline somewhat and be calculated based on invested capital. Less frequently, management fees may continue to be calculated based on capital commitment or net asset value.

- *Transaction fees* are fees paid to GPs in their advisory capacity when they provide investment banking services for transactions (mergers and acquisitions, IPOs) that benefit the fund. These fees may be subject to sharing agreements with LPs, typically a 50/50 split. When such fee-sharing agreements apply, they generally come as a deduction to the management fees.

- *Carried interest* represents the general partner's share of the profits generated by a private equity fund. Carried interest is frequently in the range of 20% of the fund's profits (after management fees).

- *Ratchet* is a mechanism that determines the allocation of equity between shareholders and the management team of the PE-controlled company. A ratchet enables the management team to increase its equity allocation depending on the company's actual performance and the return achieved by the PE firm.

- *Hurdle rate* is the internal rate of return that a private equity fund must achieve before the GP receives any carried interest. The hurdle rate is typically in the range of 7%–10%. The objective is to align the interests of the GP with those of LPs by giving additional incentives to the GP to outperform traditional investment benchmarks and to protect against LP downside.

### EXAMPLE 1

#### Calculation of Carried Interest

Suppose that a LBO fund has committed capital of US$100 million, carried interest of 20%, and a hurdle rate of 8%. The fund called 75% of its commitments from investors at the beginning of Year 1, which was invested at the beginning of Year 1 in target company A for $40 million and target company B for $35 million. Suppose that at the end of Year 2, a profit of $5 million has been realized by the GP upon exit of the investment in company A, and the value of the investment in company B has remained unchanged. Suppose also that the GP is entitled to carried interest on a deal-by-deal basis; that is, the IRR used to calculate carried interest is calculated for each investment upon exit. A theoretical carried interest

> of $1 million (20% of $5 million) could be granted to the GP, but the IRR upon exit of investment in company A is only 6.1%. Unless the IRR exceeds the hurdle rate, no carried interest may be paid to the GP.

- *Target fund size* is expressed as an absolute amount in the fund prospectus or information memorandum (also called the private placement memorandum, or PPM; offering memorandum, or OM; or offering circular, or OC). Target fund size is critical investor information because it signals the GP's capacity to manage a portfolio of a predefined size and also the GP's ability to raise funds. A fund that closed with a significantly lower size relative to the target size is perceived as a negative signal.
- *Vintage year* is the year the private equity fund is launched. Reference to the vintage year allows performance comparison of funds operating at the same stage and under the same market conditions.
- *Term of the fund* is typically 10 years, which is extendable for additional shorter periods by agreement with the investors. Although infrequently observed, funds can also be of unlimited duration, and in this case they are often quoted on stock markets—for example, investment trusts.

## Corporate Governance Terms

- *Key man clause.* Under the key man clause, a certain number of key named executives are expected to play an active role in the management of the fund. In case of the departure of such a key executive or insufficient time spent in the management of the fund, the clause provides that the GP may be prohibited from making any new investments until a new key executive is appointed.
- *Disclosure and confidentiality.* Private equity firms have no obligations to publicly disclose their financial performance. Following a 2002 court ruling requiring the California Public Employees' Retirement System (CalPERS) to publicly report its returns on private equity investments, the Freedom of Information Act (FOIA) in the United States and similar legislation in some European countries led public pension funds to report on their private equity investments. Disclosable information relates to the financial performance of the underlying funds but does not extend to information on the companies in which the funds invest, which is not typically disclosed. The reporting by CalPERS is a prominent example of the application of this clause. Some PE fund terms may be more restrictive on confidentiality and disclosure, subject to FOIA.
- *Distribution waterfall.* This is a mechanism that delineates how distributions are allocated to LPs and GPs. The predominant mechanisms are deal-by-deal waterfalls, which allow earlier distribution of carried interest to the GP after each individual deal (also known as an American waterfall), and total return waterfalls, which result in earlier distributions to LPs because carried interest is calculated on the profits of the entire portfolio (also known as a European waterfall). Two alternatives for calculating carried interest exist under the total return method: In the first alternative, the GP receives carried interest only after the fund has returned the entire committed capital to LPs; in the second alternative, the GP receives carried interest on any distribution as long as the value of the investment portfolio exceeds

a certain threshold above invested capital, usually 20%. The European waterfall has become prevalent among large funds marketed to institutional investors.

- *Clawback provision.* A clawback provision requires the GP to return a portion or all of the carried interest to LPs if it turns out the GP has received more than its share of profits. This provision ensures that when an LP exits a highly profitable investment early in the fund's life and subsequent exits are less profitable, the GP pays back capital contributions, fees, expenses, and carried interest profits to the LPs in order to ensure that the profit split is in line with the fund's prospectus. The clawback is normally due on termination of the fund but may be subject to an annual reconciliation (or true-up).

### EXAMPLE 2

### Distribution Waterfalls

Suppose a private equity fund has committed capital of £300 million and a carried interest of 20%. After a first investment of £30 million, the fund exits the investment nine months later with a £15 million profit. Under the deal-by-deal method, the GP would be entitled to 20% of the profit—that is, £3 million. In the first alternative for calculating carried interest under the total return method, the LPs are entitled to the entire proceeds of the sale—that is, £45 million—and the GP is entitled to nothing (yet). Under the second alternative, the exit value of £45 million exceeds the invested value of £30 million by more than 20%. The GP would thus be entitled to £3 million.

Continuing this example with a clawback provision with an annual true-up, suppose that the deal-by-deal method applies and that a second investment of £25 million is concluded with a loss of £5 million one year later. At the annual true-up, the GP would have to pay back £1 million to LPs. In practice, an escrow account is used to regulate these fluctuations until termination of the fund.

- *Tag-along, drag along rights* are contractual provisions in share-purchase agreements. Tag-along rights ensure that minority shareholders have the right to join in a sale entered into by a majority shareholder at the same terms offered to the majority shareholder. Essentially the buyer cannot acquire control without extending its offer to all shareholders, including the management of the company. Drag-along rights allow majority shareholders who have negotiated an exit to require the minority investors to participate in the sale at the same terms, preventing minority investors from vetoing a sale.
- *No-fault divorce.* A GP may be removed both with and without cause provided that a supermajority (generally above 75%) of LPs approve the removal. In practice it is unusual for investors to succeed in removing the GP.
- *Removal for cause* is a clause that allows for removal of the GP or an earlier termination of the fund for "cause." Cause may include gross negligence on the part of the GP, a key person event, the felony conviction of a key person, bankruptcy of the GP, or a material breach of the fund prospectus. It is difficult for LPs to remove the GP for cause because when there is an allegation of wrongdoing, the GP will often agree to an out-of-court settlement and pay a fine without having to admit guilt. Moreover, it may be many years until a final court hearing takes place.

- *Investment restrictions* generally impose a minimum level of diversification on the fund's investments, a geographic and/or sector focus, or limits on borrowing.
- *Co-investment.* LPs generally have a first right of co-investing along with the GP. This can be advantageous for the LPs as fees and profit share are likely to be lower (or zero) on co-invested capital. The GP and affiliated parties are also typically restricted in their co-investments to prevent conflicts of interest with their LPs. Crossover co-investments are a classic example of a conflict of interest. A crossover co-investment occurs when a subsequent fund launched by the same GP invests in a portfolio company that has received funding from a previous fund.

## Due Diligence Investigations by Potential Investors

Prior to investing in a private equity fund, prospective investors generally conduct thorough due diligence. Outlining several fundamental characteristics of PE funds will underline how important the due diligence process is:

- Private equity funds tend to exhibit a strong persistence of returns over time. This means that, typically, top-performing funds continue to outperform and poorly performing funds continue to perform poorly or disappear.
- The performance range between funds varies widely. For example, the difference between top-quartile and third-quartile fund IRRs can be 20 percentage points.
- Liquidity in private equity is typically very limited, and thus LPs are locked in for the long term. However, when private equity funds exit an investment, they return the cash to the investors immediately. Therefore, the duration of an investment in private equity is typically shorter than the maximum life of the fund.

Standard due diligence questionnaires (DDQs) have been developed by numerous international and country trade organizations. The Institutional Limited Partners Association (ILPA) publishes and makes available a DDQ on its website. These guides are not a substitute for the due diligence process that is conducted by LPs before investing in a venture capital or private equity fund.

## Private Equity Fund Valuation

The description of private equity valuation in a fund prospectus is generally associated with the fund's calculation of net asset value (NAV), which itself is generally defined as the value of the fund assets less liabilities corresponding to the accrued expenses of the fund. The fund's assets are frequently valued by GPs, depending on their valuation policies, in the following ways:

1. At cost with significant adjustments for subsequent financing events or deterioration
2. At the lower of cost or market value
3. By the revaluation of a portfolio company whenever a new financing round involving new investors takes place
4. At cost with no interim adjustment until the exit
5. With a discount for restricted securities—for example, Reg. 144 securities
6. More rarely, marked to market by reference to a peer group of public comparables and applying illiquidity discounts

Private equity valuation standards, such as those originally produced by British, French, and European industry associations, have been adopted by funds operating in numerous jurisdictions.

Because the fund's valuation is adjusted with each new round of financing, the NAV may be more stale in down markets when there is a long gap between funding rounds. This mechanism is similar to the valuation of investment funds of publicly quoted securities. There is thus a fundamental implicit break-up assumption whereby the fund may be broken up at any time, the funds underlying investments may be liquidated individually and immediately, and the proceeds returned to LPs. Whereas this fundamental break-up assumption may hold for publicly traded securities, which are marked to market, this assumption may be more questionable for private equity investment portfolios typically held over a long period of time. At what value should investments in portfolio companies be reported prior to the private equity fund exiting the investment and returning the proceeds to the LPs? There is no clear answer to that question, because there is no market for securities issued by private equity companies.

Undrawn LP commitments represent legal obligations to meet capital calls in the future. They are not accounted for in the NAV calculation and should be viewed as unfunded liabilities by each LP for as long as they are callable.

Given that PE funds have different investment strategies, an understanding of their respective valuation policies will prevent biases. Whereas an early-stage VC fund may record its investments at cost, a late-stage VC fund may mark its portfolio companies to market by reference to public market comparables. When market bubbles form, as they did in the year leading up to the GFC, public market comparables may distort the valuation of portfolio companies and thus reported fund returns.

Private equity valuations are mostly performed by GPs. Under pressure from LPs, an increasing number of annual and semi-annual valuations are performed by independent valuers that are mandated by GPs. Although auditors sign off on annual results, their responsibility does not extend much beyond testing the reasonableness and allocation of the GP's model for illiquid investment values.

# EVALUATING A PRIVATE EQUITY FUND

- [ ] interpret and compare financial performance of private equity funds from the perspective of an investor
- [ ] calculate management fees, carried interest, net asset value, distributed to paid in (DPI), residual value to paid in (RVPI), and total value to paid in (TVPI) of a private equity fund

Because each private equity fund is unique, assessing financial performance depends on good knowledge of a fund's objectives, structure, terms, and valuation policies. Typically an analysis of a private equity fund's financial performance includes a detailed examination of each investment's and the fund's return using IRR and multiples.

## Analysis of IRR since Inception

Here, *net of fees* means net of management fees, carried interest, or any other financial arrangements that accrue to the GP. The IRR, a cash flow–weighted rate of return, is deemed the most appropriate measure of private equity performance by the Global Investment Performance Standards (GIPS), by the International Private Equity and

Venture Capital Valuation Guidelines (2018 Guidelines), and by other venture capital and private equity standards. The interpretation of IRR in private equity is subject to caution, however, because an implicit assumption behind the IRR calculation is that the fund is fully liquid, whereas a significant portion of the fund's underlying investments is illiquid during much of a private equity fund's life. Therefore, valuation of portfolio companies according to industry standards is important to ensure the quality of the IRR figures.

Gross IRR is a function of the cash flows between the portfolio companies and the PE fund and is often considered a good measure of the PE firm's track record in creating value. Net IRR is a function of the cash flows between the PE fund and LPs, capturing the returns to investors. Fees and profit sharing create significant deviations between gross and net IRR. IRR analysis is often combined with a benchmark IRR analysis—that is, the median IRR for the relevant peer group of comparable private equity funds operating with a similar investment strategy and vintage year. This is particularly important because there are clear trends in private equity returns, with some vintage years producing much higher returns than others.

Despite the widespread prevalence of IRR as a performance measure and a hurdle for GP profit participation, it has its drawbacks. One drawback is that it can be easily manipulated. Imagine that a GP delays investor capital calls by using a fund's line of credit or bridge financing to make an initial investment instead or that the GP refinances an investment in order to return capital to investors prior to an exit. Both strategies reduce the time that investors' capital is outstanding, which boosts IRR independently of the investment holding period. In some cases, the only reason the GP may be entitled to its carried interest in the end is the manipulation and timing of leverage. Another problem with IRR is that it provides no information about the size of the return.

## Analysis of Return Multiples

Return multiples simply measure the total return to investors relative to the total sum invested. Although multiples ignore the time value of money, their ease of calculation and their ability to differentiate between "realized" actual proceeds from divestments and the "unrealized" portfolio subject to the GP's valuation make these ratios very popular among LPs. The return multiples used most frequently by LPs and also defined by GIPS that provide additional information about fund performance are as follows:

- PIC (paid-in capital): The ratio of paid-in capital, which is the proportion of the LPs' total committed capital that the GP has so far deployed following any capital calls, to total committed capital.
- DPI (distributed to paid-in): The ratio of the cumulative distributions, which is the amount of cash and stock that has already been paid out to LPs from the fund, to the paid-in capital. This ratio indicates the fund's realized return on investment and is often called the cash-on-cash return. DPI is presented net of management fees and carried interest.
- RVPI (residual value to paid-in): This is the value of LPs' shareholding held with the private equity fund as a proportion of the cumulative invested capital (i.e., the paid-in capital). The numerator is the value that the GP assigns to the remaining portfolio companies. This ratio is a measure of the private equity fund's unrealized return on investment. RVPI is presented net of management fees and carried interest.
- TVPI (total value to paid-in): This ratio is the portfolio companies' distributed (or realized) and undistributed (or unrealized) value as a proportion of the cumulative invested capital. TVPI is the sum of DPI and RVPI and is presented net of management fees and carried interest.

In addition to quantitative measures of return, an analysis of fund financial performance includes

- an analysis of realized investments since inception, with comments on all successes and failures;
- an analysis of unrealized investments, highlighting all red flags in the portfolio and the expected time to exit for each portfolio company;
- a cash flow forecast for each portfolio company and for the aggregate portfolio; and
- an analysis of portfolio valuation, audited financial statements, and the NAV.

### EXAMPLE 3

#### Calculating and Interpreting Private Equity Fund Performance

Suppose that a private equity fund has a DPI of 0.07 and an RVPI of 0.62 after five years. The IRR is −17%. The fund follows a venture capital strategy in high technology and has a vintage year of 2006 and a term of 10 years. A DPI of 7% indicates that few successful exits were made. An RVPI of 62% points to an extended J-curve effect for the fund, as TVPI amounts to 69% at the midlife of the fund. A vintage year of 2006 hints that the fund was started before the 2007 global financial crisis and that the routes to exit for portfolio companies have been dramatically changed. During the financial crisis, the investment portfolio probably suffered a number of complete write-offs. LPs should thus consider the state of the portfolio and examine the number of write-offs and other signals of ailing companies. The risk of not recovering the invested amount at termination of the fund is significant. The GP's compliance with valuation policies should also be closely monitored by LPs in order to ensure that the GP's expectations are not excessive given the state of the portfolio.

With increased allocations to private equity, performance comparisons across asset classes are often misinterpreted. The IRR, a standard measure of private equity returns, is cash flow weighted, whereas the performance of most other asset classes is measured in terms of a time-weighted rate of return.

There have been ongoing attempts to solve performance-comparison issues. The Public Market Equivalent (PME) compares a fund's IRR to a public market index (e.g., the MSCI World, the S&P 500 Index, and the FTSE All-Share Index) by assuming the fund's cash flows were invested and disinvested in the public index at the same amount and time. The PME, sometimes referred to as the Long Nickels PME for its developers Austin Long and Craig Nickels or as the Index Comparison Method (ICM), often calculates the IRR based on public index values. The PME facilitates a direct comparison of the fund's IRR to public markets, but it breaks down when the fund significantly outperforms the public index, resulting in a negative NAV and IRR. The PME+ (developed by Christophe Rouvinez in 2003), the modified PME (created by Cambridge Associates in 2013), and several other approaches attempt to address the shortcomings of the Long Nickels PME.

## Concept in Action: Evaluating Private Equity Fund Performance

Michael Hornsby, CFA, is a senior investment officer at Icarus, a UK-based institutional investor in private equity. He is contemplating an investment in Europa Venture Partners III, a new late-stage technology venture capital fund, after thorough due diligence was performed both on the fund and on the GP. Icarus has been an investor in Europa Venture Partners' (EVPs') previous two funds, EVP I and EVP II, and has been satisfied with performance so far. Icarus is seeking to further expand its relationship with this GP because it sees it as a niche venture capital firm operating in a less crowded segment of the pan-European technology markets. In light of its past success, EVP is increasing its carried interest for the third fund to 25% from 20% for the previous two funds. Hornsby has received information about the fund's financial performance and is seeking assistance in calculating and interpreting financial performance for a number of specific queries as outlined below.

### Europa Venture Partners (EVP)

General Partner: Europa Venture Partners (EVP) was established to provide equity financing to later-stage European technology companies in need of development capital. The GP seeks to provide strategic support to seasoned entrepreneurial teams and to bring proven new technologies to the market. The GP targets investment in portfolio companies between €2 million and €10 million.

**Established in 2012 — Type: Development Capital**

| Fund | Vintage | Actual Fund Size (€ Millions) | Capital Called (%) | Mgmt. Fees (%) | Carried Interest (%) | Hurdle Rate (%) | Term | Report Date |
|---|---|---|---|---|---|---|---|---|
| EVP I | 2014 | 125 | 92 | 2 | 20 | 8 | 2012 | 31 Dec 2019 |
| EVP II | 2016 | 360 | 48 | 2 | 20 | 8 | 2025 | 31 Dec 2019 |

The financial performance for Icarus' investments in EVP funds follows.

| Fund | Committed Capital (€ Millions) | Capital Called Down (€ Millions) | Gross IRR (%) | Net IRR (%) | DPI (×) | RVPI (×) | TVPI (×) | Quartile |
|---|---|---|---|---|---|---|---|---|
| EVP I | 10 | 9.2 | 16.1 | 11.3 | 1.26 | 1.29 | 2.55 | 1 |
| EVP II | 25 | 12.0 | 1.6 | (0.4) | 0.35 | 1.13 | 1.48 | 2 |

Hornsby is also interested in verifying management fees, carried interest, and the NAV of EVP I. He has the following information about yearly capital calls (assumed to occur on 1 January of the given year), operating results, and annual distributions (as of 31 December of the given year).

**Calls, Operating Results, and Distributions (€ Millions)**

|  | 2014 | 2015 | 2016 | 2017 | 2018 | 2019 |
|---|---|---|---|---|---|---|
| Called down | 50 | 15 | 10 | 25 | 10 | 5 |
| Realized results | 0 | 0 | 10 | 35 | 40 | 80 |
| Unrealized results | −5 | −15 | 15 | 10 | 15 | 25 |

**Evaluating a Private Equity Fund**

|               | 2014 | 2015 | 2016 | 2017 | 2018 | 2019 |
|---------------|------|------|------|------|------|------|
| Distributions | —    | —    | —    | 25   | 45   | 75   |

Operating results are the sum of realized results from exiting portfolio companies and unrealized results from the revaluation of investments presently held in portfolio companies. In addition to the information available on EVP I, Hornsby also knows from the fund prospectus that the distribution waterfall is calculated according to the total return method, in which the GP receives carried interest only after the fund has returned the entire committed capital to LPs. Management fees are calculated on the basis of the paid-in capital. Hornsby also wants to calculate DPI, RVPI, and TVPI of EVP I for 2019, and he is interested in understanding how to calculate gross and net IRRs.

1. Interpret and compare the financial performance of EVP I and EVP II.
2. Calculate the management fees, the carried interest, and the NAV of EVP I. Also calculate DPI, RVPI, and TVPI of EVP I for 2019. Explain on the basis of EVP I how gross and net IRRs are calculated.

### Solution to 1

In the table above, the first venture capital fund (EVP I) made its initial capital call in 2014 and returned to LPs €1.26 (all amounts in millions) for every €1 that had been drawn down two years ahead of the termination of the fund. EVP I residual value remains high, at 1.29 times capital drawn down, which is a good signal about the profitability of the fund at termination. The fund ranks in the first quartile, which means it belongs to the best-performing funds of that category and vintage year. Gross IRR of 16.1% after six years of operations and 11.3% net of fees represents good performance.

The second fund exhibits very modest performance to date in terms of gross and net IRR, which indicates that the fund is still experiencing the J-curve effect. EVP II has returned to LPs 35% of capital drawn down and a residual value of 113% of the capital drawn down, which indicates that despite the fund being in its early years, the GP has already managed a number of profitable exits and increased the value of the investment portfolio halfway through the termination of the fund. Actual fund size significantly exceeds previous fund size and is an indication that the GP is gaining momentum in terms of fundraising, probably partly attributable to the strong performance of the first fund.

### Solution to 2

**Cash Flows and Distributions (€ Millions)**

| Year | Called Down (1) | Paid-In Capital (2) | Mgmt. Fees (3) | Operating Results (4) | NAV before Distributions (5) | Carried Interest (6) | Distributions (7) | NAV after Distributions (8) |
|------|-----|-----|-----|-----|-------|------|----|-------|
| 2014 | 50  | 50  | 1.0 | −5  | 44.0  |      |    | 44.0  |
| 2015 | 15  | 65  | 1.3 | −15 | 42.7  |      |    | 42.7  |
| 2016 | 10  | 75  | 1.5 | 25  | 76.2  |      |    | 76.2  |
| 2017 | 25  | 100 | 2.0 | 45  | 144.2 | 3.8  | 25 | 115.4 |
| 2018 | 10  | 110 | 2.2 | 55  | 178.2 | 6.8  | 45 | 126.4 |
| 2019 | 5   | 115 | 2.3 | 105 | 234.1 | 11.2 | 75 | 147.9 |

Based on this table, the calculations of DPI, RVPI, and TVPI can be derived as follows:

- Paid-in capital = Cumulative capital called down (Column 2).
- Management fees = (2%) × (Column 2).
- Carried interest: The first year that NAV is higher than committed capital (€125 million), carried interest is 20% of the excess, or (20%) [(NAV in Column 5) − €125 million]. Thereafter, provided that NAV before distribution exceeds committed capital, carried interest is (20%) × (Increase in NAV before distributions). Carried interest in 2019 is calculated as follows: (20%) × (€234.1 million − €178.2 million).
- NAV before distributions = NAV after distributions$_{t-1}$ + (Column 1) − (Column 3) + (Column 4).
- NAV after distributions = (Column 5) − (Column 6) − (Column 7).
- DPI = (€25 + €45 + €75)/€115, or 1.26×.
- RVPI = €147.9/€115, or 1.29×.
- TVPI = 1.26× + 1.29× = 2.55×.

The IRRs may be developed as follows:

- Gross IRRs are estimated by calculating the internal rate of return for the following cash flows: called-down capital at the beginning of period (Column 1) and the previous year's operating results (Column 4).
- Net IRRs are estimated by calculating the internal rate of return for the following cash flows: called-down capital at the beginning of period (Column 1) and the previous year's operating results (Column 4), net of management fees (Column 3) and carried interest (Column 6). Cash flows for gross and net IRRs are shown in the following table. Gross IRR and net IRR are shown in the bottom row.

| Year End | Called Down | Operating Results | Cash Flows Gross IRR | Mgmt. Fees | Carried Interest | Cash Flows Net IRR |
|---|---|---|---|---|---|---|
| 2013 | 50 | | −50 | | | −50.0 |
| 2014 | 15 | −5 | −20 | 1.0 | | −21.0 |
| 2015 | 10 | −15 | −25 | 1.3 | | −26.3 |
| 2016 | 25 | 25 | 0 | 1.5 | | −1.5 |
| 2017 | 10 | 45 | 35 | 2.0 | 3.8 | 29.2 |
| 2018 | 5 | 55 | 50 | 2.2 | 6.8 | 41.0 |
| 2019 | | 105 | 105 | 2.3 | 11.2 | 91.5 |
| IRR | | | 16.1% | | | 11.3% |

# SUMMARY

- Private equity funds seek to add value by various means, including optimizing financial structures, incentivizing management, and creating operational improvements.

- Private equity can be thought of as an alternative system of governance for corporations: Rather than ownership and control being separated as in most publicly quoted companies, private equity concentrates ownership and control. Many view the combination of ownership and control as a fundamental source of the returns earned by the best private equity funds.
- A critical role for the GP is valuation of potential investments. But because these investments are usually privately owned, valuation encounters many challenges.
- Valuation techniques differ according to the nature of the investment. Early-stage ventures require very different techniques than leveraged buyouts. Private equity professionals tend to use multiple techniques when performing a valuation, and they explore many different scenarios for the future development of the business.
- In buyouts, the availability of debt financing can have a big impact on the scale of private equity activity, and it seems to impact valuations observed in the market.
- Because private equity funds are incentivized to acquire, add value, and then exit within the lifetime of the fund, they are considered buy-to-sell investors. Planning the exit route for the investment is a critical role for the GP, and a well-timed and well-executed investment can be a significant source of realized value.
- In addition to the problems encountered by the private equity funds in valuing potential portfolio investments, challenges exist in valuing the investment portfolio on an ongoing basis. This is because the investments have no easily observed market value and there is a large element of judgment involved in valuing each of the portfolio companies prior to their sale by the fund.
- The two main metrics for measuring the ongoing and ultimate performance of private equity funds are IRR and multiples. Comparisons of PE returns across funds and with other assets are demanding because it is important to control for the timing of cash flows, differences in risk and portfolio composition, and vintage-year effects.

# REFERENCES

Jensen, M. 1986. "Agency Costs of Free Cash Flow, Corporate Finance, and Takeovers." American Economic Review 76 (2): 323–29.

Jensen, M. 1989. "Eclipse of the Public Corporation." Harvard Business Review 67 (September–October).

# PRACTICE PROBLEMS

1. Discuss the ways that private equity funds can create value.

2. Jean-Pierre Dupont is the chief investment officer (CIO) of a French pension fund that allocates a substantial portion of its assets to private equity. The fund's PE portfolio comprises mainly large buyout funds and mezzanine funds with a limited allocation to a special situations fund. A decision has been made to increase allocations to European venture capital. The investment committee of the pension fund requested that Dupont present an analysis of five key investment characteristics specific to venture capital relative to buyout investing. Can you assist Dupont in this request?

## The following information relates to questions 3-8

Martha Brady is the CIO of the Upper Darby County (UDC) public employees' pension system. Brady is considering an allocation of the pension system's assets to private equity. She has asked two of her analysts, Jennifer Chau, CFA, and Matthew Hermansky, to provide more information about the workings of the private equity market.

Brady recognizes that the private equity asset class covers a broad spectrum of equity investments that are not traded in public markets. She asks Chau to describe the major differences between assets within this asset class. Chau notes that private equity ranges from venture capital financing of early-stage companies to complete buyouts of large publicly traded or even privately held companies. Chau describes some of the characteristics of venture capital and buyout investments.

Chau mentions that private equity firms take care to align the economic interests of the managers of the investments they control with their own. Various contractual clauses are inserted in the compensation contracts of the management team in order to reward or punish managers who meet or do not meet agreed-upon target objectives.

One concern Chau highlights is the illiquidity of private equity investments over time. Some funds are returned to investors, however, over the life of the fund because a number of investment opportunities are exited early. Provisions in a fund's prospectus describe the distribution of returns to investors, some of which favor the limited partners. One such provision is the distribution waterfall mechanism that provides distributions to limited partners (LPs) before the general partner (GP) receives the carried interest. This distribution mechanism is called the total return waterfall.

Chau prepares the following data to illustrate the distribution waterfall mechanism and the funds provided to limited partners when a private equity fund with a zero hurdle rate exits from its first three projects during a three-year period.

**Exhibit 1: Investment Returns and Distribution Waterfalls**

| | |
|---|---|
| Private equity committed capital | $400 million |
| Carried interest | 20% |

| | |
|---|---|
| First project investment capital | $20 million |
| Second project investment capital | $45 million |
| Third project investment capital | $50 million |
| Proceeds from first project | $25 million |
| Proceeds from second project | $35 million |
| Proceeds from third project | $65 million |

Chau cautions that investors must understand the terminology used to describe the performance of private equity funds. Interpretation of performance numbers should be made with the awareness that much of the fund assets are illiquid during a substantial part of the fund's life. She provides the latest data in Exhibit 2 for the Alpha, Beta, and Gamma Funds, diversified high-technology venture capital funds formed five years ago, each with five years remaining to termination.

**Exhibit 2: Financial Performance of Alpha, Beta, and Gamma Funds**

| Fund | PIC | DPI | RVPI |
|---|---|---|---|
| Alpha | 0.30 | 0.10 | 0.65 |
| Beta | 0.85 | 0.10 | 1.25 |
| Gamma | 0.85 | 1.25 | 0.75 |

Chau studies the data and comments,

Of the three funds, the Alpha Fund has the best chance to outperform over the remaining life. First, it's because the management has earned such a relatively high residual value on capital and will be able to earn a high return on the remaining funds called down. At termination, the RVPI will be double the 0.65 value when the rest of the funds are called down. Second, its cash-on-cash return as measured by DPI is already as high as that of the Beta Fund. The PIC (or paid-in capital) ratio indicates the proportion of capital already called by the GP. The PIC of Alpha is relatively low relative to Beta and Gamma.

Hermansky notes that a private equity fund's ability to properly plan and execute its exit from an investment is vital for the fund's success. Venture funds, such as Alpha, Beta, and Gamma, take special care to plan their exits.

Brady then asks the analysts what procedures private equity firms would use to value investments in their portfolios as well as investments that are added later. She is concerned about buying into a fund with existing assets that do not have public market prices that can be used to ascertain value. In such cases, she worries, what if a GP overvalues the assets and new investors in the fund pay more for the fund assets than they are worth?

Hermansky makes three statements regarding the valuation methods used in private equity transactions during the early stages of selling a fund to investors.

Statement 1   For venture capital investment in the early stages of analysis, emphasis is placed on the discounted cash flow approach to valuation.

Statement 2   For buyout investments, income-based approaches are used frequently as a primary method of valuation.

**Practice Problems**

Statement 3   If a comparable group of companies exist, multiples of revenues or earnings are used frequently to derive a value for venture capital investments.

3. The characteristic that is *most likely* common to both the venture capital and buyout private equity investment is:

   A. measurable and assessable risk.

   B. the extensive use of financial leverage.

   C. the strength of the individual track record and ability of members of management.

4. The contractual term enabling management of the private equity–controlled company to be rewarded with increased equity ownership as a result of meeting performance targets is called:

   A. a ratchet.

   B. the tag-along right.

   C. the clawback provision.

5. For the projects described in Exhibit 8, under a deal-by-deal method with a clawback provision and true-up every three years, the cumulative dollar amount the GP receives by the end of the three years is equal to:

   A. 1 million.

   B. 2 million.

   C. 3 million.

6. Are Chau's two reasons for interpreting Alpha Fund as the best-performing fund over the remaining life correct?

   A. No

   B. Yes

   C. The first reason is correct, but the second reason is incorrect.

7. The exit route for a venture capital investment is *least likely* to be in the form of a(n):

   A. initial public offering (IPO).

   B. sale to other venture funds targeting the same sector.

   C. buyout by the management of the venture investment.

8. Which statement by Hermansky is the *least* valid?

   A. Statement 1

   B. Statement 2

   C. Statement 3

## The following information relates to questions 9-14

Daniel Collin is a junior analyst at JRR Equity Partners (JRR), a private equity firm. Collin is assigned to work with Susan Tseng, a senior portfolio manager. Tseng and Collin meet to discuss existing and potential investments.

Tseng starts the meeting with a discussion of LBO firms and VC firms. Collin tells Tseng,

LBO firms tend to invest in companies with predictable cash flows and experienced management teams, whereas VC firms tend to invest in companies with high EBITDA or EBIT growth and where an exit is fairly predictable.

Tseng and Collin next analyze a potential investment in the leveraged buyout of Stoneham Industries. Specifically, they assess the expected gain if they elect to purchase all of the preference shares and 90% of the common equity through the LBO. Details of the LBO include the following:

- The buyout requires an initial investment of $10 million.
- Financing for the deal includes $6 million in debt, $3.6 million in preference shares that promise a 15% annual return paid at exit, and $0.4 million in common equity.

The expected exit value in six years is $15 million, with an estimated reduction in debt of $2.8 million over the six years prior to exit.

Tseng and Collin next discuss JRR's investment in Venture Holdings, a private equity fund. Selected details on the Venture Holdings fund include the following:

- Total committed capital is $115 million.
- The distribution waterfall follows the deal-by-deal method, and carried interest is 20%.
- On its first exit event a few years ago, the fund generated a $10 million profit.
- At the end of the most recent year, cumulative paid-in capital was $98 million, cumulative distributions paid out to LPs were $28 million, and the year-end NAV, before and after distributions, was $170.52 million and $131.42 million, respectively.
- Tseng and Collin estimate that the fund's NAV before distributions will be $242.32 million at the end of next year.

Finally, Tseng and Collin evaluate two venture capital funds for potential investment: the Squire Fund and the Treble Fund. Both funds are in Year 7 of an estimated 10-year term. Selected data for the two funds are presented in Exhibit 1.

**Exhibit 1: Selected Data for the Squire Fund and the Treble Fund**

|  | Squire Fund | Treble Fund |
|---|---|---|
| DPI | 0.11 | 0.55 |
| RVPI | 0.95 | 0.51 |
| Gross IRR | −11% | 10% |
| Net IRR | −20% | 8% |

## Practice Problems

After reviewing the performance data in Exhibit 1, Collin draws the following conclusions:

Conclusion 1   The unrealized return on investment for the Squire Fund is greater than the unrealized return on investment for the Treble Fund.

Conclusion 2   The TVPI for the Treble Fund is higher than the TVPI for the Squire Fund because the Treble Fund has a higher gross IRR.

9. Is Collin's statement about LBO firms and VC firms correct?

   A. Yes

   B. No, because he is wrong with respect to VC firms

   C. No, because he is wrong with respect to LBO firms

10. The multiple of expected proceeds at exit to invested funds for JRR's Stoneham LBO investment is *closest* to:

    A. 2.77.

    B. 2.89.

    C. 2.98.

11. The distribution available to the limited partners of the Venture Holdings fund from the first exit is *closest* to:

    A. $2 million.

    B. $8 million.

    C. $10 million.

12. At the end of the most recent year, the ratio of total value to paid-in capital (TVPI) for the Venture Holdings fund was *closest* to:

    A. 0.29.

    B. 1.34.

    C. 1.63.

13. Based on Tseng and Collin's estimate of NAV next year, the estimate of carried interest next year is *closest* to:

    A. $14.36 million.

    B. $22 million.

    C. $25.46 million.

14. Which of Collin's conclusions regarding the Squire Fund and the Treble Fund is correct?

    A. Only Conclusion 1

B. Only Conclusion 2

C. Both Conclusion 1 and Conclusion 2

15. What problems are encountered when using comparable publicly traded companies to value private acquisition targets?

16. Jo Ann Ng is a senior analyst at SING INVEST, a large regional mid-market buyout manager in Singapore. She is considering the exit possibilities for an existing investment in a mature automotive parts manufacturer that was acquired three years ago at a multiple of 7.5 times EBITDA. SING INVEST originally anticipated exiting its investment in China Auto Parts, Inc., within three to six years. Ng noted that market conditions have deteriorated and that companies operating in a similar business trade at an average multiple of 5.5 times EBITDA. She expects, however, based on analyst reports and industry knowledge, that the market will recover strongly within the next two years because of the fast-increasing demand for cars in emerging markets. Upon review of market opportunities, Ng also noted that China Gear Box, Inc., a smaller Chinese automotive parts manufacturer that presents strong potential synergies with China Auto Parts, Inc., is available for sale at an EBITDA multiple of 4.5. Exits by means of an IPO or a trade sale to a financial or strategic (company) buyer are possible in China. How would you advise Ng to enhance value upon exit of China Auto Parts?

17. Wenda Lee, CFA, is a portfolio manager at a UK-based private equity institutional investor. She is considering an investment in a mid-market European buyout fund to achieve better diversification for her firm's private equity portfolio. She short-listed two funds that she sees as having similar risk–return profiles. Before deciding which one to invest in, she is carefully reviewing and comparing the terms of each fund.

|  | Mid-Market Fund A | Mid-Market Fund B |
| --- | --- | --- |
| Management fees | 2.5% | 1.5% |
| Transaction fees | 100% to the GP | 50–50% split |
| Carried interest | 15% | 20% |
| Hurdle rate | 6% | 9% |
| Clawback provision | No | Yes |
| Distribution waterfall | Deal-by-deal | Total return |

Based on the analysis of terms, which fund would you recommend to Lee?

18. What are the main ways that the performance of private equity limited partnerships can be measured (A) during the life of the fund and (B) once all investments have been exited?

# SOLUTIONS

1. The main ways that private equity funds can create value include the following:

    - Operational improvements and clearly defined strategies: In the case of later-stage companies and buyouts, private equity owners can often create value by focusing the business on its most profitable opportunities and providing strategic direction for the business. In the case of venture capital deals, the private equity funds provide valuable business experience, mentor management, and offer access to their network of contacts and other portfolio companies.

    - Creating incentives for managers and aligning their goals with the investors: This is often achieved by providing significant monetary rewards to management if the private equity fund secures a profitable exit. In the case of buyouts, the free cash flow available to management is minimized by taking on significant amounts of debt financing.

    - Optimizing the financial structure of the company: In the case of buyouts, the use of debt can reduce the tax payments made by the company and also reduce the cost of capital. There may also be opportunities in certain market conditions to take advantage of any mispricing of risk by lenders, which can allow the private equity funds to take advantage of interest rates that do not fully reflect the risks being carried by the lenders. Many would point to various periods from 2015 to 2019 when government interest rates were low, debt spreads were tight, and/or lender covenants were loose as examples of such prevailing conditions.

2.

| Venture Capital | Buyout |
| --- | --- |
| Primarily equity funded. Use of leverage is rare and very limited. | Extensive use of leverage consisting of a large proportion of senior debt and a significant layer of junior and/or mezzanine debt. |
| Returns of investment portfolios are generally characterized by very high returns from a limited number of highly successful investments and a significant number of write-offs from low performing investments or failures. | Returns of investment portfolios are generally characterized by lower variance across returns from underlying investments. Bankruptcies are rare events. |
| Venture capital firm monitors achievement of milestones defined in business plan and growth management. | Buyout firm monitors cash flow management and strategic and business planning. |
| Expanding capital requirement if in the growth phase. | Low working capital requirement. |
| Assessment of risk is difficult because of new technologies, new markets, and lack of operating history. | Risk is measurable (e.g., mature businesses, long operating history, etc.). |

3. C is correct. Members of both the firm being bought out and the venture capital investment usually have strong individual management track records. Extensive financial leverage is common in buyouts but not venture capital investments, whereas measurable risk is more common in buyouts than in venture capital situations.

4. A is correct.

5. B is correct. On a cumulative basis for three years, the fund earns $10 million, of which $2 million goes to the GP. The $2 million earned by the GP corresponds to 20% of the difference between total three-year proceeds and three-year invested capital, or 0.2 × [(25 + 35 + 65) − (20 + 45 + 50)].

6. A is correct. Chau misinterprets DPI, RVPI, and PIC. The returns earned to date are for each dollar of invested capital—that which has been drawn down—not total returns. Chau mistakenly believes (assuming the same management skill) the result for Alpha Fund at termination will be on the order of 3 × 0.65 = 1.95, instead of 0.65. In both cases, Alpha Fund has underperformed relative to the other two funds.

7. C is correct. Leverage needed to finance a management buyout is not readily available to firms with limited history.

8. A is correct. Statement 1 is the least likely to be valid.

9. B is correct. LBO firms generally invest in firms with a predictable cash flow pattern (EBITDA or EBIT growth) and experienced management teams. In contrast, venture capital firms tend to invest in new firms and new technologies with high revenue growth. Also, VC investments tend to be characterized as having exits that are difficult to anticipate.

10. B is correct. The investment exit value is $15 million. The expected payoff to JRR is calculated as follows (all amounts in millions):

    | | |
    |---|---:|
    | Expected exit value: | $15.00 |
    | Debt remaining at exit: ($6.0 − 2.8) | 3.20 |
    | Preference shares: [$3.60 × $(1.15)^6$] | 8.33 |
    | Common equity: ($15 exit − 3.2 debt − 8.33 preference) | 3.47 |

    Initial investment: $3.6 (preference) + 0.9 × $0.4 (common) = $3.96.

    Proceeds at exit: $8.33 (preference) + 0.9 × $3.47 (common) = $11.45.

    Multiple of expected proceeds to invested funds: $11.45 exit value/$3.96 initial investment
    = 2.89×.

11. B is correct. The distribution waterfall for the Venture Holdings fund follows the deal-by-deal method. The investment generated a profit of $10 million, and with carried interest of 20%, the general partner would receive $2 million ($10 million × 20%), leaving $8 million for the limited partners.

12. C is correct. Total value to paid-in capital (TVPI) represents the fund's distributed value and undistributed value as a proportion of the cumulative invested capital. TVPI is the sum of distributed to paid-in capital (DPI) and residual value to paid-in capital (RVPI):

$$DPI = \frac{\text{Cumulative distributions}}{\text{Cumulative invested capital}} = \frac{\$28 \text{ million}}{\$98 \text{ million}} = 0.29\times$$

$$RVPI = \frac{\text{NAV (after distributions)}}{\text{Cumulative invested capital}} = \frac{\$131.42 \text{ million}}{\$98 \text{ million}} = 1.34\times$$

$$\text{TVPI} = \frac{\text{Cumulative distribution} + \text{NAV (after distributions)}}{\text{Cumulative invested capital}}$$

$$= \frac{\$28 \text{ million} + 131.42 \text{ million}}{\$98 \text{ million}} = 1.63\times$$

13. A is correct. Provided that NAV before distribution exceeds committed capital, the general partner is entitled to carried interest, calculated as the 20% multiplied by the increase in NAV before distributions. So, the carried interest is calculated as follows:

    Carried interest = 20% × ($242.32 − $170.52) = $14.36 million.

14. A is correct. DPI provides an indication of a fund's realized return, whereas RVPI provides an indication of a fund's unrealized return. The Squire Fund has a higher RVPI (0.95) than the Treble Fund (0.51). TVPI, which is the sum of DPI and RVPI, is the same for both funds: 0.11 + 0.95 = 1.06 for the Squire Fund and 0.55 + 0.51 = 1.06 for the Treble Fund.

15. There are many complexities in using comparable companies to value private targets, including the following:

    - The lack of public comparison companies operating in the same business, facing the same risks, and at the same stage of development. It is often possible to identify "approximate" comparisons but very rare to find an exact match. It is essential, therefore, to use judgment when using comparison company information, rather than just taking the average multiples derived from a sample of disparate companies.

    - Comparison companies may have different capital structures, so estimated beta coefficients and some financial ratios should be adjusted accordingly.

    - Reported accounting numbers for earnings must be chosen carefully and adjusted for any exceptional items, atypical revenues, and costs in the reference year. Care must also be taken to decide which earnings figures to compare; the main choices are trailing earnings (the last 12 months), earnings from the last audited accounts, or prospective year-ahead earnings.

16. The exit strategies available to SING INVEST to divest their holding in China Auto Parts, Inc., will largely depend on the following two factors:

    - Time remaining until the fund's term expires: If the time remaining is sufficiently long, the fund's manager has more flexibility to work out an exit at more favorable market circumstances and terms.

    - Amount of undrawn commitments from LPs in the fund: If sufficient LP commitments can be drawn, the fund manager may take advantage of current investment opportunities at depressed market prices to enhance returns upon exit in a more favorable market environment.

    In the case of China Auto Parts, Inc., depending on an analysis of the factors discussed, Ng could offer an opinion to support the acquisition of China Gear Box, Inc., subject to an in-depth analysis of potential synergies with China Auto Parts, Inc. The objective here may thus be twofold: to benefit from short-term market conditions and to enhance the value of existing investments by reinforcing their market potential with a strategic merger.

17. Assuming that both funds have similar risk–return characteristics, a closer analysis of economic and corporate governance terms should be instrumental in

determining which fund to select.

In economic terms, Mid-Market Fund B has a higher carried interest than Mid-Market Fund A, but Mid-Market Fund B has a fee structure that is better aligned with the interests of LPs. A larger proportion of Mid-Market Fund B's fees (through the carried interest) will come from achieving successful exits, whereas Mid-Market Fund A will earn relatively larger fees on running the fund (management fees and transaction fees) without necessarily achieving high performance. In addition, the 9% hurdle rate of Mid-Market Fund B is indicative of confidence in the fund manager's ability to achieve a minimum compounded 9% return to LPs for which no carried interest will be paid.

In corporate governance terms, Mid-Market Fund B is far better aligned with the interests of LPs as a result of a clawback provision and a more favorable distribution waterfall that will allow payment of carried interest on a total return basis instead of deal by deal.

The conclusion is that Mid-Market Fund B appears better aligned with the interests of LPs.

18. In the early years of a fund, all measures of return are of little relevance because fees drag down the reported returns and investments are initially valued at cost. This produces the J-curve effect. After a few years (or longer in the case of venture capital investments), performance measures become more meaningful, and the two main measures used by investors are IRR and return multiples (of the initial sum invested). During the life of the fund, it is necessary to value the non-exited investments and add them to the realized returns. The former inevitably involves an element of judgment on the part of the General Partner, especially when it is difficult to estimate the likely market value of the investment. Once all the investments have been exited, the multiples and IRR can be estimated easily, taking account of the exact timing of the cash flows into and out of the fund. The most relevant measures for investors are computed net of management fees and any carried interest earned by the general partner.

# LEARNING MODULE 5

## Introduction to Commodities and Commodity Derivatives

by David Burkart, CFA, and James Alan Finnegan, CAIA, RMA, CFA.

*David Burkart, CFA, is at Coloma Capital Futures, LLC (USA). James Alan Finnegan, CAIA, RMA, CFA at American Century Investments (USA).*

| LEARNING OUTCOMES | |
|---|---|
| Mastery | The candidate should be able to: |
| ☐ | compare characteristics of commodity sectors |
| ☐ | compare the life cycle of commodity sectors from production through trading or consumption |
| ☐ | contrast the valuation of commodities with the valuation of equities and bonds |
| ☐ | describe types of participants in commodity futures markets |
| ☐ | analyze the relationship between spot prices and futures prices in markets in contango and markets in backwardation |
| ☐ | compare theories of commodity futures returns |
| ☐ | describe, calculate, and interpret the components of total return for a fully collateralized commodity futures contract |
| ☐ | contrast roll return in markets in contango and markets in backwardation |
| ☐ | describe how commodity swaps are used to obtain or modify exposure to commodities |
| ☐ | describe how the construction of commodity indexes affects index returns |

## 1. INTRODUCTION

In the upcoming sections, we present the characteristics and valuation of commodities and commodity derivatives. Given that investment in commodities is conducted primarily through futures markets, the concepts and theories behind commodity futures is a primary focus of the reading. In particular, the relationship between spot and futures prices, as well as the underlying components of futures returns, are key analytical considerations.

What do we mean when we talk about investing in commodities? A basic economic definition is that a commodity is a physical good attributable to a natural resource that is tradable and supplied without substantial differentiation by the general public.

Commodities trade in physical (spot) markets and in futures and forward markets. Spot markets involve the physical transfer of goods between buyers and sellers; prices in these markets reflect current (or very near term) supply and demand conditions. Global commodity futures markets constitute financial exchanges of standardized futures contracts in which a price is established in the market today for the sale of some defined quantity and quality of a commodity at a future date of delivery; completion of the contract may permit cash settlement or require physical delivery.

Commodity futures exchanges allow for risk transfer and provide a valuable price discovery mechanism that reflects the collective views of all market participants with regard to the future supply and demand prospects of a commodity. Given the financial (versus physical) nature of their contract execution, commodity exchanges allow important parties beyond traditional suppliers and buyers—speculators, arbitrageurs, private equity, endowments, and other institutional investors—to participate in these price discovery and risk transfer processes. Standardized contracts and organized exchanges also offer liquidity (i.e., trading volumes) to facilitate closing, reducing, expanding, or opening new hedges or exposures as circumstances change on a daily basis.

Forward markets exist alongside futures markets in certain commodities for use by entities that require customization in contract terms. Forwards are largely outside the scope of this reading and are discussed only briefly. Exposure to commodities is also traded in the swap markets for both speculative and hedging purposes. Investment managers may want to establish swap positions to match certain portfolio needs, whereas producers may want to more precisely adjust their commodity risk (e.g., the origin of their cattle or the chemical specifications of their crude oil).

Commodities offer the potential for diversification benefits in a multi-asset class portfolio because of historically low average return correlation with stocks and bonds. In addition, certain academic studies (e.g., Gorton and Rouwenhorst 2006; Erb and Harvey 2006) demonstrate that some commodities have historically had inflation hedging qualities.

Our coverage of the commodities topic is organized as follows: We provide an overview of physical commodity markets, including the major sectors, their life cycles, and their valuation. We then describe futures market participants, commodity futures pricing, and the analysis of commodity returns, including the concepts of contango and backwardation. The subsequent section reviews the use of swap instruments rather than futures to gain exposure to commodities. We then review the various commodity indexes given their importance as benchmarks for the asset class and investment vehicles. Finally, we conclude with a summary of the major points.

# 2 COMMODITY SECTORS

- [ ] compare characteristics of commodity sectors

**Commodity Sectors**

Commodities are an asset class inherently different from traditional financial assets, such as equities and bonds. These latter assets are securities that are claims on productive capital assets and/or financial assets and thus are expected to generate cash flows for their owners. The intrinsic value of these securities is the present discounted value of their expected future cash flows. Commodities are valued differently. Commodities' value derives from either their use as consumables or as inputs to the production of goods and services. Because a number of commodities need to be processed or have a limited life before spoiling or decaying, an astute analyst will take into account the growth and extraction patterns of the various commodities as well as the logistics associated with transporting these physical goods. Therefore, commodities, while seemingly familiar from everyday life, offer distinct sets of risk exposures for investors.

Fundamental analysis of commodities relies on analyzing supply and demand for each of the products as well as estimating the reaction to the inevitable shocks to their equilibrium or underlying direction. For example, a growing world population demands more crude oil or related products as transportation of goods and people increases. However, technological improvements (e.g., shale drilling or electric vehicles) can disrupt that trend and in the case of armed conflict or adverse weather, for example, may alter it on very short notice! This means that the quantitative analysis of commodities is often imperfect because of high degrees of non-normalcy and shifting correlations. Furthermore, the coefficients to underlying variables are often non-stationary; for example, much corn today is genetically modified to resist heat, rendering drought impact estimates derived from history less predictive. Much of the raw data are held off market by private firms engaged in the commodity industry (such as oil or agricultural companies), which also hinders a purely quantitative approach. Therefore, the framework offered here will be at a high level. We will later provide a breakdown of individual areas for the investor to apply discretionary or quantitative techniques, as circumstances allow. Because the framework can be applied to both supply and demand, we shall set that distinction aside until we focus on individual sectors and commodities. The tools and considerations in fundamental analysis are as follows:

a. Direct announcements: Various government agencies and private companies broadcast production and inventory data that can be used to infer demand, which is often unobservable. Possible public sources include the USDA (US Department of Agriculture), OPEC (Organization of the Petroleum Exporting Countries), the NBS (National Bureau of Statistics of China), and the IEA (International Energy Agency). Setting aside questions of reliability, sometimes estimating current conditions is as straightforward as monitoring official announcements, even with a lag.

b. Component analysis: The more diligent analyst will attempt to break down high-level supply and demand into various components. Applying a stock and flow approach is a logical method. The stock or potential production or demand attempts to set boundaries around what is actually produced or wanted. This can be as general as the amount of arable land in all of Europe or as specific as the current capacity of the Ghawar oil field in Saudi Arabia. The flow considers the utilization of that stock of raw material. Examples include understanding the oil tanker traffic heading to China, estimating the historical yields of US cotton (the amount of fiber per unit of land) in various weather conditions, and estimating the number of piglets per mother hog in Canada.

These examples lend themselves to historical quantitative or conditional analysis. However, care needs to be taken regarding the qualitative aspects of supply and demand; a new policy such as stricter emissions standards can affect both supply (higher standards often strand lower-quality materials) and demand (not all consumers may be properly equipped to utilize a changing standard). Political unrest may not touch an isolated farm but may disrupt consumption.

c. Timing considerations: Stocks and flows from (b) can be further affected by timing issues—such as seasonality and logistics—and, therefore, price reaction. A shock, by definition, is a sudden timing switch; an earthquake that destroys a pipeline does not affect the stock, but it does halt the flow. A more common consideration is seasonality, such as the growing period for crops and people's demand for winter heat generated from natural gas. This last aspect in particular feeds into the shape of the commodity futures curve, as discussed later.

d. Money flow: Short-term and long-term prices can be affected by sentiment and macro monetary conditions, such as inflation. If investor risk tolerance is particularly high or low, then expecting exaggerated price movements would be rational as fundamental conditions are hyped up or beaten down. Alternatively, capital availability from low interest rates can help trigger the building of new mines and affect future supply. Government subsidies of substitute technologies can limit commodity price appreciation (e.g., available funds for electric cars indirectly affect the price of gasoline).

In summary, although the casual investor can perhaps focus solely on public summary statements, the engaged researcher will apply a framework of examining the stock and flow components and their related timing to better understand and weigh the pressures leading to higher or lower prices.

## Commodity Sectors

The world of commodities is relatively broad but can be defined and separated in a reasonable manner. Although there are several ways to segment the asset class by sector, here we use the approach that is the basis for the Bloomberg Commodity Index: energy, grains, industrial (base) metals, livestock, precious metals, and softs (cash crops). This segmentation is more granular than some other indexes but is reasonably consistent with the breakdown in the specialties of most market participants. As noted previously, each sector has a number of individual characteristics that are important in determining the supply and demand for each commodity. A key concept is how easily and cost-effectively the commodity can be produced and stored, as well as such related issues as frequency/timing of consumption, spoilage, insurance, and ease of transportation to consumers. Note that many commodities, such as uranium or water, are traded only in thin, private markets. They are really just individual transactions, as opposed to the markets we are discussing. For the purposes of our coverage, we have to constrain ourselves to primary commodities, recognizing that there are many others that may offer investment opportunities or require hedging. Exhibit 1 reviews each sector and its main characteristics and influences.

### Exhibit 1: A Description of Commodity Sectors and Factors

**Energy:** Fuel transportation, industrial production, and electrical generation. Primary commodities include crude oil, natural gas, coal, and refined products, such as gasoline and heating oil.

| Primary Influences | Stocks: Discovery and depletion of new fields, economic and political costs/certainty of access to those fields, refinery technology and maintenance, power plant type and construction, economic (GDP) size | Flows: Pipeline and tanker reliability, seasonality (summer/winter), adverse weather (cold, hurricanes), automobile/truck sales, geopolitical instability, environmental requirements, economic (GDP) growth |
|---|---|---|
| | **Grains:** Provide human and animal sustenance but also can be distilled into fuel (e.g., ethanol). Primary commodities include corn, soy, wheat, and rice. | |
| Primary Influences | Stocks: Arable farmland, storage/port facilities (infrastructure), human and animal population size | Flows: Weather (moisture, temperature), disease, consumer preferences, genetic modification, biofuel substitution, population growth |
| | **Industrial/Base Metals:** Materials for durable consumer goods, industry, and construction. Primary commodities include copper, aluminum, nickel, zinc, lead, tin, and iron. | |
| Primary Influences | Stocks: Mined acreage, smelter capacity, economic (GDP) stage of industrial/consumer development | Flows: Government industrial and environmental policies, economic (GDP) growth, automobile/truck sales, infrastructure investment |
| | **Livestock:** Animals raised for human consumption. Primary commodities include hogs, cattle, sheep, and poultry. | |
| Primary Influences | Stocks: Herd size, processing plant capacity, consumer preferences, feed availability/cost | Flows: Speed of maturation to slaughter weight, economic (GDP) growth/consumer income, disease, adverse weather |
| | **Precious Metals:** Certain metals that act as monetary stores of value (as well as industrial uses). Primary commodities include gold, silver, and platinum. | |
| Primary Influences | Stocks: Mined acreage, smelter capacity, fiat money supply/banking development | Flows: Central bank monetary policy, geopolitics, economic (GDP) growth |
| | **Softs (Cash Crops):** Crops sold for income—as opposed to consumed for subsistence—and often originally seen as luxuries. Primary commodities include cotton, cocoa, sugar, and coffee. | |
| Primary Influences | Stocks: Arable farmland, storage/port facilities (infrastructure), economic (GDP) size | Flows: Weather (moisture, temperature), disease, consumer preferences, biofuel substitution, economic (GDP) growth/consumer income |

As noted in this section, each commodity sector is unique in its fundamental drivers but with the overlapping context of economic and monetary data. With this context in mind, we will now examine the life cycle of the sectors from production to consumption—and their interaction—in more detail.

### EXAMPLE 1

## Commodity Sector Demand

1. Industrial activity *most likely* affects the demand for which of the following commodities?

    **A.** Copper

    **B.** Natural gas

C. Softs (e.g., cotton, coffee, sugar and cocoa)

**Solution:**

A is correct. Copper is used for construction, infrastructure development, and the manufacture of durable goods, all of which are economically sensitive. B is incorrect because demand for natural gas is driven primarily by weather conditions (heating or cooling) and only secondarily by industrial activity. C is incorrect because demand for softs is driven primarily by global income.

**EXAMPLE 2**

## Commodity Sector Risks

1. Which of the following commodity sectors are *least* affected in the short term by weather-related risks?

    A. Energy
    B. Livestock
    C. Precious metals

**Solution:**

C is correct. Weather has very little impact on the availability of precious metals given their ease of storage. Inflation expectations, fund flows, and industrial production are more important factors. A is incorrect because energy demand is strongly influenced by weather (e.g., heating demand in the winter or transportation demand in the summer). B is incorrect because the health of livestock is vulnerable to unfavorable weather conditions increasing the risks of death and disease by extreme cold, wet, and heat.

# 3 LIFE CYCLE OF COMMODITIES

> compare the life cycle of commodity sectors from production through trading or consumption

The life cycle of commodities varies considerably depending on the economic, technical, and structural (i.e., industry, value chain) profile of each commodity, as well as the sector. Conceptually, the commodity production life cycle reflects and amplifies the changes in storage, weather, and political/economic events that shift supply and demand. Recall from the earlier discussion that timing/seasonality is, in effect, an overlay on top of the underlying supply/demand factors. A short life cycle allows for relatively rapid adjustment to outside events, whereas a long life cycle generally limits the ability of supply or demand to react to new conditions. These shifts, in turn, feed into the economics for the valuation and shape of the commodity supply and demand curves, plus their respective price elasticities of demand and supply. Understanding the life cycle builds understanding of, and ideally ability to forecast, what drives market actions and commodity returns.

Among the food commodities, agriculture and livestock have well-defined seasons and growth cycles that are specific to geographic regions. For example, by March of each year, corn planting may be finished in the southern United States but not yet started in Canada. Meanwhile, the corn harvest may be underway in Brazil and Argentina given their reverse seasonal cycle in the Southern Hemisphere. Each geographic location also represents local markets that have different domestic and export demand. These differences affect the nature (level and reliability) of demand and the power of buyers to extend or contract the life cycle.

In comparison, commodities in the energy and metals sectors are extracted all year round. Their life cycle changes are generally at the margin of a continuous process, as opposed to being centered at a discrete time or season. But the products from crude oil and metal ore have seasonal demands depending on weather (e.g., gasoline demand in the summer and heating oil demand in the winter) that affect the life cycle and usage of the underlying commodity. And with all the differences between the varieties even within the same sector, the life cycles depicted have to be representative and selective. The life cycles of several key commodity sectors are as follows.

## Energy

For an example of the differences within a sector, one need look no further than energy. Natural gas can be consumed almost immediately after extraction from the ground. Crude oil, in contrast, has to be transformed into something else; crude is useless in its innate form. The refined products (e.g., gasoline and heating oil), in turn, have a number of potential processing steps depending on the quality of crude oil input and the relative demand for the various products. The steps for the energy complex can be summarized as shown in Exhibit 2.

### Exhibit 2: Steps for the Energy Complex

| Step | Title | Description |
| --- | --- | --- |
| 1. | Extraction | A drilling location is selected after surveys, and the well is dug. Enough underground pressure for the hydrocarbons to come out naturally may exist, or water or other tools may be required to create such pressure. Water is also used for the fracturing process known as "fracking," which breaks up shale formations to allow for oil or gas to be extracted. |
| 2. | Storage | After extraction, crude oil is commercially stored for a few months on average in the United States, Singapore, and northern Europe and is strategically stored by many countries. In addition, oil may temporarily be stored on tanker ships. Natural gas may be delivered directly to the end consumer. Summer-extracted natural gas is often injected into storage for the winter months. |
| 3. | Consumption Stage | Only natural gas is consumed at this stage because it does not need to be refined. Crude oil requires further processing. |
| 4. | Refining | Crude oil is distilled into its component parts via a process called "cracking." Heat is used to successively boil off the components that are, in turn, cooled down and collected (e.g., gasoline, kerosene), until only the remnants (e.g., asphalt) are left. |
| 5. | Consumption Stage | The distilled products are separated and shipped to their various locations—by ship, pipe, train, or truck—for use by the end consumer. |

*Sources:* Based on information from www.eia.gov/energyexplained/index.php?page=oil_refining#tab1, https://en.wikipedia.org/wiki/Petroleum_refining_processes (accessed 23 April 2019), and authors' research.

Refineries are extraordinarily expensive to build—typically costing several billion US dollars—depending on the processes required to purify and distill the oil. Part of the cost depends on the expected specifications of the crude oil input. Generally speaking, a low-grade, high sulfur source would require more investment than one with an assured lighter, "sweeter" source. Pipelines are also very costly: For example, the Keystone XL pipeline expansion between Canada and the United States was originally estimated to cost $5 billion in 2010, but the estimate was doubled to $10 billion in 2014. Even in countries dealing with violent insurrections (e.g., Libya, Iraq, Nigeria), damage to refineries has been generally modest because of their value to all parties. Pipelines, however, are often destroyed or cut off. Although these costs may appear staggering, they actually pale in comparison with the costs (and risks) of oil exploration, especially in deep offshore locations or geographically remote (or geopolitically risky) regions.

The crude oil market has a number of futures contracts and indexes that follow local grades and origins, but the two most commonly traded set of contracts follow the US-based crude oil (West Texas Intermediate, or WTI, crude oil) and the UK-located Brent crude oil from the North Sea. Likewise, there are futures for natural gas, gasoil, gasoline, and heating oil. Each has different delivery locations and standards, but the WTI and Brent contracts represent a high-quality refinery input that exploration and production companies can use as a hedging device.

### EXAMPLE 3

### Energy Life Cycle

1. Which of the following is a primary difference in the production life cycle between crude oil and natural gas?

    A. Only crude oil needs to be stored.

    B. European companies are the only ones that store crude oil.

    C. Natural gas requires very little additional processing after extraction compared with crude oil.

### Solution:

C is correct. Natural gas can be used after it is extracted from the ground upon delivery, but crude oil must first be processed for later use. A is incorrect because both oil and natural gas are stored before usage. B is incorrect because many countries around the world store crude oil, both commercially and strategically.

## Industrial/Precious Metals

The life cycle of both precious and industrial metals is probably the most flexible because the ore, as well as the finished products, can be stored for months (if not years) given the relative resistance to spoilage of metals (assuming proper storage). Otherwise, the life cycle parallels the energy one outlined previously, as shown in Exhibit 3.

## Life Cycle of Commodities

**Exhibit 3: Copper Purification Process**

| | Step Name | Description |
|---|---|---|
| 1. | Extracting and Preparing | Ore (raw earth with ~2% metal content) is removed via a mine or open pit. Ore is then ground into powder and concentrated to roughly 25% purity. |
| 2. | Smelting | The purified ore is heated, and more impurities are removed as slag, increasing the metal content to 60%. Further processes increase the concentration to 99.99%. |
| 3. | Storage/Logistics | The purified metal is held typically in a bonded warehouse until it is shipped to an end user. |

*Sources:* Based on information from http://resources.schoolscience.co.uk/CDA/14-16/cumining/copch2pg1.html (accessed 23 April 2019), www.madehow.com/Volume-4/Copper.html (accessed 23 April 2019), and authors' research.

Similar to refining crude oil, creating the economies of scale involved in the smelter and ore processing plants is critical. These are huge facilities for which marginal costs (i.e., the cost to convert the last pound or kilogram of processed ore into a useful metal) decline substantially with both the scale of the facility and its utilization (output as a percentage of capacity). As a result, when supply exceeds demand for a given industrial metal, it is difficult for suppliers to either cut back production or halt it entirely. Overproduction often continues until smaller or financially weaker competitors are forced to shut down. Because demand for industrial metals fluctuates with overall economic growth, as was discussed previously, there are substantial incentives for metals producers to invest in new capacity when their utilization (and profit) is high but huge economic and financial penalties for operating these facilities when demand falls off during an economic downturn. Ironically, given the typical economic cycle and the time lag involved after deciding to expand capacity, new supply often arrives just as demand is declining—which exacerbates pricing and profit declines.

With the lack of annual seasonality in the production of metals and ease of storage without spoilage, much of time variability comes from the demand side of the equation (e.g., construction and economic growth).

### EXAMPLE 4

### Industrial Metals Life Cycle

1. Because of large economies of scale for processing industrial metals, producers:

    A. immediately shut down new capacity when supply exceeds demand.

    B. have an incentive to maintain maximum operating production levels when demand declines.

    C. find it difficult to cut back production or capacity even when supply exceeds demand or demand slows.

### Solution:

C is correct. Given the sizable facilities in which metals are produced and their capital requirements, reducing capacity is difficult when demand slows. A is incorrect because of the time lag involved in responding to reduced demand conditions. B is incorrect because producers would face financial losses if they maintained maximum production levels when there is a decline in demand.

## Livestock

Livestock grows year round, but good weather and access to high-quality pasture and feed accelerate weight gain. As a result, there is fluctuation in the availability of animals ready for slaughter. The timing to maturity typically increases with size, with poultry maturing in a matter of weeks, hogs in months, and cattle in a few years. Taking the example of a hog, the life cycle begins with a sow (female hog) giving birth. Normally it takes about six months to raise a piglet to slaughter weight, and during that time it can be fed almost anything to get it up to proper bulk. In mass-scale production, soymeal and cornmeal are the most common foods. In contrast, cattle take longer to raise. For mass-scale breeding, the first one to two years are spent as "feeder cattle," first eating a grass diet in pasture. The next phase covers an additional 6–12 months whereby cattle are in a feed lot being fattened to slaughter weight, generally on a corn-based diet. Note that the various types of feed for these animals are other traded commodities.

The livestock industry in the United States has historically been among the least export-oriented of all the commodities because of the high risk of spoilage once an animal is slaughtered. However, advances in cryogenics (freezing) technologies with regard to chicken, beef, and pork mean that increasingly these products are moving from one part of the world to another in response to differences in production costs and demand. And as emerging and frontier market countries develop middle class consumers capable of purchasing meat protein as a regular part of their diet, there has been increased investment in the livestock and meatpacking industries in such countries as the United States and Brazil. These industries combine low-cost sources of animal feed, large grazing acreage, and strong domestic demand (leading to facilities with substantial economies of scale) as key export points to supply global demand.

Ranchers and slaughterhouses trade hog and cattle futures to hedge against their commitments. Ranchers can hedge both young cattle that are still in pasture (called feeder cattle) and animals being fattened for butchering (called live cattle).

### EXAMPLE 5

### Livestock Life Cycle

1. The US livestock sector has been among the least export-oriented commodity sectors because of:

    **A.** low technological innovation in the sector.

    **B.** high risk of spoilage once animals are slaughtered.

    **C.** little or no demand for US livestock from outside the United States.

### Solution:

B is correct. Livestock incur a high risk of spoilage once they are slaughtered unless the meat is frozen. A is incorrect because advances in cryogenics have improved the ability to export from the United States. C is incorrect because demand for US livestock has expanded internationally, particularly in emerging market countries that are experiencing economic growth.

## Grains

Grains in the Northern Hemisphere follow a similar growth cycle, with an analogous but opposite growth cycle in the Southern Hemisphere. Plants mature according to the following steps: (1) planting (placing the seeds in the ground after preparation/

fertilization work); (2) growth (the emerging of the seedling to full height); (3) pod/ear/head formation (the food grain is created by the plant); and (4) harvest (the collection of the grain by the farmer). The timing in North America is shown in Exhibit 4 to illustrate the time it takes to grow each crop.

**Exhibit 4: Timing for Grain Production in North America**

|  | Corn | Soybeans | Wheat* |
| --- | --- | --- | --- |
| Planting | April–May | May–June | Sep.–Oct. |
| Growth | June–Aug. | July–Aug. | Nov.–March |
| Pod/Ear/Head Formation | Aug.–Sep. | Sep. | April–May |
| Harvest | Sep.–Nov. | Sep.–Oct. | June–July |

*The hard winter wheat variety, which has a higher protein content, is used here.*
*Source:* Authors' research.

Because demand for grains is year round, they are regularly stored in silos and warehouses globally. Some countries have a central purchasing bureau, and others depend on local or international trading companies to maintain stockpiles. Poor hygienic standards and logistics can result in a substantial loss of value to grains due to mold or insect/animal infestation. Monitoring the purchasing patterns of these government tenders can assist a research analyst in determining grain demand.

Farmers and consumers can trade futures to hedge their exposure to the crop in question, and the contract delivery months reflect the different times of the growing cycle outlined earlier. Ranchers also can use grain futures to hedge against the cost of feeding an animal.

## Softs

Coffee, cocoa, cotton, and sugar are very different soft commodities in this sector, so we will focus on one that is grown and enjoyed broadly—coffee. Coffee is harvested somewhere all year round in the various countries that circle the Equator. After the coffee cherries are picked (still often by hand, to ensure that only ripe ones are taken), the husk and fruit are removed and the remaining bean dried. More than half of coffee uses the dry method in which the harvested cherries are laid out in the sun for two to three weeks. The wet method uses fresh water to soak the cherries, the soft pulp is removed, the bean is fermented for 12–48 hours, and then the bean is dried. The "green" beans are then hulled, sorted, and bagged for their final markets. With most of the consumption in faraway foreign markets, ships are commonly used to transport the beans to their buyer, which may store them in a bonded warehouse. The local buyer roasts the beans and ships them to the retail location (e.g., coffee house or supermarket) for purchase or brewing.

Coffee comes in two main varieties, robusta and arabica, although there are many others. Generally speaking, robusta beans are lower quality with less flavor than the arabica. There are two futures contracts associated with coffee: The robusta variety is traded in London, and the arabica variety is traded in New York. Note that the contracts are for the unroasted or "green" beans. The physical delivery aspect of these contracts allows for sellers to deliver the beans to an authorized bonded warehouse as fulfillment of the contract at expiration. Therefore, farmers and distributors can sell futures contracts to hedge the sales price of production, and coffee roasters can buy futures contracts to hedge coffee bean purchase costs; contract maturities can be selected by each to match their product delivery schedules.

## 4. VALUATION OF COMMODITIES

☐ contrast the valuation of commodities with the valuation of equities and bonds

The valuation of commodities compared with that of equities and bonds can be summarized by the fact that stocks and bonds represent financial assets and are claims on the economic output of a business, a government, or an individual. Commodities, however, are almost always physical assets. We say "almost always" because some newer classes of commodities, such as electricity or weather, are not physical assets in the sense that you can touch or store them.

Commodities are typically tangible items with an intrinsic (but variable) economic value (e.g., a nugget of gold, a pile of coal, a bushel of corn). They do not generate future cash flows beyond what can be realized through their purchase and sale. In addition, the standard financial instruments that are based on commodities are not financial assets (like a stock or bond) but are derivative contracts with finite lifetimes, such as futures contracts. As with other types of derivatives, commodity derivative contracts can and do have value, but they are contingent on some other factors, such as the price of the underlying commodity. Hence, the valuation of commodities is based not on the estimation of future profitability and cash flows but on a discounted forecast of future possible prices based on such factors as the supply and demand of the physical item or the expected volatility of future prices. On the one hand, this forecast may be quite formal and elaborately estimated by a producer or consumer. One can imagine the detailed inputs available to an oil company based on the labor and capital expenses needed to extract oil, refine it, and transport it to final sale as gasoline in your automobile. On the other hand, this forecast may be instinctively made by a floor trader with little fundamental analysis but instead with professional judgment based on years of experience and perhaps some technical analysis.

As opposed to a stock or bond that receives periodic income, owning a commodity incurs transportation and storage costs. These ongoing expenditures affect the shape of the forward price curve of the commodity derivative contracts with different expiration dates. If storage and transportation costs are substantial, the prices for a commodity futures contract will likely be incrementally higher as one looks farther into the future. However, sometimes the current demand for the commodity can move the spot price higher than the futures price. The spot price reflects the fact that, instead of going long a futures contract, one could buy the commodity today and store it until a future date for use. The expenditure would be the outlay/investment at today's spot price for the commodity along with (or net of) the future costs one would incur to store and hold it. This time element of commodity storage and supply and demand can generate "roll return" and affect investment returns. These and other factors figure into the assessment of futures pricing, which we will cover later.

Some commodity contracts require actual delivery of the physical commodity at the end of the contract versus settlement in a cash payment (based on the difference between the contract futures price and the spot price prevailing at the time of contract expiration). The force of arbitrage—which reflects the law of one price—may not be entirely enforced by arbitrageurs because some participants do not have the ability to make or take delivery of the physical commodity. In these situations, the relationships that link spot and futures prices are not an equality but are a range that only indicates the limit or boundary of value differences that can occur.

There is an important additional consideration concerning the link between spot and futures prices in commodities. Some of the largest users of commodity futures are businesses seeking to hedge price risk when that price is a critical source of either revenue or cost in their business operations. For example, the airline industry is very dependent on the cost of jet fuel for operating planes. The highly competitive nature of the industry results in tremendous price pressure on airfares, with a need for airlines to fill each flight with as many passengers as possible. The futures and swap markets for jet fuel allow airlines to lower the risk of higher fuel costs by hedging the price of future fuel purchases (particularly against surprise shocks in oil prices).

In addition, the price discovery process of the commodity futures markets provides airlines with insights about future fuel prices that help determine what prices to offer their customers for future flights while still making a profit. In fact, airline ticket sales are—in effect—selling a contract at a price set today for future delivery of a service—namely, a plane flight. In this case, the airlines will typically hedge their price risk and uncertainty about future fuel costs by purchasing ("going long") energy futures contracts.

### EXAMPLE 6

### Commodities versus Stocks and Bonds

1. In contrast to financial assets, such as stocks and bonds:

    **A.** commodities are always physical goods.

    **B.** commodities generate periodic cash flows.

    **C.** commodity investment is primarily via derivatives.

### Solution:

C is correct. The most common way to invest in commodities is via derivatives. A is incorrect because although most commodities are physical goods, certain newer classes, such as electricity or weather, are not tangible. B is incorrect because commodities may incur, rather than generate, periodic cash flow through transportation and storage costs (when the commodities are physically owned).

### EXAMPLE 7

### Spot Commodity Valuation

1. What is a key distinction between the valuation of commodities compared with the valuation of stocks and bonds?

    **A.** Valuation of commodities cannot be conducted using technical analysis.

    **B.** Valuation of commodities focuses on supply and demand, whereas valuation of stocks and bonds focuses on discounted cash flows.

    **C.** Valuation of stocks and bonds focuses on future supply and demand, whereas commodity valuation focuses on future profit margins and cash flow.

### Solution:

B is correct. The valuation of commodities is based on a forecast of future prices based on supply and demand factors, as well as expected price volatility. In contrast, the valuation of stocks and bonds is based on estimating future profitability and/or cash flow. A is incorrect because technical analysis is sometimes applied to valuing commodities. C is incorrect for the reasons stated for choice B.

## 5. COMMODITIES FUTURES MARKETS: PARTICIPANTS

☐ describe types of participants in commodity futures markets

Public commodity markets are structured as futures markets—that is, as a central exchange where participants trade standardized contracts to make and take delivery at a specified place at a specified future time. As mentioned, futures contracts are derivatives because the value of the contract is derived from another asset. Both futures and forward contracts are binding agreements that establish a price today for delivery of a commodity in the future (or settlement of the contract in cash at expiration). As mentioned at the beginning of the reading, the focus of this reading is on futures, with forwards discussed only briefly.

### Futures Market Participants

The key differences between futures and forward contracts is that futures contracts are standardized agreements traded on public exchanges, such as the Chicago Mercantile Exchange (CME), Intercontinental Exchange (ICE), and the Shanghai Futures Exchange (SHFE), and gains/losses are marked to market every day. Standardization allows a participant to enter into a contract without ever knowing who the counterparty is. In addition, the exchange oversees trading and margin requirements and provides some degree of self-imposed regulatory oversight. In contrast, forward contracts are commonly bilateral agreements between a known party that wants to go long and one that wants to go short. Because of their bilateral nature, forwards are considered to be OTC (over the counter) contracts with less regulatory oversight and much more customization to the specific needs of the hedging (or speculating) party. Often, the counterparty for a forward contract is a financial institution that is providing liquidity or customization in exchange for a fee. Although futures markets require that daily cash movements in the futures price be paid from the losing positions to the winning positions, forward contracts are usually only settled upon expiration or with some custom frequency dictated by the contract.

Early commodity exchanges operated as forward markets, but too often participants would go bankrupt when unrealized losses became realized at the end of the contract. The futures process was introduced to minimize this risk, with the exchange acting as payment guarantor. The first modern organized futures exchange was the Dojima Rice Exchange in Osaka, Japan, which was founded in 1710, although futures contracts were traded in England during the 16th century. The structure of futures markets is important to understand as a way of understanding the goals and roles of the various participants. When we consider any commodity, for every producer of that commodity there is a consumer. Thus, for participants who are long the physical commodity and want to sell it, there are also participants who are short the physical commodity and want to buy it. Therefore, for fairness between the two sets of participants, longs and shorts need to operate on an equal basis. As a coincident observation, the commodity markets are net zero in terms of aggregate futures positions (futures contract longs equal futures contract shorts). In contrast, in markets for stocks and bonds, there is a net long position because the issued stocks' and bonds' market values are equal to the net aggregate positions at the end of each day. Shorting an equity is constrained by the short seller's need to locate shares to short, the requirement to reimburse dividends on borrowed shares, and requirements to post and pay interest on margin that generally exceeds the margin required for long equity positions (as in the United States under Regulation T). In contrast, shorting commodity futures is much simpler, with short investors selling to long investors directly, and thus short investors post the same margin required of long investors.

There are a number of participants in commodity futures markets. First are *hedgers*, who trade in the markets to hedge their exposures related to the commodity. The second are long-term and short-term *traders* and *investors* (including index investors), who speculate on market direction or volatility and provide liquidity and price discovery for the markets in exchange for the expectation of making a profit. Third are the *exchanges* (or clearing houses), which set trading rules and provide the infrastructure of transmitting prices and payments. Fourth are *analysts*, who use the exchange information for non-trading purposes, such as evaluating commodity businesses, creating products that are based on commodity futures (e.g., exchange-traded funds, swaps, and notes), and making public policy decisions. Analysts also include brokers and other financial intermediaries who participate in the markets but do not take a position. Finally, *regulators* of both the exchange and traders exist to monitor and police the markets, investigate malfeasance, and provide a venue for complaints.

### Commodity Hedgers

Hedgers tend to be knowledgeable market participants: One would expect that a company that drills for oil knows something about the supply and demand for oil and related forms of energy (at least in the long run). However, hedgers may not be accurate predictors of the future supply and demand for their product. Consider a baker who buys wheat for future delivery and benefits from a surprise drought (has locked in a low price in a supply-constrained market). However, the baker is hurt if the weather is beneficial (has effectively overpaid during a bumper crop). Given that a hedger can make delivery (if short the futures contract) or take delivery (if long the futures contract), he or she is generally motivated by risk mitigation with regard to cash flow, so the risk is more of an opportunity cost than an actual one.

It is important to keep in mind that hedging and speculating are not synonymous with being (respectively) long or short. As Exhibit 5 illustrates with some examples, both long and short positions can be associated with either hedging or speculating.

**Exhibit 5: Examples of Hedging and Speculating Positions**

|  | Long Position | Short Position |
| --- | --- | --- |
| Hedging | Food manufacturer seeking to hedge the price of corn needed for snack chips | Gold mining company seeking to hedge the future price of gold against potential declines |
| Speculating | Integrated oil company seeking to capitalize on its knowledge of physical oil markets by making bets on future price movements | Commodity trading adviser (CTA) seeking to earn a profit for clients via a macro-commodity investment fund |

Note also that hedgers tend to speculate based on their perceived unique insight into market conditions and determine the amount of hedging that is appropriate. From a regulatory standpoint in the United States, the difficulty in clearly distinguishing between hedging and speculating, therefore, has resulted in the separation of commodity producers and consumers from other trading participants regardless of whether commercial participants are actually speculating.

### Commodity Traders and Investors

The commodity trading community, like other groups of traders, consists of three primary types: (1) informed investors, (2) liquidity providers, and (3) arbitrageurs. Informed investors largely represent the aforementioned hedgers and speculators, including index and institutional investors. With regard to the hedger, as mentioned previously, a company that drills for oil clearly is familiar with the supply and demand for oil and related forms of energy (at least in the long run). But hedgers may not be accurate predictors of the *future* supply and demand for their product.

Speculators, who believe that they have an information advantage, seek to outperform the hedger by buying or selling futures contracts in conjunction with—or opposite from—the hedger. This trading may be on a micro-second time scale or a multi-month perspective. For example, if a speculator has a superior weather prediction process, he or she has an information advantage and will trade accordingly. Alternatively, a speculator may be willing to act as a liquidity provider, knowing that producers and consumers may not be in the market at the same time. By buying when the producer wants to sell and selling when the consumer is ready to buy, speculators may be able to make a profit. In this sense, speculators are willing to step in, under the right pricing circumstances, to provide insurance to hedgers in return for an expected (albeit not guaranteed) profit.

Finally, arbitrageurs who have the ability to inventory physical commodities can attempt to capitalize on mispricing between the commodity (along with related storage and financing cost) and the futures price. They may own the storage facilities (bonded warehouses, grain silos, feedlots) and work to manage that inventory in conjunction with the futures prices to attempt to make arbitrage-style profits.

### Commodity Exchanges

Commodity futures markets are found throughout the world. The CME and ICE are the primary US markets, having consolidated the bulk of the various specialist exchanges. Elsewhere in the Americas, the primary commodity exchange is in Brazil, where B3 trades softs, grains, and livestock. In Europe, the London Metal Exchange (owned by Hong Kong Exchanges and Clearing Limited (HKEX) is the main industrial metals location globally. Energy and shipping are also traded out of London. In Asia, major commodity exchanges include China's Dalian Commodity Exchange and Shanghai Futures Exchange and Japan's Tokyo Commodity Exchange, among others. Finally, Indonesia (palm oil), Singapore (rubber), and Australia (energy, grains, wool) have supplementary commodity futures markets. Given that people all over the world need food, energy, and materials, exchanges have formed globally to meet those needs.

### Commodity Market Analysts

Non-market participants use the exchange information to perform research and conduct policy as well as to facilitate market participation. Their activities affect market behavior, albeit in an indirect manner. Research may be commercially based. For example, a manufacturer may want to project and forecast the energy cost of a new process or product as part of an academic study comparing one market structure with another. Commodity prices are a key component in understanding sources of inflation and are used in other indexes that indicate quality of life for consumers and households. Governments that control natural resource extraction (e.g., nationalized oil companies) or tax commodity extraction by private entities are also interested in understanding futures markets to promote or discourage investment and/or raise revenue.

### Commodity Regulators

Finally, various regulatory bodies monitor the global commodity markets. In the United States, commodity and futures regulation falls under the Commodity Futures Trading Commission (CFTC), which is a regulatory body separate from the better-known Securities and Exchange Commission. The CFTC delegates much of the direct monitoring to the National Futures Association (NFA)—a self-regulatory body—whose members are the authorized direct participants in the markets with customer responsibilities (e.g., clearing firms, brokers, advisers).

Outside the United States, most other countries have a unified regulatory structure. For example, the China Securities Regulatory Commission regulates both futures and securities (i.e., stocks and bonds). In Europe, most legislation in the area of financial services is initiated at the European Union (EU) level primarily through the European Securities and Markets Authority (ESMA). The Markets in Financial Instruments Directive (MiFID, and subsequently MiFID II), which first came into force in 2007, was a key element of EU financial market integration that focused largely on deregulation (MiFID II took effect in January 2018). Since 2009, existing legislative instruments, particularly for commodity derivative markets, have been revised and new regulations have been introduced with the aim to strengthen oversight and regulation, and they are subject to G–20 commitments. Harmonizing these different regulatory bodies is the International Organization of Securities Commissions (IOSCO), which is the international association of the world's securities and futures markets.

In all regions, the interests of the financial sector strongly influence debates and legislation on financial market regulation, including that of commodities.

### EXAMPLE 8

#### Commodity Market Participants

1. Commodity traders that often provide insurance to hedgers are *best* described as:

    A. arbitrageurs.
    B. liquidity providers.
    C. informed investors.

### Solution:

B is correct. Liquidity providers often play the role of providing an insurance service to hedgers who need to unload and transfer price risk by entering into futures contracts. A is incorrect because arbitrageurs typically seek to capitalize and profit on mispricing due to a lack of information in the marketplace. C is incorrect because informed investors predominantly keep commodity futures markets efficient by capitalizing on mispricing attributable to a lack of information in the marketplace.

## 6. COMMODITY SPOT AND FUTURES PRICING

☐ analyze the relationship between spot prices and futures prices in markets in contango and markets in backwardation

Commodity prices are typically represented by (1) spot prices in the physical markets and (2) futures prices for later delivery. The **spot price** is simply the current price to deliver a physical commodity to a specific location or purchase it and transport it away from a designated location. Examples of a spot price may be the price quoted at a grain silo, a natural gas pipeline, an oil storage tank, or a sugar refinery.

A **futures price** is a price agreed on to deliver or receive a defined quantity (and often quality) of a commodity at a future date. Although a producer and a consumer can enter into a bilateral contract to exchange a commodity for money in the future, there are (conveniently) many standardized contracts that trade on exchanges for buyers and sellers to use. Recall that a bilateral agreement is a forward contract, compared with a futures contract that is standardized and trades on a futures exchange. One benefit of futures markets is that information regarding contracts (number, price, etc.) is publicly available. In this way, the price discovery process that brings buyers and sellers into agreement is shared broadly and efficiently (in real time) with a global marketplace among the aforementioned market participants. The longest-maturity futures contract outstanding can have maturity extending from about a year (e.g., livestock) to several years (e.g., crude oil).

The difference between spot and futures prices is generally called the **basis**. Depending on the specified commodity and its current circumstances (e.g., supply and demand outlook), the spot price may be higher or lower than the futures price. When the spot price exceeds the futures price, the situation is called **backwardation**, and the opposite case is called **contango**. The origin of the word "contango" is a bit murky, but one theory is that it came from the word "continuation" used in the context of the London Stock Exchange in the mid-1800s. During this period, contango was a fee paid by the buyer to the seller to defer settlement of a trade (hence the near-term price would be less expensive than the longer-term price). The term "backwardation" describes the same arrangement if it were "backward," or reversed (i.e., payment to defer settlement was made by the seller to the buyer).

Backwardation and contango are also used to describe the relationship between two futures contracts of the same commodity. When the near-term (i.e., closer to expiration) futures contract price is higher than the longer-term futures contract price, the futures market for the commodity is in backwardation. In contrast, when the near-term futures contract price is lower than the longer-term futures contract price, the futures market for the commodity is in contango. The price difference (whether in backwardation or contango) is called the calendar spread. Generally speaking and assuming stable spot prices, the producer is willing to take a price in the future that is lower than the current spot price because it provides a level of certainty for the producer's business. The seller of that insurance on the other side of the trade profits because the lower futures price converges to the higher spot price over time. This relationship occurs when future commodity prices are expected to be higher because of a variety of reasons related to economic growth, weather, geopolitical risks, supply disruptions, and so on. As a long owner of a futures contract in contango, value will erode over time as the contract pricing moves closer to the spot price, assuming all else is unchanged. This relationship can be very costly for long holders of contracts if they roll futures positions over time. Although backwardation is "normal" for some contracts, there are other commodities that often trade in contango.

Exhibit 6 is a stylized representation of backwardation in West Texas Intermediate crude oil on CME Group's New York Mercantile Exchange (NYMEX).

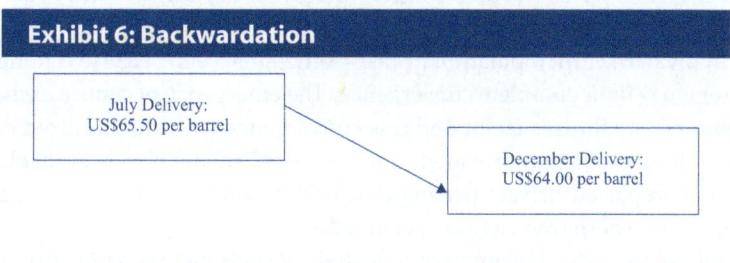

For contracts in a single (common) commodity, such as lean hogs or crude oil, the price differences may be traded as a spread rather than individually.

Exhibit 7 is a stylized representation of contango in lean hogs on the CME.

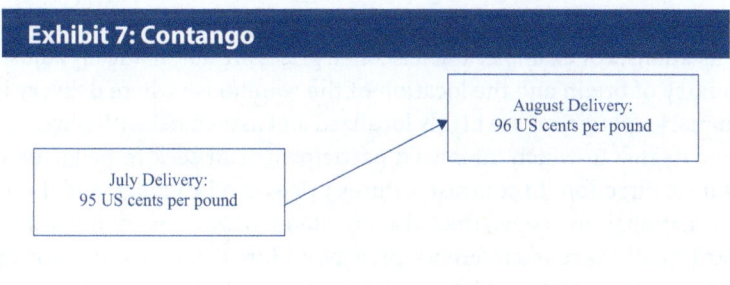

From these examples, the lean hogs July–August calendar spread is –1.0 cent per pound (95 – 96) and the crude oil July–December calendar spread is $1.50 per barrel (65.50 – 64.00).

A positive calendar spread is associated with futures markets that are in backwardation, whereas a negative calendar spread in commodities is associated with futures markets that are in contango. These calendar spreads are traded with their own bid–ask prices, trading range, and order book, similar to the single-month (i.e., nearest to expiration) futures contracts. Note that from this one trade, two contracts (one for each side, or "leg", of the spread) appear on an exchange's trading account and use their respective closing prices to determine profit or loss. Therefore, in the end, all trades and positions are valued at the close-of-day prices.

Commodity futures are settled by either cash or physical delivery. Cash-settled contracts, such as feeder cattle traded on the CME, have no value after the maturity date. Cash settlement is an important innovation in the evolution and development of commodity futures markets. To a certain extent, cash settlement enabled more involvement of two key participants in today's futures markets: speculators and arbitrageurs. It also introduced an entirely new way that hedgers (long or short) could participate in the market to transfer the future price risk of having to sell or buy a commodity without the complications associated with requiring physical delivery. Physical-settled commodity futures contracts require that the title of the actual commodity be transferred by the seller of the futures contract to the buyer at a particular place, on or by a particular date, and of a particular quality specification. For example, under a futures contract with West Texas Intermediate crude oil as the underlying physical commodity, crude oil meeting minimum specifications must be delivered to a particular set of tanks at Cushing, Oklahoma, in the United States. Meanwhile, a similar futures contract with Brent crude oil as the underlying physical commodity has delivery points in the North Sea off the coast of the United Kingdom and Norway. Supply and demand differences at these two faraway geographic locations can cause price divergences despite otherwise similar specifications.

Physical delivery also ensures a convergence of the futures and spot markets, which may not necessarily occur in a cash-settled market. Note that this statement does not imply market manipulation in cash-settled markets, because trading costs or other factors may limit complete convergence. The emergence of central exchanges for trading commodity futures facilitated this convergence with standardized contracts. In addition, these exchanges provided centrally established, publicly available pricing, which quickly replaced private pricing that was dependent on both contract terms and the location where transactions occurred.

Physical delivery can become complicated by such factors as quality or variety differences in the commodity. For example, robusta coffee (traded in the United Kingdom) cannot be delivered for arabica coffee (traded in the United States) because it is a different variety of coffee with a different venue for delivery. Likewise, raw (or unprocessed) sugar that is traded in the United States cannot be delivered for white processed sugar that is traded in the United Kingdom. Futures markets can address some of these peculiarities involving quality or differences in supply. When physical delivery is required, some futures contracts require a premium or discount associated with specifications. For example, arabica coffee prices are automatically adjusted based on the country of origin and the location of the warehouse where delivery is made.

In summary, spot prices are highly localized and associated with physical delivery, limiting the degree to which interested participants can seek to hedge or speculate on their future direction. In contrast, futures prices can be global (and if not, at least regional or national) in scope. They also are standardized for trading on exchanges to promote liquidity; act as a reference price point for customized (i.e., forward) contracts; and generate widely available, minimally biased data for market participants and governments to judge supply and demand and to make planning decisions.

In this manner, futures can be used to allocate risk and generate returns for market participants. On the surface, futures trading may seem muddled and chaotic on a micro level but serves as an overall social benefit by sending signals to producers and consumers for hedging and inventory-sizing purposes and to governments for the potential impact of policy decisions.

> ### EXAMPLE 9
>
> ### Spot and Futures Pricing (1)
>
> 1. The current price of the futures contract nearest to expiration for West Texas Intermediate (WTI) crude oil is $65.00 per barrel, whereas the six-month futures contract for WTI is priced at $60.75 per barrel. Based on this information:
>
>     **A.** the futures market for WTI crude oil is currently in a state of contango.
>
>     **B.** the futures market for WTI crude oil is currently in a state of backwardation.
>
>     **C.** the shipping and delivery cost of WTI crude oil for a futures contract expiring in six months with physical delivery to Cushing, Texas, is $4.25 per barrel.

## Solution:

B is correct. Commodity futures markets are in a state of backwardation when the spot price is greater than the price of near-term (i.e., nearest to expiration) futures contracts, and correspondingly, the price of near-term futures contracts is greater than longer-term contracts. A is incorrect because the market would be in contango only if the deferred futures price exceeded that of the nearby futures price. C is incorrect because the shipping and delivery costs associated with physical delivery of a commodity are only one component in determining a commodity futures contract price. Geopolitical, seasonal, and other factors also influence the difference in delivery months.

### EXAMPLE 10

## Spot and Futures Pricing (2)

1. An important distinction between spot and futures prices for commodities is that:

    A. spot prices are universal across regions, but futures prices vary by location.
    B. futures prices do not reflect differences in quality or composition for a commodity.
    C. spot prices vary across region based on quality/composition and local supply and demand factors.

## Solution:

C is correct. Spot prices of commodities vary across regions, reflecting logistical constraints and supply and demand imbalances that hinder the movement of materials. A is incorrect because spot prices tend to vary by region while futures are purposely standardized to facilitate trading. B is incorrect because while futures contracts are based on standardized specifications, composition and quality can be assigned premiums or discounts for delivery.

### EXAMPLE 11

## Spot and Futures Pricing (3)

1. An arbitrageur has two active positions in the commodity futures markets—one for lean hogs and the other for natural gas. The calendar spread on the lean hogs contract is quoted at −50 cents per pound, and the calendar spread on the natural gas contract is +$1.10 per million BTU (British thermal units). Based on this information, we can say that:

    A. only the spreads of these commodities, and not the individual prices, can be traded in commodity markets.
    B. the lean hogs futures market is in a state of backwardation and the natural gas futures market is in a state of contango.
    C. the lean hogs futures market is in a state of contango and the natural gas futures market is in a state of backwardation.

**Solution:**

C is correct. The spread is the difference between the current spot price for a commodity and the futures contract price. Because futures markets in a state of contango will have futures prices that exceed the spot price, the spread for these markets is negative. Conversely, in a state of backwardation, the spread is positive. A is incorrect because either the individual contract prices or the combined spreads can be traded. B is incorrect because, as mentioned earlier, the negative sign of the spread of lean hogs futures indicates a state of contango, whereas the positive sign of the spread of natural gas futures indicates a state of backwardation.

### EXAMPLE 12

### Spot and Futures Pricing (4)

1. A futures price curve for commodities in backwardation:
   - **A.** always remains in backwardation in the long term.
   - **B.** can fluctuate between contango and backwardation in the long term.
   - **C.** reflects structural long-term industry factors, as opposed to dynamic market supply and demand pressures.

**Solution:**

B is correct. During periods of market stress or fundamental structural change in market conditions, some commodity futures price curves can rapidly shift from contango to backwardation or vice versa. A is incorrect because futures price curves can vacillate between contango and backwardation. C is incorrect because the shape of a commodity futures price curve reflects both long-term industry factors as well as market expectations of future supply and demand of the underlying commodity(ies).

## 7 THEORIES OF FUTURES RETURNS

☐ compare theories of commodity futures returns

Commodity futures markets have a reputation for volatility, but similar to other asset classes, there are theoretical bases for their long-run behavior. The original purpose of futures markets is for producers and consumers to hedge physical raw materials. In this section, we will discuss the underpinning theories of commodity futures returns, deconstruct the components of futures returns (i.e., at an index level), and close with thoughts on term structure (i.e., contango versus backwardation and implications of rolling futures contracts).

## Theories of Futures Returns

Several theories have been proposed to explain the shape of the futures price curve, which has a dramatic impact on commodity futures returns. This reading covers three of the most important theories: (1) insurance theory, (2) hedging pressure hypothesis, and (3) theory of storage.

### Insurance Theory

Keynes (1930), the noted economist and market speculator, proposed one of the earliest known theories on the shape of a commodity futures price curve. Also known as his theory of "normal backwardation," Keynes, in his 1930 tome *A Treatise on Money*, proposed that producers use commodity futures markets for insurance by locking in prices and thus make their revenues more predictable. A commodity producer is long the physical good and thus would be motivated to sell the commodity for future delivery to hedge its sales price. Imagine a farmer who thinks that next year she will grow a certain amount of soybeans on her land. She can sell a portion of her crop today that will be harvested months later to lock in those prices. She can then spend money on fertilizer and seed with more confidence about her budget. She may not be locking in a profit, but she would better understand her financial condition. Keynes's theory assumes that the futures curve is in backwardation "normally" because our farmer would persistently sell forward, pushing down prices in the future. Alternatively, this theory posits that the futures price has to be lower than the current spot price as a form of payment or remuneration to the speculator who takes on the price risk and provides price insurance to the commodity seller. The concept of normal backwardation is illustrated in Exhibit 8, using cotton prices pre- and post-harvest.

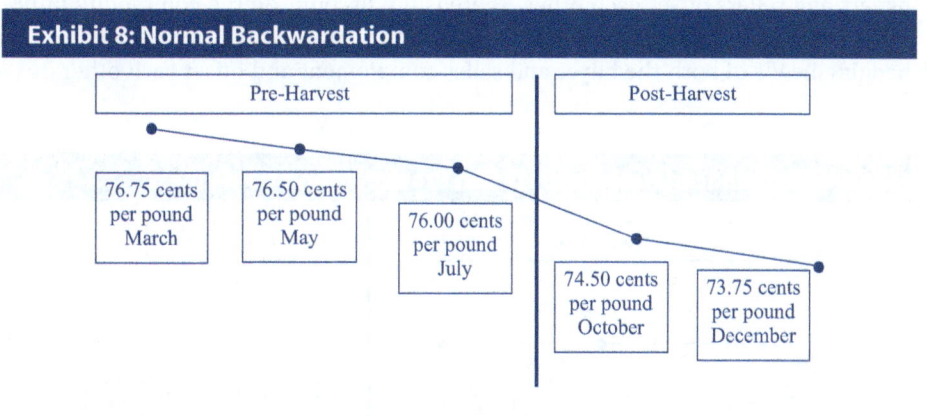

**Exhibit 8: Normal Backwardation**

In terms of returns, if the front price is stable (in our example, 76.75 cents), then an investor can buy a further-dated contract (e.g., October) at 74.50 cents and wait for that contract to become the current contract. As the month of October approaches (and assuming no change in front prices), the October contract will reach 76.75 cents at maturity, and the speculator will make a profit of 2.25 cents per pound (note that a contract is 50,000 pounds, so that is a total profit of $1,125 per contract). Even if the contract does not fully converge, this theory holds that there should be positive excess returns (sometimes referred to as the risk premium) via this process to induce buying. As noted earlier, this process acts as a type of insurance for the farmer as well as a return for the investor providing such insurance.

Looking at the evidence, however, markets failed to match Keynes's hypothesis. Kolb (1992) looked at 29 futures contracts and concluded (with some humor) that "normal backwardation is not normal." That is, the presence of backwardation does not necessarily generate positive returns in a statistically significant fashion for the investor (or that contango leads to negative returns, for that matter). This result confirmed other studies, including one by Fama and French (1987). Therefore, a more sophisticated view developed to explain futures markets in contango (i.e., when the shape of the futures price curve is upward sloping with more distant contract dates), recognizing that certain commodity futures markets often show persistently higher prices in the future as opposed to the backwardation outlined by Keynes. This view is called the hedging pressure hypothesis.

### Hedging Pressure Hypothesis

This perspective stemmed from multiple works, most notably outlined by De Roon, Nijman, and Veld (2000), who drew from Cootner (1960). Their research analyzed 20 futures markets from 1986 to 1994 and concluded that hedging pressure plays an important role in explaining futures returns. Hedging pressure occurs when both producers and consumers seek to protect themselves from commodity market price volatility by entering into price hedges to stabilize their projected profits and cash flow. Producers of commodities will tend or want to sell commodities forward and thus sell commodity futures. On the other side, consumers of commodities want to lock in prices of their commodity purchases and buy commodity futures. This theory applies to the aforementioned farmer selling a portion of next year's crop today. It can also apply to a central bank that wants to buy gold during each of the next 12 months as part of its monetary operations or a refinery that may want to lock in the price of its oil purchases and, conversely, the prices of its gasoline and heating oil production.

If the two forces of producers and consumers both seeking price protection are equal in weight, then one can envision a flat commodity curve, such as Exhibit 9 illustrates. In this idealized situation, the natural needs for price insurance by commodity buyers and sellers offset each other. There is no discount on the commodity futures price required to induce speculators to accept the commodity price risk because the hedging needs of both the buyer and seller complement and offset each other.

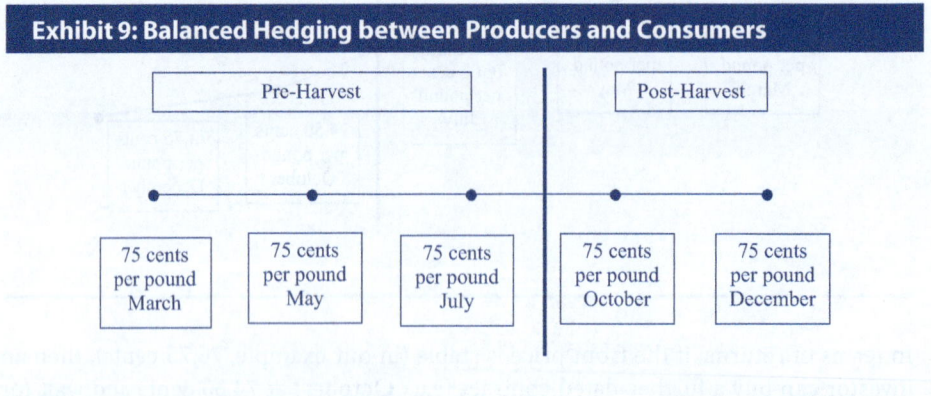

**Exhibit 9: Balanced Hedging between Producers and Consumers**

To use a different example, consider the problem of snowfall in the New England region of the United States. On one hand, small municipalities in Vermont, New Hampshire, or Maine may experience high levels of annual snowfall that are a risk to their snow removal budgets. On the other hand, ski resorts in New England have an opposite risk challenge: Low snowfall creates skiing revenue shortfalls (or adds to costs because of the need for man-made snow), whereas high snowfall winters are a potential bonanza for both higher revenue and lower operating costs. This situation is another example of when the hedging needs of two parties can offset each other and create a mutually beneficial outcome.

If commodity producers as a group are more interested in selling forward (seeking price insurance) than commodity consumers (as per the concept of normal backwardation), then the relative imbalance in demand for price protection will lead to the need for speculators to complete the market. But speculators will only do so when futures prices trade at a sufficient discount to compensate for the price risk they will take on. In this case, the shape and structure of the futures price curve can be illustrated as backwardation, as shown in Exhibit 10, which is consistent with Keynes's insurance theory.

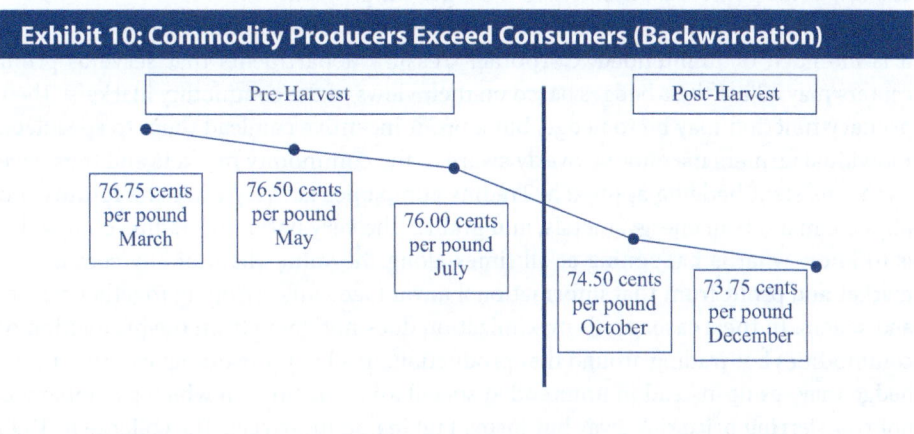

Exhibit 10: Commodity Producers Exceed Consumers (Backwardation)

Finally, if the buyers of soybeans (as a group) are especially worried about the availability of the crop in the next harvest but producers of soybeans are less concerned about crop prices, there would be an imbalance in the demand for price insurance away from producers and toward buyers. This situation would lead to a futures price curve that represents a market in contango, as illustrated in Exhibit 11. In this case, the additional demand for price insurance among buyers (versus sellers) of the commodity will lead them to bid up the futures price to induce speculators to take on this price uncertainty risk.

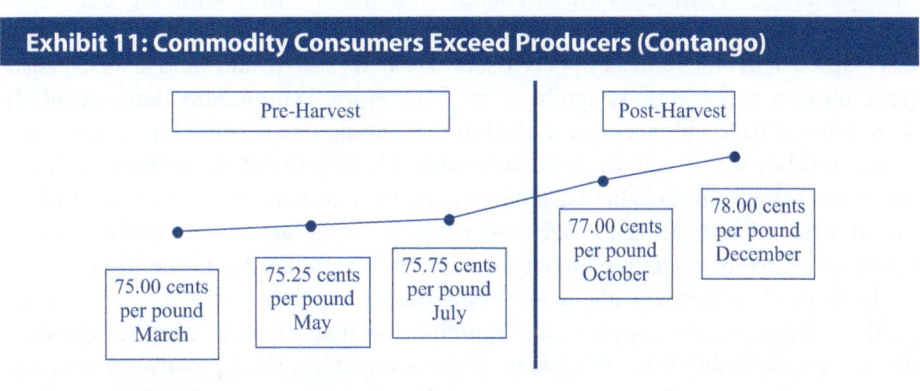

Exhibit 11: Commodity Consumers Exceed Producers (Contango)

Although this theory is more robust than the Keynes's insurance theory, it is still incomplete. One issue is that producers generally have greater exposure to commodity price risk than consumers do (Hicks 1939). There are companies (as well as countries) that are almost entirely dependent on commodity production and thus are very concentrated in one sector, such as energy (e.g., British Petroleum, ExxonMobil), grains (e.g., Cargill, Louis Dreyfus), and metals (e.g., BHP Billiton, Vale, Rio Tinto, Shenhua).

Commodity consumers, in contrast, are very diffuse and often have other priorities (i.e., few if any individual people hedge their meat consumption or gasoline spending). Companies that purchase and use commodities in their products have a mixed record of price hedging, depending on the importance of the commodities in their cost structure. Clothing companies (e.g., Gap) generally do not hedge cotton because the spending is only a few percentage points of their expense base. Marketing and store experience (seen in rent, occupancy, and depreciation expenses) are much more important. But fast food companies hedge a wide variety of commodity inputs (e.g., livestock, grains, energy) because of the high degree of competition for prepared food at a low price point (e.g., McDonald's, Burger King, Wendy's).

In addition, both producers and consumers speculate on commodity prices, whether it is intended or unintended. Corporate treasury departments that serve as profit centers may adjust their hedges based on their views of the commodity markets. Their primary function may be to hedge, but a profit incentive can lead them to speculate. Individual farmers may not be overly aware of the commodity markets and thus have an inconsistent hedging approach. Trading companies actively trade the futures and physical markets in energy, metals, and grains. The very nature of trading companies is to know what is happening at all times along the value chain of any commodity market and profit from that informational advantage while bringing together buyers and sellers. In their case, profit maximization does not come from the production of commodities but trading around that production. In all of these examples, attempts to hedge may result instead in unintended speculative positions in which a company is not transferring price risk away but instead taking on more risk. The collapse in 1993 of Metallgesellschaft AG, one of Germany's largest industrial conglomerates at the time, from a poorly constructed gasoline, fuel oil, and heating oil hedge is a defining example of flawed commercial hedging.

In summary, despite its intuitive logic, applying the hedging pressure hypothesis remains a challenge because measuring the asymmetry in hedging pressure between buyers and sellers of a commodity is very difficult.

### *Theory of Storage*

This theory, originally postulated by Kaldor (1939), focuses on how the level of commodity inventories helps shape commodity futures price curves. The key issue this theory attempts to address is whether supply or demand of the commodity dominates in terms of its price economics. Recall that commodities are physical assets, not virtual assets like stocks and bonds. Physical assets have to be stored, and storage incurs costs (rent, insurance, inspections, spoilage, etc.). Therefore, a commodity that is regularly stored should have a higher price in the future (contango) to account for those storage costs. In other words, supply dominates demand. In contrast, a commodity that is consumed along a value chain that allows for just-in-time delivery and use (i.e., minimal inventories and storage) can avoid these costs. In this situation, demand dominates supply and current prices are higher than futures prices (i.e., backwardation).

In theoretical terms, available inventory generates a benefit called a convenience yield. Having a physical supply of the commodity available is convenient for consumers of the commodity (e.g., individuals, bread companies, meat processors, refiners) because it acts as a buffer to a potential supply disruption that could otherwise force a shutdown of their operations. Because this type of risk/concern is inversely related to the inventory size and the general availability of the commodity (and confidence in its continued availability), the convenience yield is low when stock is abundant. However, the yield rises as inventories diminish and concerns regarding future availability of the commodity increase.

As a result, the theory of storage states that futures prices can be written this way:

Futures price

= Spot price of the physical commodity + Direct storage costs (such as rent and insurance) − Convenience yield.

This equation indicates that price returns and the shape of the curve can move in conjunction with the changes in the available inventory as well as actual and expected supply and demand. For example, when civil war broke out in Libya in 2011, the production of that country's high-quality crude oil was placed in jeopardy, constricting supply. In reaction, the spot price for high-quality crude oil increased. At the same time, the convenience yield increased in the futures contracts closer to expiration because there was a scramble to tap into alternative oil supplies for European refiners. The high quality of Libyan crude oil also restricted which substitute crude oil supplies could be used to replace production from the blocked oil fields and how soon these replacements could be available. The real-world constraints and complications imposed by geography and the logistics of the oil industry resulted in a multi-month delay for replacement supplies. As a result, in the further-out (i.e., longer time to expiration) futures contracts, the reaction was muted as traders assumed that such replacement supplies would be available. Thus the convenience yield remained lower in the deferred months. For this and other reasons, crude oil was pressured to trade in backwardation during 2011.

Unfortunately, while all these theories are reasonable and attractive, they have components that are unobservable or highly volatile and, therefore, not reliably calculable. Commodity producers and consumers regard storage costs as proprietary information. Events (weather, war, technology) can radically adjust convenience yield in a short time with unknown magnitude. Corn suitable for feed may not be suitable for human consumption, so defining inventories is tricky. In the end, we have frameworks and theories, but they are not easily applied and require judgment and analysis by a trader or a valuation system.

### EXAMPLE 13

### Theories of Commodity Futures Returns (1)

1. Which of the following *best* describes the insurance theory of futures returns?

   **A.** Speculators will not provide insurance unless the futures price exceeds the spot price.

   **B.** Producers of a commodity will accept a lower future price (versus the spot price) in exchange for the certainty of locking in that price.

   **C.** Commodity futures markets result in a state of contango because of speculators insisting on a risk premium in exchange for accepting price risk.

### Solution:

B is correct. Under the insurance theory of futures returns, Keynes stated that producers of a commodity would prefer to accept a discount on the potential future spot price in return for the certainty of knowing the future selling price in advance. A is incorrect because the futures price must be below the spot price (normal backwardation) under the insurance theory of futures returns. C is incorrect because the insurance theory of futures returns implies markets are in backwardation, not contango.

## EXAMPLE 14

### Theories of Commodity Futures Returns (2)

1. Under the hedging pressure hypothesis, when hedging activity of commodity futures buyers exceeds that of commodity futures sellers, that futures market is *most likely*:

   A. flat.
   B. in contango.
   C. in backwardation.

### Solution:

B is correct. Under the hedging pressure hypothesis, a market in contango typically results when excess demand for price insurance among commodity futures buyers drives up the futures price to induce speculators to take on price uncertainty risk. A is incorrect because a flat market would likely exist if futures demand activity largely equaled that of supply. C is incorrect because under this scenario, the futures market would be in contango, not backwardation.

## EXAMPLE 15

### Theories of Commodity Futures Returns (3)

1. Under the theory of storage, the convenience yield is:

   A. not affected by the supply of a commodity.
   B. typically low when the supply of a commodity is scarce.
   C. typically high when the supply of a commodity is scarce.

### Solution:

C is correct. Under the theory of storage, the convenience yield of a commodity increases as supply (inventories) diminish and concerns about the future availability increase. A is incorrect because supply levels have a discernible effect on the convenience yield, as mentioned. B is incorrect because the convenience yield would likely be high, as opposed to low, when supply is limited.

## EXAMPLE 16

### Theories of Commodity Futures Returns (4)

1. Which of the following represents the formula for a futures price according to the theory of storage?

   A. Futures price = Spot price of the physical commodity + Direct storage costs − Convenience yield.
   B. Futures price = Spot price of the physical commodity + Direct storage costs + Convenience yield.

C. Futures price = Spot price of the physical commodity − Direct storage costs + Convenience yield.

**Solution:**

A is correct. According to the theory of storage, the futures price reflects the current spot price as well as costs incurred in actually holding the commodity until its delivery. Such costs include direct storage, such as inventory and insurance costs. Finally, because there is a convenience yield (or benefit) to owning a commodity as a form of insurance against potential supply disruptions, this term is subtracted from the current price of the commodity.

## COMPONENTS OF FUTURES RETURNS

8

☐ describe, calculate, and interpret the components of total return for a fully collateralized commodity futures contract

☐ contrast roll return in markets in contango and markets in backwardation

The total return on a commodity investment in futures is different from a total return on the physical assets. So, why do investors tend to use futures to gain their exposure to commodities? Building on the previous section, one can see that physical commodities need to be stored, fed, or perhaps treated against spoilage. Each commodity can be very different in its maintenance requirements; sustaining a hog in Mexico would be very different from storing crude oil in Nigeria.

The total return on commodity futures is traditionally broken into three components:

- the price return (or spot yield),
- the roll return (or roll yield), and
- the collateral return (or collateral yield).

The price return is the change in commodity futures prices, generally the front month contract. Note that this change is different from the change in the price of the physical commodity because lack of standardization of the physical markets makes that a difficult task. Calculating the price return is straightforward, as shown in the following equation:

Price return = (Current price − Previous price)/Previous price.

In addition, as investors move from futures contract to futures contract, they must "roll" that exposure by selling the current contract as it approaches expiration and buying the next contract (assuming a long position). Depending on the shape of the futures curve, there is likely a difference between the two prices. Thus, a portfolio may require buying more far contracts than the near contracts being sold. Investors can observe this scenario if backwardation is driving the shape of the commodity futures price curve.

Example (stylized): Assume an investor has £110 of exposure in wheat futures and the near contract is worth £10 of exposure (so, the investor has £110 exposure divided by £10 per contract, or 11 contracts), but the far (i.e., longer expiration date) contract is worth only £9 of exposure. Therefore, for the investor to roll forward his contracts and maintain a constant level of exposure, he needs to roll the 11 contracts forward and also buy an additional 1 contract to keep the post-roll exposure close to the pre-roll exposure (£110 exposure divided by £9 per contract equals 12.2, or 12 contracts rounded).

In the opposite case, if the futures price curve shape is being driven by contango—with a higher futures price in the far contract—this scenario will require the purchase of fewer commodity contracts than in the near position.

Example: Assume an investor has £108 of exposure in regular unleaded gasoline (or petrol) futures and the near contract is worth £9 of exposure (so, the investor has £108 exposure divided by £9 per contract, or 12 contracts), but the far contract is worth £10 of exposure. Therefore, for the investor to roll forward her contracts and maintain a constant level of exposure, she needs to roll only 11 contracts and sell the extra 1 near contract to keep the post-roll exposure close to the pre-roll exposure (£108 exposure divided by £10 per contract equals 10.8, or 11 contracts rounded).

Note that this roll return is not a return in the sense that it can be independently captured; investors cannot construct a portfolio consisting of only roll returns. Instead, **roll return** is an accounting calculation used to replicate a portion of the total return for a fully collateralized (i.e., with no leverage) commodity index. As defined, the roll return is effectively the accounting difference (in percentage terms) between the near-term commodity futures contract price and the farther-term commodity futures contract price (note that roll return is sometimes defined in monetary terms rather than as a percentage):

Roll return

= [(Near-term futures contract closing price − Farther-term futures contract closing price)/Near-term futures contract closing price] × Percentage of the position in the futures contract being rolled.

As an example, consider the roll from the March contract to the April contract for WTI crude oil on 7 February 2019 using the S&P GSCI methodology, which rolls its positions over a five-day period (so 1/5 = 20% per day):

March contract closing price: $52.64/barrel

April contract closing price: $53.00/barrel

($52.64 − $53.00)/$52.64 = −0.68% gross roll return × 20% rollover portion

= −0.13% net roll return (note the negative return in contango).

Note that different indexes use different periods and/or weights in their "rolling methodology." In Section 5, we will further discuss the rolling methodology of various indexes.

In his book *Expected Returns*, Ilmanen (2011) made the argument (challenged by others) that roll return is approximately equal to a risk premium. This concept relates back to Keynes and his theory of "normal backwardation." Keynes proposed that speculators take the other side of the transaction from commodity producers—who sell forward to lock in their cash flows—in an attempt to earn an excess return as compensation for providing price insurance to producers. Ilmanen attempted to demonstrate that positive long-run average returns are associated with positive roll return (i.e., in commodities for which futures prices are in backwardation) and negative long-run average returns are associated with negative roll return. However, because 40% of the commodities examined by Ilmanen (p. 255) had negative roll returns but positive total returns, one cannot directly conclude that backwardation earns a positive total return.

The **collateral return** is the yield (e.g., interest rate) for the bonds or cash used to maintain the investor's futures position(s). The minimum amount of funds is called the initial margin. If an investor has less cash than required by the exchange

## Components of Futures Returns

to maintain the position, the broker who acts as custodian will require more funds (a margin call) or close the position (buying to cover a short position or selling to eliminate a long position). Collateral thus acts as insurance for the exchange that the investor can pay for losses.

For return calculations on indexed investments, the amount of cash would be considered equal to the notional value of the futures. This approach means no leverage. For expected returns, commonly, investors should use a risk-free government bond that most closely matches the term projected. Most commodity indexes use short-term US Treasury bills, but if one is forecasting 10-year returns, then for collateral return purposes, a 10-year constant maturity government bond would have a more appropriate term.

Although indexes will be discussed more fully later in the reading, to illustrate the commodity return elements just discussed, one can use an index—in this case, the aforementioned S&P GSCI, which has one of the longest backtested and live history of the investable commodity indexes. Exhibit 12 shows the disaggregation of its return components.

### Exhibit 12: Average Annual Return Components of the S&P GSCI, January 1970–March 2019

| S&P GSCI Return | Total Return | Spot Return | Roll Return[1] | Collateral Return[1] |
|---|---|---|---|---|
| Return[2] | 6.8% | 3.0% | −1.3% | 5.0% |
| Risk[3] | 19.8% | 19.8% | 4.2% | 1.1% |
| Correlation[4] |  | 0.97 | −0.11 | −0.14 |

[1] Roll return is defined as the excess return on the S&P GSCI minus the spot of the S&P GSCI. Collateral return is defined as the total return on the S&P GSCI minus the excess return of the S&P GSCI. The excess return measures the returns accrued from investing in uncollateralized nearby commodity futures.
[2] Monthly returns are used.
[3] Risk is defined as annualized standard deviation.
[4] Correlation with the S&P GSCI Total Return.
Source: Author's research based on data from S&P Dow Jones Indices.

As can be seen in the table, over the past 40+ years, the S&P GSCI generated 6.8% in geometrically compounded annualized returns, with about three-quarters derived from interest rates (collateral return). The commodity price spot return component of the index (which has varied over time) contributed to approximately 45% of the total return (3.0% out of 6.8%), whereas the roll return subtracted from the overall return by −1.3% (or 130 bps) on an annualized basis. Investors can see the effect of commodities on inflation via the price return.

The volatility and correlations of the components of index returns are driven by the changes in the spot price return (effectively the same annualized standard deviation of 19.8% as the S&P GSCI with a 97% correlation). The roll return and collateral return do not drive, in general, the monthly returns historically. This link between commodity futures prices and commodity total return indexes helps to define commodities as a separate and investable asset class.

In summary, the total return on a fully collateralized commodity futures contract can be described as the spot price return plus the roll return plus collateral return (risk-free rate return). With an index, a return from rebalancing the index's component weights—a **rebalance return**—would also be added. Using historical data (at the risk of it becoming outdated over time), one can demonstratively use the total return deconstruction to analyze commodities.

### EXAMPLE 17

### Total Returns for Futures Contracts (1)

1. A commodity futures market with pricing in backwardation will exhibit which of the following characteristics?
    - **A.** The roll return is usually negative.
    - **B.** Rolling an expiring futures contract forward will require buying more contracts in order to maintain the same dollar position in the futures markets.
    - **C.** Rolling an expiring futures contract forward will require buying fewer contracts in order to maintain the same dollar position in the futures markets.

### Solution:

B is correct. Commodity futures markets in backwardation exhibit price curves in which longer-dated futures prices are priced lower than near-dated contracts and the nearest-dated contract is priced lower than the current spot price. With a lower futures price on the futures curve, rolling contracts forward in backwardation would require purchasing more contracts to maintain the same dollar position. A is incorrect because the roll return is usually positive, not negative, in markets in backwardation. C is incorrect because an investor would need to purchase more, not fewer, contracts in markets in backwardation to maintain his or her total dollar position.

### EXAMPLE 18

### Total Returns for Futures Contracts (2)

1. An investor has realized a 5% price return on a commodity futures contract position and a 2.5% roll return after all her contracts were rolled forward. She had held this position for one year with collateral equal to 100% of the position at a risk-free rate of 2% per year. Her total return on this position (annualized excluding leverage) was:
    - **A.** 5.5%.
    - **B.** 7.3%.
    - **C.** 9.5%.

### Solution:

C is correct. Total return on a commodity futures position is expressed as

Total return = Price return + Roll return + Collateral return.

In this case, she held the contracts for one year, so the price return of 5% is an annualized figure. In addition, the roll return is also an annual 2.5%. Her collateral return equals 2% per year × 100% initial collateral investment = 2%.
So, her total return (annualized) is

Total return = 5% + 2.5% + 2% = 9.5%.

## EXAMPLE 19

### Total Returns for Futures Contracts (3)

1. An investor has a $10,000 position in long futures contracts (for a hypothetical commodity) that he wants to roll forward. The current contracts, which are close to expiration, are valued at $4.00 per contract, whereas the longer-term contract he wants to roll into is valued at $2.50 per contract. What are the transactions—in terms of buying and selling new contracts—he needs to execute in order to maintain his current exposure?

   **A.** Close out (sell) 2,500 near-term contracts and initiate (buy) 4,000 of the longer-term contracts.

   **B.** Close out (buy) 2,500 near-term contracts and initiate (sell) 4,000 of the longer-term contracts.

   **C.** Let the 2,500 near-term contracts expire and use any proceeds to purchase an additional 2,500 of the longer-term contracts.

### Solution:

A is correct. To roll over the same level of total exposure ($10,000), he will need to do the following:

Sell

$10,000/$4.00 per contract = 2,500 existing contracts.

And replace this position by purchasing

$10,000/$2.50 per contract = 4,000 existing contracts.

# CONTANGO, BACKWARDATION, AND THE ROLL RETURN

9

☐ | contrast roll return in markets in contango and markets in backwardation

To reiterate, contango and backwardation—and the resulting roll return—fundamentally reflect underlying supply and demand expectations and are accounting mechanisms for the commodity term structure. We can gain a sense of these patterns by again examining the history of an index. Recall that from January 1970 to March 2019, the historical roll return of the S&P GSCI subtracted 1.3% from the average annual total return, with a standard deviation of 4.7%. That historical roll return varied over this time period, as depicted in Exhibit 13.

### Exhibit 13: Historical One-Year S&P GSCI Price and Roll Return (Monthly Returns, January 1970–December 2019)

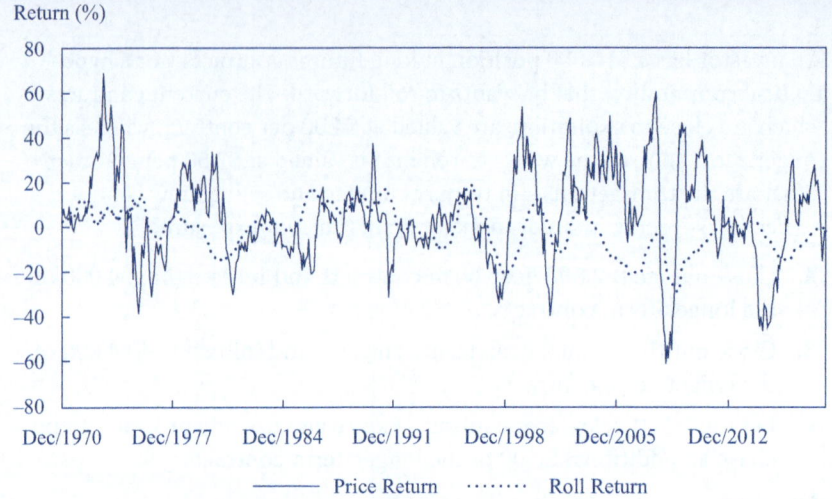

*Note*: The roll return is rolling monthly.

As the graph shows, periods of either backwardation or contango do not persist indefinitely. A simple review of the Exhibit 13 history demonstrates as much. Furthermore, with a correlation of 3%, roll return is not very indicative of price return, also contrary to popular belief. Positive price returns are associated with negative roll returns as well as positive roll returns. In some cases, certain sectors are indeed associated with contango, as can be seen in Exhibit 14.

### Exhibit 14: Average Annual Sector Roll Return and Standard Deviation[a]

|  | S&P GSCI Total | Energy | Industrial Metals | Agriculture | Livestock | Precious Metals | Softs |
|---|---|---|---|---|---|---|---|
| Mean roll return (annual)[b] | −1.3% | −1.5% | −1.3% | −4.5% | −1.1% | −5.1% | −5.5% |
| Standard deviation of the mean (annual)[b] | 0.4% | 0.8% | 0.5% | 0.4% | 0.5% | 0.2% | 0.6% |
| Maximum roll return (annual)[b] | 18.9% | 31.5% | 45.9% | 29.2% | 35.5% | −0.4% | 25.6% |
| Minimum roll return (annual)[b] | −29.6% | −39.5% | −16.6% | −18.6% | −31.2% | −15.4% | −24.9% |

[a] *The periods covered vary by sector:*

- S&P GSCI total: December 1969–March 2019
- Energy: December 1982–March 2019
- Industrial metals: December 1976–March 2019
- Agriculture: December 1969–March 2019
- Livestock: December 1969–March 2019
- Precious metals: December 1972–March 2019

# Contango, Backwardation, and the Roll Return

- Softs: December 1994–March 2019

[b] *Calculated using rolling 12-month periods of monthly data.*
*Sources:* Based on data from Bloomberg and Coloma Capital Futures.

Exhibit 14 highlights a few important factors. First, industrial metals, agriculture, livestock, precious metals, and softs have statistically strong negative mean roll returns. Only energy has a statistical possibility of a positive mean roll return, but that opportunity has diminished after 2010. Note from our comparison of the commodity sectors that industrial metals, agriculture, livestock, precious metals, and softs are stored for extended periods in warehouses, silos, and feedlots. In fact, precious metals historically have had negative roll returns because of gold's perpetual storage as an alternative currency. Historically, energy is consumed on a real-time basis apart from various strategic reserves, with the minimal storage buffer thus creating a lower or negative convenience yield. However, since 2010, the emergence of shale oil production in the United States has increased oil's convenience yield to the point that historical scarcity risk is much lower than before. Also, oil supply risk has shifted to China during this period as that country took over the United States' position as the lead oil importer. Finally, OPEC (with the inclusion of Russia and a few other non-OPEC members) regained some pricing power as the cartel achieved some success with supply restriction. Bringing it all together, one can conclude that indexes and long-only strategies that overweight agriculture, livestock, precious metals, and softs should expect to see negative roll returns (or roll yields). Energy commodities (apart from natural gas) have an opportunity for positive roll return, assuming producers successfully withhold supply from the market.

In conclusion, roll return can have an important impact on any single period return but overall has been relatively modest compared with price return. Furthermore, roll return is very sector dependent, which leads to a conclusion that sector diversification or concentration will have a profound impact on an investor's overall roll return based on a diversified portfolio of commodity futures.

### EXAMPLE 20

### Roll Return

1. When measuring its contribution to the total return of a commodity futures position, the roll return:
    - **A.** typically has a significant contribution to total return over both single and multiple periods.
    - **B.** typically has a modest contribution to total return in any single period but can be significant over multiple periods.
    - **C.** is always close to zero.

### Solution:

B is correct. Historically, the roll return has had a relatively modest impact on overall commodity futures return in the short term but can be meaningful over longer time periods. A is incorrect because the roll return is typically modest over shorter periods of time, as noted earlier. C is incorrect because futures contracts generate positive or negative roll returns, depending on the commodity and prevailing market conditions.

## 10. COMMODITY SWAPS

> describe how commodity swaps are used to obtain or modify exposure to commodities

Instead of futures, some investors can gain market exposure to or hedge risk of commodities via swaps. A **commodity swap** is a legal contract involving the exchange of payments over multiple dates as determined by specified reference prices or indexes relating to commodities. In the world of commodities, a series of futures contracts often forms the basis of the reference prices. For example, an independent oil refiner may want to hedge its oil purchases over an extended period. The refiner may not want to manage a large number of futures contracts but maintain flexibility with regard to its oil supply source. By entering into a swap contract—particularly one that is cash settled instead of physically settled—the refiner can be protected from a price spike and yet maintain flexibility of delivery.

Based on this example, one can see why commercial participants use swaps: The instrument provides both risk management and risk transfer while eliminating the need to set up and manage multiple futures contracts. Swaps also provide a degree of customization not possible with standardized futures contracts. The refiner in the example may negotiate a swap for a specific quality of crude oil (e.g., Heavy Louisiana Sweet instead of West Texas Intermediate, or WTI) as its reference price or a blend of crudes that shifts throughout the year depending on the season. Customization through the use of a swap may also have value by changing the quantity of crude oil hedged over time, such as lowering the exposure during the planned shutdown and maintenance periods at the refinery.

On the other side of the transaction from the refiner (or other hedging or speculating entity) would be a swap dealer, typically a financial intermediary, such as a bank or trading company. The dealer, in turn, may hedge its price risk exposure assumed in the swap through the futures market or, alternatively, negotiate its own swap with another party or arrange an oil purchase contract with a crude oil producer. The dealer may also choose to keep the price risk exposure, seeking to profit from its market information. A diagram demonstrating this swap transaction is shown in Exhibit 15.

### Exhibit 15: Swap Market Participant Structure

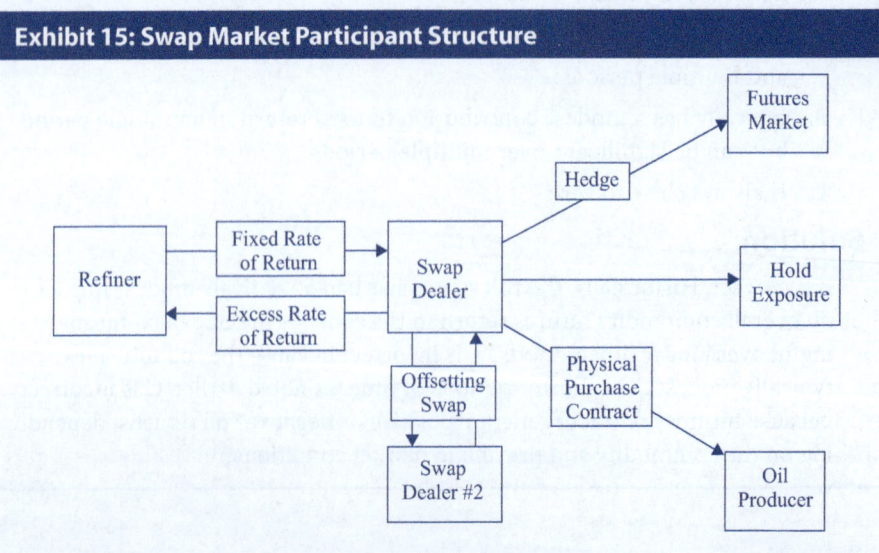

# Commodity Swaps

To further understand the diagram in Exhibit 15, assume we had the following scenario:

1. An oil refiner goes long a swap at the end of December that pays the amount exceeding $70 per barrel every month-end through September.
2. The oil refiner would pay a swap counterparty a premium (in this example, $25) for this privilege because it is effectively long a series of call options.

The flow of funds in the swap transaction would be as shown in Exhibit 16.

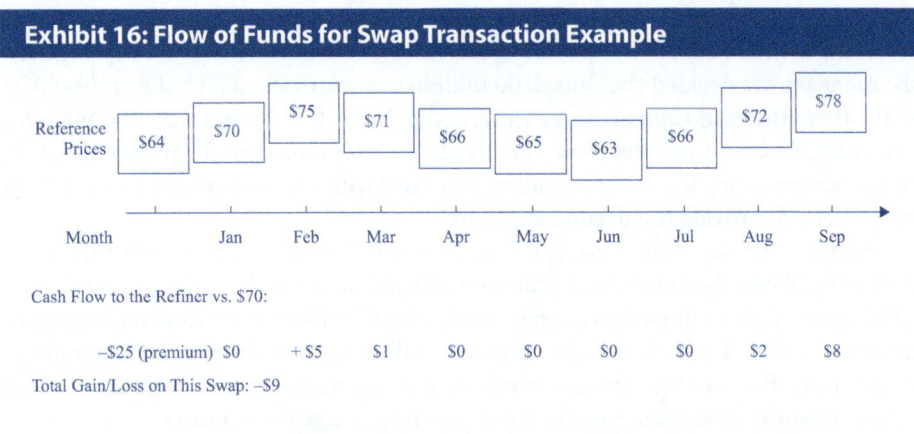

**Exhibit 16: Flow of Funds for Swap Transaction Example**

Reference Prices: $64, $70, $75, $71, $66, $65, $63, $66, $72, $78

Month: Jan, Feb, Mar, Apr, May, Jun, Jul, Aug, Sep

Cash Flow to the Refiner vs. $70:

−$25 (premium)  $0  +$5  $1  $0  $0  $0  $0  $2  $8

Total Gain/Loss on This Swap: −$9

Total gain/loss on this swap to the refiner is −$9 (found by summing the cash flows and ignoring present value calculations or other considerations).

Although this example of a swap lost money and effectively increased the refiner's cost of a barrel of oil by $1 for this time period (given that the net loss on the swap was $9 over nine months), the swap protected the company against the risk of a cash squeeze during those months when an oil price spike could have impaired the liquidity of the company. The swap also defined the cost up front, giving a measure of cash flow predictability. Note that accounting standards and practices for swaps may also have an impact on the attractiveness of swaps. Given that oil prices are subject to many events beyond a company's control, a company looking to protect itself from financing risk may find that a swap can be a valuable tool.

There are many types of swaps available in the marketplace because they are not standardized, exchange-traded contracts like futures. The previous example of the refiner is an example of an "excess return swap." In an excess return swap, the payments to either party are driven primarily by the changes in price of each of the futures contracts that make up the index. The net change in the prices of the underlying futures contracts is defined as the "excess" return, and the excess return is multiplied by the contract's notional amount to determine the payments between buyer and seller.

## Total Return Swap

Another common swap in commodities is a "total return swap." In a total return swap, the change in the level of the index will be equal to the returns generated by the change in price of each of the futures contracts that make up the index plus a return based on interest earned on any cash collateral posted on the purchase of the futures contracts that make up the index. If the level of the index increases, the swap buyer receives payment net of the fee paid to the seller; if the level of the index decreases between two valuation dates, the swap seller receives payment (plus the fee charged to the buyer). This type of swap is generally used by large institutional investors (e.g., pension plans) as opposed to commodity producers or buyers. With a total return swap, the investor seeks exposure to commodity returns, often because of the low return correlation of commodities with other asset classes (e.g., stocks or bonds) or as a reflection of the view that commodities provide a valuable inflation hedge for asset/liability matching (ALM). Therefore, such investors would engage in a total return swap that provides them with long exposure to the future returns from a commodity index that is used as the reference price. Again, accounting treatment with respect to futures often drives these decisions.

As an example of a total return swap, assume an investor who manages a defined benefit retirement plan desires commodity exposure for the reasons noted earlier. Given the size of the portfolio manager's plan assets (assume £2 billion), the manager is seeking approximately 5% exposure of plan assets to commodities. More specifically, the manager has decided that this £100 million exposure (5% of £2 billion) should be to the (hypothetical) China Futures Commodity Index (CFCI) and should remain for five years. Based on this decision, the manager issues a request for proposals (RFP) and, after evaluating the various bidders, contracts with a Swiss bank for a total return swap that will provide the desired exposure.

If on the first day of the swap agreement the CFCI increased by 1%, then the swap dealer would owe the manager £1 million (£100 million × 1%). If on the second day the CFCI declined by 5%, then the manager would owe £5 million to the dealer. Commonly, the dealer will hedge its short index exposure with futures or the physical commodity investments. Because the manager would be seeking the risk–return exposure offered by commodities, the manager would not generally hedge its exposure.

### Basis Swap

Another common commodity swap is a basis swap, in which periodic payments are exchanged based on the values of two related commodity reference prices that are not perfectly correlated. These swaps are often used to adjust for the difference (called the basis) between a highly liquid futures contract in a commodity and an illiquid but related material. For example, a swap may pay the difference between the average daily prices of Brent crude oil (very liquid) and heavy crude oil available for delivery in the Gulf of Mexico (less liquid). This can be a very valuable arrangement for, in this example, refineries on the US Gulf Coast that have heavily invested in processing cheaper heavy crudes that come from such countries as Mexico or Venezuela. Because prices of these crudes do not always move in tandem with more common crudes, such as Brent, they derive a price basis between the two. It should be noted that "basis" has other meanings as well, depending on the commodity in question. For example, in grains, the basis may refer to the difference between the soybean contract and physical soybeans available for delivery at the Mississippi River.

### Variance Swaps and Volatility Swaps

Two final types of relatively common commodity swaps are variance swaps and volatility swaps. Variance swaps of commodities are similar in concept to variance swaps of equities in that there is a variance buyer and a variance seller. Two parties agree to periodically exchange payments based on the proportional difference between an observed/actual variance in the price levels of a commodity (over consecutive time periods), and some fixed amount of variance established at the outset of the contract. If this difference is positive, the variance swap buyer receives a payment; if it is negative, the variance swap seller receives payment. Often the variance differences (observed versus fixed) are capped to limit upside and losses.

Volatility commodity swaps are very similar to variance swaps, with the exception that the direction and amount of payments are determined relative to the observed versus expected volatility for a reference price commodity. In this arrangement, the

## Commodity Swaps

two sides are not speculating on the level or direction of prices but instead on how volatile prices will be versus expectations. A volatility seller will profit if realized volatility is lower than expectations, whereas the counterparty volatility buyer anticipates higher than expected volatility.

### EXAMPLE 21

### Commodity Swaps (1)

1. A portfolio manager enters into a $100 million (notional) total return commodity swap to obtain a long position in commodity exposure. The position is reset monthly against a broad-based commodity index. At the end of the first month, the index is up 3%, and at the end of the second month, the index declines 2%. What are two payments that would occur between the portfolio manager and the swap dealer on the other side of the swap transaction?

    **A.** No payments are exchanged because a net cash flow only occurs when the swap agreement expires.

    **B.** $3 million would be paid by the swap dealer to the portfolio manager (after Month 1), and $2 million would be paid by the portfolio manager to the swap dealer (after Month 2).

    **C.** $3 million would be paid by the portfolio manager to the swap dealer (after Month 1), and $2 million would be paid by the swap dealer to the portfolio manager (after Month 2).

**Solution:**

B is correct. Because the portfolio manager has a long position in the total return commodity swap, he or she will receive payments when the commodity index rises and make payments when the commodity index declines. The payment calculations after the first two months are as follows:

Month 1: $100 million × 3% = $3 million.

Month 2: $100 million × −2% = −$2 million.

A is incorrect because swap payments are made periodically (in this case monthly) and not withheld to the end of the contract. C is incorrect because the payments would be in the opposite direction for each month.

### EXAMPLE 22

### Commodity Swaps (2)

1. In a commodity volatility swap, the direction and amount of payments are determined relative to the observed versus reference:

    **A.** direction in the price of a commodity.

    **B.** variance for the price of a commodity.

    **C.** volatility for the price of a commodity.

> **Solution:**
>
> C is correct. In a commodity volatility swap, the two sides of the transaction are speculating on expected volatility. A volatility seller will profit if realized volatility is lower than expectations, whereas the volatility buyer benefits from higher than expected volatility. A is incorrect because a volatility swap is based on price volatility, not direction. B is incorrect because a volatility swap is based on price volatility as opposed to price variance (price volatility squared).

## 11. COMMODITY INDEXES

☐ describe how the construction of commodity indexes affects index returns

As in other parts of the investment universe, indexes have been created to portray the aggregate movement of commodity prices, investment vehicles, and investing approaches. In fact, one could say that an asset class does not exist without the presence of at least one representative index.

Commodity indexes play three primary roles in commodity sector investments. First, an index can be used as a benchmark to evaluate broader moves in commodity pricing. Second, as a broad indicator, an index can be used for macroeconomic or forecasting purposes by examining statistically significant relationships between movements in the commodity index and other macroeconomic variables. Finally, an index can act as the basis for an investment vehicle or contract providing the information needed to record, monitor, and evaluate price changes that affect contract value.

Although there are a number of commodity indexes, the following are used most frequently for the purposes just mentioned: (1) the S&P GSCI; (2) the Bloomberg Commodity Index (BCOM), formerly known as the Dow Jones–UBS Commodity Index (DJ–UBS); (3) the Deutsche Bank Liquid Commodity Index (DBLCI); (4) the Thomson Reuters/CoreCommodity CRB Index (TR/CC CRB); and (5) the Rogers International Commodities Index (RICI). The following are key characteristics that differentiate each of these indexes:

- The *breadth* of coverage (number of commodities and sectors) included in each index, noting that some commodities have multiple reference contracts (e.g., for crude oil, the common contracts are for West Texas Intermediate in the United States and Brent crude for Europe).
- The relative *weightings* assigned to each component/commodity and the related methodology for how these weights are determined.
- The *rolling methodology* for determining how those contracts that are about to expire are rolled over into future months. This decision has a direct impact on the roll return (or yield) of the overall commodity. Recall that roll return is one of the three key components of overall commodity returns.
- The methodology and frequency for *rebalancing* the weights of the individual commodities, sectors, and contracts in the index to maintain the relative weightings assigned to each investment. As with stocks and bonds within a portfolio, the opportunity to earn positive rebalance returns for commodities depends on the correlation of the underlying components of the index

and the propensity of underperforming components to revert back to the mean. For example, a drought may cause cotton prices to increase, but a strong crop the following year will cause prices to collapse. A rebalance sale of the overvalued cotton exposure into an undervalued exposure should "lock in" some of that gain. The rebalance return will likely vary depending on the methodology used by the index.

- The *governance* of indexes is important because it is the process by which all the aforementioned rules are implemented. For example, some indexes are rules-based, whereas others are selection-based. The rules-based indexes follow a quantitative methodology, whereas selection-based indexes are more qualitative in that an index committee picks the commodities. Also, governance oversees the independence of index providers so that, according to best practices of the Index Industry Association, the asset price should be independent from the index provider, which, in turn, should be independent from the product provider (e.g., the exchange-traded fund or swap provider).

For the index to be a viable and useful construct, it should be investable; that is, investors or their agents should be able to replicate the methodology outlined to translate the index concept into a representation of the asset class. For this reason, index providers and investors must be mindful of the venues (physical or electronic) for trading each commodity index, the liquidity and turnover of contracts based on each commodity index, and the term structure of each index (i.e., how far into the future the index extends and which months it covers). The weighting method for components in an index is key to diversification and—combined with rebalancing frequency—influences the opportunity to earn positive rebalance returns.

An index that requires investments in exchanges all over the world is more difficult and expensive for an investor to replicate. An emphasis on illiquid contracts has a negative impact on transaction costs. Contracts without a full yield curve may be a challenge to analyze and trade. In other words, seemingly small execution concerns are magnified when constructing a benchmark that represents an entire asset class, such as commodities. And indexes that choose (perhaps inadvertently) contracts that more commonly trade in backwardation may appear to improve forward-looking performance (because this generates a positive roll return), whereas those that more commonly trade in contango may hurt performance. Exhibit 17 summarizes the various elements of the main indexes discussed.

### Exhibit 17: Overview of Major Commodity Indexes

| | Index | | | | |
|---|---|---|---|---|---|
| Element | S&P GSCI | BCOM | DBLCI | TR/CC CRB | RICI |
| Adoption date | 1991 | 1998 | 2003 | 2005 (current version) | 1998 |
| Number of commodities | 24 | 23 | 14 | 19 | 38 |
| Weighting method | Production weighted | Production and liquidity weighted | Fixed weight | Fixed weight | Fixed weight |
| Rolling methodology | Nearby most liquid contract, monthly | Front month to next or second month | Optimized on roll return | Front month to next month | Front month to next month |
| Rebalancing frequency | Annually | Annually | Annually | Monthly | Monthly |

|  | Index |  |  |  |  |
| --- | --- | --- | --- | --- | --- |
| Individual investor funds available? | Yes | Yes | Yes | Yes in some jurisdictions as well as an exchange-traded fund on a related index | Yes |

*Note:* Information is as of 30 April 2019.
*Sources:* Information from respective sponsor websites, Bloomberg, and authors' research.

Exhibit 17 helps distinguish the key characteristics that differentiate these five commercially important commodity indexes. In terms of coverage (the number of commodities and sectors included in the index), all five of these indexes have broad sector coverage, including energy, grains, livestock, precious metals, industrial metals, and softs. The only exception is the DBLCI, which does not have any livestock exposure. At the other extreme, the RICI includes relatively exotic (and thus illiquid) commodities, such as lumber, oats, and rubber. As a further example of its unique nature, the RICI once included adzuki beans (the red beans found in many Asian cuisines) and palm oil.

## S&P GSCI

The S&P GSCI is the second oldest of the selected commodity indexes. The index is based on 24 commodities and applies liquidity screens to include only those contracts with an established minimum level of trading volume and available historical pricing. It uses a world production value-weighting scheme that gives the largest weight to the most valuable commodity on the basis of physical trade value. It should be no surprise that crude oil has the highest single weight and energy has the highest sector weight (historically as high as 80%) in this index. This approach is most similar to a market-capitalization weighted index of nearly all major bond and stock market indexes. Like some market-capitalization indexes (particularly in emerging or frontier markets), the resulting weights of the S&P GSCI can be highly concentrated. The rolling methodology focuses on owning the front (i.e., near-term) contracts to address the highest liquidity and where supply and demand shocks are most likely to have an impact.

## Bloomberg Commodity Index

The BCOM (formerly the DJ–UBS) is based on 23 commodities. It includes liquidity as both a weighting factor and a screening factor, although the index is selection-based, meaning a committee uses judgment to pick the included commodities. The rules of index construction also place caps on the size of the sectors (33% maximum) and floors on individual commodities (2% minimum). These differences mean that very different index composition and weights can occur. For example, the energy sector currently dominates the S&P GSCI (as high as 80% weight), whereas the BCOM's exposure is much lower (approximately 30%). However, exposure to natural gas as a single component of energy is higher in the BCOM (approximately 9%) than in the S&P GSCI (approximately 3%). Given that natural gas had an annualized roll cost of about 19% (often the highest roll cost of all the commodities), the higher weighting of natural gas in the BCOM implies that the index has to find other sources of return (e.g., price return and rebalance return) to overcome the drag that natural gas inventory storage creates through negative roll return. The rolling methodology focuses on owning the front (i.e., near-term) contracts.

## Deutsche Bank Liquid Commodity Index

The DBLCI uses a fixed-weighting scheme to allocate exposure. The most notable/unique feature of this index is its rolling methodology. Instead of focusing on near-term contracts, it is optimized based on the time value of maximized backwardation/minimized contango for the contracts that fall within the next 12 calendar months. As an example, a June 2014 copper futures contract may be at 1% backwardation versus a May 2014 copper contract. But if the July 2014 copper contract is at a 3% backwardation (1.5% per month, or 3% divided by two months) versus the 1% backwardation per month on the June 2014 contract, then the DBLCI will roll to the July 2014 contract in preference to the June 2014 contract. Therefore, one could argue the DBLCI takes an active decision with regard to roll return positioning as compared with the other indexes.

## Thomson Reuters/CoreCommodity CRB Index

The TR/CC CRB consists of 19 commodities and is a continuation of the first investable commodity index published by the Commodities Research Bureau in 1978 (although an earlier iteration started in 1957). It uses a fixed-weighting scheme to allocate exposure. An index management committee decides the weights based on a number of factors, including diversification, sector representation, liquidity, and economic importance. It also clusters the fixed weights into a number of tiers. As a result, constituents are moved from tier to tier. The rolling methodology focuses on owning the front (i.e., near-term) contracts that mechanically focus on the front month or second front month and do not require a particular calculation.

## Rogers International Commodity Index

The RICI uses a fixed-weighting scheme to allocate exposure among 38 different commodities and was designed by investor Jim Rogers in the late 1990s. An index management committee decides the weights based on a number of factors, including diversification, sector representation, liquidity, and economic importance. Like the TR/CC CRB Index, it also clusters the fixed weights into a number of tiers. As a result, constituents are moved from tier to tier as they gain or lose relative importance as seen by the committee. Energy is the largest weight but is still a highly diversified basket. Some energy constituents are denominated in non-US dollar terms—such as rubber (traded in Japan in Japanese yen) and cocoa (traded in London in British pounds)—which potentially adds a foreign exchange exposure element to the index returns.

## Rebalancing Frequency

Rebalancing frequency plays a role in index returns, especially for those indexes that rebalance more frequently, such as the TR/CC CRB and RICI. Theoretically, from portfolio management theory, rebalancing is more important if a market is frequently mean reverting because there are more peaks to sell and valleys to buy. However, frequent rebalancing can lead to underperformance in a trending market because the outperforming assets are sold but continue up in price, whereas the underperforming assets are purchased but still drift lower.

The relative performance of the monthly rebalanced indexes (TR/CC CRB and RICI) versus the annual rebalance of the other indexes will depend on the length of time of price trends: More frequent mean reversions should favor the former two indexes, but a longer-term trend will more likely favor the annually rebalancing indexes. If an index uses a floating weighting scheme, such as production value (fully or partially), then the higher (lower) futures prices usually coincide with higher (lower) physical prices. Therefore, with this kind of approach, the magnitude of rebalancing weights is generally lower than for a fixed-weight scheme because the post-rebalance weights will generally drift in line with the current portfolio weights. As a result, the S&P GSCI and BCOM indexes typically have lower rebalancing costs and—in a trending market—have an opportunity to outperform their fixed-weight index counterparts, particularly those that have a relatively frequent rebalance period.

### Commodity Index Summary

There is no dominant index based on a particular methodology. Relative performance will occur based on the circumstances of the markets and the time period examined. Evaluating which index is superior for a *long-term* investment generates modest if any value. Per the authors' research, these indexes all have been highly correlated (well above 70%) with each other and have had low (roughly 0%) correlations with traditional asset classes (e.g., US large-cap stocks, US bonds, international stocks). As with equities, for which there are many different index providers, commodity indexes act in parallel even when their returns (and Sharpe ratios) frequently differ dramatically over time.

> **EXAMPLE 23**
>
> ### Commodity Indexes (1)
>
> 1. All else being equal, compared with an equally weighted commodity index, a production value-weighted index (such as the S&P GSCI) will be:
>    - **A.** less sensitive to energy sector returns.
>    - **B.** more sensitive to energy sector returns.
>    - **C.** equally sensitive to energy sector returns.
>
> **Solution:**
>
> B is correct. The energy sector will make up a sizable portion of a production value-weighted index and thus will be a meaningful driver of returns for such an index. A is incorrect because a production value-weighted index will be more, not less, sensitive to the energy sector. C is incorrect because a production value-weighted index will be more, not equally, sensitive to the energy sector.

> **EXAMPLE 24**
>
> ### Commodity Indexes (2)
>
> 1. Which of the following statements is *not* correct regarding commodity futures indexes?
>    - **A.** Commodity sectors in backwardation typically improve index returns.
>    - **B.** An index that invests in several futures exchanges provides a high degree of diversification.
>    - **C.** Total returns of the major commodity indexes have low correlation with traditional asset classes, such as equities and bonds.

> **Solution:**
>
> B is correct. Commodity futures exchanges throughout the world are highly correlated and thus provide little diversification benefits. A is incorrect because markets in backwardation typically have positive roll yields and thus will likely improve index returns (although the price return may still not be positive and thus the total return may still be negative). C is incorrect because commodity index returns do indeed have historically low correlation with equities and bonds.

# SUMMARY

- Commodities are a diverse asset class comprising various sectors: energy, grains, industrial (base) metals, livestock, precious metals, and softs (cash crops). Each of these sectors has a number of characteristics that are important in determining the supply and demand for each commodity, including ease of storage, geopolitics, and weather.

- Fundamental analysis of commodities relies on analyzing supply and demand for each of the products as well as estimating the reaction to the inevitable shocks to their equilibrium or underlying direction.

- The life cycle of commodities varies considerably depending on the economic, technical, and structural (i.e., industry, value chain) profile of each commodity as well as the sector. A short life cycle allows for relatively rapid adjustment to outside events, whereas a long life cycle generally limits the ability of the market to react.

- The valuation of commodities relative to that of equities and bonds can be summarized by noting that equities and bonds represent financial assets whereas commodities are physical assets. The valuation of commodities is not based on the estimation of future profitability and cash flows but rather on a discounted forecast of future possible prices based on such factors as the supply and demand of the physical item.

- The commodity trading environment is similar to other asset classes, with three types of trading participants: (1) informed investors/hedgers, (2) speculators, and (3) arbitrageurs.

- Commodities have two general pricing forms: spot prices in the physical markets and futures prices for later delivery. The spot price is the current price to deliver or purchase a physical commodity at a specific location. A futures price is an exchange-based price agreed on to deliver or receive a defined quantity and often quality of a commodity at a future date.

- The difference between spot and futures prices is generally called the basis. When the spot price is higher than the futures price, it is called backwardation, and when it is lower, it is called contango. Backwardation and contango are also used to describe the relationship between two futures contracts of the same commodity.

- Commodity contracts can be settled by either cash or physical delivery.

- There are three primary theories of futures returns.

- In insurance theory, commodity producers who are long the physical good are motived to sell the commodity for future delivery to hedge their production price risk exposure.
- The hedging pressure hypothesis describes when producers along with consumers seek to protect themselves from commodity market price volatility by entering into price hedges to stabilize their projected profits and cash flow.
- The theory of storage focuses on supply and demand dynamics of commodity inventories, including the concept of "convenience yield."

- The total return of a fully collateralized commodity futures contract can be quantified as the spot price return plus the roll return plus the collateral return (risk-free rate return).
- The roll return is effectively the weighted accounting difference (in percentage terms) between the near-term commodity futures contract price and the farther-term commodity futures contract price.
- A commodity swap is a legal contract between two parties calling for the exchange of payments over multiple dates as determined by several reference prices or indexes.
- The most relevant commodity swaps include excess return swaps, total return swaps, basis swaps, and variance/volatility swaps.
- The five primary commodity indexes based on assets are (1) the S&P GSCI; (2) the Bloomberg Commodity Index, formerly the Dow Jones–UBS Commodity Index; (3) the Deutsche Bank Liquid Commodity Index; (4) the Thomson Reuters/CoreCommodity CRB Index; and (5) the Rogers International Commodities Index.
- The key differentiating characteristics of commodity indexes are
  - the breadth and selection methodology of coverage (number of commodities and sectors) included in each index, noting that some commodities have multiple reference contracts,
  - the relative weightings assigned to each component/commodity and the related methodology for how these weights are determined,
  - the methodology and frequency for rolling the individual futures contracts,
  - the methodology and frequency for rebalancing the weights of the individual commodities and sectors, and
  - the governance that determines which commodities are selected.

# PRACTICE PROBLEMS

## The following information relates to questions 1-8

Raffi Musicale is the portfolio manager for a defined benefit pension plan. He meets with Jenny Brown, market strategist with Menlo Bank, to discuss possible investment opportunities. The investment committee for the pension plan has recently approved expanding the plan's permitted asset mix to include alternative asset classes.

Brown proposes the Apex Commodity Fund (Apex Fund) offered by Menlo Bank as a potentially suitable investment for the pension plan. The Apex Fund attempts to produce trading profits by capitalizing on the mispricing between the spot and futures prices of commodities. The fund has access to storage facilities, allowing it to take delivery of commodities when necessary. The Apex Fund's current asset allocation is presented in Exhibit 1.

### Exhibit 1: Apex Fund's Asset Allocation

| Commodity Sector | Allocation (%) |
| --- | --- |
| Energy | 31.9 |
| Livestock | 12.6 |
| Softs | 21.7 |
| Precious metals | 33.8 |

Brown explains that the Apex Fund has had historically low correlations with stocks and bonds, resulting in diversification benefits. Musicale asks Brown, "Can you identify a factor that affects the valuation of financial assets like stocks and bonds but does not affect the valuation of commodities?"

Brown shares selected futures contract data for three markets in which the Apex Fund invests. The futures data are presented in Exhibit 2.

### Exhibit 2: Selected Commodity Futures Data*

| Month | Gold Price | Coffee Price | Gasoline Price |
| --- | --- | --- | --- |
| July | 1,301.2 | 0.9600 | 2.2701 |
| September | 1,301.2 | 0.9795 | 2.2076 |
| December | 1,301.2 | 1.0055 | 2.0307 |

* *Gold:* US$/troy ounce; coffee: US$/pound; gasoline: US$/gallon.

Menlo Bank recently released a report on the coffee market. Brown shares the key conclusion from the report with Musicale: "The coffee market had a global harvest that was greater than expected. Despite the large harvest, coffee futures trading activity is balanced between producers and consumers. This balanced condition is not expected to change over the next year."

Brown shows Musicale the total return of a recent trade executed by the Apex Fund. Brown explains that the Apex Fund took a fully collateralized long futures position in nearby soybean futures contracts at the quoted futures price of 865.0 (US cents/bushel). Three months later, the entire futures position was rolled when the near-term futures price was 877.0 and the farther-term futures price was 883.0. During the three-month period between the time that the initial long position was taken and the rolling of the contract, the collateral earned an annualized rate of 0.60%.

Brown tells Musicale that the pension fund could alternatively gain long exposure to commodities using the swap market. Brown and Musicale analyze the performance of a long position in an S&P GSCI total return swap having monthly resets and a notional amount of $25 million. Selected data on the S&P GSCI are presented in Exhibit 3.

**Exhibit 3: Selected S&P GSCI Data**

| Reference Date | Index Level |
| --- | --- |
| April (swap initiation) | 2,542.35 |
| May | 2,582.23 |
| June | 2,525.21 |

1. The Apex Fund is *most likely* to be characterized as:
   - **A.** a hedger.
   - **B.** a speculator.
   - **C.** an arbitrageur.

2. Which factor would *most likely* affect the supply or demand of all four sectors of the Apex Fund?
   - **A.** Weather
   - **B.** Spoilage
   - **C.** Government actions

3. The *most appropriate* response to Musicale's question regarding the valuation factor is:
   - **A.** storage costs.
   - **B.** transportation costs.
   - **C.** expected future cash flows.

4. Which futures market in Exhibit 2 is in backwardation?
   - **A.** Gold
   - **B.** Coffee
   - **C.** Gasoline

5. Based on the key conclusion from the Menlo Bank coffee market report, the

## Practice Problems

shape of the coffee futures curve in Exhibit 2 is *most consistent* with the:

- A. insurance theory.
- B. theory of storage.
- C. hedging pressure hypothesis.

6. Based on Exhibit 2, which commodity's roll returns will *most likely* be positive?
   - A. Gold
   - B. Coffee
   - C. Gasoline

7. The Apex Fund's three-month total return on the soybean futures trade is *closest* to:
   - A. 0.85%.
   - B. 1.30%.
   - C. 2.22%.

8. Based on Exhibit 3, on the June settlement date, the party that is long the S&P GSCI total return swap will:
   - A. owe a payment of $552,042.23.
   - B. receive a payment of $1,502,621.33.
   - C. receive a payment of $1,971,173.60.

## The following information relates to questions 9-15

Mary McNeil is the corporate treasurer at Farmhouse, which owns and operates several farms and ethanol production plants in the United States. McNeil's primary responsibility is risk management. Katrina Falk, a recently hired junior analyst at Farmhouse, works for McNeil in managing the risk of the firm's commodity price exposures. Farmhouse's risk management policy requires the use of futures to protect revenue from price volatility, regardless of forecasts of future prices, and prohibits risk managers from taking speculative positions.

McNeil meets with Falk to discuss recent developments in two of Farmhouse's commodity markets, grains and livestock. McNeil asks Falk about key characteristics of the two markets that affect revenues and costs. Falk tells McNeil the following:

Statement 1  The life cycle for livestock depends on the product and varies widely by product.

Statement 2  Grains have uniform, well-defined seasons and growth cycles specific to geographic regions.

A material portion of Farmhouse's revenue comes from livestock exports, and a major input cost is the cost of grains imported from outside the United States. Falk and McNeil next discuss three conclusions that Falk reached in an analysis of the grains and livestock markets:

Conclusion 1   Assuming demand for grains remains constant, extreme heat in the regions from which we import our grains will result in a benefit to us in the form of lower grain prices.

Conclusion 2   New tariffs on cattle introduced in our primary export markets will likely result in higher prices for our livestock products in our local market.

Conclusion 3   Major improvements in freezing technology allowing for longer storage will let us better manage the volatility in the prices of our livestock products.

McNeil asks Falk to gather spot and futures price data on live cattle, wheat, and soybeans, which are presented in Exhibit 1. Additionally, she observes that (1) the convenience yield of soybeans exceeds the costs of its direct storage and (2) commodity producers as a group are less interested in hedging in the forward market than commodity consumers are.

**Exhibit 1: Selected Commodity Price Data***

| Market | Live Cattle Price | Wheat Price | Soybeans Price |
| --- | --- | --- | --- |
| Spot | 109 | 407 | 846 |
| Futures | 108 | 407 | 850 |

*\* Live cattle:* US cents per pound; wheat and soybeans: US cents per bushel.

A key input cost for Farmhouse in producing ethanol is natural gas. McNeil uses positions in natural gas (NG) futures contracts to manage the risk of natural gas price volatility. Three months ago, she entered into a long position in natural gas futures at a futures price of $2.93 per million British thermal units (MMBtu). The current price of the same contract is $2.99. Exhibit 2 presents additional data about the three-month futures position.

**Exhibit 2: Selected Information—Natural Gas Futures Three-Month Position***

| | | | Prices | |
| --- | --- | --- | --- | --- |
| Commodity | Total Current $ Exposure | Position | Near-Term Futures (Current Price) | Farther-Term Futures |
| Natural Gas (NG) | 5,860,000 | Long | 2.99 | 3.03 |

*\* NG:* $ per MMBtu; 1 contract = 10,000 MMBtu.

The futures position is fully collateralized earning a 3% rate. McNeil decides to roll forward her current exposure in the natural gas position.

Each month, McNeil reports the performance of the energy futures positions, including details on price returns, roll returns, and collateral returns, to the firm's executive committee. A new committee member is concerned about the negative roll returns on some of the positions. In a memo to McNeil, the committee member asks her to explain why she is not avoiding positions with negative roll

## Practice Problems

returns.

9. With respect to its risk management policy, Farmhouse can be *best* described as:

   A. a trader.

   B. a hedger.

   C. an arbitrageur.

10. Which of Falk's statements regarding the characteristics of the grains and livestock markets is correct?

    A. Only Statement 1

    B. Only Statement 2

    C. Both Statement 1 and Statement 2

11. Which of Falk's conclusions regarding commodity markets is correct?

    A. Conclusion 1

    B. Conclusion 2

    C. Conclusion 3

12. Which commodity market in Exhibit 1 is currently in a state of contango?

    A. Wheat

    B. Soybeans

    C. Live cattle

13. Based on Exhibit 1 and McNeil's two observations, the futures price of soybeans is *most* consistent with the:

    A. insurance theory.

    B. theory of storage.

    C. hedging pressure hypothesis.

14. Based on Exhibit 2, the total return from the long position in natural gas futures is *closest* to:

    A. 1.46%.

    B. 3.71%.

    C. 4.14%.

15. The *most appropriate* response to the new committee member's question is that:

    A. roll returns are negatively correlated with price returns.

    B. such roll returns are the result of futures markets in backwardation.

    C. such positions may outperform other positions that have positive roll returns.

## The following information relates to questions 16-22

Jamal Nabli is a portfolio manager at NextWave Commodities (NWC), a commodity-based hedge fund located in the United States. NWC's strategy uses a fixed-weighting scheme to allocate exposure among 12 commodities, and it is benchmarked against the Thomson Reuters/CoreCommodity CRB Index (TR/CC CRB). Nabli manages the energy and livestock sectors with the help of Sota Yamata, a junior analyst.

Nabli and Yamata meet to discuss a variety of factors that affect commodity values in the two sectors they manage. Yamata tells Nabli the following:

| | |
|---|---|
| Statement 1 | Storage costs are negatively related to futures prices. |
| Statement 2 | In contrast to stocks and bonds, most commodity investments are made by using derivatives. |
| Statement 3 | Commodities generate future cash flows beyond what can be realized through their purchase and sale. |

Nabli and Yamata then discuss potential new investments in the energy sector. They review Brent crude oil futures data, which are presented in Exhibit 1.

**Exhibit 1: Selected Data on Brent Crude Oil Futures**

| Spot Price | Near-Term Futures Price | Longer-Term Futures Price |
|---|---|---|
| 77.56 | 73.64 | 73.59 |

Yamata presents his research related to the energy sector, which has the following conclusions:

- Consumers have been more concerned about prices than producers have.
- Energy is consumed on a real-time basis and requires minimal storage.

After concluding the discussion of the energy sector, Nabli reviews the performance of NWC's long position in lean hog futures contracts. Nabli notes that the portfolio earned a –12% price return on the lean hog futures position last year and a –24% roll return after the contracts were rolled forward. The position was held with collateral equal to 100% of the position at a risk-free rate of 1.2% per year.

Yamata asks Nabli to clarify how the state of the futures market affects roll returns. Nabli responds as follows:

| | |
|---|---|
| Statement 1 | Roll returns are generally negative when a futures market is in contango. |
| Statement 2 | Roll returns are generally positive when a futures market is in backwardation. |

As part of their expansion into new markets, NWC is considering changing its benchmark index. Nabli investigates two indexes as a possible replacement. These indexes both use similar weighting and rebalancing schemes. Index A includes contracts of commodities typically in contango, whereas Index B includes contracts of commodities typically in backwardation. Nabli asks Yamata how the two indexes perform relative to each other in a market that is trending upward. Because of a substantial decline in drilling activity in the North Sea, Nabli believes the price of Brent crude oil will increase more than that of heavy crude oil. The actual price volatility of Brent crude oil has been lower than its expected volatility, and Nabli expects this trend to continue. Nabli also expects the level of the ICE Brent Index to increase from its current level. Nabli and Yamata discuss how to use swaps to take advantage of Nabli's expectations. The possible positions are (1) a basis swap long on Brent crude oil and short on heavy crude oil, (2) a long volatility swap on Brent crude oil, and (3) a short position in an excess return swap that is based on a fixed level (i.e., the current level) of the ICE Brent Index.

16. Which of Nabli's statements regarding the valuation and storage of commodities is correct?

    A. Statement 1

    B. Statement 2

    C. Statement 3

17. Based on Exhibit 1, Yamata should conclude that the:

    A. calendar spread for Brent crude oil is $3.97.

    B. Brent crude oil futures market is in backwardation.

    C. basis for the near-term Brent crude oil futures contract is $0.05 per barrel.

18. Based on Exhibit 1 and Yamata's research on the energy sector, the shape of the futures price curve for Brent crude oil is most consistent with the:

    A. insurance theory.

    B. theory of storage.

    C. hedging pressure hypothesis.

19. The total return (annualized excluding leverage) on the lean hog futures contract is:

    A. −37.2%.

    B. −36.0%.

    C. −34.8%.

20. Which of Nabli's statements about roll returns is correct?

    A. Only Statement 4

    B. Only Statement 5

    C. Both Statement 4 and Statement 5

21. The *best* response to Nabli's question about the relative performance of the two indexes is that Index B is *most likely* to exhibit returns that are:

    A. lower than those of Index A.

    B. the same as those of Index A.

C. higher than those of index A.

22. Given Nabli's expectations for crude oil, the *most appropriate* swap position is the:
   A. basis swap.
   B. volatility swap.
   C. excess return swap.

# SOLUTIONS

1. C is correct. Commodity arbitrage involves an ability to inventory physical commodities and the attempt to capitalize on mispricing between the commodity (along with related storage and financing costs) and the futures price. The Apex Fund has access to storage facilities and uses these facilities in the attempt to capitalize on mispricing opportunities.

2. C is correct. Government actions can affect the supply or demand of all four sectors of the Apex Fund. With respect to energy, environmental mandates imposed by governments have tightened pollution standards, which have led to increasing processing costs that negatively affect demand. The supply of livestock, such as hogs and cattle, is affected by government-permitted use of drugs and growth hormones. Softs, or cash crops, can be affected by government actions, such as the attempt to maintain strategic stockpiles to control domestic prices. The level of demand and relative value of a precious metal, such as gold, is directly linked to government actions associated with managing to inflation targets.

3. C is correct. Expected future cash flows affect the valuation of financial assets, such as stocks and bonds, but do not affect the valuation of commodities. Financial assets (stocks and bonds) are valued based on expected future cash flows. In contrast, the valuation of a commodity is based on a discounted forecast of a future commodity price, which incorporates storage and transportation costs.

4. C is correct. When the near-term (i.e., closer to expiration) futures contract price is higher than the longer-term futures contract price, the futures market for the commodity is in backwardation. Because gasoline is the only one of the three futures markets in Exhibit 2 in which the near-term futures contract price ($2.2701) is higher than the longer-term contract price ($2.0307), the gasoline futures market is the only one in backwardation.

5. B is correct. The theory of storage focuses on the level of commodity inventories and the state of supply and demand. A commodity that is regularly stored should have a higher price in the future (contango) to account for those storage costs. Because coffee is a commodity that requires storage, its higher future price is consistent with the theory of storage.

6. C is correct. Roll returns are generally positive (negative) when the futures market is in backwardation (contango) and zero when the futures market is flat. Because the gasoline market is in backwardation, its roll returns will most likely be positive.

7. A is correct. The total return on the trade represents the sum of three components: price return, roll return, and collateral return.

    Price return = (Current price − Previous price)/Previous price = (877.0 − 865.0)/865.0

    = 1.387%.

    Roll return

    = [(Near-term futures contract closing price − Farther-term futures contract closing price)/Near-term futures contract closing price] × Percentage of the position in the futures contract being rolled.

    Because the entire position is being rolled, the percentage of the position in the futures contract being rolled is equal to 100%. So:

Roll return = [(877.0 − 883.0)/877.0] × 100% = −0.684%.

Collateral return = [3 months/12 months] × 0.60% = 0.15%.

Total return = 1.387% − 0.684% + 0.15% = 0.853%.

8. A is correct. The total return swap involves a monthly cash settlement (reset) based on the performance of the underlying reference asset (S&P GSCI) given a notional amount of $25 million. If the level of the index increases between the two valuation dates (in this case, May and June), the long position (the swap buyer) receives payment. If the level of the index decreases between the two valuation dates, the swap seller receives payment.

    The return on the reference index for the month of June is [(2,525.21 − 2,582.23)/2,582.23], which is equivalent to −2.2082%. Therefore, the swap buyer (long position) must pay the swap seller a cash settlement for the month of June. The June payment calculation is equal to $25,000,000 × −2.2082%, or −$552,042.23.

9. B is correct. Hedgers trade in the futures markets to hedge their exposures related to the commodity, as stated in Farmhouse's risk management policy.

10. C is correct. The life cycle of livestock does vary widely by product. Grains have uniform, well-defined seasons and growth cycles specific to geographic regions. Therefore, both statements are correct.

11. C is correct. Commodity prices are affected by supply and demand, and improvements in freezing technology can improve the firm's ability to store its products for longer periods and manage the volatility of supply and demand. For example, during times of excess supply, a livestock producer, such as Farmhouse, can freeze its products and offer them during better market supply conditions.

12. B is correct. The futures market for soybeans is in a state of contango because the spot price is lower than the futures price.

13. C is correct. In Exhibit 1, the spot price of soybeans is less than the futures price. This observation can be explained only by the hedging pressure hypothesis. According to this hypothesis, hedging pressure occurs when both producers and consumers seek to protect themselves from commodity market price volatility by entering into price hedges to stabilize their projected profits and cash flows. If consumers are more interested in hedging than producers are, the futures price will exceed the spot price.

    In contrast, the insurance theory predicts that the futures price has to be lower than the current spot price as a form of payment or remuneration to the speculator who takes on the price risk and provides price insurance to the commodity seller. Similarly, the theory of storage also predicts that when a commodity's convenience yield is greater than its direct storage costs, the futures price will be lower than the spot price.

14. A is correct. The total return for a fully collateralized position is the sum of the price return, the roll return, and the collateral return:

    Price return = (Current price − Previous price)/Previous price

    = (2.99 − 2.93)/2.93

    = 2.05%.

    Roll return

## Solutions

= (Near-term futures closing price − Farther-term futures closing price)/Near-term futures closing price × Percentage of position in futures contract being rolled

= [(2.99 − 3.03)/2.99] × 100%

= −1.34%.

Collateral return = Annual rate × Period length as a fraction of the year

= 3% × 0.25

= 0.75%.

Therefore, the total return for three months = 2.05% − 1.34% + 0.75% = 1.46%.

15. C is correct. Investment positions are evaluated on the basis of total return, and the roll return is part of the total return. Even though negative roll return negatively affects the total return, this effect could be more than offset by positive price and collateral returns. Therefore, it is possible that positions with negative roll returns outperform positions with positive roll returns, depending on the price and collateral returns.

16. B is correct. The most common way to invest in commodities is via derivatives, and commodities do not generate future cash flows beyond what can be realized through their purchase and sale. Also, storage costs are positively related to futures prices. Physical assets have to be stored, and storage incurs costs (rent, insurance, spoilage, etc.). Therefore, a commodity that is regularly stored should have a higher price in the future to account for those storage costs.

17. B is correct. The Brent crude oil futures market is in a state of backwardation. Commodity futures markets are in a state of backwardation when the spot price is greater than the price of near-term (i.e., nearest-to-expiration) futures contracts and, correspondingly, the price of near-term futures contracts is greater than that of longer-term contracts. The calendar spread is the difference between the near-term futures contract price and the longer-term futures contract price, which is $73.64 − $73.59 = $0.05. The basis for the near-term Brent crude oil futures contract is the difference between the spot price and the near-term futures price: $77.56 − $73.64 = $3.92.

18. B is correct. The Brent crude oil futures market is in a state of backwardation: The spot price is greater than the price of near-term (i.e., nearest-to-expiration) futures contracts. Commodities (in this case, Brent crude oil) are physical assets, not virtual assets, such as stocks and bonds. Physical assets have to be stored, and storage incurs costs (rent, insurance, inspections, spoilage, etc.). According to the theory of storage, a commodity that is consumed along a value chain that allows for just-in-time delivery and use (i.e., minimal inventories and storage) can avoid these costs. Yamata's research concluded that energy is consumed on a real-time basis and requires minimal storage. In this situation, demand dominates supply, and current prices are higher than futures prices (state of backwardation).

19. C is correct. The contract was held for one year, so the price return of −12% is an annualized figure. Additionally, the −24% roll return is also annualized. Nabli's collateral return equals 1.2% per year × 100% initial collateral investment = 1.2%. Therefore, the total return (annualized) is calculated as follows:

Total return = Price return + Roll return + Collateral return.

Total return = −12% + (−24%) + 1.2% = −34.8%.

20. C is correct. Roll returns are generally negative (positive) when the futures market is in contango (backwardation) and zero when the futures market is flat.

21. C is correct. Index B is likely to have higher performance than Index A in a market that is trending upward. Indexes that (perhaps inadvertently) contain contracts that more commonly trade in backwardation may improve forward-looking performance because this generates a positive roll return. Similarly, indexes that contain contracts that more commonly trade in contango may hurt performance for the same reason (i.e., negative roll return).

22. A is correct. Nabli expects the price of Brent crude oil to increase more than that of heavy crude oil, and Nabli can take advantage of this prediction by entering into a basis swap that is long Brent crude oil and short heavy crude oil. Nabli should take a short (not long) position in a volatility swap to take advantage of his prediction that Brent crude oil's price volatility will be lower than its expected volatility. Nabli should take a long (not short) position in an excess return swap to take advantage of his expectation that the level of the ICE Brent Index will increase faster than leading oil benchmarks.

# Portfolio Management

# LEARNING MODULE 1

# Exchange-Traded Funds: Mechanics and Applications

by Joanne M. Hill, PhD, and Dave Nadig.

*Joanne M. Hill, PhD (USA). Dave Nadig is CIO and Director of Research at ETFTrends.com and etfdb.com (USA).*

| LEARNING OUTCOMES | |
|---|---|
| Mastery | The candidate should be able to: |
| ☐ | explain the creation/redemption process of ETFs and the function of authorized participants |
| ☐ | describe how ETFs are traded in secondary markets |
| ☐ | describe sources of tracking error for ETFs |
| ☐ | describe factors affecting ETF bid–ask spreads |
| ☐ | describe sources of ETF premiums and discounts to NAV |
| ☐ | describe costs of owning an ETF |
| ☐ | describe types of ETF risk |
| ☐ | identify and describe portfolio uses of ETFs |

## INTRODUCTION

Exchange-traded funds (ETFs) have grown rapidly since their invention in the early 1990s, in large part because of their low associated cost, exchange access, holdings transparency, and range of asset classes available. Growth in ETFs has also been driven by the increased use of index-based investing. ETF investors need to understand how these products work and trade and how to choose from the numerous options available. Although many ETFs are organized under the same regulation as mutual fund products, there are important differences related to trading and tax efficiency. ETFs have features that can make them more tax efficient than traditional mutual funds, and not all ETFs are organized like mutual funds. ETFs can be based on derivative strategies, use leverage and shorting, and be offered in alternate structures, such as exchange-traded notes (ETNs), which have their own unique risks.

Understanding how ETF shares are created and redeemed is key to understanding how these products can add value in a portfolio. Because so many ETFs track indexes, understanding their index tracking or tracking error is also critical. Investors should also understand how to assess an ETF's trading costs, including differences between the ETF's market price and the fair value of its portfolio holdings.

We start with a discussion of the primary and secondary markets for ETFs, including the creation/redemption process, before moving on to important investor considerations, such as costs and risks. We then explain how ETFs are use in strategic, tactical, and portfolio efficiency applications.

## 2. ETF MECHANICS

☐ explain the creation/redemption process of ETFs and the function of authorized participants

☐ describe how ETFs are traded in secondary markets

Exchange-traded funds function differently from mutual funds because of their structure, with the key difference in an ETF's method of share creation and redemption. Mutual fund shares must be purchased or sold at the end of the day from the fund manager (or via a broker) at the closing net asset value (NAV) of the fund's holdings, in a cash-for-shares or shares-for-cash swap. In contrast, an ETF trades intraday, or during the trading day, just like a stock. ETF shares are created or redeemed in kind, in a shares-for-shares swap.

ETFs are intrinsically linked to the creation/redemption process. Creation/redemption enables ETFs to operate at lower cost and with greater tax efficiency than mutual funds and generally keeps ETF prices in line with their NAVs. Unlike stocks, which come to market via an initial public offering of fixed size, ETFs can be created or redeemed continuously. ETF transactions take place in two interrelated markets. Understanding how this mechanism works is key to understanding both the benefits and potential risks of ETFs.

The primary market for ETF trading is that which exists on an over-the-counter (OTC) basis between **authorized participants** (APs), a special group of institutional investors, and the ETF issuer, or sponsor. This process is referred to as **creation/redemption**. These primary market transactions are the only way that shares of the ETF can be created or redeemed. The "trade" in this market is in kind: A pre-specified basket of securities (which can include cash) is exchanged for a certain number of shares in the ETF.

ETF shares trade in the secondary market on exchanges. For investors, exchange trading is the only way to buy or sell ETFs. Like stocks, ETFs are bought and sold on exchanges through a brokerage account. This secondary market trading is perhaps the most novel feature of ETFs.

In-kind creation/redemption creates the unique benefits ETFs offer—as well as some of their risks. Here we explain ETFs' unique creation/redemption mechanism, the role of APs, and how the creation/redemption mechanism affects ETF design. ETF trading and settlement on primary and secondary markets is also covered.

## The Creation/Redemption Process

The best way to understand the creation/redemption process is to step through the process from an investor's perspective.

Imagine you're an investor and you want to invest in an ETF. The process is simple: You place a buy order in your brokerage account the same way you would place an order to buy any publicly listed equity security, and your broker submits that order to the public market to find a willing seller: another investor or a market maker (i.e., a broker/dealer who stands ready to take the opposite side of the transaction). The order is executed, and you receive shares of the ETF in your brokerage account just as if you transacted in a stock.

At this point, the ETF manager (also referred to as the ETF issuer or sponsor) is not involved in the transaction. The ETF issuer does not know that you have bought these shares, nor does it receive an inflow of money to invest. Shares simply transfer in the open market, the secondary market for ETF shares, from one investor (the seller) to another (the buyer) and go through a settlement process based on the local exchange where the transaction took place. The process sounds simple, but if you can only buy ETF shares from another investor, where do the shares come from initially? How does money get invested into the fund?

The only investors who can create or redeem new shares of an ETF are a special group of institutional investors called *authorized participants*. APs are large broker/dealers, often market makers, who are authorized by the ETF issuer to participate in the creation/redemption process. The AP creates new ETF shares by transacting in kind with the ETF issuer. This in-kind swap happens off the exchange, in the primary market for the ETF, where APs transfer securities to (for creations) or receive securities from (for redemptions) the ETF issuer, in exchange for ETF shares. This is a prescribed, structured transaction with its own set of rules.

Each business day, the ETF manager publishes a list of required in-kind securities for each ETF. For instance, an S&P 500 Index ETF will typically list the index securities in quantities that reflect the index weighting. The list of securities specific to each ETF and disclosed publicly each day is called the **creation basket**. This basket also serves as the portfolio for determining the intrinsic net asset value of the ETF based on prices during the trading day.

To create new shares, an AP acquires the securities in the creation basket in the specified share amounts (generally by transacting in the public markets or using securities the AP happens to have in inventory). The AP then delivers this basket of securities to the ETF manager in exchange for an equal value in ETF shares. This exchange of shares happens after markets are closed through the settlement process. Importantly, the pricing of both the ETF and the basket is of minimal concern in this exchange: If the issuer receives 100 shares of a certain stock as part of the creation basket, the price the AP might have paid to acquire that stock or what its price happens to be at the end of the day is not relevant to the exchange taking place. Because it is an in-kind transaction, all that matters is that 100 shares of the required stock move from the AP's account to the ETF's account. Similarly, when the issuer delivers ETF shares to an AP, the ETF's closing NAV is not relevant.

These transactions between the AP and the ETF manager are done in large blocks called **creation units**, usually but not always equal to 50,000 shares of the ETF. This in-kind exchange involves the basket of underlying securities in exchange for a number of ETF shares of equal value.

The process also works in reverse: If the AP has a block of ETF shares it no longer wants (usually because it bought them from other market participants), the AP presents these shares for redemption to the ETF manager and receives in return the basket of underlying securities, which the AP can then sell in the market if it chooses. This basket often has the same security composition as the creation basket, but it may be different if the ETF portfolio manager is trying to sell particular securities for tax, compliance, or investment reasons. The basket of securities the AP receives when it redeems the ETF shares is called the **redemption basket**.

Although the actual process of exchanging baskets and blocks of ETF shares happens after the markets are closed, the AP is able to execute ETF trades throughout the trading day because the AP knows the security composition of the basket needed for ETF share creation or redemption, because of the fund's daily holdings disclosure to APs. If, during the course of the trading day, the AP wants to sell 50,000 shares of an ETF to investors in the secondary market, the AP can do so while simultaneously buying the securities in the creation basket. If the ETF and the securities in the creation basket are fairly priced, the AP faces no economic exposure in this transaction, because the value of the ETF shares sold and the value of the creation basket purchased are identical.

Why would APs engage in these transactions? Because there's a financial incentive to do so. The creation/redemption mechanism is key to keeping the price of an ETF in a tight range around the NAV of the portfolio of securities it holds, and it rewards the AP for this activity.

When the value of the security basket is different from the value of the corresponding ETF shares it represents, a potential arbitrage opportunity exists for APs to step in and transact in the ETF market. If the current per-share market value of the basket of underlying securities is greater than the quoted price of the ETF shares, the AP can simultaneously sell (or short) the basket of securities and buy ETF shares, to make a profit. In this situation, where the ETF share is undervalued, the ETF is said to be trading at a discount. If shares of the ETF are quoted at a higher price than the per-share market value of the basket of securities, the ETF is trading at a premium, and the AP can make a profit by simultaneously selling the ETF shares in the market and buying the basket of securities.

Because prices of the ETF and the basket securities are continuously changing on the basis of market conditions, APs monitor both for discrepancies, looking for opportunities to make arbitrage profits. The factors that drive the width of the ETF's bid–ask spread and trading range around intraday NAV include the cost of arbitrage (buying the securities and selling the ETF) and a risk premium to compensate for volatility and liquidity risk (ongoing volume in the securities and the ETF).

The *arbitrage gap*—the price(s) at which it makes sense for ETF market makers to step in and create or redeem shares—vary with the liquidity of the underlying securities and a variety of related costs; in some ETFs, the gap can be as small as the minimum tick size in the local market (e.g., ~$0.01 in the US markets), whereas for other ETFs with underlying securities that are hard to trade (e.g., high-yield bonds), the arbitrage gap can be more than 1% wide. For any ETF, however, the gap creates a band or range around its fair value inside which the ETF will trade. In other words, arbitrage keeps the ETF trading at or near its fair value.

### ETF share creation.

Let us examine how this works in practice. In the scenario shown in Exhibit 1, the ETF is trading in the market at $25.10. The fair value of the ETF based on its underlying securities, however, is only $25.00. So, an AP will step in to transact and buy the basket of securities (at ETF fair value of $25.00) and simultaneously sell ETF shares on the open market for $25.10, realizing the $0.10 per share difference. (The AP may choose to create additional ETF shares by exchanging the basket securities for ETF shares with the fund's issuer).

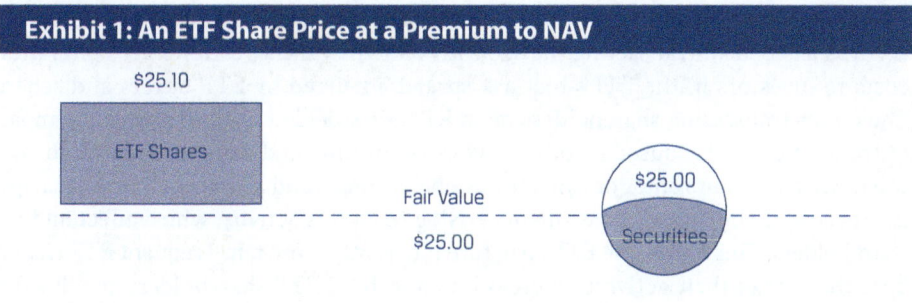

**Exhibit 1: An ETF Share Price at a Premium to NAV**

This action puts downward pressure on the ETF price because the AP is selling shares out into the market and puts upward pressure on the prices of the underlying securities because the AP went out into the market and bought the underlying shares. APs will repeat this process until no further arbitrage opportunity exists.

*ETF share redemption*

As shown in Exhibit 2, the price of the ETF is $24.90. The fair value of the underlying stocks is $25.00. Here, the AP market maker steps in and purchases ETF shares on the open market while simultaneously selling the stocks on the exchange, realizing the $0.10 per share price difference. Once again, if the share price continues to be at a discount, the AP will continue this process until no further arbitrage opportunity exists. (The AP may choose to redeem ETF shares by exchanging them for the basket securities with the fund's issuer).

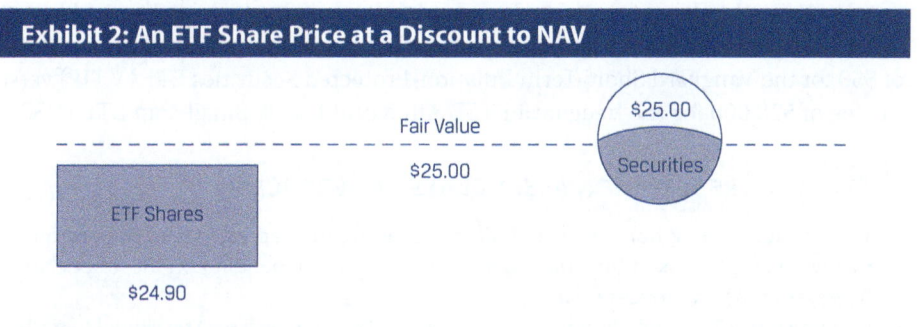

**Exhibit 2: An ETF Share Price at a Discount to NAV**

These profit-making scenarios do not include the costs that the APs incur related to ETF trading or any fees the issuer may charge for creating or redeeming shares. The AP generally pays all trading costs associated with buying or selling the securities in the baskets or the ETF shares and pays an additional fee to the ETF provider to cover processing fees associated with creation/redemption activities. APs may also have settlement costs, taxes, or other expenses based on their local markets and the markets for the underlying securities of the ETF.

The scenarios also do not account for risks in trading the basket of securities. If the underlying securities are difficult to access contemporaneously (for instance, if a US-listed ETF holds Japanese securities), then the AP will have to wait before completing one half of the transaction (e.g., selling the ETF shares but waiting until the Japanese market opens to buy the basket securities). These timing differences create uncertainty, which will generally cause the AP to wait for a wider arbitrage gap before stepping in. Similarly, if the basket securities are illiquid (such as high-yield bonds), the AP may need additional time to buy or sell the holdings. In both cases, the AP bears the market risk of the basket transaction.

A significant advantage of the ETF creation/redemption process is that the AP absorbs all costs of transacting the securities for the fund's portfolio. APs pass these costs to investors in the ETF's bid–ask spread, incurred by ETF buyers and sellers. Thus, non-transacting shareholders of an ETF are shielded from the negative impact of transaction costs caused by other investors entering and exiting the fund. In contrast, when investors enter or exit a traditional mutual fund, the mutual fund manager incurs costs to buy or sell investments arising from this activity, which affect all fund shareholders. This makes the ETF structure inherently more fair: Frequent ETF traders bear the cost of their activity, whereas buy-and-hold ETF shareholders are shielded from those costs.

Additionally, because creation and redemption happen in kind, they allow the ETF's portfolio managers to manage the cost basis of their holdings by selecting low-basis holdings for redemptions, leading to greater tax efficiency. Put simply, when an issuer is presented with a redemption request from an AP, the issuer can select which tax lots of the underlying securities to deliver. In addition, issuers may choose to publish customized redemption baskets, which allows them to target specific low-basis securities for removal from the portfolio. By delivering out shares that were originally acquired at low costs, the issuer can continuously raise the average acquired cost (or cost basis) of each position, thereby minimizing the position's unrealized gains.

The ETF issuer has the ability to determine how the process works for a fund. If the issuer requires that a creation basket be 200,000 shares instead of 50,000 shares, the AP will have less incentive to step in to arbitrage when net new demand is lower than 200,000 shares per day. Basket sizes range from 10,000 shares to 600,000 shares. If the ETF holds highly illiquid securities, the issuer can alter the basket that APs must deliver, thereby lowering the costs of creation. In the most extreme case, the fund may allow for the creation of ETF shares in exchange for cash. Issuers can also charge minimal or large fees for creation and redemption, which affect an AP's profit consideration and transactions, to keep prices in line with fair value. Consider the fee of $50 for the Vanguard Short-Term Inflation-Protected Securities ETF (VTIP) versus the fee of $28,000 for the Vanguard FTSE All-World Ex-US Small-Cap ETF (VSS).

> **CREATION/REDEMPTION ASSET CLASS DIFFERENCES**
>
> The creation/redemption mechanism described is broadly representative of how most ETFs work, regardless of their particular legal structure. Depending on the asset class, however, some differences exist.
>
> Fixed-income ETFs generally hold large amounts of bonds, which may be illiquid to trade (for example, a high-yield municipal bond ETF holds securities that might trade only every few days). Because of this, ETF issuers may choose not to do in-kind creations and redemptions but instead accept equivalent cash value. This makes the process easier for APs, encouraging greater ETF activity, but does result in trading costs and tax impact for the ETF. ETF issuers must balance those costs against the benefit of having the AP participate more actively in the market, keeping spreads tight and the price of the ETF close to fair value.
>
> Similarly, many leveraged and inverse ETFs and commodity ETFs may use cash creation/redemption because it makes managing their underlying swap positions easier. Because swaps are generally negotiated OTC transactions, it would be difficult to have APs participate in increasing or decreasing those swap positions.

## Trading and Settlement

There is much confusion in the investor community regarding the underlying mechanics of ETF trading and settlement. Whether this confusion relates to shorting, how shares are created/redeemed or settled, or how they trade, ETFs are potentially confusing to many investors. From the perspective of an investor buying on the open market, ETFs go through the same settlement and clearing process as other listed stocks. This section explains that process as it applies in two regions.

***US settlement: National Security Clearing Corporation and Depository Trust Company.***

In the United States, all trades that have been entered into on a given business day are submitted at the end of the day to the National Security Clearing Corporation (NSCC). As long as both parties of a transaction agree that Party 1 sold to Party 2 $N$ shares of XYZ stock, the NSCC becomes the guarantor of that transaction—the entity that ensures all parties are immunized against the financial impact of any operational problems—on the evening of the trade, and the trade is considered "cleared." After this point, the buyer is guaranteed beneficial ownership in the stock (or ETF) as of the time the trade was marked "executed," even if something (e.g., bankruptcy) happens to the seller before the trade is settled.

The Depository Trust Company (DTC), of which the NSCC is a subsidiary, holds the book of accounts—the actual list of security holders and ownership. This information is aggregated at the member firm level, rather than at the individual investor level. For instance, the DTC keeps track of how many shares of Microsoft are currently held by J.P. Morgan or Charles Schwab, but Charles Schwab is responsible for keeping track of which of its customers own how many shares.

After each trade is cleared, the DTC then adds up the total of all trades in a process of continuous net settlement. For example, suppose at the end of a trading day the following is true:

- E*TRADE owes Schwab 1,000 shares of SPY.
- Schwab owes Bank of America Merrill Lynch 1,000 shares of SPY.

Then, from the DTC's perspective, Schwab is "whole": It both is owed and owes 1,000 shares of SPY. To settle the day's transactions, E*TRADE's account will be debited the 1,000 shares of SPY and Bank of America Merrill Lynch will be credited 1,000 shares.

The NSCC has two days to complete this process and have each firm review its records and correct any discrepancies. We refer to this two-day period as T+2 (trade date + 2 days). This T+2 settlement process works for the vast majority of ETF transactions.

Market makers receive special treatment on settlement requirements. Because the role of market makers is to make a continuous market in a given security by standing ready to buy or sell the security on the basis of demand/supply imbalances, they are more likely to end up truly short at the end of a given day. Because of the time required to create or borrow ETF shares, market makers are given up to six days to settle their accounts.

***European trading and settlement.***

In Europe, the majority of ETF owners are institutional investors. Additionally, the market is fragmented across multiple exchanges, jurisdictions, and clearinghouses. This fragmentation results in the use of many different trading strategies by investors in both the primary and secondary markets for ETFs. Fundamentally, trading works the same as in the United States: An investor purchases shares in the secondary market from a market maker or other counterparty. APs use the creation/redemption mechanism, which helps keep the ETF share price in line with its fair value.

The majority of trading happens in negotiated OTC trades between large institutions, and although those trades are reported, they do not appear as "live" or published bids and asks on the public markets prior to their execution. Most ETFs in Europe are also cross-listed on multiple exchanges and may have different share classes available that vary in their treatment of distributions or currency hedging. The fragmented

European settlement process means that trades are cleared to one of 29 central securities depositories (or CSDs). This has no direct impact on investors other than the inherent complexity of such a system, which may result in wider spreads and higher local market trading costs.

## 3. UNDERSTANDING ETFS

- [ ] describe sources of tracking error for ETFs
- [ ] describe factors affecting ETF bid–ask spreads
- [ ] describe sources of ETF premiums and discounts to NAV
- [ ] describe costs of owning an ETF

Among the most important questions an investor can ask about an ETF is, Does the fund deliver on its promise? The best-managed ETFs charge low and predictable investment costs, closely track the indexes on which they are based, and provide investors with the lowest possible tax exposure for the investment objective. Additionally, these funds provide complete, accurate information in their prospectuses and marketing materials and explain the fund's structure, composition, performance, and risks. To best understand an ETF's ability to meet expectations, its expense ratio, index tracking, tax treatment, and potential costs and risks should be considered.

### Expense Ratios

Fund expense ratios are often one of the first factors investors look at when evaluating ETFs. ETFs generally charge lower fees than mutual funds, in part because ETF providers do not have to keep track of individual investor accounts, since ETF shares are held by and transacted through brokerage firms. Nor do ETF issuers bear the costs of communicating directly with individual investors. In addition, index-based portfolio management, used by most ETFs, does not require the security and macroeconomic research carried out by active managers, which increases fund operating costs.

The actual costs to manage an ETF vary, depending on portfolio complexity (number of securities held, frequency of rebalancing or strategy implementation, difficulty in maintaining portfolio exposures), issuer size (economies of scale apply), and the competitive landscape.

ETF expense ratios have been one of the most visible areas of competitive differentiation for issuers, which has led to an overall decline in fees. Exhibit 3 shows average US-domiciled ETF expense ratios by asset class at the end of 2018.

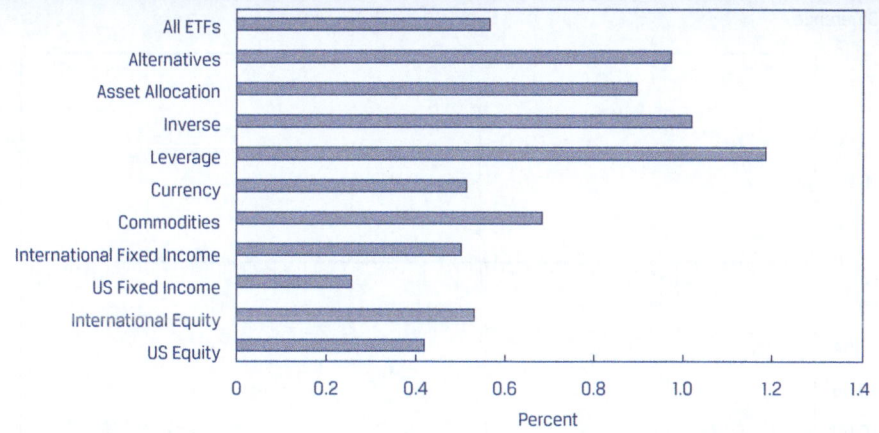

**Exhibit 3: Average US-Domiciled ETF Expense Ratios by Asset Class at the End of 2018**

*Sources*: ETF.com and FactSet, as of 31 December 2018.

Because the average numbers include complex and expensive funds, they dramatically overstate the cost of accessing the most common ETF investment strategies and indexes.

As of the end of 2018, expense ratios for broad-based, capitalization-weighted indexes were as low as 0.03% for US equities, 0.11% for emerging market equities, and 0.04% for US bonds.

## Index Tracking/Tracking Error

Even though an ETF's expense ratio is useful, it does not fully reflect the cost of holding an ETF. To understand how well an ETF delivers on its mandate, it is critical to assess the ETF's ability to track its underlying index.

For index-tracking ETFs, which represented 98% of the US ETF market as measured by assets under management (AUM) as of December 2018, ETF managers attempt to deliver performance that tracks the fund's benchmark as closely as possible (after subtracting fees). This can be measured by comparing ETF performance with index returns. The comparison can be done using daily or periodic returns but should always include both a central tendency, such as mean or median, and an expression of variability, such as standard deviation or range.

### Daily differences.

Index tracking is often evaluated using the one-day difference in returns between the fund, as measured by its NAV, and its index. Exhibit 4 shows the daily tracking difference between the iShares MSCI Emerging Markets ETF (EEM) and its underlying index, the MSCI Emerging Markets Index (EMI), for a one-year period. EMI is a multicurrency international index containing hundreds of illiquid securities in more than 20 emerging markets. The index represents large- and mid-cap stocks in each of these markets. At the end of November 2018, EEM held approximately 900 of the 1,150 constituents in EMI.

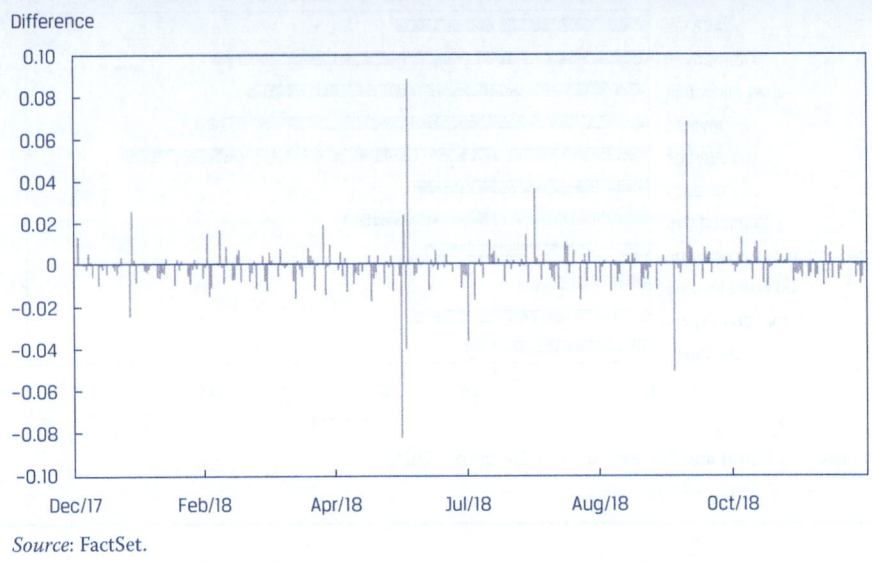

Exhibit 4: EEM Daily Tracking Difference Relative to EMI, One-Year Period Ending 30 November 2018

Source: FactSet.

**Periodic tracking.**

Tracking error is defined as the standard deviation of differences in daily performance between the index and the fund tracking the index, and a reported tracking error number is typically for a 12-month period. Over the period shown, EEM's standard deviation of daily performance differences to its index was 0.012%.

But importantly, tracking error does not reveal the extent to which the fund is under- or overperforming its index or anything about the distribution of errors. Daily tracking error could be concentrated over a few days or more consistently experienced. Therefore, tracking error should be assessed with the mean or median values.

An alternative approach is to look at tracking differences calculated over a longer holding period. A series of rolling holding periods can be used to represent both central tendencies and variability. This approach allows investors to see the cumulative effect of portfolio management and expenses over an extended period. Exhibit 5 shows the 12-month rolling return (or cumulative annual) tracking difference between EEM and its index.

**Exhibit 5: EEM 12-Month Rolling Tracking Difference Relative to EMI, One-Year Periods Ending 30 November 2018**

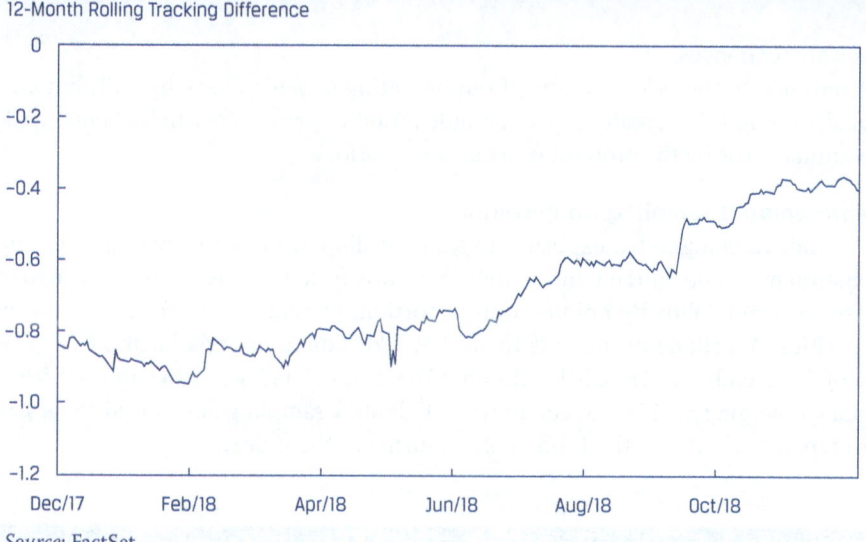

*Source*: FactSet.

One benefit of the rolling annual analysis is that it allows for comparison with other annual metrics, such as the fund's expense ratio. All else equal, one would normally expect an index fund to underperform its benchmark on an annual basis by the amount of its expense ratio. In Exhibit 5, EEM's median tracking difference of 0.79% exceeded its 0.69% expense ratio by 0.10%. Notably, the range of EEM's annual tracking difference showed some variability, with underperformance as low as 0.38% and as high as 0.95%.

**Sources of tracking error.**
Numerous factors can account for differences between an ETF's expected and actual performance and the range of results with respect to its index. Because of this, funds tracking the same underlying index can have very different index tracking results. Sources of benchmark tracking error include the following:

- Fees and expenses—Index calculation generally assumes that trading is frictionless and occurs at the closing price. A fund's operating fees and expenses reduce the fund's return relative to the index.

- Representative sampling/optimization—Rather than fully replicate the index, funds may hold only a subset of index securities to track the benchmark index.

- Depositary receipts and other ETFs—Funds may hold securities that are different from those in the index, such as American depositary receipts (ADRs), global depositary receipts (GDRs), and other ETFs.

- Index changes—Funds may trade index changes at times and prices that are different from those of the benchmark tracked.

- Fund accounting practices—Fund accounting practices may differ from the index calculation methodology—for example, valuation practices for foreign exchange and fixed income.

- Regulatory and tax requirements—Funds may be subject to regulatory and tax requirements that are different from those assumed in index methodology, such as with foreign dividend withholding.

- Asset manager operations—ETF issuers may attempt to offset costs through security lending and foreign dividend recapture. These act as "negative" costs, which enhance fund performance relative to the index.

**Fees and expenses.**

As outlined in the prior sections, fund operating expenses vary by ETF, but all else equal, one would normally expect an index fund to underperform its benchmark on an annual basis by the amount of its expense ratio.

**Representative sampling/optimization.**

For funds tracking index exposure to small or illiquid markets, owning every index constituent can be difficult and costly. Therefore, fund managers may choose to optimize their portfolios by holding only a portion, or representative sample, of index securities. A striking example is the SPDR S&P Emerging Asia Pacific ETF (GMF). As of 7 December 2018, GMF held only 763 of the 2,342 securities in the S&P Asia Pacific Emerging BMI Index. As shown in Exhibit 6, sampling has caused some sizable discrepancies between the fund's daily return and the index.

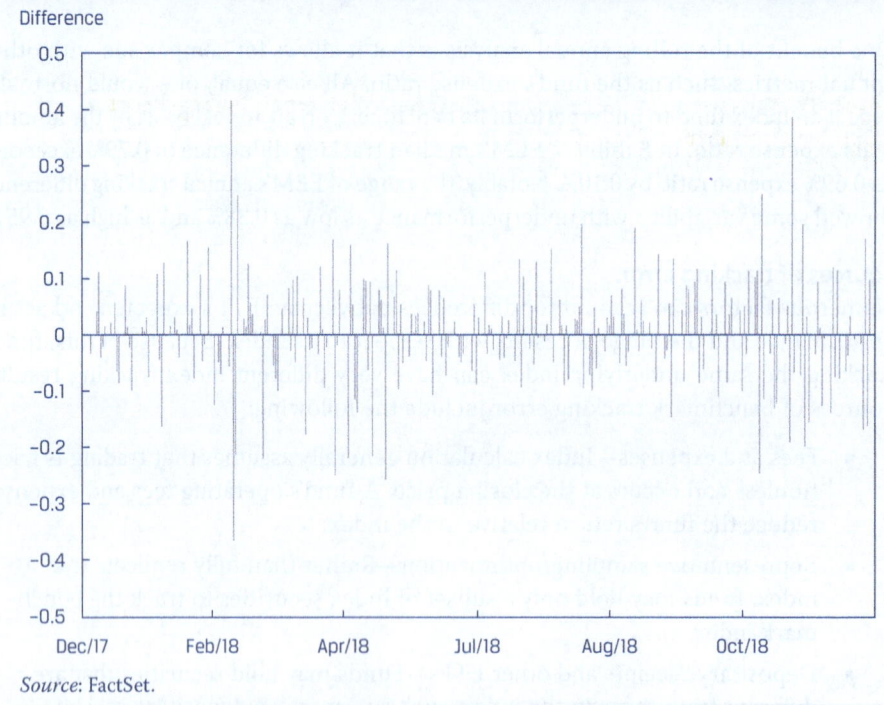

**Exhibit 6: GMF Daily Tracking Difference Relative to the S&P Asia Pacific Emerging BMI Index, One-Year Period Ending 30 November 2018**

Source: FactSet.

Sampling, or optimization, can affect long-term tracking in two ways. First, it can make the median value unpredictive of future median values, especially if market regimes shift. Second, it dramatically expands the range of results. Exhibit 7 and the table below illustrate these effects, using trailing 12-month (TTM) rolling comparisons. Exhibit 7 contrasts EEM's median trailing 12-month tracking difference with GMF's more variable results.

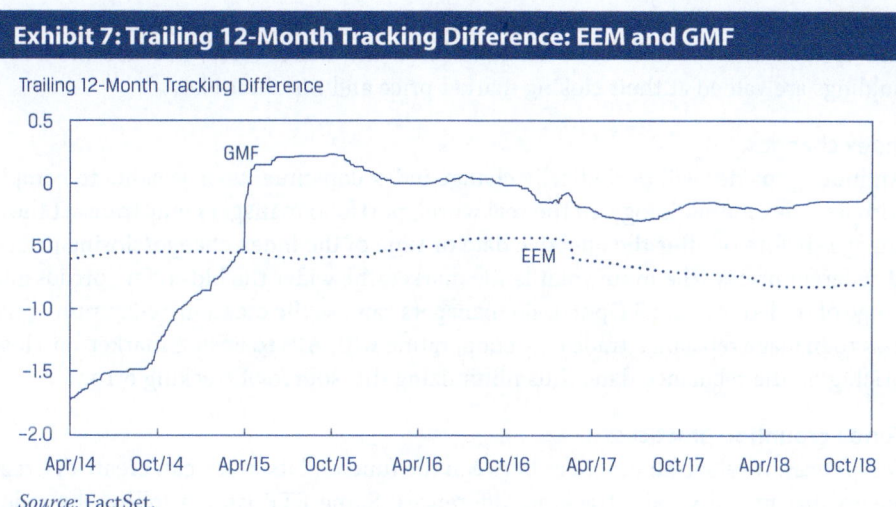

Exhibit 7: Trailing 12-Month Tracking Difference: EEM and GMF

*Source*: FactSet.

A high level of optimization causes GMF's portfolio to underperform in certain market regimes and outperform in others. Looking at the differences between GMF and its underlying index explains why. As of 30 November 2018, GMF's median constituent market cap was $2.8 billion, whereas the S&P Asia Pacific Emerging BMI's was $0.695 billion, indicating that by holding approximately one-third of index constituents, GMF's portfolio omits many of the index's mid-caps and small-caps. Therefore, GMF will likely underperform the index during times when emerging market mid-caps and small-caps outperform emerging market large-caps, and vice versa.

As illustrated in the following table, GMF's tracking range—the spread between its maximum and minimum trailing 12-month tracking difference—is nearly 4 times that of EEM. A higher level of optimization within GMF causes it to have a wider range of tracking difference relative to its index.

| EEM and GMF Tracking Range, One Year Ending 30 November 2018 | | |
| --- | --- | --- |
|  | EEM | GMF |
| Maximum TTM | −0.38% | 1.14% |
| Minimum TTM | −0.95% | −0.81% |
| Range | 0.57% | 1.95% |

*Source:* FactSet.

Representative sampling/optimization, therefore, enhances or detracts from fund returns relative to the index depending on whether ETF portfolio holdings outperform or underperform those in the index. Compared with a full replication approach, representative sampling/optimization introduces greater potential for tracking error.

**Depositary receipts and ETFs.**
When local market shares are illiquid, ETF portfolio managers may choose to hold depositary receipts instead of local constituent shares. Although the economic exposure is equivalent, exchange trading hours for these securities differ. Differences in trading hours and security prices create discrepancies between portfolio and index

values. Similarly, ETF issuers may choose to hold ETFs as underlying holdings. This also creates discrepancies between fund NAV and index value, because the ETFs' holdings are valued at their closing market price and not their NAV.

### Index changes.

An index provider will periodically change index constituents or weights to comply with its index methodology. In the real world, portfolio managers may transact these changes before or after the effective date or time of the index change/closing prices, at different prices. The more volatile the market, the wider the bid–offer spreads and range of traded prices. ETF portfolio managers can use the creation/redemption process to manage rebalance trades, by cooperating with APs to ensure market-on-close pricing on the rebalance date, thus minimizing this source of tracking error.

### Fund accounting practices.

Differences in valuation practices between the fund and its index can create discrepancies that magnify daily tracking differences. Some ETF issuers follow the index industry's convention of establishing (striking) currency valuations using WM/Reuters rates, which are set at 4:00 p.m. GMT (11:00 a.m. EST), whereas others conform to established mutual fund industry practices of striking currency valuations at the close of ETF trading. In the United States, equity markets close at 4:00 p.m. ET. Many fixed-income ETF portfolios value bond positions at the time of the equity market close, in keeping with ETF industry custom. However, fixed-income indexes often follow the bond market's practice of valuing bonds at an earlier time. These practices may create valuation discrepancies between the ETF's NAV and the index value, particularly in volatile segments of the bond market, such as long-dated maturities. Valuation discrepancies can also occur for ETFs holding futures, foreign securities, physical metals, and currencies held in specie.

### Regulatory and tax requirements.

Regulatory and tax requirements may cause a fund to mis-track its index. For example, non-domestic holders of a nation's securities owe tax on distributions received from securities of companies domiciled in that nation. The tax withholding rate charged is determined by treaty and investor domicile. Index providers who offer a "net" return series adjust the dividends received to account for the tax charged, usually from the point of view of US-domiciled investors. Index providers may use rates different from those experienced by the ETF, however, which can create return differences between the ETF and its index. For many years, Brazil imposed a tax on foreign investments coming into the country. Although this tax did not affect the closing prices of the local stocks and, therefore, was not reflected in index calculation methodology, non-local ETFs domiciled outside Brazil paid this tax whenever they acquired Brazilian stocks. This caused fund underperformance relative to the index.

### Asset manager operations.

ETF issuers may engage in security lending or foreign dividend recapture to generate additional income to offset fund expenses. These can be considered "negative" costs. Many ETFs (and mutual funds) lend a portion of their portfolio holdings to short sellers. In exchange, the ETF receives a fee and earns interest on the collateral posted by the borrower (generally, overnight fixed-income securities), which creates income for the portfolio. Because the index calculation does not account for securities-lending income, it is a source of tracking error. Asset managers may work with foreign governments to minimize tax paid on distributions received.

## Tax Issues

Two kinds of tax-based evaluations must be made for all ETFs: First, the investor must consider the likelihood of an ETF distributing capital gains to shareholders. Second, the investor must consider what happens when the investor sells the ETF. These two actions are distinct; the tax efficiency of a fund regarding its capital gains distributions has no relation to its tax efficiency at the time of investor sale.

### Capital Gains Distributions

The issue of capital gains distributions affects all investors in taxable accounts. In general, funds must distribute any capital gains realized during the year. Funds typically make these distributions at year-end, although they may make them quarterly or on another periodic schedule.

ETFs are said to be "tax fair" and "tax efficient" because they have certain advantages over traditional mutual funds regarding capital gains distributions. On average, they distribute less in capital gains than competing mutual funds for two primary reasons.

### Tax fairness.

In a traditional mutual fund, when an investor sells, the fund must (with a few exceptions) sell portfolio securities to raise cash to pay the investor. Any securities sold at a profit incur a capital gains charge, which is distributed to remaining shareholders. Put another way, in a traditional mutual fund, shareholders may have to pay tax liabilities triggered by other shareholders redeeming out of the fund.

In contrast, an investor sells ETF shares to another investor in the secondary market. The ETF manager typically does not know that the sale is occurring and does not need to alter the portfolio to accommodate this transaction. Thus, the selling activities of individual investors in the secondary market do not require the fund to trade out of its underlying positions. If an AP redeems ETF shares, this redemption occurs in kind. In markets where redemptions in kind are allowed, this is not a taxable event. Thus, redemptions do not trigger capital gain realizations. This aspect is why ETFs are considered "tax fair": The actions of investors selling shares of the fund do not influence the tax liabilities for remaining fund shareholders.

### Tax efficiency.

The redemption process allows portfolio managers to manage the fund's tax liability. When an authorized participant submits shares of an ETF for redemption, the ETF manager can choose which underlying share lots to deliver in the redemption basket. By choosing shares with the largest unrealized capital gains—that is, those acquired at the lowest cost basis—ETF managers can use the in-kind redemption process to reduce potential capital gains in the fund. Tax lot management allows portfolio managers to limit the unrealized gains in a portfolio.

### Other Distributions

Other events, such as security dividend distributions, can trigger tax liabilities for investors but the treatment varies by region, so investors must ensure they understand the tax treatment specific to each fund's domicile, legal structure, and portfolio type.

### Taxes on Sale

In most jurisdictions, ETFs are taxed according to their underlying holdings. For example, in the United States, an ETF holding equities or bonds will itself be subject to the same capital gain, dividend, and return-of-capital tax rules that apply to its underlying stock or bond holdings. There can be nuances in individual tax jurisdictions, however, that require investor analysis. For example, in the United States, exchange-traded notes tracking commodity indexes are treated differently from exchange-traded funds holding commodity futures contracts, creating a preferential tax treatment. A thorough analysis of ETF efficiency should take into account the ETF structure, the local market's taxation regime, and the individual tax situation of the end investor.

## ETF Trading Costs

In comparing ETF and mutual fund costs, the usual starting point is management fees, which are often lower for an ETF because most are index based and traded in a highly competitive market. Other important costs should be considered, however.

An ETF has the advantage that it can be purchased whenever exchanges are open—as well as at closing NAV of the fund (similar to mutual fund purchases and sales) when a transaction is large enough to qualify for a creation or redemption. ETF investors usually pay a commission and incur a trading cost related to the liquidity factors associated with the ETF. The trading, or market impact, costs are influenced by the bid–ask spread of the ETF, the size of the trade relative to the normal trading activity of the ETF, and the ease of hedging the ETF by the market-making community. The closing price of the ETF on the exchange may include a premium or discount to the NAV, driven by supply and demand factors on the exchange and the market impact costs of executing an exchange transaction.

### ETF Bid–Ask Spreads

One of the most important drivers of ETF bid–ask spreads and liquidity is the market structure and liquidity of the underlying securities held. Fixed-income securities, which trade in a dealer market, tend to have much wider bid–ask spreads than large-capitalization stocks. The bid–ask spread of an ETF holding stocks traded in other markets and time zones is influenced by whether the markets for the underlying stocks are open during the hours in which the ETF trades. For specialized ETFs—such as those tracking commodities, volatility futures, or even small-cap stocks—bid–ask spreads can be wide simply because the risk of holding a position even for a short period of time can be high. For some ETFs, even though the underlying securities are liquid, bid–ask spreads may be wide simply because the ETF trades so infrequently the market maker or liquidity provider may need to carry ETF positions for some time before they accumulate sufficient size to create or redeem. Generally, as long as the liquidity in the underlying securities is adequate or hedging instruments can be easily sourced, an ETF trade can usually be executed in a cost-effective manner.

The primary factors that determine the width of the quoted bid–ask spread for a particular transaction size are the amount of ongoing order flow in the ETF, as measured by daily share volume ; the amount of competition among market makers for that ETF ; and the actual costs and risks for the liquidity provider. The bid–ask spread represents the market maker's price for taking the other side of the ETF transaction, which includes the costs and risks to carry the position on his books or to hedge the position using underlying securities or closely related ETFs or derivatives.

More specifically, ETF bid–ask spreads are generally less than or equal to the combination of the following:

- ± Creation/redemption fees and other direct trading costs, such as brokerage and exchange fees
- + Bid–ask spreads of the underlying securities held in the ETF
- + Compensation (to market maker or liquidity provider) for the risk of hedging or carrying positions for the remainder of the trading day
- + Market maker's desired profit spread, subject to competitive forces
- − Discount related to the likelihood of receiving an offsetting ETF order in a short time frame

Large, actively traded ETFs have narrow bid–offer spreads and the capacity (or liquidity) for large transaction sizes. For very liquid US-listed ETFs, such as SPY (the SPDR S&P 500 ETF), or EEM (the iShares MSCI Emerging Markets ETF), buyers and sellers are active throughout the trading day and market makers have a high likelihood of finding the other side or hedging larger orders. Therefore, because most of these ETF trades are matched quickly and never involve the creation/redemption process, the first three factors do not contribute heavily in their spreads. For liquid ETFs, the bid–ask spread can be significantly tighter than the spreads on the underlying securities.

The quoted ETF bid–ask spread, however, is generally for a specific, usually small, trade size and does not always reflect ETF liquidity for larger transactions (more than 10% of average daily volume). Larger trades may best be handled by negotiation, involving work with capital market specialists at ETF managers and broker/dealer ETF desks to understand the various ETF execution options and associated trading costs.

Exhibit 8 shows the asset-weighted average and median bid–ask spreads for various ETF categories traded in the United States.

### Exhibit 8: Average and Median Bid–Ask Spreads for US-Traded ETFs

| US-Traded ETF Category | AUM ($ millions) | Average Spread ($ asset-weighted) | Median Spread |
|---|---|---|---|
| US Equity | 1,871,942 | 0.03% | 0.16% |
| International Equity | 731,251 | 0.05% | 0.24% |
| US Fixed Income | 589,851 | 0.02% | 0.14% |
| International Fixed Income | 65,159 | 0.06% | 0.24% |
| Commodities | 62,620 | 0.05% | 0.24% |
| Leveraged | 29,633 | 0.29% | 0.32% |
| Inverse | 11,315 | 0.10% | 0.21% |
| Asset Allocation | 9,318 | 0.21% | 0.29% |
| Alternatives | 4,388 | 0.18% | 0.38% |
| All US-Traded ETFs* | 3,377,276 | 0.04% | 0.20% |

*Includes currency ETFs in addition to ETFs listed. Total currency ETF assets are $1,799 million.
Source: FactSet, as of the end of December 2018, based on 60-day averages.

US equity and fixed-income ETFs have the tightest asset-weighted spreads. International equity and international fixed-income spreads are wider, because the underlying securities trade in different market structures, making it difficult to price simultaneously, and because the underlying security exchanges may be closed during a portion of the US trading day. ETF categories representing longer-term strategies, such as asset allocation and alternatives, are less actively traded and have lower asset levels and wider spreads, in part because they have less ongoing two-way order flow and, therefore, depend more on market makers to source liquidity through the underlying securities. Bid–ask spreads are dynamic, vary by trade, and tend to widen when market volatility increases or when significant information relating to the underlying index securities is expected.

Understanding spreads for non-equity ETFs is more complex. Although the fixed-income ETFs give investors access to a portfolio of debt securities trading with transparent bid–ask spreads in the stock market (via the ETF), the actual market for the underlying bonds is far less transparent with OTC trading, in which traders at banks and large bond desks offering quotes on demand without posting bids or offers on an exchange.

Unlike actively traded US Treasury securities, both corporate debt and high-yield bonds, as well as some municipals and international bonds, trade actively only around the time of issuance, after which they may be held until maturity. Therefore, bond ETFs that track indexes containing corporate and high-yield debt often invest only in a subset of the most liquid high-yield securities. Their bid–ask spreads tend to be wider than those of ETFs based on stocks or US Treasuries because of the risk to dealers in hedging inventory and the default risk of the securities, especially in periods of weak economic conditions.

### Premiums and Discounts

In addition to commissions and bid–ask spreads, ETF premiums and discounts are also important components of ETF trading costs.

At the end of the trading day, each ETF has an end-of-day NAV at which shares can be created or redeemed and with which the ETF's closing price can be compared. Most investors rely on return calculations based on this closing NAV. NAV is intended to be an accurate assessment of the ETF's fair value. This is the case when the underlying securities trade on the same exchange as the one where the ETF is listed (or trades), because these securities trade in the same market structure and have the same closing price time as the ETF.

During the trading day, exchanges disseminate ETF **iNAVs**, or "indicated" NAVs; iNAVs are intraday "fair value" estimates of an ETF share based on its creation basket composition for that day. An ETF is said to be trading at a premium when its share price is higher than iNAV and at a discount if its price is lower than iNAV.

The calculation for end-of-day and intraday premiums/discounts is as follows:

End-of-day ETF premium or discount (%)

= (ETF price − NAV per share)/NAV per share.

Intraday ETF premium or discount (%)

= (ETF price − iNAV per share)/iNAV per share.

Like tracking error, premiums/discounts are driven by a number of factors, including timing differences and stale pricing.

**Timing differences.**

NAV is often a poor fair value indicator for ETFs that hold foreign securities because of differences in exchange closing times between the underlying (e.g., foreign stocks, bonds, or commodities) and the exchange where the ETF trades. For example, if a commodity held in the fund stops trading in the futures market at 3:00 p.m., the issuer may elect to retain that price for a 4:00 p.m. valuation. If a fund holds securities in a different currency, it may choose to "strike" or value the currency at 4:00 p.m. ET—or occasionally, at 4:00 p.m. London time. In the case where international stocks are held in US-traded ETFs, the NAV may be based on a market closing price in Asia or Europe that occurred hours ahead of when the ETF stops trading on the US exchange.

Because bonds do not trade on an exchange, no true "closing prices" are available for valuing the bonds in a portfolio. Instead, ETF issuers rely on bids from bond desks or pricing services for proxy prices. In the case of bonds that have not traded near the close of the dealer market, index providers and bondholders typically use pricing services for bond valuation. These pricing services often use more liquid bonds that have similar features to estimate where the non-traded bond would have closed.

Sometimes, bond pricing model inputs reflect the price at which a dealer is willing to buy the bonds and the risk and cost to a dealer in carrying the bonds in inventory. In such cases, the ETF's closing price is often higher than the bid prices of the underlying bond holdings used to calculate NAV, making it appear that the ETF is at a premium. During times of market stress, few bonds may trade, leaving pricing services without updated inputs for their models. Like ETFs holding foreign securities, this causes NAVs to be "stale" and, in this case, with possibly too high a valuation given market conditions. In this case, fixed-income ETFs with sufficient trading volume may appear to be trading at discounts to NAV. In these cases, by reflecting the market's most current assessment of value, liquid ETFs become "price discovery" vehicles.

ETFs also provide price discovery for after-hours markets. For example, US-listed ETFs holding European stocks trade until 4:00 p.m. ET, hours after European markets have closed. In these cases, premiums or discounts resulting from closed underlying markets are not mispricing; rather, they are the market's best estimate as to where the fund holdings would trade if the underlying markets were open.

**Stale pricing.**
ETFs that trade infrequently may also have large premiums or discounts to NAV. If the ETF has not traded in the hours leading up to the market close, NAV may have significantly risen or fallen during that time owing to market movement. In this case, comparing the last ETF trade price—for example, at 1:00 p.m.—with the end-of-day 4:00 p.m. NAV would result in a premium (or discount) if the market and corresponding NAV fell (or rose) sharply between 1:00 and 4:00 p.m.

This situation can be compounded if days or weeks elapse between the ETF's trades. Some premium/discount calculations use a strict last price input, whereas others use a closing midpoint. The strict pricing will quote the last trade price, no matter how distant the ETF trade date, which can lead to severe premiums or discounts because NAVs are updated on the basis of the latest market closing prices while the ETF price remains unchanged at last trade.

> **EXAMPLE 1**
>
> ### Comparison of US ETF Trading Costs
>
> A good way to assess the liquidity and potential trading costs of ETFs is to compare various measures of trading activity among similar funds. Exhibit 9 shows trading measures for some of the most liquid ETFs—the SPDR S&P 500 ETF (SPY), the iShares Core S&P 500 ETF (IVV), and the Vanguard S&P 500 ETF (VOO) benchmarked to the S&P 500 Index; another large-cap ETF, the iShares MSCI USA Equal Weighted ETF (EUSA), benchmarked to the MSCI USA Equal Weighted Index; and a liquid small-cap ETF, the iShares Russell 2000 ETF (IWM), benchmarked to the Russell 2000 Index.

**Exhibit 9: Selected US Equity Index ETF Trading Measure Comparison**

| ETF Ticker | SPY | IVV | VOO | EUSA | IWM |
|---|---|---|---|---|---|
| Benchmark Index | S&P 500 | S&P 500 | S&P 500 | MSCI USA Equal Weighted | Russell 2000 |
| *Volume in US dollars* | | | | | |
| Daily average volume | 24.47 billion | 1.22 billion | 819.28 million | 1.32 million | 3.90 billion |
| Median volume | 20.23 billion | 1.08 billion | 739.69 million | 0.94 million | 3.81 billion |
| *Other trading characteristics* | | | | | |

| ETF Ticker | SPY | IVV | VOO | EUSA | IWM |
|---|---|---|---|---|---|
| Benchmark Index | S&P 500 | S&P 500 | S&P 500 | MSCI USA Equal Weighted | Russell 2000 |
| Average spread (%) | 0.00% | 0.01% | 0.01% | 0.12% | 0.01% |
| Average spread ($) | $0.01 | $0.03 | $0.03 | $0.07 | $0.01 |
| Median premium/discount (%)[a] | 0.00% | 0.00% | 0.00% | 0.04% | 0.01% |
| Maximum premium (%)[a] | 0.12% | 0.13% | 0.18% | 0.96% | 0.12% |
| Maximum discount (%)[a] | −0.19% | −0.11% | −0.08% | −0.38% | −0.13% |

[a] Over previous 12 months.

Source: FactSet, as of 7 November 2018.

SPY, the largest ETF by AUM and the first ETF traded in the United States, is one of the most liquid securities in the world. IVV and VOO, with the same benchmark, are used more by intermediate- and longer-horizon investors but also have very tight spreads because of liquidity in the underlying securities and ease of hedging for market makers. SPY trades a median of $20 billion a day, compared with a median of $1 billion for IVV. The average bid–ask spread shows that both are highly liquid. In addition, both have tight premiums and discounts to NAV.

In contrast, EUSA has a larger spread, 0.12%. The lower liquidity and higher trading cost for EUSA can be attributed to the fact that the benchmark index does not have futures and other index products available for hedging use by market makers. The MSCI USA Equal Weighted Index also includes close to 600 stocks—100 more than the S&P 500 Index has.

IWM, benchmarked to the Russell 2000 Index of US small-cap stocks, holds far more securities than any of the previously mentioned ETFs, and many are small-cap stocks that have wide spreads. IWM, however, trades with spreads and premiums/discounts close to those of SPY.

How is that possible? First, trading activity in IWM is high (median daily dollar volume of $4 billion) and continuous throughout the trading day. Second, the Russell 2000 Index has an active futures market, making it easy for market makers and APs to quickly hedge the risk of large trades.

Exhibit 10 shows three US fixed-income ETFs—one US-Treasury based and two benchmarked to US high-Yield indexes. All three are among the most liquid fixed-income ETFs and have tight average bid–ask spreads. The iShares iBoxx $ High Yield Corporate Bond ETF (HYG) is the most liquid, with median daily volume of $1.4 billion and a higher median premium (0.20%) than the iShares 20+ Year Treasury Bond ETF (TLT). These positive median premiums indicate that the SPDR Bloomberg Barclays High Yield Bond ETF (JNK) and HYG have been in a net demand position over most of the 12-month period covered in Exhibit 10 and investors have typically paid above fair value for ETF access to a high-yield portfolio.

The maximum premium and discount have generally been much larger for bond ETFs compared with the equity ETFs shown in Exhibit 9. This is because the underlying fixed-income securities trade in a dealer market and are not continuously priced. In this case, the fixed-income ETFs, which trade on an exchange with more continuous pricing, may be a better reflection of true supply and demand for the portfolio because the underlying bonds may not trade as frequently, particularly in extreme market conditions.

### Exhibit 10: Selected US Fixed-Income ETF Trading Measure Comparison

| ETF Ticker | TLT | JNK | HYG |
|---|---|---|---|
| Benchmark Index | ICE US Treasury 20+ Year Bond Index | Bloomberg Barclays High Yield Very Liquid Index | Markit iBoxx USD Liquid High Yield Index |
| *Volume in US dollars* | | | |
| Daily average volume | 1.04 billion | 0.46 billion | 1.50 billion |
| Median volume | 0.97 billion | 0.41 billion | 1.44 billion |
| *Other trading characteristics* | | | |
| Average spread (%) | 0.01% | 0.03% | 0.01% |
| Average spread ($) | $0.01 | $0.01 | $0.01 |
| Median premium/discount (%)[a] | 0.03% | 0.10% | 0.20% |
| Maximum premium (%)[a] | 0.68% | 0.41% | 0.59% |
| Maximum discount (%)[a] | −0.52% | −0.67% | −0.75% |

[a] *Over the previous 12 months.*

*Source:* FactSet, as of 7 November 2018.

## Total Costs of ETF Ownership

Exhibit 11 provides a summary of cost factors when considering ETFs and mutual funds. Some of these costs are explicit, whereas others are implicit and reflected in net investment returns. Both ETFs and mutual funds typically pay lower institutional commission rates for trades because of their asset size. ETF transaction costs are incurred at purchase and sale regardless of holding period, whereas other costs, such as management fees, increase as the holding period lengthens. Ongoing costs, such as management fees, portfolio turnover, and security lending proceeds, have a consistent impact on investment returns based on holding period. ETF trading costs, such as commissions and bid–ask spreads, are incurred only at purchase and sale, and their return impact diminishes over longer holding periods, whereas management fees and other ongoing costs become a more significant proportion of total costs. Tracking error can be considered a positive or negative implicit cost.

For active short-term ETF investors who trade frequently, the cost of entering and exiting their ETF positions (commissions, bid–ask spreads, premiums/discounts) is a far more significant consideration than management fees, tracking error, and other costs that accumulate over longer holding periods.

ETFs may trade at market prices higher (premiums) or lower (discounts) than NAV, which is based on closing prices for the fund's underlying securities. Premiums and discounts may reflect a lag in the timing of the underlying security valuations relative to current market conditions and can be considered positive costs (in the case of premiums) or negative costs (in the case of discounts).

There are additional implicit trading costs of fund management, such as portfolio turnover costs that are reflected in fund returns. These are incurred within the fund as the portfolio manager buys and sells securities to execute the investment strategy and manage fund cash flows. Portfolio turnover costs reduce returns and affect performance for all investors in the fund. Many ETFs are based on indexes that have lower portfolio turnover than actively managed funds. Taxable gains incurred upon sale can be considered positive costs for the investor, whereas taxable losses represent negative costs. Security lending income for the fund represents negative costs.

### Exhibit 11: Cost Factor Comparison—ETFs and Mutual Funds

| Fund Cost Factor | Function of Holding Period? | Explicit/Implicit | ETFs | Mutual Funds |
|---|---|---|---|---|
| Management fee | Y | E | X (often less) | X |
| Tracking error | Y | I | X (often less than comparable index mutual funds) | (index funds only) |
| Commissions | N | E | X (some free) | |
| Bid–ask spread | N | I | X | |
| Premium/discount to NAV | N | I | X | |
| Portfolio turnover (from investor flows and fund management) | Y | I | X (often less) | X |
| Taxable gains/losses to investors | Y | E | X (often less) | X |
| Security lending | Y | I | X (often more) | X |

*Trading costs vs. management fees.*

To illustrate the effect of management fees versus trading costs, consider an investor who pays a commission of $10 on a $20,000 trade (0.05% each way) combined with a 0.15% bid–ask spread on purchase and sale. The round-trip trading cost is, therefore, 0.25% and is calculated as follows:

Round-trip trading cost (%)

= (One-way commission % × 2) + (½ Bid–ask spread % × 2)

= (0.05% × 2) + (½ × 0.15% × 2)

= 0.10% + 0.15%

= 0.25%.

For a round-trip trade that happens over a year, 0.25% can be larger than the annual expense ratios of many ETFs. If held for less than a year, the trading costs may be far larger than the expense ratio paid on the ETF.

To see the impact of holding period, consider the 3-month versus 12-month versus 3-year holding period costs for an ETF with a 0.15% annual fee, one-way commissions of 0.05%, and a bid–ask spread of 0.15%. Holding period costs can be calculated as follows:

Holding period cost (%)

= Round-trip trade cost (%) + Management fee for period (%).

Specific holding period costs can be calculated as follows:

3-month holding period cost (%) = 0.25% + 3/12 × 0.15%

= 0.29%.

12-month holding period cost (%) = 0.25% + 12/12 × 0.15%

= 0.40%.

3-year holding period cost (%) = 0.25% + 36/12 × 0.15%

= 0.70%.

Exhibit 12 illustrates that for holding periods of 3 and 12 months, trading costs represent the largest proportion of annual holding costs (0.86% and 0.625%, respectively). Excluding the compounding effect, for a three-year holding period, management fees represent a much larger proportion of holding costs (0.64%).

**Exhibit 12: ETF Management Fee and Trading Cost Comparison**

| Holding Period: | 3 Months | 12 Months | 3 Years |
|---|---|---|---|
| Commission | 0.10% | 0.10% | 0.10% |
| Bid–ask spread | 0.15% | 0.15% | 0.15% |
| Management fee | 0.0375% | 0.15% | 0.45% |
| **Total** | **0.29%** | **0.40%** | **0.70%** |
| Trading costs (% of total) | 0.86% | 0.625% | 0.36% |
| Management fees (% of total) | 0.14% | 0.375% | 0.64% |

For broad-based, capitalization-weighted equity index ETFs that have the lowest fees, trading costs represent the largest cost in using an ETF. The longer an ETF is held, the greater the proportion of total costs represented by the management fee component.

Tactical traders will generally choose an ETF on the basis of its liquidity and trading costs (e.g., commissions, bid–ask spreads). In many cases, shorter-term tactical traders may use an ETF with a higher management fee but a tighter bid–ask spread and more active or continuous two-way trading flow to avoid incurring the capital commitment cost of a market maker or the cost of arbitrage for the ETF versus the underlying securities. The size of the management fee is typically a more significant consideration for longer-term buy-and-hold investors.

# ETF RISKS

describe types of ETF risk

ETFs introduce several unique risks because of their structure, fund holdings, and underlying exposure.

## Counterparty Risk

Some ETP (exchange-traded product) legal structures involve dependence on a counterparty. A counterparty failure can put the investor's principal at risk of default or affect a portion of the assets via settlement risk. Likewise, counterparty activity can affect a fund's economic exposure. Therefore, investors should carefully assess counterparty risk.

Although exchange-traded notes (ETNs) trade on exchanges and have a creation/redemption mechanism, they are not truly funds because they do not hold underlying securities. ETNs are unsecured debt obligations of the institution that issues them and are structured as a promise to pay a pattern of returns based on the return of the stated index minus fund expenses. The issuer of the note takes responsibility for setting up the counterbalancing hedges it believes necessary to meet the obligations.

In the United States, ETNs are registered under the Securities Act of 1933 because they are general obligation debt securities of a bank and are not managed by an investment firm for a fee. Similar ETN structures exist in most markets where ETFs are listed.

ETNs have the largest potential counterparty risk of all exchange-traded products because they are unsecured, unsubordinated debt notes and, therefore, are subject to default by the ETN issuer. Theoretically, an ETN's counterparty risk is 100% in the event of an instantaneous default by the underwriting bank, and should an issuing bank declare bankruptcy, any ETNs issued by the bank would effectively be worthless. Because baskets of notes may be redeemed back to the issuer at NAV, however, it is likely that only an extremely rapid and catastrophic failure would take investors by surprise. This happened once, in 2008, with three Lehman Brothers–backed ETNs, but it has not happened since.

In the United States, some funds offering exposure to non-US-dollar currencies achieve this via offshore bank deposits. These funds bear default risk at the deposit-holding bank.

Because ETNs and deposit-based ETFs are backed by banks, their default risk can be monitored via the issuing bank's credit default swap (CDS) pricing.

The credit spreads for one-year CDSs by issuer at the end of October 2018 are shown in Exhibit 13.

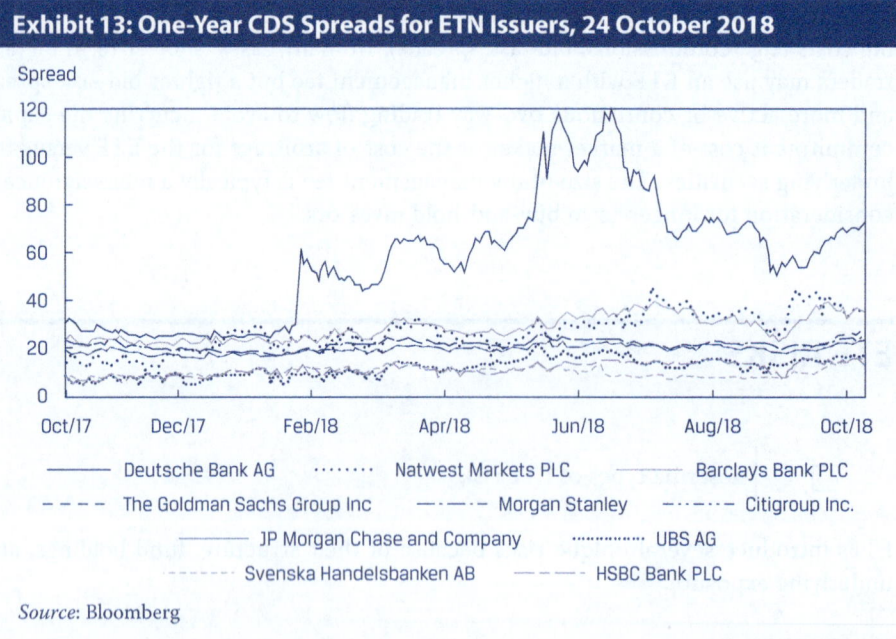

**Exhibit 13: One-Year CDS Spreads for ETN Issuers, 24 October 2018**

Source: Bloomberg

The quoted CDS rates represent the cost to insure debt, in basis points per year; so, for example, investors could "insure" $1 million in Goldman Sachs bonds for just under $30,000 per year. Although the insurance rate should never be considered an estimate of actual default risk for a 12-month period, it does provide a reasonable gauge of the relative risk of the various issuers. In general, a one-year CDS rate above 5% should raise significant concerns among investors because it foretells a significant default risk in the year to come.

*Settlement risk.*

A fund that uses OTC derivatives, such as swaps, to gain market exposure has settlement risk; that is, mark-to-market (unrealized) gains are subject to counterparty default. Such ETFs include many European swap-based funds (or synthetic ETFs), funds using leverage (or geared funds), some currency funds, and some actively managed portfolios. To minimize settlement risk, OTC contracts are typically settled frequently—usually on a daily or weekly basis. This frequent settlement reduces the exposure the swap partners face if a company goes bankrupt, but there is a theoretical risk of counterparty default between settlement periods. In addition, the majority of the contract collateral is held in low-risk instruments, such as US T-bills, at a custodian bank.

Swap exposures are not unique to ETFs. Many mutual funds also use swaps and other derivatives to gain exposure. With ETFs, swap exposures are somewhat transparent because these holdings are disclosed daily by the ETF provider, although full information on counterparties and terms may not be disclosed.

*Security lending.*

ETF issuers (in addition to traditional mutual fund managers and institutions) lend their underlying securities to short sellers, earning additional income for the fund's investors. Securities lent are generally overcollateralized, to 102% (domestic) or 105% (international), so that the risk from counterparty default is low. Cash collateral is usually reinvested into extremely short-term fixed-income securities with minimal associated risk. At the time of writing, there has been no instance of shareholder loss resulting from security lending in an ETF since ETF product inception in the early 1990s. A well-run security lending program can generate significant income for the ETF issuer, sometimes entirely offsetting the fund's operating expenses. Most ETF issuers credit all profits from this activity back to shareholders, although information about issuer lending programs is sometimes not well disclosed.

## Fund Closures

Similar to mutual fund closures, ETF issuers may decide to close an ETF. In such a case, the fund generally sells its underlying positions and returns cash to investors. This activity can trigger capital gain events for investors and the need to find a replacement investment. Primary reasons for a fund to close include regulation, competition, and corporate activity. "Soft" closures—which do not involve an actual fund closing—include creation halts and changes in investment strategy.

*Regulations.*

Security regulators can change the regulations governing certain types of funds, resulting in forced closure of those funds. For example, commodity futures are under constant regulatory scrutiny, and position limits can make it impossible for some funds to function. In 2018, the Israeli security regulator banned the ETN structure, forcing over 700 products to close and reopen as traditional ETFs.

*Competition.*

Investors have benefited from a growing number of ETFs and increased competition. As ETFs proliferate, some funds fail to attract sufficient assets and are shut down by the ETF issuer. A fund's assets under management, in addition to those of any competitor, and the ETF's average daily liquidity are indications of market support. Low AUM and trading volumes over a significant period could indicate potential fund closure.

*Corporate actions.*

Mergers and acquisitions between ETF providers can prompt fund closures. When ETF families merge or are sold to other ETF providers, new ETF owners may close underperforming ETFs (from an asset-gathering perspective) and invest in new, higher-growth opportunities.

*Creation and redemption halts.*

ETN issuers may halt creations and redemptions. An example of this scenario is when an ETN issuer no longer wants to add debt to its balance sheet related to the index on which the ETN is based. This situation occurred in September 2018, when ETN issuer UBS issued a "sales halt" for its ETRACS Monthly Pay 2xLeveraged Mortgage REIT ETN (MORL), effectively suspending further sales from its outstanding inventory of the ETN and preventing new shares from being created. When creations are halted, the ETN can trade at a substantial premium over fair value, as the arbitrage mechanism breaks down. In this case, MORL traded at a premium of more than 5%. Although all ETFs can theoretically close creations in extraordinary situations, in practice, it happens more commonly with ETNs.

*Change in investment strategy.*

Some ETF issuers find it easier to repurpose a low-asset ETF from their existing lineup than to close one fund and open another. Issuers simply announce a change in the fund's underlying index—a common occurrence in the ETF industry. Although most index changes result in small adjustments to an ETF's portfolio and economic exposure, these "soft closures" can sometimes result in a complete overhaul, changing exposures to countries, industries, or even asset classes.

## Investor-Related Risk

ETFs provide access to sometimes complex asset classes and strategies. For all ETFs, it is important that investors understand the underlying exposure provided by the ETF; otherwise, ETFs may introduce risks to investors who do not fully understand them. For many investors, leveraged and inverse ETFs fall into this category by failing to meet investor expectations. Index methodology (e.g., constituent universe, weighting approach) and the fund's portfolio construction approach are central to understanding an ETF's underlying exposure and related performance.

Leveraged and inverse funds generally offer levered (or geared), inverse, or levered and inverse exposure to a given index and have a daily performance objective that is a multiple of index returns. These products must reset or adjust their exposure daily to deliver the target return multiple each day.

For example, consider a fund offering 300% exposure (3 times, or 3×) to the FTSE 100 Index with a net asset value of £100. It uses swaps to obtain a notional exposure of £300. If the one-day FTSE 100 Index return is 5%, the £300 in exposure becomes £315 (a 5% increase), and the ETF's end-of-day NAV is £115: 100 × (1 + 3 × 5%).

In order to deliver 300% of the index's daily performance for the following day, the ETF, now valued at £115, requires notional exposure of £345 for 3 times exposure. Because at the end of the day the ETF has only £315 in exposure, it must reset its exposure—in this case, increasing notional swap exposure by £30.

Exhibit 14 outlines this example.

### Exhibit 14: Example of Levered 3× ETF Exposure

| | Index Level | One-Day Index Return (%) | 3× ETF NAV (£) | Notional Swap Exposure (£) | 3× Swap Exposure (£) | Swap Exposure Adjustment (£) |
|---|---|---|---|---|---|---|
| Day 1 | 100 | — | 100 | 300 | 300 | 0 |
| Day 2 | 105 | 5% | 115 | 315 | 345 | 30 |

If these ETFs are held for longer than a one-day period, the math of compounding and resetting exposure is such that an investor will not see the return multiple—for example, a 200% or –100% return in the case of a 2× ETF or inverse ETF, respectively—over her holding period.

Exhibit 15 presents a levered, inverse fund offering 2 times (–200%) exposure to the S&P 500 Index. The fund (–2× ETF) has a starting net asset value of $100 and uses swaps to obtain notional exposure.

### Exhibit 15: Example of Levered and Inverse 2× ETF Daily Return vs. Holding Period Return

| | Index Level | One-Day Index Return (%) | Index Period Return (%) | –2× ETF NAV | One-Day ETF Return (%) | 2× ETF Holding Period Return (%) |
|---|---|---|---|---|---|---|
| Day 1 | 100 | — | — | 100 | — | — |
| Day 2 | 110 | 10% | 10% | 80 | –20% | –20% |
| Day 3 | 99 | –10% | –1% | 96 | 20% | –4% |

Day 1: Both the index and the –2× fund are at a starting level of 100.
Day 2: The index increases to 110, a one-day return of 10%.

The –2× ETF daily return is calculated as follows:

$$= -2 \times [(110 - 100)/100]$$

$$= -2 \times (10\%)$$

$$= -20\%.$$

The –2× ETF NAV is calculated as follows:

$$= 100 \times (1 + -0.2)$$

$$= 80.$$

Day 3: The index falls to 99, a one-day return of –10%.

The 2× ETF daily return is calculated as follows:

$$= -2 \times [(99 - 110)/110]$$

$$= -2 \times (-10\%)$$

$$= 20\%.$$

The −2× ETF NAV is calculated as follows:

$= 80 \times (1 + 0.2).$

$= 96.$

This example shows the fund delivering its promised performance, −2× the daily index return, but it also shows how the return may not be what is naively expected over periods longer than a day.

Over the three days, the index return is −1%: (99 − 100)/100. A naive expectation might assume that over the same period, the −2× ETF would return 2% (= −2 × −1%). Over the three days, the fund's actual return was −4%: (96 − 100)/100.

Because of these compounding effects in leveraged ETFs, the funds are generally not intended to be buy-and-hold products for more than a one-month horizon. If investors are planning to hold them long term, they must rebalance the funds periodically to maintain the desired net exposure.

## 5. ETFS IN PORTFOLIO MANAGEMENT

> identify and describe portfolio uses of ETFs

ETFs have become valuable tools for both institutional and retail investors. Available on a wide range of passive, systematic (rules-based) active, and traditional active strategies and segments of the stock, bond, and commodity markets, ETFs are used for both top-down (based on macro views) and bottom-up (focused on security selection) investment approaches. In addition to their use in implementing long-term strategic exposure to asset classes and risk factors, ETFs are used for tactical tilts, portfolio rebalancing, and risk management.

### ETF Strategies

Most institutional asset managers and hedge fund managers, Registered Investment Advisers (RIAs), and financial advisers use ETFs for a wide range of strategies. These strategies serve many different investment objectives—some strategic, some tactical, and some dynamic, where the timing of changes is based on market conditions. Other ETF applications help in managing portfolios more efficiently and are used primarily for operational purposes. As we discuss the diverse set of strategies that can be found in an ETF structure, it is apparent that they are not easily classified as either active or passive. Except for core asset class and portfolio efficiency investment applications that use ETFs based on market-capitalization weighted benchmarks, almost all ETF-related strategies have some component of active investing, either within the ETF strategy or in the way the ETF is used.

Not all strategies are suitable in an ETF structure. The disclosure of holdings may be undesirable for an active manager who invests in less liquid securities or pursues either a concentrated investment strategy or one that relies on an approach that cannot be easily described (such as a "black box" methodology) or disclosed without compromising the strategy. The liquidity of the underlying investments must also be high enough to accommodate daily creations and redemptions. Such factors as tax efficiency, low fees, and available product make ETFs competitive alternatives to traditional mutual funds and active managers. The primary applications in which ETFs are used include the following:

**Portfolio efficiency:** The use of ETFs to better manage a portfolio for efficiency or operational purposes. Applications include cash or liquidity management, rebalancing, portfolio completion, and active manager transition management.

**Asset class exposure management:** The use of ETFs to achieve or maintain core exposure to key asset classes, market segments, or investment themes on a strategic, tactical, or dynamic basis.

**Active and factor investing:** The use of ETFs to target specific active or factor exposures on the basis of an investment view or risk management need.

## Efficient Portfolio Management

ETFs are useful tools for managing portfolio activity necessitated by cash flows and changes in external managers. In addition, ETFs can be used to easily accommodate portfolio rebalancing needs and unwanted gaps in portfolio exposure.

### *Portfolio liquidity management.*

One of the primary institutional applications of ETFs is cash flow management. ETFs can be used to invest excess cash balances quickly (known as cash equitization), enabling investors to remain fully invested in target benchmark exposure, thereby minimizing potential cash drag. Cash drag refers to a fund's mis-tracking relative to its index that results from holding uninvested cash. Managers may also use ETFs to transact small cash flows originating from dividends, income, or shareholder activity. Some portfolio managers hold small portions of their funds in ETFs in anticipation of future cash outflows. Transacting the ETF may incur lower trading costs and be easier operationally than liquidating underlying securities or requesting funds from an external manager.

### *Portfolio rebalancing.*

Many investors rebalance portfolios on the basis of a specified time interval, usually at least quarterly, and some may adjust whenever the market value of a portfolio segment, or allocation, deviates from its target weight by a threshold, such as 2%. For tighter rebalancing thresholds and more frequent rebalancing time intervals, using liquid ETFs with tight bid–ask spreads allows the portfolio manager to execute the rebalance in a single ETF trade and ensures the portfolio remains fully invested according to its target weights. For investors who have the ability to sell short, reducing exposure associated with a rebalance can be done quickly using an ETF, and as the underlying securities are sold off, the short position can be covered.

### *Portfolio completion strategies.*

ETFs can also be used for completion strategies to fill a temporary gap in exposure to an asset class, sector, or investment theme or factor. Gaps may arise with changes in external managers or when an existing manager takes an active view that moves the portfolio out of a market segment to which the investor wishes to have continued exposure. The investor may want to retain the manager but use a tactical ETF strategy to maintain exposure to the desired market segment. If external managers are collectively underweighting or overweighting an industry or segment, such as technology, international small-cap stocks, or high-yield bonds, ETFs can be used to adjust exposure up or down to the desired level without making changes to underlying external manager allocations.

*Transition management.*

Transition management refers to the process of hiring and firing managers—or making changes to allocations with existing managers—while trying to keep target allocations in place. Because ETFs exist on most domestic, international, and global equity benchmarks, a newly appointed transition manager can invest in an ETF to maintain market exposure as she undergoes the process of selling the unwanted positions of the manager she is replacing (the terminated manager). The new transition manager can then take her time to invest in positions for her strategy and gradually reduce the ETF holding.

Asset owners can use ETFs to maintain desired market or asset class exposure in the absence of having an external manager in place. For example, if a fixed-income manager benchmarked to the Bloomberg Barclays US Aggregate Bond Index is terminated, the asset owner may wish to invest in the iShares Core US Aggregate Bond ETF (AGG) to maintain benchmark exposure until a replacement manager can be hired. In some cases, asset owners will "fund" new managers with ETF positions. The new manager will then sell off his ETF positions in the benchmark index as he invests in the underlying securities that meet his desired investment objectives and valuation criteria.

For very large asset owners, there are three potential drawbacks to using ETFs for portfolio management: (1) Given the asset owner size, they may be able to negotiate lower fees for a dedicated separately managed account (SMA) or find lower-cost commingled trust accounts that offer lower fees for large investors, (2) an SMA can be customized to the investment goals and needs of the investor, and (3) many regulators require large ETF holdings (as a percentage of ETF assets) to be disclosed to the public. This can detract from the flexibility in managing the ETF position and increase the cost of shifting investment holdings.

Exhibit 16 provides a summary of ETF portfolio efficiency applications, covering their roles in the portfolio, and examples by benchmark type. Applications include (1) transacting cash flows for benchmark exposure, (2) rebalancing to target asset class or risk factor weights, (3) filling exposure gaps in portfolio holdings of other strategies and funds, and (4) temporarily holding during transitions of strategies or managers.

**Exhibit 16: ETF Portfolio Applications—Portfolio Efficiency**

| Portfolio Application | Role in Portfolio | Examples of ETFs by Benchmark Type |
|---|---|---|
| Cash Equitization/Liquidity Management | Minimize cash drag by staying fully invested to benchmark exposure, transact small cash flows | Liquid ETFs benchmarked to asset category |
| Portfolio Rebalancing | Maintain exposure to target weights (asset classes, sub-asset classes) | Domestic equity, international equity, domestic fixed income |
| Portfolio Completion | Fill gaps in strategic exposure (countries, sectors, industries, themes, factors) | International small cap, Canada, bank loans, real assets, health care, technology, quality, ESG |
| Manager Transition Activity | Maintain interim benchmark exposure during manager transitions | ETFs benchmarked to new manager's target benchmark |

## Asset Class Exposure Management

Investors have used index exposure in core asset classes for decades, but one of the fastest-growing areas of ETF usage, especially by institutional investors, is fixed income. Since the financial crisis of 2008, the reduced capital available for banks (to participate in dealer bond markets) has contributed to greater use of fixed-income ETFs for core exposure. Except for the largest institutional investors, trading portfolios of bonds is much more difficult and expensive than similar portfolio trades in stocks. Fixed-income ETFs, especially those benchmarked to indexes containing corporates and high-yield securities, provide bond investors with a more efficient (lower cost, more continuous pricing, agency market) and liquid means of obtaining core fixed-income exposure.

*Core exposure to an asset class or sub-asset class.*

The primary strategic use of ETFs is to gain core index exposure to various asset classes and sub-asset classes. ETFs make doing so easy—across global equities, bonds, commodities, and currencies—and investors regularly use ETFs for broad portfolio diversification. Investors also use ETFs for more targeted strategic exposure to such segments as high-yield debt, bank loans, and commodities (including crude oil, gold and other metals, and agricultural products).

A financial adviser can use ETFs to build a diversified portfolio on the basis of ETF recommendations from his firm's wealth management research team. Benchmarked to broad asset classes, portfolio choices for equity ETF exposure might include domestic large- and small-cap equities, sectors, such risk factors as dividend growth or momentum, industries, and international regions or countries with or without currency exposure. Choices for fixed-income ETF exposure might include government and corporate debt of various maturities, emerging market debt, bank loans, and possibly floating interest rate strategies. Commodity ETF exposure could include gold and other metals, broad commodity indexes, agriculture products, and oil. Similarly, brokerage firms and robo-advisers may offer more-automated solutions that select an ETF allocation based on the investor's risk and return profile. These firms offer a range of ETF investment choices from a preapproved product list to fit different asset class and risk factor categories.

*Tactical strategies.*

ETFs can also be used to implement market views and adjust portfolio risk on a more short-term, tactical basis. Some financial advisers and institutional investors allocate a portion of their portfolios for opportunistic trading based on their firm's (or strategist's) research or short-term outlook. Others make tactical adjustments in a range around target weights for asset classes or categories within an asset class. ETFs based on risk factors, country exposure, credit or duration exposure, currencies, or even volatility, crude oil, or metals can be used to express tactical views. To profit from an expected price decline, investors can sell ETFs short in a margin account.

Thematic ETFs are also used to implement investment views. Thematic ETFs hold stocks passively but allow investors to take an active view on a market segment they believe will deliver strong returns. These ETFs typically cover a narrow or niche area of the market not well represented by an industry. Examples include focused areas of technology, such as cybersecurity and robotics. Other themes accessed via ETFs are global infrastructure, regional banks, semiconductors, and gold mining. Generally, thematic ETFs are tactical tools that serve as substitutes for buying individual stocks or an industry ETF that is too broad to adequately represent the investor's investment view. Holdings may overlap with those of other ETFs or other portfolio positions but play a role when the investor wants to overweight this segment in the portfolio. Thematic ETFs should be evaluated similarly to stocks because they tend to have comparable levels of volatility and represent specialized active views.

ETFs that have the highest trading volumes in their asset class category are generally preferred for tactical trading applications, and the liquidity in many of the largest ETFs offered in each region makes them well suited for this purpose. Trading costs and liquidity, rather than management fees, are the important criteria in selecting an ETF for tactical adjustments. To identify the most commonly used ETFs for tactical strategies, one can look at the ratio of average dollar volume to average assets for the ETF.

Exhibit 17 provides a summary of ETF asset class exposure applications, covering their roles in the portfolio, categories of use, and examples by benchmark type. These applications relate to using ETFs for strategic, tactical, and dynamic asset class exposure.

### Exhibit 17: ETF Portfolio Applications—Asset Class Exposure Management

| Portfolio Application | Category | Role in Portfolio | Examples of ETFs by Benchmark Type |
|---|---|---|---|
| Core asset class or market | Strategic or tactical | Core long-term, strategic weighting; Tactical tilt to enhance returns or modify risk; Ease of access vs. buying underlying securities | Domestic equity, international equity, fixed income, commodities |
| Equity style, country, or sector; fixed income or commodity segment | Strategic or tactical | Tactical tilt to enhance returns or modify risk depending on short-term views; Hedge index exposure of active stocks or bond strategy; Ease of access vs. buying underlying securities | Value, growth, Japanese, Chinese, UK, Canadian, or Mexican equities; corporate or high-yield debt; gold; oil; agriculture |
| Equity sector, industry, investment theme | Dynamic or tactical | Tactical or dynamic active tilt to enhance returns or modify risk; Efficient implementation of a thematic/industry vs. single-stock view; Capture performance on an emerging theme or innovation not reflected in industry categories | Technology, financials, oil and gas, biotech, infrastructure, robotics, gold mining, buybacks, internet innovation, cybersecurity |

## Active and Factor Investing

In the mid-2000s, quantitative or rules-based strategies became available in ETFs. These strategies had "active" weights different from market capitalization and were able to disclose holdings because the stock selection and weighting was not chosen by a discretionary portfolio manager but, rather, by a set of quantitative rules, disclosed in the index methodology.

The first smart beta ETFs were indexes weighted by company fundamentals, such as dividends, or quantitatively screened on stock features. Although adoption was initially slow, institutional investors and RIAs now use smart beta ETF strategies to gain systematic active exposure to persistent common return drivers or factors. Global assets in smart beta equity funds, including both single-factor and multi-factor strategies, now represent approximately 20% of ETF assets.

Active ETFs, where the investment strategy is benchmarked but managed with discretion, have also gained assets, especially in fixed income, but they still represent a relatively small percentage of global ETF assets, at 2%–3%.

### Factor (smart beta) ETFs.

Factor ETFs are usually benchmarked to an index created with predefined rules for screening and/or weighting constituent holdings. The strategy index rules are structured around return drivers or factors, such as value, dividend yield, earnings or dividend growth, quality, stock volatility, or momentum. Some of these factors, such as size, value, and momentum, have academic support as equity risk premiums that may be rewarded over the long term. Within each single factor category, a range of offerings from competing ETF providers exists, differentiated by the criteria used to represent the factor and the weights applied to constituent holdings (equal, factor, or cap weighted). Their application is typically in providing longer-term, buy-and-hold exposure to a desired factor based on an investment view. Factor ETFs can be used to add risk factor allocations that might not be present in a benchmark or portfolio—for example, adding an equity index ETF with stocks screened for quality to add desired exposure to a quality factor.

Multi-factor ETFs that combine several factors also exist. They may adjust their weights dynamically as market opportunities and risk change. In a multi-factor ETF, strategy design involves factor selection, factor strategy construction, and a weighting scheme across factors that is managed over time. A multi-factor approach typically has lower return volatility than a single-factor approach over time but may also have less return potential for investors who want to capitalize on factor timing.

The success of active strategy ETFs is related to (1) whether the factor, as represented by a target benchmark factor index, performs well relative to expectations and (2) how effective the selected ETF is at delivering the benchmark factor return. Just as with traditional active investing, the success of active investing with ETFs depends on the skill of the ETF portfolio manager as well as the end investor's decision to undertake the investment strategy.

*Risk management.*

Some smart beta ETFs are constructed to deliver lower or higher risk than that of their asset class benchmark. For example, low-volatility factor ETFs select stocks on the basis of their relative return volatility and seek to represent a portfolio that offers a lower or target volatility return profile. These low-volatility rules-based factor ETFs have gained assets within each segment of the global equity market (domestic, developed international, and emerging markets) as investors have moved to lower volatility in portfolios. Other ETFs based on the beta characteristics of the constituent stocks can be used to adjust the portfolio's beta profile to desired levels.

ETFs are also used to manage other portfolio risks, such as currency and duration risk. ETFs that provide international exposure with a hedge on all or part of the associated currency risk are available. With respect to interest rate risk management, several smart beta fixed-income ETFs hold long positions in corporate or high-yield bonds and hedge out the duration risk of these bonds with futures or short positions in government bonds. These ETFs enable investors to add a position to their portfolio that seeks returns from taking credit risk with minimal sensitivity to movements in interest rates. Active investors with a negative macro view can use inverse asset class or factor ETF exposure to temporarily reduce benchmark holding risk. Doing so allows them to implement a macro view on a short-term basis and minimize turnover in underlying portfolio holdings.

*Alternatively weighted ETFs.*

ETFs that weight their constituents by means other than market capitalization, such as equal weighting or weightings based on fundamentals, can also be used to implement investment views—for example, ETFs that weight constituent stocks on the basis of their dividend yields. These ETFs select or overweight stocks with higher dividend yields, subject to other fundamental criteria or constraints, and are used by investors seeking income-generating strategies.

*Discretionary active ETFs.*

The largest active ETFs are in fixed income, where passive management is much less prominent than in equities. The PIMCO Active Bond ETF (BOND) launched in 2012 with an investment objective similar to that of the world's largest mutual fund at that time, the PIMCO Total Return Fund. Shorter-maturity, actively managed ETFs are also available in fixed income. Other active ETFs include exposure to senior bank loans, floating rate debt, and mortgage securities. Active equity ETFs have also been launched in areas of the technology industry.

"Liquid alternative" ETFs are based on strategy indexes that attempt to deliver absolute return performance and/or risk diversification of stock and bond holdings. Some of the first liquid alternative ETFs used rules-based strategies to replicate broad hedge fund indexes. Other strategy indexes offer transparent, rules-based, "hedge fund–like" strategies in specific types of alternatives. Such strategies include long–short, managed futures, private equity, and merger arbitrage.

### *Dynamic asset allocation and multi-asset strategies.*

ETF availability across a wide range of equity and bond risk exposures has fostered greater use of dynamic, top-down investment strategies based on return and risk forecasts. Asset managers, hedge funds, and asset owners have increasingly used ETFs for discretionary asset allocation or global macro strategies. Dynamic asset allocation ETF strategies are also available in commodities. Although some strategies allocate holdings on the basis of their relative risk contribution and others are return focused, all involve adjustments back to target weights, as defined by a dynamic investment process. Some pension and sovereign wealth funds implement these strategies in house, whereas other investors hire asset managers that offer multi-asset strategies. Implementation is done using ETFs, along with futures and swaps where available and when they are more efficient to trade.

Proper use of an active or factor strategy ETF requires investors to research and assess the index construction methodology and performance history and to ensure consistency with their investment view.

Exhibit 18 provides a summary of active and factor ETF portfolio applications, covering their roles in the portfolio, categories of use, and examples by benchmark type. These applications relate to ETFs as alternatives to other fund products, such as active mutual funds. In these cases, ETF evaluation is based on features of the investment approach, holdings, cost, risk, and return potential, as well as the impact to the portfolio's overall risk and return.

### Exhibit 18: ETF Portfolio Applications—Active and Factor Investing

| Portfolio Application | Category | Role in Portfolio | Examples of ETFs by Benchmark Type |
|---|---|---|---|
| Factor exposure | Strategic, dynamic, or tactical | Capture risk premium for one or more factors driving returns or risk<br>Overweight or underweight depending on factor return or risk outlook<br>Seek to capture alpha from rules-based screening and rebalancing (systematic active) | Quality, dividend growth, value, momentum, low volatility, liquidity screen, multi-factor |
| Risk management | Dynamic or tactical | Adjust equity beta, duration, credit, or currency risk | Currency-hedged, low-volatility, or downside-risk-managed ETFs |
| Leveraged and inverse exposure | Tactical | Access leveraged or short exposure for short-term tilts or risk management<br>Limit losses on shorting to invested funds | ETFs representing asset classes, countries, or industries with leveraged or inverse daily return targets |
| Alternative weighting | Strategic, dynamic, or tactical | Seek outperformance from weighting based on one or more fundamental factors<br>Balance or manage risk of security holdings | ETFs weighted by fundamentals, dividends, or risk; equal-weighted ETFs |

| Portfolio Application | Category | Role in Portfolio | Examples of ETFs by Benchmark Type |
|---|---|---|---|
| Active strategies within an asset class | Strategic | Access discretionary active management in an ETF structure | ETFs from reputable fixed income or equity managers with active approach or theme |
| Dynamic asset allocation and multi-asset strategies | Dynamic or tactical | Seek returns from active allocation across asset classes or factors based on return or risk outlook<br>Invest in a multi-asset-class strategy in single product | ETFs that allocate across asset categories or investment themes based on quantitative or fundamental factors |

# SUMMARY

We have examined important considerations for ETF investors, including how ETFs work and trade, tax efficient attributes, and key portfolio uses. The following is a summary of key points:

- ETFs rely on a creation/redemption mechanism that allows for the continuous creation and redemption of ETF shares.
- The only investors who can create or redeem new ETF shares are a special group of institutional investors called authorized participants.
- ETFs trade on both the primary market (directly between APs and issuers) and on the secondary markets (exchange-based or OTC trades, such as listed equity).
- End investors trade ETFs on the secondary markets, like stocks.
- Holding period performance deviations (tracking differences) are more useful than the standard deviation of daily return differences (tracking error).
- ETF tracking differences from the index occur for the following reasons:
  - fees and expenses,
  - representative sampling/optimization,
  - use of depositary receipts and other ETFs,
  - index changes,
  - fund accounting practices,
  - regulatory and tax requirements, and
  - asset manager operations.
- ETFs are generally taxed in the same manner as the securities they hold, with some nuances:
  - ETFs are more tax fair than traditional mutual funds, because portfolio trading is generally not required when money enters or exits an ETF.
  - Owing to the creation/redemption process, ETFs can be more tax efficient than mutual funds.
  - ETF issuers can redeem out low-cost-basis securities to minimize future taxable gains.
  - Local markets have unique ETF taxation issues that should be considered.

- ETF bid–ask spreads vary by trade size and are usually published for smaller trade sizes. They are tightest for ETFs that are very liquid and have continuous two-way order flow. For less liquid ETFs, the following factors can determine the quoted bid–ask spread of an ETF trade:
  - Creation/redemption costs, brokerage and exchange fees
  - Bid–ask spread of underlying securities held by the ETF
  - Risk of hedging or carry positions by liquidity provider
  - Market makers' target profit spread
- ETF bid–ask spreads on fixed income relative to equity tend to be wider because the underlying bonds trade in dealer markets and hedging is more difficult. Spreads on ETFs holding international stocks are tightest when the underlying security markets are open for trading.
- ETF premiums and discounts refer to the difference between the exchange price of the ETF and the fund's calculated NAV, based on the prices of the underlying securities and weighted by the portfolio positions at the start of each trading day. Premiums and discounts can occur because NAVs are based on the last traded prices, which may be observed at a time lag to the ETF price, or because the ETF is more liquid and more reflective of current information and supply and demand than the underlying securities in rapidly changing markets.
- Costs of ETF ownership may be positive or negative and include both explicit and implicit costs. The main components of ETF cost are
  - the fund management fee;
  - tracking error;
  - portfolio turnover;
  - trading costs, such as commissions, bid–ask spreads, and premiums/discounts;
  - taxable gains/losses; and
  - security lending.
- Trading costs are incurred when the position is entered and exited. These one-time costs decrease as a portion of total holding costs over longer holding periods and are a more significant consideration for shorter-term tactical ETF traders.
- Other costs, such as management fees and portfolio turnover, increase as a proportion of overall cost as the investor holding period lengthens. These costs are a more significant consideration for longer-term buy-and-hold investors.
- ETFs are different from exchange-traded notes, although both use the creation/redemption process.
  - Exchange-traded notes carry unique counterparty risks of default.
  - Swap-based ETFs may carry counterparty risk.
  - ETFs, like mutual funds, may lend their securities, creating risk of counterparty default.
  - ETF closures can create unexpected tax liabilities.

- ETFs are used for core asset class exposure, multi-asset, dynamic, and tactical strategies based on investment views or changing market conditions; for factor or smart beta strategies with a goal to improve return or modify portfolio risk; and for portfolio efficiency applications, such as rebalancing, liquidity management, completion strategies, and transitions.
- ETFs are useful for investing cash inflows, as well as for raising proceeds to provide for client withdrawals. ETFs are used for rebalancing to target asset class weights and for "completion strategies" to fill a temporary gap in an asset class category, sector, or investment theme or when external managers are underweight. When positions are in transition from one external manager to another, ETFs are often used as the temporary holding and may be used to fund the new manager.
- All types of investors use ETFs to establish low-cost core exposure to asset classes, equity style benchmarks, fixed-income categories, and commodities.
- For more tactical investing, thematic ETFs are used in active portfolio management and represent narrow or niche areas of the equity market not well represented by industry or sector ETFs.
- Systematic, active strategies that use rules-based benchmarks for exposure to such factors as size, value, momentum, quality, or dividend tilts or combinations of these factors are frequently implemented with ETFs.
- Multi-asset and global asset allocation or macro strategies that manage positions dynamically as market conditions change are also areas where ETFs are frequently used.
- Proper utilization requires investors to carefully research and assess the ETF's index construction methodology, costs, risks, and performance history.

## PRACTICE PROBLEMS

1. Which of the following statements regarding exchange-traded funds (ETFs) is correct? ETFs:

    A. disclose their holdings on a quarterly basis.

    B. trade in both primary and secondary markets.

    C. offer a creation/redemption mechanism that allows any investor to create or redeem shares.

2. The list of securities that a particular ETF wants to own, which is disclosed daily by all ETFs, is referred to as the:

    A. creation unit.

    B. creation basket.

    C. redemption basket.

3. When an authorized participant transacts to create or redeem ETF shares, the related costs are ultimately borne:

    A. solely by the ETF sponsor.

    B. solely by the AP.

    C. proportionally by all existing ETF shareholders.

4. Assuming arbitrage costs are minimal, which of the following is *most likely* to occur when the share price of an ETF is trading at a premium to its intraday NAV?

    A. New ETF shares will be created by the ETF sponsor.

    B. Redemption baskets will be received by APs from the ETF sponsor.

    C. Retail investors will exchange baskets of securities that the ETF tracks for creation units.

## The following information relates to questions 5-10

Howie Rutledge is a senior portfolio strategist for an endowment fund. Rutledge meets with recently hired junior analyst Larry Stosur to review the fund's holdings.

Rutledge asks Stosur about the mechanics of exchange-traded funds (ETFs). Stosur responds by making the following statements:

| | |
|---|---|
| Statement 1 | Unlike mutual fund shares that can be shorted, ETF shares cannot be shorted. |
| Statement 2 | In the ETF creation/redemption process, the authorized participants (APs) absorb the costs of transacting securities for the ETF's portfolio. |

## Practice Problems

Statement 3  If ETF shares are trading at a discount to NAV and arbitrage costs are sufficiently low, APs will buy the securities in the creation basket and exchange them for ETF shares from the ETF sponsor.

Rutledge notes that one holding, ETF 1, is trading at a premium to its intraday NAV. He reviews the ETF's pricing and notes that the premium to the intraday NAV is greater than the expected arbitrage costs.

Stosur is evaluating three ETFs for potential investment. He notes that the ETFs have different portfolio characteristics that are likely to affect each ETF's tracking error. A summary of the characteristics for the ETFs is presented in Exhibit 1.

### Exhibit 1: ETF Characteristics Affecting Tracking Error

|  | ETF 2 | ETF 3 | ETF 4 |
|---|---|---|---|
| Portfolio Construction Approach | Full Replication | Representative Sampling | Full Replication |
| Type of Foreign Holdings | Local shares | ADRs* | ADRs* |
| Engagement in Securities Lending | Yes | Yes | No |

*ADRs are American Depositary Receipts.

Rutledge and Stosur discuss the factors that influence ETF bid–ask spreads. Stosur tells Rutledge that quoted bid–ask spreads for a particular transaction size are (1) negatively related to the amount of the ongoing order flow in the ETF, (2) positively related to the costs and risks for the ETF liquidity provider, and (3) positively related to the amount of competition among market makers for the ETF.

As ETF shares may trade at prices that are different from the NAV, Rutledge examines selected data in Exhibit 2 for three ETFs that might have this problem.

### Exhibit 2: Selected Data on ETFs

|  | ETF 5 | ETF 6 | ETF 7 |
|---|---|---|---|
| Percentage of Foreign Holdings | 10% | 50% | 90% |
| Trading Frequency | High | Low | Low |

Rutledge considers a new ETF investment for the fund. He plans to own the ETF for nine months. The ETF has the following trading costs and management fees:

- Annual management fee of 0.32%
- Round-trip trading commissions of 0.20%
- Bid–offer spread of 0.10% on purchase and sale

Rutledge asks Stosur to compute the expected total holding period cost for investing in the ETF.

5. Which of Stosur's statements regarding ETF mechanics is correct?

   A. Statement 1

   B. Statement 2

   C. Statement 3

6. Given the current pricing of ETF 1, the *most likely* transaction to occur is that:
   A. new ETF shares will be created by the APs.
   B. redemption baskets will be received by APs from the ETF sponsor.
   C. retail investors will exchange baskets of securities that the ETF tracks for creation units.

7. Which ETF in Exhibit 1 is *most likely* to have the lowest tracking error?
   A. ETF 2
   B. ETF 3
   C. ETF 4

8. Stosur's statement about quoted bid–ask spreads is *incorrect* with respect to the:
   A. amount of the ongoing order flow in the ETF.
   B. costs and risks for the ETF liquidity providers.
   C. amount of competition among market makers for the ETF.

9. Which ETF in Exhibit 2 is *most likely* to trade at the largest premium or discount relative to NAV?
   A. ETF 5
   B. ETF 6
   C. ETF 7

10. Excluding the compounding effect, the expected total holding period cost for investing in the ETF over a nine-month holding period is *closest* to:
    A. 0.54%.
    B. 0.62%.
    C. 0.64%.

11. An ETF's reported tracking error is typically measured as the:
    A. standard deviation of the difference in daily returns between an ETF and its benchmark.
    B. difference in annual return between an ETF and its benchmark over the past 12 months.
    C. annualized standard deviation of the difference in daily returns between an ETF and its benchmark.

12. To best assess an ETF's performance, which reflects the impact of portfolio rebalancing expenses and other fees, an investor should:
    A. review daily return differences between the ETF and its benchmark.
    B. perform a rolling return assessment between the ETF and its benchmark.

C. compare the ETF's annual expense ratio with that of other ETFs in its asset class category.

13. An ETF's tracking error, as traditionally reported, indicates to investors:

    A. whether the ETF is underperforming or outperforming its underlying index.

    B. the magnitude by which an ETF's returns deviate from its benchmark over time.

    C. the distribution of differences in daily returns between the ETF and its benchmark.

14. For a typical ETF, which of the following sources of tracking error is *most likely* to be the smallest contributor to tracking error?

    A. Representative sampling

    B. Fees and expenses incurred by the ETF

    C. Changes to the underlying index securities

15. Which of the following statements relating to capital gains in ETFs and mutual funds is correct?

    A. ETFs tend to distribute less in capital gains than mutual funds do.

    B. Mutual funds may elect not to distribute all realized capital gains in a given year.

    C. The selling of ETF shares by some investors may create capital gains that affect the remaining ETF investors in terms of taxes.

16. Which of the following statements regarding distributions made by ETFs is correct?

    A. Return-of-capital (ROC) distributions are generally not taxable.

    B. ETFs generally reinvest any dividends received back into the ETF's holdings.

    C. A dividend distribution is a distribution paid to investors in excess of an ETF's earnings.

17. Investors buying ETFs:

    A. incur management fees that decrease with the length of the holding period.

    B. are assured of paying a price equal to the NAV if they purchase shares at the market close.

    C. incur trading costs in the form of commissions and bid–ask spreads at the time of purchase.

18. Consider an ETF with the following trading costs and management fees:

    - Annual management fee of 0.40%
    - Round-trip trading commissions of 0.55%

- Bid–offer spread of 0.20% on purchase and sale

Excluding compound effects, the expected total holding-period cost for investing in the ETF over a nine-month holding period is *closest* to:

A. 1.05%.

B. 1.15%.

C. 1.25%.

19. The bid–ask spread for very liquid, high-volume ETFs will be *least* influenced by the:

A. market maker's desired profit spread.

B. creation/redemption fees and other direct costs.

C. likelihood of receiving an offsetting ETF order in a short time frame.

20. Such factors as regulations, competition, and corporate actions relate to:

A. fund-closure risk.

B. counterparty risk.

C. expectation-related risk.

21. John Smith has invested in an inverse ETF. Smith is a novice investor who is not familiar with inverse ETFs, and therefore, he is unsure how the ETF will perform because of a lack of understanding of the ETF's risk and return characteristics. This risk is *best* described as:

A. counterparty risk.

B. holdings-based risk.

C. expectation-related risk.

22. Factor (smart beta) strategy ETFs are *least likely* to be used by investors:

A. to modify portfolio risk.

B. for tactical trading purposes.

C. to seek outperformance versus a benchmark.

23. Which of the following statements regarding applications of ETFs in portfolio management is correct?

A. Equity ETFs tend to be more active than fixed-income ETFs.

B. The range of risk exposures available in the futures market is more diverse than that available in the ETF space.

C. ETFs that have the highest trading volumes in their asset class category are generally preferred for tactical trading applications.

## SOLUTIONS

1. B is correct. ETFs trade in both primary and secondary markets. The primary market for ETF trading is that which exists on an over-the-counter basis between authorized participants (APs), a special group of institutional investors, and the ETF issuer or sponsor. This process is referred to as creation/redemption, and it is only through these primary market transactions that shares of the ETF can be created or destroyed. ETFs also trade in the secondary market on exchanges. Secondary market trading happens between any pair of market participants—individual or institutional investors, market makers, and so on.

2. B is correct. Each day, ETF managers publicly disclose a list of securities that they want to own, which is referred to as the creation basket. This basket also serves as the portfolio for determining the intrinsic net asset value (NAV) of the ETF on the basis of prices during the trading day.

3. B is correct. The AP generally absorbs all the costs associated with buying or selling the securities in the baskets or the ETF shares and pays an additional fee to the ETF provider to cover processing fees associated with creation/redemption activities. APs pass these costs to investors in the ETF's bid–ask spread, which is incurred by investors entering (ETF share buyers) and exiting (ETF share sellers) the fund.

4. A is correct. When the share price of an ETF is trading at a premium to its intraday NAV and assuming arbitrage costs are minimal, APs will step in and take advantage of the arbitrage. Specifically, APs will step in and buy the basket of securities that the ETF tracks (the creation basket) and exchange it with the ETF provider for new ETF shares (a creation unit). These new shares received by APs can then be sold on the open market to realize arbitrage profits.

5. B is correct. Statement 2 is correct. A significant advantage of the ETF creation/redemption process is that the AP absorbs all costs of transacting the securities for the fund's portfolio. APs pass these costs to investors in the ETF's bid–ask spread, incurred by ETF buyers and sellers. Thus, non-transacting shareholders of an ETF are shielded from the negative impact of transaction costs caused by other investors entering and exiting the fund. In contrast, when investors enter or exit a traditional mutual fund, the mutual fund manager incurs costs to buy or sell investments arising from this activity, which affects all fund shareholders. This makes the ETF structure inherently fairer: Frequent ETF traders bear the cost of their activity, while buy-and-hold ETF shareholders are shielded from those costs. Investors cannot short mutual fund shares, but they can short ETF shares. Also, if ETF shares are trading at a discount to NAV and arbitrage costs are sufficiently low, APs will buy ETF shares and exchange them for the securities in the redemption basket. Statement 3 describes the scenario that would occur if the ETF shares are trading at a premium to NAV.

   A is incorrect because Statement 1 is incorrect. Investors cannot short mutual fund shares, but they can short ETF shares.

   C is incorrect because Statement 3 is incorrect. If ETF shares are trading at a discount to NAV and arbitrage costs are sufficiently low, APs will buy ETF shares and exchange them for the securities in the redemption basket. Statement 3 describes the scenario that would occur if ETF shares are trading at a premium to NAV.

6. A is correct. When the share price of an ETF is trading at a premium to its intraday NAV and arbitrage costs are minimal, APs will step in and take advantage

of the arbitrage. Specifically, APs will buy the basket of securities that the ETF tracks (the creation basket) and exchange it with the ETF sponsor for new ETF shares (a creation unit). These new ETF shares received by APs can then be sold on the open market to realize arbitrage profits.

B is incorrect because in the case of an ETF trading at a premium to NAV, the APs will not receive redemption baskets of securities. Instead, the APs will deliver creation baskets to the ETF sponsor and receive new ETF shares.

C is incorrect because only APs can deliver creation baskets or receive redemption baskets from the ETF sponsors. Retail investors can buy and sell ETF shares on the open market.

7. A is correct. Compared with a full replication approach, ETF portfolios managed using a representative sampling/optimization approach are likely to have greater tracking error. Also, differences in trading hours for depositary receipts and local constituent shares create discrepancies between the portfolio and index values. These discrepancies can lead to greater tracking error for portfolios holding ADRs in lieu of the underlying local shares. Further, ETF sponsors that engage in securities lending can generate additional portfolio income to help offset fund expenses, thereby lowering tracking error. ETF 2 uses a full replication approach, holds only local foreign shares, and engages in securities lending. Therefore, ETF 2 will likely have the lowest tracking error out of the ETFs in Exhibit 1. ETF 3 will likely have greater tracking error than ETF 2 because it is managed using a representative sampling approach and is invested in depositary receipts in lieu of local shares. ETF 4 will likely have greater tracking error than ETF 2 because it is invested in depositary receipts in lieu of local shares and does not engage in securities lending.

8. C is correct. Several factors determine the width of an ETF's quoted bid–ask spread. First, the amount of ongoing order flow in the ETF is negatively related to the bid–ask spread (more flow means lower spreads). Second, the actual costs and risks for the liquidity provider are positively related to spreads (more costs and risks mean higher spreads); the spread is compensation to the liquidity provider for incurring these costs and risks. Finally, the amount of competition among market makers for that ETF is negatively related to the bid–ask spread (more competition means lower spreads).

A is incorrect because Stosur is correct in stating that the quoted bid–ask spread for a particular transaction size is negatively related to the amount of the ongoing order flow in the ETF (more flow means lower spreads).

B is incorrect because Stosur is correct in stating that the quoted bid–ask spread for a particular transaction size is positively related to the costs and risks for the ETF liquidity provider (more costs and risks mean higher spreads). The bid–ask spread represents the market maker's price for taking the other side of the ETF transaction, which includes the costs and risks to carry the position on its books and/or to hedge the position using underlying securities or closely related ETFs or derivatives.

9. C is correct. ETFs that trade infrequently may have large premiums or discounts to NAV, because the ETF may not have traded in the hours leading up to the market close and NAV may have significantly risen or fallen during that time because of market movement. Furthermore, NAV is often a poor fair value indicator for ETFs holding foreign securities because of differences in exchange closing times between the underlying (e.g., foreign stocks, bonds, or commodities) and the exchange where the ETF trades. Therefore, ETF 7 is most likely to have the largest discount or premium because it has a low trading frequency and has the highest

percentage of foreign holdings among the three ETFs.

A is incorrect because ETF 5 has the lowest percentage of foreign holdings among the three ETFs and is the one ETF with a high trading frequency. Therefore, relative to ETF 7, with its low trading frequency and high foreign holdings, ETF 5 is likely to trade at smaller premiums or discounts.

B is incorrect because ETF 6 has a lower percentage of foreign holdings than ETF 7. Even though both ETF 6 and ETF 7 have the same low trading frequency, the lower percentage of foreign holdings for ETF 6 is likely to result in it trading at smaller premiums or discounts.

10. A is correct. The expected total holding period cost for investing in the ETF over the nine-month holding period is calculated as follows:

    Total expected holding period cost

    = Annual management fee + Round-trip trading commissions + Bid–offer spread on purchase/sale.

    Total expected holding period cost = (9/12) × (0.32%) + 0.20% + 0.10% = 0.54%.

11. C is correct. An ETF's tracking error is typically reported as the annualized standard deviation of the daily differential returns of the ETF and its benchmark.

12. B is correct. A rolling return assessment, referred to in the ETF industry as the "tracking difference," provides a more informative picture of the investment outcome for an investor in an ETF. Such an analysis allows investors to see the cumulative effect of portfolio management and expenses over an extended period. It also allows for comparison with other annual metrics such as a fund's expense ratio. Tracking error, as a statistic, reveals only ETF tracking variability; it does not reveal to investors whether the fund is over- or underperforming its index or whether that tracking error is concentrated over a few days or is more consistently experienced. An ETF's expense ratio does not fully reflect the investor experience. That is, the expense ratio does not reflect the cost of portfolio rebalancing or other fees, making it an inferior assessment measure relative to a rolling return assessment.

13. B is correct. An ETF's tracking error is typically reported as the annualized standard deviation of the daily differential returns of the ETF and its benchmark. Therefore, an ETF's reported tracking error indicates to investors the magnitude by which an ETF's returns deviate from those of its benchmark over time.

14. C is correct. Although additions and deletions of securities from the underlying benchmark index may occur and result in tracking error, such index changes generally occur infrequently (often quarterly). In addition, ETF portfolio managers may work with APs for index rebalance trades to ensure market-on-close pricing to minimize this source of tracking error. Therefore, the resulting tracking error caused by index changes will not likely be as large as the tracking error caused by representative sampling or by fees and expenses incurred by the ETF.

15. A is correct. ETFs tend to distribute far less in capital gains relative to mutual funds. This is mostly due to the fact that ETFs have historically had significantly lower turnover than mutual funds have had.

16. A is correct. Return-of-capital distributions are amounts paid out in excess of an ETF's earnings and serve to reduce an investor's cost basis by the amount of the distribution. These distributions are generally not taxable.

17. C is correct. ETF trading costs in the form of commissions and bid–ask spreads

are paid by investors buying or selling ETF shares on an exchange. These trading costs are influenced by the bid–ask spread of the ETF, the size of the trade relative to the normal trading activity of the ETF, and the ease of hedging the ETF by the market-making community. Even the closing price of the ETF on the exchange includes a premium or discount to the NAV, driven by supply and demand factors on the exchange and the market impact costs of executing an exchange transaction. The purchase and sale trading costs of an ETF are paid regardless of holding period, whereas other costs, such as management fees, increase as the holding period lengthens.

18. A is correct. The expected total holding-period cost for investing in the ETF over a nine-month holding period is calculated as follows:

Total holding-period cost = Annual management fee + Round-trip trading commissions + Bid–offer spread on purchase/sale.

Total holding-period cost = (9/12) × (0.40%) + 0.55% + 0.20% = 1.05%.

19. B is correct. ETF bid–ask spreads are generally less than or equal to the combination of the following:

- ± Creation/redemption fees and other direct costs, such as brokerage and exchange fees
- + Bid–ask spread of the underlying securities held by the ETF
- + Compensation for the risk of hedging or carrying positions by liquidity providers (market makers) for the remainder of the trading day
- + Market maker's desired profit spread
- − Discount related to the likelihood of receiving an offsetting ETF order in a short time frame

For very liquid and high-volume ETFs, buyers and sellers are active throughout the trading day. Therefore, because most of these ETF trades are matched extremely quickly and never involve the creation/redemption process, the first three factors listed do not contribute heavily to their bid–ask spreads. So, creation/redemption fees and other direct costs are not likely to have much influence on these ETFs' bid–ask spreads.

20. A is correct. Fund-closure risk is the risk that an ETF may shut down. The reasons that lead to an ETF closing down often have to do with changes in regulations, increased competition, and corporate activity (merger and acquisition activity within the ETF industry).

21. C is correct. Expectation-related risk is the risk that some ETF investors may not fully understand how more complex ETFs will perform because of a lack of understanding of sophisticated assets classes and strategies.

22. B is correct. Factor strategy ETFs are usually benchmarked to an index created with predefined rules for screening and/or weighting stock holdings and are considered longer-term, buy-and-hold investment options rather than tactical trading instruments. The strategy index rules are structured around return drivers or factors, such as value, dividend yield, earnings or dividend growth, quality, stock volatility, or momentum. Investors using factor-based investing seek outperformance versus a benchmark or portfolio risk modification.

23. C is correct. ETFs that have the highest trading volumes in their asset class category are generally preferred for tactical trading applications.

# LEARNING MODULE 2

## Using Multifactor Models

by Jerald E. Pinto, PhD, CFA, and Eugene L. Podkaminer, CFA.

*Jerald E. Pinto, PhD, CFA, is at CFA Institute (USA). Eugene L. Podkaminer, CFA, is at Franklin Templeton Investments (USA).*

| LEARNING OUTCOMES | |
|---|---|
| Mastery | The candidate should be able to: |
| ☐ | describe arbitrage pricing theory (APT), including its underlying assumptions and its relation to multifactor models |
| ☐ | define arbitrage opportunity and determine whether an arbitrage opportunity exists |
| ☐ | calculate the expected return on an asset given an asset's factor sensitivities and the factor risk premiums |
| ☐ | describe and compare macroeconomic factor models, fundamental factor models, and statistical factor models |
| ☐ | describe uses of multifactor models and interpret the output of analyses based on multifactor models |
| ☐ | describe the potential benefits for investors in considering multiple risk dimensions when modeling asset returns |
| ☐ | explain sources of active risk and interpret tracking risk and the information ratio |

## 1. BACKGROUND AND USES

As used in investments, a **factor** is a variable or a characteristic with which individual asset returns are correlated. Models using multiple factors are used by asset owners, asset managers, investment consultants, and risk managers for a variety of portfolio construction, portfolio management, risk management, and general analytical purposes. In comparison to single-factor models (typically based on a market risk factor), multifactor models offer increased explanatory power and flexibility. These comparative strengths of multifactor models allow practitioners to

- build portfolios that replicate or modify in a desired way the characteristics of a particular index;

- establish desired exposures to one or more risk factors, including those that express specific macro expectations (such as views on inflation or economic growth), in portfolios;
- perform granular risk and return attribution on actively managed portfolios;
- understand the comparative risk exposures of equity, fixed-income, and other asset class returns;
- identify active decisions relative to a benchmark and measure the sizing of those decisions; and
- ensure that an investor's aggregate portfolio is meeting active risk and return objectives commensurate with active fees.

Multifactor models have come to dominate investment practice, having demonstrated their value in helping asset managers and asset owners address practical tasks in measuring and controlling risk. We explain and illustrate the various practical uses of multifactor models.

We first describe the modern portfolio theory background of multifactor models. We then describe arbitrage pricing theory and provide a general expression for multifactor models. We subsequently explore the types of multifactor models and certain applications. Lastly, we summarize major points.

## Multifactor Models and Modern Portfolio Theory

In 1952, Markowitz introduced a framework for constructing portfolios of securities by quantitatively considering each investment in the context of a portfolio rather than in isolation; that framework is widely known today as modern portfolio theory (MPT). Markowitz simplified modeling asset returns using a multivariate normal distribution, which completely defines the distribution of returns in terms of mean returns, return variances, and return correlations. One of the key insights of MPT is that any value of correlation among asset returns of less than one offers the potential for risk reduction by means of diversification.

In 1964, Sharpe introduced the capital asset pricing model (CAPM), a model for the expected return of assets in equilibrium based on a mean–variance foundation. The CAPM and the literature that developed around it has provided investors with useful and influential concepts—such as alpha, beta, and systematic risk—for thinking about investing. The concept of systematic risk, for example, is critical to understanding multifactor models: An investment may be subject to many different types of risks, but they are generally not equally important so far as investment valuation is concerned. Risk that can be avoided by holding an asset in a portfolio, where the risk might be offset by the various risks of other assets, should not be compensated by higher expected return, according to theory. By contrast, investors would expect compensation for bearing an asset's non-diversifiable risk: **systematic risk**. Theory indicates that only systematic risk should be **priced risk**. In the CAPM, an asset's systematic risk is a positive function of its beta, which measures the sensitivity of an asset's return to the market's return. According to the CAPM, differences in mean return are explained by a single factor: market portfolio return. Greater risk with respect to the market factor, represented by higher beta, is expected to be associated with higher return.

The accumulation of evidence from the equity markets during the decades following the CAPM's development have provided clear indications that the CAPM provides an incomplete description of risk and that models incorporating multiple sources of systematic risk more effectively model asset returns. Bodie, Kane, and Marcus (2017) provide an introduction to the empirical evidence. There are, however, various perspectives in practice on how to model risk in the context of multifactor models. We will examine some of these—focusing on macroeconomic factor models and fundamental factor models—in subsequent sections.

## ARBITRAGE PRICING THEORY AND MULTIFACTOR MODELS

- describe arbitrage pricing theory (APT), including its underlying assumptions and its relation to multifactor models
- define arbitrage opportunity and determine whether an arbitrage opportunity exists
- calculate the expected return on an asset given an asset's factor sensitivities and the factor risk premiums

In the 1970s, Ross (1976) developed the arbitrage pricing theory (APT) as an alternative to the CAPM. APT introduced a framework that explains the expected return of an asset (or portfolio) in equilibrium as a linear function of the risk of the asset (or portfolio) with respect to a set of factors capturing systematic risk. Unlike the CAPM, the APT does not indicate the identity or even the number of risk factors. Rather, for any multifactor model assumed to generate returns ("return-generating process"), the theory gives the associated expression for the asset's expected return.

Suppose that $K$ factors are assumed to generate returns. Then the simplest expression for a multifactor model for the return of asset $i$ is given by

$$R_i = a_i + b_{i1}I_1 + b_{i2}I_2 + \ldots + b_{iK}I_K + \varepsilon_i, \tag{1}$$

where

$R_i$ = the return to asset $i$

$a_i$ = an intercept term

$I_k$ = the return to factor $k$, $k = 1, 2, \ldots, K$

$b_{ik}$ = the sensitivity of the return on asset $i$ to the return to factor $k$, $k = 1, 2, \ldots, K$

$\varepsilon_i$ = an error term with a zero mean that represents the portion of the return to asset $i$ not explained by the factor model

The intercept term $a_i$ is the expected return of asset $i$ given that all the factors take on a value of zero. Equation 1 presents a multifactor return-generating process (a time-series model for returns). In any given period, the model may not account fully for the asset's return, as indicated by the error term. But error is assumed to average to zero. Another common formulation subtracts the risk-free rate from both sides of Equation 1 so that the dependent variable is the return in excess of the risk-free rate and one of the explanatory variables is a factor return in excess of the risk-free rate. (The Carhart model described next is an example.)

Based on Equation 1, the APT provides an expression for the expected return of asset $i$ assuming that financial markets are in equilibrium. The APT is similar to the CAPM, but the APT makes less strong assumptions than the CAPM. The APT makes just three key assumptions:

1. A factor model describes asset returns.
2. With many assets to choose from, investors can form well-diversified portfolios that eliminate asset-specific risk.
3. No arbitrage opportunities exist among well-diversified portfolios.

**Arbitrage** is a risk-free operation that requires no net investment of money but earns an expected positive net profit. (Note that "arbitrage," or the phrase "risk arbitrage," is also sometimes used in practice to describe investment operations in which significant risk is present). An **arbitrage opportunity** is an opportunity to conduct an arbitrage—an opportunity to earn an expected positive net profit without risk and with no net investment of money.

In the first assumption, the number of factors is not specified. The second assumption allows investors to form portfolios with factor risk but without asset-specific risk. The third assumption is the condition of financial market equilibrium.

Empirical evidence indicates that Assumption 2 is reasonable (Fabozzi, 2008). When a portfolio contains many stocks, the asset-specific or non-systematic risk of individual stocks makes almost no contribution to the variance of portfolio returns.

According to the APT, if these three assumptions hold, the following equation holds:

$$E(R_p) = R_F + \lambda_1 \beta_{p,1} + \ldots + \lambda_K \beta_{p,K}, \tag{2}$$

where

$E(R_p)$ = the expected return to portfolio $p$

$R_F$ = the risk-free rate

$\lambda_j$ = the expected reward for bearing the risk of factor $j$

$\beta_{p,j}$ = the sensitivity of the portfolio to factor $j$

$K$ = the number of factors

The APT equation, Equation 2, says that the expected return on any well-diversified portfolio is linearly related to the factor sensitivities of that portfolio. The equation assumes that a risk-free rate exists. If no risk-free asset exists, in place of $R_F$ we write $\lambda_0$ to represent the expected return on a risky portfolio with zero sensitivity to all the factors. The number of factors is not specified but must be much lower than the number of assets, a condition fulfilled in practice.

The **factor risk premium** (or **factor price**), $\lambda_j$, represents the expected reward for bearing the risk of a portfolio with a sensitivity of 1 to factor $j$ and a sensitivity of 0 to all other factors. The exact interpretation of "expected reward" depends on the multifactor model that is the basis for Equation 2. For example, in the Carhart four-factor model, shown later in Equation 3 and Equation 4, the risk premium for the market factor is the expected return of the market in excess of the risk-free rate. Then, the factor risk premiums for the other three factors are the mean returns of the specific portfolios held long (e.g., the portfolio of small-cap stocks for the "small minus big" factor) minus the mean return for a related but opposite portfolio (e.g., a portfolio of large-cap stocks, in the case of that factor). A portfolio with a sensitivity of 1 to factor $j$ and a sensitivity of 0 to all other factors is called a **pure factor portfolio** for factor $j$ (or simply the **factor portfolio** for factor $j$).

# Arbitrage Pricing Theory and Multifactor Models

For example, suppose we have a portfolio with a sensitivity of 1 with respect to Factor 1 and a sensitivity of 0 to all other factors. Using Equation 2, the expected return on this portfolio is $E_1 = R_F + \lambda_1 \times 1$. If $E_1 = 0.12$ and $R_F = 0.04$, then the risk premium for Factor 1 is

$0.12 = 0.04 + \lambda_1 \times 1$.

$\lambda_1 = 0.12 - 0.04 = 0.08$, or 8%.

### EXAMPLE 1

### Determining the Parameters in a One-Factor APT Model

Suppose we have three well-diversified portfolios that are each sensitive to the same single factor. Exhibit 1 shows the expected returns and factor sensitivities of these portfolios. Assume that the expected returns reflect a one-year investment horizon. To keep the analysis simple, all investors are assumed to agree upon the expected returns of the three portfolios as shown in the exhibit.

**Exhibit 1: Sample Portfolios for a One-Factor Model**

| Portfolio | Expected Return | Factor Sensitivity |
|---|---|---|
| A | 0.075 | 0.5 |
| B | 0.150 | 2.0 |
| C | 0.070 | 0.4 |

We can use these data to determine the parameters of the APT equation. According to Equation 2, for any well-diversified portfolio and assuming a single factor explains returns, we have $E(R_p) = R_F + \lambda_1 \beta_{p,1}$. The factor sensitivities and expected returns are known; thus there are two unknowns, the parameters $R_F$ and $\lambda_1$. Because two points define a straight line, we need to set up only two equations. Selecting Portfolios A and B, we have

$E(R_A) = 0.075 = R_F + 0.5\lambda_1$

and

$E(R_B) = 0.150 = R_F + 2\lambda_1$.

From the equation for Portfolio A, we have $R_F = 0.075 - 0.5\lambda_1$. Substituting this expression for the risk-free rate into the equation for Portfolio B gives

$0.15 = 0.075 - 0.5\lambda_1 + 2\lambda_1$.

$0.15 = 0.075 + 1.5\lambda_1$.

So, we have $\lambda_1 = (0.15 - 0.075)/1.5 = 0.05$. Substituting this value for $\lambda_1$ back into the equation for the expected return to Portfolio A yields

$0.075 = R_F + 0.05 \times 0.5$.

$R_F = 0.05$.

So, the risk-free rate is 0.05 or 5%, and the factor premium for the common factor is also 0.05 or 5%. The APT equation is

$E(R_p) = 0.05 + 0.05\beta_{p,1}$.

From Exhibit 1, Portfolio C has a factor sensitivity of 0.4. Therefore, according to the APT, the expected return of Portfolio C should be

$$E(R_B) = 0.05 + (0.05 \times 0.4) = 0.07,$$

which is consistent with the expected return for Portfolio C given in Exhibit 1.

### EXAMPLE 2

### Checking Whether Portfolio Returns Are Consistent with No Arbitrage

In this example, we examine how to tell whether expected returns and factor sensitivities for a set of well-diversified portfolios may indicate the presence of an arbitrage opportunity. Exhibit 2 provides data on four hypothetical portfolios. The data for Portfolios A, B, and C are repeated from Exhibit 1. Portfolio D is a new portfolio. The factor sensitivities given relate to the one-factor APT model $E(R_p) = 0.05 + 0.05\beta_{p,1}$ derived in Example 1. As in Example 1, all investors are assumed to agree upon the expected returns of the portfolios. The question raised by the addition of this new Portfolio D is whether the addition of this portfolio created an arbitrage opportunity. If a portfolio can be formed from Portfolios A, B, and C that has the same factor sensitivity as Portfolio D but a different expected return, then an arbitrage opportunity exists: Portfolio D would be either undervalued (if it offers a relatively high expected return) or overvalued (if it offers a relatively low expected return).

**Exhibit 2: Sample Portfolios for a One-Factor Model**

| Portfolio | Expected Return | Factor Sensitivity |
|---|---|---|
| A | 0.0750 | 0.50 |
| B | 0.1500 | 2.00 |
| C | 0.0700 | 0.40 |
| D | 0.0800 | 0.45 |
| 0.5A + 0.5C | 0.0725 | 0.45 |

Exhibit 2 gives data for an equally weighted portfolio of A and C. The expected return and factor sensitivity of this new portfolio are calculated as weighted averages of the expected returns and factor sensitivities of A and C. Expected return is thus (0.50)(0.0750) + (0.50)(0.07) = 0.0725, or 7.25%. The factor sensitivity is (0.50)(0.50) + (0.50)(0.40) = 0.45. Note that the factor sensitivity of 0.45 matches the factor sensitivity of Portfolio D. In this case, the configuration of expected returns in relation to factor risk presents an arbitrage opportunity involving Portfolios A, C, and D. Portfolio D offers, at 8%, an expected return that is too high given its factor sensitivity. According to the assumed APT model, the expected return on Portfolio D should be $E(R_D) = 0.05 + 0.05\beta_{D,1} = 0.05 + (0.05 \times 0.45) = 0.0725$, or 7.25%. Portfolio D is undervalued relative to its factor risk. We will buy D (hold it long) in the portfolio that exploits the arbitrage opportunity (the **arbitrage portfolio**). We purchase D using the proceeds from selling short an equally weighted portfolio of A and C with exactly the same 0.45 factor sensitivity as D.

The arbitrage thus involves the following strategy: Invest $10,000 in Portfolio D and fund that investment by selling short an equally weighted portfolio of Portfolios A and C; then close out the investment position at the end of one year (the investment horizon for expected returns). Exhibit 3 demonstrates the arbitrage profits to the arbitrage strategy. The final row of the exhibit shows the net cash flow to the arbitrage portfolio.

### Exhibit 3: Arbitrage Opportunity within Sample Portfolios

|  | Initial Cash Flow | Final Cash Flow | Factor Sensitivity |
|---|---|---|---|
| Portfolio D | −$10,000.00 | $10,800.00 | 0.45 |
| Portfolios A and C | $10,000.00 | −$10,725.00 | −0.45 |
| Sum | $0.00 | $75.00 | 0.00 |

As Exhibit 3 shows, if we buy $10,000 of Portfolio D and sell $10,000 of an equally weighted portfolio of Portfolios A and C, we have an initial net cash flow of $0. The expected value of our investment in Portfolio D at the end of one year is $10,000(1 + 0.08) = $10,800. The expected value of our short position in Portfolios A and C at the end of one year is −$10,000(1.0725) = −$10,725. So, the combined expected cash flow from our investment position in one year is $75.

What about the risk? Exhibit 3 shows that the factor risk has been eliminated: Purchasing D and selling short an equally weighted portfolio of A and C creates a portfolio with a factor sensitivity of 0.45 − 0.45 = 0. The portfolios are well diversified, and we assume any asset-specific risk is negligible.

Because an arbitrage is possible, Portfolios A, C, and D cannot all be consistent with the same equilibrium. If Portfolio D actually had an expected return of 8%, investors would bid up its price until the expected return fell and the arbitrage opportunity vanished. Thus, arbitrage restores equilibrium relationships among expected returns.

The Carhart four-factor model, also known as the four-factor model or simply the Carhart model, is a frequently referenced multifactor model in current equity portfolio management practice. Presented in Carhart (1997), it is an extension of the three-factor model developed by Fama and French (1992) to include a momentum factor. According to the model, three groups of stocks tend to have higher returns than those predicted solely by their sensitivity to the market return:

- Small-capitalization stocks
- Low price-to-book stocks, commonly referred to as "value" stocks
- Stocks whose prices have been rising, commonly referred to as "momentum" stocks

On the basis of that evidence, the Carhart model posits the existence of three systematic risk factors beyond the market risk factor. They are named, in the same order as above, the following:

- Small minus big (SMB)
- High minus low (HML)
- Winners minus losers (WML)

Equation 3 is the Carhart model, in which the excess return on the portfolio is explained as a function of the portfolio's sensitivity to a market index (RMRF), a market capitalization factor (SMB), a book-to-market factor (HML), which is essentially the reciprocal of the aforementioned price-to-book ratio, and a momentum factor (WML).

$$R_p - R_F = a_p + b_{p1}\text{RMRF} + b_{p2}\text{SMB} + b_{p3}\text{HML} + b_{p4}\text{WML} + \varepsilon_p, \qquad (3)$$

where

$R_p$ and $R_F$ = the return on the portfolio and the risk-free rate of return, respectively

$a_p$ = "alpha" or return in excess of that expected given the portfolio's level of systematic risk (assuming the four factors capture all systematic risk)

$b_p$ = the sensitivity of the portfolio to the given factor

RMRF = the return on a value-weighted equity index in excess of the one-month T-bill rate

SMB = small minus big, a size (market capitalization) factor; SMB is the average return on three small-cap portfolios minus the average return on three large-cap portfolios

HML = high minus low, the average return on two high book-to-market portfolios minus the average return on two low book-to-market portfolios

WML = winners minus losers, a momentum factor; WML is the return on a portfolio of the past year's winners minus the return on a portfolio of the past year's losers. (Note that WML is an equally weighted average of the stocks with the highest 30% 11-month returns lagged 1 month minus the equally weighted average of the stocks with the lowest 30% 11-month returns lagged 1 month.)

$\varepsilon_p$ = an error term that represents the portion of the return to the portfolio, $p$, not explained by the model

Following Equation 2, the Carhart model can be stated as giving equilibrium expected return as

$$E(R_p) = R_F + \beta_{p,1}\text{RMRF} + \beta_{p,2}\text{SMB} + \beta_{p,3}\text{HML} + \beta_{p,4}\text{WML} \qquad (4)$$

because the expected value of alpha is zero.

The Carhart model can be viewed as a multifactor extension of the CAPM that explicitly incorporates drivers of differences in expected returns among assets variables that are viewed as anomalies from a pure CAPM perspective. (The term "anomaly" in this context refers to an observed capital market regularity that is not explained by, or contradicts, a theory of asset pricing.) From the perspective of the CAPM, there are size, value, and momentum anomalies. From the perspective of the Carhart model, however, size, value, and momentum represent systematic risk factors; exposure to them is expected to be compensated in the marketplace in the form of differences in mean return.

Size, value, and momentum are common themes in equity portfolio construction, and all three factors continue to have robust uses in active management risk decomposition and return attribution.

# 3  TYPES OF MULTIFACTOR MODELS

- [ ] describe and compare macroeconomic factor models, fundamental factor models, and statistical factor models
- [ ] describe uses of multifactor models and interpret the output of analyses based on multifactor models

# Types of Multifactor Models

Having introduced the APT, it is appropriate to examine the diversity of multifactor models in current use.

In the following sections, we explain the basic principles of multifactor models and discuss various types of models and their application. We also expand on the APT, which relates the expected return of investments to their risk with respect to a set of factors.

## Factors and Types of Multifactor Models

Many varieties of multifactor models have been proposed and researched. We can categorize most of them into three main groups according to the type of factor used:

- In a **macroeconomic factor model**, the factors are surprises in macroeconomic variables that significantly explain returns. In the example of equities, the factors can be understood as affecting either the expected future cash flows of companies or the interest rate used to discount these cash flows back to the present. Among macroeconomic factors that have been used are interest rates, inflation risk, business cycle risk, and credit spreads.

- In a **fundamental factor model**, the factors are attributes of stocks or companies that are important in explaining cross-sectional differences in stock prices. Among the fundamental factors that have been used are the book-value-to-price ratio, market capitalization, the price-to-earnings ratio, and financial leverage.

- In a **statistical factor model**, statistical methods are applied to historical returns of a group of securities to extract factors that can explain the observed returns of securities in the group. In statistical factor models, the factors are actually portfolios of the securities in the group under study and are therefore defined by portfolio weights. Two major types of factor models are factor analysis models and principal components models. In factor analysis models, the factors are the portfolios of securities that best explain (reproduce) historical *return covariances*. In principal components models, the factors are portfolios of securities that best explain (reproduce) the historical *return variances*.

A potential advantage of statistical factor models is that they make minimal assumptions. But the interpretation of statistical factors is generally difficult in contrast to macroeconomic and fundamental factors. A statistical factor that is a portfolio with weights that are similar to market index weights might be interpreted as "the market factor," for example. But in general, associating a statistical factor with economic meaning may not be possible. Because understanding statistical factor models requires substantial preparation in quantitative methods, a detailed discussion of statistical factor models is outside the scope of our coverage.

Our discussion concentrates on macroeconomic factor models and fundamental factor models. Industry use has generally favored fundamental and macroeconomic models, perhaps because such models are much more easily interpreted and rely less on data-mining approaches. Nevertheless, statistical factor models have proponents and are also used in practical applications.

## The Structure of Fundamental Factor Models

We earlier gave the equation of a macroeconomic factor model as

$$R_i = a_i + b_{i1}F_1 + b_{i2}F_2 + \ldots + b_{iK}F_K + \varepsilon_i.$$

We can also represent the structure of fundamental factor models with this equation, but we need to interpret the terms differently.

In fundamental factor models, the factors are stated as *returns* rather than return *surprises* in relation to predicted values, so they do not generally have expected values of zero. This approach changes the meaning of the intercept, which is no longer interpreted as the expected return. Note that if the coefficients were not standardized, as described in the following paragraph, the intercept could be interpreted as the risk-free rate because it would be the return to an asset with no factor risk (zero factor betas) and no asset-specific risk (with standardized coefficients, the intercept is not interpreted beyond being an intercept in a regression included so that the expected asset-specific risk equals zero).

Factor sensitivities are also interpreted differently in most fundamental factor models. In fundamental factor models, the factor sensitivities are attributes of the security. An asset's sensitivity to a factor is expressed using a **standardized beta**: the value of the attribute for the asset minus the average value of the attribute across all stocks divided by the standard deviation of the attribute's values across all stocks.

$$b_{ik} = \frac{\text{Value of attribute } k \text{ for asset } i - \text{Average value of attribute } k}{\sigma(\text{Values of attribute } k)}. \quad (5)$$

Consider a fundamental model for equities that uses a dividend yield factor. After standardization, a stock with an average dividend yield will have a factor sensitivity of 0; a stock with a dividend yield one standard deviation above the average will have a factor sensitivity of 1; and a stock with a dividend yield one standard deviation below the average will have a factor sensitivity of −1. Suppose, for example, that an investment has a dividend yield of 3.5% and that the average dividend yield across all stocks being considered is 2.5%. Further, suppose that the standard deviation of dividend yields across all stocks is 2%. The investment's sensitivity to dividend yield is (3.5% − 2.5%)/2% = 0.50, or one-half standard deviation above average. The scaling permits all factor sensitivities to be interpreted similarly, despite differences in units of measure and scale in the variables. The exception to this interpretation is factors for binary variables, such as industry membership. A company either participates in an industry or does not. The industry factor is represented by dummy variables: The value of the variable is 1 if the stock belongs to the industry and 0 if it does not.

A second distinction between macroeconomic multifactor models and fundamental factor models is that with the former, we develop the factor (surprise) series first and then estimate the factor sensitivities through regressions. With the latter, we generally specify the factor sensitivities (attributes) first and then estimate the factor returns through regressions.

Financial analysts use fundamental factor models for a variety of purposes, including portfolio performance attribution and risk analysis. (*Performance attribution* consists of return attribution and risk attribution. *Return attribution* is a set of techniques used to identify the sources of the excess return of a portfolio against its benchmark. *Risk attribution* addresses the sources of risk, identifying the sources of portfolio volatility for absolute mandates and the sources of tracking risk for relative mandates.) Fundamental factor models focus on explaining the returns to individual stocks using observable fundamental factors that describe either attributes of the securities themselves or attributes of the securities' issuers. Industry membership, price-to-earnings ratio, book-value-to-price ratio, size, and financial leverage are examples of fundamental factors.

Example 4 discusses a study that examined macroeconomic, fundamental, and statistical factor models.

We encounter a range of distinct representations of risk in the fundamental models that are currently used in practical applications. Diversity exists in both the identity and exact definition of factors as well as in the underlying functional form and estimation procedures. Despite the diversity, we can place the factors of most fundamental factor models for equities into three broad groups:

- **Company fundamental factors**. These are factors related to the company's internal performance. Examples are factors relating to earnings growth, earnings variability, earnings momentum, and financial leverage.
- **Company share-related factors**. These factors include valuation measures and other factors related to share price or the trading characteristics of the shares. In contrast to the previous category, these factors directly incorporate investors' expectations concerning the company. Examples include price multiples, such as earnings yield, dividend yield, and book to market. Market capitalization falls under this heading. Various models incorporate variables relating to share price momentum, share price volatility, and trading activity that fall in this category.
- **Macroeconomic factors**. Sector or industry membership factors fall under this heading. Various models include such factors as CAPM beta, other similar measures of systematic risk, and yield curve level sensitivity—all of which can be placed in this category.

For global factor models, in particular, a classification of country, industry, and style factors is often used. In that classification, country and industry factors are dummy variables for country and industry membership, respectively. Style factors include those related to earnings, risk, and valuation that define types of securities typical of various styles of investing.

## Fixed-Income Multifactor Models

While the previous discussion focuses on equity applications, similar approaches are equally suited to fixed income. In addition, some of the same broad factor groupings are relevant for bonds.

### Macroeconomic Multifactor Models

Macroeconomic models, as discussed earlier, are easily translatable to fixed-income investing. For instance, surprises to economic growth, interest rates, and inflation will impact bond pricing, often mechanically.

Consider a bond factor model in which the returns are correlated with two factors. Following our earlier discussion, returns for bonds are assumed to be correlated with surprises in inflation rates and surprises in GDP growth. The return to *bond i*, $R_i$, can be modeled as

$$R_i = a_i + b_{i1}F_{INFL} + b_{i2}F_{GDP} + \varepsilon_i,$$

where

$R_i$ = the return to bond $i$

$a_i$ = the expected return to bond $i$

$b_{i1}$ = the sensitivity of the return on bond $i$ to inflation rate surprises

$F_{INFL}$ = the surprise in inflation rates

$b_{i2}$ = the sensitivity of the return on bond $i$ to GDP growth surprises

$F_{GDP}$ = the surprise in GDP growth (assumed to be uncorrelated with $F_{INFL}$)

$\varepsilon_i$ = an error term with a zero mean that represents the portion of the return to bond $i$ not explained by the factor model

### Fundamental Multifactor Models

Fundamental factor approaches have been developed to address the unique aspects of fixed income by using, for example, the following categories:

- Duration (ranging from cash to long-dated bonds)
- Credit (ranging from government securities to high yield)
- Currency (ranging from home currency to foreign developed and emerging market currencies)
- Geography (specific developed and emerging markets)

A simplified structure, shown in Exhibit 4, divides the US Barclays Bloomberg Aggregate index, a standard bond benchmark, into sectors, where each has such unique factor exposures as spread or duration. This factor model was developed by Dopfel (2004), and the factors have been chosen to cover three macro sectors plus high yield. The government sector is further broken down into three maturity buckets to help explain duration exposures.

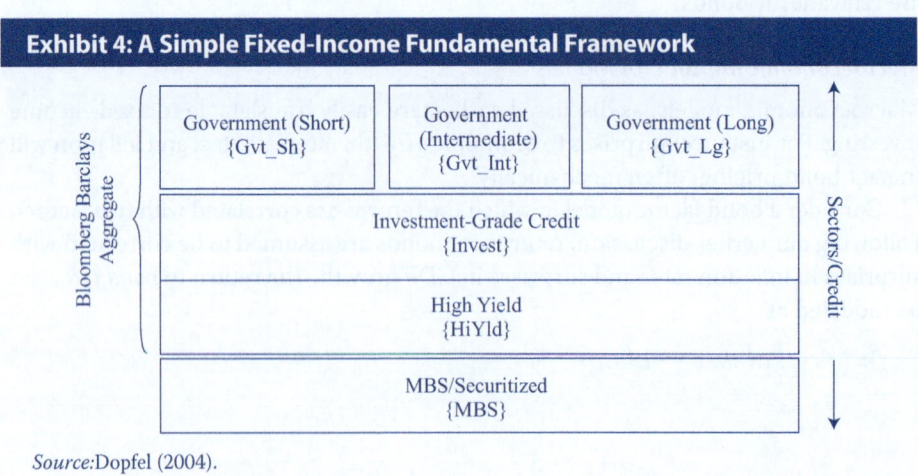

**Exhibit 4: A Simple Fixed-Income Fundamental Framework**

Source: Dopfel (2004).

These components can be thought of as both macroeconomic and fundamental. They are macroeconomically oriented because spread, or expected return above similar duration government bonds, is closely related to the growth factor and is sometimes expressed as simply credit spread. Fundamentally, duration can also be thought of as a factor. This simplistic approach can be extended to encompass global fixed-income markets or adapted to a specific country's market:

$$R_i = a_i + b_{i1}F_{Gvt\_Sh} + b_{i2}F_{Gvt\_Int} + b_{i3}F_{Gvt\_Lg} + b_{i4}F_{Invest} + b_{i5}F_{HiYld} + b_{i6}F_{MBS} + \varepsilon_i, \text{where}$$

$R_i$ = the return to bond $i$

$a_i$ = the expected return to bond $i$

$b_{ik}$ = the sensitivity of the return on bond $i$ to factor $k$

$F_k$ = factor $k$, where $k$ represents "Gov't (Short)," "Gov't (Long)," and so on

$\varepsilon_i$ = an error term with a zero mean that represents the portion of the return to bond $i$ not explained by the factor model

The historic style factor weights, $b_{ik}$, are determined by a constrained regression (the constraint being that the total "weights" add up to 100%) of the portfolio returns against the listed style factors.

This framework lends itself readily to performance and risk attribution, along with portfolio construction. When evaluating a fixed-income manager, such characteristics as spread, duration, yield, and quality can be incorporated. This type of framework can also be extended to ESG (environmental, social, and governance) considerations as these should be generally unrelated to the basic duration and spread foundation presented. For instance, each box in Exhibit 4 could also contain E, S, and G scores, which after the initial disaggregation of a fixed-income return stream into duration and spread components could be used to model the overall portfolio's aggregate scores. For forward-looking portfolio construction purposes, a desired loading on duration, spread, and ESG scores could be handled with a quantitative objective function.

### Risk and Style Multifactor Models

Another category of multifactor approach incorporates risk, or style, factors, several of which can thematically apply across asset classes. Examples of such factors include momentum, value, carry, and volatility. Many of these are similar in construction to those commonly used in equity portfolios. Examples include defining value as real (inflation-adjusted) yield, momentum as the previous 12-month excess return, and carry as the term spread. An illustrative example of risk factor approaches, in this case across asset classes, can be found in Exhibit 5.

**Exhibit 5: An Illustration of Factor Approaches across Asset Classes**

|       | Factor/Asset Class | Equity | Credit | Treasury | Commodities | Currency |
|-------|--------------------|--------|--------|----------|-------------|----------|
| Macro | Economic Growth    | xx     | x      |          |             |          |
|       | Rates              |        | x      | xx       |             |          |
|       | Inflation          |        |        | x        | xx          | x        |

| | Factor/Asset Class | Equity | Credit | Treasury | Commodities | Currency |
|---|---|---|---|---|---|---|
| Style | Value | xx | x | | x | x |
| | Size | xx | | | | |
| | Momentum | xx | xx | xx | xx | xx |
| | Carry | x | xx | xx | xx | xx |
| | Low-Volume | xx | x | | | |

*Note:* Double check marks denote strong alignment between risk factor and asset class; single check marks denote moderate alignment.
*Source:* Podkaminer (2017).

Of the three types of multifactor models (macroeconomic, fundamental, and statistical), statistical models can be most easily applied to various asset classes, including fixed income, as no asset-class-specific tuning is required given the minimal required assumption set. This is in contrast to macroeconomic and fundamental models, which both require adjustments and repurposing to ensure the frameworks are fit for the specifics of bond investing. Example 3 shows how expected return could be expressed.

### EXAMPLE 3

### Calculating Factor-Based Expected Returns at the Portfolio Level

1. A fixed-income portfolio has the following estimated exposures: 35% intermediate government bonds, 40% investment-grade credit, 5% securitized, and 20% high yield. The expected component returns are

    A. Short government bonds: 0.25%
    B. Intermediate government bonds: 1.50%
    C. Long government bonds: 3.00%
    D. Investment-grade credit: 4.25%
    E. MBS/Securitized: 1.75%
    F. High yield: 5.75%
    G. Express the expected return of the portfolio.

### Solution

Expected return could be expressed as

$E(R) = 3.46\%$
$= (0.35)(1.50\%) + (0.40)(4.25\%) + (0.05)(1.75\%) + (0.20)(5.75\%)$.

### EXAMPLE 4

### Reconciling Bond Portfolio Characteristics Using Style Factors

Talia Ayalon is evaluating intermediate duration (between 5 and 7 years) investment-grade fixed-income strategies using the framework presented in Exhibit 4. One of the strategies has the following sector attribution (totaling to 100%):

| | | |
|---|---|---|
| Gov't (Short) 2% | Gov't (Intermediate) 4% | Gov't (Long) 14% |
| Investment-Grade Credit 56% | | |
| MBS/Securitized 6% | | |
| High Yield 18% | | |

Are these sector exposures consistent with an intermediate duration investment-grade approach? Why or why not?

**Suggested answer:**

No, the sector exposures are inconsistent with the stated approach for two reasons: 1) The 18% exposure to high yield constitutes a significant amount of below investment-grade exposure. A true investment-grade portfolio would, for example, not have exposure to high yield. 2) The loading to longer duration sectors implies a longer-than-intermediate duration for the portfolio.

# MACROECONOMIC FACTOR MODELS

- [ ] calculate the expected return on an asset given an asset's factor sensitivities and the factor risk premiums
- [ ] describe and compare macroeconomic factor models, fundamental factor models, and statistical factor models

The representation of returns in macroeconomic factor models assumes that the returns to each asset are correlated with only the surprises in some factors related to the aggregate economy, such as inflation or real output. We can define *surprise* in general as the actual value minus predicted (or expected) value. A factor's surprise is the component of the factor's return that was unexpected, and the factor surprises constitute the model's independent variables. This idea contrasts with the representation of independent variables as returns in Equation 2, reflecting the fact that how the independent variables are represented varies across different types of models.

Suppose that $K$ macro factors explain asset returns. Then in a macroeconomic factor model, Equation 6 expresses the return of asset $i$:

$$R_i = a_i + b_{i1}F_1 + b_{i2}F_2 + \ldots + b_{iK}F_K + \varepsilon_i, \tag{6}$$

where

$R_i$ = the return to asset $i$

$a_i$ = the expected return to asset $i$   *The intercept is the expected return*

$b_{ik}$ = the sensitivity of the return on asset $i$ to a surprise in factor $k$, $k = 1, 2, \ldots, K$

$F_k$ = the surprise in the factor $k$, $k = 1, 2, \ldots, K$   *Surprise = actual − expected*

$\varepsilon_i$ = an error term with a zero mean that represents the portion of the return to asset $i$ not explained by the factor model

Surprise in a macroeconomic factor can be illustrated as follows: Suppose we are analyzing monthly returns for stocks. At the beginning of each month, we have a prediction of inflation for the month. The prediction may come from an econometric model or a professional economic forecaster, for example. Suppose our forecast at the beginning of the month is that inflation will be 0.4% during the month. At the end of the month, we find that inflation was actually 0.5% during the month. During any month,

Actual inflation = Predicted inflation + Surprise inflation.

In this case, actual inflation was 0.5% and predicted inflation was 0.4%. Therefore, the surprise in inflation was 0.5% − 0.4% = 0.1%.

What is the effect of defining the factors in terms of surprises? Suppose we believe that inflation and gross domestic product (GDP) growth are two factors that carry risk premiums; that is, inflation and GDP represent priced risk. (GDP is a money measure of the goods and services produced within a country's borders.) We do not use the predicted values of these variables because the predicted values should already be reflected in stock prices and thus in their expected returns. The intercept $a_i$, the expected return to asset $i$, reflects the effect of the predicted values of the macroeconomic variables on expected stock returns. The surprise in the macroeconomic variables during the month, however, contains new information about the variable. As a result, this model structure analyzes the return to an asset in three components: the asset's expected return, its unexpected return resulting from new information about the factors, and an error term.

Consider a factor model in which the returns to each asset are correlated with two factors. For example, we might assume that the returns for a particular stock are correlated with surprises in inflation rates and surprises in GDP growth. For stock $i$, the return to the stock can be modeled as

$$R_i = a_i + b_{i1}F_{INFL} + b_{i2}F_{GDP} + \varepsilon_i,$$

where

$R_i$ = the return to stock $i$

$a_i$ = the expected return to stock $i$

$b_{i1}$ = the sensitivity of the return on stock $i$ to inflation rate surprises

$F_{INFL}$ = the surprise in inflation rates

$b_{i2}$ = the sensitivity of the return on stock $i$ to GDP growth surprises

$F_{GDP}$ = the surprise in GDP growth (assumed to be uncorrelated with $F_{INFL}$)

$\varepsilon_i$ = an error term with a zero mean that represents the portion of the return to asset $i$ not explained by the factor model

Consider first how to interpret $b_{i1}$. The factor model predicts that a 1 percentage point surprise in inflation rates will contribute $b_{i1}$ percentage points to the return to stock $i$. The slope coefficient $b_{i2}$ has a similar interpretation relative to the GDP growth factor. Thus, slope coefficients are naturally interpreted as the factor sensitivities of the asset. A *factor sensitivity* is a measure of the response of return to each unit of increase in a factor, holding all other factors constant. (Factor sensitivities are sometimes called *factor betas* or *factor loadings*.)

Now consider how to interpret the intercept $a_i$. Recall that the error term has a mean or average value of zero. If the surprises in both inflation rates and GDP growth are zero, the factor model predicts that the return to asset $i$ will be $a_i$. Thus, $a_i$ is the expected value of the return to stock $i$.

Finally, consider the error term, $\varepsilon_i$. The intercept $a_i$ represents the asset's expected return. The term $(b_{i1}F_{INFL} + b_{i2}F_{GDP})$ represents the return resulting from factor surprises, and we have interpreted these as the sources of risk shared with other assets. The term $\varepsilon_i$ is the part of return that is unexplained by expected return or the factor surprises. If we have adequately represented the sources of common risk (the factors), then $\varepsilon_i$ must represent an asset-specific risk. For a stock, it might represent the return from an unanticipated company-specific event.

The risk premium for the GDP growth factor is typically positive. The risk premium for the inflation factor, however, is typically negative. Thus, an asset with a positive sensitivity to the inflation factor—an asset with returns that tend to be positive in response to unexpectedly high inflation—would have a lower required return than if its inflation sensitivity were negative; an asset with positive sensitivity to inflation would be in demand for its inflation-hedging ability.

This discussion has broader applications. It can be used for various asset classes, including fixed income and commodities. It can also be used in asset allocation, where asset classes can be examined in relation to inflation and GDP growth, as illustrated in the following exhibit. In Exhibit 6, each quadrant reflects a unique mix of inflation and economic growth expectations. Certain asset classes or securities can be expected to perform differently in various inflation and GDP growth regimes and can be plotted in the appropriate quadrant, thus forming a concrete illustration of a two-factor model.

**Exhibit 6: Growth and Inflation Factor Matrix**

|  | *Inflation* | |
|---|---|---|
| **Growth** | **Low Inflation/Low Growth**<br>- Cash<br>- Government bonds | **High Inflation/Low Growth**<br>- Inflation-linked bonds<br>- Commodities<br>- Infrastructure |
|  | **Low Inflation/High Growth**<br>- Equity<br>- Corporate debt | **High Inflation/High Growth**<br>- Real assets (real estate, timberland, farmland, energy) |

*Note:* Entries are assets likely to benefit from the specified combination of growth and inflation.

In macroeconomic factor models, the time series of factor surprises are constructed first. Regression analysis is then used to estimate assets' sensitivities to the factors. In practice, estimated sensitivities and intercepts are often acquired from one of the many consulting companies that specialize in factor models. When we have the parameters for the individual assets in a portfolio, we can calculate the portfolio's parameters as a weighted average of the parameters of individual assets. An individual asset's weight in that calculation is the proportion of the total market value of the portfolio that the individual asset represents.

### EXAMPLE 5

### Estimating Returns for a Two-Stock Portfolio Given Factor Sensitivities

Suppose that stock returns are affected by two common factors: surprises in inflation and surprises in GDP growth. A portfolio manager is analyzing the returns on a portfolio of two stocks, Manumatic (MANM) and Nextech (NXT). The following equations describe the returns for those stocks, where the factors $F_{INFL}$ and $F_{GDP}$ represent the surprise in inflation and GDP growth, respectively:

$$R_{MANM} = 0.09 - 1F_{INFL} + 1F_{GDP} + \varepsilon_{MANM}.$$

$$R_{NXT} = 0.12 + 2F_{INFL} + 4F_{GDP} + \varepsilon_{NXT}.$$

One-third of the portfolio is invested in Manumatic stock, and two-thirds is invested in Nextech stock.

In evaluating the equations for surprises in inflation and GDP, convert amounts stated in percentage terms to decimal form.

1. Formulate an expression for the return on the portfolio.

### Solution to 1:

The portfolio's return is the following weighted average of the returns to the two stocks:

$$R_P = (1/3)(0.09) + (2/3)(0.12) + [(1/3)(-1) + (2/3)(2)]F_{INFL} + [(1/3)(1) + (2/3)(4)]F_{GDP} + (1/3)\varepsilon_{MANM} + (2/3)\varepsilon_{NXT}$$

$$= 0.11 + 1F_{INFL} + 3F_{GDP} + (1/3)\varepsilon_{MANM} + (2/3)\varepsilon_{NXT}.$$

2. State the expected return on the portfolio.

### Solution to 2:

The expected return on the portfolio is 11%, the value of the intercept in the expression obtained in the solution to 1.

3. Calculate the return on the portfolio given that the surprises in inflation and GDP growth are 1% and 0%, respectively, assuming that the error terms for MANM and NXT both equal 0.5%.

### Solution to 3:

$$R_P = 0.11 + 1F_{INFL} + 3F_{GDP} + (1/3)\varepsilon_{MANM} + (2/3)\varepsilon_{NXT}$$

$$= 0.11 + 1(0.01) + 3(0) + (1/3)(0.005) + (2/3)(0.005)$$

$$= 0.125, \text{ or } 12.5\%.$$

# FUNDAMENTAL FACTOR MODELS

5

- [ ] calculate the expected return on an asset given an asset's factor sensitivities and the factor risk premiums
- [ ] describe and compare macroeconomic factor models, fundamental factor models, and statistical factor models

### EXAMPLE 6

### Comparing Types of Factor Models

Connor (1995) contrasted a macroeconomic factor model with a fundamental factor model to compare how well the models explain stock returns.

Connor reported the results of applying a macroeconomic factor model to the returns for 779 large-cap US stocks based on monthly data from January 1985 through December 1993. Using five macroeconomic factors, Connor was able to explain approximately 11% of the variance of return on these stocks. Exhibit 7 shows his results.

#### Exhibit 7: The Explanatory Power of the Macroeconomic Factors

| Factor | Explanatory Power from Using Each Factor Alone | Increase in Explanatory Power from Adding Each Factor to All the Others |
|---|---|---|
| Inflation | 1.3% | 0.0% |
| Term structure | 1.1% | 7.7% |
| Industrial production | 0.5% | 0.3% |
| Default premium | 2.4% | 8.1% |
| Unemployment | −0.3% | 0.1% |
| All factors (total explanatory power) | | 10.9% |

*Notes:* The explanatory power of a given model was computed as 1 − [(Average asset −Specific variance of return across stocks)/(Average total variance of return across stocks)]. The variance estimates were corrected for degrees of freedom, so the marginal contribution of a factor to explanatory power can be zero or negative. Explanatory power captures the proportion of the total variance of return that a given model explains for the average stock.

*Source:* Connor (1995).

Connor also reported a fundamental factor analysis of the same companies. The factor model employed was the BARRA US-E2 model (as of 2019, the current version is E4). Exhibit 8 shows these results. In the exhibit, "variability in markets" represents the stock's volatility, "success" is a price momentum variable, "trade activity" distinguishes stocks by how often their shares trade, and "growth" distinguishes stocks by past and anticipated earnings growth (explanations of variables are from Grinold and Kahn 1994).

### Exhibit 8: The Explanatory Power of the Fundamental Factors

| Factor | Explanatory Power from Using Each Factor Alone | Increase in Explanatory Power from Adding Each Factor to All the Others |
|---|---|---|
| Industries | 16.3% | 18.0% |
| Variability in markets | 4.3% | 0.9% |
| Success | 2.8% | 0.8% |
| Size | 1.4% | 0.6% |
| Trade activity | 1.4% | 0.5% |
| Growth | 3.0% | 0.4% |
| Earnings to price | 2.2% | 0.6% |
| Book to price | 1.5% | 0.6% |
| Earnings variability | 2.5% | 0.4% |
| Financial leverage | 0.9% | 0.5% |
| Foreign investment | 0.7% | 0.4% |
| Labor intensity | 2.2% | 0.5% |
| Dividend yield | 2.9% | 0.4% |
| All factors (total explanatory power) | | 42.6% |

*Source:* Connor (1995).

As Exhibit 8 shows, the most important fundamental factor is "industries," represented by 55 industry dummy variables. The fundamental factor model explained approximately 43% of the variation in stock returns, compared with approximately 11% for the macroeconomic factor model. Because "industries" must sum to the market and the market portfolio is not incorporated in the macroeconomic factor model, some advantage to the explanatory power of the fundamental factor may be built into the specific models being compared. Connor's article also does not provide tests of the statistical significance of the various factors in either model; however, Connor's research is strong evidence for the usefulness of fundamental factor models. Moreover, this evidence is mirrored by the wide use of those models in the investment community. For example, fundamental factor models are frequently used in portfolio performance attribution. Typically, fundamental factor models employ many more factors than macroeconomic factor models, giving a more detailed picture of the sources of an investment manager's returns.

We cannot conclude from this study, however, that fundamental factor models are inherently superior to macroeconomic factor models. Each major type of model has its uses. The factors in various macroeconomic factor models are individually backed by statistical evidence that they represent systematic risk (i.e., risk that cannot be diversified away). The same may not be true of each factor in a fundamental factor model. For example, a portfolio manager can easily construct a portfolio that excludes a particular industry, so exposure to a particular industry is not systematic risk.

The two types of factors, macroeconomic and fundamental, have different implications for measuring and managing risk, in general. The macroeconomic factor set is parsimonious (five variables in the model studied) and allows a portfolio manager to incorporate economic views into portfolio construction by adjustments to portfolio exposures to macro factors. The fundamental factor set examined by Connor is large (67 variables, including the 55 industry dummy variables); at the expense of greater complexity, it can give a more detailed picture of risk in terms that are easily related to company and security characteristics. Connor found that the macroeconomic factor model had no marginal explanatory power when added to the fundamental factor model, implying that the fundamental risk attributes capture all the risk characteristics represented by the macroeconomic factor betas. Because the fundamental factors supply such a detailed description of the characteristics of a stock and its issuer, however, this finding is not necessarily surprising.

## FACTOR MODELS IN RETURN ATTRIBUTION

6

- [ ] calculate the expected return on an asset given an asset's factor sensitivities and the factor risk premiums
- [ ] describe uses of multifactor models and interpret the output of analyses based on multifactor models
- [ ] describe the potential benefits for investors in considering multiple risk dimensions when modeling asset returns

The following sections present selected applications of multifactor models in investment practice. The applications discussed are return attribution, risk attribution, portfolio construction, and strategic portfolio decisions. We begin by discussing portfolio return attribution and risk attribution, focusing on the analysis of benchmark-relative returns. After discussing performance attribution and risk analysis, we explain the use of multifactor models in creating a portfolio with a desired set of risk exposures.

Additionally, multifactor models can be used for asset allocation purposes. Some large, sophisticated asset owners have chosen to define their asset allocation opportunity sets in terms of macroeconomic or thematic factors and aggregate factor exposures (represented by pure factor portfolios as defined earlier). Many others are examining their traditionally derived asset allocation policies using factor models to map asset class exposure to factor sensitivities. The trend toward factor-based asset allocation has two chief causes: First is the increasing availability of sophisticated factor models (like the BARRA models used in the following examples); second is the more intense focus by asset owners on the many dimensions of risk.

### Factor Models in Return Attribution

Multifactor models can help us understand in detail the sources of a manager's returns relative to a benchmark. For simplicity, in this section we analyze the sources of the returns of a portfolio fully invested in the equities of a single national equity market, which allows us to ignore the roles of country selection, asset allocation, market timing, and currency hedging. The same methodology can, however, be applied across asset classes and geographies.

Analysts often favor fundamental multifactor models in decomposing (separating into basic elements) the sources of returns. In contrast to statistical factor models, fundamental factor models allow the sources of portfolio performance to be described using commonly understood terms. Fundamental factors are also thematically understandable and can be incorporated into simple narratives for clients concerning return or risk attribution.

Also, in contrast to macroeconomic factor models, fundamental models express investment style choices and security characteristics more directly and often in greater detail.

We first need to understand the objectives of active managers. As mentioned previously, managers are commonly evaluated relative to a specified benchmark. Active portfolio managers hold securities in different-from-benchmark weights in an attempt to add value to their portfolios relative to a passive investment approach. Securities held in different-from-benchmark weights reflect portfolio manager expectations that differ from consensus expectations. For an equity manager, those expectations may relate to common factors driving equity returns or to considerations unique to a company. Thus, when we evaluate an active manager, we want to ask such questions as, Did the manager have insights that were effectively translated into returns in excess of those that were available from a passive alternative? Analyzing the sources of returns using multifactor models can help answer these questions.

The return on a portfolio, $R_p$, can be viewed as the sum of the benchmark's return, $R_B$, and the **active return** (portfolio return minus benchmark return):

$$\text{Active return} = R_p - R_B. \tag{7}$$

With the help of a factor model, we can analyze a portfolio manager's active return as the sum of two components. The first component is the product of the portfolio manager's factor tilts (over- or underweights relative to the benchmark factor sensitivities) and the factor returns; we call this component the return from factor tilts. The second component of active return reflects the manager's skill in individual asset selection (ability to overweight securities that outperform the benchmark or underweight securities that underperform the benchmark); we call this component security selection. Equation 8 shows the decomposition of active return into those two components, where $k$ represents the factor or factors represented in the benchmark portfolio:

$$\text{Active return} = \sum_{k=1}^{K} \left[ (\text{Portfolio sensitivity})_k - (\text{Benchmark sensitivity})_k \right] \\ \times (\text{Factor return})_k + \text{Security selection} \tag{8}$$

In Equation 8, the portfolio's and benchmark's sensitivities to each factor are calculated as of the beginning of the evaluation period.

> **EXAMPLE 7**
>
> ### Four-Factor Model Active Return Decomposition
>
> As an equity analyst at a pension fund sponsor, Ronald Service uses the Carhart four-factor multifactor model of Equation 3a to evaluate US equity portfolios:
>
> $$R_p - R_F = a_p + b_{p1}\text{RMRF} + b_{p2}\text{SMB} + b_{p3}\text{HML} + b_{p4}\text{WML} + \varepsilon_p.$$
>
> Service's current task is to evaluate the performance of the most recently hired US equity manager. That manager's benchmark is an index representing the performance of the 1,000 largest US stocks by market value. The manager describes himself as a "stock picker" and points to his performance in beating the benchmark as evidence that he is successful. Exhibit 9 presents an analysis based on the Carhart model of the sources of that manager's active return during the year, given an assumed set of factor returns. In Exhibit 9, the entry "A. Return from Factor Tilts = 2.1241%" is the sum of the four numbers above

it. The entry "B. Security Selection" gives security selection as equal to −0.05%. "C. Active Return" is found as the sum of these two components: 2.1241% + (−0.05%) = 2.0741%.

### Exhibit 9: Active Return Decomposition

| Factor | Factor Sensitivity | | | Factor Return (4) | Contribution to Active Return | |
|---|---|---|---|---|---|---|
| | Portfolio (1) | Benchmark (2) | Difference (3) = (1) − (2) | | Absolute (3) × (4) | Proportion of Total Active |
| RMRF | 0.95 | 1.00 | −0.05 | 5.52% | −0.2760% | −13.3% |
| SMB | −1.05 | −1.00 | −0.05 | −3.35% | 0.1675% | 8.1% |
| HML | 0.40 | 0.00 | 0.40 | 5.10% | 2.0400% | 98.4% |
| WML | 0.05 | 0.03 | 0.02 | 9.63% | 0.1926% | 9.3% |
| | | | | A. Return from Factor Tilts = | 2.1241% | 102.4% |
| | | | | B. Security Selection = | −0.0500% | −2.4% |
| | | | | C. Active Return (A + B) = | 2.0741% | 100.0% |

From his previous work, Service knows that the returns to growth-style portfolios often have a positive sensitivity to the momentum factor (WML). By contrast, the returns to certain value-style portfolios, in particular those following a contrarian strategy, often have a negative sensitivity to the momentum factor. Using the information given, address the following questions (assume the benchmark chosen for the manager is appropriate):

1. Determine the manager's investment mandate and his actual investment style.

### Solution to 1:

The benchmarks chosen for the manager should reflect the baseline risk characteristics of the manager's investment opportunity set and his mandate. We can ascertain whether the manager's actual style follows the mandate by examining the portfolio's actual factor exposures:

- The sensitivities of the benchmark are consistent with the description in the text. The sensitivity to RMRF of 1 indicates that the assigned benchmark has average market risk, consistent with it being a broad-based index; the negative sensitivity to SMB indicates a large-cap orientation. The mandate might be described as large-cap without a value/growth bias (HML is zero) or a momentum bias (WML is close to zero).

- Stocks with high book-to-market ratios are generally viewed as value stocks. Because the equity manager has a positive sensitivity to HML (0.40), it appears that the manager has a value orientation. The manager is approximately neutral to the momentum factor, so the equity manager is not a momentum investor and probably not a contrarian value investor. In summary, these considerations suggest that the manager has a large-cap value orientation.

2. Evaluate the sources of the manager's active return for the year.

### Solution to 2:

The dominant source of the manager's positive active return was his positive active exposure to the HML factor. The bet contributed approximately 98% of the realized active return of about 2.07%. The manager's active exposure to the overall market (RMRF) was unprofitable, but his active exposures to small stocks (SMB) and to momentum (WML) were profitable. The magnitudes of the manager's active exposures to RMRF, SMB, and WML were relatively small, however, so the effects of those bets on active return were minor compared with his large and successful bet on HML.

3. What concerns might Service discuss with the manager as a result of the return decomposition?

### Solution to 3:

Although the manager is a self-described "stock picker," his active return from security selection in this period was actually negative. His positive active return resulted from the concurrence of a large active bet on HML and a high return to that factor during the period. If the market had favored growth rather than value without the manager doing better in individual security selection, the manager's performance would have been unsatisfactory. Service's conversations with the manager should focus on evidence that he can predict changes in returns to the HML factor and on the manager's stock selection discipline.

## 7. FACTOR MODELS IN RISK ATTRIBUTION

☐ explain sources of active risk and interpret tracking risk and the information ratio

☐ describe uses of multifactor models and interpret the output of analyses based on multifactor models

☐ describe the potential benefits for investors in considering multiple risk dimensions when modeling asset returns

Building on the discussion of active returns, this section explores the analysis of active risk. A few key terms are important to the understanding of how factor models are used to build an understanding of a portfolio manager's risk exposures. We will describe them briefly before moving on to the detailed discussion of risk attribution.

**Active risk** can be represented by the standard deviation of active returns. A traditional term for that standard deviation is **tracking error** (TE). **Tracking risk** is a synonym for tracking error that is often used in the CFA Program curriculum. We will use the abbreviation TE for the concept of active risk and refer to it usually as tracking error:

$$TE = s(R_p - R_B). \tag{9}$$

# Factor Models in Risk Attribution

In Equation 9, $s(R_p - R_B)$ indicates that we take the sample standard deviation (indicated by $s$) of the time series of differences between the portfolio return, $R_p$, and the benchmark return, $R_B$. We should be careful that active return and tracking error are stated on the same time basis. As an approximation assuming returns are serially uncorrelated, to annualize a daily TE based on daily returns, we multiply daily TE by $(250)^{1/2}$ based on 250 trading days in a year. To annualize a monthly TE based on monthly returns, we multiply monthly TE by $(12)^{1/2}$.

As a broad indication of the range for tracking error, in US equity markets a well-executed passive investment strategy can often achieve a tracking error on the order of 0.10% or less per year. A low-risk active or enhanced index investment strategy, which makes tightly controlled use of managers' expectations, often has a tracking error goal of 2% per year. A diversified active large-cap equity strategy that might be benchmarked to the S&P 500 Index would commonly have a tracking error in the range of 2%–6% per year. An aggressive active equity manager might have a tracking error in the range of 6%–10% or more.

Somewhat analogous to the use of the traditional Sharpe measure in evaluating absolute returns, the **information ratio** (IR) is a tool for evaluating mean active returns per unit of active risk. The historical or *ex post* IR is expressed as follows:

$$IR = \frac{\overline{R}_p - \overline{R}_B}{s(R_p - R_B)}. \tag{10}$$

In the numerator of Equation 10, $\overline{R}_p$ and $\overline{R}_B$ stand for the sample mean return on the portfolio and the sample mean return on the benchmark, respectively. The equation assumes that the portfolio being evaluated has the same systematic risk as its benchmark. To illustrate the calculation, if a portfolio achieved a mean return of 9% during the same period that its benchmark earned a mean return of 7.5% and the portfolio's tracking error (the denominator) was 6%, we would calculate an information ratio of (9% − 7.5%)/6% = 0.25. Setting guidelines for acceptable active risk or tracking error is one of the methods that some investors use to ensure that the overall risk and style characteristics of their investments are in line with their chosen benchmark.

Note that in addition to focusing exclusively on *active* risk, multifactor models can also be used to decompose and attribute sources of *total* risk. For instance, a multi-asset class multi-strategy long/short fund can be evaluated with an appropriate multifactor model to reveal insights on sources of total risk.

### EXAMPLE 8

#### Creating Active Manager Guidelines

The framework of active return and active risk is appealing to investors who want to manage the risk of investments. The benchmark serves as a known and continuously observable reference standard in relation to which quantitative risk and return objectives may be stated and communicated. For example, a US public employee retirement system invited investment managers to submit proposals to manage a "low-active-risk US large-cap equity fund" that would be subject to the following constraints:

- Shares must be components of the S&P 500.
- The portfolio should have a minimum of 200 issues. At time of purchase, the maximum amount that may be invested in any one issuer is 5% of the portfolio at market value or 150% of the issuers' weight within the S&P 500, whichever is greater.
- The portfolio must have a minimum information ratio of 0.30 either since inception or over the last seven years.

> - The portfolio must also have tracking risk of less than 3% with respect to the S&P 500 either since inception or over the last seven years.
>
> Once a suitable active manager is found and hired, these requirements can be written into the manager's guidelines. The retirement system's individual mandates would be set such that the sum of mandates across managers would equal the desired risk exposures.

Analysts use multifactor models to understand a portfolio manager's risk exposures in detail. By decomposing active risk, the analyst's objective is to measure the portfolio's active exposure along each dimension of risk—in other words, to understand the sources of tracking error. This can even be done at the level of individual holdings. Among the questions analysts will want to answer are the following:

- What active exposures contributed most to the manager's tracking error?
- Was the portfolio manager aware of the nature of his active exposures, and if so, can he articulate a rationale for assuming them?
- Are the portfolio's active risk exposures consistent with the manager's stated investment philosophy?
- Which active bets earned adequate returns for the level of active risk taken?

In addressing these questions, analysts often choose fundamental factor models because they can be used to relate active risk exposures to a manager's portfolio decisions in a fairly direct and intuitive way. In this section, we explain how to decompose or explain a portfolio's active risk using a multifactor model.

We previously addressed the decomposition of active return; now we address the decomposition of active risk. In analyzing risk, it is more convenient to use variances rather than standard deviations because the variances of uncorrelated variables are additive. We refer to the variance of active return as **active risk squared**:

$$\text{Active risk squared} = s^2(R_p - R_B). \tag{11}$$

We can separate a portfolio's active risk squared into two components:

- **Active factor risk** is the contribution to active risk squared resulting from the portfolio's different-from-benchmark exposures relative to factors specified in the risk model.
- **Active specific risk** or **security selection risk** measures the active non-factor or residual risk assumed by the manager. Portfolio managers attempt to provide a positive average return from security selection as compensation for assuming active specific risk.

As we use the terms, "active specific risk" and "active factor risk" refer to variances rather than standard deviations. When applied to an investment in a single asset class, active risk squared has two components:

$$\text{Active risk squared} = \text{Active factor risk} + \text{Active specific risk}. \tag{12}$$

Active factor risk represents the part of active risk squared explained by the portfolio's active factor exposures. Active factor risk can be found indirectly as the risk remaining after active specific risk is deducted from active risk squared. Active specific risk can be expressed as

$$\text{Active specific risk} = \sum_{i=1}^{n} (w_i^a)^2 \sigma_{\varepsilon_i}^2,$$

where $w_i^a$ is the $i$th asset's active weight in the portfolio (that is, the difference between the asset's weight in the portfolio and its weight in the benchmark) and $\sigma_{\varepsilon_i}^2$ is the residual risk of the $i$th asset (the variance of the $i$th asset's returns left unexplained by the factors).

# Factor Models in Risk Attribution

The direct procedure for calculating active factor risk is as follows. A portfolio's active factor exposure to a given factor $j$, $b_j^a$, is found by weighting each asset's sensitivity to factor $j$ by its active weight and summing the terms:

$$b_j^a = \sum_{i=1}^{n} w_i^a b_{ji}.$$

Then active factor risk equals

$$\sum_{i=1}^{K}\sum_{j=1}^{K} b_i^a b_j^a \operatorname{cov}(F_i, F_j).$$

## EXAMPLE 9

### A Comparison of Active Risk

Richard Gray is comparing the risk of four US equity managers who share the same benchmark. He uses a fundamental factor model, the BARRA US-E4 model, which incorporates 12 style factors and a set of 60 industry factors. The style factors measure various fundamental aspects of companies and their shares, such as size, liquidity, leverage, and dividend yield. In the model, companies have non-zero exposures to all industries in which the company operates. Exhibit 10 presents Gray's analysis of the active risk squared of the four managers, based on Equation 12 (note that there is a covariance term in active factor risk, reflecting the correlation of industry membership and the risk indexes, which we assume is negligible in this example). In Exhibit 10, the column labeled "Industry" gives the portfolio's active factor risk associated with the industry exposures of its holdings; the "Style Factor" column gives the portfolio's active factor risk associated with the exposures of its holdings to the 12 style factors.

#### Exhibit 10: Active Risk Squared Decomposition

| Portfolio | Active Factor | | | Active Specific | Active Risk Squared |
|---|---|---|---|---|---|
| | Industry | Style Factor | Total Factor | | |
| A | 12.25 | 17.15 | 29.40 | 19.60 | 49 |
| B | 1.25 | 13.75 | 15.00 | 10.00 | 25 |
| C | 1.25 | 17.50 | 18.75 | 6.25 | 25 |
| D | 0.03 | 0.47 | 0.50 | 0.50 | 1 |

*Note:* Entries are in % squared.

Using the information in Exhibit 10, address the following:

1. Contrast the active risk decomposition of Portfolios A and B.

### Solution to 1:

Exhibit 11 restates the information in Exhibit 10 to show the proportional contributions of the various sources of active risk. (e.g., Portfolio A's active risk related to industry exposures is 25% of active risk squared, calculated as 12.25/49 = 0.25, or 25%).

The last column of Exhibit 11 now shows the square root of active risk squared—that is, active risk or tracking error.

**Exhibit 11: Active Risk Decomposition (restated)**

| Portfolio | Active Factor (% of total active) | | | Active Specific (% of total active) | Active Risk |
|---|---|---|---|---|---|
| | Industry | Style Factor | Total Factor | | |
| A | 25% | 35% | 60% | 40% | 7% |
| B | 5% | 55% | 60% | 40% | 5% |
| C | 5% | 70% | 75% | 25% | 5% |
| D | 3% | 47% | 50% | 50% | 1% |

Portfolio A has assumed a higher level of active risk than B (7% versus 5%). Portfolios A and B assumed the same proportions of active factor and active specific risk, but a sharp contrast exists between the two in the types of active factor risk exposure. Portfolio A assumed substantial active industry risk, whereas Portfolio B was approximately industry neutral relative to the benchmark. By contrast, Portfolio B had higher active bets on the style factors representing company and share characteristics.

2. Contrast the active risk decomposition of Portfolios B and C.

### Solution to 2:

Portfolios B and C were similar in their absolute amounts of active risk. Furthermore, both Portfolios B and C were both approximately industry neutral relative to the benchmark. Portfolio C assumed more active factor risk related to the style factors, but B assumed more active specific risk. It is also possible to infer from the greater level of B's active specific risk that B is somewhat less diversified than C.

3. Characterize the investment approach of Portfolio D.

### Solution to 3:

Portfolio D appears to be a passively managed portfolio, judging by its negligible level of active risk. Referring to Exhibit 11, Portfolio D's active factor risk of 0.50, equal to 0.707% expressed as a standard deviation, indicates that the portfolio's risk exposures very closely match the benchmark.

The discussion of performance attribution and risk analysis has used examples related to common stock portfolios. Multifactor models have also been effectively used in similar roles for portfolios of bonds and other asset classes. For example, such factors as duration and spread can be used to decompose the risk and return of a fixed-income manager.

## FACTOR MODELS IN PORTFOLIO CONSTRUCTION

- [ ] describe uses of multifactor models and interpret the output of analyses based on multifactor models
- [ ] describe the potential benefits for investors in considering multiple risk dimensions when modeling asset returns

Equally as important to the use of multifactor models in analyzing a portfolio's active returns and active risk is the use of such multifactor models in portfolio construction. At this stage of the portfolio management process, multifactor models permit the portfolio manager to make focused bets or to control portfolio risk relative to the benchmark's risk. This greater level of detail in modeling risk that multifactor models afford is useful in both passive and active management.

- *Passive management.* In managing a fund that seeks to track an index with many component securities, portfolio managers may need to select a sample of securities from the index. Analysts can use multifactor models to replicate an index fund's factor exposures, mirroring those of the index tracked.
- *Active management.* Many quantitative investment managers rely on multifactor models in predicting alpha (excess risk-adjusted returns) or relative return (the return on one asset or asset class relative to that of another) as part of a variety of active investment strategies. In constructing portfolios, analysts use multifactor models to establish desired risk profiles.
- *Rules-based active management (alternative indexes).* These strategies routinely tilt toward such factors as size, value, quality, or momentum when constructing portfolios. As such, alternative index approaches aim to capture some systematic exposure traditionally attributed to manager skill, or "alpha," in a transparent, mechanical, rules-based manner at low cost. Alternative index strategies rely heavily on factor models to introduce intentional factor and style biases versus capitalization-weighted indexes.

In the following, we explore some of these uses in more detail. As indicated, an important use of multifactor models is to establish a specific desired risk profile for a portfolio. In the simplest instance, the portfolio manager may want to create a portfolio with sensitivity to a single factor. This particular (pure) factor portfolio would have a sensitivity of 1 for that factor and a sensitivity (or weight) of 0 for all other factors. It is thus a portfolio with exposure to only one risk factor and exactly represents the risk of that factor. As a pure bet on a source of risk, factor portfolios are of interest to a portfolio manager who wants to hedge that risk (offset it) or speculate on it. This simple case can be expanded to multiple factors where a factor replication portfolio can be built based either on an existing target portfolio or on a set of desired exposures. Example 10 illustrates the use of factor portfolios.

> **EXAMPLE 10**
>
> ### Factor Portfolios
>
> Analyst Wanda Smithfield has constructed six portfolios for possible use by portfolio managers in her firm. The portfolios are labeled A, B, C, D, E, and F in Exhibit 12. Smithfield adapts a macroeconomic factor model based on research presented in Burmeister, Roll, and Ross (1994). The model includes five factors:
>
> - Confidence risk, based on the yield spread between corporate bonds and government bonds. A positive surprise in the spread suggests that investors are willing to accept a smaller reward for bearing default risk and so that confidence is high.
> - Time horizon risk, based on the yield spread between 20-year government bonds and 30-day Treasury bills. A positive surprise indicates increased investor willingness to invest for the long term.
> - Inflation risk, measured by the unanticipated change in the inflation rate.
> - Business cycle risk, measured by the unexpected change in the level of real business activity.
> - Market timing risk, measured as the portion of the return on a broad-based equity index that is unexplained by the first four risk factors.
>
> **Exhibit 12: Factor Portfolios**
>
> | Risk Factor | Portfolios | | | | | |
> |---|---|---|---|---|---|---|
> | | A | B | C | D | E | F |
> | Confidence risk | 0.50 | 0.00 | 1.00 | 0.00 | 0.00 | 0.80 |
> | Time horizon risk | 1.92 | 0.00 | 1.00 | 1.00 | 1.00 | 1.00 |
> | Inflation risk | 0.00 | 0.00 | 1.00 | 0.00 | 0.00 | −1.05 |
> | Business cycle risk | 1.00 | 1.00 | 0.00 | 0.00 | 1.00 | 0.30 |
> | Market timing risk | 0.90 | 0.00 | 1.00 | 0.00 | 0.00 | 0.75 |
>
> *Note:* Entries are factor sensitivities.
>
> 1. A portfolio manager wants to place a bet that real business activity will increase.
>
>    Determine and justify the portfolio among the six given that would be most useful to the manager.
>
> ### Solution:
>
> Portfolio B is the most appropriate choice. Portfolio B is the factor portfolio for business cycle risk because it has a sensitivity of 1 to business cycle risk and a sensitivity of 0 to all other risk factors. Portfolio B is thus efficient for placing a pure bet on an increase in real business activity.

2. Would the manager take a long or short position in the portfolio chosen in Part A?

**Solution:**

The manager would take a long position in Portfolio B to place a bet on an increase in real business activity.

3. A portfolio manager wants to hedge an existing positive (long) exposure to time horizon risk.

Determine and justify the portfolio among the six given that would be most useful to the manager.

**Solution:**

Portfolio D is the appropriate choice. Portfolio D is the factor portfolio for time horizon risk because it has a sensitivity of 1 to time horizon risk and a sensitivity of 0 to all other risk factors. Portfolio D is thus efficient for hedging an existing positive exposure to time horizon risk.

4. What type of position would the manager take in the portfolio chosen in Part A?

**Solution:**

The manager would take a short position in Portfolio D to hedge the positive exposure to time horizon risk.

## CONSTRUCTING MULTIFACTOR PORTFOLIOS

In practice, most stock selection models use some common multifactor structure. Here, we describe constructing two types of multifactor portfolios—a benchmark portfolio and a risk parity portfolio—that target desired risk exposures to eight fundamental factors. The benchmark portfolio equally weights the pure factors, whereas the risk parity portfolio weights the pure factors based on equal risk contribution. We focus on the benchmark and risk parity portfolios because their factor weighting schemes are clear and objective.

### Setting the Scene: Pure Factor Portfolios

For demonstration purposes, we use fundamental factor models and choose common company- and company share–related factors from each main investment style (i.e., value, growth, price momentum, analyst sentiment, and quality):

1. *Defensive value*: Trailing earnings yield—companies with high earnings yield are preferred.
2. *Cyclical value*: Book-to-market ratio—companies with high book-to-market ratios (i.e., cheap stock valuations) are bought.
3. *Growth*: Consensus FY1/FY0 EPS growth—companies with high expected earnings growth are preferred.
4. *Price momentum*: 12M total return excluding the most recent month—companies with positive price momentum are preferred.
5. *Analyst sentiment*: 3M EPS revision—companies with positive earnings revisions are bought.
6. *Profitability*: Return on equity (ROE)—companies with high ROEs are bought.

7. *Leverage*: Debt/equity ratio—companies with low financial leverage are preferred.
8. *Earnings quality*: Non-cash earnings—companies with low accruals are bought. Research suggests that net income with low levels of non-cash items (i.e., accruals) is less likely to be manipulated.

The stock universe for this demonstration consists of the Russell 3000 Index (US), the S&P/TSX Composite Index (Canada), the MSCI China A Index (China), and the S&P Global Broad Market Index (all other countries). A pure factor portfolio is formed for each of the eight factors by buying the top 20% of stocks and shorting the bottom 20% of stocks ranked by the factor. Stocks held long and short are equally weighted, and the eight factor portfolios are each rebalanced monthly. Note that this demonstration does not account for transaction costs or other portfolio constraints. Other methods for forming pure factor portfolios include ranking stocks by Pearson IC (correlation between prior period factor scores and current period stock returns) or by Spearman Rank IC (correlation between prior period ranked factor scores and current period ranked stock returns), as well as ranking by other univariate regression methods. However, for simplicity, we follow the long–short portfolio approach.

A straightforward way to combine these pure factor portfolios into a multifactor portfolio is equal weighting. We call the equally weighted multifactor portfolio the "benchmark (BM) portfolio." The experience in practice is that portfolios constructed using this simple weighting scheme typically perform at least as well as those using more sophisticated optimization techniques.

Risk parity is a common alternative portfolio construction technique used in the asset allocation space. Risk parity accounts for the volatility of each factor and the correlations of returns among all factors to be combined into the multifactor portfolio. The objective is for each factor to contribute equally to the overall (or targeted) risk of the portfolio. Thus, a risk parity (RP) multifactor portfolio can be created by equally weighting the risk contribution of each of the eight pure factors mentioned.

## Constructing and Backtesting Benchmark and Risk Parity Multifactor Portfolios

To create a successful multifactor portfolio strategy, the investment manager needs to perform backtesting to assess factor performance and effectiveness. In a typical backtest, a manager first forms her investment hypothesis, determines her investment rules and processes, collects the required data, and creates the portfolio, and then she periodically rebalances and evaluates the portfolio.

In the rolling window backtesting methodology, analysts use a rolling window framework, fit factors based on the rolling window, rebalance the portfolio periodically, and then track performance. Thus, backtesting is a proxy for actual investing. As new information arrives, investment managers readjust their models and rebalance their stock positions, typically monthly. Thus, they repeat the same in-sample training/out-of-sample testing process. If the investment strategy's performance in out-of-sample periods is desirable and the strategy makes intuitive sense, then it is deemed successful.

The following exhibit illustrates rolling window backtesting of the defensive value factor from November 2011 to April 2012. On 30 November 2011, we compute each stock's trailing 12-month earnings yield, then buy the 20% of stocks with the highest earnings yield and short the bottom quintile of stocks, and assess performance using returns in the next month, December 2011, the out-of-sample (OOS) period. The process is repeated on 31 December 2011, and so on, and finally, we compute the average monthly return, volatility, Sharpe ratio, and drawdown from the test results of the six OOS periods.

## An Example of Rolling Window Backtesting of the Defensive Value Factor

| | 2010:12 | 2011:01 | 2011:02 | 2011:03 | 2011:04 | 2011:05 | 2011:06 | 2011:07 | 2011:08 | 2011:09 | 2011:10 | 2011:11 | 2011:12 | 2012:01 | 2012:02 | 2012:03 | 2012:04 | 2012:05 |
|---|---|---|---|---|---|---|---|---|---|---|---|---|---|---|---|---|---|---|
| 11/30/2011 | | | | | | | | | | | | In-Sample (Last 12M EPS/Price) | | OOS | | | | |
| 12/31/2011 | | | | | | | | | | | | | In-Sample (Last 12M EPS/Price) | | OOS | | | |
| 1/31/2012 | | | | | | | | | | | | | | In-Sample (Last 12M EPS/Price) | | OOS | | |
| 2/29/2012 | | | | | | | | | | | | | | | In-Sample (Last 12M EPS/Price) | | OOS | |
| 3/31/2012 | | | | | | | | | | | | | | | | In-Sample (Last 12M EPS/Price) | | OOS |
| 4/30/2012 | | | | | | | | | | | | | | | | | In-Sample (Last 12M EPS/Price) | OOS |

*Source:* Wolfe Research Luo's QES.

Constructing and backtesting multifactor portfolios is similar to the method just described, except that the rolling window procedure is implemented twice. First, we form the eight pure factor portfolios for each month from 1988 until May 2019 by implementing the rolling window procedure. Then, we combine the underlying factor portfolios into the multifactor portfolios using the two approaches—equally weighting all factors (i.e., benchmark, or BM, allocation) and equally risk weighting all factors (i.e., risk parity, or RP, allocation).

Importantly, the process for creating the multifactor portfolios requires a second implementation of the rolling window procedure to avoid look-ahead bias; note this second rolling window covers the same time span as the first one (i.e., 1988 until May 2019). At each month-end, the previous five years of monthly data are used to estimate the variance–covariance matrix for the eight factor portfolios. Once the covariance matrix is estimated, we optimize and compute the weights for each of the eight pure factor portfolios and then form the RP portfolio. Finally, we compute the returns of the two multifactor portfolios (BM and RP) during this out-of-sample period using the weights at the end of the previous month and the returns of the eight underlying factor portfolios for the current month. This process is repeated every month over the entire horizon of 1988 until May 2019.

We created and backtested the multifactor portfolios using both the equal weighting (BM) scheme and risk parity (RP) scheme for each of 10 markets, including the United States. Both multifactor portfolios are rebalanced monthly to maintain equal factor weights or equal factor risk contributions. As noted previously, the key input to the RP allocation is the monthly variance–covariance matrix for the eight underlying factor portfolios derived from the rolling (five-year) window procedure. To be clear, each of the eight factor portfolios is a long–short portfolio. However, our factor allocation strategies to form the BM and RP multifactor portfolios are long only, meaning the weights allocated to each of the eight factor portfolios are restricted to be non-negative. Therefore, factor weights for the BM and RP portfolios are positive and add to 100%.

In the United States over the period 1993–2019, the weights of the eight factor portfolios in the RP allocation are relatively stable. Interestingly, book-to-market and earnings quality factor portfolios receive the largest allocations, whereas ROE and price momentum factor portfolios have the lowest weights. The RP multifactor portfolio provides a lower cumulative return than does the BM multifactor portfolio; however, the RP portfolio's volatility is substantially lower than that of the BM portfolio. Consequently, in the United States, the RP portfolio's Sharpe ratio is nearly double that of the BM portfolio, as shown in the following exhibit. Outperformance of the RP portfolio in terms of Sharpe ratio is also apparent across most markets examined.

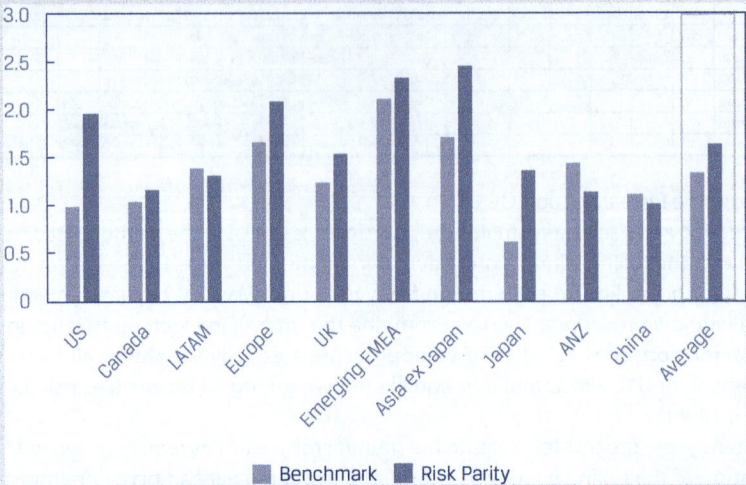

**Average Sharpe Ratios for Multifactor Portfolios: Equally Weighted vs. Risk Parity Weighted (1993–2019)**

*Sources:* Bloomberg Finance LLP, FTSE Russell, S&P Capital IQ, Thomson Reuters, Wolfe Research Luo's QES.

*The following case was written by Yin Luo, CPA, PStat, CFA, and Sheng Wang, both of Wolfe Research LLC (USA).*

## 9. FACTOR MODELS IN STRATEGIC PORTFOLIO DECISIONS

> ☐ describe uses of multifactor models and interpret the output of analyses based on multifactor models
>
> ☐ describe the potential benefits for investors in considering multiple risk dimensions when modeling asset returns

Multifactor models can help investors recognize considerations that are relevant in making various strategic decisions. For example, given a sound model of the systematic risk factors that affect assets' mean returns, the investor can ask, relative to other investors,

- What types of risk do I have a comparative advantage in bearing?
- What types of risk am I at a comparative disadvantage in bearing?

For example, university endowments, because they typically have very long investment horizons, may have a comparative advantage in bearing business cycle risk of traded equities or the liquidity risk associated with many private equity investments. They may tilt their strategic asset allocation or investments within an asset class to capture the associated risk premiums for risks that do not much affect them. However, such investors may be at a comparative disadvantage in bearing inflation risk to the extent that the activities they support have historically been subject to cost increases running above the average rate of inflation.

This is a richer framework than that afforded by the CAPM, according to which all investors optimally should invest in two funds: the market portfolio and a risk-free asset. Practically speaking, a CAPM-oriented investor might hold a money market fund and a portfolio of capitalization-weighted broad market indexes across many asset classes, varying the weights in these two in accordance with risk tolerance. These types of considerations are also relevant to individual investors. An individual investor who depends on income from salary or self-employment is sensitive to business cycle risk, in particular to the effects of recessions. If this investor compared two stocks with the same CAPM beta, given his concern about recessions, he might be very sensitive to receiving an adequate premium for investing in procyclical assets. In contrast, an investor with independent wealth and no job-loss concerns would have a comparative advantage in bearing business cycle risk; his optimal risky asset portfolio might be quite different from that of the investor with job-loss concerns in tilting toward greater-than-average exposure to the business cycle factor, all else being equal. Investors should be aware of which priced risks they face and analyze the extent of their exposure.

A multifactor approach can help investors achieve better-diversified and possibly more-efficient portfolios. For example, the characteristics of a portfolio can be better explained by a combination of SMB, HML, and WML factors in addition to the market factor than by using the market factor alone.

Thus, compared with single-factor models, multifactor models offer a richer context for investors to search for ways to improve portfolio selection.

## SUMMARY

In our coverage of multifactor models, we have presented concepts, models, and tools that are key ingredients to quantitative portfolio management and are used to both construct portfolios and to attribute sources of risk and return.

- Multifactor models permit a nuanced view of risk that is more granular than the single-factor approach allows.
- Multifactor models describe the return on an asset in terms of the risk of the asset with respect to a set of factors. Such models generally include systematic factors, which explain the average returns of a large number of risky assets. Such factors represent priced risk—risk for which investors require an additional return for bearing.
- The arbitrage pricing theory (APT) describes the expected return on an asset (or portfolio) as a linear function of the risk of the asset with respect to a set of factors. Like the CAPM, the APT describes a financial market equilibrium; however, the APT makes less strong assumptions.
- The major assumptions of the APT are as follows:
  - Asset returns are described by a factor model.
  - With many assets to choose from, asset-specific risk can be eliminated.
  - Assets are priced such that there are no arbitrage opportunities.
- Multifactor models are broadly categorized according to the type of factor used:
  - Macroeconomic factor models
  - Fundamental factor models
  - Statistical factor models

- In *macroeconomic* factor models, the factors are surprises in macroeconomic variables that significantly explain asset class (equity in our examples) returns. Surprise is defined as actual minus forecasted value and has an expected value of zero. The factors can be understood as affecting either the expected future cash flows of companies or the interest rate used to discount these cash flows back to the present and are meant to be uncorrelated.

- In *fundamental* factor models, the factors are attributes of stocks or companies that are important in explaining cross-sectional differences in stock prices. Among the fundamental factors are book-value-to-price ratio, market capitalization, price-to-earnings ratio, and financial leverage.

- In contrast to macroeconomic factor models, in fundamental models the factors are calculated as returns rather than surprises. In fundamental factor models, we generally specify the factor sensitivities (attributes) first and then estimate the factor returns through regressions. In macroeconomic factor models, however, we first develop the factor (surprise) series and then estimate the factor sensitivities through regressions. The factors of most fundamental factor models may be classified as company fundamental factors, company share-related factors, or macroeconomic factors.

- In *statistical* factor models, statistical methods are applied to a set of historical returns to determine portfolios that explain historical returns in one of two senses. In factor analysis models, the factors are the portfolios that best explain (reproduce) historical return covariances. In principal-components models, the factors are portfolios that best explain (reproduce) the historical return variances.

- Multifactor models have applications to return attribution, risk attribution, portfolio construction, and strategic investment decisions.

- A factor portfolio is a portfolio with unit sensitivity to a factor and zero sensitivity to other factors.

- Active return is the return in excess of the return on the benchmark.

- Active risk is the standard deviation of active returns. Active risk is also called tracking error or tracking risk. Active risk squared can be decomposed as the sum of active factor risk and active specific risk.

- The information ratio (IR) is mean active return divided by active risk (tracking error). The IR measures the increment in mean active return per unit of active risk.

- Factor models have uses in constructing portfolios that track market indexes and in alternative index construction.

- Traditionally, the CAPM approach would allocate assets between the risk-free asset and a broadly diversified index fund. Considering multiple sources of systematic risk may allow investors to improve on that result by tilting away from the market portfolio. Generally, investors would gain from accepting above average (below average) exposures to risks that they have a comparative advantage (comparative disadvantage) in bearing.

# REFERENCES

Bodie, Zvi, Alex Kane, Alan J. Marcus. 2017. Investments. 11th ed. New York: McGraw-Hill Education.

Burmeister, Edwin, Richard Roll, Stephen A. Ross. 1994. "A *Practitioner's* Guide to Arbitrage Pricing Theory." In A Practitioner's Guide to Factor Models. Charlottesville, VA: Research Foundation of the Institute of Chartered Financial Analysts.

Carhart, Mark M. 1997. "On Persistence in Mutual Fund Performance." Journal of Finance 52 (1): 57–82. 10.1111/j.1540-6261.1997.tb03808.x

Connor, Gregory. 1995. "The Three Types of Factor Models: A Comparison of Their Explanatory Power." Financial Analysts Journal 51 (3): 42–46. 10.2469/faj.v51.n3.1904

Dopfel, Frederick E. 2004. "Fixed-Income Style Analysis and Optimal Manager Structure." Journal of Fixed Income 14 (2): 32–43. 10.3905/jfi.2004.439835

Fabozzi, Frank J. 2008. Handbook of Finance, Financial Markets and Instruments. Wiley.

Fama, Eugene F., Kenneth R. French. 1992. "The Cross-Section of Expected Stock Returns." Journal of Finance 47 (2): 427–65. 10.1111/j.1540-6261.1992.tb04398.x

Grinold, Richard, Ronald N. Kahn. 1994. "Multi-Factor Models for Portfolio Risk." In A Practitioner's Guide to Factor Models. Charlottesville, VA: Research Foundation of the Institute of Chartered Financial Analysts.

Podkaminer, Eugene L. 2017. "Smart Beta Is the Gateway Drug to Risk Factor Investing." Journal of Portfolio Management 43 (5): 130–34. 10.3905/jpm.2017.43.5.130

Ross, S. A. 1976. "The Arbitrage Theory of Capital Asset Pricing." Journal of Economic Theory 13 (3): 341–60. 10.1016/0022-0531(76)90046-6

# PRACTICE PROBLEMS

1. Compare the assumptions of the arbitrage pricing theory (APT) with those of the capital asset pricing model (CAPM).

2. Assume that the following one-factor model describes the expected return for portfolios:

   $E(R_p) = 0.10 + 0.12\beta_{p,1}$

   Also assume that all investors agree on the expected returns and factor sensitivity of the three highly diversified Portfolios A, B, and C given in the following table:

   | Portfolio | Expected Return | Factor Sensitivity |
   |---|---|---|
   | A | 0.196 | 0.80 |
   | B | 0.156 | 1.00 |
   | C | 0.244 | 1.20 |

   Assuming the one-factor model is correct and based on the data provided for Portfolios A, B, and C, determine if an arbitrage opportunity exists and explain how it might be exploited.

## The following information relates to questions 3-8

Carlos Altuve is a manager-of-managers at an investment company that uses quantitative models extensively. Altuve seeks to construct a multi-manager portfolio using some of the funds managed by portfolio managers within the firm. Maya Zapata is assisting him.

Altuve uses arbitrage pricing theory (APT) as a basis for evaluating strategies and managing risks. From his earlier analysis, Zapata knows that Funds A and B in Exhibit 1 are well diversified. He has not previously worked with Fund C and is puzzled by the data because it is inconsistent with APT. He asks Zapata gather additional information on Fund C's holdings and to determine if an arbitrage opportunity exists among these three investment alternatives. Her analysis, using the data in Exhibit 1, confirms that an arbitrage opportunity does exist.

| Exhibit 1: Expected Returns and Factor Sensitivities (One-Factor Model) | | |
|---|---|---|
| Fund | Expected Return | Factor Sensitivity |
| A | 0.02 | 0.5 |
| B | 0.04 | 1.5 |
| C | 0.03 | 0.9 |

Using a two-factor model, Zapata now estimates the three funds' sensitivity to inflation and GDP growth. That information is presented in Exhibit 2. Zapata assumes a zero value for the error terms when working with the selected two-factor model.

## Practice Problems

**Exhibit 2: Expected Returns and Factor Sensitivities (Two-Factor Model)**

| Fund | Expected Return | Factor Sensitivity | |
|---|---|---|---|
| | | Inflation | GDP Growth |
| A | 0.02 | 0.5 | 1.0 |
| B | 0.04 | 1.6 | 0.0 |
| C | 0.03 | 1.0 | 1.1 |

Altuve asks Zapata to calculate the return for Portfolio AC, composed of a 60% allocation to Fund A and 40% allocation to Fund C, using the surprises in inflation and GDP growth in Exhibit 3.

**Exhibit 3: Selected Data on Factors**

| Factor | Research Staff Forecast | Actual Value |
|---|---|---|
| Inflation | 2.0% | 2.2% |
| GDP Growth | 1.5% | 1.0% |

Finally, Altuve asks Zapata about the return sensitivities of Portfolios A, B, and C given the information provided in Exhibit 3.

3. Which of the following is *not* a key assumption of APT, which is used by Altuve to evaluate strategies and manage risks?

   A. A factor model describes asset returns.

   B. Asset-specific risk can be eliminated through diversification.

   C. Arbitrage opportunities exist among well-diversified portfolios.

4. The arbitrage opportunity identified by Zapata can be exploited with:

   A. Strategy 1: Buy $50,000 Fund A and $50,000 Fund B; sell short $100,000 Fund C.

   B. Strategy 2: Buy $60,000 Fund A and $40,000 Fund B; sell short $100,000 Fund C.

   C. Strategy 3: Sell short $60,000 of Fund A and $40,000 of Fund B; buy $100,000 Fund C.

5. The two-factor model Zapata uses is a:

   A. statistical factor model.

   B. fundamental factor model.

   C. macroeconomic factor model.

6. Based on the data in Exhibits 2 and 3, the return for Portfolio AC, given the surprises in inflation and GDP growth, is *closest* to:

   A. 2.02%.

   B. 2.40%.

   C. 4.98%.

7. The surprise in which of the following had the greatest effect on fund returns?

   A. Inflation on Fund B

   B. GDP growth on Fund A

   C. GDP growth on Fund C

8. Based on the data in Exhibit 2, which fund is most sensitive to the combined surprises in inflation and GDP growth in Exhibit 3?

   A. Fund A

   B. Fund B

   C. Fund C

## The following information relates to questions 9-14

Hui Cheung, a portfolio manager, asks her assistant, Ronald Lam, to review the macroeconomic factor model currently in use and to consider a fundamental factor model as an alternative.

The current macroeconomic factor model has four factors:

$$R_i = a_i + b_{i1}F_{GDP} + b_{i2}F_{CAP} + b_{i3}F_{CON} + b_{i4}F_{UNEM} + \varepsilon_i,$$

Where $F_{GDP}$, $F_{CAP}$, $F_{CON}$, and $F_{UNEM}$ represent unanticipated changes in four factors: gross domestic product, manufacturing capacity utilization, consumer spending, and the rate of unemployment, respectively. Lam assumes the error term is equal to zero when using this model.

Lam estimates the current model using historical monthly returns for three portfolios for the most recent five years. The inputs used in and estimates derived from the macroeconomic factor model are presented in Exhibit 1. The US Treasury bond rate of 2.5% is used as a proxy for the risk-free rate of interest.

### Exhibit 1: Inputs for and Estimates from the Current Macroeconomic Model

| Factor | Factor Sensitivities and Intercept Coefficients | | | | Factor Surprise (%) |
|---|---|---|---|---|---|
| | Portfolio 1 | Portfolio 2 | Portfolio 3 | Benchmark | |
| Intercept (%) | 2.58 | 3.20 | 4.33 | | |
| $F_{GDP}$ | 0.75 | 1.00 | 0.24 | 0.50 | 0.8 |
| $F_{CAP}$ | −0.23 | 0.00 | −1.45 | −1.00 | 0.5 |
| $F_{CON}$ | 1.23 | 0.00 | 0.50 | 1.10 | 2.5 |

## Practice Problems

| | Factor Sensitivities and Intercept Coefficients | | | | Factor |
|---|---|---|---|---|---|
| Factor | Portfolio 1 | Portfolio 2 | Portfolio 3 | Benchmark | Surprise (%) |
| $F_{UNEM}$ | −0.14 | 0.00 | −0.05 | −0.10 | 1.0 |

| Annual Returns, Most Recent Year | | | | |
|---|---|---|---|---|
| Return (%) | 6.00 | 4.00 | 5.00 | 4.50 |

Lam uses the macroeconomic model to calculate the tracking error and the mean active return for each portfolio. He presents these statistics in Exhibit 2.

### Exhibit 2: Macroeconomic Factor Model Tracking Error and Mean Active Return

| Portfolio | Tracking Error | Mean Active Return |
|---|---|---|
| Portfolio 1 | 1.50% | 1.50% |
| Portfolio 2 | 1.30% | −0.50% |
| Portfolio 3 | 1.00% | 0.50% |

Lam considers a fundamental factor model with four factors:

$R_i = a_j + b_{j1}F_{LIQ} + b_{j2}F_{LEV} + b_{j3}F_{EGR} + b_{j4}F_{VAR} + \varepsilon_j$,

where $F_{LIQ}$, $F_{LEV}$, $F_{EGR}$, and $F_{VAR}$ represent liquidity, financial leverage, earnings growth, and the variability of revenues, respectively.

Lam and Cheung discuss similarities and differences between macroeconomic factor models and fundamental factor models, and Lam offers a comparison of those models to statistical factor models. Lam makes the following statements.

Statement 1   The factors in fundamental factor models are based on attributes of stocks or companies, whereas the factors in macroeconomic factor models are based on surprises in economic variables.

Statement 2   The factor sensitivities are generally determined first in fundamental factor models, whereas the factor sensitivities are estimated last in macroeconomic factor models.

Lam also tells Cheung:

An advantage of statistical factor models is that they make minimal assumptions, and therefore, statistical factor model estimation lends itself to easier interpretation than macroeconomic and fundamental factor models.

Lam tells Cheung that multifactor models can be useful in active portfolio management, but not in passive management. Cheung disagrees; she tells Lam that multifactor models can be useful in both active and passive management.

9. Based on the information in Exhibit 1, the expected return for Portfolio 1 is *closest* to:

   A. 2.58%.

   B. 3.42%.

   C. 6.00%.

10. Based on Exhibit 1, the active risk for Portfolio 2 is explained by surprises in:

    A. GDP.

    B. consumer spending.

    C. all four model factors.

11. Based on Exhibit 2, which portfolio has the best information ratio?

    A. Portfolio 1

    B. Portfolio 2

    C. Portfolio 3

12. Which of Lam's statements regarding macroeconomic factor models and fundamental factor models is correct?

    A. Only Statement 1

    B. Only Statement 2

    C. Both Statements 1 and 2

13. Is Lam's comment regarding statistical factor models correct?

    A. Yes

    B. No, because he is incorrect with respect to interpretation of the models' results

    C. No, because he is incorrect with respect to the models' assumptions

14. Whose statement regarding the use of multifactor models in active and passive portfolio management is correct?

    A. Lam only

    B. Cheung only

    C. Both Lam and Cheung

15. Last year the return on Harry Company stock was 5 percent. The portion of the return on the stock not explained by a two-factor macroeconomic factor model was 3 percent. Using the data given below, calculate Harry Company stock's expected return.

| Macroeconomic Factor Model for Harry Company Stock | | | |
|---|---|---|---|
| Variable | Actual Value (%) | Expected Value (%) | Stock's Factor Sensitivity |
| Change in interest rate | 2.0 | 0.0 | −1.5 |
| Growth in GDP | 1.0 | 4.0 | 2.0 |

16. Which type of factor model is most directly applicable to an analysis of the style orientation (for example, growth vs. value) of an active equity investment manag-

er? Justify your answer.

17. Suppose an active equity manager has earned an active return of 110 basis points, of which 80 basis points is the result of security selection ability. Explain the likely source of the remaining 30 basis points of active return.

## The following information relates to questions 18-19

Address the following questions about the information ratio.

18. What is the information ratio of an index fund that effectively meets its investment objective?

19. What are the two types of risk an active investment manager can assume in seeking to increase his information ratio?

20. A wealthy investor has no other source of income beyond her investments and that income is expected to reliably meet all her needs. Her investment advisor recommends that she tilt her portfolio to cyclical stocks and high-yield bonds. Explain the advisor's advice in terms of comparative advantage in bearing risk.

# SOLUTIONS

1. APT and the CAPM are both models that describe what the expected return on a risky asset should be in equilibrium given its risk. The CAPM is based on a set of assumptions including the assumption that investors' portfolio decisions can be made considering just returns' means, variances, and correlations. The APT makes three assumptions:

    1. A factor model describes asset returns.
    2. There are many assets, so investors can form well-diversified portfolios that eliminate asset-specific risk.
    3. No arbitrage opportunities exist among well-diversified portfolios.

2. According to the one-factor model for expected returns, the portfolio should have these expected returns if they are correctly priced in terms of their risk:

    Portfolio 1  $E(R_A) = 0.10 + 0.12\beta_{A,1} = 0.10 + (0.12)(0.80) = 0.10 + 0.10 = 0.20$

    Portfolio 2  $E(R_B) = 0.10 + 0.12\beta_{B,1} = 0.10 + (0.12)(1.00) = 0.10 + 0.12 = 0.22$

    Portfolio 3  $E(R_C) = 0.10 + 0.12\beta_{C,1} = 0.10 + (0.12)(1.20) = 0.10 + 0.14 = 0.24$

    In the table below, the column for expected return shows that Portfolios A and C are correctly priced but Portfolio B offers too little expected return for its risk, 0.15 or 15%. By shorting Portfolio B (selling an overvalued portfolio) and using the proceeds to buy a portfolio 50% invested in A and 50% invested in C with a sensitivity of 1 that matches the sensitivity of B, for each monetary unit shorted (say each euro), an arbitrage profit of €0.22 − €0.15 = €0.07 is earned.

    | Portfolio | Expected Return | Factor Sensitivity |
    |---|---|---|
    | A | 0.196 | 0.80 |
    | B | 0.156 | 1.00 |
    | C | 0.244 | 1.20 |
    | 0.5A + 0.5C | 0.22 | 1.00 |

3. C is correct. Arbitrage pricing theory (APT) is a framework that explains the expected return of a portfolio in equilibrium as a linear function of the risk of the portfolio with respect to a set of factors capturing systematic risk. A key assumption of APT is that, in equilibrium, there are no arbitrage opportunities.

4. C is correct. The expected return and factor sensitivities of a portfolio with a 60% weight in Fund A and a 40% weight in Fund B are calculated as weighted averages

of the expected returns and factor sensitivities of Funds A and B:

Expected return of Portfolio 60/40 = (0.60)(0.02) + (0.40)(0.04)

= 0.028, or 2.8%

Factor sensitivity of Portfolio 60/40 = (0.60)(0.5) + (0.40)(1.5)

= 0.9

| Fund | Expected Return | Factor Sensitivity |
|---|---|---|
| A | 0.02 | 0.5 |
| B | 0.04 | 1.5 |
| C | 0.03 | 0.9 |
| **Portfolio 60/40** | | |
| 60%A + 40%B | 0.028 | 0.900 |
| **Portfolio 50/50** | | |
| 50%A + 50%B | 0.030 | 1.000 |

The factor sensitivity of Portfolio 60/40 is identical to that of Fund C; therefore, this strategy results in no factor risk relative to Portfolio C. However, Fund C's expected return of 3.0% is higher than Portfolio 60/40's expected return of 2.8%. This difference supports Strategy 3: buying Fund C and selling short Portfolio 60/40 to exploit the arbitrage opportunity.

5. C is correct. In a macroeconomic factor model, the factors are surprises in macroeconomic variables, such as inflation risk and GDP growth, that significantly explain returns.

6. A is correct. The macroeconomic two-factor model takes the following form:

$R_i = a_i + b_{i1}F_{INF} + b_{i2}F_{GDP} + \varepsilon_i$,

where $F_{INF}$ and $F_{GDP}$ represent surprises in inflation and surprises in GDP growth, respectively, and $a_i$ represents the expected return to asset $i$. Using this model and the data in Exhibit 2, the returns for Fund A and Fund C are represented by the following:

$R_A = 0.02 + 0.5F_{INF} + 1.0F_{GDP} + \varepsilon_A$

$R_C = 0.03 + 1.0F_{INF} + 1.1F_{GDP} + \varepsilon_C$

Surprise in a macroeconomic model is defined as actual factor minus predicted factor. The surprise in inflation is 0.2% (= 2.2% − 2.0%). The surprise in GDP growth is −0.5% (= 1.0% − 1.5%). The return for Portfolio AC, composed of a 60% allocation to Fund A and 40% allocation to Fund C, is calculated as the following:

$R_{AC}$ = (0.6)(0.02) + (0.4)(0.03) + [(0.6)(0.5) + (0.4)(1.0)](0.002)+ [(0.6)(1.0) + (0.4)(1.1)](−0.005) + 0.6(0) + 0.4(0)

= 2.02%

7. C is correct. Surprise in a macroeconomic model is defined as actual factor minus predicted factor. For inflation, the surprise factor is 2.2% − 2.0% = 0.2%; for

GDP growth, the surprise factor is 1.0% − 1.5% = −0.5%. The effect on returns is the product of the surprise and the factor sensitivity.

| | Change in Portfolio Return due to Surprise in | |
|---|---|---|
| Fund | Inflation | GDP Growth |
| A | 0.5 × 0.2% = 0.10% | 1.0 × −0.5% = −0.50% |
| B | 1.6 × 0.2% = 0.32% | 0.0 × −0.5% = 0.00% |
| C | 1.0 × 0.2% = 0.20% | 1.1 × −0.5% = −0.55% |

The effect of the GDP growth surprise on Fund C was the largest single-factor effect on Fund returns (−0.55%).

8. A is correct. The effect of the surprises in inflation and GDP growth on the returns of the three funds is calculated as the following.

| | Change in Portfolio Return Because of Surprise in | |
|---|---|---|
| Fund | Inflation | GDP Growth |
| A | 0.5 × 0.2% = 0.10% | 1.0 × −0.5% = −0.50% |
| B | 1.6 × 0.2% = 0.32% | 0.0 × −0.5% = 0.00% |
| C | 1.0 × 0.2% = 0.20% | 1.1 × −0.5% = −0.55% |

The combined effects for the three funds are the following.

Fund A: 0.10% + (−0.50%) = −0.40%

Fund B: 0.32% + (0.00%) = 0.32%

Fund C: 0.20% + (−0.55%) = −0.35%

Therefore, Fund A is the most sensitive to the surprises in inflation and GDP growth in Exhibit 3.

9. A is correct. When using a macroeconomic factor model, the expected return is the intercept (when all model factors take on a value of zero). The intercept coefficient for Portfolio 1 in Exhibit 1 is 2.58.

10. C is correct. Active risk, also referred to as tracking risk or tracking error, is the sample standard deviation of the time series of active returns, where the active returns consist of the differences between the portfolio return and the benchmark return. Whereas GDP is the only portfolio non-zero sensitivity for Portfolio 2, the contribution to the portfolio's active return is the sum of the differences between the portfolio's and the benchmark's sensitivities multiplied by the factor return. Because all four of the factor sensitivities of Portfolio 2 are different from the factor sensitivities of the benchmark, all four factors contribute to the portfolio's active return and, therefore, to its active risk.

11. A is correct. Portfolio 1 has the highest information ratio, 1.0, and thus has the best mean active return per unit of active risk:

$$IR = \frac{\bar{R}_P - \bar{R}_B}{s(R_P - R_B)}$$
$$= \frac{1.50\%}{1.50\%}$$
$$= 1.00$$

This information ratio exceeds that of Portfolio 2 (−0.38) or Portfolio 3 (0.50).

# Solutions

12. C is correct. In a macroeconomic factor model, the factors are surprises in macroeconomic variables that significantly explain returns. Factor sensitivities are generally specified first in fundamental factor models, whereas factor sensitivities are estimated last in macroeconomic factor models.

13. B is correct. An advantage of statistical factor models is that they make minimal assumptions. However, the interpretation of statistical factors is generally more difficult than the interpretation of macroeconomic and fundamental factor models.

14. B is correct. Analysts can use multifactor models in passively managed portfolios to replicate an index fund's factor exposures.

15. In a macroeconomic factor model, the surprise in a factor equals actual value minus expected value. For the interest rate factor, the surprise was 2 percent; for the GDP factor, the surprise was −3 percent. The intercept represents expected return in this type of model. The portion of the stock's return not explained by the factor model is the model's error term.

    5% = Expected return − 1.5(Interest rate surprise) + 2(GDP surprise) + Error term

    = Expected return − 1.5(2%) + 2(−3%) + 3%

    = Expected return − 6%

    Rearranging terms, the expected return for Harry Company stock equals 5% + 6% = 11%.

16. A fundamental factor model. Such models typically include many factors related to the company (e.g., earnings) and to valuation that are commonly used indicators of a growth orientation. A macroeconomic factor model may provide relevant information as well, but typically indirectly and in less detail.

17. This remainder of 30 basis points would be attributable to the return from factor tilts. A portfolio manager's active return is the sum of two components, factor tilts and security selection. Factor tilt is the product of the portfolio manager's higher or lower factor sensitivities relative to the benchmark's factor sensitivities and the factor returns. Security selection reflects the manager's ability to overweight securities that outperform or underweight securities that underperform.

18. An index fund that effectively meets its investment objective is expected to have an information ratio of zero, because its active return should be zero.

19. The active manager may assume active factor risk and active specific risk (security selection risk) in seeking a higher information ratio.

20. This wealthy investor has a comparative advantage in bearing business cycle risk compared with the average investor who depends on income from employment. Because the average investor is sensitive to the business cycle and in particular the risk of recession, we would expect there to be a risk premium to hold recession-sensitive securities. Cyclical stocks and high-yield bonds are both very sensitive to the risk of recessions. Because the welfare of the wealthy investor is not affected by recessions, she can tilt her portfolio to include cyclical stocks and high yield bonds to attempt to capture the associated risk premiums.

# LEARNING MODULE

# 3

## Measuring and Managing Market Risk

by Don M. Chance, PhD, CFA, and Michelle McCarthy Beck.

*Don M. Chance, PhD, CFA, is at Louisiana State University (USA). Michelle McCarthy Beck is at TIAA (USA).*

| LEARNING OUTCOMES | |
|---|---|
| Mastery | *The candidate should be able to:* |
| ☐ | explain the use of value at risk (VaR) in measuring portfolio risk |
| ☐ | compare the parametric (variance–covariance), historical simulation, and Monte Carlo simulation methods for estimating VaR |
| ☐ | estimate and interpret VaR under the parametric, historical simulation, and Monte Carlo simulation methods |
| ☐ | describe advantages and limitations of VaR |
| ☐ | describe extensions of VaR |
| ☐ | describe sensitivity risk measures and scenario risk measures and compare these measures to VaR |
| ☐ | demonstrate how equity, fixed-income, and options exposure measures may be used in measuring and managing market risk and volatility risk |
| ☐ | describe the use of sensitivity risk measures and scenario risk measures |
| ☐ | describe advantages and limitations of sensitivity risk measures and scenario risk measures |
| ☐ | explain constraints used in managing market risks, including risk budgeting, position limits, scenario limits, and stop-loss limits |
| ☐ | explain how risk measures may be used in capital allocation decisions |
| ☐ | describe risk measures used by banks, asset managers, pension funds, and insurers |

# 1 INTRODUCTION

☐ explain the use of value at risk (VaR) in measuring portfolio risk

This reading is an introduction to the process of measuring and managing market risk. Market risk is the risk that arises from movements in stock prices, interest rates, exchange rates, and commodity prices. Market risk is distinguished from credit risk, which is the risk of loss from the failure of a counterparty to make a promised payment, and also from a number of other risks that organizations face, such as breakdowns in their operational procedures. In essence, market risk is the risk arising from changes in the markets to which an organization has exposure.

Risk management is the process of identifying and measuring risk and ensuring that the risks being taken are consistent with the desired risks. The process of managing market risk relies heavily on the use of models. A model is a simplified representation of a real world phenomenon. Financial models attempt to capture the important elements that determine prices and sensitivities in financial markets. In doing so, they provide critical information necessary to manage investment risk. For example, investment risk models help a portfolio manager understand how much the value of the portfolio is likely to change given a change in a certain risk factor. They also provide insight into the gains and losses the portfolio might reasonably be expected to experience and the frequency with which large losses might occur.

Effective risk management, though, is much more than just applying financial models. It requires the application of judgment and experience not only to know how to use the models appropriately but also to appreciate the strengths and limitations of the models and to know when to supplement or substitute one model with another model or approach.

Financial markets operate more or less continuously, and new prices are constantly being generated. As a result, there is a large amount of data on market risk and a lot of collective experience dealing with this risk, making market risk one of the easier financial risks to analyze. Still, market risk is not an easy risk to capture. Although a portfolio's exposures can be identified with some certainty, the potential losses that could arise from those exposures are unknown. The data used to estimate potential losses are generated from past prices and rates, not the ones to come. Risk management models allow the experienced risk manager to blend that historical data with their own forward-looking judgment, providing a framework within which to test that judgment.

We first lay a foundation for understanding value at risk, discuss three primary approaches to estimating value at risk, and cover the primary advantages and limitations as well as extensions of value at risk. We then address the sensitivity measures used for equities, fixed-income securities, and options and also cover historical and hypothetical scenario risk measures. Next, we discuss the use of constraints in risk management, such as risk budgeting, position limits, scenario limits, stop-loss limits, and capital allocation as risk management tools. Lastly, we describe various applications and limitations of risk measures as used by different types of market participants and summarize our discussion.

## Understanding Value at Risk

**Value at risk (VaR)** was developed in the late 1980s, and over the next decade, it emerged as one of the most important risk measures in global financial markets.

## Introduction

### Value at Risk: Formal Definition

*Value at risk is the minimum loss that would be expected a certain percentage of the time over a certain period of time given the assumed market conditions.* It can be expressed in either currency units or as a percentage of portfolio value. Although this statement is an accurate definition of VaR, it does not provide sufficient clarity to fully comprehend the concept. To better understand what VaR means, let us work with an example. Consider the statement:

> *The 5% VaR of a portfolio is €2.2 million over a one-day period.*

The following three points are important in understanding the concept of VaR:

- VaR can be measured in either currency units (in this example, the euro) or in percentage terms. In this example, if the portfolio value is €400 million, the VaR expressed in percentage terms would be 0.55% (€2.2 million/€400 million = 0.0055).

- VaR is a *minimum* loss. This point cannot be emphasized enough. VaR is often mistakenly assumed to represent *how much one can lose*. If the question is, "how much can one lose?" there is only one answer: *the entire portfolio*. In a €400 million portfolio, assuming no leverage, the most one can lose is €400 million.

- A VaR statement references a time horizon: losses that would be expected to occur over a given period of time. In this example, that period of time is one day. (If VaR is measured on a daily basis, and a typical month has 20–22 business days, then 5% of the days equates to about one day per month.)

These are the explicit elements of a VaR statement: the *frequency* of losses of a given *minimum magnitude* expressed either in *currency* or *percentage* terms. Thus, the VaR statement can be rephrased as follows: A loss of at least €2.2 million would be expected to occur about once every month.

A 5% VaR is often expressed as its complement—a 95% level of confidence. In this reading, we will typically refer to the notion as a 5% VaR, but we should be mindful that it does imply a 95% level of confidence.

---

Using the example given, it is correct to say any of the following:

- €2.2 million is the minimum loss we would expect 5% of the time.
- 5% of the time, losses would be at least €2.2 million.
- We would expect a loss of no more than €2.2 million 95% of the time.

The last sentence is sometimes mistakenly phrased as "95% of the time we would expect to lose less than €2.2 million," but this statement could be taken to mean that 95% of the time we would incur losses, although those losses would be less than €2.2 million. In fact, a large percentage of the time we will make money.

---

Exhibit 1 illustrates the concept of VaR using the 5% case. It depicts a probability distribution of returns from a hypothetical portfolio. The distribution chosen is the familiar normal distribution, known sometimes as the bell curve, but that distribution is only one curve that might be used. In fact, there are compelling arguments that the normal distribution is not the right one to use for financial market returns. We discuss these arguments later.

### Exhibit 1: Illustration of 5% VaR in the Context of a Probability Distribution

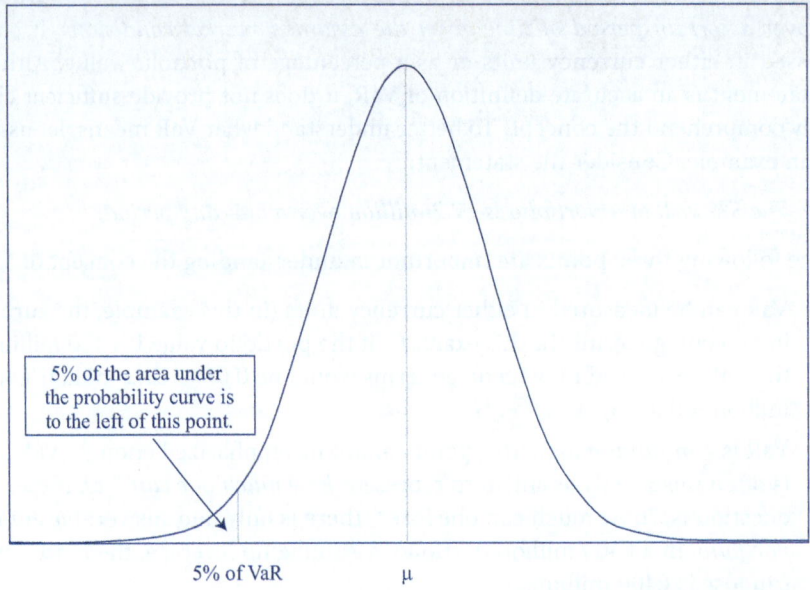

Note that the distribution in Exhibit 1 is centered on the value μ. [The symbol μ (Greek: *mu*) is a common symbol used to represent an expected value.] Near the left tail of the distribution is the notation "5% VaR," indicating that 5% of the area under the curve is to the left of the point of the VaR (i.e., the probability of observing a value less than the VaR is 5%).

Thus, it is apparent that VaR is simply a point on the probability distribution of profits or returns from a portfolio. Given the characteristics of the normal distribution, a 5% VaR is equivalent to the point on the distribution that is 1.65 standard deviations below the expected value. Although the concept of VaR can be easily visualized in this manner, actually measuring the VaR is a challenge.

Before we take on that challenge, however, note that there is no formal requirement that VaR be measured at a 5% threshold. It is also common to use a 1% threshold (2.33 standard deviations from the expected value), and some investment managers use a one standard deviation movement (equal to a 16% VaR)—both assuming a normal distribution. There is no definitive rule for what VaR cutoff should be used. A specification with a higher confidence level will produce a higher VaR. It is up to the decision maker to choose an appropriate level.

### VaR and Standard Deviations

The 16% VaR relates to a one standard deviation move as follows: In a normal distribution, 50% of the outcomes are to the right of the expected value and 50% are to the left. A one standard deviation interval implies that 68% of the outcomes lie within one standard deviation of the expected value; thus, 34% of the outcomes lie one standard deviation to the left of the expected value and 34% of the outcomes one standard deviation to the right. Adding the 50% of the outcomes that lie to the right of the expected value to the 34% of the outcomes that lie one standard deviation below the expected value means that 84% of all outcomes lie to the right of the point that is one standard deviation to the left of the expected value. Therefore, 16% of all outcomes lie below this point. Thus, a one standard deviation movement is equivalent to a 16% VaR (or an 84% level of confidence).

Just as there is no formal requirement that VaR be measured at a 5% cutoff, there is also no formal requirement that VaR be measured using a daily loss estimate. One could reasonably measure VaR on a weekly, bi-weekly, monthly, quarterly, semiannually, or annual basis. Choosing the VaR threshold and the time horizon are examples of why VaR is not a precise measure but in fact entails considerable judgment.

We should also reiterate that VaR can be expressed as a rate of return or in monetary terms. It is typically easier to process the data necessary to estimate VaR in terms of returns, but VaR is most frequently expressed in terms of profits or losses. This point will become clearer as we work through examples.

---

**EXAMPLE 1**

### Definition of VaR

1. Given a VaR of $12.5 million at 5% for one month, which of the following statements is correct?

   A. There is a 5% chance of losing $12.5 million over one month.

   B. There is a 95% chance that the expected loss over the next month is less than $12.5 million.

   C. The minimum loss that would be expected to occur over one month 5% of the time is $12.5 million.

**Solution to 1:**

C is correct because it is the only statement that accurately expresses the VaR. A is incorrect because VaR does not give the likelihood of losing a specific amount. B is incorrect because VaR is not an expected loss; rather, it is a minimum loss.

2. Which of the following statements is **not** correct?

   A. A 1% VaR implies a downward move of 1%.

   B. A one standard deviation downward move is equivalent to a 16% VaR.

   C. A 5% VaR implies a move of 1.65 standard deviations less than the expected value.

**Solution to 2:**

A is correct. A 1% VaR (99% confidence) is the point on the distribution 2.33 standard deviations below the expected value. Answers B and C correctly describe a 16% and 5% VaR, respectively.

---

To this point, we have given only the conceptual definition of VaR. Defining something is one thing; measuring it can be quite challenging. Such is the case for VaR.

## ESTIMATING VAR

Three methods are typically used to estimate VaR: the parametric (variance–covariance) method, the historical simulation method, and the Monte Carlo simulation method. Each of these will be discussed in turn.

The first step of every VaR calculation, regardless of the VaR method used, is to convert the set of holdings in the portfolio into a set of exposures to **risk factors**, a process called **risk decomposition**. In some instances, this process can be very simple: An equity security can be the risk factor itself. In other instances, the process can be highly complex. For example, a convertible bond issued by a foreign entity has both currency and equity risk factors as well as exposures to multiple points on a yield curve of a given credit quality. Fixed-income instruments and derivatives products often contain distinct risk exposures that require decomposition in order to accurately capture their loss potential.

The second step of VaR estimation requires gathering a data history for each of the risk factors in the VaR model. The three methods use different approaches to specifying these inputs, which will be discussed in the following sections. We will see that the parametric and Monte Carlo methods do not formally require a data history. They require only that the user enter estimates of certain parameters into the computational procedure (expected return, standard deviation, and for some models, skewness and kurtosis). One of the most common sources for estimating parameter inputs for any financial model is historical data, but the user could substitute estimates based on judgement or alternative forecasting models. Indeed, shortly we will override some historical estimates with our own judgement. Nonetheless, the collection of a data history is typically used at least as a starting point in the parametric and Monte Carlo methods, and it is absolutely required for the historical simulation method.

The third step of each method is where the differences between the three VaR methods are most apparent: how each method uses the data to make an estimate of the VaR.

Although most portfolios contain a large number of individual securities and other assets, we will use a two-asset portfolio to illustrate the three VaR methods. Using a limited number of assets permits us to closely observe the essential elements of the VaR estimation procedure without getting mired in the complex mathematics required to accommodate a large number of assets. The objective is to understand the concept of VaR, be aware of how it is estimated, know how it is used, appreciate the benefits of VaR, and be attentive to its limitations. We can achieve these objectives by keeping the portfolio fairly simple.

Our example portfolio has a market value of $150 million and consists of two ETFs—SPDR S&P 500 ETF (SPY), representing the US equity exposure, and SPDR Portfolio Long-Term Corporate Bond ETF (SPLB), representing a corporate bond exposure. We will allocate 80% of the portfolio to SPY and 20% of the portfolio to SPLB. For the sake of simplicity, the two securities will represent the risk factors and the return history of each ETF will serve as the risk factor history used in the VaR model. We have collected a set of two years of daily total return data, reflecting both capital appreciation and dividends on each ETF. The period used for this historical data set is called the **lookback period**. The question of exactly how much data are required to be a representative data set is a complex question that is common to all estimation problems in economics and finance. We will discuss some of the issues on this matter later in this reading.

Exhibit 2 provides statistical summary information based on the two years of daily data in the lookback period, covering the period of 1 July 2015 through 28 June 2019.

## Exhibit 2: Statistical Estimates from Daily Return Data, 1 July 2015–28 June 2019

|  | Daily | | Annualized | |
|---|---|---|---|---|
|  | Average Return | Standard Deviation | Average Return | Standard Deviation |
| SPY | 0.047% | 0.86% | 12.51% | 13.64% |
| SPLB | 0.031% | 0.49% | 8.03% | 7.73% |

*Note:* The correlation of SPLB and SPY = –0.0607.

SPY produced an annualized average return of about 12.5% with a standard deviation of 13.6%, significantly different from the long-term historical performance of the S&P 500 Index of approximately 10.5% average return and 20% standard deviation. SPLB produced an annualized average return of 8% with a standard deviation of about 7.7%. These numbers compare with an average annual return for long-term corporate bonds of slightly more than 6% and a standard deviation of about 8.5% (historical data are drawn from Malkiel 2007). Although the average return of SPLB in the last four years was higher than that of the overall long-term corporate bond sector, the standard deviations were similar.

The risk and return parameters for each risk factor in Exhibit 2 illustrate how one might collect historical data. It is necessary, however, to critically assess the data and apply judgment to modify the inputs if the lookback period is not representative of the expected performance of the securities (or risk factors) going forward. Exercising our judgment, and believing that we have no information to suggest that future performance will deviate from the long-run historical performance, we adjust our inputs and use returns of 10.5% for SPY and 6% for SPLB, with standard deviations of 20% for SPY and 8.5% for SPLB. These adjustments align the inputs more closely with the long-run historical performance of each sector. In practice, users will want to use estimates they believe are reflective of current expectations, though clearly one user's estimates could differ widely from another's.

Although the returns and standard deviations experienced over the lookback period have been adjusted to more closely align with long-run historical experience, we will use a correlation estimate approximately equal to the observed correlation over our lookback period. We are assuming that the recent historical relationship of equity and fixed-income returns is a reasonable assumption moving forward. To keep the numbers simple, we round the observed correlation of –0.0607 to –0.06.

Exhibit 3 illustrates our input assumptions for the VaR estimations.

## Exhibit 3: Input Assumptions, 1 July 2015–28 June 2019

|  |  | Annualized | |
|---|---|---|---|
|  | Allocation | Return | Standard Deviation |
| SPY | 80% | 10.5% | 20.0% |
| SPLB | 20% | 6.0% | 8.5% |

*Note:* The correlation of SPLB and SPY = –0.06.

## 3. THE PARAMETRIC METHOD OF VAR ESTIMATION

- [ ] compare the parametric (variance–covariance), historical simulation, and Monte Carlo simulation methods for estimating VaR
- [ ] estimate and interpret VaR under the parametric, historical simulation, and Monte Carlo simulation methods

The **parametric method** of estimating VaR is sometimes referred to as the analytical method and sometimes the variance–covariance method. The parametric method begins, as does each method, with a risk decomposition of the portfolio holdings. It typically assumes that the return distributions for the risk factors in the portfolio are normal. It then uses the expected return and standard deviation of return for each risk factor to estimate the VaR.

Note that we said that this method *typically* uses the normal distribution. Indeed, that is the common case in practice, but there is no formal requirement that the normal distribution be used. The normal distribution conveniently requires only two parameters—the expected value and standard deviation—to encompass everything there is to know about it. If other distributions are used, additional parameters of the distribution, such as skewness and kurtosis, would be required. We will limit the presentation here to the normal distribution, but be aware that other, more accurately representative distributions could be used but would add complexity to the VaR estimation process.

Recall that in defining VaR, we identified a VaR threshold—a point in the left tail of the distribution, typically either the 5% left tail, the 1% left tail, or a one standard deviation move (16%). If the portfolio is characterized by normally distributed returns and the expected value and standard deviation are known, it is a simple matter to identify any point on the distribution. A normal distribution with expected value $\mu$ and standard deviation $\sigma$ can be converted to a standard normal distribution, which is a special case of the normal distribution in which the expected value is zero and the standard deviation is one. A standard normal distribution is also known as a $z$-distribution. If we have observed a return $R$ from a normal distribution, we can convert to its equivalent $z$-distribution value by the transformation:

$$z = \frac{R - \mu}{\sigma}.$$

In a standard normal ($z$) distribution, a 5% VaR is 1.65 standard deviations below the expected value of zero. A 1% VaR is 2.33 standard deviations below the expected value of zero. A 16% VaR is one standard deviation below the expected value of zero. Thus, in our example, for a 5% VaR, we wish to know the return that is 1.65 standard deviations to the left of the expected return.

To estimate this VaR, we need the expected return and volatility of the portfolio. The expected return is estimated from the following equation:

$$E(R_p) = w_{SPY} E(R_{SPY}) + w_{SPLB} E(R_{SPLB}), \tag{1}$$

where the expected return of the portfolio, $E(R_p)$, is equal to the portfolio weights of SPY ($w_{SPY}$) and SPLB ($w_{SPLB}$) multiplied by the expected return of each asset, $E(R_{SPY})$ and $E(R_{SPLB})$.

The volatility of the portfolio, $\sigma_p$, is estimated from the following equation:

$$\sigma_p = \sqrt{w_{SPY}^2 \sigma_{SPY}^2 + w_{SPLB}^2 \sigma_{SPLB}^2 + 2 w_{SPY} w_{SPLB} \rho_{SPY,SPLB} \sigma_{SPY} \sigma_{SPLB}}, \tag{2}$$

# The Parametric Method of VaR Estimation

where $\sigma_{SPY}$ and $\sigma_{SPLB}$ are the standard deviations (volatilities) of SPY and SPLB, respectively; $\rho_{SPY,SPLB}$ is the correlation between the returns on SPY and SPLB, respectively; and $\rho_{SPY,SPLB}\sigma_{SPY}\sigma_{SPLB}$ is the covariance between SPY and SPLB.

Recall that we estimated these parameters from the historical data, with some modifications to make them more consistent with long-run values. The formal calculations for our portfolio based on these adjusted estimates are as follows:

$$E(R_p) = 0.8(0.105) + 0.2(0.06) = 0.096000$$

$$\sigma_p = \sqrt{(0.8)^2(0.2)^2 + (0.2)^2(0.085)^2 + 2(0.8)(0.2)(-0.06)(0.2)(0.085)}$$

$$= 0.159883.$$

Thus, our portfolio, consisting of an 80% position in SPY and a 20% position in SPLB, is estimated to have an expected return of 9.6% and a volatility of approximately 15.99%. But these inputs are based on annual returns. If we want a one-day VaR, we should adjust the expected returns and volatilities to their daily counterparts. Assuming 250 trading days in a year, the expected return is adjusted by dividing by 250 and the standard deviation is adjusted by dividing by the square root of 250. (Note that the variance is converted by dividing by time, 250 days; thus, the standard deviation must be adjusted by using the square root of time, 250 days.) Thus, the daily expected return and volatility are

$$E(R_p) = \frac{0.096}{250} = 0.000384 \qquad (3)$$

and

$$\sigma_p = \frac{0.159883}{\sqrt{250}} = 0.010112 \qquad (4)$$

It is important to note that we have assumed that the statistical properties of the return distribution are constant across the year. Earlier, we annualized the daily data in Exhibit 2 in order to see how our estimates compared with long-term estimates. We made some modest adjustments to the annualized data and then, in Equations 3 and 4, returned to using daily data. To estimate an annual VaR, we would need to use annual data, but we would need a longer lookback period in order to have sufficient data points.

> It is important to note that we cannot estimate a daily VaR and annualize it to arrive at an annual VaR estimate. First, to assume that a daily distribution of returns can be extrapolated to an annual distribution is a bold assumption. Second, annualizing the daily VaR is not the same as adjusting the expected return and the standard deviation to annual numbers and then calculating the annual VaR. The expected return is annualized by multiplying the daily return by 250, and the standard deviation is annualized by multiplying the daily standard deviation by the square root of 250. Thus, we can annualize the data and estimate an annual VaR, but we cannot estimate a daily VaR and annualize it without assuming a zero expected return.

Having calculated the daily expected return and volatility, the parametric VaR is now easily obtained. With the distribution centered at the expected return of 0.0384% and a one standard deviation move equal to 0.996%, a 5% VaR is obtained by identifying the point on the distribution that lies 1.65 standard deviations to the left of the mean. It is now easy to see why parametric VaR is so named: The expected values, standard deviations, and covariances are the *parameters* of the distributions.

The following step-by-step procedure shows how the VaR is derived:

$$\{[E(Rp) - 1.65\sigma_p](-1)\}(\$150{,}000{,}000)$$

Step 1      Multiply the portfolio standard deviation by 1.65.

0.010112 × 1.65 = 0.016685

Step 2      Subtract the answer obtained in Step 1 from the expected return.

0.000384 − 0.016685 = −0.016301

Step 3      Because VaR is expressed as an absolute number (despite representing an expected loss), change the sign of the value obtained in Step 2.

Change −0.016301 to 0.016301

Step 4      Multiply the result in Step 3 by the value of the portfolio.

$150,000,000 × 0.016301 = $2,445,150

Thus, using the parametric method, our estimate of VaR is $2,445,150, meaning that on 5% of trading days the portfolio would be expected to incur a loss of at least $2,445,150. Note that asset managers may stop at Step 3 because at that point the measure is expressed as a percentage of the value of the portfolio, which is the unit this group more commonly uses.

### EXAMPLE 2

### Parametric VaR

1. The parameters of normal distribution required to estimate parametric VaR are:

   A. expected value and standard deviation.

   B. skewness and kurtosis.

   C. standard deviation and skewness.

### Solution to 1:

A is correct. The parameters of a normal distribution are the expected value and standard deviation. Skewness, as mentioned in B and C, and kurtosis, as mentioned in B, are characteristics used to describe a *non*-normal distribution.

2. Assuming a daily expected return of 0.0384% and daily standard deviation of 1.0112% (as in the example in the text), which of the following is *closest* to the 1% VaR for a $150 million portfolio? Express your answer in dollars.

   A. $3.5 million

   B. $2.4 million

   C. $1.4 million

### Solution to 2:

A is correct and is obtained as follows:

Step 1      2.33 × 0.010112 = 0.023561

Step 2      0.000384 − 0.023561 = −0.023177

> Step 3             Convert −0.023177 to 0.023177
>
> Step 4             0.023177 × $150 million = $3,476,550
>
> B is the estimated VaR at a 5% threshold, and C is the estimated VaR using a one standard deviation threshold.

---

> 3. Assuming a daily expected return of 0.0384% and daily standard deviation of 1.0112% (as in the example in the text), the daily 5% parametric VaR is $2,445,150. Rounding the VaR to $2.4 million, which of the following values is *closest* to the annual 5% parametric VaR? Express your answer in dollars.
>
>    A. $38 million
>    B. $25 million
>    C. $600 million
>
> ## Solution to 3:
>
> B is correct. It is found by annualizing the daily return and standard deviation and using these figures in the calculation. The annual return and standard deviation are, respectively, 0.096000 (0.000384 × 250) and 0.159885 (0.010112 × $\sqrt{250}$).
>
> Step 1             0.159885 × 1.65 = 0.263810
>
> Step 2             0.096000 − 0.263810 = −0.167810
>
> Step 3             Convert −0.167810 to 0.167810
>
> Step 4             0.167810 × $150 million = $25,171,500
>
> A incorrectly multiplies the daily VaR by the square root of the number of trading days in a year ($\sqrt{250}$), and C incorrectly multiplies the daily VaR by the approximate number of trading days in a year (250). Neither A nor C make the appropriate adjustment to annualize the standard deviation.

---

To recap, we see that the parametric VaR method generally makes the assumption that the distribution of returns on the risk factors is normal. Under that assumption, all of the information about a normal distribution is contained in the expected value and standard deviation. Therefore, finding the 5% VaR requires only that we locate the point in the distribution beyond which 5% of the outcomes occur. Although normality is the general assumption of the parametric method, it is not an absolute requirement. Other distributions could be accommodated by incorporating skewness and kurtosis, the third and fourth parameters of the distribution, but that added complexity is not needed to demonstrate the general approach to parametric VaR and is rarely done in practice.

The major advantage of the parametric method is its simplicity and straightforwardness. The assumption of the normal distribution allows us to easily estimate the parameters using historical data, although judgment is required to adjust the parameters when the historical data may be misleading. The parametric method is best used in situations in which one is confident that the normal distribution can be applied as a reasonable approximation of the true distribution and the parameter estimates are reliable or can be turned into reliable estimates by suitable adjustments. It is important to understand that VaR under the parametric method is very sensitive to the parameter estimates, especially the covariances.

One of the major weaknesses of the parametric method is that it can be difficult to use when the investment portfolio contains options. When options are exercised, they pay off linearly with the underlying; however, if never exercised, an option loses 100% of its value. This characteristic leads to a truncated, non-normal distribution that does not lend itself well to the parametric method. But some adjustments can render options more responsive to the parametric method. These adjustments are helpful but not perfect, limiting the usefulness of the parametric method when options are in the portfolio. Additionally, although the expected return and volatility of the underlying fixed income or equity security may be stable over the life of the option, the distribution of the option changes continuously as the value of the underlying, the volatility of the underlying, and the time to expiration all change.

# 4. THE HISTORICAL SIMULATION METHOD OF VAR ESTIMATION

- [ ] compare the parametric (variance–covariance), historical simulation, and Monte Carlo simulation methods for estimating VaR
- [ ] estimate and interpret VaR under the parametric, historical simulation, and Monte Carlo simulation methods

The **historical simulation method** of VaR uses the *current* portfolio and reprices it using the actual *historical* changes in the key factors experienced during the lookback period. We begin, as with the parametric method, by decomposing the portfolio into risk factors and gathering the historical returns of each risk factor from the chosen lookback period. Unlike the parametric method, however, we do not characterize the distribution using estimates of the mean return, the standard deviation, or the correlations among the risk factors in the portfolio. Instead, we reprice the current portfolio given the returns that occurred on each day of the historical lookback period and sort the results from largest loss to greatest gain. To estimate a one-day VaR at a 5% confidence interval, we choose the point on the resulting distribution beyond which 5% of the outcomes result in larger losses.

Illustrating this point using a full four years of daily observations would be tedious and consume a great deal of space, so we will condense the process quite a bit and then extrapolate the methodology. Exhibit 4 shows the daily returns on the SPY, the SPLB, and our 80% SPY/20% SPLB portfolio over the first five days of our historical data set. Please note that fixed weights are assumed for all days. Neither historical simulation nor Monte Carlo simulation is intended to be a replication of sequences of prices. They are intended to create a sample of one-day returns for a portfolio of given weights.

**Exhibit 4: First Five Days of Historical Returns on the SPY/SPLB Portfolio Using the 1 July 2015–28 June 2019 Data**

| Day | SPY Return | SPLB Return | Portfolio Return |
|---|---|---|---|
| 1 | 0.80% | −0.53% | 0.53% |
| 2 | −0.09% | 0.45% | 0.02% |
| 3 | −0.28% | 1.47% | 0.07% |
| 4 | −0.63% | 0.28% | 0.56% |
| 5 | −1.68% | −0.23% | −1.39% |

*Notes:* The Day 1 portfolio return is obtained by multiplying each holding (SPY, SPLB) by its respective

## The Historical Simulation Method of VaR Estimation

weight in the portfolio (80%/20%) and adding the two results together: 0.80(0.008) + 0.20(–0.0053). Although Exhibit 4 shows only five days of returns, we would, of course, use all of the data at our disposal that is reasonably representative of possible future outcomes.

The historical simulation VaR extracts the portfolio return that lies at the appropriate confidence interval along the distribution. Using Excel's "=percentile(x,y)" function, we calculated the following historical simulation VaRs for our sample portfolio:

- 1% VaR (99% confidence) $2,643,196
- 5% VaR (95% confidence) $1,622,272
- 16% VaR (84% confidence) $880,221

Now, it will be interesting to compare this result with the parametric VaR estimates. Exhibit 5 shows the results side-by-side with the parameters used. The historical simulation method does not directly use these parameters but uses the data itself, and these numbers are the parameters implied by the data itself.

### Exhibit 5: Comparison of Historical and Parametric VaR Estimates Using 1 July 2015–28 June 2019 Data

|  | Historical Simulation Method | Parametric Method |
|---|---|---|
| 1% VaR | $2,643,196 | $3,476,550 |
| 5% VaR | $1,622,272 | $2,445,150 |
| 16% VaR | $880,221 | $1,459,200 |

|  | Average Return | Standard Deviation | Average Return | Standard Deviation |
|---|---|---|---|---|
| SPY | 12.51% | 13.64% | 10.50% | 20.00% |
| SPLB | 8.03% | 7.73% | 6.00% | 8.50% |
| Correlation of SPY and SPLB | –0.061 |  | –0.06 |  |

The historical simulation VaRs are much smaller, and the differences stem primarily from the adjustments we made to the historical parameters. We adjusted the volatility and the average return estimates of SPY to more closely reflect the historical norms and slightly raised the volatility of SPLB. Recall, in particular, that our factor history for the S&P 500 exhibited abnormally low volatility relative to the long-run experience.

Additionally, our calculations using the historical simulation method were not constrained by the assumption of a normal distribution as was the case with the parametric method. Exhibit 6 is a histogram of the portfolio returns used in the historical simulation results, overlaid with a normal distribution.

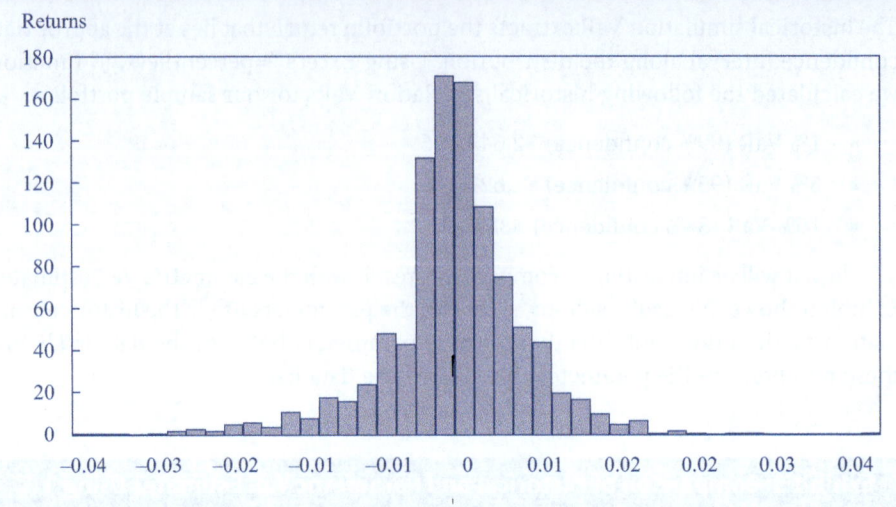

**Exhibit 6: Histogram of Historical Portfolio Returns (80% SPY and 20% SPLB) Using 1 July 2015–28 June 2019 Data**

As can be seen, the resulting distribution under the historical simulation method is a departure from a normal distribution. This point again highlights the importance of understanding the underlying assumptions of any VaR model.

There is *no single right way* of estimating VaR. Each method provides an estimate of VaR and is highly sensitive to the input parameters, and similar to many estimation models, they will disagree.

Both the parametric and historical simulation methods in their most basic forms have the limitation that, as with most samples, all observations are weighted equally. The historical simulation method can adjust for this problem, however, by using a weighting methodology that gives more weight to more recent observations and less weight to more distant observations.

The primary advantage of the historical simulation method compared with the parametric method is that the historical simulation method estimates VaR based on what actually happened, so it cannot be dismissed as introducing impossible outcomes. Yet, therein also lies the primary weakness of the historical simulation method: There can be no certainty that a historical event will re-occur or that it would occur in the same manner or with the same likelihood as represented by the historical data. If one uses a relatively short historical data set, such as from January 1987 through December 1988 (a period encompassing the "Black Monday" of 19 October 1987, when stock markets around the world collapsed in a very short time), an occurrence of this magnitude might be projected to occur once every two years, surely an overstatement of its probability. Thus, the historical simulation method is best used when the distribution of returns during the lookback period are expected to be representative of the future.

The historical method is capable of handling the adjustment of one time horizon to another; that is, the information derived from daily data can be extrapolated to estimate an annual VaR, provided the distribution can be assumed to be stationary. In other words, one can convert each daily return to an annual return and then estimate the annual VaR. Although using annual data to estimate an annual VaR is always preferred, that would require a much longer lookback period.

We noted earlier that the parametric method is not well suited for options. Because the historical simulation method captures the returns that actually occurred regardless of the type of financial instrument used, it can accommodate options.

> **EXAMPLE 3**
>
> ### Historical Simulation VaR
>
> 1. Which of the following statements about the historical simulation method of estimating VaR is *most* correct?
>
>    **A.** A 5% historical simulation VaR is the value that is 5% to the left of the expected value.
>
>    **B.** A 5% historical simulation VaR is the value that is 1.65 standard deviations to the left of the expected value.
>
>    **C.** A 5% historical simulation VaR is the fifth percentile, meaning the point on the distribution beyond which 5% of the outcomes result in larger losses.
>
> **Solution to 1:**
>
> C is correct. In the historical method, the portfolio returns are arrayed lowest to highest and the observation at the fifth percentile (95% of the outcomes are better than this outcome) is the VaR. A is not correct because it draws a point on the distribution relative to the expected value rather than using the 5% of the outcomes that are in the left-most of the distribution. B confuses the parametric and historical methods. In the parametric method, the 5% VaR lies 1.65 standard deviations below the mean.
>
> 2. Which of the following is a limitation of the historical simulation method?
>
>    **A.** The past may not repeat itself.
>    **B.** There is a reliance on the normal distribution.
>    **C.** Estimates of the mean and variance could be biased.
>
> **Solution to 2:**
>
> A is correct. The historical simulation method estimates VaR based on the historical distribution of the risk factors. B is not correct; the historical simulation method does not rely on any particular distribution because it simply uses whatever distribution applied in the past. C is not correct because the historical distribution does not formally estimate the mean and variance.

# THE MONTE CARLO SIMULATION METHOD OF VAR ESTIMATION    5

☐ compare the parametric (variance–covariance), historical simulation, and Monte Carlo simulation methods for estimating VaR

☐ estimate and interpret VaR under the parametric, historical simulation, and Monte Carlo simulation methods

**Monte Carlo simulation** is a method of estimating VaR in which the user develops his own assumptions about the statistical characteristics of the distribution and uses those characteristics to generate random outcomes that represent hypothetical returns to a portfolio with the specified characteristics. This method is widely used in the sciences to estimate the statistical distribution of scientific phenomena and has many applications in business and finance. For example, a corporation considering the investment of a large amount of capital in a new project with many uncertain variables could simulate the possible values of these variables and thus gain an understanding of the distribution of the possible returns from this investment. Or, complex options can often be priced by simulating outcomes of the underlying, determining the payoffs of the option, and then averaging the option payoffs and discounting that value back to the present. The reference to the famous Mediterranean casino city allegedly came from an observation made by a scientist that the method is similar to tossing dice at a casino.

Monte Carlo simulation avoids the complexity inherent in the parametric method when the portfolio has a large number of assets. (A large number of assets makes the parameters of the distribution difficult to extract.) There can be many risk factors, and the interactions among these risk factors can be too complex to specify. Moreover, Monte Carlo simulation does not need to be constrained by the assumption of normal distributions. Rather than attempt to determine the expected return and volatility of a combination of multiple statistical processes, one would simply simulate these processes, tabulate the statistical results of the simulations, and thereby gain a measure of the combined effects of these complex component processes on the overall risk.

Monte Carlo simulation requires the generation of random values of the underlying unknowns. In our example, the unknowns are the returns on the two risk factors, represented by the SPY and SPLB ETFs. We can, of course, assume that the statistical properties of the historical returns—their averages, volatilities, and correlation—are appropriate for use in a simulation, or we can modify those values to conform to what we expect to be relevant for the future. For illustrative purposes here, we will simply use the inputs we used in the parametric method.

Recall that we previously assumed for the sake of simplicity that the two securities represent the risk factors. We now decompose the portfolio holdings into these risk factors. First we simulate the returns of these two risk factors, and then we re-price our exposures to the risk factors under the range of simulated returns, recording the results much as we do in the historical simulation method. We then sort the results in order from worst to best. A 5% Monte Carlo VaR would simply be the fifth percentile of the simulated values instead of the historical values.

Yet, it is not quite that simple. We must first decide how many random values to generate. There is no industry standard. The more values we use, the more reliable our answers are but the more time-consuming the procedure becomes. In addition, we cannot just simulate values of two random variables without accounting for the correlation between the two. For example, if you spin two roulette wheels, you can assume they are independent of each other in much the same manner as are two uncorrelated assets. But most assets have at least a small degree of correlation. In our example, we used the historical correlation of about −0.06. Monte Carlo simulation must take that relationship into account.

For simplicity, this reading will not go into detail on either the mathematical techniques that can account for the correlations among risk factor returns or the specific method used to simulate outcomes given average values and volatilities for each risk factor. Both are beyond the scope of this reading.

For this example, we will use 10,000 simulated returns on SPY and SPLB drawn from a normal distribution. Of course, non-normal distributions can be used—and they commonly are in practice—but we want to keep the illustration simple to facilitate comparisons between methods. Each set of simulated returns combines to produce a sample with the expected returns and volatilities as we specified. In addition, the returns will have the pre-specified correlation of −0.06. Each pair of returns is weighted 80/20 as desired. We generate the 10,000 outcomes, sort them from worst to best, and

# The Monte Carlo Simulation Method of VaR Estimation

either select the outcome at the 5th percentile for a 5% VaR, the outcome at the 1st percentile for a 1% VaR, or the outcome at the 16th percentile if we want to evaluate the impact of a one standard deviation move. Using the parameters specified in our example, the simulation returns a distribution from which we can draw the following VaR numbers:

1% VaR = $3,541,035

5% VaR = $2,517,702

16% VaR = $1,524,735

Note that these results are fairly close to VaR under the parametric VaR method, where the 5% VaR was $2,445,150. The slight difference arises from the fact that Monte Carlo simulation only *samples* from a population with certain parameters while the parametric method *assumes* those parameters. A sample of a distribution will not produce statistics that match the parameters precisely except in extremely large sample sizes, much larger than the 10,000 used here. Exhibit 7 displays a histogram of the simulated returns overlaid with a bell curve representing a normal distribution. Note how the simulated returns appear more normally distributed than do the historical values, as illustrated in Exhibit 6. This is because we explicitly assumed a normal distribution when running the simulation to generate the values in our example.

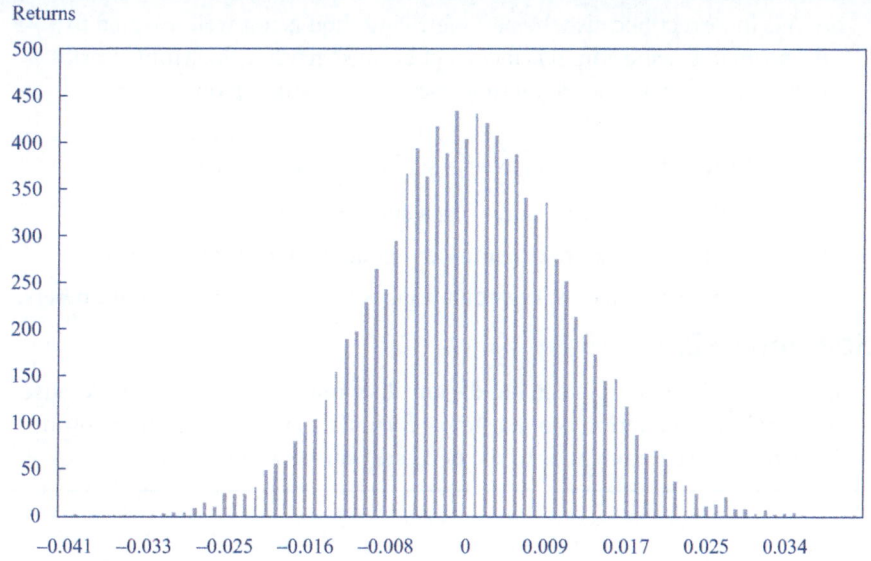

Exhibit 7: Monte Carlo Simulated Returns 80/20 Portfolio of SPY and SPLB

Although we conveniently assumed a normal distribution, one of the advantages of the Monte Carlo method is that it can accommodate virtually *any* distribution. In fact, the flexibility of the Monte Carlo method to handle more complex distributions is its primary attraction. The Monte Carlo and historical simulation methods are much more capable than the parametric method of accurately incorporating the effects of option positions or bond positions with embedded options.

Similar to the historical simulation method, you can scale daily returns to annual returns and extrapolate an estimate of the annual VaR by running a Monte Carlo simulation on these annual returns.

At one time, calculating VaR using the Monte Carlo simulation method was slow, but with the speed of today's computers, it is relatively easy and fast to simulate extremely complex processes for portfolios with thousands of exposures.

> **EXAMPLE 4**
>
> ### Monte Carlo Simulation VaR
>
> 1. When will the Monte Carlo method of estimating VaR produce virtually the same results as the parametric method?
>     - **A.** When the Monte Carlo method assumes a non-normal distribution.
>     - **B.** When the Monte Carlo method uses the historical return and distribution parameters.
>     - **C.** When the parameters and the distribution used in the parametric method are the same as those used in the Monte Carlo method and the Monte Carlo method uses a sufficiently large sample.
>
> ### Solution to 1:
>
> C is correct. The Monte Carlo method simulates outcomes using whatever distribution is specified by the user. *If* a normal distribution is used *and* a sufficiently large number of simulations are run, the parameters of the Monte Carlo sample will converge with those used in the parametric method and the overall VaR should be very close to that of the parametric method. A is incorrect because the parametric method is not well-adapted to a non-normal distribution. B is incorrect because neither the Monte Carlo method nor the parametric method focuses on historical outcomes.
>
> 2. Which of the following is an advantage of the Monte Carlo method?
>     - **A.** The VaR is easy to calculate with a simple formula.
>     - **B.** It is flexible enough to accommodate many types of distributions.
>     - **C.** The number of necessary simulations is determined by the parameters.
>
> ### Solution to 2:
>
> B is correct. The method can handle any distribution. A is incorrect because Monte Carlo simulation is not a simple formula. C is incorrect; there is no industry-wide agreement as to the necessary number of simulations.

## 6. ADVANTAGES, LIMITATIONS, AND EXTENSIONS OF VAR

- [ ] describe advantages and limitations of VaR
- [ ] describe extensions of VaR

# Advantages, Limitations, and Extensions of VaR

The concept of VaR is solidly grounded in modern portfolio analysis. Nonetheless, the implementation of VaR, both in the estimation procedure and in the application of the concept, presents a number of advantages and limitations.

## Advantages of VaR

The use of VaR as a risk measure has the following advantages:

- *Simple concept.* VaR is relatively easy to understand. Although the methodology is fairly technical, the concept itself is not very difficult. So, decision makers without technical backgrounds should be able to grasp the likelihood of possible losses that might endanger the organization. Reporting that a daily 5% VaR is, for example, €2.2 million allows the user to assess the risk in the context of the capital deployed. If a portfolio is expected to incur losses of a minimum of €2.2 million on 5% of the trading days, about once a month, this information is valuable in the context of the size of the portfolio.

- *Easily communicated concept.* VaR captures a considerable amount of information into a single number. If the recipient of the information fully understands the meaning and limitations of VaR, it can be a very significant and practical piece of information.

- *Provides a basis for risk comparison.* VaR can be useful in comparing risks across asset classes, portfolios, and trading units—giving the risk manager a better picture of which constituents are contributing the least and the most to the overall risk. As such, the risk manager can be better informed as he looks for potential hot spots in the organization. This point will be discussed further in a later section.

- *Facilitates capital allocation decisions.* The ability to compare VaR across trading units or portfolio positions provides management with a benchmark that can be used in capital allocation decisions. A proprietary trading firm, for example, can find that its VaR in equity trading is $20 million and its VaR in fixed-income trading is $10 million. If its equity trading portfolio is not expected to take more risk than its fixed-income trading portfolio, then the equity trading activities are taking too much risk or there is too much capital allocated to equity trading. The firm should either make adjustments to realign its VaR or allocate capital in proportion to the relative risks. If a firm is looking to add a position to a portfolio or change the weights of existing portfolio positions, certain extensions of VaR allow the manager to assess the risk of these changes. This topic will be covered in more detail later.

- *Can be used for performance evaluation.* Risk-adjusted performance measurement requires that return or profit be adjusted by the level of risk taken. VaR can serve as the basis for risk adjustment. Without this adjustment, more profitable units could be perceived as more successful; however, when adjusted by VaR, a less profitable unit that poses less risk of loss may be judged more desirable.

- *Reliability can be verified.* VaR is easily capable of being verified, a process known as backtesting. For example, if the daily VaR is $5 million at 5%, we would expect that on 5% of trading days a loss of at least $5 million would be incurred. To determine whether a VaR estimate is reliable, one can determine over a historical period of time whether losses of at least $5 million were incurred on 5% of trading days, subject to reasonable statistical variation.

- *Widely accepted by regulators.* In the United States, the SEC requires that the risk of derivatives positions be disclosed either in the form of a summary table, by sensitivity analysis (a topic we cover later), or by VaR. Thus, VaRs are frequently found in annual reports of financial firms. Global banking regulators also encourage banks to use VaR. These regulations require or encourage the use of VaR, but they do not prescribe how it should be implemented, which estimation method to use, or the maximum acceptable VaR.

## Limitations of VaR

Despite its many advantages, users of VaR must also understand its limitations. The primary limitations of VaR are the following:

- *Subjectivity.* In spite of the apparent scientific objectivity on which it is based, VaR is actually a rather subjective method. As we saw in the descriptions of the three methods of estimating VaR, there are many decisions to make. At the fundamental level, decisions must be made as to the desired VaR cutoff (5%, 1%, or some other cutoff); over what time horizon the VaR will be measured; and finally, which estimation method will be used. As we have seen here, for each estimation method, there are numerous other discretionary choices to make about inputs, source of data, and so on.

- *Underestimating the frequency of extreme events.* In particular, use of the normal distribution in the parametric method and sometimes in the Monte Carlo method commonly underestimates the likelihood of extreme events that occur in the left tail of the distribution. In other words, there are often more extreme adverse events, called "left-tail events," than would be expected under a normal distribution. As mentioned previously, there is no particular requirement that one use the normal distribution. The historical simulation method uses whatever distribution the data produce. We chose to illustrate the Monte Carlo method with a normal distribution, and it is virtually always used in the parametric method. Nonetheless, the tendency to favor the normal distribution and other simple and symmetrical distributions often leads to an understatement of the frequency of left-tail events.

- *Failure to take into account liquidity.* If some assets in a portfolio are relatively illiquid, VaR could be understated, even under normal market conditions. Additionally, liquidity squeezes are frequently associated with tail events and major market downturns, thereby exacerbating the risk. Although illiquidity in times of stress is a general problem that affects virtually all of a firm's financial decisions, reliance on VaR in non-normal market conditions will lead the user to underestimate the magnitude of potential losses.

- *Sensitivity to correlation risk.* Correlation risk is the risk that during times of extreme market stress, correlations among all assets tend to rise significantly. Thus, markets that provide a reasonable degree of diversification under normal conditions tend to decline together under stressed market conditions, thereby no longer providing diversification.

- *Vulnerability to trending or volatility regimes.* A portfolio might remain under its VaR limit every day but lose an amount approaching this limit each day. Under such circumstances, the portfolio could accumulate substantial losses without technically breaching the VaR constraint. Also, during periods of low volatility, VaR will appear quite low, underestimating the losses that could occur when the environment returns to a normal level of volatility.

# Advantages, Limitations, and Extensions of VaR

- *Misunderstanding the meaning of VaR.* VaR is not a worst-case scenario. Losses can and will exceed VaR.
- *Oversimplification.* Although we noted that VaR is an easily communicated concept, it can also oversimplify the picture. And although VaR does indeed consolidate a considerable amount of information into a single number, that number should be interpreted with caution and an awareness of the other limitations as well as supported by additional risk measures.
- *Disregard of right-tail events.* VaR focuses so heavily on the left tail (the losses) that the right tail (potential gains) are often ignored. By examining both tails of the distribution, the user can get a better appreciation of the overall risk–reward trade-off, which is often missed by concentrating only on VaR.

These limitations are not unique to VaR; they apply equally to any technique or measure used to quantify the expected rewards and risks of investing.

### EXAMPLE 5

### Advantages and Limitations of VaR

1. Which of the following is **not** an advantage of VaR?
    - **A.** It is a simple concept to communicate.
    - **B.** There is widespread agreement on how to calculate it.
    - **C.** It can be used to compare risk across portfolios or trading units.

### Solution to 1:

B is correct. There is no consensus on how to calculate VaR. A and C are both advantages of VaR, as we noted that VaR is fairly simple to communicate and it can show the contribution of each unit to the overall VaR.

2. Which of the following is a limitation of VaR?
    - **A.** It requires the use of the normal distribution.
    - **B.** The maximum VaR is prescribed by federal securities regulators.
    - **C.** It focuses exclusively on potential losses, without considering potential gains.

### Solution to 2:

C is correct. VaR deals exclusively with left-tail or adverse events. A is wrong because although parametric VaR does generally use the normal distribution, the historical simulation method uses whatever distribution occurred in the past and Monte Carlo simulation uses whatever distribution the user chooses. B is incorrect because regulators do not specify maximum VaRs, although they may encourage and require that the measure be used.

## Extensions of VaR

Clearly no single risk model can answer all of the relevant questions a risk manager may have. As a result, VaR has laid a foundation for a number of variations, each of which provides additional information.

As discussed previously, VaR is a minimum loss and is typically expressed as the minimum loss that can be expected to occur 5% of the time. An important and related measure can determine the average loss that would be incurred if the VaR cutoff is exceeded. This measure is sometimes referred to as the **conditional VaR (CVaR)**, although it is not technically a VaR measure. It is the average loss conditional on exceeding the VaR cutoff. So, VaR answers the question, "What is the minimum loss I can expect at a certain confidence?" And CVaR answers the question, "How much can I expect to lose if VaR is exceeded?" CVaR is also sometimes referred to as the **expected tail loss** or **expected shortfall**. CVaR is best derived using the historical simulation and Monte Carlo methods, in which one can observe all of the returns throughout the distribution and calculate the average of the losses beyond the VaR cutoff. The parametric method uses a continuous distribution, so obtaining the average loss beyond the VaR cutoff would require a level of mathematics beyond the scope of this reading.

Using our earlier example, in the historical simulation method, our sample of 500 historical returns was sorted from lowest to highest and the 5% VaR was $1,622,272. With 1,006 returns in the sample, 50 observations (5% of 1,006) lie below the VaR estimate. The average of these losses is $2,668,389. Thus, when the VaR is exceeded, we would expect an average loss of about $2.7 million.

For the Monte Carlo method, we generated 10,000 random values and obtained a 5% VaR of $2,517,705. Given 10,000 random values, 500 observations are in the lowest 5% of the VaR distribution. The CVaR using the Monte Carlo method would be the average of the 500 lowest values, which is $4,397,756.

Note that once again, the CVaR derived using the historical simulation method is lower than the CVaR derived using the Monte Carlo method. As explained earlier, this result can largely be attributed to the lower volatility of the S&P 500 component in the historical data series.

Beyond assessing tail loss, a risk manager often wants to know how the portfolio VaR will change if a position size is changed relative to the remaining positions. This effect can be captured by a concept called **incremental VaR (IVaR)**. Using our example, suppose the portfolio manager is contemplating increasing the risk by increasing the investment in SPY to 90% of the portfolio. We recalculate the VaR under the proposed allocation, and the incremental VaR is the difference between the "before" and "after" VaR. As an example, using the parametric method, the VaR would be expected to increase from $2,445,150 to $2,752,500; thus, the IVaR for the 5% case would be $307,350. Or, the portfolio manager might wish to add a new asset, thereby reducing the exposure to the existing assets. The risk manager would calculate the VaR under the assumption that the change is made, and then the difference between the new VaR and the old VaR is the IVaR. This measure is useful because it reflects the effect of an anticipated change on the VaR. The risk manager could find that the new VaR will be unacceptably high or that it has possibly even decreased.

A related concept is called **marginal VaR (MVaR)**. It is conceptually similar to incremental VaR in that it reflects the effect of an anticipated change in the portfolio, but it uses formulas derived from calculus to reflect the effect of a very small change in the position. Some people interpret MVaR as a change in the VaR for a $1 or 1% change in the position, although that is not strictly correct. Nonetheless, this interpretation is a reasonable approximation of the concept behind marginal VaR, which is to reflect the impact of a small change. In a diversified portfolio, marginal VaR may be used to determine the contribution of each asset to the overall VaR; the marginal VaRs for all positions may be proportionately weighted to sum to the total VaR.

# Advantages, Limitations, and Extensions of VaR

Both incremental and marginal VaR address the question of what impact a change in the portfolio holdings might have on the total VaR of the portfolio. Both take into account the potential diversifying effects of various positions or subportfolios, and thus they both can be useful in evaluating the potential effect of a trade before the trade is done.

Another related measure is **ex ante tracking error**, also known as **relative VaR**, which is a measure of the degree to which the performance of a given investment portfolio might deviate from its benchmark. It is computed using any of the standard VaR models, described earlier, but the portfolio to which VaR is applied contains the portfolio's holdings *minus* the holdings in the specified benchmark. In other words, the benchmark's holdings, weighted in proportion to the value of the subject portfolio, are entered into the VaR modeling process as short positions. VaR for this measure is typically expressed as a one standard deviation annualized measure. If the portfolio is a perfect match to the benchmark, *ex ante* tracking error will be at or near zero. The more the portfolio differs from the benchmark, the larger the *ex ante* tracking error will be.

---

**EXAMPLE 6**

## Extensions of VaR

1. Conditional VaR measures the:

    A. VaR over all possible losses.

    B. VaR under normal market conditions.

    C. average loss, given that VaR is exceeded.

### Solution to 1:

C is correct. Conditional VaR is the average loss conditional on exceeding the VaR. A is not correct because CVaR is not concerned with losses that do not exceed the VaR threshold, and B is incorrect because VaR does not distinguish between normal and non-normal markets.

2. Which of the following correctly identifies incremental VaR?

    A. The change in VaR from increasing a position in an asset.

    B. The increase in VaR that might occur during extremely volatile markets.

    C. The difference between the asset with the highest VaR and the asset with the second highest VaR.

### Solution to 2:

A correctly defines incremental VaR. Incremental VaR is the change in VaR from increasing a position in an asset, not a change in VaR from an increase in volatility. B is not correct because incremental VaR reflects the results of intentional changes in exposure, not uncontrollable market volatility. C is not correct because incremental VaR is not the difference in the VaRs of the assets with the greatest and second greatest VaRs.

3. Which of the following statements is correct about marginal VaR?

    A. The marginal VaR is the same as the incremental VaR.

    B. The marginal VaR is the VaR required to meet margin calls.

C. Marginal VaR estimates the change in VaR for a small change in a given portfolio holding.

**Solution to 3:**

C is correct. In A, marginal VaR is a similar concept to incremental VaR in that they both deal with the effect of changes in VaR, but they are not the same concept. B is incorrect because marginal VaR has nothing to do with margin calls.

## 7. OTHER KEY RISK MEASURES

> *Handwritten note: Although gamma and convexity can be used with delta and duration to estimate the impact of extreme market movements, they are not suited for scenario analysis related to option-embedded bonds.*

- [ ] describe sensitivity risk measures and scenario risk measures and compare these measures to VaR
- [ ] demonstrate how equity, fixed-income, and options exposure measures may be used in measuring and managing market risk and volatility risk
- [ ] describe the use of sensitivity risk measures and scenario risk measures

Just as no single measure of a person's health gives a complete picture of that person's physical condition, no single risk measure gives a full picture of a portfolio's risk profile. As we saw, although VaR has many advantages, it also has many limitations. Therefore, good risk managers will use a comprehensive set of risk tools. In this section, we will look at two additional classes of risk measures: those based on sensitivity analysis and those based on the use of hypothetical or historical scenarios. The former enable us to estimate how our estimated gains and losses change with changes in the underlying risk factors, whereas the latter are based on situations involving considerable market stress from which we estimate how our portfolio will perform.

### Sensitivity Risk Measures

Equity, fixed-income, and options positions can be characterized by a number of exposure measures that reflect the sensitivities of these positions to movements in underlying risk factors. Sensitivity measures examine how performance responds to a single change in an underlying risk factor. Understanding and measuring how portfolio positions respond to the underlying sources of risk are primary objectives in managing risk.

#### Equity Exposure Measures

The primary equity exposure measure is the beta. In a simple world, a single market factor drives equity returns. The return on a stock is given by the familiar capital asset pricing model (CAPM):

$$E(R_i) = R_F + \beta_i[E(R_M) - R_F],$$

where $E(R_i)$ is the expected return on the asset or portfolio $i$, $R_F$ is the risk-free rate, $E(R_m)$ is the expected return on the market portfolio, and $\beta_i$ is the beta, which is the risk measure. The expression $E(R_m) - R_F$ is the equity risk premium, which is the return investors demand for investing in equities rather than risk-free instruments. It

## Other Key Risk Measures

should be apparent from this often-used equation that beta measures the sensitivity of the security's expected return to the equity risk premium. The beta is defined as the covariance of the asset return with the market return divided by the variance of the market return. The broad market beta, which is an average of all individual betas, is 1.0. Assets with betas more (less) than 1 are considered more (less) volatile than the market as a whole. The CAPM has a number of extensions, including multifactor models, and risk measures derived from those models can also provide more nuanced information on equity risk exposures.

### Fixed-Income Exposure Measures

The primary sensitivity exposure measures for fixed-income investments are duration and convexity. (Note that credit, a major factor driving non-government fixed-income markets, is covered elsewhere.) **Duration** is sometimes described as the weighted-average time to maturity of a bond, in which the bond is treated as partially maturing on each coupon payment date. Duration is a sensitivity measure. Under the assumption that all interest rates that affect a bond change by the same percentage, the duration is a measure of the sensitivity of the bond price to the interest rate change that characterizes all rates. This single rate can be viewed as the bond's yield, $y$. Given a bond priced at $B$ and yield change of $\Delta y$, the rate of return or percentage price change for the bond is approximately given as follows:

$$\frac{\Delta B}{B} \approx -D\frac{\Delta y}{1+y},$$

where $D$ is the duration. (The $\approx$ sign stands for the phrase "approximately equal" and reflects the fact that the relationship is not exact.) In this expression, it is easy to see that duration does reflect the sensitivity of a bond's price to its yield, although under the restrictive assumption of a single change to all rates. The assumption of a single change to all rates may seem fairly restrictive, but ultimately the assumption is encapsulated by assuming that a single discount rate, the yield, drives the bond price. Duration is considered to be a fairly good sensitivity measure. As previously mentioned, duration is a time measure, the weighted-average maturity of a bond, in which the bond is viewed as maturing progressively as it makes its coupon payments.

The relationship shown here is approximate. The formula is derived under the assumption that the yield change is infinitesimally small, and duration fails to accurately capture bond price movements when yield changes are relatively large. Thus, in the above expression, $\Delta y$ is for small yield changes. It is not possible, however, to say how small a yield change must be before it is small enough for the expression to hold true. In addition, the expression holds only at any instant in time and only for that instant. Over longer periods, the relationship will be less accurate because of the passage of time and because $\Delta y$ is likely to be larger. To accommodate longer periods of time and larger yield changes, we can incorporate a second factor called **convexity**, which is denoted $C$. Convexity describes the sensitivity of a bond's duration to changes in interest rates. Adding convexity to the expression, we obtain the following formula:

$$\frac{\Delta B}{B} \approx -D\frac{\Delta y}{1+y} + \frac{1}{2}C\frac{\Delta y^2}{(1+y)^2}.$$

Convexity can play an important role as a risk measure for large yield changes and long holding periods.

Duration and convexity are essential tools in fixed-income risk management. They allow the risk manager to assess the potential losses to a fixed-income portfolio or position under a given change in interest rates.

### Options Risk Measures

Derivatives have their own unique exposure measures. Because forwards, futures, and swaps have payoffs that are linear in relation to their underlying, they can often be evaluated using the same exposure measures as their underlying. Options, however, have non-linear payoffs, which result in them having their own family of exposure measures that incorporate this non-linear behavior.

Although options can be very risky instruments in and of themselves, they are a critical tool for effective risk management and are often used to create an exposure to offset an existing risk in the portfolio. The relative riskiness of an option arises from the high degree of leverage embedded in most options. An additional and very important risk can also arise from the sensitivity of an option to the volatility of the underlying security. We will expand on these points in the next few paragraphs.

The most fundamental risk of an option is its sensitivity to the price of the underlying. This sensitivity is called the option's **delta**. Although delta is derived by using mathematics beyond the scope of this reading, we can provide a simple and reasonably effective definition as follows:

$$\Delta \text{ (delta)} \approx \frac{\text{Change in value of option}}{\text{Change in value of underlying}}.$$

Call option deltas range from a value of 0 to a value of 1, whereas put option deltas range from a value of 0 to a value of −1. A value of 0 means that the option value does not change when the value of the underlying changes, a condition that is never absolutely true but can be roughly true for a very deep out-of-the-money option. A call delta of 1 means that the price of the call option changes in unison with the underlying, a condition that is also never absolutely true but is *approximately* true for very deep in-the-money calls. A put delta of −1 means that the price of the put option changes in unison with the underlying but in the opposite direction, a condition that is also never absolutely true but is *approximately* true for very deep in-the-money puts. As expiration approaches, an in-the-money call (put) delta approaches 1 (−1) and an out-of-the-money call (put) delta approaches 0.

Delta can be used to approximate the new price of an option as the underlying changes. For a call option, we can use the following formula:

$$c + \Delta c \approx c + \Delta_c \Delta S.$$

Here, $c$ is the original price of the option and $\Delta c$ is the change in the price. We approximate the change in the price as the product of the call's delta, $\Delta_c$, and the change in the value of the underlying, $\Delta S$. The same relationship would hold for puts, simply changing the $c$'s to $p$'s.

The delta of an option is somewhat analogous to the duration of a fixed-income security. It is a first-order effect, reflecting the direct change in the value of the option or fixed-income security when the underlying price or yield, respectively, changes. Just as duration captures the effect of only small changes in the yield over a short period of time, delta captures the effect of only small changes in the value of the underlying security over a short period of time. Similar to duration, which has the second-order effect of convexity, we can add a second-order effect for options called **gamma**. Gamma is a measure of how sensitive an option's delta is to a change in the underlying. It is a second-order effect in that it is measuring the sensitivity of the first-order effect, delta. Gamma can be interpreted in several ways. The delta reflects the direct change in the value of the underlying position, whereas gamma reflects the indirect change (i.e., the change in the change). Technically, it reflects the change in the delta, as indicated by the following:

$$\Gamma \text{ (gamma)} \approx \frac{\text{Change in delta}}{\text{Change in value of underlying}}.$$

As with convexity, gamma itself is not simple to interpret. For example, a call option might have a delta of 0.6 and a gamma of 0.02. It is not easy to determine whether the gamma is large or small. Using the equation just given, if the value of the underlying increases by 0.10 and the gamma is 0.02, then the delta would increase by 0.002 (0.10 × 0.02), from 0.6 to 0.602. Gammas get larger as the option approaches at-the-money, and they are large when options approach expiration, unless the option is deeply in or out of the money. Gamma reflects the uncertainty of whether the option will expire in or out of the money. When an option is close to expiration and roughly at the money, a small change in the price of the underlying will determine whether the option expires worthless or in the money. The uncertainty associated with this win-or-lose situation over a very short time frame leads to a large gamma.

Using delta and gamma, the new call price is

$$c + \Delta c \approx c + \Delta_c \Delta S + \tfrac{1}{2}\Gamma_c(\Delta S)^2,$$

where $\Gamma_c$ is the gamma of the call. This equation is similar to the corresponding expression that relates yield changes to bond price changes through duration and convexity. Indeed, as we said, gamma is a second-order effect, like convexity.

A third important sensitivity measure for options is **vega**, and it reflects the effect of volatility. Vega is a first-order effect reflecting the relationship between the option price and the volatility of the underlying. Vega is expressed by the following relationship:

$$\text{Vega} \approx \frac{\text{Change in value of option}}{\text{Change in volatility of underlying}}.$$

Most options are very sensitive to the volatility of the underlying security. The effect of changing volatility can have a material impact on the value of the option, even when the value of the underlying is not changing.

Using delta, gamma, and vega, the new value of an option given an old value, a change in the value of the underlying, and a change in the volatility can be estimated as follows:

$$c + \Delta c \approx c + \Delta_c \Delta S + \tfrac{1}{2}\Gamma_c(\Delta S)^2 + \text{vega}(\Delta \sigma),$$

where $\Delta \sigma$ is the change in volatility.

The expression represents a composite sensitivity relationship for options. It reflects the expected response of an option value to changes in the value and volatility of the underlying, the two primary factors that change in an unpredictable manner and influence the option value. For portfolios that contain options, understanding these relationships and using them to assess the portfolio's response to market movements are essential elements of effective risk management.

These option measures are applicable not only to options but also to portfolios that contain options. For example, the delta of a portfolio consisting of a long position in an S&P 500 ETF and a short position in a call option on the ETF has a delta that is determined by both the ETF and the option. The ETF has a delta of 1; it changes one-for-one with the S&P 500. The option delta, as noted, has a delta between 0 and 1, though technically 0 and –1 because the option position is short. The ETF has no gamma or vega, so the portfolio gamma and vega are determined by the option. The overall deltas, gammas, and vegas are sums of the deltas, gammas, and vegas of the component positions, taking into account the relative amounts of money invested in each position. Risk managers need to know the overall deltas, gammas, vegas, durations, convexities, and betas to get a comprehensive picture of the sensitivity of the entire portfolio to the prices and volatilities of the underlying.

**EXAMPLE 7**

### Sensitivity Risk Measures

1. Which of the following *most* accurately characterizes duration and convexity?
   
   **A.** Sensitivity of bond prices to interest rates
   
   **B.** First- and second-order effects of yield changes on bond prices
   
   **C.** Weighted-average time to maturity based on the coupon payments and principal

### Solution to 1:

B is correct. Duration is the first-order effect and convexity the second-order effect of a change in interest rates on the value of a bond. A and C are correct with respect to duration, but not for convexity.

2. Which of the following statements about the delta of a call option is **not** correct?
   
   **A.** It ranges between 0 and 1.
   
   **B.** It precisely captures the change in the call value when the underlying changes.
   
   **C.** It approaches 1 for an in-the-money option and 0 for an out-of-the-money option.

### Solution to 2:

B is correct. A and C correctly characterize delta, whereas B states that delta is precise, which is incorrect because it gives an approximate relationship.

3. Which of the following statements about gamma and vega are correct?
   
   **A.** Gamma is a second-order effect, and vega is a first-order effect.
   
   **B.** Gamma is the effect of volatility, and vega is the effect of changes in volatility.
   
   **C.** Gamma is a second-order effect arising from changes in the sensitivity of volatility to the underlying price.

### Solution to 3:

A is correct. B is not correct because gamma does not capture the effect of volatility. Vega is the effect of volatility, but it relates to the level and not the change in volatility. C is incorrect because although gamma is a second-order effect on the option value, it is not related to the sensitivity of volatility to the underlying price.

# SCENARIO RISK MEASURES

8

☐ describe sensitivity risk measures and scenario risk measures and compare these measures to VaR

☐ describe the use of sensitivity risk measures and scenario risk measures

A scenario risk measure estimates the portfolio return that would result from a hypothetical change in markets (a hypothetical scenario) or a repeat of a historical event (a historical scenario). As an example, the risk manager might want to understand how her current portfolio would perform if an event, such as the Black Monday of October 1987, were to reoccur. The factor movements that characterized the historical event would be applied to the factor exposures of the current portfolio. Alternatively, the risk manager may develop a hypothetical scenario to describe a market event that has not occurred in the past but which he or she believes has some probability of occurring in the future. The two elements of scenario risk measures that set them apart from sensitivity risk measures are (1) the use of multiple factor movements used in the scenario measures versus the single factor movements typically used in risk sensitivity measures and (2) the typically larger size of the factor movement used in the scenario measures. Scenario risk measures are related to VaR in that they focus on extreme outcomes, but they are not bound by either recent historical events or assumptions about parameters or probability distributions. **Stress tests**, which apply extreme negative stress to a particular portfolio exposure, are closely related to scenario risk measures. Scenario analysis is an open-ended exercise that could look at positive or negative events, although its most common application is to assess the negative outcomes. Stress tests intentionally focus on extreme negative events to assess the impact of such an event on the portfolio.

The two types of scenario risk measures—historical scenarios and hypothetical scenarios—are discussed in the following sections.

## Historical Scenarios

Historical scenarios are scenarios that measure the portfolio return that would result from a repeat of a particular period of financial market history. Historical scenarios used in risk management include such events as the currency crisis of 1997–1998, the market dislocation surrounding the failure of Long-Term Capital Management, the market rout of October 1987, the bursting of the technology bubble in 2001, and the financial crisis of 2008–2009. In order to create a historical scenario, the current set of portfolio holdings is placed into the appropriate valuation models.

Equity positions can often be modeled using their price histories as proxies for their expected behavior, although some practitioners model equities using factor analysis. Valuation models are needed for fixed-income and derivatives products because they have a maturity or an expiration feature that must be accommodated when modeling the portfolio. Historical prices for the fixed-income and derivatives positions currently held in the portfolio may not exist, as in the case of a bond that was issued after the historical period being modeled. Even when historical prices for specific instruments do exist, they may not be relevant to the current characteristics of the instrument. Take the case of a 5-year historical price series for a 10-year bond with 1 year remaining to maturity; the historical price series reflects the price volatility of what used to be a longer bond (e.g., five years ago, the bond had six years remaining to maturity; three years ago, the bond had four years remaining to maturity). The volatility of the bond when it had six years remaining to maturity would be higher than it is today, with only one year remaining to maturity. Using its historical price history would mischaracterize the risk of the current portfolio holding. For this reason, the historical yields, spreads, implied volatilities, prices of the underlying assets in derivatives contracts, and the other input parameters that drive the pricing of these instruments are more important in explaining the risks of these instruments than the price history of the instrument itself.

Some examples may help to show how fixed-income or derivatives valuation models are used in a historical scenario. In the case of a convertible bond, the bond's terms and conditions (e.g., coupon, conversion ratio, maturity) are entered into a convertible bond pricing model. In the case of standard bonds, the terms and conditions of these instruments (e.g., coupon, call features, put features, any amortization or sinking fund features, maturity) are entered into fixed-income pricing models. These modeled fixed-income or derivatives holdings, together with the equity holdings, are then re-priced under the conditions that prevailed during the "scenario period"—a given set of dates in the past. Changes in interest rates, credit spreads, implied volatility levels, and any asset underlying a derivatives product, as well as the historical price changes in the equity portfolio, would all be reflected in the re-priced portfolio. The value of each position is recorded before and after these changes in order to arrive at the gain or loss that would occur under the chosen scenario. Historical scenario events are specifically chosen to represent extreme market dislocations and often exhibit abnormally high correlations among asset classes. It is most common to run the scenario or stress test as if the total price action movement across the period occurs instantaneously, before any rebalancing or management action is possible. The output of the scenario can include

- the total return of the portfolio;
- for long-only asset managers, the total return of the portfolio relative to its benchmark;
- for pensions, insurers, and others whose liabilities are not already incorporated into the portfolio, the total return of the portfolio relative to the change in liabilities under the scenario; and
- any collateral requirements and other cash needs that will be driven by the changes specified in the scenario.

One variation of the historical scenario approach includes running the scenario over multiple days and incorporating actions that the manager might be expected to take during the period. Instead of assuming the shock is a single instant event, this approach assumes it takes place over a number of days and that on each day the portfolio manager can take such actions as selling assets or rebalancing hedges.

Many risk managers are skeptical of this approach because it produces smaller potential loss measures (by design) and does not answer important questions that have been relevant in real crises, such as, "What if the severe price action happens so quickly that the portfolio manager cannot take remedial actions?" Generally, risk managers prefer that a stress testing exercise be tailored to the *initial outcome of a large shock*, to ensure that the event is survivable by a portfolio that uses leverage, and that there will be no unacceptable counterparty exposures or portfolio concentrations before action can be taken to improve the situation. This method also helps to simulate the possibility that liquidity may be unavailable.

Risk managers seeking to measure the impact of a historical scenario need to ensure all relevant risk factors are included. For instance, foreign equities will need to be decomposed into foreign exchange exposure and equity exposure in the analysis. Stress tests typically take the explicit currency approach, which measures the currency exposure of each foreign equity. Alternatively, the risk manager may use an approach that incorporates implicit currency risks, such as companies that may be registered in one country but have earnings flowing in from other countries, and may hedge some of those revenues back to their base currency.

When the historical simulation fully revalues securities under rate and price changes that occurred during the scenario period, the results should be highly accurate. Sometimes, however, scenarios are applied to risk sensitivities rather than the securities themselves. This approach is a simpler form of analysis, but it should not be used for options or option-embedded securities. Although it may be tempting to use delta and gamma or duration and convexity to estimate the impact of a scenario on options or option-embedded securities, these measures are not suited for handling the kinds of extreme movements analyzed in scenario analysis. Although gamma and convexity are second-order adjustments that work with delta and duration to estimate extreme movements, they are inadequate for scenario analysis.

Even in simpler fixed-income cases in which no options are present, care needs to be taken to ensure the analysis does not oversimplify. Duration sensitivities can be used as the inputs to a scenario analysis for straightforward fixed-income instruments, but these sensitivities need to be mapped to the most relevant sectors, credit curves, and yield curve segments before beginning the analysis. If assets are mapped too broadly, the analysis will miss the important differences that could drive the most meaningful outcomes in a given scenario.

It is also important to pay careful attention to how securities or markets that did not yet exist at the time of the scenario are modeled. If, for instance, an analyst is measuring a current portfolio's sensitivity to a recurrence of the 1987 US stock market crash, the analyst needs to determine how to treat stocks in the portfolio that had an initial public offering after 1987. They may need to be mapped to a relevant index or to a similar company or be decomposed into the relevant statistical factors (such as growth, value, volatility, or momentum) by using a factor model before beginning the analysis. Similarly, because credit default swaps did not come into widespread use until 2002, historical scenarios for dates preceding this time would need to be adapted to appropriately reflect the impact of a repeat of that scenario on these new securities.

## Hypothetical Scenarios

Scenarios have a number of benefits. They can reflect the impact of extreme market movements, and they make no specific assumptions regarding normality or correlation. Historical scenarios have the extra benefit of being uncontroversial; no one can claim it is impossible for such events to occur, because they did. One problem with scenario analysis, however, lies in ascribing the probability of a given scenario. Most would agree that it is improbable to assume that the exact historical scenario specified will actually occur in precisely the same way in the future. Another potential problem is that, because it has happened (particularly when it has happened recently), risk managers or portfolio managers are inclined to take precautions that make their portfolios safer for a replay of that historical crisis—and, in the process, make their portfolios more vulnerable to a crisis that has not yet happened.

For that reason, risk managers also use hypothetical scenarios—extreme movements and co-movements in different markets that have not necessarily previously occurred. The scenarios used are somewhat difficult to believe, and it is difficult to assess their probability. Still, they represent the only real method to assess portfolio outcomes under market movements that might be imagined but that have not yet been experienced.

To design an effective hypothetical scenario, it is necessary to identify the portfolio's most significant exposures. Targeting these material exposures and assessing their behavior in various environments is a process called **reverse stress testing**. The risk manager is seeking answers to such questions as the following: What are the top 10 exposures or risk drivers in my portfolio? What would make them risky? What are the top 10 benchmark-relative exposures? Under what scenario would hedges not hedge? Under what scenario would my securities lending activity, ordinarily thought to be riskless, be risky? The ideal use of hypothetical scenarios is, then, not to model every possible future state of every market variable, but rather to target those that are highly significant to the portfolio in order to assess, and potentially address, vulnerabilities.

Reverse stress testing is particularly helpful in estimating potential losses if more than one important exposure is affected in a market crisis, as often happens when participants "crowd" into the same exposures. Sometimes, apparently unrelated markets experience stress at the same time.

The risk manager might also choose to design a hypothetical geopolitical event, estimating its potential effect on markets and the resulting impact on the portfolio. To develop these scenarios, individuals with varying areas of expertise posit an event—such as an earthquake in Country Y, or Country X invades Country Z, or the banking system implodes in Region A. The group conducting the analysis identifies which markets are most likely to be affected as well as any identifiable secondary effects. The next step is to establish a potential range of movement for the affected markets. The final scenario is intended to meet the standard of "rare, but not impossible." The exercise is unlikely to be truly accurate in the face of the real event, but it will often help to identify unexpected portfolio vulnerabilities and outcomes and to think through counterparty credit and operational considerations that could exacerbate or accelerate the scenario.

Hypothetical scenarios are particularly beneficial in being able to stress correlation parameters. The scenario is not constrained to assume that assets will co-move as they have done in the past, which can help identify dangers that other forms of risk analysis may miss. Scenarios can be designed to highlight that correlations often increase in times of stress. This is often achieved by subjecting markets that typically have little or no correlation with one another to the same or similar movements, thereby simulating a temporarily higher correlation. Scenarios can also be devised to pinpoint times when hedging might work poorly—when assets, such as a bond and the credit default swap used to hedge it, that normally have a high correlation might temporarily decouple and move by different percentages or even in different directions. This often occurs when markets experience a "flight to quality"; the swap rate may move down as a result of their relative credit strength, whereas the bond yield might increase given its perceived credit risk.

Once a risk manager has completed a scenario analysis, common questions may be, "What do you do with a scenario analysis? What are the action steps?" If the portfolios are within all other rules and guidelines—their exposures have been kept within desired limits and their VaR or *ex ante* tracking error is within the desired range—scenario analysis provides one final opportunity to assess the potential for negative surprises during a given stress event. The action steps might be to trim back positions that are otherwise within all limits and that appear to present comfortable risk exposures under the current environment but would perform unacceptably during a plausible stress environment. In the case of asset management, where clients have elected to be in a given asset class and the asset manager is constrained by that investment mandate, action steps may include adjusting benchmark-relative risk, disclosing to clients the manager's concerns regarding the risks in the portfolio, or changing counterparty or operational procedures to avoid an unwanted event.

But a caution is in order: A portfolio that has no sensitivity to any stress event is unlikely to earn more than the risk-free rate, or in the case of long-only asset managers, outperform the benchmark index. Stress tests and scenarios analyses are best used in the effort to *understand* a portfolio's risk exposures, not to eliminate them. Effective risk management sets a tolerance range for a stress test or scenario that reflects a higher loss possibility than the investment manager would normally find acceptable.

Scenarios should be periodically run again, and action should be taken only if the portfolio exceeds this relatively high tolerance level. It is also important to continually evaluate new threats and new market developments and to periodically refresh the set of scenarios, removing scenarios that are no longer meaningful for the portfolio.

Note also that scenario risk measures and stress tests are best used as the final screen in a series of position constraints that include position size limits, exposure limits, and VaR or *ex ante* tracking error limits. They do not serve well as the initial or primary screen, for reasons that will be discussed shortly.

Parties that use leverage, such as banks and hedge funds, are more likely to use single-factor stress tests rather than multifactor scenario analyses. The focus on a single factor helps in assessing whether a given exposure is likely to impair their capital under a given stress movement; these are pass/fail tests. If capital falls below an acceptable level, it could set off a chain reaction of margin calls, withdrawal of financing, and other actions that threaten the viability of the business.

### EXAMPLE 8

#### Scenario Analysis

1. Which of the following is an example of a reverse stress test?

    **A.** Identify the top 10 exposures in the portfolio, and then generate a hypothetical stress that could adversely affect all 10 simultaneously.

    **B.** Find the worst single day's performance that could have occurred for the current portfolio had it been held throughout the past five years.

    **C.** Find the returns that occurred in all risk factors in the 2008 global financial crisis, reverse the sign on these, and apply them to today's portfolio.

#### Solution to 1:

A is correct. B is not a reverse stress test because reverse stress tests focus more narrowly on trouble spots for a specific portfolio. C would illustrate how the portfolio would have performed in an extremely strong market, quite unlike what occurred in 2008.

2. Which kind of market participant is *least likely* to use scenario analysis as a pass/fail stress test?

    **A.** Bank

    **B.** Long-only asset manager

    **C.** Hedge fund using leverage

#### Solution to 2:

B is correct. Long-only asset managers do not typically use leverage and are thus less likely to become insolvent, making a pass/fail test for solvency less relevant to them. A and C are not correct because parties that use leverage, such as hedge funds and banks, are likely to use stress tests to determine what market movements could impair their capital and lead to insolvency.

3. What is the *most* accurate approach to scenario analysis for a portfolio that uses options?

    **A.** Apply the scenario to option delta.

    **B.** Apply the scenario to option delta + gamma.

C. Fully reprice the options using the market returns specified under the scenario.

**Solution to 3:**

C is correct. Both A and B risk misestimating the actual results of the scenario because both delta and gamma estimate how an option's value might change for a small move in the underlying asset, not the large movements typically used in a scenario analysis.

## 9. SENSITIVITY AND SCENARIO RISK MEASURES AND VAR

- [ ] describe sensitivity risk measures and scenario risk measures and compare these measures to VaR
- [ ] describe advantages and limitations of sensitivity risk measures and scenario risk measures

Although both VaR and sensitivity risk measures deal with related concepts, they have their own distinctions. VaR is a measure of losses and the probability of large losses. Sensitivity risk measures capture changes in the value of an asset in response to a change in something else, such as a market index, an interest rate, or an exchange rate; they do not, however, tell us anything about the probability of a given change in value occurring. For example, we could use duration to measure the change in a bond price for an instantaneous 1 bp change in the yield, but duration does not tell us anything about the likelihood of such a change occurring. Similar statements could be made about equities and the various option measures: Betas and deltas do not tell us how likely a change might be in the underlying risk factors, but given a change, they tell us how responsive the asset or derivative would be.

VaR gives us a broader picture of the risk in the sense that it accounts for the probability of losses of certain amounts. In this sense, it incorporates what we know about the probability of movements in the risk factors. Nonetheless, these sensitivity measures are still very useful in that they allow us to take a much more detailed look at the relationships driving the risk. It is one thing to say that a VaR is $2 million for one day at 5%. We know what that means. But it is equally important to understand what is driving the risk. Is it coming from high beta stocks, high duration bonds, or high delta options? If we find our VaR unacceptable, we have to know where to look to modify it. If we simply use VaR by itself, we will blindly rely on a single number without understanding what factors are driving the number.

VaR has much in common with scenario risk measures in that both types of measures estimate potential loss. VaR tends to do so using a model for which input parameters are created based on market returns from a particular time in history. Thus, the VaR estimate is vulnerable if correlation relationships and market volatility during the period in question are not representative of the conditions the portfolio may face in the future. VaR does, however, allow a disciplined method for stressing all factors in the portfolio. Scenario analysis allows either the risk assessment to be fully hypothetical or to be linked to a different and more extreme period of history, helping reduce some of the biases imposed by the VaR model. But there is no guarantee that the scenario chosen will be the "right" one to estimate risk for future markets. Moreover, it is particularly difficult to stress all possible risk factors in a hypothetical scenario in a way that does not embed biases similar to those that occur in VaR modeling.

Each of these measures—sensitivity risk measures, scenario risk measures, and VaR—has distinct limitations and distinct benefits. They are best used in combination because no one measure has the answer, but all provide valuable information that can help risk managers understand the portfolio and avoid unwanted outcomes and surprises.

## Advantages and Limitations of Sensitivity Risk Measures and Scenario Risk Measures

Before portfolios began using risk measures based on modern portfolio theory, the very first risk measure was "position size"—the value invested in a given type of asset. Position size is a very effective risk measure for homogeneous, long-only portfolios, particularly for those familiar with the homogenous asset class in question; an experienced person can assess what the loss potential of such a portfolio is just by knowing its size. But position size is less useful for assessing interest rate risk, even less useful for summarizing the risk of a multi-asset class portfolio, and less useful still at assessing net risk in a portfolio that uses hedging instruments, short positions, and liabilities.

Sensitivity measures address some of the shortcomings of position size measures. Duration, for example, addresses the difference between a 1-year note and a 30-year note; it measures the level of interest rate risk. Option delta and duration (for fixed income) help to display net risk in a portfolio that has hedging or short positions with optionality or interest rate risk.

Sensitivities typically do not often distinguish assets by volatility, though. When measured as the sensitivity to a 1 bp or 1% move, they do not tell the user which portfolio has greater loss potential any more than position size measures do. A high-yield bond portfolio might have the same sensitivity to a 0.01% credit spread movement as an investment-grade portfolio, but they do not have the same risk because the credit spreads of the high-yield portfolio are more likely to move 0.01%, or more, than the credit spreads of the investment-grade bonds. Sensitivity measures do not distinguish by standard deviation/volatility or other higher confidence loss measures. Measuring sensitivity to a one standard deviation movement in an asset's price or yield, however, is one way to overcome this shortcoming of sensitivity.

### Granularity: Too Much or Too Little?

Sensitivity measures are aggregated in categories or "buckets." (A bucket is a risk factor description such as "one- to five-year French sovereign debt.") When a number of fixed-income positions are assigned to the same bucket, the effect is an assumption of perfect correlation across the risks encompassed by that bucket. For the "one- to five-year French sovereign debt" risk factor, a short duration position in four-year French sovereign debt will be assumed to fully offset a long duration position in two-year French sovereign debt. However, this may not be true in the case of a non-parallel interest rate change; these points on the yield curve do not have a correlation coefficient of 1 to one another. The broader the buckets used, the more they can hide this kind of correlation risk; but the narrower the buckets used, the greater the complexity and thus the more difficult to portray portfolios in simple, accessible ways. The width or the narrowness of the risk-factor buckets used to portray sensitivity measures is referred to as granularity.

Scenario analysis and stress testing have well-deserved popularity, and they address many of the shortcomings of VaR described earlier. Sensitivity and scenario risk measures can complement VaR in the following ways:

- They do not need to rely on history. Sensitivity and scenario risk measures can be constructed to test the portfolio's vulnerability to a truly never-before-seen market movement. In this way, they can be free of the volatility and correlation behavior of recent market history, which may simply not be representative of stress conditions. In a scenario analysis, assets that typically have a low correlation with one another can be modeled under an assumption of perfect positive correlation simply by simulating an identical price movement for these assets. Alternatively, they can be modeled under an assumption of perfect negative correlation by simulating identical price movements (i.e., in the opposite direction). A scenario might be designed in which a market that typically exhibits an annual standard deviation of 15% moves by 20% in a single day.

- Scenarios can be designed to overcome any assumption of normal distributions; the shock used could be the equivalent of 1, 10, or 1,000 standard deviations, at the choice of the analyst—or as provided by an actual moment in history.

- Scenarios can be tailored to expose a portfolio's most concentrated positions to even worse movement than its other exposures, allowing liquidity to be taken into account.

But scenario measures are not without their own limitations:

- Historical scenarios are interesting, and illuminating, but are not going to happen in exactly the same way again, making hypothetical scenarios necessary to truly fill the gaps identified with the other risk measures listed.

- Hypothetical scenarios may incorrectly specify how assets will co-move, they may get the magnitude of movements wrong, and they may incorrectly adjust for the effects of liquidity and concentration.

- Hypothetical scenarios can be very difficult to create and maintain. Getting all factors and their relationships accurately represented in the suite of scenarios is a painstaking and possibly never-ending exercise. Accordingly, it is necessary to draw a line of "reasonableness" at which to curtail the scenario analysis, and by the very act of being curtailed, the scenario might miss the real risk.

- It is very difficult to know how to establish the appropriate limits on a scenario analysis or stress test. Because we are proposing hypothetical movements in markets and risk factors, we cannot use history to assign a probability of such a move occurring. What if rates rise instantaneously 0.50%, 1.00%, or 3.00%? How should the short end of the yield curve move versus the long end? How much should credit spreads of different qualities move? It is difficult to choose.

The more extreme the scenario, and the farther from historical experience, the less likely it is to be found believable or actionable by management of a company or a portfolio. This issue tends to lead scenario constructors to underestimate movement in order to appear credible. As an example, prior to the very large drop in real estate values that prevailed in the United States from 2008 to 2010, no similar nationwide price decline had occurred in history. Risk measurement teams at a number of firms did prepare scenarios that estimated the potential outcome if real estate prices declined meaningfully, but their scenarios in many cases were only half as large as the movements that subsequently occurred. Because these large market movements had never before occurred, there was no historical basis for estimating them, and to do so appeared irresponsible. This is an additional risk of scenario analysis: The need to keep the scenario plausible may lead to it being incorrect.

In sum, scenario analyses and stress tests have the opportunity to correct the failings of probabilistic risk measures, such as VaR and *ex ante* tracking error; however, because the version of the future they suggest may be no more accurate than that used in VaR, they may also fail to predict potential loss accurately.

As we can see, each risk measure has elements that are better than the others, and each has important failings. No one measure is the "solution" to risk management. Each is useful and necessary to answer certain questions but not sufficient to answer all possible questions—or to prevent all forms of unexpected loss. Using the measures in combination, to correct each other's failings, is as close to a solution as we come. Designing constraints by using multiple measures is the key practice used by successful risk managers. Viewing a portfolio through these multiple lenses provides a more solid framework for a risk manager or an investor to exercise judgment and can help reduce conceptual bias in portfolio management.

### EXAMPLE 9

### Limitations of Risk Measures

1. Which of the following is **not** a limitation of VaR?

   A. It does not adjust for bonds of different durations.

   B. It largely relies on recent historical correlations and volatilities.

   C. It can be inaccurate if the size of positions held is large relative to available liquidity.

### Solution to 1:

A is correct. Well-executed VaR measures do adjust for bonds of differing duration, and therefore it is not a limitation of VaR. B is incorrect because VaR ordinarily uses some period of recent history as part of the calculation, and this reliance on history is one of its limitations. C is incorrect because VaR can be inaccurate and underestimate risk if portfolio positions are too large relative to the available market liquidity, and this inability to account for the illiquidity of an individual investor's position is an additional limitation of VaR.

2. Which of the following statements about sensitivities is true?

   A. When duration is measured as the sensitivity to a 1 bp change in interest rates, it can be biased by choice of the historical period preceding this measure.

   B. Sensitivity measures are the best way to determine how an option can behave under extreme market movements.

   C. Duration effectively assumes that the correlation between a fixed-income exposure and the risk-free rate is 1, whereas beta takes into account the historical correlation between an equity and its comparison index.

### Solution to 2:

C is correct. Duration assumes that all interest rates that affect a bond change by the same percentage (an effective correlation of 1). A is incorrect because the 1 bp change in rates is applied to current rates, not historical rates. B is incorrect because sensitivity measures are often too small to reveal the most extreme movements for option positions; the larger shocks used in scenario measures are preferable to reveal option characteristics.

3. Which of the following is **not** a limitation of scenario measures?

   A. It is difficult to ascribe probability to a given scenario.
   B. Scenario measures assume a normal distribution, and market returns are not necessarily normal.
   C. They risk being an infinite task; one cannot possibly measure all of the possible future scenarios.

### Solution to 3:

B is correct. Scenario measures do not assume any given distribution, and thus this is not a limitation of scenario analysis. A is incorrect because it is in fact difficult to ascribe probability to many scenarios, and thus this is a limitation of scenario analysis. C is also incorrect because it is in fact impossible to measure all possible future scenarios, and this is a limitation of scenario analysis.

4. Which measures are based on market returns during a particular historical period?

   A. Hypothetical scenario analysis and duration sensitivity
   B. Historical scenario analysis and VaR
   C. Option delta and vega

### Solution to 4:

B is correct. Historical scenarios apply market returns from a particular period to the portfolio, and virtually all VaR methodologies use a historical period to underpin the VaR model (although certain methods may make adjustments if this historical period is seen to be anomalous in some way). A is incorrect because a hypothetical scenario is not based on an actual historical period, and duration sensitivity measures change in value for a given small change in rates, not for a given historical period. C is incorrect because option delta and vega measure how much an option's value will change for a given change in the price of the underlying (delta) or implied volatility (vega), and these are sensitivity measures, not measures based on a particular historical period.

## 10 USING CONSTRAINTS IN MARKET RISK MANAGEMENT

- [ ] explain constraints used in managing market risks, including risk budgeting, position limits, scenario limits, and stop-loss limits
- [ ] explain how risk measures may be used in capital allocation decisions

# Using Constraints in Market Risk Management

Designing suitable constraints to be used in market risk management is essential to managing risk effectively. Risk *measurements* in and of themselves cannot be said to be restrictive or unrestrictive: The *limits* placed on the measures drive action. VaR can be measured to a very high confidence level (for example, 99%) or to a low level (for example, 84%). But placing a loose limit on a 99% confidence VaR measure could be less of a constraint than placing a tight limit on an 84% confidence measure. It is not the confidence interval that drives conservatism as much as the limit that is placed on it.

If constraints are too tight, they may limit the pursuit of perceived opportunities and shrink returns or profitability to a sub-optimal level. If constraints are too loose, outsized losses can occur, threatening the viability of the portfolio or business. The concept of "restrictive" or "unrestrictive" relates to the risk appetite of the firm or portfolio and the sizes of losses it can tolerate. Unrestrictive limits are typically set far from current risk levels and permit larger losses than restrictive limits. As an example, for a leveraged portfolio in which insolvency could occur if cumulative daily losses exceed $10 million and the portfolio's current two week, 1% VaR measure is $3 million, an unrestrictive limit might be one set at $10 million. If the portfolio increased positions and went right up to its limit, a misestimation of VaR could result in insolvency; moreover, the fact that losses are expected to exceed the measure at least 1% of the time could mean disaster. But if the limit were set at $4 million, the portfolio might under-allocate the capital it has to invest and fail to make a high enough return on equity to thrive in a competitive environment.

Before applying constraints, particularly those involving such potential loss measures as VaR or a scenario analysis, it is worth considering how far down in the organizational hierarchy to impose them. If applied exclusively to lower level business units, the firm's aggregate risk exposure fails to take advantage of offsetting risks that may occur at higher levels of the organization. As a result, the overall company may never be able to invest according to its risk tolerance because it is "stopped out" by rules lower in the organization. For example, imagine a bank with five trading desks: It might have an overall VaR tolerance of €10 million and might set each trading desk's limit for its standalone VaR at €2 million, which seems reasonable. If there is anything lower than perfect correlation across these desks' positions, however—and particularly if one desk has a short position that to some degree serves as an offset to another desk's long position—the firm will never be able to use its €10 million risk appetite in full. The cure for this problem is over-allocation, with the caveat that a given desk might need to be cut back to its pro rata share in the event that correlations among trading desks are higher than, or the short positions across the different portfolios are not as offsetting as, the over-allocation assumes. Alternatively, some firms might use marginal VaR for each trading desk, allocating each desk a VaR budget such that the total VaR is the sum of each individual desk's marginal VaR. This approach permits each trading desk to "reinvest" the diversification benefits obtained at the aggregate level.

Among the constraints most often used in risk management are risk budgeting, position limits, scenario limits, and stop-loss limits. As is the case in risk measurement, for which multiple measures work better than any one measure alone does, so it is in risk constraints. No one approach on its own works perfectly; they are most effective in combination.

## Risk Budgeting

In **risk budgeting**, the total risk appetite of the firm or portfolio is agreed on at the highest level of the entity and then allocated to sub-activities. Risk budgeting typically rests on a foundation of VaR or *ex ante* tracking error.

A bank might establish a limit on total economic capital or VaR and describe this limit as its risk appetite. Next, it might allocate this risk appetite among the basic risk types (market, credit, and operational) and different business units, geographies, and activities. It allocates to the business unit and/or risk type by specifying a limit, using its chosen measure, for that given activity. For example, it might allow its European business to use 20% of its market risk capital (the portion of its economic capital expected to be used to support market risk taking) and 40% of its credit risk capital, whereas its Asian business might have a different limit. It will set these limits based on the expected long-term profitability of the opportunity set and the demonstrated skill of a business at delivering profitable results, taking into consideration shareholders' expectations regarding the activities the bank is engaged in. As an example of potential shareholder expectations, consider a case in which a firm's shareholder disclosure suggests that the firm's predominant market risk-taking activities are in the Asian markets and that less risk-taking activity is in Europe. Shareholders will be surprised if greater losses are incurred from its European business than its Asian business. Market risk capital limits for the European business should be lower than for the Asian business to be consistent with shareholder disclosures.

A pension fund sponsor might begin with its tolerance for how much of a mismatch it is willing to tolerate overall between the total value of assets and its liabilities—its surplus at risk. Surplus at risk can be the starting point for its asset allocation decision making. Once the broad asset allocation is established, usually expressed via a set of benchmarks, the pension fund sponsor might further establish its tolerance for underperformance in a given asset class and allocate that tolerance to the asset managers selected to manage the assets by assigning each an *ex ante* tracking error budget.

A portfolio manager might have an *ex ante* tracking error budget explicitly provided by the client, or if none is provided by the client, it might instead develop a tracking error budget based on her investment philosophy and market practice. Given this budget, she will seek to optimize the portfolio's exposures relative to the benchmark to ensure that the strategies that generate the most tracking error for the portfolio are those for which she expects the greatest reward.

## Position Limits

Risk budgeting follows a clear logic; but as we have noted, VaR-based measures have a number of drawbacks. One of them is that they perform poorly if portfolios are unusually concentrated, particularly with respect to market liquidity.

Position limits are limits on the market value of any given investment, or the notional principal amount for a derivatives contract. They can be expressed in currency units or as a percentage of some other value, such as net assets. Position limits do not take into account duration, volatility, and correlation, as VaR does, but they are excellent controls on overconcentration. Like risk budgeting, position limits need to be used carefully; if every asset type that a portfolio manager could invest in is constrained, he will have no room to succeed in outperforming the benchmark or generating absolute returns, assuming that is the mandate. Position limits should not be overly prescriptive but should address the event risk and single name risk that VaR handles so poorly, such as

- limits per issuer;
- limits per currency or country;
- limits on categories expected to be minimized in a given strategy, such as high-yield credit or emerging market equities;
- limits on gross size of long–short positions or derivatives activity; and
- limits on asset ownership that correspond to market liquidity measures, such as daily average trading volume.

## Scenario Limits

A scenario limit is a limit on the estimated loss for a given scenario, which if exceeded, would require corrective action in the portfolio.

As discussed in Section 3.3, scenarios also address shortcomings of VaR, such as the potential for changes in correlation or for extreme movements that might not be predicted using a normal distribution or the historical lookback period used for the VaR measure. Just producing scenario analysis, however, without having any related action steps is not a very valuable exercise.

The action steps that generally follow a scenario analysis are to examine (1) whether the results are within risk tolerance and, in the case of asset managers, (2) whether the results are well incorporated into investor disclosures. To determine whether results are within the established risk tolerance, a tolerance level for each scenario must be developed. It is better to establish a higher tolerance for potential loss under the most extreme scenarios. If the same limit is applied to all scenarios, even extremely unlikely scenarios (e.g., "interest rates rise 1,000,000%"), then the portfolio will simply not be able to take any risk. The risk manager then observes over time whether the portfolio's sensitivity to the scenario is increasing or crosses this high-tolerance bound.

## Stop-Loss Limits

A **stop-loss limit** requires a reduction in the size of a portfolio, or its complete liquidation, when a loss of a particular size occurs in a specified period.

One of the limitations of VaR described in Section 2.3.2 was "trending," in which a portfolio remains under its VaR limit each day but cumulatively loses more than expected. This trending can be managed by imposing and monitoring stop-loss limits in addition to the VaR constraints. In one form of a stop-loss limit, the portfolio's positions are unwound if its losses over a pre-specified period exceed a pre-specified level. (Those levels are typically defined to align with the overall risk tolerance.) As an example, a portfolio might have a 10-day, 1% VaR limit of $5 million, but it will be liquidated if its cumulative monthly loss ever exceeds $8 million. The relationship between the stop-loss and the VaR measure can vary depending on management preferences as well as the differing time periods with which the measures are specified.

An alternative approach to a stop-loss limit might instead be to impose a requirement to undertake hedging activity, which may include purchases of protective options, after losses of a given magnitude, with the magnitude of the hedge increasing as losses increase. This approach, called drawdown control or portfolio insurance, is more dynamic and more sophisticated than the simpler stop-loss limit.

## Risk Measures and Capital Allocation

In market risk management, capital allocation is the practice of placing limits on each of a company's activities in order to ensure that the areas in which it expects the greatest reward and has the greatest expertise are given the resources needed to accomplish their goals. Allocating capital wisely ensures that an unproven strategy does not use up all of the firm's risk appetite and, in so doing, deprive the areas most likely to be successful of the capital they need to execute on their strategy.

Economic capital is often used to estimate how much of shareholders' equity could be lost by the portfolio under very unfavorable circumstances. Capital allocation may start with a measurement of economic capital (the amount of capital a firm needs to hold if it is to survive severe losses from the risks in its businesses). The company's actual, physical on-balance-sheet capital must exceed the measure of economic capital, and a minimum level of economic capital must be established to ensure that the company does not take on a risk of loss that will exceed its available capital. The company first establishes its overall risk appetite in economic capital terms, and then it subdivides this appetite among its units. This exercise is similar to risk budgeting, but in the case of corporations, banks, insurers, or hedge funds, it is more likely to be called "capital allocation." Capital allocation is often used in cases in which leverage is used by the portfolio or in which the strategy has meaningful **tail risk**, meaning that losses in extreme events could be far greater than would be expected for a portfolio of assets with a normal distribution. Economic capital is designed to measure how much shareholders' equity could be required to meet tail risk losses. Strategies that have greater-than-expected tail risk include those that sell options, sell insurance, take substantial credit risk, or have unique liquidity or exposure concentration risks. Although risk budgeting more commonly focuses on losses at the one standard deviation level, capital allocation focuses on losses at a very high confidence level in order to capture the magnitude of capital that is placed at risk by the strategy. Capital allocation seeks to understand how much of an investor's scarce resources are, or could be, used by a given portfolio, thereby making it unavailable to other portfolios.

Because a company's capital is a scarce resource and relatively expensive, it should be deployed in activities that have the best chance of earning a superior rate of return. It also should be deployed in a way that investors expect, in activities in which the company has expertise, and in strategies that investors believe the company can successfully execute.

To optimize the use of capital, the "owner" of the capital will typically establish a hurdle rate over a given time horizon; this is often expressed as the expected rate of return per unit of capital allocated. Two potential activities, Portfolio A and Portfolio B, might require different amounts of capital. Portfolio A might require €325,000, and its expected return might be €50,000 per year (15.4%). Portfolio B might have a reasonable expectation of earning €100,000 per year, but it might require €1,000,000 in capital (a 10% return). If the investor has an annualized hurdle rate of 15%, Portfolio A will exceed the hurdle rate and appear a better user of capital than Portfolio B, even though the absolute income for Portfolio B is higher.

Beyond measuring and limiting economic capital, capital allocation is sometimes used as a broad term for allocating costly resources. In some cases, the costly resource is cash; if, for instance, the portfolio has invested in options and futures trading strategies that require heavy use of margin and overcollateralization, its use of economic capital could be low and available cash may be the constraining factor. For other types of investors, such as banks or insurance companies, the capital required by regulatory bodies could be relatively large; as a result, these capital measures may be the most onerous constraint and thus the basis of capital allocation.

When the current measure of economic capital is a smaller number than the portfolio's cash or regulatory capital needs, it may not be the binding constraint. But when it is higher than other measures, it can become the binding constraint, and the one to which hurdle rates should be applied.

> **EXAMPLE 10**
>
> ### Creating Constraints with Risk Measures
>
> 1. Which of the following is **not** an example of risk budgeting?
>    - **A.** Giving a foreign exchange trading desk a VaR limit of $10 million
>    - **B.** Allowing a portfolio manager to have an *ex ante* tracking error up to 5% in a given portfolio
>    - **C.** Reducing the positions in a portfolio after a loss of a 5% of capital has occurred in a single month

### Solution to 1:

C is correct. This is an example of a stop-loss limit, not risk budgeting. The other choices are both examples of risk budgeting.

2. Which statement is true regarding risk budgeting in cases in which marginal VaR is used?

   **A.** The total risk budget is never equal to the sum of the individual sub-portfolios' risk budgets.

   **B.** The total risk budget is always equal to the sum of the individual sub-portfolios' risk budgets.

   **C.** If the total risk budget is equal to the sum of the individual sub-portfolios' risk budgets, there is a risk that this approach may cause capital to be underutilized.

### Solution to 2:

B is correct. When using marginal VaR, the total risk budget will be equal to the sum of the individual risk budgets. Choice A is not correct. C is also incorrect; it would be correct if each sub-portfolio's individual VaR measure, not adjusted for its marginal contribution, were used, which could lead to underutilization of capital.

# MARKET PARTICIPANTS AND THE RISK MEASURES THEY USE

## 11

☐ describe risk measures used by banks, asset managers, pension funds, and insurers

In this section, we examine the practical applications of risk measures. First, we will look at how different types of market participants use risk measures. An understanding of how various market participants use these measures will help as we move to a discussion of their limitations.

### Market Participants and the Different Risk Measures They Use

Three factors tend to greatly influence the types of risk measures used by different market participants:

- The degree to which the market participant is leveraged and the resulting need to assess minimum capitalization/maximum leverage ratios;
- The mix of risk factors to which their business is exposed (e.g., the degree of equity or fixed-income concentration in their portfolios);
- The accounting or regulatory requirements that govern their reporting.

Market participants who use a high degree of leverage typically need to assess their sensitivity to shocks to ensure that they will remain a going concern under very severe, but foreseeable, stresses. This leads them to focus on potential loss measures with a high confidence interval or to focus on rare events that might occur in a short period of time, such as two weeks. Those who use minimal (or no) leverage, such as long-only asset managers, are interested in shock sensitivity as well, but they are likely less concerned with trying to discern the difference between a 99.99% (0.01% VaR) worst case and a 99.95% (0.05% VaR) worst case. Their focus is more likely on avoiding underperformance—for example, failing to keep pace with their market benchmark when markets are doing well. For this reason, they are often more interested in lower confidence intervals—events that are more likely to occur and lead to underperformance for a given strategy. Unleveraged asset managers may also prefer to measure potential underperformance over longer periods of time, such as a quarter or a year, rather than shorter periods.

For portfolios dominated by fixed-income investments, risk managers focus on how sensitive the portfolios are to instantaneous price and yield changes in a variety of categories and typically emphasize duration, credit spread duration, and key rate duration measures. Credit spread duration measures the impact on an instrument's value if credit spreads move while risk-free rates remain unchanged. Key rate duration (sometimes called partial duration) measures the sensitivity of a bond's price to changes in specific maturities on the benchmark yield curve. Risk measurement for fixed-income portfolios is conducted using bond pricing models and by shifting each market rate assumption in the model and aggregating their portfolio's sensitivity to these market rates. Often, these factors are combined into scenarios representing expected central bank policies, inflation expectations, and/or anticipated fiscal policy changes. When portfolios are dominated by equities, risk managers typically categorize the equities by broad country markets, industries, and market capitalization levels. Also, they may additionally regress the returns of their portfolios against fundamental factor histories (such as those for growth, value, momentum, and capitalization size) to understand their exposure to such factors.

Portfolios with full fair value accounting (also called mark-to-market accounting), such as US mutual funds, European UCITS funds, and the held-for-sale portfolios of banks, are very well suited to such risk measures as VaR, economic capital (the amount of capital a firm needs to hold if it is to survive severe losses from the risks in its businesses), duration, and beta—all of which rely on measuring the changes in the fair values of assets. Asset/liability gap models are more meaningful when portfolios are subject to book value accounting in whole or in part.

### Banks

Banks need to balance a number of sometimes competing aspects of risk to manage their business and meet the expectations of equity investors/equity analysts, bond investors, credit rating agencies, depositors, and regulatory entities. Some banks apply risk measures differently depending on whether the portfolio being assessed is designated as a "held-to-maturity" portfolio, which requires book value accounting, or a "held-for-sale" or "trading book" portfolio, which requires fair value accounting. Other banks will use fair value measures for all risk assessments regardless of the designation used for accounting purposes. In the following list are some of the factors that banks seek to address through their use of risk tools. In compiling this list, we have assumed that banks may treat measures differently depending on accounting treatment.

- *Liquidity gap:* The extent of any liquidity and asset/liability mismatch. The ability to raise sufficient cash for foreseeable payment needs; a view of the liquidity of assets, as well as the expected repayment date of debt.
- *VaR:* The value at risk for the held-for-sale or trading (fair value) portion of the balance sheet.
- *Leverage:* A leverage ratio is typically computed, sometimes according to a regulatory requirement or to an internally determined measure. Leverage ratios will weight risk assets using a variety of methods and rules and divide

this weighted asset figure by equity. The result is that riskier assets will be assigned a greater weighting and less risky assets a lower weighting so that more equity is required to support riskier assets.

- *Sensitivities:* For the held-for-sale portion of their balance sheet, banks measure duration, key rate duration or partial duration, and credit spread duration for interest rate risk positions. Banks will also measure foreign exchange exposure and any equity or commodity exposures. All these exposure measures will include the delta sensitivities of options with any other exposures to the same underlying asset and will also monitor gamma and vega exposures of options. Gamma and vega exposures can be broken out by term to identify how much of these risks come from long-dated versus short-dated options.

- *Economic capital:* This is measured by blending the company's market, credit, and operational risk measures to estimate the total loss the company could suffer at a very high level of confidence (e.g., 99% to 99.99%), usually in one year's time. Economic capital measures are applied to the full balance sheet, including both the held-for-sale and held-for-investment portfolios, and include market, credit, and operational risk capital.

- *Scenario analysis:* Stress tests are applied to the full balance sheet and augment economic capital and liquidity; they are used to identify whether capital is sufficient for targeted, strong negative shocks. Outside of stress testing, significant scenario analysis takes places. Scenario analysis is used to examine how the full balance sheet might be affected by different interest rate, inflation, and credit environments, such as unemployment levels for credit card lenders, home price appreciation/depreciation for mortgage lenders, and business cycle stresses for corporate lenders.

It is common for banks to compute risk measures in distinct business units and geographies and then aggregate these measures to the parent company entity.

### Asset Managers

Asset managers are not typically regulated with regard to sufficient capital or liquidity; they are more commonly regulated for fair treatment of investors—that disclosures are full and accurate, that marketing is not misleading, that one client is not favored over the other. In some jurisdictions, certain market risk measures may be used to define risk limits for different fund types.

In asset management portfolios, risk management efforts are focused primarily on volatility, probability of loss, or probability of underperforming a benchmark rather than insolvency. A diversified, unleveraged, long-only fund is unlikely to see asset values decline below zero in the absence of a wholesale withdrawal of assets by the firm's clients. Although service costs and other items make insolvency a technical possibility, in practice, insolvency is a much higher threat for leveraged portfolios. Although derivatives use by asset managers can create effective leverage, these positions are often balanced by an amount of cash in the portfolio equal to the notional exposure created by the derivatives mitigating, if not fully eliminating, the impact of leverage.

Asset managers typically measure and view each portfolio separately with respect to its own constraints and limits. However, there are a few exceptions:

- Long-only asset managers: If the adviser has invested its own capital in any of the funds that it manages, these investments may need to be aggregated for the firm to assess its risk exposures across portfolios.

- Hedge funds: A hedge fund manager needs to aggregate the adviser's side-by-side investment in the various funds it advises.

- Funds of funds: Risk measures for these portfolios typically aggregate the risks of the underlying hedge funds to the master fund level.

An asset manager may choose to aggregate exposures across all funds and strategies to determine if there are unusual concentrations in individual securities or counterparties that would make management actions across all portfolios difficult to carry out (e.g., a single portfolio's holdings in a given security may not pose a liquidity risk, but if the firm were to aggregate all of its holdings in that security, it may find that the portfolio fails to meet the desired liquidity target).

It is important when observing risk measures for asset managers to determine whether the measures represent the backward-looking variability of realized returns in the portfolio as it was then constituted or use the current portfolio and measure its potential loss. Backward-looking returns-based measures (typically including standard deviation, *ex post* tracking error, Sharpe ratio, information ratio, and historical beta) have the value of showing the fund's behavior over time and help assess the skill of the manager. Only an analysis of the current holdings, however, will reveal current risk exposures. Measures that use current holdings typically include VaR, *ex ante* tracking error, duration and forward-looking beta, stress tests, and scenario analyses. All risk and performance measures can be conducted on past portfolio holdings or current portfolio holdings; it is important for the user of any measure to determine which ingredients (which set of portfolio holdings, and for market history, what length and smoothing techniques) have been used in order to use it correctly. Assessing the trends in risk exposures, including whether risk has recently risen or if other important changes have taken place in the strategy, can be accomplished by tracking the risk measures through time.

**Traditional Asset Managers**

Asset managers that use little leverage typically find relative risk measures most meaningful and actionable. The decision to invest in a given asset class is normally the client's, not the adviser's. The adviser seeks to outperform the benchmark representative of the asset class. Exceptions include absolute return funds and asset allocation strategies, but even these can be measured relative to a benchmark. For absolute return strategies, the benchmark is typically cash or a cash-like hurdle rate. When cash is the benchmark, VaR and *ex ante* tracking error will be effectively the same if measured using the same holding period and confidence interval. (Cash has no volatility, so adding a cash benchmark into a relative VaR calculation does not affect the calculation because its zero volatility cancels out its impact; thus, the resulting calculation is the same as the VaR of the portfolio.) Asset allocation funds can use an asset allocation index as the benchmark for a relative risk measure, or they can use a custom combination of market benchmarks.

Although banks, insurers, and other market participants favor measuring VaR in currency terms relevant for the institution (e.g., dollars for a US-based insurer, yen for a Japanese bank) and measure duration and similar statistics as the value change for a 1 bp interest rate change, long-only asset managers generally prefer to express VaR in percentage terms and will divide VaR and duration by the net assets of the portfolio being analyzed. (Note that using returns as the fundamental source of data removes the last step in calculating VaR: multiplying by the size of the portfolio.)

A typical sample of risk measures used by asset managers includes the following:

- *Position limits:* Asset managers use position limits as the most frequent form of risk control for the portfolios they manage, particularly in fund offering documents that need to be understandable to a broad range of investors. Position limits include restrictions on country, currency, sector, and asset class. They may measure them in absolute terms or relative to a benchmark, and they are almost always expressed as a percentage of the portfolio's value.

- *Sensitivities:* Asset managers use the full range of sensitivity measures, including option-adjusted duration, key rate duration, and credit spread duration, and they will typically include the delta exposure of options in these measures. Measures can be expressed in absolute terms as well as relative to a benchmark.

- *Beta sensitivity:* Beta is frequently used for equity-only accounts.

- *Liquidity:* Asset managers often look at the liquidity characteristics of the assets in their portfolios. For equity portfolios, it is common to measure what percentage of daily average trading volume the portfolio holds of each equity security and how many days it would take to liquidate a security if the manager did not want it to be too large a portion of trading volume to avoid taking a price concession.

- *Scenario analysis:* Long-only asset managers typically use stress tests or scenario analyses to verify that the risks in the portfolio are as they have been disclosed to investors and to identify any unusual behavior that could arise in stressed markets.

- *Redemption risk:* Open-end fund managers often assess what percentage of the portfolio could be redeemed at peak times and track this behavior across the funds and asset classes they manage.

- *Ex post versus ex ante tracking error:* Limits on *ex ante* tracking error are often used by traditional asset managers as a key risk metric for the portfolios they manage. It provides an estimate of the degree to which the current portfolio could underperform its benchmark. It is worth noting the distinction between *ex post* tracking error and *ex ante* tracking error: Asset managers use *ex post* tracking error to identify sources of performance and manager skill and *ex ante* tracking error to identify whether today's positions could give rise to unexpected potential performance. *Ex post* tracking error measures the historical deviation between portfolio returns and benchmark returns, and thus both the portfolio holdings and market returns are historical in this measure. *Ex ante* tracking error takes today's benchmark-relative position and exposes it to the variability of past markets to estimate what kind of benchmark-relative performance could arise from the current portfolio. *Ex post* tracking error is a useful tool for assessing manager skill and behavior. The day after a large change in portfolio strategy, *ex ante* tracking will immediately reflect the portfolio's new return profile, whereas *ex post* tracking error will not do so until the new strategy has been in place long enough to dominate the data history. (If *ex post* tracking error is computed using 200 days of history, the day after a large strategy change, only 1 of the 200 data points will reflect the current risk positioning.) Some asset managers focus on maintaining *ex ante* tracking error boundaries for the portfolios they manage to monitor and balance the potential performance impact of the active risks they are taking. **Active share** is a measure of that percentage of the portfolio that differs from the benchmark (i.e., a deviation from the benchmark). It is often monitored to help limit tracking error of the portfolio.

- *VaR:* VaR is less commonly used as a risk measure than *ex ante* tracking error by traditional asset managers, but it is used by some—particularly for portfolios that are characterized as "absolute return" strategies for which a given market benchmark may not serve as the portfolio objective.

### Hedge Funds

Similar to banks, hedge funds that use leverage need to observe sources and uses of cash through time, including when credit lines could be withdrawn, and need to simulate the interplay between market movements, margin calls, and the redemption rights of investors in order to understand worst-case needs for cash. A sample of the typical range of hedge fund market risk measures includes the following:

- *Sensitivities:* All hedge fund strategies will display some form of sensitivity or exposure, so the full range of sensitivity measures are useful for hedge fund risk management.

- *Gross exposure:* Long–short, market neutral, and arbitrage strategies will typically measure long exposure, short exposure, and gross exposure (the sum of the absolute value of long plus short positions) separately. Gross position risk is an important guide to the importance of correlation risk for the portfolio.

- *Leverage:* Leverage measures are common for hedge funds. It is important to understand how the measure is treating derivatives and what elements appear in the numerator versus the denominator because there are many different ways to execute the measure.

- *VaR:* Hedge funds that use VaR measures tend to focus on high confidence intervals (more than 90%) and short holding periods, and they rarely use a benchmark-relative measure.

- *Scenarios:* Hedge funds commonly use scenario/stress tests that are well tuned to the specific risks of their strategy—in merger arbitrage strategies, for example, the chance that the merger will not take place.

- *Drawdown:* In the case of the following types of hedge fund strategies, standard deviation and historical beta measures can be particularly misleading when seeking to understand what the more extreme risks can be. This is because the strategies listed frequently display decidedly non-normal return distributions, and when this is true, standard deviation is not a good guide to worst-case outcomes. For the following strategies, any historical standard deviation or historical beta measures should be supplemented by a measure of what has been the **maximum drawdown**, often defined as the worst-returning month or quarter for the portfolio or the worst peak-to-trough decline in a portfolio's returns:

  - Strategies that focus on credit risk taking, such as long–short credit, credit arbitrage, or bankruptcy investing
  - Strategies that focus on events, such as merger arbitrage
  - Strategies that make meaningful investments in non-publicly issued assets or other assets that do not reliably have a daily, independent fair value determination
  - Strategies that invest in illiquid asset classes or take large positions relative to market size in any asset class
  - Strategies that sell options or purchase bonds with embedded options
  - Strategies that are highly reliant on correlation relationships, such as equity market neutral

In addition, it is not uncommon for those investing in hedge funds to look at the returns of the hedge fund during a relevant historical period, such as the 2008 financial crisis.

# PENSION FUNDS AND INSURERS

☐ describe risk measures used by banks, asset managers, pension funds, and insurers

A defined benefit pension plan is required to make payments to its pensioners in the future that are typically determined as a function of a retiree's final salary. This differs from a defined contribution plan, in which the plan's sponsor may be required to make contributions currently but is not responsible to ensure that they grow to a particular future amount. To meet the required payouts, defined benefit plans have significant market risk management responsibilities. This section describes the practices of defined benefit pension plans only; all mentions in this section of "pension funds" or "pension plans" refer to defined benefit pensions.

The risk management goal for pension funds is to be sufficiently funded to make future payments to pensioners. The requirements for sufficient funding vary from country to country. Different jurisdictions will have regulations concerning such items as how to compute the present value of pension liabilities (including which interest rates are permitted to be used as a discount rate) and what the sponsor of the pension plan is required to contribute when the assets in the pension fund are lower than the present value of the liabilities. In addition, some jurisdictions impose taxes when surplus—the value of the assets less the value of the liabilities—is withdrawn for other use by the plan sponsor. Although these regional differences will shape the practice of pension plan risk management in different countries, it is typically an exercise in ensuring that the plan is not likely to become significantly under- or overfunded. Overfunding occurs when the funding ratio (the assets divided by the present value of the liabilities) is greater than 100%; underfunding occurs when the funding ratio is under 100%. Overfunding may be cured over time by the plan sponsor not needing to make regular contributions to the plan because the number of employees and their salary levels, which drive the pension benefit, are growing. Underfunding, if not cured by growth in the assets in the fund over a suitable time horizon as permitted by regulation, is cured by the plan sponsor contributing to the fund. The pension plan's actions will also vary depending on its age (whether it is a new or established plan) and whether it is currently meaningfully under- or overfunded. Important market risk measures or methods for pension funds often include the following:

- *Interest rate and curve risk:* The first step of risk measurement for pension funds is the analysis of expected payments to pensioners in the future. The expected future cash flows are grouped by maturity. In the case of an international pension fund that must make future payouts in multiple currencies, they may also be grouped by currency. In cases in which the jurisdiction requires a particular fixed-income instrument or curve be used to provide the discount rate for arriving at the present value of the pension liability (such as corporate bonds in the United States, inflation-linked gilts in the United Kingdom, or government bonds in the Netherlands), the liability cash flows will be expressed as a short position at the relevant points on the curve.

- *Surplus at risk:* This measure is an application of VaR. It is computed by entering the assets in the portfolio into a VaR model as long positions and the pension liabilities as short fixed-income positions. It estimates how much the assets might underperform the liabilities, usually over one year, and pension plan sponsors may vary with respect to how high a level of confidence they choose to use (e.g., 84%, 95%, 99%). If the assets in the portfolio were invested precisely in the same fixed-income instruments to which the liabilities have been apportioned and in the same amounts, it would result in zero surplus at risk. In practice, however, it may be impossible to invest in the sizes required in the particular fixed-income instruments specified in the liability analysis, so the pension will invest in other, non-fixed-income investments, such as equities or real assets. The more volatile the investments in the pension fund and the less well correlated these assets are with the liabilities, the higher the surplus at risk. The pension fund may set a threshold level or limit on surplus at risk; when the pension fund's surplus at risk exceeds this limit, pension staff will change the fund's asset allocation to make the assets in the fund better match the liabilities. This liability-focused form of pension investing is commonly referred to as "liability driven investing."

- *Liability hedging exposures versus return generating exposures:* Although matching liabilities is an important goal of pension fund management, it is not the only goal. Pension staff may separate their investment portfolio into investments designed to match the pension liability versus those meant to generate excess returns. The precise instruments linked to the liability cannot always be directly invested in, so a separate portion of the portfolio may be necessary and should perform the function of earning returns that can minimize the chance of having an over- or underfunded status greater than the pension fund's risk tolerance. The return-generating portion of the portfolio also helps to hedge the potential for future changes in the size of the liability that could be caused by longevity risk or by wage growth that exceeds the forecasts currently used to compute the liability.

## Insurers

Insurers in the largest global economies are subject to significant regulation and accounting oversight regarding how they must retain reserves and reflect their liabilities. Regulation may also affect the pricing permitted by product line. It is common for insurers to aggregate risk from underlying business units to arrive at a firm-wide view of risk.

Insurance liabilities vary in their correlation with financial markets. The risk metrics of property and casualty insurance differ significantly from those used for life insurance and annuity products. Property and casualty insurance, including home, auto, corporate liability insurance, and health insurance, are typically not highly correlated with financial asset markets.

Insurers focus on managing a number of forms of insurance risk, for which they may use such tools as reinsurance and geographic dispersion. The market risk management measures in the property and casualty lines of business include the following:

- *Sensitivities and exposures:* Insurers often design an asset allocation for these portfolios and monitor current exposures to remain within the target ranges set forth in the target asset allocation.
- *Economic capital and VaR:* The risk measurement focus for these lines of business is capital at risk and VaR. The premiums earned in these areas are typically set to compensate for the expected payouts (usually defined as a range of possible payouts), so it is only in cases of greater-than-expected payouts that capital is tapped. The risk modeling effort is to estimate what that catastrophic loss amount could be at a given level of probability.

Assessment of the risk to economic capital will include the market risks in the portfolio as well as characteristics of the insurance exposures and reinsurance coverage.

- *Scenario analysis:* Insurers use scenario analysis like other market participants that have capital at risk, such as banks and hedge funds. For the property and casualty lines, these scenarios may stress the market risks and the insurance risks in the same scenario.

Insurers do not focus on matching assets with liabilities in their property and casualty lines of business. Investment portfolios are not designed to pay out insurance claims in property and casualty insurance businesses; the premium income is primarily used for that purpose. These investments are designed to achieve a good absolute return within the constraints imposed under regulatory reserve requirements. Riskier assets are discounted relative to safer, fixed-income assets in measuring required reserves.

Life insurance and annuities have stronger ties to the financial markets, even while retaining distinct mortality-based risk profiles. Life liabilities are very long, and the reserves that insurers are required to maintain by insurance regulators are highly dependent on discount rate assumptions. Non-financial inputs include assumptions about mortality and which policyholders will either tap into options in their policy to add coverage at a given level or cancel their policy. Annuities produce returns based on financial assets, with some extra optionality driven by any life insurance elements embedded in the policy. These activities are paired with long-term investment portfolios in a variety of assets that are designed to help the insurer meet future claims.

For life portfolios, market risk measures include the following:

- *Sensitivities:* The exposures of the investment portfolio and the annuity liability are measured and monitored.
- *Asset and liability matching:* The investment portfolio is not designed to be a perfect match to the liabilities, but it is more closely matched to liabilities than is the case in property and casualty insurance.
- *Scenario analysis:* The main focus of risk measurement for the life lines of insurance are measures of potential stress losses based on the differences between the assets in which the insurance company has invested and the liabilities driven by the insurance contracts it has written to its customers. Scenario analyses need to stress both market and non-market sources of cash flow change (in which non-market changes can include changes in longevity).

### EXAMPLE 11

### Uses of Risk Measures by Market Participants

1. Which type of market participant is *most likely* to consistently express risk measures as a percentage of assets and relative to a benchmark?

    **A.** Banks
    **B.** Corporations
    **C.** Long-only asset managers

### Solution to 1:

C is correct. Long-only asset managers most commonly express risk measures in percentage terms and relative to a benchmark, whereas the entities in answers A and B measure risk more commonly in currency units and in absolute terms (not relative to a benchmark). Banks occasionally express risk measures, such as economic capital, as a percentage of assets or other balance sheet measures, but bank risk measures are typically expressed in currency units.

2. How does *ex ante* tracking error differ from *ex post* tracking error?

    **A.** *Ex ante* tracking error takes into account the behavior of options, whereas *ex post* tracking error does not.

    **B.** *Ex post* tracking error uses a more accurate forecast of future markets than the forecast used for *ex ante* tracking error.

    **C.** *Ex ante* tracking error uses *current* portfolio holdings exposed to the variability of historical markets, whereas *ex post* tracking error measures the variability of *historical* portfolio holdings in historical markets.

### Solution to 2:

C is correct. A is incorrect because although *ex post* tracking error accounts for the options that were in the portfolio in the past, *ex ante* tracking error might actually misstate the risk of options if it is computed using the parametric method. B is incorrect because *ex post* tracking error is not aiming to forecast the future; it is only measuring the variability of past results.

## SUMMARY

This reading on market risk management models covers various techniques used to manage the risk arising from market fluctuations in prices and rates. The key points are summarized as follows:

- Value at risk (VaR) is the minimum loss in either currency units or as a percentage of portfolio value that would be expected to be incurred a certain percentage of the time over a certain period of time given assumed market conditions.
- VaR requires the decomposition of portfolio performance into risk factors.
- The three methods of estimating VaR are the parametric method, the historical simulation method, and the Monte Carlo simulation method.
- The parametric method of VaR estimation typically provides a VaR estimate from the left tail of a normal distribution, incorporating the expected returns, variances, and covariances of the components of the portfolio.
- The parametric method exploits the simplicity of the normal distribution but provides a poor estimate of VaR when returns are not normally distributed, as might occur when a portfolio contains options.
- The historical simulation method of VaR estimation uses historical return data on the portfolio's current holdings and allocation.
- The historical simulation method has the advantage of incorporating events that actually occurred and does not require the specification of a distribution or the estimation of parameters, but it is only useful to the extent that the future resembles the past.

- The Monte Carlo simulation method of VaR estimation requires the specification of a statistical distribution of returns and the generation of random outcomes from that distribution.
- The Monte Carlo simulation method is extremely flexible but can be complex and time consuming to use.
- There is no single right way to estimate VaR.
- The advantages of VaR include the following: It is a simple concept; it is relatively easy to understand and easily communicated, capturing much information in a single number. It can be useful in comparing risks across asset classes, portfolios, and trading units and, as such, facilitates capital allocation decisions. It can be used for performance evaluation and can be verified by using backtesting. It is widely accepted by regulators.
- The primary limitations of VaR are that it is a subjective measure and highly sensitive to numerous discretionary choices made in the course of computation. It can underestimate the frequency of extreme events. It fails to account for the lack of liquidity and is sensitive to correlation risk. It is vulnerable to trending or volatility regimes and is often misunderstood as a worst-case scenario. It can oversimplify the picture of risk and focuses heavily on the left tail.
- There are numerous variations and extensions of VaR, including conditional VaR (CVaR), incremental VaR (IVaR), and marginal VaR (MVaR), that can provide additional useful information.
- Conditional VaR is the average loss conditional on exceeding the VaR cutoff.
- Incremental VaR measures the change in portfolio VaR as a result of adding or deleting a position from the portfolio or if a position size is changed relative to the remaining positions.
- MVaR measures the change in portfolio VaR given a small change in the portfolio position. In a diversified portfolio, MVaRs can be summed to determine the contribution of each asset to the overall VaR.
- *Ex ante* tracking error measures the degree to which the performance of a given investment portfolio might deviate from its benchmark.
- Sensitivity measures quantify how a security or portfolio will react if a single risk factor changes. Common sensitivity measures are beta for equities; duration and convexity for bonds; and delta, gamma, and vega for options. Sensitivity measures do not indicate which portfolio has greater loss potential.
- Risk managers can use deltas, gammas, vegas, durations, convexities, and betas to get a comprehensive picture of the sensitivity of the entire portfolio.
- Stress tests apply extreme negative stress to a particular portfolio exposure.
- Scenario measures, including stress tests, are risk models that evaluate how a portfolio will perform under certain high-stress market conditions.
- Scenario measures can be based on actual historical scenarios or on hypothetical scenarios.
- Historical scenarios are scenarios that measure the portfolio return that would result from a repeat of a particular period of financial market history.
- Hypothetical scenarios model the impact of extreme movements and co-movements in different markets that have not previously occurred.
- Reverse stress testing is the process of stressing the portfolio's most significant exposures.

- Sensitivity and scenario risk measures can complement VaR. They do not need to rely on history, and scenarios can be designed to overcome an assumption of normal distributions.
- Limitations of scenario measures include the following: Historical scenarios are unlikely to re-occur in exactly the same way. Hypothetical scenarios may incorrectly specify how assets will co-move and thus may get the magnitude of movements wrong. And, it is difficult to establish appropriate limits on a scenario analysis or stress test.
- Constraints are widely used in risk management in the form of risk budgets, position limits, scenario limits, stop-loss limits, and capital allocation.
- Risk budgeting is the allocation of the total risk appetite across sub-portfolios.
- A scenario limit is a limit on the estimated loss for a given scenario, which, if exceeded, would require corrective action in the portfolio.
- A stop-loss limit either requires a reduction in the size of a portfolio or its complete liquidation (when a loss of a particular size occurs in a specified period).
- Position limits are limits on the market value of any given investment.
- Risk measurements and constraints in and of themselves are not restrictive or unrestrictive; it is the limits placed on the measures that drive action.
- The degree of leverage, the mix of risk factors to which the business is exposed, and accounting or regulatory requirements influence the types of risk measures used by different market participants.
- Banks use risk tools to assess the extent of any liquidity and asset/liability mismatch, the probability of losses in their investment portfolios, their overall leverage ratio, interest rate sensitivities, and the risk to economic capital.
- Asset managers' use of risk tools focuses primarily on volatility, probability of loss, or the probability of underperforming a benchmark.
- Pension funds use risk measures to evaluate asset/liability mismatch and surplus at risk.
- Property and casualty insurers use sensitivity and exposure measures to ensure exposures remain within defined asset allocation ranges. They use economic capital and VaR measures to estimate the impairment in the event of a catastrophic loss. They use scenario analysis to stress the market risks and insurance risks simultaneously.
- Life insurers use risk measures to assess the exposures of the investment portfolio and the annuity liability, the extent of any asset/liability mismatch, and the potential stress losses based on the differences between the assets in which they have invested and the liabilities resulting from the insurance contracts they have written.

# REFERENCES

Malkiel, Burton. 2007. A Random Walk Down Wall Street. New York: W.W. Norton.

# PRACTICE PROBLEMS

## The following information relates to questions 1-5

Randy Gorver, chief risk officer at Eastern Regional Bank, and John Abell, assistant risk officer, are currently conducting a risk assessment of several of the bank's independent investment functions. These reviews include the bank's fixed-income investment portfolio and an equity fund managed by the bank's trust department. Gorver and Abell are also assessing Eastern Regional's overall risk exposure.

### Eastern Regional Bank Fixed-Income Investment Portfolio

The bank's proprietary fixed-income portfolio is structured as a barbell portfolio: About half of the portfolio is invested in zero-coupon Treasuries with maturities in the 3- to 5-year range (Portfolio $P_1$), and the remainder is invested in zero-coupon Treasuries with maturities in the 10- to 15-year range (Portfolio $P_2$). Georges Montes, the portfolio manager, has discretion to allocate between 40% and 60% of the assets to each maturity "bucket." He must remain fully invested at all times. Exhibit 1 shows details of this portfolio.

**Exhibit 1: US Treasury Barbell Portfolio**

|  | Maturity | |
| --- | --- | --- |
|  | $P_1$ | $P_2$ |
|  | 3–5 Years | 10–15 Years |
| Average duration | 3.30 | 11.07 |
| Average yield to maturity | 1.45% | 2.23% |
| Market value | $50.3 million | $58.7 million |

### Trust Department's Equity Fund

a. **Use of Options:** The trust department of Eastern Regional Bank manages an equity fund called the Index Plus Fund, with $325 million in assets. This fund's objective is to track the S&P 500 Index price return while producing an income return 1.5 times that of the S&P 500. The bank's chief investment officer (CIO) uses put and call options on S&P 500 stock index futures to adjust the risk exposure of certain client accounts that have an investment in this fund. The portfolio of a 60-year-old widow with a below-average risk tolerance has an investment in this fund, and the CIO has asked his assistant, Janet Ferrell, to propose an options strategy to bring the portfolio's delta to 0.90.

# Practice Problems

    **b. Value at Risk**: The Index Plus Fund has a value at risk (VaR) of $6.5 million at 5% for one day. Gorver asks Abell to write a brief summary of the portfolio VaR for the report he is preparing on the fund's risk position.

## Combined Bank Risk Exposures

The bank has adopted a new risk policy, which requires forward-looking risk assessments in addition to the measures that look at historical risk characteristics. Management has also become very focused on tail risk since the subprime crisis and is evaluating the bank's capital allocation to certain higher-risk lines of business. Gorver must determine what additional risk metrics to include in his risk reporting to address the new policy. He asks Abell to draft a section of the risk report that will address the risk measures' adequacy for capital allocation decisions.

1. If Montes is expecting a 50 bp increase in yields at all points along the yield curve, which of the following trades is he *most likely* to execute to minimize his risk?

   A. Sell $35 million of $P_2$ and reinvest the proceeds in three-year bonds

   B. Sell $15 million of $P_2$ and reinvest the proceeds in three-year bonds

   C. Reduce the duration of $P_2$ to 10 years and reduce the duration of $P_1$ to 3 years

2. Which of the following options strategies is Ferrell *most likely* to recommend for the client's portfolio?

   A. Long calls

   B. Short calls

   C. Short puts

3. Which of the following statements regarding the VaR of the Index Plus Fund is correct?

   A. The expected maximum loss for the portfolio is $6.5 million.

   B. Five percent of the time, the portfolio can be expected to experience a loss of at least $6.5 million.

   C. Ninety-five percent of the time, the portfolio can be expected to experience a one-day loss of no more than $6.5 million.

4. To comply with the new bank policy on risk assessment, which of the following is the *best* set of risk measures to add to the chief risk officer's risk reporting?

   A. Conditional VaR, stress test, and scenario analysis

   B. Monte Carlo VaR, incremental VaR, and stress test

   C. Parametric VaR, marginal VaR, and scenario analysis

5. Which of the following statements should *not* be included in Abell's report to management regarding the use of risk measures in capital allocation decisions?

   A. VaR measures capture the increased liquidity risk during stress periods.

**B.** Stress tests and scenario analysis can be used to evaluate the effect of outlier events on each line of business.

**C.** VaR approaches that can accommodate a non-normal distribution are critical to understand relative risk across lines of business.

## The following information relates to questions 6-13

Tina Ming is a senior portfolio manager at Flusk Pension Fund (Flusk). Flusk's portfolio is composed of fixed-income instruments structured to match Flusk's liabilities. Ming works with Shrikant McKee, Flusk's risk analyst.

Ming and McKee discuss the latest risk report. McKee calculated value at risk (VaR) for the entire portfolio using the historical method and assuming a lookback period of five years and 250 trading days per year. McKee presents VaR measures in Exhibit 1.

**Exhibit 1: Flusk Portfolio VaR (in $ millions)**

| Confidence Interval | Daily VaR | Monthly VaR |
|---|---|---|
| 95% | 1.10 | 5.37 |

After reading McKee's report, Ming asks why the number of daily VaR breaches over the last year is zero even though the portfolio has accumulated a substantial loss.

Next, Ming requests that McKee perform the following two risk analyses on Flusk's portfolio:

Analysis 1　Use scenario analysis to evaluate the impact on risk and return of a repeat of the last financial crisis.

Analysis 2　Estimate over one year, with a 95% level of confidence, how much Flusk's assets could underperform its liabilities.

Ming recommends purchasing newly issued emerging market corporate bonds that have embedded options. Prior to buying the bonds, Ming wants McKee to estimate the effect of the purchase on Flusk's VaR. McKee suggests running a stress test using a historical period specific to emerging markets that encompassed an extreme change in credit spreads.

At the conclusion of their conversation, Ming asks the following question about risk management tools: "What are the advantages of VaR compared with other risk measures?"

6. Based on Exhibit 1, Flusk's portfolio is expected to experience:

   **A.** a minimum daily loss of $1.10 million over the next year.

   **B.** a loss over one month equal to or exceeding $5.37 million 5% of the time.

   **C.** an average daily loss of $1.10 million 5% of the time during the next 250 trading days.

7. The number of Flusk's VaR breaches *most likely* resulted from:
   A. using a standard normal distribution in the VaR model.
   B. using a 95% confidence interval instead of a 99% confidence interval.
   C. lower market volatility during the last year compared with the lookback period.

8. To perform Analysis 1, McKee should use historical bond:
   A. prices.
   B. yields.
   C. durations.

9. The limitation of the approach requested for Analysis 1 is that it:
   A. omits asset correlations.
   B. precludes incorporating portfolio manager actions.
   C. assumes no deviation from historical market events.

10. The estimate requested in Analysis 2 is *best* described as:
    A. liquidity gap.
    B. surplus at risk.
    C. maximum drawdown.

11. Which measure should McKee use to estimate the effect on Flusk's VaR from Ming's portfolio recommendation?
    A. Relative VaR
    B. Incremental VaR
    C. Conditional VaR

12. When measuring the portfolio impact of the stress test suggested by McKee, which of the following is *most likely* to produce an accurate result?
    A. Marginal VaR
    B. Full revaluation of securities
    C. The use of sensitivity risk measures

13. The risk management tool referenced in Ming's question:
    A. is widely accepted by regulators.
    B. takes into account asset liquidity.
    C. usually incorporates right-tail events.

## The following information relates to questions 14-20

Carol Kynnersley is the chief risk officer at Investment Management Advisers (IMA). Kynnersley meets with IMA's portfolio management team and investment advisers to discuss the methods used to measure and manage market risk and how risk metrics are presented in client reports.

The three most popular investment funds offered by IMA are the Equity Opportunities, the Diversified Fixed Income, and the Alpha Core Equity. The Equity Opportunities Fund is composed of two exchange-traded funds: a broadly diversified large-cap equity product and one devoted to energy stocks. Kynnersley makes the following statements regarding the risk management policies established for the Equity Opportunities portfolio:

Statement 1     IMA's preferred approach to model value at risk (VaR) is to estimate expected returns, volatilities, and correlations under the assumption of a normal distribution.

Statement 2     In last year's annual client performance report, IMA stated that a hypothetical $6 million Equity Opportunities Fund account had a daily 5% VaR of approximately 1.5% of portfolio value.

Kynnersley informs the investment advisers that the risk management department recently updated the model for estimating the Equity Opportunities Fund VaR based on the information presented in Exhibit 1.

### Exhibit 1: Equity Opportunities Fund—VaR Model Input Assumptions

|  | Large-Cap ETF | Energy ETF | Total Portfolio |
|---|---|---|---|
| Portfolio weight | 65.0% | 35.0% | 100.0% |
| Expected annual return | 12.0% | 18.0% | 14.1% |
| Standard deviation | 20.0% | 40.0% | 26.3% |

Correlation between ETFs: 0.90
Number of trading days/year: 250

For clients interested in fixed-income products, IMA offers the Diversified Fixed-Income Fund. Kynnersley explains that the portfolio's bonds are all subject to interest rate risk. To demonstrate how fixed-income exposure measures can be used to identify and manage interest rate risk, Kynnersley distributes two exhibits featuring three hypothetical Treasury coupon bonds (Exhibit 2) under three interest rate scenarios (Exhibit 3).

### Exhibit 2: Fixed-Income Risk Measure

| Hypothetical Bond | Duration |
|---|---|
| Bond 1 | 1.3 |
| Bond 2 | 3.7 |
| Bond 3 | 10.2 |

## Practice Problems

**Exhibit 3: Interest Rate Scenarios**

| Scenario | Interest Rate Environment |
| --- | --- |
| Scenario 1 | Rates increase 25 bps |
| Scenario 2 | Rates increase 10 bps |
| Scenario 3 | Rates decrease 20 bps |

One of the investment advisers comments that a client recently asked about the performance of the Diversified Fixed-Income Fund relative to its benchmark, a broad fixed-income index. Kynnersley informs the adviser as follows:

Statement 3  The Diversified Fixed-Income Fund manager monitors the historical deviation between portfolio returns and benchmark returns. The fund prospectus stipulates a target deviation from the benchmark of no more than 5 bps.

Kynnersley concludes the meeting by reviewing the constraints IMA imposes on securities included in the Alpha Core Equity Fund. The compliance department conducts daily oversight using numerous risk screens and, when indicated, notifies portfolio managers to make adjustments. Kynnersley makes the following statement:

Statement 4  It is important that all clients investing in the fund be made aware of IMA's compliance measures. The Alpha Core Equity Fund restricts the exposure of individual securities to 1.75% of the total portfolio.

14. Based on Statement 1, IMA's VaR estimation approach is *best* described as the:
    A. parametric method.
    B. historical simulation method.
    C. Monte Carlo simulation method.

15. In Statement 2, Kynnersley implies that the portfolio:
    A. is at risk of losing $4,500 each trading day.
    B. value is expected to decline by $90,000 or more once in 20 trading days.
    C. has a 5% chance of falling in value by a maximum of $90,000 on a single trading day.

16. Based *only* on Statement 2, the risk measurement approach:
    A. ignores right-tail events in the return distribution.
    B. is similar to the Sharpe ratio because it is backward looking.
    C. provides a relatively accurate risk estimate in both trending and volatile regimes.

17. Based on Exhibit 1, the daily 5% VaR estimate is *closest* to:
    A. 1.61%.
    B. 2.42%.
    C. 2.69%.

18. Based *only* on Exhibits 2 and 3, it is *most likely* that under:
    A. Scenario 1, Bond 2 outperforms Bond 1.
    B. Scenario 2, Bond 1 underperforms Bond 3.
    C. Scenario 3, Bond 3 is the best performing security.

19. The risk measure referred to in Statement 3 is:
    A. active share.
    B. beta sensitivity
    C. *ex post* tracking error.

20. In Statement 4, Kynnersley describes a constraint associated with a:
    A. risk budget.
    B. position limit.
    C. stop-loss limit.

## The following information relates to questions 21-26

Hiram Life (Hiram), a large multinational insurer located in Canada, has received permission to increase its ownership in an India-based life insurance company, LICIA, from 26% to 49%. Before completing this transaction, Hiram wants to complete a risk assessment of LICIA's investment portfolio. Judith Hamilton, Hiram's chief financial officer, has been asked to brief the management committee on investment risk in its India-based insurance operations.

LICIA's portfolio, which has a market value of CAD260 million, is currently structured as shown in Exhibit 1. Despite its more than 1,000 individual holdings, the portfolio is invested predominantly in India. The Indian government bond market is highly liquid, but the country's mortgage and infrastructure loan markets, as well as the corporate bond market, are relatively illiquid. Individual mortgage and corporate bond positions are large relative to the normal trading volumes in these securities. Given the elevated current and fiscal account deficits, Indian investments are also subject to above-average economic risk.

Hamilton begins with a summary of the India-based portfolio. Exhibit 1 presents the current portfolio composition and the risk and return assumptions used to estimate value at risk (VaR).

## Practice Problems

### Exhibit 1: Selected Assumptions for LICIA's Investment Portfolio

| | Allocation | Average Daily Return | Daily Standard Deviation |
|---|---|---|---|
| India government securities | 50% | 0.015% | 0.206% |
| India mortgage/infrastructure loans | 25% | 0.045% | 0.710% |
| India corporate bonds | 15% | 0.025% | 0.324% |
| India equity | 10% | 0.035% | 0.996% |

Infrastructure is a rapidly growing asset class with limited return history; the first infrastructure loans were issued just 10 years ago.

Hamilton's report to the management committee must outline her assumptions and provide support for the methods she used in her risk assessment. If needed, she will also make recommendations for rebalancing the portfolio to ensure its risk profile is aligned with that of Hiram.

Hamilton develops the assumptions shown in Exhibit 2, which will be used for estimating the portfolio VaR.

### Exhibit 2: VaR Input Assumptions for Proposed CAD260 Million Portfolio

| Method | Average Return Assumption | Standard Deviation Assumption |
|---|---|---|
| Monte Carlo simulation | 0.026% | 0.501% |
| Parametric approach | 0.026% | 0.501% |
| Historical simulation | 0.023% | 0.490% |

Hamilton elects to apply a one-day, 5% VaR limit of CAD2 million in her risk assessment of LICIA's portfolio. This limit is consistent with the risk tolerance the committee has specified for the Hiram portfolio.

The markets' volatility during the last 12 months has been significantly higher than the historical norm, with increased frequency of large daily losses, and Hamilton expects the next 12 months to be equally volatile.

She estimates the one-day 5% portfolio VaR for LICIA's portfolio using three different approaches:

### Exhibit 3: VaR Results over a One-Day Period for Proposed Portfolio

| Method | 5% VaR |
|---|---|
| Monte Carlo simulation | CAD2,095,565 |
| Parametric approach | CAD2,083,610 |
| Historical simulation | CAD1,938,874 |

The committee is likely to have questions in a number of key areas—the limitations of the VaR report, potential losses in an extreme adverse event, and the reliability of the VaR numbers if the market continues to exhibit higher-than-normal volatility. Hamilton wants to be certain that she has thoroughly evaluated the risks inherent in the LICIA portfolio and compares them with the risks in Hiram's present portfolio.

Hamilton believes the possibility of a ratings downgrade on Indian sovereign debt is high and not yet fully reflected in securities prices. If the rating is lowered, many of the portfolio's holdings will no longer meet Hiram's minimum ratings requirement. A downgrade's effect is unlikely to be limited to the government bond portfolio. All asset classes can be expected to be affected to some degree. Hamilton plans to include a scenario analysis that reflects this possibility to ensure that management has the broadest possible view of the risk exposures in the India portfolio.

21. Given Hamilton's expectations, which of the following models is *most appropriate* to use in estimating portfolio VaR?

    A. Parametric method

    B. Historical simulation method

    C. Monte Carlo simulation method

22. Which risk measure is Hamilton *most likely* to present when addressing the committee's concerns regarding potential losses in extreme stress events?

    A. Relative VaR

    B. Incremental VaR

    C. Conditional VaR

23. The scenario analysis that Hamilton prepares for the committee is *most likely* a:

    A. stress test.

    B. historical scenario.

    C. hypothetical scenario.

24. The scenario analysis that Hamilton prepares for the committee is a valuable tool to supplement VaR *because* it:

    A. incorporates historical data to evaluate the risk in the tail of the VaR distribution.

    B. enables Hamilton to isolate the risk stemming from a single risk factor—the ratings downgrade.

    C. allows the committee to assess the effect of low liquidity in the event of a ratings downgrade.

25. Using the data in Exhibit 2, the portfolio's annual 1% parametric VaR is *closest* to:

    A. CAD17 million.

    B. CAD31 million.

    C. CAD48 million.

**Practice Problems** 519

26. What additional risk measures would be most appropriate to add to Hamilton's risk assessment?

    A. Delta

    B. Duration

    C. Tracking error

# SOLUTIONS

1. B is correct. Duration is a measure of interest rate risk. To reduce risk in anticipation of an increase in interest rates, Montes would seek to shorten the portfolio's duration. He is limited, however, in the amount he can shift from $P_2$ to $P_1$. Selling $15 million of $P_2$ reduces that portfolio to the lower end of the permitted 40% to 60% range. By reinvesting the proceeds at the shortest maturities allowed, Montes substantially reduces the portfolio duration.

2. B is correct. An index-tracking portfolio without options has a delta of 1. To achieve a delta of 0.9, the delta of the options position must be negative. Of the three choices, only short calls have a negative delta. Long call options have deltas ranging from 0 to 1. Short calls, therefore, have deltas ranging from 0 to –1. The short call position lowers the portfolio's overall delta as desired.

3. B is correct. VaR measures the frequency of losses of a given minimum magnitude. Here the VaR indicates that on 5% of trading days, the portfolio will experience a loss of at least $6.5 million. (Although C may appear to say the same thing as B, it actually implies that the portfolio will experience a loss on 95% of trading days.) The correct interpretation is that returns will be equal to or greater than –$6.5 million on 95% of trading days; those returns include gains as well as losses.

4. A is correct. The bank policy requires the addition of forward-looking risk assessments, and management is focused on tail risk. Conditional VaR measures tail risk, and stress tests and scenario analysis subject current portfolio holdings to historical or hypothetical stress events.

5. A is correct. VaR measures do *not* capture liquidity risk. "If some assets in a portfolio are relatively illiquid, VaR could be understated, even under normal market conditions. Additionally, liquidity squeezes are frequently associated with tail events and major market downturns, thereby exacerbating the risk."

6. B is correct. VaR is the minimum loss that would be expected a certain percentage of the time over a specified period of time given the assumed market conditions. A 5% VaR is often expressed as its complement—a 95% level of confidence. Therefore, the monthly VaR in Exhibit 5 indicates that $5.37 million is the minimum loss that would be expected to occur over one month 5% of the time. Alternatively, 95% of the time, a loss of more than $5.37 million would not be expected.

7. C is correct. Flusk experienced zero daily VaR breaches over the last year yet incurred a substantial loss. A limitation of VaR is its vulnerability to different volatility regimes. A portfolio might remain under its VaR limit every day but lose an amount approaching this limit each day. If market volatility during the last year is lower than in the lookback period, the portfolio could accumulate a substantial loss without technically breaching the VaR constraint.

    A is incorrect because VaR was calculated using historical simulation, so the distribution used was based on actual historical changes in the key risk factors experienced during the lookback period. Thus, the distribution is not characterized using estimates of the mean return, the standard deviation, or the correlations among the risk factors in the portfolio. In contrast, the parametric method of estimating VaR generally assumes that the distribution of returns for the risk factors is normal.

    B is incorrect because a specification with a higher confidence level will produce a higher VaR. If a 99% confidence interval was used to calculate historical VaR,

# Solutions

the VaR would be larger (larger expected minimum loss). During the last year, none of Flusk's losses were substantial enough to breach the 5% VaR number (95% confidence interval); therefore, if McKee used a 1% VaR (99% confidence interval), the number of VaR breaches would not change.

8. B is correct. In order to simulate the impact of the latest financial crisis on the current bond portfolio holdings, McKee's valuation model for bonds should use the historical yields of bonds with similar maturity. Historical yields drive the pricing of bonds more than the price history or the current duration. Historical prices for the fixed-income positions currently held in the portfolio may not exist, and even when historical prices do exist, they may not be relevant to the current characteristics (e.g., maturity) of the instrument. Even if the same bonds existed at the time of the latest financial crisis, their durations would change because of the passage of time.

    A is incorrect because using a bond's past price history would mischaracterize the risk of the current portfolio holdings. For this reason, the historical yields are more important in explaining the risks. Historical prices for the fixed-income positions currently held in the portfolio may not exist, and even when historical prices do exist, they may not be relevant to the current characteristics (e.g., maturity) of the instrument.

    C is incorrect because historical bond durations would not capture the current characteristics of the bonds in the portfolio. Duration is a sensitivity measure and is the weighted-average time to maturity of a bond. Even if the same bonds existed at the time of the latest financial crisis, their remaining time to maturity and durations would change because of the passage of time.

9. C is correct. Ming suggested in Analysis 1 to use a historical scenario that measures the hypothetical portfolio return that would result from a repeat of a particular period of financial market history. Historical scenarios are complementary to VaR but are not going to happen in exactly the same way again, and they require additional measures to overcome the shortcomings of the VaR.

10. B is correct. Analysis 2 describes surplus at risk. Surplus at risk is an application of VaR; it estimates how much the assets might underperform the liabilities with a given confidence level, usually over a year.

11. B is correct. Incremental VaR measures the change in a portfolio's VaR as a result of adding or removing a position from the portfolio or if a position size is changed relative to the remaining positions.

12. B is correct. McKee suggests running a stress test using a historical scenario specific to emerging markets that includes an extreme change in credit spreads. Stress tests, which apply extreme negative stress to a particular portfolio exposure, are closely related to scenario risk measures. A scenario risk measure estimates the portfolio return that would result from a hypothetical change in markets (hypothetical scenario) or a repeat of a historical event (historical scenario). When the historical simulation fully revalues securities under rate and price changes that occurred during the scenario period, the results should be highly accurate.

    A is incorrect because marginal VaR measures the change in portfolio VaR given a very small change in a portfolio position (e.g., change in VaR for a $1 or 1% change in the position). Therefore, marginal VaR would not allow McKee to estimate how much the value of the option-embedded bonds would change under an extreme change in credit spreads.

    C is incorrect because sensitivity risk measures use sensitivity exposure measures, such as first-order (delta, duration) and second-order (gamma, convexity) sensitivity, to assess the change in the value of a financial instrument. Although gamma and convexity can be used with delta and duration to estimate the impact of extreme market movements, they are not suited for scenario analysis related to option-embedded bonds.

13. A is correct. VaR has emerged as one of the most popular risk measures because global banking regulators require or encourage the use of it. VaR is also frequently found in annual reports of financial firms and can be used for comparisons.

14. A is correct. VaR is an estimate of the loss that is expected to be exceeded with a given level of probability over a specified time period. The parametric method typically assumes that the return distributions for the risk factors in the portfolio are normal. It then uses the expected return and standard deviation of return for each risk factor and correlations to estimate VaR.

15. B is correct. Value at risk is the minimum loss that would be expected a certain percentage of the time over a certain period of time. Statement 2 implies that there is a 5% chance the portfolio will fall in value by $90,000 (= $6,000,000 × 1.5%) or more in a single day. If VaR is measured on a daily basis and a typical month has 20–22 business days, then 5% of the days equates to about 1 day per month or once in 20 trading days.

16. A is correct. Statement 2 indicates that the Equity Opportunities Fund reported a daily VaR value. One of the limitations of VaR is that it focuses so heavily on left-tail events (the losses) that right-tail events (potential gains) are often ignored.

    B is incorrect because VaR is viewed as forward looking in that it uses the current portfolio holdings and measures its potential loss. The Sharpe ratio represents a backward-looking, return-based measure and is used to assess the skill of the manager.

    C is incorrect because VaR does not provide an accurate risk estimate in either trending or volatile regimes. A portfolio might remain under its VaR limit every day but lose an amount approaching this limit each day. Under such circumstances, the portfolio could accumulate substantial losses without technically breaching the VaR constraint. Also, during periods of low volatility, VaR will appear quite low, underestimating the losses that could occur when the environment returns to a normal level of volatility.

17. C is correct. Measuring VaR at a 5% threshold produces an estimated value at risk of 2.69%.

    From Exhibit 6, the expected annual portfolio return is 14.1% and the standard deviation is 26.3%. Annual values need to be adjusted to get their daily counterparts. Assuming 250 trading days in a year, the expected annual return is adjusted by dividing by 250 and the standard deviation is adjusted by dividing by the square root of 250.

    Thus, the daily expected return is 0.141/250 = 0.000564, and volatility is $0.263/\sqrt{250}$ = 0.016634.

    5% daily VaR = $E(R_p) - 1.65\sigma_p$ = 0.000564 − 1.65(0.016634) = −0.026882. The portfolio is expected to experience a potential minimum loss in percentage terms of 2.69% on 5% of trading days.

18. C is correct. The change in value of a bond is inversely related to a change in yield. Given a bond priced at $B$ with duration $D$ and yield change of $\Delta y$, the rate of return or percentage price change for the bond is approximately given as follows: $\Delta B/B \approx -D\Delta y/(1 + y)$. Under Scenario 3, interest rates decrease by 20 bps. In an environment of decreasing interest rates, the bond with the highest dura-

## Solutions

tion will have the greatest positive return. Bond 3 has a duration of 10.2, which is greater than that of both Bond 1 (duration = 1.3) and Bond 2 (duration = 3.7).

19. C is correct. A traditional asset manager uses *ex post* tracking error when analyzing backward-looking returns. The Diversified Fixed-Income Fund prospectus stipulates a target benchmark deviation of no more than 5 bps. Tracking error is a measure of the degree to which the performance of a given investment deviates from its benchmark.

20. B is correct. Position limits are limits on the market value of any given investment; they are excellent controls on overconcentration. Position limits can be expressed in currency units or as a percentage of net assets. The Alpha Core Equity Fund restricts the exposure of individual securities to 1.75% of the total portfolio.

21. C is correct. The Monte Carlo simulation method can accommodate virtually any distribution, an important factor given the increased frequency of large daily losses. This method can also more easily accommodate the large number of portfolio holdings. The Monte Carlo method allows the user to develop her own forward-looking assumptions about the portfolio's risk and return characteristics, unlike the historical simulation method, which uses the current portfolio and re-prices it using the actual historical changes in the key factors experienced during the lookback period. Given the limited return history for infrastructure investments and Hamilton's expectations for higher-than-normal volatility, the historical simulation method would be a suboptimal choice.

22. C is correct. Conditional VaR is a measure of tail risk that provides an estimate of the average loss that would be incurred if the VaR cutoff is exceeded.

23. C is correct. A hypothetical scenario analysis allows the risk manager to estimate the likely effect of the scenario on a range of portfolio risk factors. A sovereign ratings downgrade would affect Hiram's India equity and corporate bond exposures as well as the government bond exposure. In addition, the assumptions used in constructing the scenario analysis can specifically address the effect of a need to sell large position sizes under decreased liquidity conditions resulting from a ratings downgrade. VaR alone does not accurately reflect the risk of large position sizes, which may be difficult to trade.

24. C is correct. A hypothetical scenario analysis allows Hamilton to estimate the direct effect of a ratings downgrade on the portfolio's government bond holdings and the resulting need to sell a number of the portfolio's holdings because they no longer meet the ratings guidelines. VaR alone does not accurately reflect the risk of large position sizes, which may be difficult to trade. The hypothetical scenario analysis will also highlight the effect of increased economic turmoil on all of the portfolio's exposures, not only the government bond exposures.

25. B is correct. The VaR is derived as follows:

$$\text{VaR} = \{[E(Rp) - 2.33\sigma_p](-1)\}(\text{Portfolio value}),$$

where

$E(R_p)$ = Annualized daily return = $(0.00026 \times 250) = 0.065$

250 = Number of trading days annually

2.33 = Number of standard deviations to attain 1% VaR

$\sigma_p$ = Annualized standard deviation = $(0.00501 \times \sqrt{250}) = 0.079215$

Portfolio value = CAD260,000,000

VaR = $-(0.065 - 0.184571) \times$ CAD260,000,000

= CAD31,088,460.

26. B is correct. Given the large fixed-income exposure in the LICIA portfolio, examining the portfolio duration more closely would be prudent. Duration is the primary sensitivity exposure measure for fixed-income investments.

# LEARNING MODULE 4

# Backtesting and Simulation

by Yin Luo, CPA, PStat, CFA, and Sheng Wang.

*Yin Luo, CPA, PStat, CFA, is at Wolfe Research LLC (USA). Sheng Wang is at Wolfe Research LLC (USA).*

| LEARNING OUTCOMES | |
|---|---|
| Mastery | The candidate should be able to: |
| ☐ | describe objectives in backtesting an investment strategy |
| ☐ | describe and contrast steps and procedures in backtesting an investment strategy |
| ☐ | interpret metrics and visuals reported in a backtest of an investment strategy |
| ☐ | identify problems in a backtest of an investment strategy |
| ☐ | evaluate and interpret a historical scenario analysis |
| ☐ | contrast Monte Carlo and historical simulation approaches |
| ☐ | explain inputs and decisions in simulation and interpret a simulation; and |
| ☐ | demonstrate the use of sensitivity analysis |

## INTRODUCTION

☐ describe objectives in backtesting an investment strategy

Sarah Koh heads the quantitative research team at Newton Research Pte. SWF Fund, one of Newton's biggest clients, has asked Koh to help develop new investment strategies by rigorously and independently evaluating their risk and return profiles. SWF Fund would like Koh to evaluate the merits of a "value" equity strategy—does owning "cheap" stocks and avoiding (or short-selling) "expensive" stocks add alpha?—as well as two multifactor

> fundamental strategies that incorporate several other factors besides value. SWF Fund's Investment Committee will use Koh's findings in its decision-making on whether to begin using these strategies.
> Koh's work and findings for SWF Fund will be illustrated throughout the reading.

This reading provides an overview of four techniques used to evaluate investment strategies. The first technique, known as **backtesting**, tests a strategy in a historical environment, usually over long periods, answering the question "How would this strategy have performed if it were implemented in the past?" The second technique, **historical scenario analysis**, also known as **historical stress testing**, examines the efficacy of a strategy in discrete historical environments, such as during recessions or periods of high inflation. The third technique, **simulation**, explores how a strategy would perform in a hypothetical environment specified by the user, rather than a historical setting; it is a useful complement to other methods because the past may not recur and only a limited number of all possible future observations for important variables (e.g., interest rates, return correlations, economic growth) is represented in history. Finally, we explore **sensitivity analysis**, which is often combined with simulation to uncover the impact of changing key assumptions.

Increasingly powerful off-the-shelf software has moved these techniques from the realm of specialists to generalists. In a CFA Institute survey of nearly 250 analysts, portfolio managers, and private wealth managers, 50% of respondents reported that they had performed backtesting analysis on an investment strategy in the past 12 months. Although performing these analyses now has fewer technical challenges than before, understanding the steps and procedures, the implicit assumptions, the pitfalls, and the interpretation of results have only increased in importance given the proliferation of these tools. This reading is a starting point on the journey to building this core professional competency.

## 2 THE OBJECTIVES OF BACKTESTING

Backtesting approximates the real-life investment process by using historical data to assess whether a strategy would have produced desirable results. Although not all strategies that perform well in a backtest will produce excess returns in the future, backtesting can offer investors insight and rigor to the investment process. Conversely, a strategy that does not show efficacy in backtesting could deliver excess returns in the future, but such a strategy is unlikely to be accepted by portfolio managers and investors alike. As a result, backtesting can be employed as a rejection or acceptance criterion for an investment strategy, depending on the investment manager's process.

Backtesting has been widely used in the investment community for many years. Although it fits quantitative and systematic investment styles more naturally, it is also widely used by fundamental managers. Before using a criterion to screen for stocks (such as a valuation metric, for example), a backtest can uncover the historical efficacy of that criterion by determining if its use would have added incremental excess return.

The implicit assumption in backtesting is that the future will at least somewhat resemble history. The reality, however, is more complicated. We attempt to account for the randomness of the future using complementary techniques discussed later in the reading.

## THE BACKTESTING PROCESS

| | |
|---|---|
| ☐ | describe and contrast steps and procedures in backtesting an investment strategy |
| ☐ | interpret metrics and visuals reported in a backtest of an investment strategy |

Backtesting consists of three steps: strategy design, historical investment simulation, and analysis of backtesting output. Exhibit 1 illustrates these steps and component procedures. We will discuss each step and illustrate them with example backtests of two investment strategies.

**Exhibit 1: Backtesting Flowchart**

**Strategy Design**
- Specify investment hypothesis and goal(s)
- Determine investment rules and process
- Decide key parameters

**Historical Investment Simulation**
- Form investment portfolios for each period according to the rules specified in the previous step
- Rebalance the portfolio periodically based on pre-determined rules

**Analysis of Backtesting Output**
- Calculate portfolio performance statistics
- Compute other key metrics (e.g., turnover, etc.)

*Source*: Wolfe Research Luo's QES.

### Step 1: Strategy Design

The first step is to identify the investment goals and hypothesis. For active strategies, the goal is typically to achieve excess returns over the relevant benchmark or superior risk-adjusted absolute return. An investment hypothesis is a method—a trading rule, security selection criterion, a portfolio, etc.—aimed at achieving the goal.

The next step is to translate the hypothesis into rules and processes and to specify several key parameters, so that the hypothesis can be backtested. The key parameters include the investment universe, specific definition of returns, frequency of portfolio rebalancing, and start and end dates.

#### Investment Universe

The investment universe refers to all of the securities in which we can potentially invest. Although academic researchers and specialists typically use the union of Compustat/Worldscope and CRSP,[1] many practitioners use the constituents of well-known broad market indexes as their investment universe. In this reading, unless specified otherwise,

---

1  CRSP (the Center for Research in Security Prices) provides high-quality data and security returns. The CRSP data series of New York Stock Exchange–listed stocks begins on 31 December 1925.

we use the Russell 3000 Index, S&P/TSX Composite Index, MSCI China A, and S&P Global Broad Market Index (BMI) for the investment universe for equity strategies in the United States, Canada, mainland China, and all other markets, respectively.

*Return Definition*

As we extend our investment universe from a single country to a global context, multiple complexities arise, such as currency, trading, and regulatory considerations. For example, we need to decide in what currency the return should be computed. The two most frequent choices are either to translate all investment returns into one single currency—typically the home country currency—or to denominate returns in local currencies. The choice of currency in backtesting often depends on whether the portfolio manager hedges their currency exposures. Managers who do not hedge their exchange rate risk often choose to backtest using single-currency-denominated returns.

If the goal of the investment strategy is excess return, a benchmark must also be specified. The benchmark used is often the benchmark for the client mandate or fund for which the investment strategy under study is applicable. The benchmark should relate to the investment universe; for example, the MSCI China A Index is a logical choice for a strategy that uses the constituents of that index as its universe.

*Rebalancing Frequency and Transaction Cost*

Practitioners often use a monthly frequency for portfolio rebalancing, although higher or lower frequencies are also common. Note that daily or higher frequency rebalancing typically incurs higher transaction costs, and price data will likely be biased by bid–ask spreads, asynchronous trading across different parts of the world, and missing days because of holidays in different countries. Consideration of transaction costs is critical, because many market anomalies simply disappear once they are included. As such, the analyst should explicitly communicate whether transaction costs are included or not in any presentation of the output.

*Start and End Date*

All else equal, investment managers prefer to backtest investment strategies using as long a history as possible, because a larger sample imparts greater statistical confidence in the results. Conversely, however, because financial data are likely to be non-stationary, performance over a long data history should be supplemented with examinations of discrete regimes within the long history (e.g., periods of high and low inflation, recessions and expansions, etc.) using historical scenario analysis, which we will discuss later in the reading.

> ### EXAMPLE 1
>
> ### Strategy Design
>
> After an initial conversation with the investment committee at SWF Fund, Sarah Ko notes the following:
>
> ### Goal:
>
> Superior risk-adjusted absolute return.
>
> ### Hypothesis:
>
> "Cheap" stocks—those with lower relative valuations—will outperform "expensive" stocks. In other words, exposure to the "value" factor will lead to outperformance.
>
> Koh must now further specify the hypothesis to allow backtesting, as well as define key parameters for the backtest.

The value factor can be described using almost any combination of market price and fundamental performance measures, on a historical (called trailing) or forward-looking basis. Koh selects a simple valuation metric—trailing earnings yield, the inverse of the P/E—to quantify the "cheapness" of a stock. Although P/E is more commonly understood than earnings yield, a serious flaw is that it cannot be computed or logically interpreted if EPS is zero or negative. Earnings yield, on the other hand, can be computed for any stock so long as EPS and price data are available.

$$\text{Trailing earnings yield} = \frac{\text{Trailing 12-month EPS}}{\text{Current share price}}. \tag{1}$$

## Specification of Key Parameters:

- Investment universe: Russell 3000 for the US market and S&P Europe BMI for the European market. Total returns will be hedged back into US dollars.
- Start and end date: Because data required for this strategy are widely available, Koh will use a long time period: January 1986–May 2019.
- Rebalancing frequency: monthly, including transaction costs, but returns on a 12-month moving average basis will be computed.

1. Given the backtesting strategy design outlined here, which of the following is a concern about which the investment committee of SWF Fund should be aware?

    **A.** The strategy assumes that the US dollar will appreciate against the euro.

    **B.** The historical period of the data includes recessions, currency regime changes, and periods of varying interest rates.

    **C.** There are serious issues with computing earnings yield for many stocks.

## Solution:

B is correct. The portfolio manager is using a long data history that includes regime changes in inflation, currencies, and interest rates, so the data is non-stationary. Consequently, backtesting performance results should be supplemented with examinations of performance during the discrete regimes.

A is incorrect because the analysis makes no assumption about exchange rates. C is incorrect because earnings yield can be computed as long as EPS and price data are available.

2. Which of the following describes the relationship between rebalancing frequency and transaction costs?

    **A.** Changing the rebalancing frequency from monthly to weekly would likely increase transaction costs.

    **B.** Changing the rebalancing frequency from monthly to quarterly would likely increase transaction costs.

    **C.** Rebalancing frequency has no effect on transaction costs.

A is correct. Rebalancing frequency refers to how often a portfolio is updated to reflect current data, such as (in this case) changes in earnings yields across the investment universe. Typically, the more frequently rebalancing is done, the more trading is required, which incurs more transaction costs. B is incorrect because it describes a decrease in rebalancing frequency, which would decrease transaction costs. C is incorrect because rebalancing frequency is the primary driver of trading volume, which incurs transaction costs.

3. Which of the following is **not** a potential concern of using a short time period for a backtest?

   **A.** The backtest will cover a limited number of business cycle, inflation, and interest rate regimes.

   **B.** The backtest may not be useful because the findings may apply only under the conditions present in the time frame.

   **C.** The backtest is likely to cover multiple business cycle, inflation, and interest rate regimes.

   C is correct. Covering multiple macroeconomic regimes *is not* a concern associated with using a short time period for a backtest, because macroeconomic regimes tend to be multi-year in length. A and B are incorrect because they *are* concerns associated with using a short time period: The backtest may capture only a limited experience, and thus the findings may be relevant for only that experience.

## Step 2: Historical Investment Simulation

The next step is constructing the portfolio to be tested and ensuring that it is rebalanced based on the pre-determined frequency.

The portfolio construction process depends primarily on the investment hypothesis under consideration (e.g., whether it is an entire portfolio, a trading strategy, or a modification of an existing strategy), the investment manager's capabilities and style, and the client's investment mandate for which the potential strategy is relevant (e.g., are there geographical limitations? Are there size and liquidity constraints? Can the manager short stocks?). Although our examples use fundamental factor-based, quantitative equity strategies in which we assume stocks can be shorted, backtesting can be applied to any kind of investment strategy.

To simulate rebalancing, analysts typically use **rolling windows**, in which a portfolio or strategy is constituted at the beginning of a period using data from a historical in-sample period, followed by testing on a subsequent, out-of-sample period. The process is repeated as time moves forward. This approach replicates the live investing process, because investment managers adjust their positions as new information arrives. For example, assume we backtest a value strategy by measuring its performance each month from December 2011 to May 2012. The process begins on 30 November 2011 by compiling every stock's trailing 12-month earnings yield using EPS reported in the previous 12 months (i.e., from December 2010 to November 2011, the in-sample months) divided by stock prices as of 30 November 2011. We then execute the investment strategy—for example, buying stocks with high earnings yields and shorting stocks with low earnings yields—as of that date. Then, we record the investment results for the month of December (i.e., the out-of-sample, OOS, month). The process is repeated at the end of each subsequent month, by rebalancing the portfolio with refreshed trailing 12-month earnings yield data and measuring the results over the ensuing (OOS) month. Exhibit 2 illustrates this process is illustrated.

## Exhibit 2: Rolling Window Backtesting of the Earnings Yield Factor

| | 2010:12 | 2011:01 | 2011:02 | 2011:03 | 2011:04 | 2011:05 | 2011:06 | 2011:07 | 2011:08 | 2011:09 | 2011:10 | 2011:11 | 2011:12 | 2012:01 | 2012:02 | 2012:03 | 2012:04 | 2012:05 |
|---|---|---|---|---|---|---|---|---|---|---|---|---|---|---|---|---|---|---|
| 11/30/2011 | | | | | | | | | In-Sample (Last 12M EPS/Price) | | | | OOS | | | | | |
| 12/31/2011 | | | | | | | | | | In-Sample (Last 12M EPS/Price) | | | | OOS | | | | |
| 1/31/2012 | | | | | | | | | | | In-Sample (Last 12M EPS/Price) | | | | OOS | | | |
| 2/29/2012 | | | | | | | | | | | | In-Sample (Last 12M EPS/Price) | | | | OOS | | |
| 3/31/2012 | | | | | | | | | | | | | In-Sample (Last 12M EPS/Price) | | | | OOS | |
| 4/30/2012 | | | | | | | | | | | | | | In-Sample (Last 12M EPS/Price) | | | | OOS |

*Source:* Wolfe Research Luo's QES.

## Step 3: Analysis of Backtesting Output

The final step in backtesting is generating results for presentation and interpretation. We care about not only the average return of the portfolio but also the risk profile (e.g., volatility and downside risk). Therefore, analysts often use metrics such as the Sharpe ratio, the Sortino ratio, volatility, and **maximum drawdown**. Maximum drawdown is the maximum loss from a peak to a trough for an asset or portfolio.

Beyond these measures, other key performance outputs are visual: for example, time series of returns as well as distributions of returns plotted against a well-known distribution, such as the normal distribution. Visuals are an intuitive way of summarizing many datapoints that often reveal more than a single number summary measure.

It is also useful to examine the backtested cumulative performance of an investment strategy over an extended history. We recommend plotting performance using a logarithmic scale, wherein equal percentage changes are presented as the same vertical distance on the $y$-axis. Using these cumulative performance graphs, one can readily identify downside risk, performance decay, and structural breaks. Structural breaks, or regime changes, are the result of many exogenous factors and are one reason why the past is not always a good guide to the future. The following are examples of structural breaks:

- Depressions and recessions, such as the 2008–09 global financial crisis;
- Geopolitical events, such as changing trade relationships involving countries representing important global equity and bond markets, as well as key countries exiting or entering major trading blocs;
- Major shifts in monetary and fiscal policies, such as the prolonged period of quantitative easing (QE) adopted by major central banks in the aftermath of the 2008 global financial crisis; and
- Major technological changes and advances, such as those that fueled the dot-com bubble and the proliferation of machine learning and artificial intelligence.

We implement our earnings yield-based value strategy as a long–short hedged portfolio, a widely used approach pioneered by Fama and French (1993). In this approach, the analyst sorts the investable stock universe by the relevant metric—trailing earnings yield, in this case—and divides the universe into quantiles (typically into quintiles or deciles) based on those metrics. A long–short hedged portfolio is then formed by going long the top quantile (i.e., the group of stocks with the highest earnings yield) and shorting the bottom quantile (i.e., the group of stocks with the lowest earnings yield). Individual stocks are either equally weighted or market capitalization weighted within each quantile. Although the quantiles may not have equal beta exposure, and they may have exposures to other common factors, the difference in the average earnings yield metric between quantiles is a reasonable and straightforward characterization of underlying performance.

We used quintiles (e.g., top and bottom 20%) and monthly rolling windows and measured the results in several ways for the strategy in the US and European markets, shown in Exhibit 3.

**Exhibit 3: Earnings Yield Factor, Long–Short Hedged Quintile Portfolio Returns (January 1986–May 2019)**

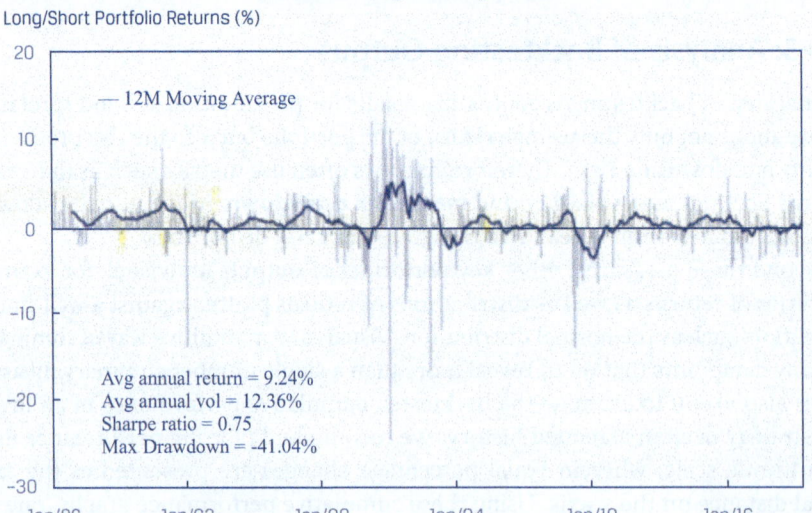

*Sources*: Bloomberg Finance LLP, FTSE Russell, S&P Capital IQ, Thomson Reuters, Wolfe Research Luo's QES.

We also examined the cumulative performance of the strategy in four different stock markets: the United States, Europe, Asia ex-Japan, and Japan, with the results shown in Exhibit 4.

### Exhibit 4: Earnings Yield Factor, Long–Short Hedged Quintile Portfolio Returns (January 1986–May 2019) in Several Markets

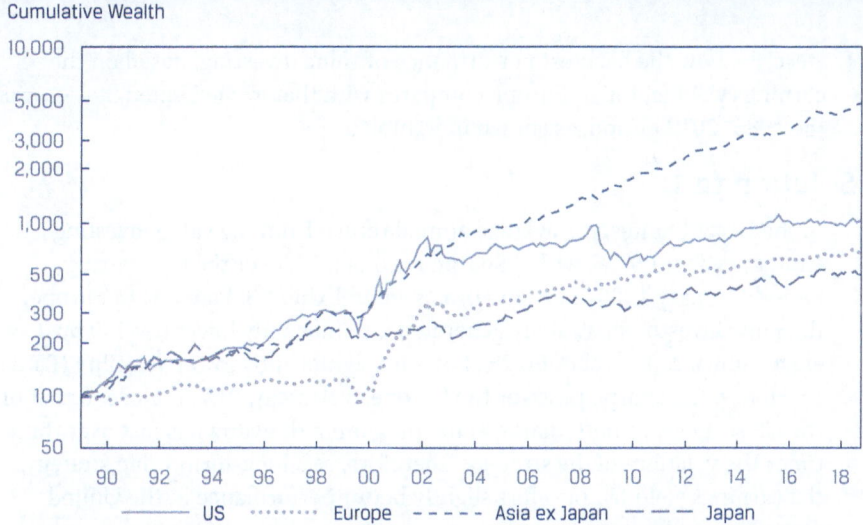

*Sources*: Bloomberg Finance LLP, FTSE Russell, S&P Capital IQ, Thomson Reuters, and Wolfe Research Luo's QES.

Finally, we show the distribution of the strategy's returns in the US market against the normal distribution in Exhibit 5.

### Exhibit 5: Distribution of Earnings Yield Returns, United States (1986–2019)

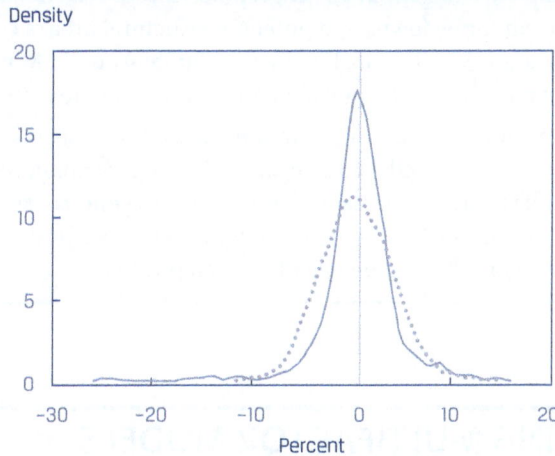

*Source*: Bloomberg Finance LLP, FTSE Russell, S&P Capital IQ, Thomson Reuters, Wolfe Research Luo's QES.

> **EXAMPLE 2**
>
> ### Historical Investment Simulation and Output Analysis
>
> 1. Describe how the backtest performance of value investing, based on the earnings yield factor, in Europe compares with that in the United States over the 1986–2019 period, as shown in Exhibit 3.
>
> ### Solution to 1:
>
> In the United States, the average annual return from the value investing strategy is about 9.2%, with a Sharpe ratio of 0.75, over the backtesting period (January 1986–May 2019), as seen in Exhibit 3, Panel A. In Europe, the same investment strategy generated a significantly lower (by 250 bps) average annual return, about 6.7%, but with significantly lower volatility (Panel B). Hence, the Sharpe ratio for the European strategy, 0.67, is close to that of the US strategy. In both markets, the maximum drawdown is just over three times the volatility of the strategy. Therefore, as a long-term value strategy, the earnings yield factor offers slightly better performance in the United States than in Europe.
>
> 2. Describe the cumulative performance of value investing across the different markets shown in Exhibit 4 and the distributions of returns in the United States from this strategy in Exhibit 5.
>
> ### Solution to 2:
>
> The value strategy has delivered strong performance over the long run across the several markets, especially in Asia ex-Japan (Exhibit 4). Performance has flattened since 2016, however, in the United States, Europe, and Japan after first leveling off in all geographies except Asia ex-Japan after 2002. Significant drawdowns and potential structural breaks can also be observed in late 1990s (i.e., during the tech bubble) and in March–May 2009 (i.e., the risk rally during the global financial crisis) in most regions.
>
> More problematically, the strategy in the United States seems to suffer from excess kurtosis (i.e., fat tails) and negative skewness (Exhibit 5). The excess kurtosis implies that this strategy is more likely to generate surprises—that is, extreme returns—whereas the negative skewness suggests that those surprises are more likely to be negative (than positive).

## 4. BACKTESTING MULTIFACTOR MODELS

- [ ] describe and contrast steps and procedures in backtesting an investment strategy
- [ ] interpret metrics and visuals reported in a backtest of an investment strategy

Few investment managers use a single signal, such as earnings yield, in an investment strategy. In practice, most quantitative stock selection models use a multifactor structure, with a linear combination of factors being the dominant framework. Similarly, most fundamental managers use multiple filters in their stock screening tools.

In this section, we introduce two multifactor equity portfolio strategies to more richly illustrate backtesting: a benchmark (BM) factor portfolio, which equally weights multiple fundamental factors, and a **risk parity** (RP) factor portfolio, which weights factors based on equal risk contribution. We chose these two approaches because their weighting schemes—equal weights and equal risk weights, respectively—are objective. We will continue to use these two portfolios throughout the reading to discuss other evaluation techniques.

To backtest these two portfolios, we follow the same three steps described previously: strategy design, historical investment simulation, and output analysis.

## Step 1: Strategy Design

We chose eight fundamental factors from common investment styles:

1. Defensive value: Trailing earnings yield
2. Cyclical value: Book-to-market ratio
3. Growth: Consensus FY1/FY0 EPS growth
4. Price momentum: 12-month total return, excluding the most recent month
5. Analyst sentiment: 3-month EPS revision
6. Profitability: Return on equity (ROE)
7. Leverage: Debt-to-equity ratio
8. Earnings quality: Non-cash earnings (proportion of accruals in earnings)

For each factor, we form a portfolio by buying the top 20% of stocks and shorting the bottom 20% of stocks ranked by the factor. Stocks within both long and short buckets are equally weighted. For illustration purposes, we do not account for transaction costs or other portfolio implementation constraints.

As shown in Exhibit 6 (which uses a logarithm scale on the $y$-axis), all eight factor portfolios have delivered positive returns over the long term (1988–2019) in the United States. Earnings revision, earnings yield, and price momentum factors produced the highest returns, and the earnings growth and debt/equity factors lagged far behind. The eight factor portfolios appear to share some commonalities. Upon visual inspection, returns seem to fall into three clusters: (1) earnings revision, earnings yield, and price momentum; (2) ROE and earnings quality; and (3) book-to-market ratio, earnings growth, and debt/equity. They also show significant dispersions at times.

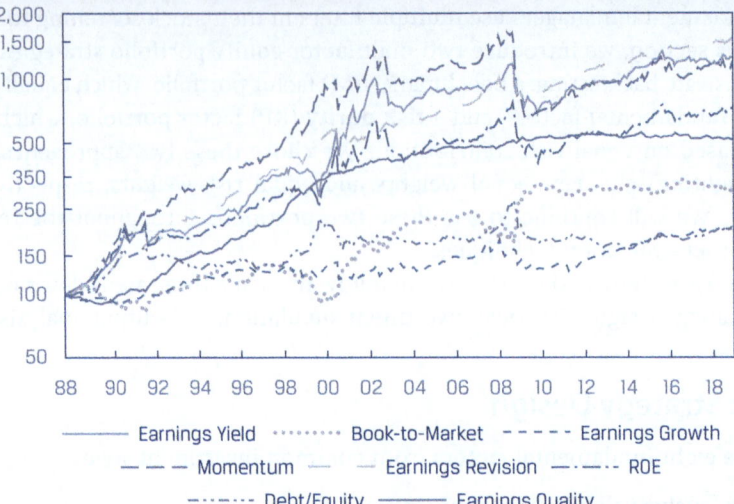

**Exhibit 6: Cumulative Return of Eight Factor Portfolios, United States (1988–2019)**

*Sources*: Bloomberg Finance LLP, FTSE Russell, S&P Capital IQ, Thomson Reuters, Wolfe Research Luo's QES.

For our benchmark portfolio, we combine these eight factor portfolios by equally weighting each one. Researchers have found that such an equally weighted portfolio either outperforms or performs in line with portfolios constructed using more sophisticated optimization techniques (e.g., DeMiguel, Garlappi, and Uppal 2007).

For our risk parity (RP) portfolio, we combine the eight factor portfolios by equally weighting them by their risk contribution. Risk parity is a popular alternative portfolio construction technique that accounts for the volatility of each factor and the correlations of returns among all factors in the portfolio. The objective is for each factor to make an equal (hence "parity") risk contribution to the overall risk of the portfolio.

We backtested our two portfolios in each of the following markets: the United States, Canada, Latin America (LATAM), Europe, the United Kingdom, emerging Europe, Middle East, and Africa (EMEA), Asia ex-Japan, Japan, Australia and New Zealand (ANZ), and mainland China. Both portfolios are rebalanced monthly to maintain equal factor weights or equal factor risk contributions (i.e., risk parity). Although each of the eight underlying factor portfolios is a long–short portfolio, our BM and RP multifactor portfolios are long only, meaning the weights allocated to each factor portfolio are restricted to be non-negative, such that weights for each of the underlying portfolios are all positive and sum to 100%.

### Step 2: Historical Investment Simulation

Backtesting a multifactor strategy is similar to the method introduced earlier, but the rolling-window procedure is implemented twice, once at each portfolio "layer."

First, we form eight factor portfolios at each given point in time (i.e., monthly) from 1988 until May 2019 using the rolling-window procedure discussed previously. We then combine these factor portfolios into two multifactor portfolios, each with different weights: equal weighted (BM portfolio) and equal risk weighted (RP portfolio).

A second rolling-window procedure over the same time span is required to avoid look-ahead bias. At each month end, the previous five years of monthly data are used to estimate the variance–covariance matrix for the eight factor portfolios. This is the most important ingredient to form the RP portfolio. Once the covariance matrix is estimated, we can optimize and compute the weights (i.e., weights for equal risk contribution) for each of the eight factor portfolios and then form the RP portfolio.

Finally, we compute the returns of the two multifactor portfolios (BM and RP) during each "out-of-sample" month from 1988 to May 2019.

## Step 3: Output Analysis

Exhibit 7, Panel A, shows that the weights of the eight factor portfolios in the RP portfolio are relatively stable over time (1993–2019) in the United States, but they are certainly not equal—so we should expect the RP portfolio's risk and return profile to differ from that of the BM portfolio. Notably, book-to-market and earnings quality factor portfolios receive the largest allocations, whereas ROE and price momentum factor portfolios have the lowest weights. Although the RP portfolio appears to deliver a lower cumulative return than does the BM portfolio (Panel B), Panel C shows that the RP portfolio's volatility is less than half the volatility of the BM portfolio. As a result, the RP portfolio's Sharpe ratio is nearly twice that of the BM portfolio (Panel D).

**Exhibit 7: Backtesting Multifactor Strategies: Equally Weighted Benchmark Portfolio vs. Risk Parity Weighted Portfolio**

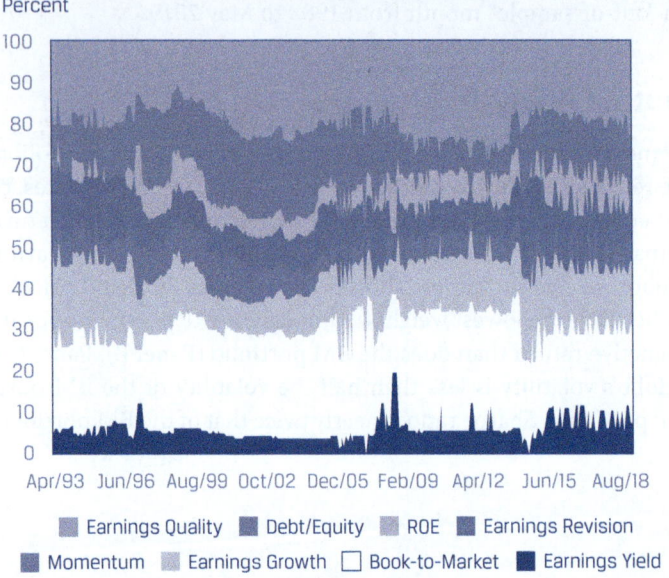

A. RP Portfolio Allocation Weights in the US

- Earnings Quality
- Debt/Equity
- ROE
- Earnings Revision
- Momentum
- Earnings Growth
- Book-to-Market
- Earnings Yield

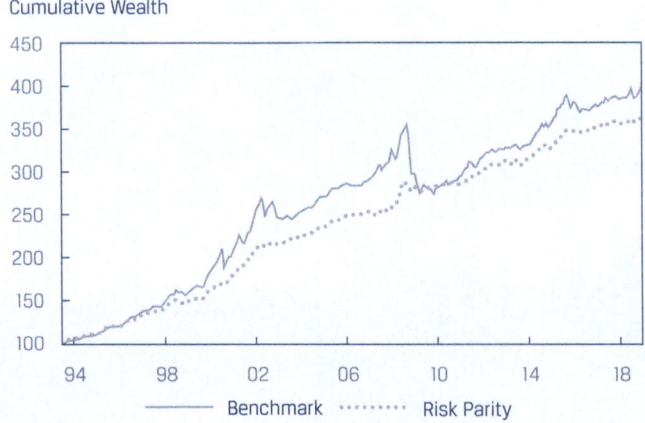

B. Cumulative Return

— Benchmark ········ Risk Parity

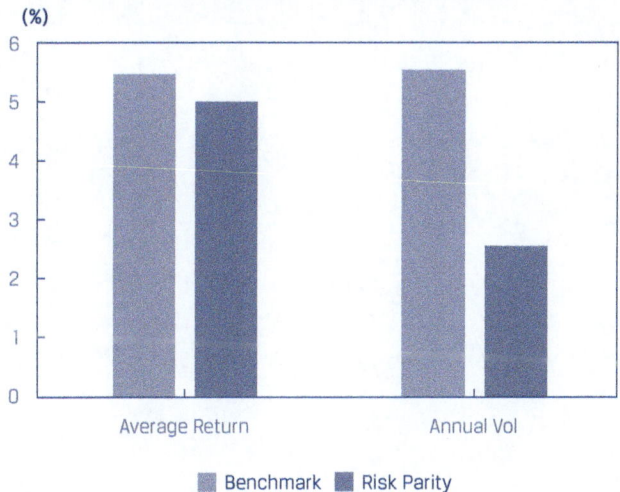

**C. Average Return and Volatility**

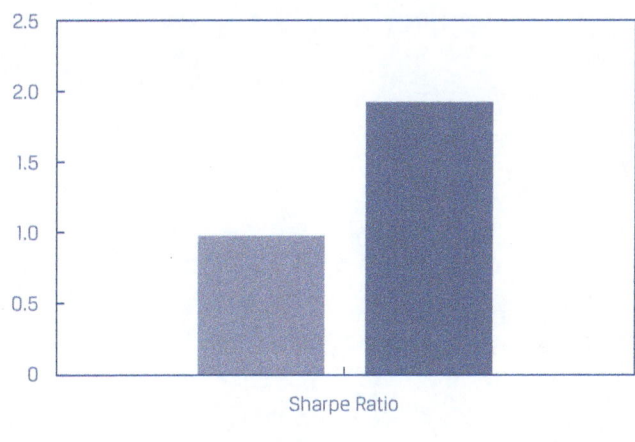

**D. Sharpe Ratio**

Sources: Bloomberg Finance LLP, FTSE Russell, S&P Capital IQ, Thomson Reuters, Wolfe Research Luo's QES.

Exhibit 8 presents statistics for the return distributions of the eight factor portfolios and the equally weighted BM and RP weighted multifactor portfolios from 1993 to 2019. Six of the eight factor portfolios have negative skewness (the BM portfolio does as well), and all factors and factor allocation portfolios show excess kurtosis (i.e., kurtosis exceeding 3.0). The downside risk (i.e., minimum monthly return) is clearly greater in magnitude than the maximum upside for most factor strategies. The two factor allocation strategy portfolios—BM and RP—both display moderate mean returns (0.5% and 0.4% per month, respectively) and low standard deviations (1.6% and 0.7% per month, respectively) compared with the eight underlying factor portfolios, highlighting the diversification benefits from factor allocation decisions. Exhibit 9 compares the various downside risk measures for the eight factor portfolios and the BM and RP portfolios from 1993 to 2019. The three downside risk measures—value at risk (VaR), conditional value at risk (CVaR), and maximum drawdown—suggest that the price momentum factor, followed by the ROE factor, has the largest downside risk. The smallest downside risk is observed for the earnings quality factor. The risk parity portfolio shows considerably less downside risk than any of the eight

### Exhibit 8: Monthly Return Distributions: Factor, BM, and RP Portfolios (1993–2019)

|  | Earnings Yield | Book-to-Market | Earnings Growth | Momentum | Earnings Revision | ROE | Debt/Equity | Earnings Quality | Benchmark | Risk Parity |
|---|---|---|---|---|---|---|---|---|---|---|
| Mean | 0.7% | 0.4% | 0.2% | 0.6% | 0.7% | 0.5% | 0.1% | 0.4% | 0.5% | 0.4% |
| Median | 0.6% | 0.1% | 0.4% | 0.8% | 0.8% | 0.6% | 0.1% | 0.4% | 0.5% | 0.4% |
| Maximum | 14.5% | 28.9% | 6.2% | 11.7% | 9.1% | 10.8% | 11.9% | 5.3% | 4.3% | 3.7% |
| Minimum | (24.0%) | (12.1%) | (15.8%) | (32.7%) | (18.7%) | (28.0%) | (17.1%) | (2.6%) | (10.9%) | (2.5%) |
| Std. Dev | 3.8% | 3.7% | 2.1% | 4.6% | 2.4% | 3.9% | 2.5% | 1.2% | 1.6% | 0.7% |
| Skewness | (1.00) | 2.82 | (2.46) | (2.36) | (2.39) | (1.92) | (0.58) | 0.41 | (2.40) | 0.51 |
| Kurtosis | 11.06 | 23.61 | 17.80 | 16.56 | 20.76 | 14.96 | 11.55 | 3.87 | 17.78 | 5.37 |

*Sources:* Bloomberg Finance LLP, FTSE Russell, S&P Capital IQ, Thomson Reuters, Wolfe Research Luo's QES.

underlying factors and the benchmark portfolio. This evidence suggests that the RP strategy benefits greatly from risk diversification, at least in the United States for the period under investigation.

> **EXAMPLE 3**
>
> ### Risk and Return beyond Normal Distribution
>
> 1. Compare return profiles for the BM and RP strategy multifactor portfolios and explain which investment strategy offers the more attractive statistical properties for risk-averse investors (refer to Exhibits 8 and 9).
>
> ### Solution:
>
> The BM and RP portfolios have nearly the same mean monthly returns, at 0.5% and 0.4%, respectively (Exhibit 8). Although the maximum returns are similar, the RP portfolio has a much smaller minimum return (−2.5%) and a significantly lower standard deviation (0.7%) compared with those of the BM portfolio (−10.9% and 1.6%, respectively). The RP portfolio is also slightly positively skewed (0.51%) and has moderate kurtosis (5.37), in contrast to the negative skew (−2.40%) and high kurtosis (17.78) of the BM portfolio.
>
> The RP portfolio offers similar returns, less downside risk (confirmed by its superior VaR, CVaR, and maximum drawdown results in Exhibit 9), lower volatility, and slightly higher probability of positive returns (i.e., positive skew) compared with the BM portfolio. It is also less fat tailed (i.e., moderate kurtosis, meaning lower probability of extreme negative surprises) than the BM portfolio. Therefore, the RP portfolio has the more attractive distribution properties for risk-averse investors.

> **EXAMPLE 4**
>
> ### Backtesting the Performance of Factor Allocation Strategies
>
> During the presentation of her backtesting results to SWF's investment committee, Koh is asked the following questions:
>
> 1. Regarding rolling-window backtesting, which one of the following statements is *inaccurate*?
>    - **A.** The data are divided into just two samples.
>    - **B.** Out-of-sample data become part of the next period's in-sample data.
>    - **C.** Repeated in-sample training and out-of-sample testing allow managers to adjust security positions on the basis of the arrival over time of new information.
>
> ### Solution to 1:
>
> A is correct, because the statement is inaccurate. B and C are incorrect, because they accurately describe the rolling-window backtesting technique.

### Exhibit 9: Downside Risk Using Monthly Returns: Factor, BM, and RP Portfolios (1993–2019)

| | Earnings Yield | Book-to-Market | Earnings Growth | Momentum | Earnings Revision | ROE | Debt/Equity | Earnings Quality | Benchmark | Risk Parity |
|---|---|---|---|---|---|---|---|---|---|---|
| VaR(95%) | (5.9%) | (0.7%) | (3.9%) | (8.4%) | (3.7%) | (6.8%) | (4.0%) | (1.3%) | (2.6%) | (0.7%) |
| CVaR(95%) | (14.3%) | (11.1%) | (10.9%) | (22.9%) | (12.8%) | (18.7%) | (8.4%) | (1.7%) | (7.9%) | (0.9%) |
| Max Drawdown | 41.0% | 35.3% | 27.2% | 59.7% | 23.9% | 47.5% | 41.8% | 8.3% | 22.6% | 3.8% |

*Sources*: Bloomberg Finance LLP, FTSE Russell, S&P Capital IQ, Thomson Reuters, Wolfe Research Luo's QES.

2. Which of the following is a drawback of the long–short hedged portfolio approach for implementing factor-based portfolios?

   A. The hedged portfolio is formed by going long the top quantile (with the best factor scores) and shorting the bottom quantile (with the worst factor scores).
   B. Securities must be ranked by the factor being scrutinized and then grouped into quantiles based on their factor scores.
   C. Not every manager can short stocks.

## Solution to 2:

C is correct, because it best describes a drawback of the long–short hedged portfolio approach. A and B are incorrect because they describe the approach itself.

3. Which one of the following is *not* a metric or visual used in assessing backtesting of a factor-based investment strategy?

   A. Distribution plots of factor returns
   B. A word cloud of text describing the characteristics of the factor
   C. Maximum drawdown

## Solution to 3:

B is correct, because a word cloud is not a visual used in assessing backtesting of a factor-based investment strategy. A and C are incorrect, because they are visuals and metrics, respectively, used to assess backtests of factor-based strategies.

4. Regarding the use of rolling-window backtesting in assessing factor allocation to a risk parity–based strategy, which statement is correct?

   A. The procedure is used once for estimating factor returns over the rolling window.
   B. The procedure is used once for dividing the data into just two samples.
   C. The procedure is used twice—once for estimating factor returns over the rolling window, and a second time for estimating the covariance matrix of factor returns (for deriving risk parity weights) over the rolling window.

## Solution to 4:

C is correct, because the procedure must be used a second time for estimating the covariance matrix of factor returns (for deriving risk parity weights) over the rolling window. A is incorrect because the procedure must be done twice: once for estimating factor returns over the rolling window and a second time for estimating the covariance matrix of factor returns (for deriving risk parity weights). B is incorrect because the rolling-window procedure divides the sample into many samples.

## 5 COMMON PROBLEMS IN BACKTESTING

☐ identify problems in a backtest of an investment strategy

In this section, we discuss some of the most common mistakes investors make when they conduct backtests. Although backtesting is the subject of the discussion, all of these mistakes are relevant to and commonly found in quantitative research generally.

### Survivorship Bias

Companies continually appear and disappear from market indexes. New firms appear via IPOs, spin-offs, and outperformance. Companies disappear for many reasons, including privatization, acquisition, bankruptcy, and prolonged under- or outperformance that results in a change in market capitalization from large to mid/small and vice versa. As shown in Panel A of Exhibit 10, fewer than 400 of the constituents of the Russell 3000 Index in 1985 (less than 13%) are still included in the index as of 31 May 2019. Similarly, the S&P BMI Europe Index, which tracks the broad European market, started with about 720 stocks in 1989 and now contains around 1,200 companies. Among the 720 stocks in the index at inception, only 142 (or about 20%) were still in the index as of May 2019 (Panel B of Exhibit 10). Stocks that have remained in the index over time are referred to as "survivors."

# Common Problems in Backtesting

**Exhibit 10: Number of Stocks in Index vs. Survivors**

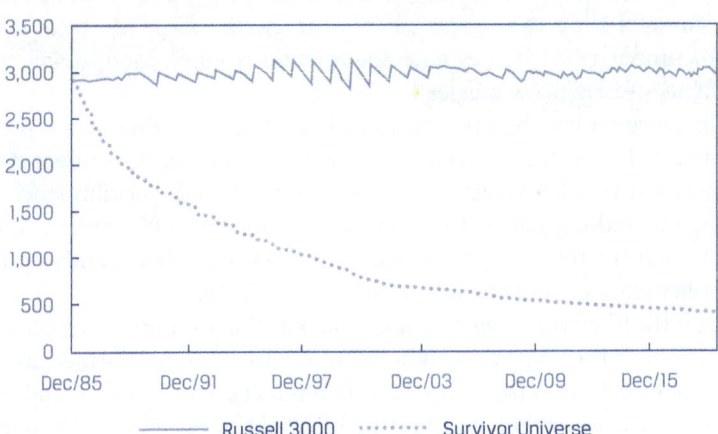

A. US (Russell 3000)

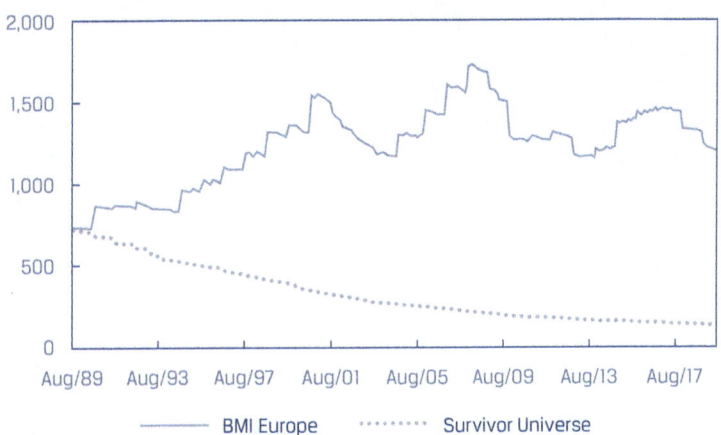

B. Europe (S&P BMI)

*Sources*: Bloomberg Finance LLP, FTSE Russell, S&P Capital IQ, Thomson Reuters, Wolfe Research Luo's QES.

---

**Survivorship bias** refers to deriving conclusions from data that reflects only those entities that have survived to that date. It is one of the most obvious but, interestingly, also one of the most common mistakes that investors make when conducting backtests. Although the problem is widely covered in the academic literature, relatively few practitioners, whether investing in equities, fixed income, hedge funds, or other asset classes, bother to quantify the implications of survivorship bias in their backtesting.

Some investors contend that because you can invest only in companies that exist today, there is nothing wrong with backtesting strategies using only the current index constituents. The problem is, however, that in the past, one could not know which companies would survive in the future, which companies would disappear, and which companies would be created and become successful enough to be added to the index. Moreover, the list of surviving firms is likely biased in one way or another—for example, it could represent primarily multinational firms, or highly innovative firms, or the most successful firms.

Although it is straightforward (but definitely not recommended) to backtest an investment strategy using only the survivors, tracking all companies that have ever existed in a correct point-in-time fashion (i.e., the casualties as well as the survivors) is strongly recommended, especially as such data becomes more available from data vendors. **Point-in-time data** allow analysts to use the most complete data for any given prior time period, thereby enabling the construction (and backtesting) of the most realistic investment strategies.

The difference between backtesting with current index constituents and point-in-time data is illustrated using the low-volatility anomaly, a popular investment strategy that argues that stocks with low volatility tend to outperform high-volatility stocks. A proper backtesting methodology using the point-in-time Russell 3000 universe in Panel A of Exhibit 11 confirms this view; low-volatility stocks have significantly outperformed high-volatility stocks over the three decades up to 2019.

Importantly, however, if we repeat the backtesting exercise using only survivors, then the result is the opposite: high-volatility stocks outperformed low-volatility stocks by about 5.5 times (see Panel B of Exhibit 11). This example underscores the importance of accounting for survivorship bias in backtesting by using point-in-time index constituent stocks and not just the current survivors.

## Exhibit 11: Survivorship Bias and the Low-Volatility Anomaly

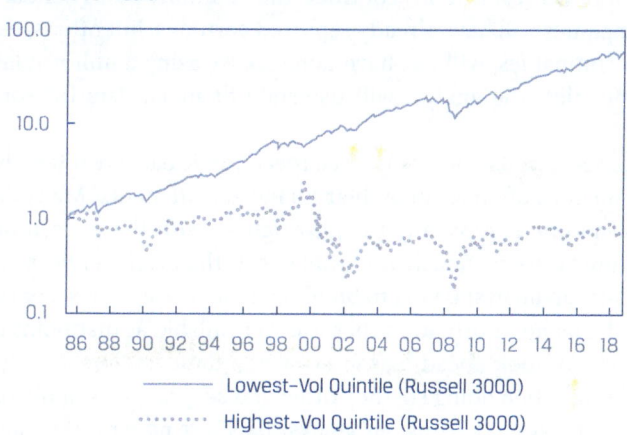

A. Using a Point-in-Time Universe

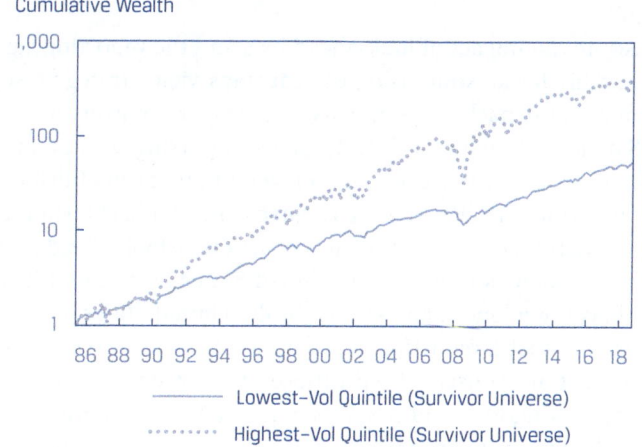

B. Using the Survived Companies

*Sources*: Bloomberg Finance LLP, FTSE Russell, S&P Capital IQ, Thomson Reuters, Wolfe Research Luo's QES.

## Look-Ahead Bias

Another common mistake investors make in backtesting is failing to recognize and account for **look-ahead bias**. This form of bias is created by using information that was unknown or unavailable during the historical periods over which the backtest is conducted. Survivorship bias is actually a type of look-ahead bias, because the question of whether a stock will survive or be added to an index in the future is unknown during the earlier periods over which the backtesting occurs. Look-ahead bias is likely the most common mistake that practitioners make when performing backtesting. It can be overcome by using point-in-time data, which, again, might not be available. Look-ahead bias has several common forms: reporting lags, revisions, and index additions.

The first common form of look-ahead bias derives from reporting lags. For example, in conducting a backtest for year-end 2018, we would not have EPS results for the quarter ending 31 December 2018 for all publicly traded companies until some point around 31 March 2019, although many larger-cap companies might report by 31 January 2019. So, to avoid look-ahead bias, analysts typically compensate by adding several months of reporting lag for every company. This process can also introduce stale information, however. If we continue the example, by 31 January 2019 many larger-cap companies will have already reported earnings, but others, especially mid- and small-cap companies, will not have done so. By using a uniform lag assumption across all companies, the analyst will use stale financial data for some larger-cap companies.

A second problem is data revisions: Macroeconomic data are often revised multiple times, and companies often re-state their financial statements. Many databases keep only the latest numbers, replacing the past figures with the revised ones, although the revised figures were obviously not available at the original release date. By using such revised data, an analyst trying to build realistic investment scenarios going back in time would be using information that was unavailable at that point in time.

Another form of look-ahead bias arises when data vendors add new companies to their databases. When doing so, they often add several years of historical financial statements into the system. Thus, an analyst backtesting with the current database would be using information on companies that were not actually in the database during the backtesting period. The consequence of this look-ahead bias is often overly optimistic results.

To demonstrate the impact of look-ahead bias and the reporting lag assumption, we conduct monthly backtesting using the earnings yield strategy discussed previously. We compared the backtest results using a proper point-in-time database with the actual EPS data as of each month end, against reporting lag assumptions ranging from zero to six months (a zero lag assumption would suffer from full look-ahead bias).

As shown in Exhibit 12, Panel A, it is clear from the backtesting results of the point-in-time scenario against the no-lag scenario that look-ahead bias inflates the performance of our value strategy in the United States by almost 100%. The impact of look-ahead bias is evident in all regions. In the United States, Canada, and Japan (Panel B), it appears that a reporting lag of between one and two months produces backtest results that are consistent with those of the proper point-in-time data. In Europe, the United Kingdom, and ANZ (Panel C), a lag assumption of between two and three months appears appropriate, whereas for Asia ex-Japan, LATAM, and emerging EMEA (Panel D), the point-in-time consistent lag assumption increases to three months. These different lag assumptions reflect the timeliness with which companies in each region report their earnings.

**Exhibit 12: Look-Ahead Bias: Impact on Backtesting of Reporting Lag Assumptions (1986–2016)**

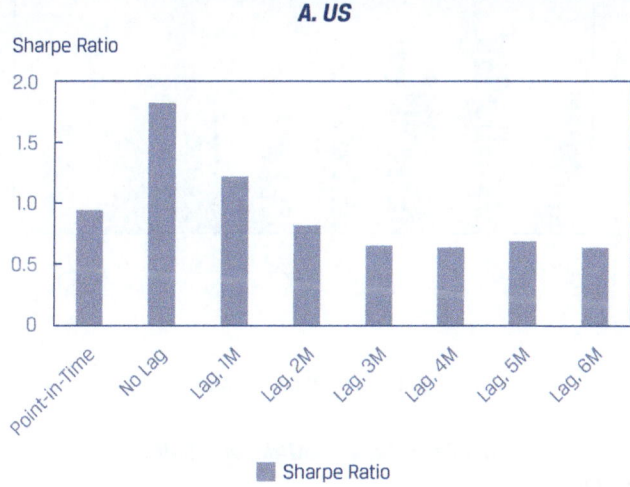

A. US

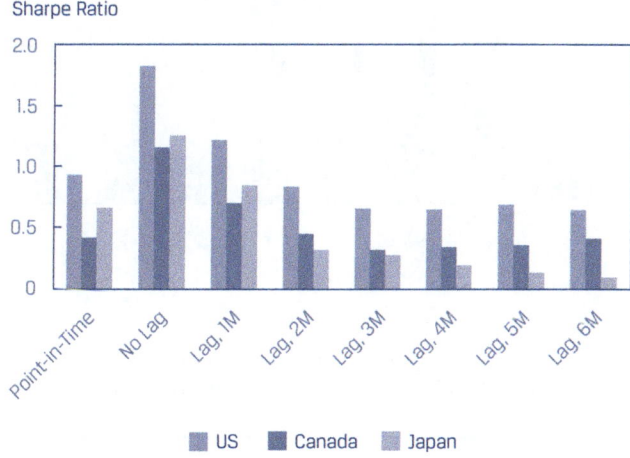

B. US, Canada, and Japan

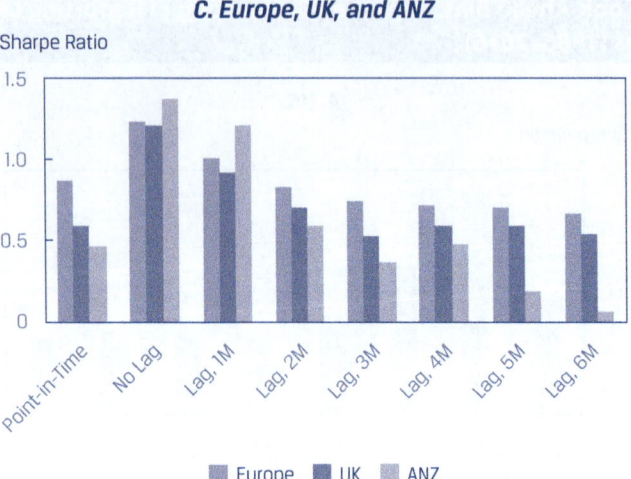

*C. Europe, UK, and ANZ*

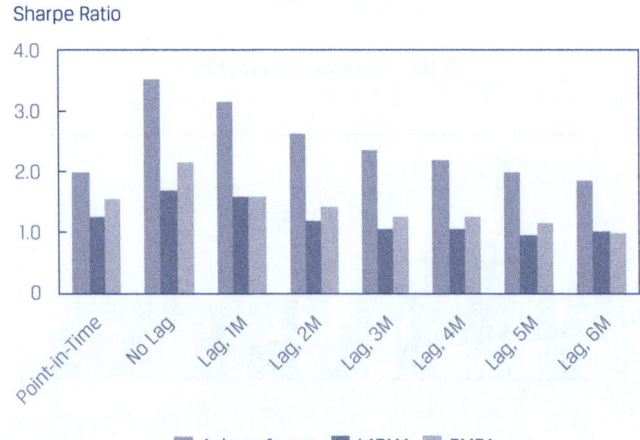

*D. Asia ex Japan, LATAM, and EMEA*

Sources: Bloomberg Finance LLP, FTSE Russell, S&P Capital IQ, Thomson Reuters, Wolfe Research Luo's QES.

## Data Snooping

There is often a temptation to substitute sound portfolio construction by simply backtesting many strategies and picking the best-performing strategy. This bias is called **data snooping**—making an inference after looking at statistical results rather than testing a prior inference. Otherwise known as "p-hacking," data snooping occurs when an analyst selects data or performs analyses until a significant result is found. It can take many forms, including performing interim analyses to decide whether to continue collecting data, using many variables and deciding which to report later; dropping outliers only after performing analyses; and so on. The ultimate results are often false positives.

Data snooping may be mitigated by setting a much higher hurdle than typical—for example, a *t*-statistic greater than 3.0—for assessing whether a newly discovered factor is indeed adding incremental value (i.e., is statistically significant). Another technique to detect and mitigate data snooping is cross validation, in which the analyst partitions the dataset into training data and testing data (i.e., "validation data") and tests a model built from the training data on the validation data. Rolling window backtesting is a form of cross-validation, albeit in a deterministic and non-random manner, as past periods (i.e., in-sample periods) are used to train a model that is applied to the next (i.e., out-of-sample) period.

---

**EXAMPLE 5**

### Data Snooping in Investment Management

1. A research analyst has just presented her risk factor–based quantitative/systematic investment model for the UK market to you and several other portfolio managers. She reports the development and backtesting of several different models: The number of factors ranged from 5 to 10, rebalancing periods were monthly and quarterly, and rolling windows were implemented for 5, 15, and 25 years of historical data. She recommends the 10-factor model (with monthly rebalancing) because backtesting of 15 years of data generated the following annualized performance metrics: Sharpe ratio of 3.0 and realized volatility of 1.0%. She also reports a $t$-statistic of 2.5 and a $p$-value of 1.3% for this model of UK market returns, which were the highest and lowest statistics, respectively, of all the models.

   Describe the concerns you should raise around the issue of data snooping for this seemingly very attractive strategy.

### Solution:

As a portfolio manager, you must be careful in assessing these performance results in light of how the analyst developed and backtested her model. For example, it is critical to know whether backtesting has incorporated transaction costs and trading liquidity. More importantly, however, you need to understand whether data snooping was involved in developing this model/strategy. Given the many variations of models developed and tested by the analyst, it is highly likely that her process suffers from model selection bias. Recommending the model with the highest $t$-statistic and lowest $p$-value also points to data snooping. One way to mitigate the problem is to raise the hurdle for an acceptable model to a $t$-statistic exceeding 3.0 (thereby lowering the $p$-value). The analyst should also consider other techniques that can be used to better understand the true performance of this model/strategy (i.e., cross-validation).

---

A common way to perform cross validation is to use data from different geographic regions. For example, if the risk parity strategy is developed and tested initially using US equities, the same strategy can be tested in other markets globally to assess whether risk parity is a robust factor allocation strategy.

As shown in Exhibit 13, Panel A, as a risk-based factor allocation technique, the RP strategy does indeed deliver a lower realized volatility (i.e., standard deviation of returns) than the benchmark (i.e., equal-weighted factor) strategy in all 10 global markets over 1993–2019. Similarly, the RP portfolios also outperform the BM portfolios in terms of Sharpe ratio (Panel B) in 7 of the 10 global markets.

### Exhibit 13: Global Cross-Validation, Equally Weighted Benchmark Portfolio vs. Risk Parity Weighted Portfolio (1993–2019)

**A. Realized Volatility**

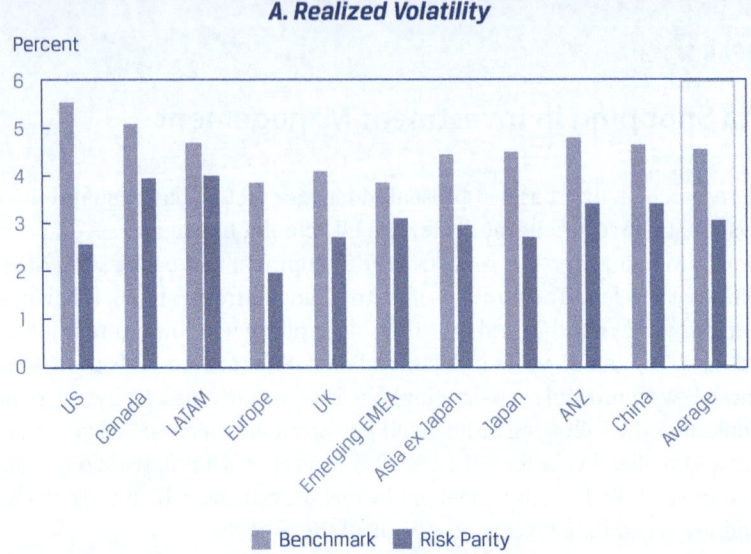

**B. Sharpe Ratio**

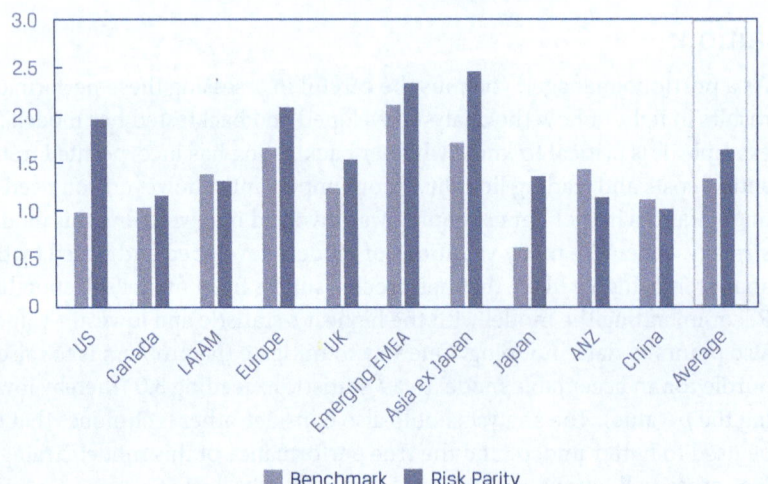

*Sources*: Bloomberg Finance LLP, FTSE Russell, S&P Capital IQ, Thomson Reuters, Wolfe Research Luo's QES.

### EXAMPLE 6

## Commons Problems in Backtesting

1. An analyst develops an investment strategy by picking the strategy with the highest *t*-statistic and lowest *p*-value after backtesting dozens of different strategies. This approach is an example of which common problem in backtesting?

    **A.** Reporting lag

**B.** Survivorship bias

**C.** Data snooping

## Solution to 1:

C is correct. Data snooping refers to making an inference—such as formulating an investment strategy—*after* looking at statistical results rather than testing a prior inference. A is incorrect because reporting lag refers to the fact that data describing a period is often available only after the period ends and is often subject to revision. B is incorrect because survivorship bias is a form of look-ahead bias in which results are based on a limited, biased sample of subjects (e.g., only surviving companies).

2. Point-in-time data are useful for avoiding the following problems that may affect backtesting *except*:

   **A.** data snooping.

   **B.** survivorship bias.

   **C.** look-ahead bias.

## Solution to 2:

A is correct. An analyst can still use a point-in-time dataset to make an inference based on statistical results rather than testing a prior inference. B and C are incorrect, because point-in-time data are useful for avoiding look-ahead bias and survivorship bias (a special case of look-ahead bias). Point-in-time data explicitly corrects for what is not known at a given point in time.

3. The fact that GDP figures for a quarter are not released by government statistical agencies until approximately 30 days after the quarter ends and often undergo several revisions thereafter creates a problem known as:

   **A.** data snooping.

   **B.** survivorship bias.

   **C.** reporting lag.

## Solution to 3:

C is correct. Reporting lag refers to the fact that data describing a period is often available only after the period ends and is often subject to revision, which certainly is true of GDP data.

4. Which of the following is an example of cross-validation?

   **A.** Maximum drawdown

   **B.** Backtesting with out-of-sample data

   **C.** Incorporating point-in-time data

## Solution to 4:

B is correct. Cross-validation is a technique that involves testing a hypothesis on a different set of data than that which was used to form the inference or initially test the hypothesis. Choice B is the definition of cross-validation.

5. An analyst performed a backtest on an investment strategy in June 2019, selecting the constituents of the Russell 3000 Index as the investment universe, and December 1985 and May 2019 as the start and end dates,

respectively. While discussing the results with some colleagues, the analyst was shown lists of the Russell 3000 Index constituents as of December 2005 and December 1995. She noticed that the lists included only 2,250 and 1,500 companies, respectively, of the Russell 3000 companies at May 2019. The analyst must correct her backtest for which problem?

**A.** Data snooping

**B.** Reporting lag

**C.** Look-ahead bias

## Solution to 5:

C is correct. The dataset the analyst uses assumes that the Russell 3000 Index constituents as of May 2019 are the same companies that constituted the index throughout the entire backtesting period. The backtest suffers from look-ahead bias, so conclusions drawn from it will be erroneous because it includes companies that did not exist (or were not index members) over the period starting in December 1985. To correct this problem, the analyst should use a dataset of point-in-time constituents of the Russell 3000 Index.

# 6. HISTORICAL SCENARIO ANALYSIS

☐ evaluate and interpret a historical scenario analysis

Rather than simply acknowledging or even ignoring structural breaks evident in backtesting results, an analyst should pay careful attention to different structural regimes and impacts to a strategy during regime changes. Historical scenario analysis is a type of backtesting that explores the performance and risk of an investment strategy in different structural regimes and at structural breaks. Two common examples of regime changes are from economic expansions to recessions and from low-volatility to high-volatility environments (and vice versa):

- *Expansions and recessions.* In the United States, since the start of our risk parity allocation strategy in 1993, the National Bureau of Economic Research (NBER) has recognized two official recessions: March 2001–November 2001 and December 2007–June 2009. These recessions are shown in Panel A of Exhibit 14. Although we ignore look-ahead bias in this brief example, it is important to note that business cycle inflection points—the beginning and end of expansions and recessions—are observed only in hindsight. For example, NBER did not identify December 2007 as the beginning of a recession in the United States until December 2008, and it did not identify June 2009 as the end of that recession until September 2010.

- *High- and low-volatility regimes.* The Chicago Board Options Exchange (CBOE) computes the VIX index, which gauges options-implied volatility on the S&P 500 Index. To transform the VIX into a volatility regime indicator, a five-year moving average is computed. Then, the periods when the VIX is above (below) its five-year moving average are defined as high-volatility (low-volatility) regime periods, as shown in Panel B of Exhibit 14 for 1993–2019.

# Historical Scenario Analysis

## Exhibit 14: Regime Changes

### A. Recession Indicator

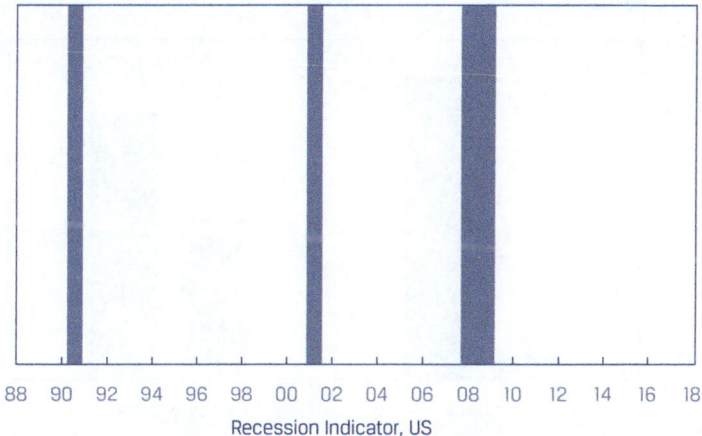

Recession Indicator, US

### B. VIX: High- vs. Low-Volatility Regimes

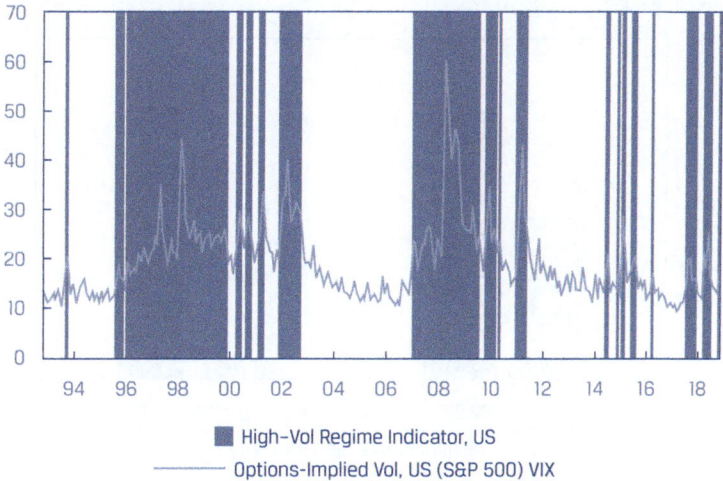

■ High-Vol Regime Indicator, US
—— Options-Implied Vol, US (S&P 500) VIX

*Sources*: Bloomberg Finance LLP, FTSE Russell, Haver, S&P Capital IQ, Thomson Reuters, Wolfe Research Luo's QES.

---

We can examine the benchmark and risk parity factor portfolios with respect to these two regimes—recession versus expansion and high volatility versus low volatility. As shown in Panel A of Exhibit 15, in terms of the Sharpe ratio, the RP strategy is quite robust to recession and the BM strategy struggles in recessions. Panel B of Exhibit 15 reveals that the BM strategy's performance is slightly worse in low-volatility regimes than in high-volatility regimes, whereas the RP strategy performs equally well in both volatility environments.

**Exhibit 15: Sharpe Ratio for BM and RP Portfolios in Different Macro Scenarios (1993–2019)**

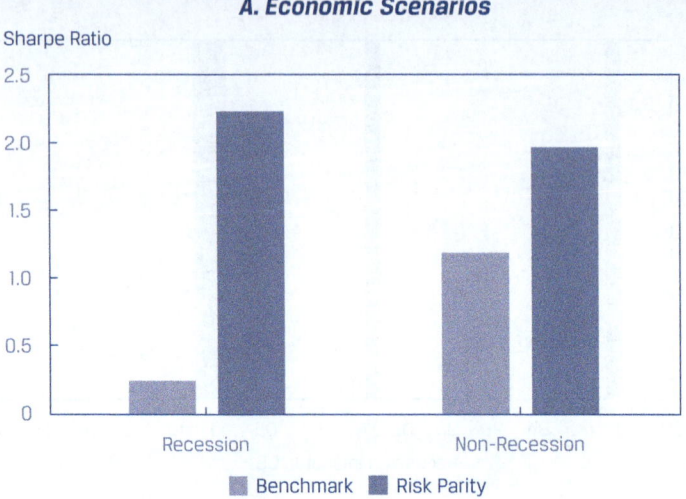

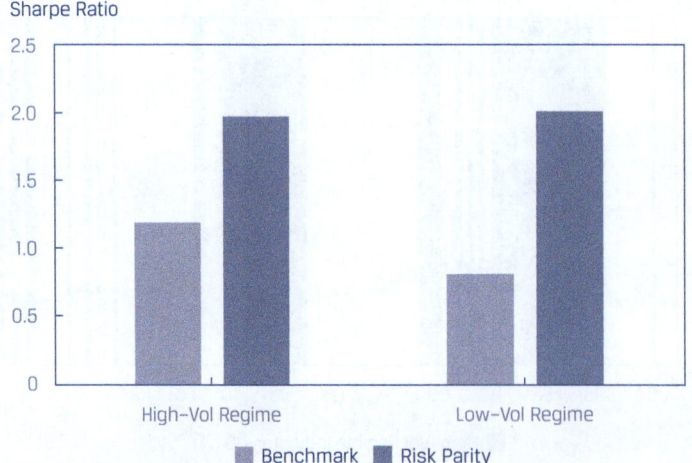

Sources: Bloomberg Finance LLP, FTSE Russell, S&P Capital IQ, Thomson Reuters, Wolfe Research Luo's QES.

In addition to the Sharpe ratio, a probability density plot can reveal additional information about the sensitivity of the return distributions of these investment strategies—for example, during recession versus non-recession periods. As shown in Exhibit 16, the distribution of returns for both the BM and RP strategies is flatter in a non-recession environment, which implies higher standard deviations during these regimes. The BM strategy suffers from negative skewness and excess kurtosis (i.e., fat tails to the left), regardless of the recession regime, but its average return is clearly lower in a recession environment (Panel A). The RP strategy also has a lower average return in the recession regime (Panel B), but its volatility and kurtosis are both also much lower compared with those of the BM strategy.

**Exhibit 16: Distribution of Returns for Factor Allocation Strategies: Recession and Non-Recession Regimes**

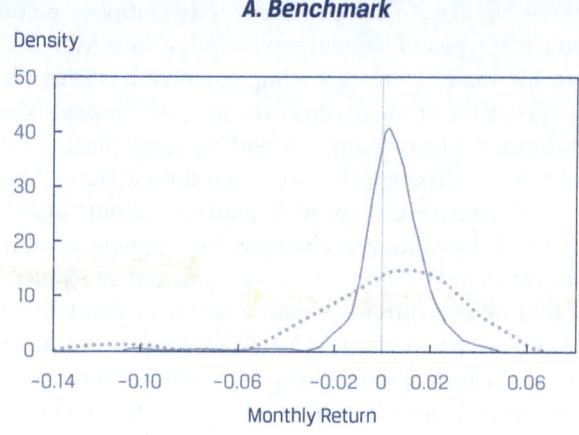

A. Benchmark

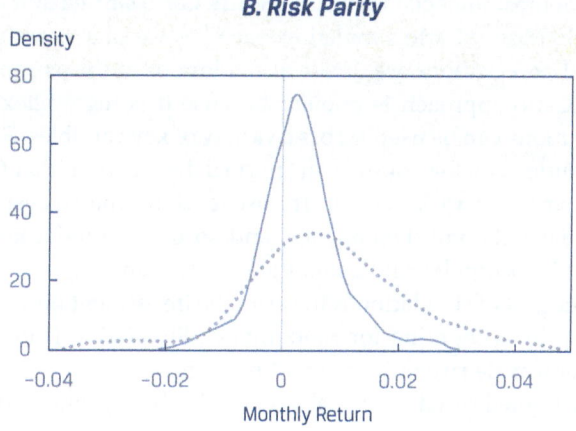

B. Risk Parity

—— Recession Regime   ......... Non-Recession Regime

Sources: Bloomberg Finance LLP, FTSE Russell, S&P Capital IQ, Thomson Reuters, Wolfe Research Luo's QES.

## SIMULATION ANALYSIS

7

☐ contrast Monte Carlo and historical simulation approaches

☐ explain inputs and decisions in simulation and interpret a simulation; and

In backtesting, we essentially assume that we can go back in time, apply our investment strategies, rebalance our portfolio(s), and measure performance. This idea is intuitive because it mimics how investing is done in reality—that is, forming our ideas, implementing our strategies, and incorporating new information as it arrives.

Backtesting implicitly assumes that the past is likely to repeat itself, however, and this assumption does not fully account for the dynamic nature of financial markets, which may include extreme upside and downside risks that have never occurred before. We now explore how simulation can provide a more complete picture.

There are two basic types of simulation: historical and Monte Carlo. In **historical simulation**, rather than assuming we implemented a strategy at some past date and collecting results as the strategy runs over time, we instead construct results by selecting returns at random from many different historical periods (windows) without regard to time-ordering. Although this approach does assume, like rolling-window backtesting, that past asset returns provide guidance about future asset returns, it relaxes a key restriction by randomly changing the sequencing of historical periods from which factor returns are drawn. As a result, historical simulation is essentially a non-deterministic rolling-window backtest. Historical simulation is widely used in investment management, particularly by banks for market risk analysis.

The problem with historical time-series data (such as factor returns) is that there is only one set of realized data to draw from—the past happened only one way. A critical assumption behind classical time-series analysis—that the data are stationary—is simply not true of most financial variables. **Monte Carlo simulation** overcomes many of these issues. In Monte Carlo simulation, each key variable is assigned a statistical distribution, and observations are drawn at random from the assigned distribution.

The Monte Carlo approach is popular because it is highly flexible; an array of different distributions can be used across a variety of key variables. Rather than using historical distributions or, for example, the normal distribution (that may only roughly approximate a particular variable's return distribution), the analyst can incorporate non-normality, fat tails, tail dependence, and so on, to model key variables. The downside is that it is complex and computationally intensive.

An important goal of simulation is to verify the investment performance obtained from backtesting by accounting for randomness. Simulation is especially useful in measuring the downside risk of investment strategies.

A properly designed simulation analysis is typically implemented in the following eight steps:

1. Determine what we want to understand: the target variable. This variable is typically the return on an investment strategy or $r_{p,t}$ (the return on portfolio $p$ at time $t$) and its distribution.

2. Specify key decision variables. Key decision variables are often the returns of each underlying asset, $r_{i,t}$ (the return on asset $i$ at time $t$), in the overall portfolio and the weight, $\omega_{i,t}$ (the weight of asset $i$ at time $t$), allocated to each asset in the portfolio. Once we know the returns and weights of all ($K$) underlying assets, we can readily compute the return of the portfolio as $r_{p,t} = \sum_{i=1}^{K} (\omega_{i,t} \times r_{i,t})$. Recall that the weight of each underlying asset is determined by the investment strategy being tested.

3. Specify the number of trials ($N$) to run. In practice, researchers typically choose between 1,000 and 10,000 simulation runs. The greater the number of trials, the more stable the predictions of performance and variance of performance. In theory, determining the optimal number of iterations is a complex topic (for an example, see Ritter, Schoelles, Quigley, and Klein 2011).

4. Define the distributional properties of the key decision variables. At this point, historical and Monte Carlo simulations diverge. In historical simulation, we draw from historical data. Conversely, in Monte Carlo simulation, we must specify a statistical distribution for each key decision variable. Although it is up to the user, the choice of distribution should be guided by

how well it has described historical observations. It might be appropriate to specify different functions (e.g., normal, lognormal, binomial) for different variables to account for the impact of correlations and tail dependence.

5. Use a random number generator to draw $N$ random numbers for each key decision variable.
6. For each set of simulated key decision variables, compute the value of the target variable. The value of the target variable is then saved for later analysis.
7. Repeat the same processes from Steps 5 and 6 until completing the desired number of trials ($N$).
8. Now we have a set of $N$ values of the target variable. In this context, it is $N$ returns of the investment strategy. The analyst can now calculate the typical metrics, such as mean return, volatility, Sharpe ratio, and the various downside risk metrics. For simulations, analysts typically use CVaR and maximum drawdown to characterize downside risk.

## Historical Simulation

Although backtesting and historical simulation rely on history to understand the future, they are different in that rolling-window backtesting is deterministic, whereas historical simulation incorporates randomness by randomly drawing returns from historical data rather than following each period chronologically.

First, a decision must be made about whether to sample from the historical returns with replacement or without replacement. Random sampling with replacement, also known as **bootstrapping**, is often used in investment research because the number of simulations needed is often larger than the size of the historical dataset.

Using the factor allocation strategies (BM and RP) for the eight factor portfolios as an example, we can perform a historical simulation as follows:

1. The target variables are the returns for the BM and RP multifactor portfolios.
2. The key decision variables are the returns of the eight underlying factor-based portfolios (the weights allocated to the eight factors are already known).
3. The simulation will be performed for $N = 1,000$ trials.
4. The historical simulation will be implemented using bootstrapped sampling. In this case, we will randomly draw a number from a uniform distribution (so there is equal probability of being selected) between 0 and 1.[2] Once a random number is generated, it is assigned to a specific historical month. Note that we have a total of 374 months of historical factor return data (April 1988–May 2019). We assign random numbers to specific months by dividing the span of the uniform distribution by the number of months ($1.0/374 = 0.00267$). Therefore, if the random number is between 0 and 0.00267, the first month is selected. Similarly, if the random number generator draws a number between 0.00267 and 0.00535 (= $2 \times 0.00267$), the second month is chosen, and so on.
5. The random number generator will then randomly draw 1,000 numbers from the uniform distribution between 0 and 1, and, as mentioned, sampling of the historical return data is with replacement. For example, as

---

[2] Technically, the random number generator will draw a random number that equals or is greater than 0 but is less than 1.

shown in Exhibit 17, the first five numbers generated are 0.59163, 0.32185, 0.76485, 0.89474, and 0.45431, which are then mapped to Months 222 (September 2006), 121 (April 1998), 287 (February 2012), 335 (February 2016), and 170 (May 2002), respectively. To be clear, months are mapped by dividing the random number by 0.00267, so Month 222 is determined as 0.59163/0.00267, Month 121 is 0.32185/0.00267, and so on.

**Exhibit 17: Factor Returns for the First Five Randomly Selected Months**

| Simulation # | Month | Random # | Month # | Earnings Yield | Book-to-Market | Earnings Growth | Momentum |
|---|---|---|---|---|---|---|---|
| 1 | 9/30/2006 | 0.59163 | 222 | 2.5% | 0.3% | (0.8%) | (0.0%) |
| 2 | 4/30/1998 | 0.32185 | 121 | 0.1% | 0.8% | (0.2%) | (0.5%) |
| 3 | 2/29/2012 | 0.76485 | 287 | (1.9%) | 0.5% | 1.7% | 1.8% |
| 4 | 2/29/2016 | 0.89474 | 335 | 2.5% | 2.4% | (0.4%) | (1.5%) |
| 5 | 5/31/2002 | 0.45431 | 170 | 6.3% | (3.3%) | 1.8% | 2.4% |

| Simulation # | Month | Random # | Month # | Earnings Revision | ROE | Debt/Equity | Earnings Quality |
|---|---|---|---|---|---|---|---|
| 1 | 9/30/2006 | 0.59163 | 222 | (0.8%) | 2.5% | 0.5% | (0.5%) |
| 2 | 4/30/1998 | 0.32185 | 121 | (0.1%) | (0.1%) | 0.3% | 1.6% |
| 3 | 2/29/2012 | 0.76485 | 287 | 1.8% | (0.5%) | (2.1%) | (0.8%) |
| 4 | 2/29/2016 | 0.89474 | 335 | (1.5%) | 1.2% | (1.2%) | 1.3% |
| 5 | 5/31/2002 | 0.45431 | 170 | 2.4% | 6.4% | (0.7%) | (1.2%) |

*Sources:* Bloomberg Finance LLP, FTSE Russell, S&P Capital IQ, Thomson Reuters, Wolfe Research Luo's QES.

6. Once a given month is selected, the returns of the corresponding eight factor portfolios represent one possible set of outcomes that we use to compute the values of our target variables—the returns of the BM and RP portfolios—using the prespecified factor weights. For example, the first trial picks the month of September 2006. The return of the benchmark portfolio is the equally weighted average of the eight factor returns, or 0.46% (= 0.125 × 2.5% + 0.125 × 0.3% + 0.125 × −0.8% + 0.125 × 0.0% + 0.125 × −0.8% + 0.125 × 2.5% + 0.125 × 0.5% + 0.125 × −0.5%).

To compute the return on the risk parity portfolio, we use the weights allocated to each of the eight factors for the final month (May 2019). As shown in Exhibit 18, for the first trial, September 2006, the weighted average return of the risk parity portfolio is 0.17%. It should be clear that each trial in the historical simulation assumes the simulated returns of the eight factors follow the same patterns observed in the sampled month—in this case, September 2006.

## Simulation Analysis

### Exhibit 18: How to Compute the Return of the Risk Parity Portfolio, Historical Simulation

| Asset (Factor) | September 2006 Return | May 2019 Weight | Weighted Return |
|---|---|---|---|
| Earnings yield | 2.5% | 6.0% | 0.2% |
| Book-to-market | 0.3% | 30.3% | 0.1% |
| Earnings growth | (0.8%) | 11.7% | (0.1%) |
| Momentum | (0.0%) | 5.2% | (0.0%) |
| Earnings revision | (0.8%) | 10.4% | (0.1%) |
| ROE | 2.5% | 6.3% | 0.2% |
| Debt/equity | 0.5% | 9.6% | 0.0% |
| Earnings quality | (0.5%) | 20.4% | (0.1%) |
| **Risk Parity Portfolio** | | | **0.17%** |

*Sources:* Bloomberg Finance LLP, FTSE Russell, S&P Capital IQ, Thomson Reuters, Wolfe Research Luo's QES.

7. The same simulation process (from Steps 5 to 6) is repeated for all 1,000 trials, generating a collection of 1,000 simulated returns for the benchmark and risk parity portfolios.

8. Finally, equipped with these 1,000 return scenarios, we can calculate performance metrics of interest (Sharpe ratio, CVaR, etc.) and plot the distributions of the *simulated* benchmark and risk parity portfolio returns.

As shown in Panel A of Exhibit 19, the results of the historical simulation (over the 1,000 iterations) suggest that the Sharpe ratios of the BM and RP strategies are largely in line with the rolling-window backtesting method demonstrated previously. In particular, the RP portfolio outperforms the BM portfolio in terms of Sharpe ratio according to both methodologies. Similarly, as shown in Panel B, both methodologies indicate that the RP portfolio carries substantially less downside risk, measured by CVaR, than the BM portfolio.

### Exhibit 19: Comparing Historical Simulation with Backtesting

#### A. Sharpe Ratio

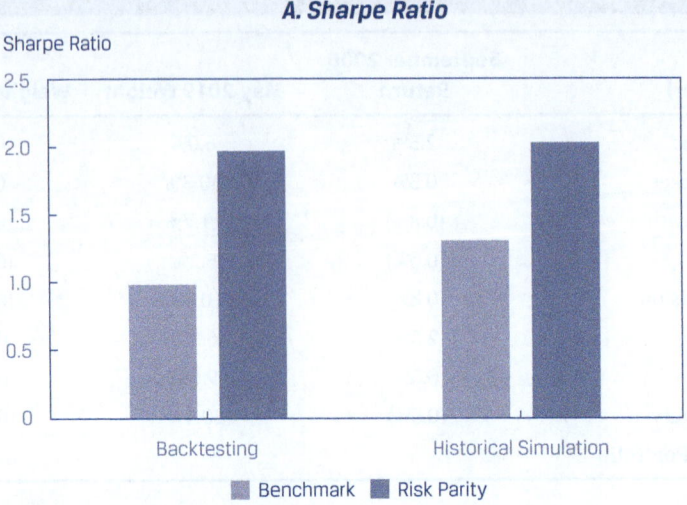

#### B. Conditonal Value-at-Risk

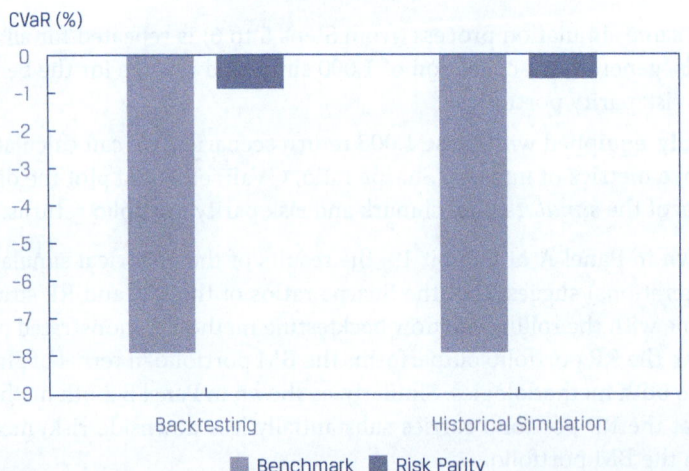

*Sources*: Bloomberg Finance LLP, FTSE Russell, S&P Capital IQ, Thomson Reuters, Wolfe Research Luo's QES.

In addition to capturing downside risk with a single number (e.g., CVaR), we can also plot the estimated probability distribution of returns for our two investment strategies. Panel A of Exhibit 20 plots the estimated probability distribution of returns for the BM and RP portfolios using backtested returns, whereas Panel B shows the estimated return distribution plots using the historical simulated returns. We can observe a broadly similar pattern between them. Both the backtesting and historical simulation approaches suggest that the RP portfolio returns are less volatile and more skewed to the right with lower downside risk (i.e., lower standard deviation and thinner tails) than the BM portfolio returns.

# Simulation Analysis

### Exhibit 20: Estimated Distribution Plots: Backtesting and Historical Simulation

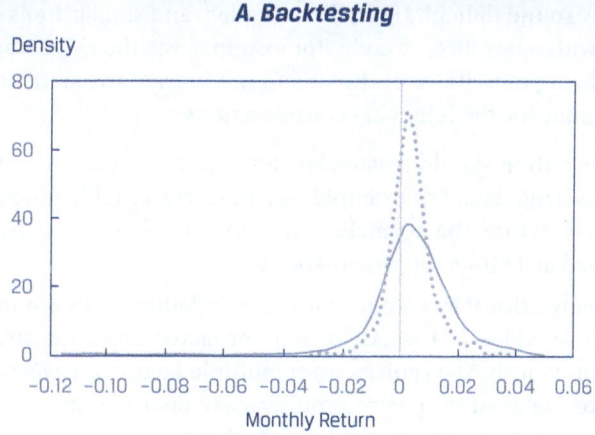

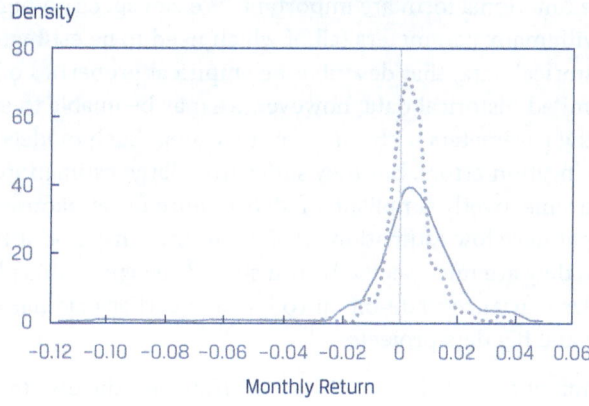

Sources: Bloomberg Finance LLP, FTSE Russell, S&P Capital IQ, Thomson Reuters, Wolfe Research Luo's QES.

## Monte Carlo Simulation

An important issue with historical simulation is that the data are limited to historical observations, which may not represent the future. This deficiency can be addressed with Monte Carlo simulation, which follows similar steps as historical simulation but with a few key differences.

First, we need to specify a functional form for each key decision variable. Exploratory data analysis—focusing on moments (i.e., mean, standard deviation, skewness, kurtosis) and tail dependence—is often crucial here. The usefulness of the Monte Carlo simulation technique critically depends on whether the functional form of the statistical distribution that we specify accurately reflects the true distribution of the underlying data. Because the data's true distribution is unknown, we need to be aware of the fact that our model, like all models, only provides guidance and will not be perfect.

Regression and distribution-fitting techniques are used to estimate the parameters (i.e., mean, standard deviation, skewness, kurtosis) underlying the statistical distributions of the key decision variables. This step is typically called model calibration. Although it may sound difficult, R, Python, Matlab, and similar tools can readily perform this task with a few lines of code (for example, see the fMultivar package in R).

Before finalizing our choice of the functional form of the statistical distribution, we need to account for the following considerations:

- The distribution should reasonably describe the key empirical patterns of the underlying data. For example, asset returns roughly follow a bell curve pattern; therefore, the normal distribution and Student's $t$-distribution are often used as first-cut approximations.
- It is equally critical to account for the correlations between multiple key decision variables. In the case of asset or factor allocation strategies, as shown previously, the returns from multiple factors are clearly correlated; therefore, we need to specify a multivariate distribution rather than modeling each factor or asset on a standalone basis.
- The complexity of the functional form and number of parameters that determine the functional form are important. We can specify a highly complex model with many parameters (all of which need to be estimated/calibrated from historical data) that describe the empirical properties of the data well. Given limited historical data, however, we may be unable to estimate all the underlying parameters with sufficient precision. Such models tend to have low specification errors, but they suffer from large estimation errors. At the other extreme, overly simplistic models require fewer parameters (therefore, they might have low estimation errors), but they may not fit the data well (because they are mis-specified). You should recognize this phenomenon as the bias–variance trade-off, introduced in earlier readings on machine learning and big data projects.

For simulation of asset or factor allocation strategies, the distribution of asset or factor returns is typically modeled as a multivariate normal distribution—as a first-cut approximation—which captures some of the key properties of the underlying data reasonably well. More importantly, a multivariate normal distribution can be fully specified with only a few key parameters—the mean, the standard deviation, and the covariance matrix. For $K$ assets, we need to estimate $K$ mean returns, $K$ standard deviations, and $[K \times (K-1)]/2$ correlations.

We have to be aware, however, that the multivariate normal distribution does not fully account for the empirical characteristics of (negative) skewness, excess kurtosis, and tail dependence apparent in the data. We will address these non-normal distribution properties shortly, when we cover sensitivity analysis.

Continuing with the same BM and RP strategies, the Monte Carlo simulation is performed as follows:

1. Our target variables are the returns for the BM and RP multifactor portfolios.
2. The key decision variables are the returns of the eight underlying factor-based portfolios.
3. We will perform the simulation using 1,000 trials.
4. We choose the multivariate normal distribution as our initial functional form. We calibrate the model—calculate the eight factor portfolio mean returns, the eight standard deviations, and the 28 elements of the covariance matrix—using the 374 months of historical factor return data (April 1988–May 2019).

5. The calibrated multivariate normal distribution is then used to simulate the future factor returns. The process by which this simulation occurs in the context of a multivariate normal distribution of eight random variables, corresponding to our eight factor portfolios, is complex. Suffice it to say, in this case, eight randomly generated numbers from the uniform distribution are mapped onto a point on the joint cumulative probability distribution function, and this point jointly determines the values of the eight factor returns in this trial.

Exhibit 21 shows the first five sets of Monte Carlo simulated returns for the eight underlying factor-based portfolios.

### Exhibit 21: Monte Carlo Simulation: First Five Simulations of Factor Returns Using a Multivariate Normal Distribution

| Simulation # | Earnings Yield | Book-to-Market | Earnings Growth | Momentum | Earnings Revision | ROE | Debt/ Equity | Earnings Quality |
|---|---|---|---|---|---|---|---|---|
| 1 | (3.2%) | (3.1%) | (0.2%) | 0.7% | 2.3% | (3.3%) | (1.7%) | 1.9% |
| 2 | (0.0%) | 3.5% | 0.9% | (0.4%) | 0.9% | (2.4%) | (3.5%) | (0.2%) |
| 3 | 0.7% | (1.8%) | 2.9% | 3.8% | 2.5% | 1.3% | (0.8%) | (0.0%) |
| 4 | 9.7% | (0.5%) | 1.2% | 3.8% | (0.9%) | 7.6% | (3.7%) | 1.6% |
| 5 | 1.7% | 0.2% | 2.9% | (0.2%) | 3.0% | 0.2% | (0.9%) | 0.2% |

*Sources:* Bloomberg Finance LLP, FTSE Russell, S&P Capital IQ, Thomson Reuters, Wolfe Research Luo's QES.

6. Once the returns of the eight factor portfolios are simulated, we can compute the values of our target variables—the returns of the BM and RP portfolios. For example, for the first simulated set of returns, the benchmark portfolio (with equally weighted factor returns) delivers a monthly return of −0.83% (= 0.125 × −3.2% + 0.125 × −3.1% + 0.125 × −0.2% + 0.125 × 0.7% + 0.125 × 2.3% + 0.125 × −3.3% + 0.125 × −1.7% + 0.125 × 1.9%).

Similarly, using the RP allocation factor weights for the final month, May 2019 (see Exhibit 18), the simulated risk parity portfolio return is −0.86% (= 0.06 × −3.2% + 0.303 × −3.1% + 0.117 × −0.2% + 0.052 × 0.7% + 0.104 × 2.3% + 0.063 × −3.3% + 0.096 × −1.7% + 0.204 × 1.9%).

7. Next, we repeat Steps 5 and 6 for all 1,000 trials to generate a collection of 1,000 returns for the benchmark and risk parity portfolios.

8. Finally, we assess the performance and risk profiles of our two investment strategies from the 1,000 simulated returns.

# EXAMPLE 7

## How to Interpret Results from Historical and Monte Carlo Simulations

1. Exhibit 22 shows the Sharpe ratios (Panel A) and downside risk measures, CVaRs (Panel B), for the returns of the benchmark and risk parity portfolios based on rolling-window backtesting, historical simulation, and Monte Carlo simulation of the returns on the eight underlying factor portfolios.

   Discuss similarities and differences among the three approaches for simulated performance of the benchmark and risk parity portfolios.

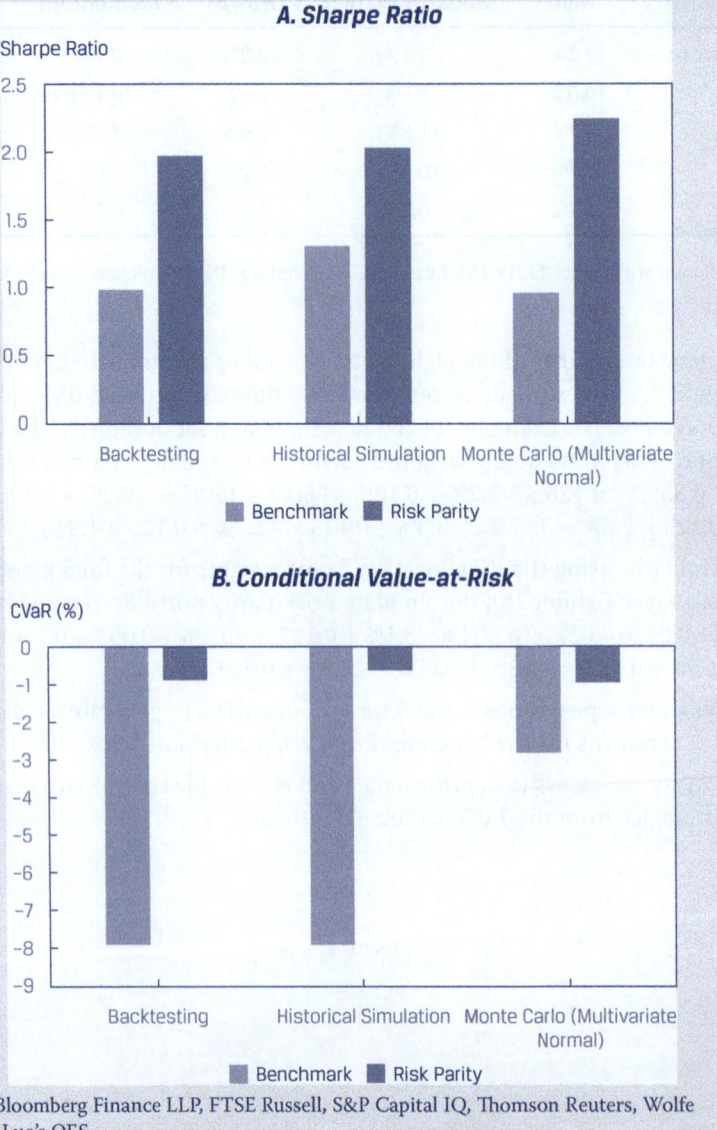

Exhibit 22: Comparing Backtesting, Historical Simulation, and Monte Carlo Simulation-Based Performance for the BM and RP Portfolios

*Sources:* Bloomberg Finance LLP, FTSE Russell, S&P Capital IQ, Thomson Reuters, Wolfe Research Luo's QES.

> **Solution:**
>
> Note that the backtesting approach provides realistic performance metrics assuming investors have been following the same trading rules throughout the past periods under investigation. The two simulation analyses are complementary to backtesting and deliver additional insights. In particular, they account for the random nature of investment data in different ways. Historical simulation randomly samples (with replacement) from the past record of asset returns, in a manner that each set of past monthly returns is equally likely to be selected. Monte Carlo simulation randomly samples from an assumed multivariate joint probability distribution (e.g., normal or another type of distribution), in a manner that the past record of asset returns is used to calibrate the parameters of the multivariate distribution. Therefore, these simulation methods are used to independently verify the results from the rolling-window backtesting.
>
> As shown in Panel A of Exhibit 22, the Sharpe ratio appears relatively insensitive to the simulation and backtesting methods used, with the RP strategy outperforming the BM strategy by nearly the same margin for each method. In contrast, CVaR seems to be sensitive to how randomness is treated. In particular, the Monte Carlo simulation appears to understate the downside risk of the BM strategy compared with both rolling-window backtesting and historical simulation methods (Panel B). Because the factor returns are negatively skewed with fat tails (i.e., excess kurtosis), the multivariate normal distribution assumption is likely to be underestimating the true downside risk of the BM strategy. This underestimation of risk appears only for the BM strategy because factor risks and correlations are not properly accounted for in the naive (equal) weighting scheme. Conversely, in this case, the risk parity strategy is robust to a non-normal factor return distribution, resulting in a portfolio with considerably lower downside risk.

# SENSITIVITY ANALYSIS

☐ demonstrate the use of sensitivity analysis

In addition to simulation, sensitivity analysis—a technique for exploring how a target variable is affected by changes in input variables (e.g., the distribution of asset or factor returns)—can be implemented to help managers further understand the potential risks and returns of their investment strategies.

The Monte Carlo simulation just described fits a multivariate normal distribution to the factor returns—a sensible first approximation because it requires relatively few parameters to be estimated from historical data. Despite the simplicity and wide adoption in practice, the multivariate normal distribution assumption fails to account for various empirical properties in the factor return distributions, including negative skewness and fat tails. Because the value of the simulation results depends crucially on whether the selected functional form is a reasonable proxy for the true distribution, we should conduct a sensitivity analysis by fitting our factor return data to a different distribution and repeating the Monte Carlo simulation accordingly. One alternative to test is a multivariate skewed Student's $t$-distribution.

The Student's *t*-distribution is a natural extension of the multivariate normal distribution, because it has the ability to account for the skewness and the excess kurtosis often observed in factor and asset return data. It is mathematically more complex, however, and requires estimating a larger number of parameters than a normal distribution.

With the goal of determining the sensitivity of our target variables (the returns of the benchmark and the risk parity portfolios) to the new factor return distribution assumption, the procedure for the new Monte Carlo simulation process is almost identical to the one performed previously. The only two exceptions are Steps 4 and 5. In Step 4, instead of fitting the data to a multivariate normal distribution, we calibrate our model to a multivariate skewed *t*-distribution. In Step 5, we simulate 1,000 sets of factor returns from this new distribution function. Then, as before, we assess the performance and risk profiles of our investment strategies from the 1,000 simulated returns.

Exhibit 23 shows the first five sets of simulated factor returns from this new model. As previously, we compute the values of our target variables for each set of simulated factor returns and then assess their performance and risk characteristics. For the first set of factor returns, the equal-weighted (i.e., 0.125 for each factor) benchmark portfolio achieves a simulated monthly return of 1.21%, and the risk parity portfolio (using May 2019 factor weights in Exhibit 18) delivers a simulated return of 0.75%.

### Exhibit 23: First Five Simulations of Factor Returns Using Multivariate Skewed *t*-Distribution

| Simulation # | Earnings Yield | Book-to-Market | Earnings Growth | Momentum | Earnings Revision | ROE | Debt/Equity | Earnings Quality |
|---|---|---|---|---|---|---|---|---|
| 1 | 2.0% | 0.3% | 1.7% | 3.1% | 2.0% | 0.9% | 0.2% | (0.5%) |
| 2 | 1.8% | (1.4%) | 0.2% | 4.9% | 1.8% | 2.7% | 0.4% | (0.1%) |
| 3 | (0.6%) | 0.2% | (1.0%) | (0.1%) | 0.4% | 1.5% | 1.6% | 0.9% |
| 4 | 11.2% | 2.6% | 1.8% | 1.5% | 2.2% | 9.6% | (2.9%) | (1.9%) |
| 5 | (3.9%) | (1.3%) | 0.9% | 0.9% | 0.8% | (3.5%) | 2.9% | 0.2% |

*Sources:* Bloomberg Finance LLP, FTSE Russell, S&P Capital IQ, Thomson Reuters, Wolfe Research Luo's QES.

Turning to the performance and risk profiles of our investment strategies, shown in Panel A of Exhibit 24, we note that the Sharpe ratio appears insensitive to any of the particular simulation methods used by consistently suggesting that the risk parity allocation strategy outperforms the benchmark strategy. Downside risk (expressed as CVaR), however, appears quite sensitive to the choice of simulation approach for the BM strategy, but not very sensitive for the RP strategy (Panel B). If we focus on the BM strategy, the CVaR results from historical simulation and rolling-window backtesting resemble each other very closely. The CVaR results of both (multivariate skewed *t*- and multivariate normal) Monte Carlo simulations are also very similar: Both underestimate the downside risk of the BM strategy. This finding suggests that additional sensitivity analyses should be run with different functional forms for the factor return distributions.

## Sensitivity Analysis

**Exhibit 24: Comparing Simulation Methods with Backtesting**

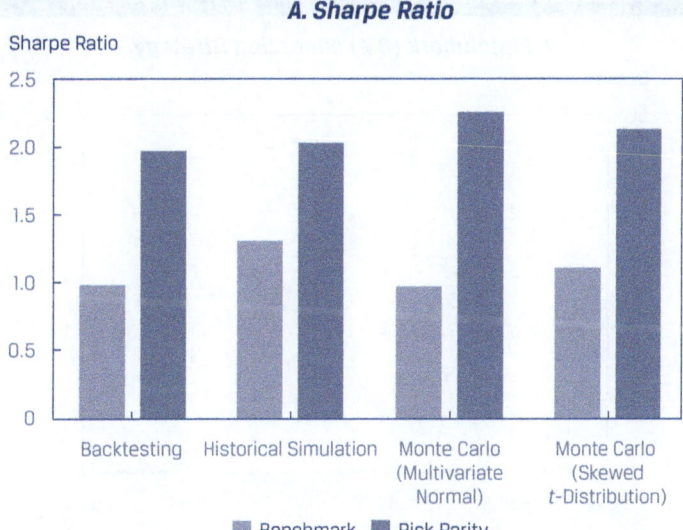

A. Sharpe Ratio

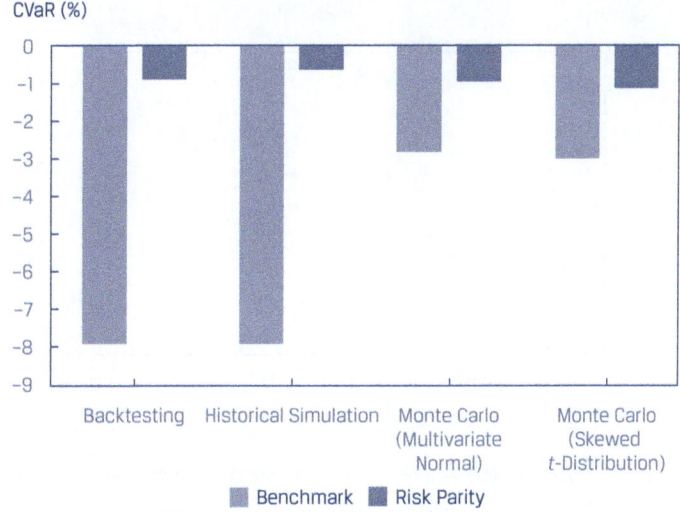

B. Conditional Value-at-Risk

*Sources*: Bloomberg Finance LLP, FTSE Russell, S&P Capital IQ, Thomson Reuters, Wolfe Research Luo's QES.

---

Estimated probability density plots, in Panel A of Exhibit 25, show that the difference between the historical simulation and the two Monte Carlo methods is rather large for the BM strategy. Given the negative skewness and excess kurtosis of the BM strategy's returns, which is apparent from the shape of the historical simulation return distribution, it is not surprising that the two Monte Carlo simulations fail to account sufficiently for this left-tail risk property. Conversely, because the distribution of the RP strategy's returns is relatively symmetric and without much excess kurtosis, all three simulation methods provide a fairly similar picture (Panel B).

### Exhibit 25: Estimated Distribution Plots for BM and RP Strategies Using Three Different Simulations

#### A. Benchmark (BM) Allocation Strategy

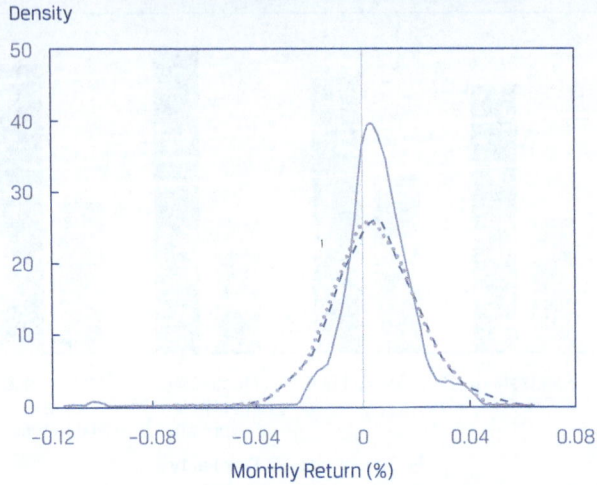

#### B. Risk Parity (RP) Allocation Strategy

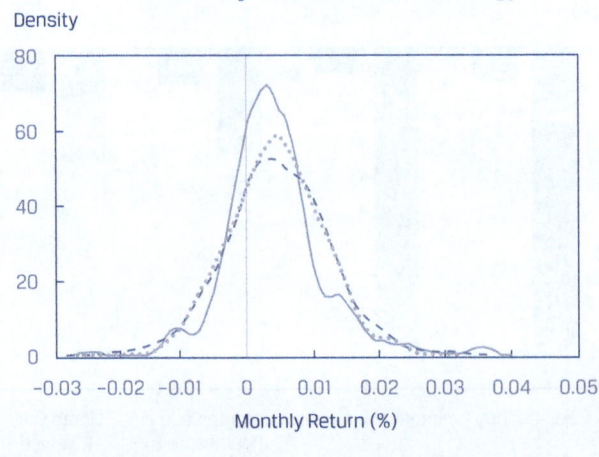

——— Historical Simulation ......... Monte Carlo (Multivariate Normal)
- - - - - Monte Carlo (Skewed *t*-Distribution)

*Sources*: Bloomberg Finance LLP, FTSE Russell, S&P Capital IQ, Thomson Reuters, Wolfe Research Luo's QES.

### EXAMPLE 8

### Simulating the Performance of Factor Allocation Strategies

Earlier, Sarah Koh presented her team's backtesting results for the factor-based allocation strategies being considered by an important client, SWF Fund. Now, while presenting the simulation results for these same strategies, SWF Fund's investment committee asks Koh the following questions:

# Sensitivity Analysis

1. The following are caveats regarding the use of rolling-window backtesting in assessing investment strategies *except*:

   **A.** this technique implicitly assumes that the same pattern of past performance is likely to repeat itself over time.

   **B.** this technique may not fully account for the dynamic nature of financial markets and potentially extreme downside risks.

   **C.** this technique is intuitive, because it mimics how investing is done in reality—that is, forming ideas, testing strategies, and implementing periodically.

## Solution to 1:

C is correct, because it is not a caveat in using rolling-window backtesting. A and B are incorrect because they are caveats in the use of this technique.

2. Which of the following situations is *most likely* to involve data snooping?

   **A.** A researcher performs rolling-window backtesting of a new momentum strategy using 20 years of point-in-time (PIT) data from the United States. She cross-validates results by similarly analyzing PIT data from the following markets: mainland China, Asia ex-Japan, Europe, the United Kingdom, and Canada.

   **B.** A researcher tries many different modeling techniques, backtesting each of them, and then picking the best-performing model without accounting for model selection bias.

   **C.** A researcher sets a relatively high hurdle, a *t*-statistic greater than 3.0, for assessing whether a newly discovered factor is statistically significant.

## Solution to 2:

B is correct, because this situation most likely involves data snooping. A and C are incorrect because these are approaches to avoiding data snooping.

3. Which of the following situations is *least likely* to involve scenario analysis?

   **A.** Simulating the performance and risk of investment strategies by first using stocks in the Nikkei 225 Index and then using stocks in the TOPIX 1000 Index.

   **B.** Simulating the performance and risk of investment strategies in both "trade agreement" and "no-trade-agreement" environments.

   **C.** Simulating the performance and risk of investment strategies in both high-volatility and low-volatility environments.

## Solution to 3:

A is correct, because there is no structural break or different structural regime. B and C are incorrect because they involve structural breaks/different structural regimes and thus represent different scenarios.

4. Which one of the following statements concerning historical simulation and Monte Carlo simulation is *false*?

   **A.** Historical simulation randomly samples (with replacement) from the past record of asset returns, where each set of past monthly returns is equally likely to be selected.

B. Neither historical simulation nor Monte Carlo simulation makes use of a random number generator.

C. Monte Carlo simulation randomly samples from an assumed multivariate joint probability distribution in which the past record of asset returns is used to calibrate the parameters of the multivariate distribution.

### Solution to 4:

B is correct, because this statement is false. A and C are incorrect because they are true statements about historical and Monte Carlo simulation, respectively.

5. Which one of the following statements concerning Monte Carlo simulation is *false*?

   A. When simulating multiple assets (factors) whose returns are correlated, it is crucial to specify a multivariate distribution rather than modeling each asset on a standalone basis.

   B. Regression and distribution-fitting techniques are used to estimate the parameters underlying the statistical distributions of the key decision variables.

   C. The Monte Carlo simulation process is deterministic and non-random in nature.

### Solution to 5:

C is correct, because this statement is false. A and B are incorrect because they are true statements about Monte Carlo simulation.

6. Which of the following situations concerning simulation of a multifactor asset allocation strategy is *most likely* to involve sensitivity analysis?

   A. Changing the specified multivariate distribution assumption from a normal to a skewed *t*-distribution to better account for skewness and fat tails

   B. Splitting the rolling window between periods of recession and non-recession

   C. Splitting the rolling window between periods of high volatility and low volatility

### Solution to 6:

A is correct, because this choice represents sensitivity analysis. B and C are incorrect because these choices represent scenario analysis.

## SUMMARY

In this reading, we have discussed how to perform rolling-window backtesting—a widely used technique in the investment industry. We also described how to use scenario analysis and simulation along with sensitivity analysis to supplement backtesting, so investors can better account for the randomness in data that may not be fully captured by backtesting.

- The main objective of backtesting is to understand the risk–return trade-off of an investment strategy by approximating the real-life investment process.

- The basic steps in rolling-window backtesting are specifying the investment hypothesis and goals, determining the rules and processes behind an investment strategy, forming an investment portfolio according to those rules, rebalancing the portfolio periodically, and computing the performance and risk profiles of the strategy.

- In the rolling-window backtesting methodology, researchers use a rolling-window (or walk-forward) framework, fit/calibrate factors or trade signals based on the rolling window, rebalance the portfolio periodically, and then track the performance over time. Thus, rolling-window backtesting is a proxy for actual investing.

- Analysts need to pay attention to several behavioral issues in backtesting, including survivorship bias and look-ahead bias.

- Asset (and factor) returns are often negatively skewed and exhibit excess kurtosis (fat tails) and tail dependence compared with a normal distribution. As a result, standard rolling-window backtesting may be unable to fully account for the randomness in asset returns, particularly on downside risk.

- Financial data often face structural breaks. Scenario analysis can help investors understand the performance of an investment strategy in different structural regimes.

- Historical simulation is relatively straightforward to perform but shares pros and cons similar to those of rolling-window backtesting. For example, a key assumption these methods share is that the distribution pattern from the historical data is sufficient to represent the uncertainty in the future. Bootstrapping (or random draws with replacement) is often used in historical simulation.

- Monte Carlo simulation is a more sophisticated technique than historical simulation. In Monte Carlo simulation, the most important decision is the choice of functional form of the statistical distribution of decision variables/return drivers. Multivariate normal distribution is often used in investment research, owing to its simplicity. However, a multivariate normal distribution cannot account for negative skewness and fat tails observed in factor and asset returns.

- Sensitivity analysis, a technique for exploring how a target variable and risk profiles are affected by changes in input variables, can further help investors understand the limitations of conventional Monte Carlo simulation (which typically assumes a multivariate normal distribution as a starting point). A multivariate skewed $t$-distribution considers skewness and kurtosis but requires estimation of more parameters and thus is more likely to suffer from larger estimation errors.

# PRACTICE PROBLEMS

## The following information relates to questions 1-8

Kata Rom is an equity analyst working for Gimingham Wealth Partners (GWP), a large investment advisory company. Rom meets with Goran Galic, a Canadian private wealth client, to explain investment strategies used by GWP to generate portfolio alpha for its clients.

Rom states that GWP is recognized in the Canadian investment industry as a leading factor-based value portfolio manager and describes how GWP creates relevant investment strategies and explains GWP's backtesting process. Rom notes the following:

| | |
|---|---|
| Statement 1 | Using historical data, backtesting approximates a real-life investment process to illustrate the risk–return tradeoff of a particular proposed investment strategy. |
| Statement 2 | Backtesting is used almost exclusively by quantitative investment managers and rarely by fundamental investment managers, who are more concerned with information such as forward estimates of company earnings, macroeconomic factors, and intrinsic values. |

Galic, who is 62 years old, decides to allocate C$2 million (representing 10% of his net worth) to an account with GWP and stipulates that portfolio assets be restricted exclusively to domestic securities. Although GWP has not backtested its strategies with such a restriction, it has backtested its strategies using a global index that includes domestic securities. Rom shows the following risk measures to Galic for three factor portfolios.

### Exhibit 1: Downside Risk Measures for Model Factors

| Risk Measure | Factor 1 | Factor 2 | Factor 3 |
|---|---|---|---|
| Value at risk (VaR) (95%) | (6.49%) | (0.77%) | (2.40%) |
| Conditional VaR (CVaR) (95%) | (15.73%) | (4.21%) | (3.24%) |
| Maximum drawdown | 35.10% | 38.83% | 45.98% |

Galic asks Rom, "What happens if the future is different from the past?" Rom gives the following replies:

| | |
|---|---|
| Statement 3 | Although backtesting can offer some comfort, you are correct that it does have a weakness: Backtesting generally does not capture the dynamic nature of financial markets and in particular may not capture extreme downside risk. |

## Practice Problems

Statement 4   As a result, we have captured extreme downside risk and the dynamic nature of financial markets by using the Value-at-Risk and Conditional Value-at-Risk measures.

In an effort to make Galic fully aware of the risks inherent in GWP's strategies, Rom describes a recent study that investigated the return distributions of value and momentum factors that GWP uses to construct portfolios. The study found that these distributions were non-normal based on their negative skewness, excess kurtosis, and tail dependence. Rom indicated that investment strategies based on this type of data are prone to significantly higher downside risk. Rom informs Galic that GWP also uses a technique commonly referred to as scenario analysis to examine how strategies perform in different structural regimes. Exhibit 2 compares the performance of two of GWP's factor allocation strategies in different regimes:

### Exhibit 2: Scenario Analysis Using the Sharpe Ratio

| Strategy/Regime | High Volatility | Low Volatility | Recession | Non-recession |
|---|---|---|---|---|
| Strategy I | 0.88 | 0.64 | 0.20 | 1.00 |
| Strategy II | 1.56 | 1.60 | 1.76 | 1.52 |

Galic is surprised to see that some of the backtest results are unfavorable. He asks, "Why has GWP not considered strategies that perform better in backtesting?" Galic recently met with Fastlane Wealth Managers, who showed much better performance results. The portfolio manager at Fastlane told Galic that the company selects the top-performing strategies after performing thousands of backtests.

1. Which of Rom's statements concerning backtesting is correct?

    A. Only Statement 1

    B. Only Statement 2

    C. Both Statement 1 and Statement 2

2. Which key parameter needs to be changed for a new backtest that includes Galic's restrictions?

    A. Start and end dates

    B. Consideration of transaction costs

    C. Investment universe

3. Galic's concern embedded in the question "What happens if the future is different from the past?" is a problem most relevant for which investment strategy evaluation technique?

    A. Sensitivity analysis

    B. Backtesting

    C. Monte Carlo simulation

4. Which of the following conclusions of Exhibit 1 is *least* likely to be true?
   A. 5% of the time, losses from Factor 1 would be at least 6.49%.
   B. When the VaR is exceeded in Factor 1, we should expect an average loss of 15.73%.
   C. 5% of the time, losses from Factor 2 are likely to be worse than losses from Factor 1.

5. Based on the statistical study performed by GWP, which of the following represents a suggested course of action if GWP were to conduct Monte Carlo simulation analyses on the factor strategies?
   A. Inverse transformation
   B. Bootstrapping
   C. Sensitivity analysis

6. Based on Exhibit 1, which factor has the smallest downside risk as measured by the weighted average of all losses that exceed a threshold?
   A. Factor 1
   B. Factor 2
   C. Factor 3

7. The approach used by Fastlane Wealth Managers *most likely* incorporates:
   A. risk parity.
   B. data snooping.
   C. cross-validation.

8. Comparing the two strategies in Exhibit 2, the *best* risk-adjusted performance is demonstrated by:
   A. Strategy II in periods of low volatility and recession.
   B. Strategy I in periods of high volatility and non-recession.
   C. Strategy II in periods of high volatility and non-recession.

## The following information relates to questions 9-16

Emily Yuen is a senior analyst for a consulting firm that specializes in assessing equity strategies using backtesting and simulation techniques. She is working with an assistant, Cameron Ruckey, to develop multifactor portfolio strategies based on nine factors common to the growth style of investing. To do so, Yuen and Ruckey plan to construct nine separate factor portfolios and then use them to create factor-weighted allocation portfolios.

Yuen tasks Ruckey with specifying the investment universe and determining the availability of appropriate reporting data in vendor databases. Ruckey selects

## Practice Problems

a vendor database that does not provide point-in-time data, so he adjusts the database to include point-in-time constituent stocks and a reporting lag of four months.

Next, Yuen and Ruckey run initial backtests on the nine factor portfolios, calculating performance statistics and key metrics for each. For backtesting purposes, the portfolios are rebalanced monthly over a 30-year time horizon using a rolling-window procedure.

Yuen and Ruckey consider a variety of metrics to assess the results of the factor portfolio backtests. Yuen asks Ruckey what can be concluded from the data for three of the factor strategies in Exhibit 1:

### Exhibit 1: Backtest Metrics for Factor Strategies

|  | Factor 1 | Factor 2 | Factor 3 |
|---|---|---|---|
| VaR (95%) | (3.9%) | (1.3%) | (8.4%) |
| Standard deviation of returns | 2.1% | 1.2% | 4.6% |
| Maximum drawdown | 27.2% | 8.3% | 59.7% |

Ruckey tells Yuen the following:

Statement 1  We do not need to consider maximum drawdown, because standard deviation sufficiently characterizes risk.

Statement 2  Factor 2 has the highest downside risk.

From her professional experience Yuen knows that benchmark and risk parity factor portfolios, in which factors are equally weighted and equally risk weighted, respectively, are popular with institutional and high-net-worth clients. To gain a more complete picture of these investment strategies' performance, Yuen and Ruckey design a Benchmark Portfolio (A) and a Risk Parity Portfolio (B), and then run two simulation methods to generate investment performance data based on the underlying factor portfolios, assuming 1,000 simulation trials for each approach:

Approach 1  Historical simulation

Approach 2  Monte Carlo simulation

Yuen and Ruckey discuss the differences between the two approaches and then design the simulations, making key decisions at various steps. During the process, Yuen expresses a number of concerns:

Concern 1: Returns from six of the nine factors are correlated.

Concern 2: The distribution of Factor 1 returns exhibits excess kurtosis and negative skewness.

Concern 3: The number of simulations needed for Approach 1 is larger than the size of the historical dataset.

For each approach, Yuen and Ruckey run 1,000 trials to obtain 1,000 returns for Portfolios A and B. To help understand the effect of the skewness and excess kurtosis observed in the Factor 1 returns on the performance of Portfolios A and B, Ruckey suggests simulating an additional 1,000 factor returns using a multivariate skewed Student's $t$-distribution, then repeating the Approach 2 simulation.

9. Following Ruckey's adjustments to the initial vendor database, backtested returns will *most likely* be subject to:
   A. stale data.
   B. data snooping
   C. p-hacking

10. Based on Exhibit 1, Ruckey should conclude that:
    A. Factor Strategy 3 has the highest portfolio turnover.
    B. Factor Strategy 2 has less downside risk than Strategy 3.
    C. Factor Strategy 2 has the highest returns.

11. Which of Ruckey's statements about Exhibit 1 is incorrect?
    A. Only Statement 1
    B. Only Statement 2
    C. Both Statement 1 and Statement 2

12. Simulation Approach 1 (historical simulation) differs from Approach 2 (Monte Carlo simulation) in that:
    A. it is deterministic.
    B. a functional form of the statistical distribution for each decision variable needs to be specified.
    C. it assumes that sampling the returns from the actual data provides sufficient guidance about future asset returns.

13. To address Concern 1 when designing Approach 2, Yuen should:
    A. model each factor or asset on a standalone basis.
    B. calculate the 15 covariance matrix elements needed to calibrate the model.
    C. specify a multivariate distribution rather than modeling each factor or asset on a standalone basis.

14. Based on Concern 2, the Factor 1 strategy is *most likely* to:
    A. be favored by risk-averse investors.
    B. generate surprises in the form of negative returns.
    C. have return data that line up tightly around a trend line.

15. To address Concern 3 when designing Approach 1, Yuen should:
    A. add monthly return observations to the dataset using interpolation.
    B. randomly sample from the historical returns with replacement.
    C. choose the multivariate normal distribution as the initial functional form.

**Practice Problems**

16. The process Ruckey suggests to better understand how the performance of Portfolios A and B using Approach 2 is affected by the distribution of Factor 1 returns is *best* described as:

    A. data snooping.

    B. sensitivity analysis.

    C. inverse transformation.

# SOLUTIONS

1. A is correct. Statement 1 is correct because the main objective of backtesting is to understand the risk–return tradeoff of an investment strategy by approximating the real-life investment process.

   B is incorrect because Statement 2 is inaccurate. Although backtesting fits quantitative and systematic investment styles more naturally, it has also been heavily used by fundamental managers.

   C is incorrect because Statement 2 is not accurate. Backtesting, used in quantitative and systematic investment styles, is also heavily used by fundamental managers.

2. C is correct. Investment universe represents the securities in which a strategy can potentially invest. Galic's restriction to exclusively own domestic securities means the investment universe of a backtest for a strategy for Galic's account should use a domestic rather than global investment universe.

   A is incorrect. Galic's restriction to domestic securities does not affect the start and end dates for a backtest.

   B is incorrect. Galic's restriction to domestic securities does not change the inclusion of transaction costs in the study.

3. B is correct. An implicit assumption of backtesting is that past returns are a guide to future asset returns.

   A is incorrect. Sensitivity analysis refers to modifying assumptions such as probability distributions of key variables in a Monte Carlo simulation, which is a non-deterministic evaluation technique that does not use historical data.

   C is incorrect. Monte Carlo simulation is a non-deterministic evaluation technique that does not use historical data.

4. C is correct. The VaR metrics in Exhibit 1 show that 5% of the time, losses will be at least 6.49% and 0.77%, respectively, for Factor 1 and Factor 2. The CVaR metrics in Exhibit 1 show that the weighted average of all loss outcomes that exceed the VaR loss are 15.73% and 4.21% for Factor 1 and Factor 2, respectively. Thus, A is true because it correctly defines VaR, and B is true because it correctly defines CVaR, whereas C is untrue because both VaR and CVaR are lower for Factor 2 than Factor 1.

5. C is correct. Performing sensitivity analysis represents best practice given these characteristics, because the user could test different probability distributions that relax the assumptions of the normal distribution, for example.

   A is incorrect. Inverse transformation is a method of random observation generation, often used in simulation.

   B is incorrect. Bootstrapping refers to random sampling with replacement, often used in historical simulation.

6. C is correct. Exhibit 1 presents three downside risk measures: VaR, CVaR, and maximum drawdown. Conditional VaR is defined as the weighted average of all loss outcomes in the return distribution that exceed the VaR loss. Thus, CVaR is a more comprehensive measure of tail loss than VaR. Based on Exhibit 1, the factor with the smallest downside risk based on CVaR is Factor 3.

7. B is correct. The fact that the two firms' investment performance results differ over similar time horizons using the same data and factors may be the result of selection bias. Data snooping is a type of selection bias. Fastlane Wealth Manag-

ers is most likely selecting the best-performing modeling approach and publishing its results (i.e., data snooping).

A is incorrect because risk parity is a portfolio construction technique that accounts for the volatility of each factor and the correlations of returns among all factors to be combined in the portfolio. It is not regarded as selection bias.

C is incorrect because cross-validation is a technique used in the machine learning field, as well as in backtesting investment strategies, to partition data for model training and testing. It is not considered selection bias.

8. A is correct. Using the Sharpe ratio, the best risk-adjusted relative performance can be determined by comparing the sensitivity of the two strategies under differing macroeconomic regimes: recession versus non-recession and high volatility versus low volatility. The best risk-adjusted return will exhibit the highest Sharpe ratio. Strategy II demonstrates higher risk-adjusted returns compared with Strategy I under all four macroeconomic conditions, particularly in periods of low volatility, when the Sharpe ratio outperformance is 0.96, and recessions, when the Sharpe ratio outperformance is 1.56.

9. A is correct. A reporting lag of four months is likely to introduce stale data into the backtest because many large-capitalization companies report earnings within 30–50 days of quarter end. Although assuming four months (120 days) of reporting lag will eliminate a source of look-ahead bias, it introduces a new problem (i.e., stale data).

    B and C are incorrect. Data snooping and p-hacking refer to the same problem: a flawed approach to using data to make decisions. Data snooping and p-hacking are not characteristics of data, nor can they be added to a dataset by making an adjustment.

10. B is correct. Both VaR and maximum drawdown are downside risk measures, and both measures are lower for Strategy 2 than Strategy 3.

    A is incorrect. We cannot deduce portfolio turnover from the metrics provided in Exhibit 1.

    C is incorrect. We cannot deduce returns from the metrics provided in Exhibit 1.

11. C is correct. Both statements are incorrect. Statement 1 is incorrect because maximum drawdown and standard deviation are different measures. Maximum drawdown is typically used to represent downside risk, because it is the minimum cumulative return observed. Standard deviation is a measure of volatility. Although the two measures may be correlated, they are not substitutes for each other. Statement 2 is incorrect because two downside risk measures are presented: VaR and maximum drawdown. Factor Strategy 2 has the lowest reading for both measures, indicating that it has the *least* downside risk among the three strategies presented in Exhibit 1.

12. C is correct. Approach 1 is a historical simulation and assumes that past asset returns provide sufficient guidance about future asset returns.

    A is incorrect because both approaches are non-deterministic and random in nature. Approach 1 is a historical simulation, and Approach 2 is a Monte Carlo simulation.

    B is incorrect because Approach 1 is a historical simulation and each random variable of interest (key driver and/or decision variable) is randomly drawn from historical data. A functional form of the statistical distribution of returns for each decision variable needs to be specified for a Monte Carlo simulation, which is Approach 2.

13. C is correct. Approach 2 is a Monte Carlo simulation. The returns of Portfolios A and B are driven by the returns of the nine underlying factor portfolios (based on nine common growth factors). In the case of asset or factor allocation strategies, the returns from six of the nine factors are correlated, and therefore it is necessary to specify a multivariate distribution rather than modeling each factor or asset on a standalone basis.

    A is incorrect because Approach 2 is a Monte Carlo simulation to generate investment performance data for the nine underlying factor portfolios. The returns of six of the nine factors are correlated, which means specifying a multivariate distribution rather than modeling each factor or asset on a standalone basis.

    B is incorrect because the analyst should calculate the elements of the covariance matrix for all factors, not only the correlated factors. Doing so entails calculating 36, not 15, elements of the covariance matrix. Approach 2 is a Monte Carlo simulation using the factor allocation strategies for Portfolios A and B for the nine factor portfolios, the returns of which are correlated, which means specifying a multivariate distribution. To calibrate the model, a few key parameters need to be calculated: the mean, the standard deviation, and the covariance matrix. For 9 assets, we need to estimate 9 mean returns, 9 standard deviations, and $\frac{9 \times (9 - 1)}{2}$ = 36 elements of the covariance matrix. Assuming just the 6 correlated assets, the calculation is $\frac{6 \times (6 - 1)}{2}$ = 15.

14. B is correct. The distribution of Factor 1 returns exhibits excess kurtosis and negative skewness (relative to the normal distribution). The excess kurtosis implies that these strategies are more likely to generate surprises, meaning extreme returns, whereas the negative skewness suggests those surprises are more likely to be negative (than positive).

    A is incorrect because risk-averse investors are more likely to prefer distribution properties such as positive skew (higher probability of positive returns) and lower to moderate kurtosis (lower probability of extreme negative surprises). The distribution of Factor 1 returns exhibits excess kurtosis and negative skewness.

    C is incorrect because the distribution of Factor 1 returns exhibits excess kurtosis and negative skewness. The joint distribution of such returns is rarely multivariate normal—so, typically the means and variances of these returns and the correlations between them are insufficient to describe the joint return distribution. In other words, the return data do not line up tightly around a trend line because of fat tails and outliers.

15. B is correct. Random sampling with replacement, also known as bootstrapping, is often used in historical simulations because the number of simulations needed is often larger than the size of the historical dataset. Because Approach 1 is a historical simulation and Concern 3 notes that the number of simulations needed is larger than the size of the historical dataset, bootstrapping should be used.

    A is incorrect because this approach would result in creating observations that do not exist in the historical record. Doing so would violate the assumption and procedures of historical simulation.

    C is incorrect because choosing the multivariate normal distribution as the initial functional form is typically done in a Monte Carlo simulation (Approach 2), not in a historical simulation (Approach 1). Historical simulation randomly samples from the historical dataset by drawing a number from a uniform distribution so that there is equal probability of being selected. Choice of distribution would not address the concern about the size of the dataset.

16. B is correct. Sensitivity analysis can be implemented to help managers understand how the target variable (portfolio returns) and risk profiles are affected by changes in input variables. Approach 2 is a Monte Carlo simulation, and the

results depend on whether the multivariate normal distribution is the correct functional form or a reasonable proxy for the true distribution. Because this information is almost never known, sensitivity analysis using a multivariate skewed Student's $t$-distribution helps to account for empirical properties such as the skewness and the excess kurtosis observed in the underlying factor return data.

A is incorrect. Data snooping is the subconscious or conscious manipulation of data in a way that produces a statistically significant result (i.e., a $p$-value that is sufficiently small or a $t$-statistic that is sufficiently large to indicate statistically significance).

C is incorrect. The inverse transformation method is the process of converting a randomly generated number into a simulated value of a random variable.

# Glossary

**Abnormal earnings**   See *residual income*.

**Abnormal return**   The amount by which a security's actual return differs from its expected return, given the security's risk and the market's return.

**Absolute convergence**   The idea that developing countries, regardless of their particular characteristics, will eventually catch up with the developed countries and match them in per capita output.

**Absolute valuation model**   A model that specifies an asset's intrinsic value.

**Absolute version of PPP**   An extension of the law of one price whereby the prices of goods and services will not differ internationally once exchange rates are considered.

**Accounting estimates**   Estimates used in calculating the value of assets or liabilities and in the amount of revenue and expense to allocate to a period. Examples of accounting estimates include, among others, the useful lives of depreciable assets, the salvage value of depreciable assets, product returns, warranty costs, and the amount of uncollectible receivables.

**Accumulated benefit obligation**   The actuarial present value of benefits (whether vested or non-vested) attributed, generally by the pension benefit formula, to employee service rendered before a specified date and based on employee service and compensation (if applicable) before that date. The accumulated benefit obligation differs from the projected benefit obligation in that it includes no assumption about future compensation levels.

**Accuracy**   The percentage of correctly predicted classes out of total predictions. It is an overall performance metric in classification problems.

**Acquisition**   When one company, the acquirer, purchases from the seller most or all of another company's (the target) shares to gain control of either an entire company, a segment of another company, or a specific group of assets in exchange for cash, stock, or the assumption of liabilities, alone or in combination. Once an acquisition is complete, the acquirer and target merge into a single entity and consolidate management, operations, and resources.

**Activation function**   A functional part of a neural network's node that transforms the total net input received into the final output of the node. The activation function operates like a light dimmer switch that decreases or increases the strength of the input.

**Active factor risk**   The contribution to active risk squared resulting from the portfolio's different-than-benchmark exposures relative to factors specified in the risk model.

**Active return**   The return on a portfolio minus the return on the portfolio's benchmark.

**Active risk**   The standard deviation of active returns.

**Active risk squared**   The variance of active returns; active risk raised to the second power.

**Active share**   A measure of how similar a portfolio is to its benchmark. A manager who precisely replicates the benchmark will have an active share of zero; a manager with no holdings in common with the benchmark will have an active share of one.

**Active specific risk**   The contribution to active risk squared resulting from the portfolio's active weights on individual assets as those weights interact with assets' residual risk.

**Adjusted funds from operations (AFFO)**   Funds from operations adjusted to remove any non-cash rent reported under straight-line rent accounting and to subtract maintenance-type capital expenditures and leasing costs, including leasing agents' commissions and tenants' improvement allowances.

**Adjusted present value**   As an approach to valuing a company, the sum of the value of the company, assuming no use of debt, and the net present value of any effects of debt on company value.

**Adjusted $R^2$**   Goodness-of-fit measure that adjusts the coefficient of determination, $R^2$, for the number of independent variables in the model.

**Administrative regulations or administrative law**   Rules issued by government agencies or other regulators.

**Advanced set**   An arrangement in which the reference interest rate is set at the time the money is deposited.

**Advanced settled**   An arrangement in which a forward rate agreement (FRA) expires and settles at the same time, at the FRA expiration date.

**Agency issues**   Conflicts of interest that arise when the agent in an agency relationship has goals and incentives that differ from the principal to whom the agent owes a fiduciary duty. Also called *agency problems* or *principal–agent problems*.

**Agglomerative clustering**   A bottom-up hierarchical clustering method that begins with each observation being treated as its own cluster. The algorithm finds the two closest clusters, based on some measure of distance (similarity), and combines them into one new larger cluster. This process is repeated iteratively until all observations are clumped into a single large cluster.

**Akaike's information criterion (AIC)**   A statistic used to compare sets of independent variables for explaining a dependent variable. It is preferred for finding the model that is best suited for prediction.

**Allowance for loan losses**   A balance sheet account; it is a contra asset account to loans.

**Alpha**   The return on an asset in excess of the asset's required rate of return; the risk-adjusted return.

**American Depositary Receipt**   A negotiable certificate issued by a depositary bank that represents ownership in a non-US company's deposited equity (i.e., equity held in custody by the depositary bank in the company's home market).

**Analysis of variance (ANOVA)**   The analysis that breaks the total variability of a dataset (such as observations on the dependent variable in a regression) into components representing different sources of variation.

**Application programming interface (API)**   A set of well-defined methods of communication between various software components and typically used for accessing external data.

**Arbitrage**   1) The simultaneous purchase of an undervalued asset or portfolio and sale of an overvalued but equivalent asset or portfolio, in order to obtain a riskless profit on the price differential. Taking advantage of a market inefficiency in a risk-free manner. 2) The condition in a financial market in which equivalent assets or combinations of assets sell for two different prices, creating an opportunity to profit at no risk with no commitment of money. In a well-functioning financial market, few arbitrage opportunities are possible. 3) A risk-free operation that earns an expected positive net profit but requires no net investment of money.

**Arbitrage-free models** Term structure models that project future interest rate paths that emanate from the existing term structure. Resulting prices are based on a no-arbitrage condition.

**Arbitrage-free valuation** An approach to valuation that determines security values consistent with the absence of any opportunity to earn riskless profits without any net investment of money.

**Arbitrage opportunity** An opportunity to conduct an arbitrage; an opportunity to earn an expected positive net profit without risk and with no net investment of money.

**Arbitrage portfolio** The portfolio that exploits an arbitrage opportunity.

**Ask price** The price at which a trader will sell a specified quantity of a security. Also called *ask*, *offer price*, or *offer*.

**Asset-based approach** Approach that values a private company based on the values of the underlying assets of the entity less the value of any related liabilities.

**Asset-based valuation** An approach to valuing natural resource companies that estimates company value on the basis of the market value of the natural resources the company controls.

**At market contract** When a forward contract is established, the forward price is negotiated so that the market value of the forward contract on the initiation date is zero.

**Authorized participants** (APs) A special group of institutional investors who are authorized by the ETF issuer to participate in the creation/redemption process. APs are large broker/dealers, often market makers.

**Autocorrelations** The correlations of a time series with its own past values.

**Autoregressive model (AR)** A time series regressed on its own past values in which the independent variable is a lagged value of the dependent variable.

**Backtesting** The process that approximates the real-life investment process, using historical data, to assess whether an investment strategy would have produced desirable results.

**Backward propagation** The process of adjusting weights in a neural network, to reduce total error of the network, by moving backward through the network's layers.

**Backwardation** A condition in the futures markets in which the spot price exceeds the futures price, the forward curve is downward sloping, and the convenience yield is high.

**Bag-of-words (BOW)** A collection of a distinct set of tokens from all the texts in a sample dataset. BOW does not capture the position or sequence of words present in the text.

**Balance sheet restructuring** Altering the composition of the balance sheet by either shifting the asset composition, changing the capital structure, or both.

**Bankruptcy** A declaration provided for by a country's laws that typically involves the establishment of a legal procedure that forces creditors to defer their claims.

**Barbell portfolio** Fixed-income portfolio that combines short and long maturities.

**Base error** Model error due to randomness in the data.

**Basic earnings per share** (EPS) Net earnings available to common shareholders (i.e., net income minus preferred dividends) divided by the weighted average number of common shares outstanding during the period.

**Basis** The difference between the spot price and the futures price. As the maturity date of the futures contract nears, the basis converges toward zero.

**Basis trade** A trade based on the pricing of credit in the bond market versus the price of the same credit in the CDS market. To execute a basis trade, go long the "underpriced" credit and short the "overpriced" credit. A profit is realized as the implied credit prices converge.

**Bearish flattening** Term structure shift in which short-term bond yields rise more than long-term bond yields, resulting in a flatter yield curve.

**Benchmark value of the multiple** In using the method of comparables, the value of a price multiple for the comparison asset; when we have comparison assets (a group), the mean or median value of the multiple for the group of assets.

**Best ask** The offer to sell with the lowest ask price. Also called *best offer* or *inside ask*.

**Best bid** The highest bid in the market.

**Best offer** The lowest offer (ask price) in the market.

**Bias error** Describes the degree to which a model fits the training data. Algorithms with erroneous assumptions produce high bias error with poor approximation, causing underfitting and high in-sample error.

**Bid price** In a price quotation, the price at which the party making the quotation is willing to buy a specified quantity of an asset or security.

**Bid–ask spread** The ask price minus the bid price.

**Bill-and-hold basis** Sales on a bill-and-hold basis involve selling products but not delivering those products until a later date.

**Blockage factor** An illiquidity discount that occurs when an investor sells a large amount of stock relative to its trading volume (assuming it is not large enough to constitute a controlling ownership).

**Bond indenture** A legal contract specifying the terms of a bond issue.

**Bond risk premium** The expected excess return of a default-free long-term bond less that of an equivalent short-term bond.

**Bond yield plus risk premium (BYPRP) approach** An estimate of the cost of common equity that is produced by summing the before-tax cost of debt and a risk premium that captures the additional yield on a company's stock relative to its bonds.

**Bonus issue of shares** A type of dividend in which a company distributes additional shares of its common stock to shareholders instead of cash.

**Book value** The net amount shown for an asset or liability on the balance sheet; book value may also refer to the company's excess of total assets over total liabilities. Also called *carrying value*.

**Book value of equity** Shareholders' equity (total assets minus total liabilities) minus the value of preferred stock; common shareholders' equity.

**Book value per share** The amount of book value (also called carrying value) of common equity per share of common stock, calculated by dividing the book value of shareholders' equity by the number of shares of common stock outstanding.

**Bootstrap aggregating (or bagging)** A technique whereby the original training dataset is used to generate $n$ new training datasets or bags of data. Each new bag of data is generated by random sampling with replacement from the initial training set.

**Bootstrapping** The use of a forward substitution process to determine zero-coupon rates by using the par yields and solving for the zero-coupon rates one by one, from the shortest to longest maturities.

**Bottom-up approach** With respect to forecasting, an approach that usually begins at the level of the individual company or a unit within the company.

**Breakup value** The value derived using a sum-of-the-parts valuation.

**Breusch–Godfrey (BG) test** A test used to detect autocorrelated residuals up to a predesignated order of the lagged residuals.

**Breusch–Pagan (BP) test** A test for the presence of heteroskedasticity in a regression.

**Bullet portfolio** A fixed-income portfolio concentrated in a single maturity.

**Bullish flattening** Term structure change in which the yield curve flattens in response to a greater decline in long-term rates than short-term rates.

**Bullish steepening** Term structure change in which short-term rates fall by more than long-term yields, resulting in a steeper term structure.

**Buy-side analysts** Analysts who work for investment management firms, trusts, bank trust departments, and similar institutions.

**Buyback** A transaction in which a company buys back its own shares. Unlike stock dividends and stock splits, share repurchases use corporate cash.

**CDS spread** A periodic premium paid by the buyer to the seller that serves as a return over a market reference rate required to protect against credit risk.

**Callable bond** A bond containing an embedded call option that gives the issuer the right to buy the bond back from the investor at specified prices on pre-determined dates.

**Canceled shares** Shares that were issued, subsequently repurchased by the company, and then retired (cannot be reissued).

**Capital asset pricing model (CAPM)** A single factor model such that excess returns on a stock are a function of the returns on a market index.

**Capital charge** The company's total cost of capital in money terms.

**Capital deepening** An increase in the capital-to-labor ratio.

**Capitalization of earnings method** In the context of private company valuation, a valuation model based on an assumption of a constant growth rate of free cash flow to the firm or a constant growth rate of free cash flow to equity.

**Capitalization rate** The divisor in the expression for the value of perpetuity. In the context of real estate, it is the divisor in the direct capitalization method of estimating value. The cap rate equals net operating income divided by value.

**Capitalized cash flow method** In the context of private company valuation, a valuation model based on an assumption of a constant growth rate of free cash flow to the firm or a constant growth rate of free cash flow to equity. Also called *capitalized cash flow model*.

**Capitalized income method** In the context of private company valuation, a valuation model based on an assumption of a constant growth rate of free cash flow to the firm or a constant growth rate of free cash flow to equity.

**Capped floater** Floating-rate bond with a cap provision that prevents the coupon rate from increasing above a specified maximum rate. It protects the issuer against rising interest rates.

**Carry arbitrage model** A no-arbitrage approach in which the underlying instrument is either bought or sold along with an opposite position in a forward contract.

**Carry benefits** Benefits that arise from owning certain underlyings; for example, dividends, foreign interest, and bond coupon payments.

**Carry costs** Costs that arise from owning certain underlyings. They are generally a function of the physical characteristics of the underlying asset and also the interest forgone on the funds tied up in the asset.

**Cash available for distribution** See *adjusted funds from operations*.

**Cash-generating unit** The smallest identifiable group of assets that generates cash inflows that are largely independent of the cash inflows of other assets or groups of assets.

**Cash settlement** A procedure used in certain derivative transactions that specifies that the long and short parties settle the derivative's difference in value between them by making a cash payment.

**Catalyst** An event or piece of information that causes the marketplace to re-evaluate the prospects of a company.

**Ceiling analysis** A systematic process of evaluating different components in the pipeline of model building. It helps to understand what part of the pipeline can potentially improve in performance by further tuning.

**Centroid** The center of a cluster formed using the $k$-means clustering algorithm.

**Chain rule of forecasting** A forecasting process in which the next period's value as predicted by the forecasting equation is substituted into the right-hand side of the equation to give a predicted value two periods ahead.

**Cheapest-to-deliver** The debt instrument that can be purchased and delivered at the lowest cost yet has the same seniority as the reference obligation.

**Classification and regression tree** A supervised machine learning technique that can be applied to predict either a categorical target variable, producing a classification tree, or a continuous target variable, producing a regression tree. CART is commonly applied to binary classification or regression.

**Clean surplus relation** The relationship between earnings, dividends, and book value in which ending book value is equal to the beginning book value plus earnings less dividends, apart from ownership transactions.

**Club convergence** The idea that only rich and middle-income countries sharing a set of favorable attributes (i.e., are members of the "club") will converge to the income level of the richest countries.

**Cluster** A subset of observations from a dataset such that all the observations within the same cluster are deemed "similar."

**Clustering** The sorting of observations into groups (clusters) such that observations in the same cluster are more similar to each other than they are to observations in other clusters.

**Cobb–Douglas production function** A function of the form $Y = K^\alpha L^{1-\alpha}$ relating output ($Y$) to labor ($L$) and capital ($K$) inputs.

**Coefficient of determination** The percentage of the variation of the dependent variable that is explained by the independent variables. Also referred to as the $R$-squared or $R^2$.

**Cointegrated** Describes two time series that have a long-term financial or economic relationship such that they do not diverge from each other without bound in the long run.

**Collateral return** The component of the total return on a commodity futures position attributable to the yield for the bonds or cash used to maintain the futures position. Also called *collateral yield*.

**Collection frequency (CF)** The number of times a given word appears in the whole corpus (i.e., collection of sentences) divided by the total number of words in the corpus.

**Commercial real estate properties** Income-producing real estate properties; properties purchased with the intent to let, lease, or rent (in other words, produce income).

**Commodity swap** A type of swap involving the exchange of payments over multiple dates as determined by specified reference prices or indexes relating to commodities.

**Company fundamental factors** Factors related to the company's internal performance, such as factors relating to earnings growth, earnings variability, earnings momentum, and financial leverage.

**Company share-related factors** Valuation measures and other factors related to share price or the trading characteristics of the shares, such as earnings yield, dividend yield, and book-to-market value.

**Comparables** Assets used as benchmarks when applying the method of comparables to value an asset. Also called *comps*, *guideline assets*, or *guideline companies*.

**Compiled financial statements** Financial statements that are not accompanied by an auditor's opinion letter.

**Complexity** A term referring to the number of features, parameters, or branches in a model and to whether the model is linear or non-linear (non-linear is more complex).

**Composite variable** A variable that combines two or more variables that are statistically strongly related to each other.

**Comprehensive income** All changes in equity other than contributions by, and distributions to, owners; income under clean surplus accounting; includes all changes in equity during a period except those resulting from investments by owners and distributions to owners. Comprehensive income equals net income plus other comprehensive income.

**Comps** Assets used as benchmarks when applying the method of comparables to value an asset.

**Concentrated ownership** Ownership structure consisting of an individual shareholder or a group (controlling shareholders) with the ability to exercise control over the corporation.

**Conditional convergence** The idea that convergence of per capita income is conditional on the countries having the same savings rate, population growth rate, and production function.

**Conditional heteroskedasticity** A condition in which the variance of residuals of a regression are correlated with the value of the independent variables.

**Conditional VaR (CVaR)** The weighted average of all loss outcomes in the statistical (i.e., return) distribution that exceed the VaR loss. Thus, CVaR is a more comprehensive measure of tail loss than VaR is. Sometimes referred to as the *expected tail loss* or *expected shortfall*.

**Confirmation bias** A belief perseverance bias in which people tend to look for and notice what confirms their beliefs, to ignore or undervalue what contradicts their beliefs, and to misinterpret information as support for their beliefs.

**Confusion matrix** A grid used for error analysis in classification problems, it presents values for four evaluation metrics including true positive (TP), false positive (FP), true negative (TN), and false negative (FN).

**Conglomerate discount** When an issuer is trading at a valuation lower than the sum of its parts, which is generally the result of diseconomies of scale or scope or the result of the capital markets having overlooked the business and its prospects.

**Constant dividend payout ratio policy** A policy in which a constant percentage of net income is paid out in dividends.

**Constant returns to scale** The condition that if all inputs into the production process are increased by a given percentage, then output rises by that same percentage.

**Contango** A condition in the futures markets in which the spot price is lower than the futures price, the forward curve is upward sloping, and there is little or no convenience yield.

**Contingent consideration** Potential future payments to the seller that are contingent on the achievement of certain agreed-on occurrences.

**Continuing earnings** Earnings excluding nonrecurring components. Also referred to as *core earnings*, *persistent earnings*, or *underlying earnings*.

**Continuing residual income** Residual income after the forecast horizon.

**Continuing value** The analyst's estimate of a stock's value at a particular point in the future.

**Control premium** An increment or premium to value associated with a controlling ownership interest in a company.

**Convergence** The tendency for differences in output per capita across countries to diminish over time. In technical analysis, the term describes the case when an indicator moves in the same manner as the security being analyzed.

**Conversion period** For a convertible bond, the period during which bondholders have the right to convert their bonds into shares.

**Conversion price** For a convertible bond, the price per share at which the bond can be converted into shares.

**Conversion rate (or ratio)** For a convertible bond, the number of shares of common stock that a bondholder receives from converting the bond into shares.

**Conversion value** For a convertible bond, the value of the bond if it is converted at the market price of the shares. Also called *parity value*.

**Convertible bond** Bond that gives the bondholder the right to exchange the bond for a specified number of common shares in the issuing company.

**Convexity** A measure of how interest rate sensitivity changes with a change in interest rates.

**Cook's distance** A metric for identifying influential data points. Also known as Cook's $D$ ($D_i$).

**Core earnings** Earnings excluding nonrecurring components. Also referred to as *continuing earnings*, *persistent earnings*, or *underlying earnings*.

**Core real estate investment style** Investing in high-quality, well-leased, core property types with low leverage (no more than 30% of asset value) in the largest markets with strong, diversified economies. It is a conservative strategy designed to avoid real estate–specific risks, including leasing, development, and speculation in favor of steady returns. Hotel properties are excluded from the core categories because of the higher cash flow volatility resulting from single-night leases and the greater importance of property operations, brand, and marketing.

**Corpus** A collection of text data in any form, including list, matrix, or data table forms.

**Cost approach** An approach that values a private company based on the values of the underlying assets of the entity less the value of any related liabilities. In the context of real estate, this approach estimates the value of a property based on what it would cost to buy the land and construct a new property on the site that has the same utility or functionality as the property being appraised.

**Cost of carry model** A model that relates the forward price of an asset to the spot price by considering the cost of carry (also referred to as future-spot parity model).

**Cost of debt** The required return on debt financing to a company, such as when it issues a bond, takes out a bank loan, or leases an asset through a finance lease.

**Cost of equity** The return required by equity investors to compensate for both the time value of money and the risk. Also referred to as the required rate of return on common stock or the required return on equity.

**Cost restructuring** Actions to reduce costs by improving operational efficiency and profitability, often to raise margins to a historical level or to those of comparable industry peers.

**Country risk premium (CRP)** The additional return required by investors to compensate for the risk associated with investing in a foreign country relative to the investor's domestic market.

**Country risk rating (CRR)** The rating of a country based on many risk factors, including economic prosperity, political risk, and ESG risk.

**Covariance stationary** Describes a time series when its expected value and variance are constant and finite in all periods and when its covariance with itself for a fixed number of periods in the past or future is constant and finite in all periods.

**Covered bonds** A senior debt obligation of a financial institution that gives recourse to the originator/issuer and a predetermined underlying collateral pool.

**Covered interest rate parity** The relationship among the spot exchange rate, the forward exchange rate, and the interest rates in two currencies that ensures that the return on a hedged (i.e., covered) foreign risk-free investment is the same as the return on a domestic risk-free investment. Also called *interest rate parity*.

**Cox-Ingersoll-Ross model** A general equilibrium term structure model that assumes interest rates are mean reverting and interest rate volatility is directly related to the level of interest rates.

**Creation basket** The list of securities (and share amounts) the authorized participant (AP) must deliver to the ETF manager in exchange for ETF shares. The creation basket is published each business day.

**Creation units** Large blocks of ETF shares transacted between the authorized participant (AP) and the ETF manager that are usually but not always equal to 50,000 shares of the ETF.

**Creation/redemption** The process in which ETF shares are created or redeemed by authorized participants transacting with the ETF issuer.

**Credit correlation** The correlation of credit (or default) risks of the underlying single-name CDS contained in an index CDS.

**Credit curve** The credit spreads for a range of maturities of a company's debt.

**Credit default swap** A derivative contract between two parties in which the buyer makes a series of cash payments to the seller and receives a promise of compensation for credit losses resulting from the default.

**Credit derivative** A derivative instrument in which the underlying is a measure of the credit quality of a borrower.

**Credit event** An event that defines a payout in a credit derivative. Events are usually defined as bankruptcy, failure to pay an obligation, or an involuntary debt restructuring.

**Credit protection buyer** One party to a credit default swap; the buyer makes a series of cash payments to the seller and receives a promise of compensation for credit losses resulting from the default.

**Credit protection seller** One party to a credit default swap; the seller makes a promise to pay compensation for credit losses resulting from the default.

**Credit risk** The risk of loss caused by a counterparty's or debtor's failure to make a promised payment. Also called *default risk*.

**Credit spread** The compensation for the risk inherent in a company's debt security.

**Credit valuation adjustment** The value of the credit risk of a bond in present value terms.

**Cross-validation** A technique for estimating out-of-sample error directly by determining the error in validation samples.

**Cumulative preferred stock** Preferred stock that requires that the dividends be paid in full to preferred stock owners for any missed dividends prior to any payment of dividends to common stock owners.

**Current exchange rate** For accounting purposes, the spot exchange rate on the balance sheet date.

**Current rate method** Approach to translating foreign currency financial statements for consolidation in which all assets and liabilities are translated at the current exchange rate. The current rate method is the prevalent method of translation.

**Curvature** One of the three factors (the other two are level and steepness) that empirically explain most of the changes in the shape of the yield curve. A shock to the curvature factor affects mid-maturity interest rates, resulting in the term structure becoming either more or less hump-shaped.

**Curve trade** Buying a CDS of one maturity and selling a CDS on the same reference entity with a different maturity.

**Customer concentration risk** The risk associated with sales dependent on a few customers.

**Cyclical businesses** Businesses with high sensitivity to business- or industry-cycle influences.

**Data preparation (cleansing)** The process of examining, identifying, and mitigating (i.e., cleansing) errors in raw data.

**Data snooping** The practice of determining a model by extensive searching through a dataset for statistically significant patterns.

**Data wrangling (preprocessing)** This task performs transformations and critical processing steps on cleansed data to make the data ready for ML model training (i.e., preprocessing), and includes dealing with outliers, extracting useful variables from existing data points, and scaling the data.

**Deep learning** Machine learning using neural networks with many hidden layers.

**Deep neural networks** Neural networks with many hidden layers—at least 2 but potentially more than 20—that have proven successful across a wide range of artificial intelligence applications.

**Default risk** See *credit risk*.

**Defined benefit pension plans** Plans in which the company promises to pay a certain annual amount (defined benefit) to the employee after retirement. The company bears the investment risk of the plan assets.

**Defined contribution pension plans** Individual accounts to which an employee and typically the employer makes contributions during their working years and expect to draw on the accumulated funds at retirement. The employee bears the investment and inflation risk of the plan assets.

**Delay costs** Implicit trading costs that arise from the inability to complete desired trades immediately. Also called *slippage*.

**Delta** The relationship between the option price and the underlying price, which reflects the sensitivity of the price of the option to changes in the price of the underlying. Delta is a good approximation of how an option price will change for a small change in the stock.

**Dendrogram** A type of tree diagram used for visualizing a hierarchical cluster analysis; it highlights the hierarchical relationships among the clusters.

**Depository Trust and Clearinghouse Corporation** A US-headquartered entity providing post-trade clearing, settlement, and information services.

**Diluted earnings per share** (Diluted EPS)Net income, minus preferred dividends, divided by the weighted average number of common shares outstanding considering all dilutive securities (e.g., convertible debt and options); the EPS that would result if all dilutive securities were converted into common shares.

**Dilution** A reduction in proportional ownership interest as a result of the issuance of new shares.

**Dimension reduction** A set of techniques for reducing the number of features in a dataset while retaining variation across observations to preserve the information contained in that variation.

**Diminishing marginal productivity** When each additional unit of an input, keeping the other inputs unchanged, increases output by a smaller increment.

**Direct capitalization method** In the context of real estate, this method estimates the value of an income-producing property based on the level and quality of its net operating income.

**Discount** To reduce the value of a future payment in allowance for how far away it is in time; to calculate the present value of some future amount. Also, the amount by which an instrument is priced below its face value.

**Discount factor** The price equivalent of a zero rate. Also may be stated as the present value of a currency unit on a future date.

**Discount for lack of control** An amount or percentage deducted from the pro rata share of 100% of the value of an equity interest in a business to reflect the absence of some or all of the powers of control.

**Discount for lack of marketability** An amount of percentage deducted from the value of an ownership interest to reflect the relative absence of marketability.

**Discount function** Discount factors for the range of all possible maturities. The spot curve can be derived from the discount function and vice versa.

**Discounted abnormal earnings model** A model of stock valuation that views intrinsic value of stock as the sum of book value per share plus the present value of the stock's expected future residual income per share.

**Discounted cash flow (DCF) method** Income approach that values an asset based on estimates of future cash flows discounted to present value by using a discount rate reflective of the risks associated with the cash flows. In the context of real estate, this method estimates the value of an income-producing property based on discounting future projected cash flows.

**Discounted cash flow method** Income approach that values an asset based on estimates of future cash flows discounted to present value by using a discount rate reflective of the risks associated with the cash flows. In the context of real estate, this method estimates the value of an income-producing property based on discounting future projected cash flows.

**Discounted cash flow model** A model of intrinsic value that views the value of an asset as the present value of the asset's expected future cash flows.

**Dispersed ownership** Ownership structure consisting of many shareholders, none of which has the ability to individually exercise control over the corporation.

**Divestiture** When a seller sells a company, segment of a company, or group of assets to an acquirer. Once complete, control of the target is transferred to the acquirer.

**Dividend** A distribution paid to shareholders based on the number of shares owned.

**Dividend coverage ratio** The ratio of net income to dividends.

**Dividend discount model** (DDM) A present value model of stock value that views the intrinsic value of a stock as present value of the stock's expected future dividends.

**Dividend discount model (DDM)** The model of the value of stock that is the present value of all future dividends, discounted at the required return on equity.

**Dividend displacement of earnings** The concept that dividends paid now displace earnings in all future periods.

**Dividend imputation tax system** A taxation system that effectively assures corporate profits distributed as dividends are taxed just once and at the shareholder's tax rate.

**Dividend index point** A measure of the quantity of dividends attributable to a particular index.

**Dividend payout ratio** The ratio of cash dividends paid to earnings for a period.

**Dividend policy** The strategy a company follows with regard to the amount and timing of dividend payments.

**Dividend rate** The annualized amount of the most recent dividend.

**Dividend recapitalization** Restructuring the mix of debt and equity, typically shifting the capital structure from equity to debt through debt-financed share repurchases. The objective is to reduce the issuer's weighted average cost of capital by replacing expensive equity with cheaper debt by purchasing equity from shareholders using newly issued debt.

**Dividend yield** Annual dividends per share divided by share price.

**Divisive clustering** A top-down hierarchical clustering method that starts with all observations belonging to a single large cluster. The observations are then divided into two clusters based on some measure of distance (similarity). The algorithm then progressively partitions the intermediate clusters into smaller ones until each cluster contains only one observation.

**Document frequency (DF)** The number of documents (texts) that contain a particular token divided by the total number of documents. It is the simplest feature selection method and often performs well when many thousands of tokens are present.

**Document term matrix (DTM)** A matrix where each row belongs to a document (or text file), and each column represents a token (or term). The number of rows is equal to the number of documents (or text files) in a sample text dataset. The number of columns is equal to the number of tokens from the BOW built using all the documents in the sample dataset. The cells typically contain the counts of the number of times a token is present in each document.

**Dominance** An arbitrage opportunity when a financial asset with a risk-free payoff in the future must have a positive price today.

**Double taxation system** Corporate earnings are taxed twice when paid out as dividends. First, corporate pretax earnings are taxed regardless of whether they will be distributed as dividends or retained at the corporate level. Second, dividends are taxed again at the individual shareholder level.

**Downstream** A transaction between two related companies, an investor company (or a parent company) and an associate company (or a subsidiary) such that the investor company records a profit on its income statement. An example is a sale of inventory by the investor company to the associate or by a parent to a subsidiary company.

**Dual-class shares** Shares that grant one share class superior or even sole voting rights, whereas the other share class has inferior or no voting rights.

**Due diligence** Investigation and analysis in support of an investment action, decision, or recommendation.

**Dummy variable** An independent variable that takes on a value of either 1 or 0, depending on a specified condition. Also known as an *indicator variable*.

**Duration** A measure of the approximate sensitivity of a security to a change in interest rates (i.e., a measure of interest rate risk).

**Durbin–Watson (DW) test** A test for the presence of first-order serial correlation.

**Dutch disease** A situation in which currency appreciation driven by strong export demand for resources makes other segments of the economy (particularly manufacturing) globally uncompetitive.

**ESG integration** An ESG investment approach that focuses on systematic consideration of material ESG factors in asset allocation, security selection, and portfolio construction decisions for the purpose of achieving the product's stated investment objectives. Used interchangeably with **ESG investing**.

**Earnings surprise** The portion of a company's earnings that is unanticipated by investors and, according to the efficient market hypothesis, merits a price adjustment.

**Earnings yield** EPS divided by price; the reciprocal of the P/E.

**Economic profit** Equal to accounting profit less the implicit opportunity costs not included in total accounting costs; the difference between total revenue (TR) and total cost (TC). Also called *abnormal profit* or *supernormal profit*.

**Economic sectors** Large industry groupings.

**Economic value added** (EVA®) A commercial implementation of the residual income concept; the computation of EVA® is the net operating profit after taxes minus the cost of capital, where these inputs are adjusted for a number of items.

**Economies of scale** A situation in which average costs per unit of good or service produced fall as volume rises. In reference to mergers, the savings achieved through the consolidation of operations and elimination of duplicate resources.

**Edwards–Bell–Ohlson model** A model of stock valuation that views intrinsic value of stock as the sum of book value per share plus the present value of the stock's expected future residual income per share.

**Effective convexity** A *curve convexity* statistic that measures the secondary effect of a change in a benchmark yield curve on a bond's price.

**Effective duration** Sensitivity of the bond's price to a 100 bps parallel shift of the benchmark yield curve, assuming no change in the bond's credit spread.

**Effective spread** Two times the difference between the execution price and the midpoint of the market quote at the time an order is entered.

**Eigenvalue** A measure that gives the proportion of total variance in the initial dataset that is explained by each eigenvector.

**Eigenvector** A vector that defines new mutually uncorrelated composite variables that are linear combinations of the original features.

**Embedded options** Contingency provisions found in a bond's indenture or offering circular representing rights that enable their holders to take advantage of interest rate movements. They can be exercised by the issuer, by the bondholder, or automatically depending on the course of interest rates.

**Ensemble learning** A technique of combining the predictions from a collection of models to achieve a more accurate prediction.

**Ensemble method** The method of combining multiple learning algorithms, as in ensemble learning.

**Enterprise value** Total company value (the market value of debt, common equity, and preferred equity) minus the value of cash and investments.

**Enterprise value multiple** A valuation multiple that relates the total market value of all sources of a company's capital (net of cash) to a measure of fundamental value for the entire company (such as a pre-interest earnings measure).

**Equity charge** The estimated cost of equity capital in money terms.

**Equity investment** A company purchasing another company's equity but less than 50% of its shares. The two companies maintain their independence, but the investor company has investment exposure to the investee and, in some cases depending on the size of the investment, can have representation on the investee's board of directors to influence operations.

**Equity REITs** REITs that own, operate, and/or selectively develop income-producing real estate.

**Equity risk premium (ERP)** Compensation for bearing market risk.

**Equity swap** A swap transaction in which at least one cash flow is tied to the return on an equity portfolio position, often an equity index.

**Error autocorrelations** The autocorrelations of the error term.

***Ex ante* tracking error** A measure of the degree to which the performance of a given investment portfolio might be expected to deviate from its benchmark; also known as *relative VaR*.

**Ex ante version of PPP**  The hypothesis that expected changes in the spot exchange rate are equal to expected differences in national inflation rates. An extension of relative purchasing power parity to expected future changes in the exchange rate.

**Ex-dividend**  Trading ex-dividend refers to shares that no longer carry the right to the next dividend payment.

**Ex-dividend date**  The first date that a share trades without (i.e., "ex") the right to receive the declared dividend for the period.

**Excess earnings method**  Income approach that estimates the value of all intangible assets of the business by capitalizing future earnings in excess of the estimated return requirements associated with working capital and fixed assets.

**Exercise date**  The date when employees actually exercise stock options and convert them to stock.

**Exercise value**  The value of an option if it were exercised. Also sometimes called *intrinsic value*.

**Expanded CAPM**  An adaptation of the CAPM that adds to the CAPM a premium for small size and company-specific risk.

**Expectations approach**  A procedure for obtaining the value of an option derived from discounting at the risk-free rate its expected future payoff based on risk neutral probabilities.

**Expected exposure**  The projected amount of money an investor could lose if an event of default occurs, before factoring in possible recovery.

**Expected shortfall**  The average loss conditional on exceeding the VaR cutoff; sometimes referred to as *conditional VaR* or *expected tail loss*.

**Expected tail loss**  See *expected shortfall*.

**Exploratory data analysis (EDA)**  The preliminary step in data exploration, where graphs, charts, and other visualizations (heat maps and word clouds) as well as quantitative methods (descriptive statistics and central tendency measures) are used to observe and summarize data.

**Exposure to foreign exchange risk**  The risk of a change in value of an asset or liability denominated in a foreign currency due to a change in exchange rates.

**Extendible bond**  Bond with an embedded option that gives the bondholder the right to keep the bond for a number of years after maturity, possibly with a different coupon.

**Extra dividend**  A dividend paid by a company that does not pay dividends on a regular schedule, or a dividend that supplements regular cash dividends with an extra payment.

**F1 score**  The harmonic mean of precision and recall. F1 score is a more appropriate overall performance metric (than accuracy) when there is unequal class distribution in the dataset and it is necessary to measure the equilibrium of precision and recall.

**FX carry trade**  An investment strategy that involves taking long positions in high-yield currencies and short positions in low-yield currencies.

**Factor**  A common or underlying element with which several variables are correlated.

**Factor betas**  An asset's sensitivity to a particular factor; a measure of the response of return to each unit of increase in a factor, holding all other factors constant.

**Factor portfolio**  See *pure factor portfolio*.

**Factor price**  The expected return in excess of the risk-free rate for a portfolio with a sensitivity of 1 to one factor and a sensitivity of 0 to all other factors.

**Factor risk premium**  The expected return in excess of the risk-free rate for a portfolio with a sensitivity of 1 to one factor and a sensitivity of 0 to all other factors. Also called *factor price*.

**Factor risk premiums**  The expected return in excess of the risk-free rate for a portfolio with a sensitivity of 1 to one factor and a sensitivity of 0 to all other factors. Also called factor price.

**Failure to pay**  When a borrower does not make a scheduled payment of principal or interest on any outstanding obligations after a grace period.

**Fair market value**  The price, expressed in terms of cash equivalents, at which a property (asset) would change hands between a hypothetical willing and able buyer and a hypothetical willing and able seller, acting at "arm's length" in an open and unrestricted market, when neither is under compulsion to buy or sell and when both have reasonable knowledge of the relevant facts. Fair market value is most often used in a tax reporting context in the United States.

**Fair value**  The amount at which an asset could be exchanged, or a liability settled, between knowledgeable, willing parties in an arm's-length transaction; the price that would be received to sell an asset or paid to transfer a liability in an orderly transaction between market participants.

**Fama–French models**  Factor models that explain the drivers of returns related to three, four, or five factors.

**Feature engineering**  A process of creating new features by changing or transforming existing features.

**Feature selection**  A process whereby only pertinent features from the dataset are selected for model training. Selecting fewer features decreases model complexity and training time.

**Features**  The independent variables ($X$'s) in a labeled dataset.

**Finance (or capital) lease**  A lease that is viewed as a financing arrangement.

**Financial contagion**  A situation in which financial shocks spread from their place of origin to other locales. In essence, a faltering economy infects other, healthier economies.

**Financial leverage**  The use of fixed sources of capital, such as debt, relative to sources without fixed costs, such as equity.

**Financial transaction**  A purchase involving a buyer having essentially no material synergies with the target (e.g., the purchase of a private company by a company in an unrelated industry or by a private equity firm would typically be a financial transaction).

**First-differencing**  A transformation that subtracts the value of the time series in period $t - 1$ from its value in period $t$.

**First-order serial correlation**  The correlation of residuals with residuals adjacent in time.

**Fitting curve**  A curve which shows in- and out-of-sample error rates ($E_{in}$ and $E_{out}$) on the $y$-axis plotted against model complexity on the $x$-axis.

**Fixed price tender offer**  Offer made by a company to repurchase a specific number of shares at a fixed price that is typically at a premium to the current market price.

**Fixed-rate perpetual preferred stock**  Nonconvertible, noncallable preferred stock that has a fixed dividend rate and no maturity date.

**Flight to quality**  During times of market stress, investors sell higher-risk asset classes such as stocks and commodities in favor of default-risk-free government bonds.

**Float**  Amounts collected as premium and not yet paid out as benefits.

**Floored floater** Floating-rate bond with a floor provision that prevents the coupon rate from decreasing below a specified minimum rate. It protects the investor against declining interest rates.

**Flotation cost** Fees charged to companies by investment bankers and other costs associated with raising new capital.

**Forced conversion** For a convertible bond, when the issuer calls the bond and forces bondholders to convert their bonds into shares, which typically happens when the underlying share price increases above the conversion price.

**Foreign currency transactions** Transactions that are denominated in a currency other than a company's functional currency.

**Forward curve** A series of forward rates, each having the same time frame.

**Forward dividend yield** A dividend yield based on the anticipated dividend during the next 12 months.

**Forward-looking estimates** Estimates based on current and expectations. Also referred to as ex ante estimates.

**Forward P/E** A P/E calculated on the basis of a forecast of EPS; a stock's current price divided by next year's expected earnings.

**Forward price** Represents the price agreed upon in a forward contract to be exchanged at the contract's maturity date, $T$. This price is shown in equations as $F_0(T)$.

**Forward pricing model** The model that describes the valuation of forward contracts.

**Forward propagation** The process of adjusting weights in a neural network, to reduce total error of the network, by moving forward through the network's layers.

**Forward rate** An interest rate determined today for a loan that will be initiated in a future period.

**Forward rate agreement** An over-the-counter forward contract in which the underlying is an interest rate on a deposit. A forward rate agreement (FRA) calls for one party to make a fixed interest payment and the other to make an interest payment at a rate to be determined at contract expiration.

**Forward rate model** The forward pricing model expressed in terms of spot and forward interest rates.

**Forward rate parity** The proposition that the forward exchange rate is an unbiased predictor of the future spot exchange rate.

**Forward value** The monetary value of an existing forward contract.

**Franchising** An owner of an asset and associated intellectual property divests the asset and licenses intellectual property to a third-party operator (franchisee) in exchange for royalties. Franchisees operate under the constraints of a franchise agreement.

**Franking credit** A tax credit received by shareholders for the taxes that a corporation paid on its distributed earnings.

**Free cash flow method** Income approach that values an asset based on estimates of future cash flows discounted to present value by using a discount rate reflective of the risks associated with the cash flows.

**Free cash flow to equity** The cash flow available to a company's common shareholders after all operating expenses, interest, and principal payments have been made and necessary investments in working and fixed capital have been made.

**Free cash flow to equity model** A model of stock valuation that views a stock's intrinsic value as the present value of expected future free cash flows to equity.

**Free cash flow to the firm** The cash flow available to the company's suppliers of capital after all operating expenses (including taxes) have been paid and necessary investments in working and fixed capital have been made.

**Free cash flow to the firm model** A model of stock valuation that views the value of a firm as the present value of expected future free cash flows to the firm.

**Frequency analysis** The process of quantifying how important tokens are in a sentence and in the corpus as a whole. It helps in filtering unnecessary tokens (or features).

**Functional currency** The currency of the primary economic environment in which an entity operates.

**Fundamental factor models** A multifactor model in which the factors are attributes of stocks or companies that are important in explaining cross-sectional differences in stock prices.

**Fundamentals** Economic characteristics of a business, such as profitability, financial strength, and risk.

**Funds available for distribution (FAD)** See *adjusted funds from operations*.

**Funds from operations (FFO)** Net income (computed in accordance with generally accepted accounting principles) *plus* (1) gains and losses from sales of properties and (2) depreciation and amortization.

**Futures price** The pre-agreed price at which a futures contract buyer (seller) agrees to pay (receive) for the underlying at the maturity date of the futures contract.

**Futures value** The monetary value of an existing futures contract.

**Gamma** A numerical measure of how sensitive an option's delta (the sensitivity of the derivative's price) is to a change in the value of the underlying.

**General linear *F*-test** A test statistic used to assess the goodness of fit for an entire regression model, so it tests all independent variables in the model.

**Generalize** When a model retains its explanatory power when predicting out-of-sample (i.e., using new data).

**Global CAPM (GCAPM)** A single-factor model with a global index representing the single factor.

**Going-concern assumption** The assumption that the business will maintain its business activities into the foreseeable future.

**Going-concern value** A business's value under a going-concern assumption.

**Goodwill** An intangible asset that represents the excess of the purchase price of an acquired company over the value of the net identifiable assets acquired.

**Gordon growth model** A DDM that assumes dividends grow at a constant rate into the future.

**Grant date** The day that stock options are granted to employees.

**Green bond** Bonds in which the proceeds are designated by issuers to fund a specific project or portfolio of projects that have environmental or climate benefits.

**Greenmail** The purchase of the accumulated shares of a hostile investor by a company that is targeted for takeover by that investor, usually at a substantial premium over market price.

**Greenwashing** The risk that a green bond's proceeds are not actually used for a beneficial environmental or climate-related project.

**Grid search**  A method of systematically training a model by using various combinations of hyperparameter values, cross validating each model, and determining which combination of hyperparameter values ensures the best model performance.

**Gross domestic product**  The market value of all final goods and services produced within the economy during a given period (output definition) or, equivalently, the aggregate income earned by all households, all companies, and the government within the economy during a given period (income definition).

**Gross lease**  A lease under which the tenant pays a gross rent to the landlord, who is responsible for all operating costs, utilities, maintenance expenses, and real estate taxes relating to the property.

**Ground truth**  The known outcome (i.e., target variable) of each observation in a labelled dataset.

**Growth accounting equation**  The production function written in the form of growth rates. For the basic Cobb–Douglas production function, it states that the growth rate of output equals the rate of technological change plus $\alpha$ multiplied by the growth rate of capital plus $(1 - \alpha)$ multiplied by the growth rate of labor.

**Growth capital expenditures**  Capital expenditures needed for expansion.

**Guideline assets**  Assets used as benchmarks when applying the method of comparables to value an asset.

**Guideline companies**  Assets used as benchmarks when applying the method of comparables to value an asset.

**Guideline public companies**  Public-company comparables for the company being valued.

**Guideline public company method**  A variation of the market approach; establishes a value estimate based on the observed multiples from trading activity in the shares of public companies viewed as reasonably comparable to the subject private company.

**Guideline transactions method**  A variation of the market approach; establishes a value estimate based on pricing multiples derived from the acquisition of control of entire public or private companies that were acquired.

**Harmonic mean**  A type of weighted mean computed as the reciprocal of the arithmetic average of the reciprocals.

**Hazard rate**  The probability that an event will occur, given that it has not already occurred.

**Hedonic index**  Unlike a repeat-sales index, a hedonic index does not require repeat sales of the same property. It requires only one sale. The way it controls for the fact that different properties are selling each quarter is to include variables in the regression that control for differences in the characteristics of the property, such as size, age, quality of construction, and location.

**Heteroskedastic**  When the variance of the residuals differs across observations in a regression.

**Heteroskedasticity**  The property of having a nonconstant variance; refers to an error term with the property that its variance differs across observations.

**Hierarchical clustering**  An iterative unsupervised learning procedure used for building a hierarchy of clusters.

**High-leverage point**  An observation of an independent variable that has an extreme value and is potentially influential.

**Highest and best use**  The concept that the best use of a vacant site is the use that would result in the highest value for the land. Presumably, the developer that could earn the highest risk-adjusted profit based on time, effort, construction and development cost, leasing, and exit value would be the one to pay the highest price for the land.

**Historical exchange rates**  For accounting purposes, the exchange rates that existed when the assets and liabilities were initially recorded.

**Historical scenario analysis**  A technique for exploring the performance and risk of investment strategies in different structural regimes.

**Historical simulation**  A simulation method that uses past return data and a random number generator that picks observations from the historical series to simulate an asset's future returns.

**Historical simulation method**  The application of historical price changes to the current portfolio.

**Historical stress testing**  The process that tests how investment strategies would perform under some of the most negative (i.e., adverse) combinations of events and scenarios.

**Ho–Lee model**  The first arbitrage-free term structure model. The model is calibrated to market data and uses a binomial lattice approach to generate a distribution of possible future interest rates.

**Holdout samples**  Data samples that are not used to train a model.

**Homoskedasticity**  The property of having a constant variance; refers to an error term that is constant across observations.

**Horizontal ownership**  Companies with mutual business interests (e.g., key customers or suppliers) that have cross-holding share arrangements with each other.

**Human capital**  An implied asset; the net present value of an investor's future expected labor income weighted by the probability of surviving to each future age. Also called *net employment capital*.

**Hybrid approach**  With respect to forecasting, an approach that combines elements of both top-down and bottom-up analyses.

**Hyperparameter**  A parameter whose value must be set by the researcher before learning begins.

**iNAVs**  "Indicated" net asset values are intraday "fair value" estimates of an ETF share based on its creation basket.

**ISDA Master Agreement**  A standard or "master" agreement published by the International Swaps and Derivatives Association. The master agreement establishes the terms for each party involved in the transaction.

**I-spreads**  Shortened form of "interpolated spreads" and a reference to a linearly interpolated yield.

**Idiosyncratic risk premium (IRP)**  The additional return required for bearing company-specific risks.

**Illiquidity discount**  A reduction or discount to value that reflects the lack of depth of trading or liquidity in that asset's market.

**Impairment**  Diminishment in value as a result of carrying (book) value exceeding fair value and/or recoverable value.

**Impairment of capital rule**  A legal restriction that dividends cannot exceed retained earnings.

**Implementation shortfall**  (IS) The difference between the return for a notional or paper portfolio, where all transactions are assumed to take place at the manager's decision price, and the portfolio's actual return, which reflects realized transactions, including all fees and costs.

**Implied volatility**  The standard deviation that causes an option pricing model to give the current option price.

**In-sample forecast errors** The residuals from a fitted time-series model within the sample period used to fit the model.

**Income approach** A valuation approach that values an asset as the present discounted value of the income expected from it. In the context of real estate, this approach estimates the value of a property based on an expected rate of return. The estimated value is the present value of the expected future income from the property, including proceeds from resale at the end of a typical investment holding period.

**Incremental borrowing rate (IBR)** The rate of interest that the lessee would have to pay to borrow using a collateralized loan over the same term as a lease.

**Incremental VaR (IVaR)** A measure of the incremental effect of an asset on the VaR of a portfolio by measuring the difference between the portfolio's VaR while including a specified asset and the portfolio's VaR with that asset eliminated.

**Indenture** A written contract between a lender and borrower that specifies the terms of the loan, such as interest rate, interest payment schedule, or maturity.

**Independent board directors** Directors with no material relationship with the company with regard to employment, ownership, or remuneration.

**Independent regulators** Regulators recognized and granted authority by a government body or agency. They are not government agencies per se and typically do not rely on government funding.

**Index CDS** A type of credit default swap that involves a combination of borrowers.

**Industry risk premium (IP)** The additional return that is required to bear industry-specific risk.

**Industry shocks** Unexpected changes to an industry from regulations or the legal environment, technology, or changes in the growth rate of the industry.

**Industry structure** An industry's underlying economic and technical characteristics.

**Influence plot** A visual that shows, for all observations, studentized residuals on the $y$-axis, leverage on the $x$-axis, and Cook's $D$ as circles whose size is proportional to the degree of influence of the given observation.

**Influential observation** An observation in a statistical analysis whose inclusion may significantly alter regression results.

**Information gain** A metric which quantifies the amount of information that the feature holds about the response. Information gain can be regarded as a form of non-linear correlation between Y and X.

**Information ratio** (IR) Mean active return divided by active risk; or alpha divided by the standard deviation of diversifiable risk.

**Informational frictions** Forces that restrict availability, quality, and/or flow of information and its use.

**Inside ask** See *best ask*.

**Inside bid** See *best bid*.

**Inside spread** The spread between the best bid price and the best ask price. Also called the *market bid-ask spread*, *inside bid-ask spread*, or *market spread*.

**Insiders** Corporate managers and board directors who are also shareholders of a company.

**Intangible assets** Assets without a physical form, such as patents and trademarks.

**Inter-temporal rate of substitution** The ratio of the marginal utility of consumption $s$ periods in the future (the numerator) to the marginal utility of consumption today (the denominator).

**Interaction term** A term that combines two or more variables and represents their joint influence on the dependent variable.

**Intercept dummy** An indicator variable that allows a single regression model to estimate two lines of best fit, each with differing intercepts, depending on whether the dummy takes a value of 1 or 0.

**Interest rate risk** The risk that interest rates will rise and therefore the market value of current portfolio holdings will fall so that their current yields to maturity then match comparable instruments in the marketplace.

**Interlocking directorates** Corporate structure in which individuals serve on the board of directors of multiple corporations.

**International CAPM (ICAPM)** A two-factor model with a global index and a wealth-weighted currency index.

**International Fisher effect** The proposition that nominal interest rate differentials across currencies are determined by expected inflation differentials.

**Intrinsic value** The amount gained (per unit) by an option buyer if an option is exercised at any given point in time. May be referred to as the exercise value of the option.

**Inverse price ratio** The reciprocal of a price multiple—for example, in the case of a P/E, the "earnings yield" E/P (where P is share price and E is earnings per share).

**Investment value** The value to a specific buyer, taking account of potential synergies based on the investor's requirements and expectations.

**Joint test of hypotheses** The test of hypotheses that specify values for two or more independent variables in the hypotheses.

**Joint venture** Two or more companies form and control a new, separate company to achieve a business objective. Each participant contributes assets, employees, know-how, or other resources to the joint venture company. The participants maintain their independence otherwise and continue to do business apart from the joint venture, but they share in the joint venture's profits or losses.

**Judicial law** Interpretations of courts.

**Justified price multiple** The estimated fair value of the price multiple, usually based on forecasted fundamentals or comparables.

**Justified (fundamental) P/E** The price-to-earnings ratio that is fair, warranted, or justified on the basis of forecasted fundamentals.

***K*-fold cross-validation** A technique in which data (excluding test sample and fresh data) are shuffled randomly and then are divided into $k$ equal sub-samples, with $k-1$ samples used as training samples and one sample, the $k$th, used as a validation sample.

***K*-means** A clustering algorithm that repeatedly partitions observations into a fixed number, $k$, of non-overlapping clusters.

***K*-nearest neighbor** A supervised learning technique that classifies a new observation by finding similarities ("nearness") between this new observation and the existing data.

**Kalotay–Williams–Fabozzi (KWF) model** An arbitrage-free term structure model that describes the dynamics of the log of the short rate and assumes constant drift, no mean reversion, and constant volatility.

**Key rate durations** Sensitivity of a bond's price to changes in specific maturities on the benchmark yield curve. Also called *partial durations*.

**kth-order autocorrelation** The correlation between observations in a time series separated by $k$ periods.

**LASSO** Least absolute shrinkage and selection operator is a type of penalized regression which involves minimizing the sum of the absolute values of the regression coefficients. LASSO can also be used for regularization in neural networks.

**Labeled dataset** A dataset that contains matched sets of observed inputs or features ($X$'s) and the associated output or target ($Y$).

**Labor force** Everyone of working age (ages 16 to 64) who either is employed or is available for work but not working.

**Labor force participation rate** The percentage of the working age population that is in the labor force.

**Labor productivity** The quantity of goods and services (real GDP) that a worker can produce in one hour of work.

**Labor productivity growth accounting equation** States that potential GDP growth equals the growth rate of the labor input plus the growth rate of labor productivity.

**Lack of marketability discount** An extra return to investors to compensate for lack of a public market or lack of marketability.

**Latency** The elapsed time between the occurrence of an event and a subsequent action that depends on that event.

**Law of one price** A principle that states that if two investments have the same or equivalent future cash flows regardless of what will happen in the future, then these two investments should have the same current price.

**Leading dividend yield** Forecasted dividends per share over the next year divided by current stock price.

**Leading P/E** A P/E calculated on the basis of a forecast of EPS; a stock's current price divided by next year's expected earnings.

**Learning curve** A curve that plots the accuracy rate (= 1 – error rate) in the validation or test samples (i.e., out-of-sample) against the amount of data in the training sample, which is thus useful for describing under- and overfitting as a function of bias and variance errors.

**Learning rate** A parameter that affects the magnitude of adjustments in the weights in a neural network.

**Level** One of the three factors (the other two are steepness and curvature) that empirically explain most yield curve shape changes. A shock to the level factor changes the yield for all maturities by an almost identical amount.

**Leverage** A measure for identifying a potentially influential high-leverage point.

**Leveraged buyout (LBO)** An acquirer (typically an investment fund specializing in LBOs) uses a significant amount of debt to finance the acquisition of a target and then pursues restructuring actions, with the goal of exiting the target with a sale or public listing.

**Libor–OIS spread** The difference between Libor and the overnight indexed swap rate.

**Likelihood ratio (LR) test** A method to assess the fit of logistic regression models and is based on the log-likelihood metric that describes the model's fit to the data.

**Limit order book** The book or list of limit orders to buy and sell that pertains to a security.

**Linear classifier** A binary classifier that makes its classification decision based on a linear combination of the features of each data point.

**Linear trend** A trend in which the dependent variable changes at a constant rate with time.

**Liquidating dividend** A dividend that is a return of capital rather than a distribution from earnings or retained earnings.

**Liquidation value** The value of a company if the company were dissolved and its assets sold individually.

**Liquidity preference theory** A term structure theory that asserts liquidity premiums exist to compensate investors for the added interest rate risk they face when lending long term.

**Liquidity premium** An extra return that compensates investors for the risk of loss relative to an investment's fair value if the investment needs to be converted to cash quickly.

**Local currency** The currency of the country where a company is located.

**Local expectations theory** A term structure theory that contends the return for all bonds over short periods is the risk-free rate.

**Log-linear model** With reference to time-series models, a model in which the growth rate of the time series as a function of time is constant.

**Log odds** The natural log of the odds of an event or characteristic happening. Also known as the *logit function*.

**Logistic regression (logit)** A regression in which the dependent variable uses a logistic transformation of the event probability.

**Logistic transformation** The log of the probability of an occurrence of an event or characteristic divided by the probability of the event or characteristic not occurring.

**Long/short credit trade** A credit protection seller with respect to one entity combined with a credit protection buyer with respect to another entity.

**Look-ahead bias** A bias caused by using information that was unavailable on the test date.

**Lookback period** The time period used to gather a historical data set.

**Loss given default** The amount that will be lost if a default occurs.

**Macroeconomic factor model** A multifactor model in which the factors are surprises in macroeconomic variables that significantly explain equity returns.

**Macroeconomic factors** Factors related to the economy, such as the inflation rate, industrial production, or economic sector membership.

**Maintenance capital expenditures** Capital expenditures needed to maintain operations at the current level.

**Majority shareholders** Shareholders that own more than 50% of a corporation's shares.

**Majority-vote classifier** A classifier that assigns to a new data point the predicted label with the most votes (i.e., occurrences).

**Marginal VaR (MVaR)** A measure of the effect of a small change in a position size on portfolio VaR.

**Market approach** Valuation approach that values an asset based on pricing multiples from sales of assets viewed as similar to the subject asset.

**Market conditions** Interest rates, inflation rates, and other economic characteristics that comprise the macroeconomic environment.

**Market conversion premium per share** For a convertible bond, the difference between the market conversion price and the underlying share price, which allows investors to identify the premium or discount payable when buying a convertible bond rather than the underlying common stock.

**Market conversion premium ratio** For a convertible bond, the market conversion premium per share expressed as a percentage of the current market price of the shares.

**Market efficiency** A finance perspective on capital markets that deals with the relationship of price to intrinsic value. The traditional efficient markets formulation asserts that an asset's price is the best available estimate of its intrinsic value. The rational efficient markets formulation asserts that investors should expect to be rewarded for the costs of information gathering and analysis by higher gross returns.

**Market fragmentation** Trading the same instrument in multiple venues.

**Market impact** The effect of the trade on transaction prices. Also called *price impact*.

**Market model** A regression model with the return on a stock as the dependent variable and the returns on a market index as the independent variable.

**Market value of invested capital** The market value of debt and equity.

**Mature growth rate** The earnings growth rate in a company's mature phase; an earnings growth rate that can be sustained long term.

**Maximum drawdown** The worst cumulative loss ever sustained by an asset or portfolio. More specifically, maximum drawdown is the difference between an asset's or a portfolio's maximum cumulative return and its subsequent lowest cumulative return.

**Maximum likelihood estimation (MLE)** A method that estimates values for the intercept and slope coefficients in a logistic regression that make the data in the regression sample most likely.

**Mean reversion** The tendency of a time series to fall when its level is above its mean and rise when its level is below its mean; a mean-reverting time series tends to return to its long-term mean.

**Metadata** Data that describes and gives information about other data.

**Method based on forecasted fundamentals** An approach to using price multiples that relates a price multiple to forecasts of fundamentals through a discounted cash flow model.

**Method of comparables** An approach to valuation that involves using a price multiple to evaluate whether an asset is relatively fairly valued, relatively undervalued, or relatively overvalued when compared to a benchmark value of the multiple.

**Midquote price** The average, or midpoint, of the prevailing bid and ask prices.

**Minority interest** The proportion of the ownership of a subsidiary not held by the parent (controlling) company.

**Minority shareholders** Particular shareholders or a block of shareholders holding a small proportion of a company's outstanding shares, resulting in a limited ability to exercise control in voting activities.

**Mispricing** Any departure of the market price of an asset from the asset's estimated intrinsic value.

**Model specification** The set of independent variables included in a model and the model's functional form.

**Molodovsky effect** The observation that P/Es tend to be high on depressed EPS at the bottom of a business cycle and tend to be low on unusually high EPS at the top of a business cycle.

**Momentum indicators** Valuation indicators that relate either price or a fundamental (such as earnings) to the time series of their own past values (or in some cases to their expected value).

**Monetary assets and liabilities** Assets and liabilities with value equal to the amount of currency contracted for, a fixed amount of currency. Examples are cash, accounts receivable, accounts payable, bonds payable, and mortgages payable. Inventory is not a monetary asset. Most liabilities are monetary.

**Monetary/non-monetary method** Approach to translating foreign currency financial statements for consolidation in which monetary assets and liabilities are translated at the current exchange rate. Non-monetary assets and liabilities are translated at historical exchange rates (the exchange rates that existed when the assets and liabilities were acquired).

**Monetizing** Unwinding a position to either capture a gain or realize a loss.

**Monte Carlo simulation** A technique that uses the inverse transformation method for converting a randomly generated uniformly distributed number into a simulated value of a random variable of a desired distribution. Each key decision variable in a Monte Carlo simulation requires an assumed statistical distribution; this assumption facilitates incorporating non-normality, fat tails, and tail dependence as well as solving high-dimensionality problems.

**Mortgage** A loan with real estate serving as collateral for the loan.

**Multicollinearity** When two or more independent variables are highly correlated with one another or are approximately linearly related.

**Multiple linear regression** Modeling and estimation method that uses two or more independent variables to describe the variation of the dependent variable. Also referred to as *multiple regression*.

**Mutual information** Measures how much information is contributed by a token to a class of texts. MI will be 0 if the token's distribution in all text classes is the same. MI approaches 1 as the token in any one class tends to occur more often in only that particular class of text.

**N-grams** A representation of word sequences. The length of a sequence varies from 1 to $n$. When one word is used, it is a unigram; a two-word sequence is a bigram; and a 3-word sequence is a trigram; and so on.

**$n$-Period moving average** The average of the current and immediately prior $n - 1$ values of a time series.

**NTM P/E** Next 12-month P/E: current market price divided by an estimated next 12-month EPS.

**Naked credit default swap** A position where the owner of the CDS does not have a position in the underlying credit.

**Name entity recognition** An algorithm that analyzes individual tokens and their surrounding semantics while referring to its dictionary to tag an object class to the token.

**Negative serial correlation** A situation in which residuals are negatively related to other residuals.

**Nested models** Models in which one regression model has a subset of the independent variables of another regression model.

**Net asset balance sheet exposure** When assets translated at the current exchange rate are greater in amount than liabilities translated at the current exchange rate. Assets exposed to translation gains or losses exceed the exposed liabilities.

**Net asset value per share (NAVPS)** Net asset value divided by the number of shares outstanding.

**Net lease** A lease under which the tenant pays a net rent to the landlord and an additional amount based on the tenant's pro rata share of the operating costs, utilities, maintenance expenses, and real estate taxes relating to the property.

**Net liability balance sheet exposure** When liabilities translated at the current exchange rate are greater assets translated at the current exchange rate. Liabilities exposed to translation gains or losses exceed the exposed assets.

**Net operating income (NOI)** Gross rental revenue minus operating costs but before deducting depreciation, corporate overhead, and interest expense. In the context of real estate, a measure of the income from the property after deducting operating expenses for such items as property taxes, insurance, maintenance, utilities, repairs, and insurance but before deducting any costs associated with financing and before deducting federal income taxes. It is similar to EBITDA in a financial reporting context.

**Net regulatory burden** The private costs of regulation less the private benefits of regulation.

**Network externalities** The impact that users of a good, a service, or a technology have on other users of that product; it can be positive (e.g., a critical mass of users makes a product more useful) or negative (e.g., congestion makes the product less useful).

**Neural networks** Computer programs based on how our own brains learn and process information.

**No-arbitrage approach** A procedure for obtaining the value of an option based on the creation of a portfolio that replicates the payoffs of the option and deriving the option value from the value of the replicating portfolio.

**No-growth company** A company without positive expected net present value projects.

**No-growth value per share** The value per share of a no-growth company, equal to the expected level amount of earnings divided by the stock's required rate of return.

**Non-cash rent** An amount equal to the difference between the average contractual rent over a lease term (the straight-line rent) and the cash rent actually paid during a period. This figure is one of the deductions made from FFO to calculate AFFO.

**Non-convergence trap** A situation in which a country remains relatively poor, or even falls further behind, because it fails to implement necessary institutional reforms and/or adopt leading technologies.

**Non-monetary assets and liabilities** Assets and liabilities that are not monetary assets and liabilities. Non-monetary assets include inventory, fixed assets, and intangibles, and non-monetary liabilities include deferred revenue.

**Non-renewable resources** Finite resources that are depleted once they are consumed; oil and coal are examples.

**Non-residential properties** Commercial real estate properties other than multi-family properties, farmland, and timberland.

**Nonearning assets** Cash and investments (specifically cash, cash equivalents, and short-term investments).

**Normal EPS** The EPS that a business could achieve currently under mid-cyclical conditions. Also called *normalized EPS*.

**Normal Q-Q plot** A visual used to compare the distribution of the residuals from a regression to a theoretical normal distribution.

**Normalized EPS** The EPS that a business could achieve currently under mid-cyclical conditions. Also called *normal EPS*.

**Normalized earnings** The expected level of mid-cycle earnings for a company in the absence of any unusual or temporary factors that affect profitability (either positively or negatively).

**Normalized P/E** P/E based on normalized EPS data.

**Notional amount** The amount of protection being purchased in a CDS.

**Off-the-run** A series of securities or indexes that were issued/created prior to the most recently issued/created series.

**Offshoring** Refers to relocating operations from one country to another, mainly to reduce costs through lower labor costs or to achieve economies of scale through centralization, but still maintaining operations within the corporation.

**Omitted variable bias** Bias resulting from the omission of an important independent variable from a regression model.

**On-the-run** The most recently issued and most actively traded sovereign securities.

**One hot encoding** The process by which categorical variables are converted into binary form (0 or 1) for machine reading. It is one of the most common methods for handling categorical features in text data.

**One-sided durations** Effective durations when interest rates go up or down, which are better at capturing the interest rate sensitivity of bonds with embedded options that do not react symmetrically to positive and negative changes in interest rates of the same magnitude.

**One-tier board** Board structure consisting of a single board of directors, composed of executive (internal) and non-executive (external) directors.

**Opportunity cost** Reflects the foregone opportunity of investing in a different asset. It is typically denoted by the risk-free rate of interest, $r$.

**Option-adjusted spread** (OAS) Constant spread that, when added to all the one-period forward rates on the interest rate tree, makes the arbitrage-free value of the bond equal to its market price.

**Orderly liquidation value** The estimated gross amount of money that could be realized from the liquidation sale of an asset or assets, given a reasonable amount of time to find a purchaser or purchasers.

**Other comprehensive income** Items of comprehensive income that are not reported on the income statement; comprehensive income minus net income.

**Other post-employment benefits** Promises by the company to pay benefits in the future, such as life insurance premiums and all or part of health care insurance for its retirees.

**Out-of-sample forecast errors** The differences between actual and predicted values of time series outside the sample period used to fit the model.

**Outlier** An observation that has an extreme value of the dependent variable and is potentially influential.

**Outsourcing** Shifting internal business services to a subcontractor that can offer services at lower costs by scaling to serve many clients.

**Overfitting** Situation in which the model has too many independent variables relative to the number of observations in the sample, such that the coefficients on the independent variables represent noise rather than relationships with the dependent variable.

**Overnight indexed swap (OIS) rate** An interest rate swap in which the periodic floating rate of the swap equals the geometric average of a daily unsecured overnight rate (or overnight index rate).

**PEG ratio** The P/E-to-growth ratio, calculated as the stock's P/E divided by the expected earnings growth rate.

**Pairs trading** An approach to trading that uses pairs of closely related stocks, buying the relatively undervalued stock and selling short the relatively overvalued stock.

**Par curve** A sequence of yields-to-maturity such that each bond is priced at par value. The bonds are assumed to have the same currency, credit risk, liquidity, tax status, and annual yields stated for the same periodicity.

**Par swap** A swap in which the fixed rate is set so that no money is exchanged at contract initiation.

**Parametric method** A method of estimating VaR that uses the historical mean, standard deviation, and correlation of security price movements to estimate the portfolio VaR. Generally assumes a normal distribution but can be adapted to non-normal distributions with the addition of skewness and kurtosis. Sometimes called the *variance–covariance method* or the *analytical method*.

**Partial regression coefficient** Coefficient that describes the effect of a one-unit change in the independent variable on the dependent variable, holding all other independent variables constant. Also known as *partial slope coefficient*.

**Parts of speech** An algorithm that uses language structure and dictionaries to tag every token in the text with a corresponding part of speech (i.e., noun, verb, adjective, proper noun, etc.).

**Payout amount** The loss given default times the notional.

**Payout policy** The principles by which a company distributes cash to common shareholders by means of cash dividends and/or share repurchases.

**Payouts** Cash dividends and the value of shares repurchased in any given year.

**Penalized regression** A regression that includes a constraint such that the regression coefficients are chosen to minimize the sum of squared residuals *plus* a penalty term that increases in size with the number of included features.

**Pension obligation** The present value of future benefits earned by employees for service provided to date.

**Perfect capital markets** Markets in which, by assumption, there are no taxes, transaction costs, or bankruptcy costs and in which all investors have equal ("symmetric") information.

**Perpetuity** A perpetual annuity, or a set of never-ending level sequential cash flows, with the first cash flow occurring one period from now.

**Persistent earnings** Earnings excluding nonrecurring components. Also referred to as *core earnings*, *continuing earnings*, or *underlying earnings*.

**Physical settlement** Involves actual delivery of the debt instrument in exchange for a payment by the credit protection seller of the notional amount of the contract.

**Point-in-time data** Data consisting of the exact information available to market participants as of a given point in time. Point-in-time data is used to address look-ahead bias.

**Portfolio balance approach** A theory of exchange rate determination that emphasizes the portfolio investment decisions of global investors and the requirement that global investors willingly hold all outstanding securities denominated in each currency at prevailing prices and exchange rates.

**Positive serial correlation** A situation in which residuals are positively related to other residuals.

**Potential GDP** The maximum amount of output an economy can sustainably produce without inducing an increase in the inflation rate. The output level that corresponds to full employment with consistent wage and price expectations.

**Precision** In error analysis for classification problems it is ratio of correctly predicted positive classes to all predicted positive classes. Precision is useful in situations where the cost of false positives (FP), or Type I error, is high.

**Preferred habitat theory** A term structure theory that contends that investors have maturity preferences and require yield incentives before they will buy bonds outside of their preferred maturities.

**Premise of value** The status of a company in the sense of whether it is assumed to be a going concern or not.

**Premium leg** The series of payments the credit protection buyer promises to make to the credit protection seller.

**Premiums** Amounts paid by the purchaser of insurance products.

**Present value model** A model of intrinsic value that views the value of an asset as the present value of the asset's expected future cash flows.

**Present value of growth opportunities** The difference between the actual value per share and the no-growth value per share. Also called *value of growth*.

**Presentation currency** The currency in which financial statement amounts are presented.

**Price improvement** When trade execution prices are better than quoted prices.

**Price momentum** A valuation indicator based on past price movement.

**Price multiples** The ratio of a stock's market price to some measure of value per share.

**Price-to-earnings ratio** (P/E) The ratio of share price to earnings per share.

**Priced risk** Risk for which investors demand compensation for bearing (e.g., equity risk, company-specific factors, macroeconomic factors).

**Principal components analysis (PCA)** An unsupervised ML technique used to transform highly correlated features of data into a few main, uncorrelated composite variables.

**Principle of no arbitrage** In well-functioning markets, prices will adjust until there are no arbitrage opportunities.

**Prior transaction method** A variation of the market approach; considers actual transactions in the stock of the subject private company.

**Private market value** The value derived using a sum-of-the-parts valuation.

**Pro forma financial statements** Financial statements that include the effect of a corporate restructuring.

**Probability of default** The likelihood that a borrower defaults or fails to meet its obligation to make full and timely payments of principal and interest.

**Probability of survival** The probability that a bond issuer will meet its contractual obligations on schedule.

**Procedural law** The body of law that focuses on the protection and enforcement of the substantive laws.

**Projection error** The vertical (perpendicular) distance between a data point and a given principal component.

**Prospective P/E** A P/E calculated on the basis of a forecast of EPS; a stock's current price divided by next year's expected earnings.

**Protection leg** The contingent payment that the credit protection seller may have to make to the credit protection buyer.

**Protection period** Period during which a bond's issuer cannot call the bond.

**Provision for loan losses** An income statement expense account that increases the amount of the allowance for loan losses.

**Prudential supervision** Regulation and monitoring of the safety and soundness of financial institutions to promote financial stability, reduce system-wide risks, and protect customers of financial institutions.

**Pruning** A regularization technique used in CART to reduce the size of the classification or regression tree—by pruning, or removing, sections of the tree that provide little classifying power.

**Purchasing power gain** A gain in value caused by changes in price levels. Monetary liabilities experience purchasing power gains during periods of inflation.

**Purchasing power loss** A loss in value caused by changes in price levels. Monetary assets experience purchasing power loss during periods of inflation.

**Purchasing power parity (PPP)** The idea that exchange rates move to equalize the purchasing power of different currencies.

**Pure expectations theory** A term structure theory that contends the forward rate is an unbiased predictor of the future spot rate. Also called the *unbiased expectations theory*.

**Pure factor portfolio** A portfolio with sensitivity of 1 to the factor in question and a sensitivity of 0 to all other factors.

**Putable bond** Bond that includes an embedded put option, which gives the bondholder the right to put back the bonds to the issuer prior to maturity, typically when interest rates have risen and higher-yielding bonds are available.

**Qualitative dependent variable** A dependent variable that is discrete (binary). Also known as a *categorical dependent variable*.

**Quality of earnings analysis** The investigation of issues relating to the accuracy of reported accounting results as reflections of economic performance. Quality of earnings analysis is broadly understood to include not only earnings management but also balance sheet management.

**Random forest classifier** A collection of a large number of decision trees trained via a bagging method.

**Random walk** A time series in which the value of the series in one period is the value of the series in the previous period plus an unpredictable random error.

**Rate implicit in the lease (RIIL)** The discount rate that equates the present value of the lease payment with the fair value of the leased asset, considering also the lessor's direct costs and the present value of the leased asset's residual value.

**Rational efficient markets formulation** See *market efficiency*.

**Readme files** Text files provided with raw data that contain information related to a data file. They are useful for understanding the data and how they can be interpreted correctly.

**Real estate investment trusts (REITs)** Tax-advantaged entities (companies or trusts) that own, operate, and—to a limited extent—develop income-producing real estate property.

**Real estate operating companies (REOCs)** Regular taxable real estate ownership companies that operate in the real estate industry in countries that do not have a tax-advantaged REIT regime in place or that are engage in real estate activities of a kind and to an extent that do not fit in their country's REIT framework.

**Real interest rate parity** The proposition that real interest rates will converge to the same level across different markets.

**Real options** Options that relate to investment decisions such as the option to time the start of a project, the option to adjust its scale, or the option to abandon a project that has begun.

**Rebalance return** A return from rebalancing the component weights of an index.

**Recall** Also known as *sensitivity*, in error analysis for classification problems it is the ratio of correctly predicted positive classes to all actual positive classes. Recall is useful in situations where the cost of false negatives (FN), or Type II error, is high.

**Recency bias** The behavioral tendency to place more relevance on recent events.

**Reconstitution** When dealers recombine appropriate individual zero-coupon securities and reproduce an underlying coupon Treasury.

**Recovery rate** The percentage of the loss recovered.

**Redemption basket** The list of securities (and share amounts) the authorized participant (AP) receives when it redeems ETF shares back to the ETF manager. The redemption basket is published each business day.

**Reference entity** The borrower (debt issuer) covered by a single-name CDS.

**Reference obligation** A particular debt instrument issued by the borrower that is the designated instrument being covered.

**Regime** With reference to a time series, the underlying model generating the times series.

**Regular expression (regex)** A series of texts that contains characters in a particular order. Regex is used to search for patterns of interest in a given text.

**Regularization** A term that describes methods for reducing statistical variability in high-dimensional data estimation problems.

**Regulatory arbitrage** Entities identify and use some aspect of regulations that allows them to exploit differences in economic substance and regulatory interpretation or in foreign and domestic regulatory regimes to their (the entities') advantage.

**Regulatory burden** The costs of regulation for the regulated entity.

**Regulatory capture** Theory that regulation often arises to enhance the interests of the regulated.

**Regulatory competition** Regulators may compete to provide a regulatory environment designed to attract certain entities.

**Reinforcement learning** Machine learning in which a computer learns from interacting with itself or data generated by the same algorithm.

**Relative-strength indicators** Valuation indicators that compare a stock's performance during a period either to its own past performance or to the performance of some group of stocks.

**Relative VaR** See *ex ante tracking error*.

**Relative valuation models** A model that specifies an asset's value relative to the value of another asset.

**Relative version of PPP** The hypothesis that changes in (nominal) exchange rates over time are equal to national inflation rate differentials.

**Renewable resources** Resources that can be replenished, such as a forest.

**Rental price of capital** The cost per unit of time to rent a unit of capital.

**Reorganization** A court-supervised restructuring process available in some jurisdictions for companies facing insolvency from burdensome debt levels. A bankruptcy court assumes control of the company and oversees an orderly negotiation process between the company and its creditors for asset sales, conversion of debt to equity, refinancing, and so on.

**Repeat sales index** As the name implies, this type of index relies on repeat sales of the same property. In general, the idea supporting this type of index is that because it is the same property that sold twice, the change in value between the two sale dates indicates how market conditions have changed over time.

**Replacement cost** In the context of real estate, the value of a building assuming it was built today using current construction costs and standards.

**Reporting unit** For financial reporting under US GAAP, an operating segment or one level below an operating segment (referred to as a component).

**Required rate of return on equity** The minimum rate of return required by an investor to invest in an asset, given the asset's riskiness. Also known as the required return on equity.

**Residential properties** Properties that provide housing for individuals or families. Single-family properties may be owner-occupied or rental properties, whereas multi-family properties are rental properties even if the owner or manager occupies one of the units.

**Residual autocorrelations** The sample autocorrelations of the residuals.

**Residual income** Earnings for a given period, minus a deduction for common shareholders' opportunity cost in generating the earnings. Also called *economic profit* or *abnormal earnings*.

**Residual income method** Income approach that estimates the value of all intangible assets of the business by capitalizing future earnings in excess of the estimated return requirements associated with working capital and fixed assets.

**Residual income model** (RIM) A model of stock valuation that views intrinsic value of stock as the sum of book value per share plus the present value of the stock's expected future residual income per share. Also called *discounted abnormal earnings model* or *Edwards–Bell–Ohlson model*.

**Restricted model** A regression model with a subset of the complete set of independent variables.

**Restructuring** Reorganizing the capital structure of a firm.

**Return on invested capital** A measure of the profitability of a company relative to the amount of capital invested by the equity- and debtholders.

**Reverse carry arbitrage** A strategy involving the short sale of the underlying and an offsetting opposite position in the derivative.

**Reverse stock split** A reduction in the number of shares outstanding with a corresponding increase in share price, but no change to the company's underlying fundamentals.

**Reverse stress testing** A risk management approach in which the user identifies key risk exposures in the portfolio and subjects those exposures to extreme market movements.

**Reviewed financial statements** A type of non-audited financial statements; typically provide an opinion letter with representations and assurances by the reviewing accountant that are less than those in audited financial statements.

**Rho** The change in a given derivative instrument for a given small change in the risk-free interest rate, holding everything else constant. Rho measures the sensitivity of the option to the risk-free interest rate.

**Risk-based models** Models of the return on equity that identify risk factors or drivers and sensitivities of the return to these factors.

**Risk budgeting** The establishment of objectives for individuals, groups, or divisions of an organization that takes into account the allocation of an acceptable level of risk.

**Risk decomposition** The process of converting a set of holdings in a portfolio into a set of exposures to risk factors.

**Risk factors** Variables or characteristics with which individual asset returns are correlated. Sometimes referred to simply as *factors*.

**Risk-free rate** The minimum rate of return expected on a security that has no default risk.

**Risk parity** A portfolio allocation scheme that weights stocks or factors based on an equal risk contribution.

**Robust standard errors** Method for correcting residuals for conditional heteroskedasticity. Also known as *heteroskedasticity-consistent standard errors* or *White-corrected standard errors*.

**Roll** When an investor moves its investment position from an older series to the most current series.

**Roll return** The component of the return on a commodity futures contract attributable to rolling long futures positions forward through time. Also called *roll yield*.

**Rolling down the yield curve** A maturity trading strategy that involves buying bonds with a maturity longer than the intended investment horizon. Also called *riding the yield curve*.

**Rolling windows** A backtesting method that uses a rolling-window (or walk-forward) framework, rebalances the portfolio after each period, and then tracks performance over time. As new information arrives each period, the investment manager optimizes (revises and tunes) the model and readjusts stock positions.

**Root mean squared error (RMSE)** The square root of the average squared forecast error; used to compare the out-of-sample forecasting performance of forecasting models.

**Sale-leaseback** A situation in which a company sells the building it owns and occupies to a real estate investor and the company then signs a long-term lease with the buyer to continue to occupy the building. At the end of the lease, use of the property reverts to the landlord.

**Sales comparison approach** In the context of real estate, this approach estimates value based on what similar or comparable properties (comparables) transacted for in the current market.

**Sales risk** The uncertainty regarding the price and number of units sold of a company's products.

**Scaled earnings surprise** Unexpected earnings divided by the standard deviation of analysts' earnings forecasts.

**Scaling** The process of adjusting the range of a feature by shifting and changing the scale of the data. Two of the most common ways of scaling are normalization and standardization.

**Scatterplot matrix** A visualization technique that shows the scatterplots between different sets of variables, often with the histogram for each variable on the diagonal. Also referred to as a *pairs plot*.

**Scenario analysis** A technique for exploring the performance and risk of investment strategies in different structural regimes.

**Schwarz's Bayesian information criterion (BIC or SBC)** A statistic used to compare sets of independent variables for explaining a dependent variable. It is preferred for finding the model with the best goodness of fit.

**Scree plots** A plot that shows the proportion of total variance in the data explained by each principal component.

**Screening** The application of a set of criteria to reduce a set of potential investments to a smaller set having certain desired characteristics.

**Seasonality** A characteristic of a time series in which the data experience regular and predictable periodic changes; for example, fan sales are highest during the summer months.

**Secured overnight financing rate (SOFR)** A daily volume-weighted index of rates on qualified cash borrowings collateralized by US Treasuries that is expected to replace Libor as a floating reference rate for swaps.

**Security selection risk** See *active specific risk*.

**Segmented markets theory** A term structure theory that contends yields are solely a function of the supply and demand for funds of a particular maturity.

**Self-regulating organizations (SROs)** Self-regulating bodies that are given recognition and authority, including enforcement power, by a government body or agency.

**Self-regulatory bodies** Private, non-governmental organizations that both represent and regulate their members. Some self-regulating organizations are also independent regulators.

**Sell-side analysts** Analysts who work at brokerages.

**Sensitivity analysis** Analysis that shows the range of possible outcomes as specific assumptions are changed.

**Sentence length** The number of characters, including spaces, in a sentence.

**Serial correlation** A condition found most often in time series in which residuals are correlated across observations. Also known as *autocorrelation*.

**Serial-correlation consistent standard errors** Method for correcting serial correlation. Also known as *serial correlation and heteroskedasticity adjusted standard errors*, *Newey–West standard errors*, and *robust standard errors*.

**Service period** For employee stock options, usually the period between the grant date and the vesting date.

**Settled in arrears** An arrangement in which the interest payment is made (i.e., settlement occurs) at the maturity of the underlying instrument.

**Settlement** The closing date at which the counterparties of a derivative contract exchange payment for the underlying as required by the contract.

**Shadow banking** Lending by financial institutions that are not regulated as banks.

**Shaping risk** The sensitivity of a bond's price to the changing shape of the yield curve.

**Share repurchase** A transaction in which a company buys back its own shares. Unlike stock dividends and stock splits, share repurchases use corporate cash.

**Shareholder activism** Strategies used by shareholders to attempt to compel a company to act in a desired manner.

**Shareholders' equity** Total assets minus total liabilities.

**Simulation** A technique for exploring how a target variable (e.g. portfolio returns) would perform in a hypothetical environment specified by the user, rather than a historical setting.

**Single-name CDS** Credit default swap on one specific borrower.

**Sinking fund bond** A bond that requires the issuer to set aside funds over time to retire the bond issue, thus reducing credit risk.

**Size premium (SP)** Additional return compensation for bearing the additional risk associated with smaller companies.

**Slope dummy** An indicator variable that allows a single regression model to estimate two lines of best fit, each with differing slopes, depending on whether the dummy takes a value of 1 or 0.

**Soft margin classification** An adaptation in the support vector machine algorithm which adds a penalty to the objective function for observations in the training set that are misclassified.

**Sovereign yield spread** The spread between the yield on a foreign country's sovereign bond and a similar-maturity domestic sovereign bond.

**Special dividend** A dividend paid by a company that does not pay dividends on a regular schedule, or a dividend that supplements regular cash dividends with an extra payment.

**Specific-company risk premium (SCRP)** Additional return required by investors for bearing non-diversifiable company-specific risk.

**Spin off** When a company separates a distinct part of its business into a new, independent company. The term is used to describe both the transaction and the separated component, while the company that conducts the transaction and formerly owned the spin off is known as the parent.

**Split-rate tax system** In reference to corporate taxes, a split-rate system taxes earnings to be distributed as dividends at a different rate than earnings to be retained. Corporate profits distributed as dividends are taxed at a lower rate than those retained in the business.

**Spot curve** A sequence of yields-to-maturity on zero-coupon bonds. Sometimes called *zero* or *strip curve* (because coupon payments are "stripped" off the bonds).

**Spot price** The current price of an asset or security. For commodities, the current price to deliver a physical commodity to a specific location or purchase and transport it away from a designated location.

**Spot rate** The interest rate that is determined today for a risk-free, single-unit payment at a specified future date.

**Spot yield curve** The term structure of spot rates for loans made today.

**Stabilized NOI** In the context of real estate, the expected NOI when a renovation is complete.

**Stable dividend policy** A policy in which regular dividends are paid that reflect long-run expected earnings. In contrast to a constant dividend payout ratio policy, a stable dividend policy does not reflect short-term volatility in earnings.

**Standardized beta** With reference to fundamental factor models, the value of the attribute for an asset minus the average value of the attribute across all stocks, divided by the standard deviation of the attribute across all stocks.

**Standardized unexpected earnings** Unexpected earnings per share divided by the standard deviation of unexpected earnings per share over a specified prior time period.

**Statistical factor model** A multifactor model in which statistical methods are applied to a set of historical returns to determine portfolios that best explain either historical return covariances or variances.

**Statutes** Laws enacted by legislative bodies.

# Glossary

**Steady-state rate of growth**  The constant growth rate of output (or output per capita) that can or will be sustained indefinitely once it is reached. Key ratios, such as the capital–output ratio, are constant on the steady-state growth path.

**Steepness**  The difference between long-term and short-term yields that constitutes one of the three factors (the other two are level and curvature) that empirically explain most of the changes in the shape of the yield curve.

**Stock dividend**  A type of dividend in which a company distributes additional shares of its common stock to shareholders instead of cash.

**Stop-loss limit**  Constraint used in risk management that requires a reduction in the size of a portfolio, or its complete liquidation, when a loss of a particular size occurs in a specified period.

**Straight bond**  An underlying option-free bond with a specified issuer, issue date, maturity date, principal amount and repayment structure, coupon rate and payment structure, and currency denomination.

**Straight debt**  Debt with no embedded options.

**Straight-line rent**  The average annual rent under a multi-year lease agreement that contains contractual increases in rent during the life of the lease.

**Straight-line rent adjustment**  See *non-cash rent*.

**Straight voting**  A shareholder voting process in which shareholders receive one vote for each share owned.

**Stranded assets**  Assets that are obsolete or not economically viable.

**Strategic transaction**  A purchase involving a buyer that would benefit from certain synergies associated with owning the target firm.

**Stress tests**  A risk management technique that assesses the portfolio's response to extreme market movements.

**Stripping**  A dealer's ability to separate a bond's individual cash flows and trade them as zero-coupon securities.

**Studentized residual**  A *t*-distributed statistic that is used to detect outliers.

**Substantive law**  The body of law that focuses on the rights and responsibilities of entities and relationships among entities.

**Succession event**  A change of corporate structure of the reference entity, such as through a merger, a divestiture, a spinoff, or any similar action, in which ultimate responsibility for the debt in question is unclear.

**Sum-of-the-parts valuation**  A valuation that sums the estimated values of each of a company's businesses as if each business were an independent going concern.

**Summation operator**  A functional part of a neural network's node that multiplies each input value received by a weight and sums the weighted values to form the total net input, which is then passed to the activation function.

**Supernormal growth**  Above-average or abnormally high growth rate in earnings per share.

**Supervised learning**  A machine learning approach that makes use of labeled training data.

**Support vector machine**  A linear classifier that determines the hyperplane that optimally separates the observations into two sets of data points.

**Survivorship bias**  The exclusion of poorly performing or defunct companies from an index or database, biasing the index or database toward financially healthy companies.

**Sustainable growth rate**  The rate of dividend (and earnings) growth that can be sustained over time for a given level of return on equity, keeping the capital structure constant and without issuing additional common stock.

**Swap curve**  The term structure of swap rates.

**Swap rate**  The fixed rate to be paid by the fixed-rate payer specified in a swap contract.

**Swap rate curve**  The term structure of swap rates.

**Swap spread**  The difference between the fixed rate on an interest rate swap and the rate on a Treasury note with equivalent maturity; it reflects the general level of credit risk in the market.

**Synergies**  The combination of two companies being more valuable than the sum of the parts. Generally, synergies take the form of lower costs ("cost synergies") or increased revenues ("revenue synergies") through combinations that generate lower costs or higher revenues, respectively.

**Systematic risk**  Risk that affects the entire market or economy; it cannot be avoided and is inherent in the overall market. Systematic risk is also known as non-diversifiable or market risk.

**Systemic risk**  Refers to risks supervisory authorities believe are likely to have broad impact across the financial market infrastructure and affect a wide swath of market participants.

**TED spread**  A measure of perceived credit risk determined as the difference between Libor and the T-bill yield of matching maturity.

**Tail risk**  The risk that losses in extreme events could be greater than would be expected for a portfolio of assets with a normal distribution.

**Takeover premium**  The amount by which the per-share takeover price exceeds the unaffected price expressed as a percentage of the unaffected price. It reflects the amount shareholders require to relinquish their control of the company to the acquirer.

**Tangible assets**  Identifiable, physical assets such as property, plant, and equipment.

**Tangible book value per share**  Common shareholders' equity minus intangible assets reported on the balance sheet, divided by the number of shares outstanding.

**Target**  In machine learning, the dependent variable (*Y*) in a labeled dataset; the company in a merger or acquisition that is being acquired.

**Target capital structure**  A company's chosen proportions of debt and equity.

**Target payout ratio**  A strategic corporate goal representing the long-term proportion of earnings that the company intends to distribute to shareholders as dividends.

**Taxable REIT subsidiaries**  Subsidiaries that pay income taxes on earnings from non-REIT-qualifying activities like merchant development or third-party property management.

**Technical indicators**  Momentum indicators based on price.

**Temporal method**  A variation of the monetary/non-monetary translation method that requires not only monetary assets and liabilities, but also non-monetary assets and liabilities that are measured at their current value on the balance sheet date to be translated at the current exchange rate. Assets and liabilities are translated at rates consistent with the timing of their measurement value. This method is typically used when the functional currency is other than the local currency.

**Term frequency (TF)** Ratio of the number of times a given token occurs in all the texts in the dataset to the total number of tokens in the dataset.

**Term premium** The additional return required by lenders to invest in a bond to maturity net of the expected return from continually reinvesting at the short-term rate over that same time horizon.

**Terminal price multiples** The price multiple for a stock assumed to hold at a stated future time.

**Terminal share price** The share price at a particular point in the future.

**Terminal value of the stock** The analyst's estimate of a stock's value at a particular point in the future. Also called *continuing value of the stock*.

**Test sample** A data sample that is used to test a model's ability to predict well on new data.

**Theta** The change in a derivative instrument for a given small change in calendar time, holding everything else constant. Specifically, the theta calculation assumes nothing changes except calendar time. Theta also reflects the rate at which an option's time value decays.

**Time series** A set of observations on a variable's outcomes in different time periods.

**Tobin's q** The ratio of the market value of debt and equity to the replacement cost of total assets.

**Token** The equivalent of a word (or sometimes a character).

**Tokenization** The process of representing ownership rights to physical assets on a blockchain or distributed ledger.

**Top-down approach** With respect to forecasting, an approach that usually begins at the level of the overall economy. Forecasts are then made at more narrowly defined levels, such as sector, industry, and market for a specific product.

**Total factor productivity (TFP)** A multiplicative scale factor that reflects the general level of productivity or technology in the economy. Changes in total factor productivity generate proportional changes in output for any input combination.

**Total invested capital** The sum of market value of common equity, book value of preferred equity, and face value of debt.

**Tracking error** The standard deviation of the differences between a portfolio's returns and its benchmark's returns; a synonym of *active risk*. Also called *tracking risk*.

**Tracking risk** The standard deviation of the differences between a portfolio's returns and its benchmarks returns. Also called *tracking error*.

**Trailing dividend yield** The reciprocal of current market price divided by the most recent annualized dividend.

**Trailing P/E** A stock's current market price divided by the most recent four quarters of EPS (or the most recent two semi-annual periods for companies that report interim data semi-annually). Also called *current P/E*.

**Training sample** A data sample that is used to train a model.

**Tranche CDS** A type of credit default swap that covers a combination of borrowers but only up to pre-specified levels of losses.

**Transaction exposure** The risk of a change in value between the transaction date and the settlement date of an asset of liability denominated in a foreign currency.

**Treasury shares/stock** Shares that were issued and subsequently repurchased by the company.

**Trend** A long-term pattern of movement in a particular direction.

**Triangular arbitrage** An arbitrage transaction involving three currencies that attempts to exploit inconsistencies among pairwise exchange rates.

**Trimming** Also called truncation, it is the process of removing extreme values and outliers from a dataset.

**Triple-net leases** Leases that require each tenant to pay its share of the following three operating expenses: common area maintenance and repair expenses; property taxes; and building insurance costs. Also known as *NNN leases*.

**Two-tier board** Board structure consisting of a supervisory board that oversees a management board.

**Unbiased expectations theory** A term structure theory that contends the forward rate is an unbiased predictor of the future spot rate. Also called the *pure expectations theory*.

**Unconditional heteroskedasticity** When heteroskedasticity of the error variance is not correlated with the regression's independent variables.

**Uncovered interest rate parity** The proposition that the expected return on an uncovered (i.e., unhedged) foreign currency (risk-free) investment should equal the return on a comparable domestic currency investment.

**Underlying earnings** Earnings excluding nonrecurring components. Also referred to as *continuing earnings*, *core earnings*, or *persistent earnings*.

**Unexpected earnings** The difference between reported EPS and expected EPS. Also referred to as an *earnings surprise*.

**Unit root** A time series that is not covariance stationary is said to have a unit root.

**Unrestricted model** A regression model with the complete set of independent variables.

**Unsupervised learning** A machine learning approach that does not make use of labeled training data.

**Upfront payment** The difference between the credit spread and the standard rate paid by the protection buyer if the standard rate is insufficient to compensate the protection seller. Also called *upfront premium*.

**Upfront premium** See *upfront payment*.

**Upstream** A transaction between two related companies, an investor company (or a parent company) and an associate company (or a subsidiary company) such that the associate company records a profit on its income statement. An example is a sale of inventory by the associate to the investor company or by a subsidiary to a parent company.

**Validation sample** A data sample that is used to validate and tune a model.

**Valuation** The process of determining the value of an asset or service either on the basis of variables perceived to be related to future investment returns or on the basis of comparisons with closely similar assets.

**Value additivity** An arbitrage opportunity when the value of the whole equals the sum of the values of the parts.

**Value at risk (VaR)** The minimum loss that would be expected a certain percentage of the time over a certain period of time given the assumed market conditions.

**Value of growth** The difference between the actual value per share and the no-growth value per share.

**Variance error** Describes how much a model's results change in response to new data from validation and test samples. Unstable models pick up noise and produce high variance error, causing overfitting and high out-of-sample error.

**Variance inflation factor (VIF)** A statistic that quantifies the degree of multicollinearity in a model.

**Vasicek model**  A partial equilibrium term structure model that assumes interest rates are mean reverting and interest rate volatility is constant.

**Vega**  The change in a given derivative instrument for a given small change in volatility, holding everything else constant. A sensitivity measure for options that reflects the effect of volatility.

**Venture capital investors**  Private equity investors in development-stage companies.

**Vertical ownership**  Ownership structure in which a company or group that has a controlling interest in two or more holding companies, which in turn have controlling interests in various operating companies.

**Vested benefit obligation**  The actuarial present value of vested benefits.

**Vesting date**  The date that employees can first exercise stock options.

**Visibility**  The extent to which a company's operations are predictable with substantial confidence.

**Voting caps**  Legal restrictions on the voting rights of large share positions.

**Web spidering (scraping or crawling) programs**  Programs that extract raw content from a source, typically web pages.

**Weighted average cost of capital (WACC)**  A weighted average of the after-tax required rates of return on a company's common stock, preferred stock, and long-term debt, where the weights are the fraction of each source of financing in the company's target capital structure.

**Weighted harmonic mean**  See *harmonic mean*.

**Winsorization**  The process of replacing extreme values and outliers in a dataset with the maximum (for large value outliers) and minimum (for small value outliers) values of data points that are not outliers.

**Write-down**  A reduction in the value of an asset as stated in the balance sheet.

**Yield curve factor model**  A model or a description of yield curve movements that can be considered realistic when compared with historical data.

**Zero**  A bond that does not pay a coupon but is priced at a discount and pays its full face value at maturity.

**Zero-coupon bond**  A bond that does not pay interest during its life. It is issued at a discount to par value and redeemed at par. Also called *pure discount bond*.